# THE POEMS AND PLAYS
## OF
## OLIVER ST JOHN GOGARTY

# THE POEMS & PLAYS

## of

## Oliver St John Gogarty

collected, edited and introduced
by
A. Norman Jeffares

COLIN SMYTHE LIMITED

This collection first published in 2001 by Colin Smythe Limited
P.O. Box 6, Gerrards Cross, Buckinghamshire SL9 8XA

**British Library Cataloguing-in-Publication Data**

A catalogue record for this book is available
from the British Library

ISBN 0-86140-404-1

Printed in Great Britain
Printed and bound by T.J. International Ltd., Padstow, Cornwall

# CONTENTS

## SATIRES AND FACETIAE

## LOVE AND BEAUTY

## LIFE AND DEATH

## ELEGIES

## PART 2: POEMS FROM OTHER COLLECTIONS – PUBLISHED AND UNPUBLISHED – NOT INCLUDED IN COLLECTED POEMS

### From *Hyperthuleana* (1916)

### From *Secret Springs of Dublin Song* (1918)

## From *The Ship and Other Poems* (1918)

## From *An Offering of Swans* (1923)

## From *An Offering of Swans and Other Poems* (1924)

## From *Wild Apples* (1928)

## From *Wild Apples* (1929)

## PART 3: POEMS PUBLISHED IN JOURNALS AND UNPUBLISHED POEMS:

## PRELUDE

## ODES AND ADDRESSES

## EARTH AND SEA

## SATIRES AND FACETIAE:

### Dislikes and Disapprobations

### Limericks

## Parodies

## Light-hearted Verses

## Some Martello Tower Poems

CONTENTS xiii

## On Drinking

## Medical Meditations

## Monto Poems

## LOVE AND BEAUTY

## APPENDICES

## ACKNOWLEDGEMENTS AND ANNOTATIONS

## ADDENDA

## INDEXES

# PREFACE

## I

### By W. B. YEATS

"TWELVE years ago Oliver Gogarty was captured by his enemies, imprisoned in a deserted house on the edge of the Liffey with every prospect of death. Pleading a natural necessity he got into the garden, plunged under a shower of revolver bullets and as he swam the ice-cold December stream promised it, should it land him in safety, two swans. I was present when he fulfilled that vow.

His poetry fits the incident, a gay, stoical – no, I will not withhold the word – heroic song. Irish by tradition and many ancestors, I love, though I have nothing to offer but the philosophy they deride, swashbucklers, horsemen, swift indifferent men; yet I do not think that is the sole reason, good reason though it is, why I gave him considerable space, and think him one of the great lyric poets of our age."

(From the Introduction to the *Oxford Book of Modern Verse*.)

# PREFACE

## II

### By A. E.

### THE POETRY OF MY FRIEND

WHEN I was young I thought of my opposites with terror, but as I grew older I transcended those hatreds, because, I hope, my mood became more spiritual. I came to feel the attraction in opposites, not that I wished to be like them but to understand them, to establish some harmony or balance between them and myself. I found this inclination in others more spiritual than myself. Emerson who could not, I think, have brought his lips to utter a Rabelaisian sentence, does twice in his journal refer almost with envy to the Rabelaisian freedom of speech of the lumbermen. This attraction to opposites may have its roots in a purely spiritual impulse to have life in all fullness, and it may have been the same impulse which made him write to Whitman telling the poet what joy he took in his free and brave thought. I found myself liking Oliver Gogarty when I knew him only as having the wildest wit in Ireland from which nothing in heaven or earth was immune, though often I had reverence for the things he assailed. I never suspected in that rich nature a poet lay hidden, though my intuition should have told me that at the root of all friendships and desires are hidden identities. For all his rich vitality the elements obvious in it seemed incongruous with delicate poetry. An athlete in his youth, an airman in later life, his mind thronged with the knowledge and technique of a specialist, his imagination brimful of Rabelaisian fantasy and that wild wit which in every poet but Heine has made timid the sensitive psyche.

All this was not congruous with poetry. But, among the multitudes he contained, there was a poet, a genie in the innermost who gradually emerged in spite of all the dragons in its path. I was astonished when he began to show us verses so finely carved that his genie seemed to have wrought with words as the Image-maker in his own verse treated the hard jade, making a transient beauty into adamant. It is easier to suggest a lovely transience than to carve it in definite forms. Monticelli in the blurred jewelry of his woodland could make glimmer a white arm, a gleaming neck, a gesture, a mothlike flutter of drapery, and leave it to our imagination to create the full riot of lovely life.

But the ideal of Oliver's genie was beauty and mystery achieved by precision. His beauty must shine in the sun not in the shade, and its mystery must be its own perfection. That I think is his genie's true intent in its art; but, when it consorts with the crowd of lusty incompatibles in the house of the soul, it is often deflected and becomes witty with the rest, or it listens to scandal and forgets for a time its own ideal. But I always assume that what is best is most real and I find what is best in lovely poems like *The Plum Tree by the House* in which the genie reveals to the poet the manner of its own artistry, to hold fast to the image, to brood on its beauty until it becomes what it contemplates and is itself a blossoming tree. It is not the secret of such art as I have myself, for my genie would melt all form into bodiless spirit. It looks with wonder on its opposite whose art is to project defined and shapely images and which gets its life from this art. That precise carving in words is in the first poem in this book, where the crab tree grows in the imagination with its stiff, twisted beauty, and, as we read, it becomes as sturdy a dweller in memory as its prototype in earth. Again in the *Coin from Syracuse* how determined the genie is to miss nothing of the hard drawing of the beauty it sees until the features

'Crowned with the thickly rolled
And corrugated gold'

are built anew in fancy with the curious hands

'lost
On the sweet Asian coast'

and then we know at last it was some Irish beauty had started the genie on its interpretation of the ancient image, some one

'Come of the old stock,
Lords of the limestone rock,
And acres fit to breed
Many a likely steed,
Straight in the back and bone,

> With head high like her own,
> And blood that, tamed and mild,
> Can suddenly grow wild.'

When I was young and saw a face that set me dreaming I tried to track it back to the Pleroma, the fountain of all beauty, to find justification for my adoration. I had not then found in Emerson the wisdom which justifies the image–maker –

> 'Tell them, dear, if eyes were made for seeing,
> That beauty is its own excuse for being,'

and I have become less timid and more gallant in my thought, accepting beauties not in my own hierarchy, and am happier being able to escape from myself and to see with the delighted, unfearing eyes of a poet who is my opposite.

Oliver Gogarty has eyes which can see what is most enchanting and alluring in women. He casts a glamour over them, the art which Gainsborough had in painting and which Reynolds, for all his mastery of his craft, had not. How few poets convey to us the enchantment of the women they adored. Their love blurs their art. I doubt if Oliver was in love with any of the women he praises, but, as we read, we feel that we could easily fall in love with the woman he depicts. His cool eye has noticed that second of illumination where the light on limb and dress becomes one with the light in the heart, and he can have no peace until he can give that transience permanence –

> 'till the cloud
> Of thought takes definite shape,
> And bodies you forth unbowed,
> Tall, on a bare landscape,
> Where earth the stone upthrusts –
> Holding your exquisite frock
> Against the morning gusts,
> And light is on half the rock.'

That is the beauty seen and drawn with precision enough to make it alluring to us. I sometimes think of Herrick after I have read one of Oliver Gogarty's lyrics. The Julia of the English poet is a lovely piece of girlhood. That is much, but she will never be more to our imagination. There is some aristocracy of vision in the Irish poet. He sees the lovely girl, but he suggests, however remotely, the psyche within the flesh. In an instant, she might be transfigured in the imagination and become the dream stuff out of which goddesses, naiads and nymphs were fashioned. That is, the images he depicts, however modern in outward fashion, are still in the divine procession and set us travelling with them to

> 'The Perfect, the Forbidden City,
> That's built – Ah, God knows where.'

From practice the art of the poet, at first a little stiff, has become supple, and the words will fly up swiftly to catch a sudden glory in their net. This must have come almost as swiftly as the vision it speaks of:

> 'I gaze and gaze when I behold
> The meadows springing green and gold.
> I gaze until my mind is naught
> But wonderful and wordless thought!
> Till, suddenly, surpassing wit,
> Spontaneous meadows spring in it:
> And I am but a glass between
> Un-walked in meadows, gold and green.'

I take so much pleasure in my friend's poetry because it is the opposite to my own. It gives to me some gay and gallant life which was not in my own birthright. He is never the professional poet made dull by the dignity of recognised genius. He has never made a business of beauty: and, because he is disinterested in his dealings with it, the Muse has gone with him on his walks and revealed to him some airs and graces she kept secret from other lovers who were too shy or too awed by her to laugh and be natural in her presence.

(From *Selected Poems of Oliver St. John Gogarty*.)

# PREFACE

## III

By Horace Reynolds

## GOGARTY IN THE FLESH

I FIRST met Oliver Gogarty in George Moore's *Salve* where he is introduced as Dublin's arch-mocker, the author of the limericks that are on the lips of all Dublin. And in Dublin, most vocal of all cities, where talk is the national art and pastime, it means much to be the crowned arch-ollave of joke and jest. In *Salve* the wicket of Moore's garden clangs, and Gogarty makes his gay entrance fanfared by Moore who cries out in welcome Gogarty's motif, 'There was a young man of St. John's,' the first line of one of the great limericks, slyly leaving the following lines to our curiosity, and thus confounds the censor, for much of Gogarty's wit necessarily bubbles in secret springs. But he gives complete Gogarty's improvisation on Sir Thornley Stoker, the Dublin surgeon, whose excursions into the suburbs of art were made possible by his skill with the scalpel, his antiquarian touch turning a cancer into a Chippendale sofa or a floating kidney into a Ming Cloisonné. And with the laughter that his sallies arouse in Moore's dinner guests Gogarty fades out of the Trilogy, a beautifully realized minor character.

My curiosity was excited. A. E. and John Eglinton, Moore's other guests, were identifiable, but who was this man whose volatile and grotesque name seemed the mirror of his mind? Like Max Beerbohm in *Enoch Soames* I went unrewarded to the index of a literary history, Ernest Boyd's *Ireland's Literary Renaissance*, a book that had stood me in good stead in my first flirtings with the literature of the Renaissance. Evidently Boyd in his perhaps too earnest quest for the meaning of Ireland's literature had had no time for personalities: he had been interested only in the written, not the spoken, word. Finally in my copy of *Dana*, a rare early journal, I found printed some of Gogarty's lyrics – the Goddess speaking where the critic was mute – and fresh surprise was added to my already aroused curiosity: this man whose wit was as Gothic as a gargoyle wrote lyrics cool and fresh as a fountain, and as delicate as a beautiful change of light.

Later when *Ulysses* fell into my hands, and it was whispered to me that Gogarty was in it, I recognized him in 'stately, plump Buck Mulligan' who comes 'from the stairhead bearing a bowl of lather on which a mirror and a razor lay crossed' to open that tragedy of the unconscious, although Gogarty is not plump, and stately, perhaps, only in repose. There in that book without reticences Gogarty piled imagination upon imagination with breath-taking invention, and I knew enough of Joyce's marvellous phonographic ear and photographic eye to know that much of it was but Gogarty printed, and I marvelled anew.

Three years passed, and it so happened that each year I met an Irish poet who had known Gogarty: Joseph Campbell, James Stephens, and Padraic Colum passed in succession through the city in which I lived, and from each I gleaned something of the famous Dublin doctor. To ask of him was to evoke a legend: his name was open sesame to the treasure-house of Gogartiana in which each one who knew him seemed to have a full share. 'He does not belong to our spindling, self-nauseated age,' cried Campbell; 'he is a Buck of the robust, devil-may-care 18th century, born out of time to our delight,' Campbell's slower, Northern blood standing momentarily still in homage before the memory of a mind which was lightning. And then to illustrate the quickness of Gogarty's wit he told how as a young poet he had walked down Grafton Street one day, proud of a new, very bright red tie. Suddenly he came face to face with Gogarty. 'Tiger! Tiger! burning bright,' cried Gogarty instantly, passing on with a swift smile and a bright nod. And I shall never forget Stephens's praise of one of Gogarty's poems, *To a Cock*, in a series of mounting phrases which exploded like a rocket in a vehement 'By God, 'tis tragic!' while we all looked at each other in wild surprise. Colum told us of Gogarty's adventures before he had hung up his tankard in stories which ranged from his pilgrimage to the top of the Featherbed Mountain to restore the snakes to Ireland to his offering of the swans to the Liffey, a gesture of gratitude to that river which, when he had been taken out by a group of Republicans to be shot, had offered him the opportunity to escape with his life. We gasped at the audacity of those stories in which man revenges himself on those two great barriers that lie athwart the highway of the mind and keep it active – sex and religion. Our pulses beat to the limericks that immortalize in oral tradition such oddly assorted personalities as the King in Sing a Song of Sixpence; Miss Horniman, patron saint of the Abbey Theatre; and Daniel O'Connell, the Irish patriot. We applauded the skill of the parodies that transubstantiates sound and sense as skilfully as Joyce, with that passion for phonetic waggery which is so large a part of *Ulysses* and the Irish mind, turned *Oliver Gogarty* into *Malachi Mulligan*, keeping the two dancing dactyls and the clash of race and mood in given name and surname. And I shall always remember one occasion in particular which Gogarty ruled superbly by proxy, transforming what might well have been just another dinner into an evening of almost Dublin brilliance. Among others, Colum was there, and Maurice Joy, once secretary to Sir Horace Plunkett, and a friend of Gogarty's youth. Scarcely had we seated ourselves when someone spoke of Gogarty, and then Colum and Joy began an antiphony of Gogartian reminiscences; first one, then the other, would remember one of Gogarty's limericks, stories, or parodies, and these quotations intoxicated, like a succession of drinks. Then when we were all a little giddy with excitement and delight, Joy arose to recite Gogarty's *The Death of Diogenes, the Doctor's Dog*, which is both a lampoon on the tongue-tied, king-loving Professor Mahaffy and a parody of Swinburne, written, when Gogarty was an undergraduate at Trinity, in the quintains that close the *Atalanta in Calydon*. I can hear Joy now chanting the lines that Mahaffy speaks over the body of the dog which had died on the voyage from Greece to Ireland, a hound especially prized because it had been given him by the niece of the King of Greece:

> As I wambled awound
>     On the gwound that was Gweece
> I was given that hound
>     By the King's little niece,
> And had rather be fined e'er I found him to gaze
>     on his saddest surcease.

And then the Chorus of Scholars in the house comments gravely on the action, with a deeper tone, *adagio pesante*:

> He was given that hound
>     By the seed of a King
> For the wisdom profound
>     Of his wide wandering.
> But was it the owner, or donor, or dog that was led
>     by a string?

As Joy spoke the last words of this threnody, I made my vow. I would make a pilgrimage to Dublin. I had not seen Shelley plain, but I would at least catch a glimpse of Gogarty in the flesh!

Two months later I found myself one afternoon before a door in which was set a large silver plate bearing the name *Oliver St. John Gogarty, M.D.* Before ringing the bell, I looked about me. This was a moment of which I had long dreamed; it was not to be hurried over; I wanted to squeeze every possible value out of it, roll it around in the mouth, taste it to the full. At last I was in Ely Place. Across the street was the row of houses, from the windows of one of which, Number 4, George Moore, surrounded by his Monets and Manets and lovingly treading his Aubusson carpet, had looked forth and seen the copy of his masterpiece, *Hail and Farewell.* At the end of the street rose the often spoken of convent wall, for Ely Place is a cul-de-sac; between it and Gogarty's house stretched the sunken garden through the wicket of which Gogarty had first walked into my mind. There was the largest apple tree in all Ireland under which Moore, an Ovid among his friends, had dined; there was the damson tree, 'coral boughs in light inurned,' of which Gogarty himself was later to sing in one of his most beautiful lyrics.

I rang the bell, I waited, I was ushered into the house, I was conducted to the drawing-room. Dr. Gogarty was engaged with a patient. And as I waited for him, I chatted with Mrs. Gogarty and some company. Mrs. Gogarty politely asked me about my stay in Ireland, and I summarized my trip up from Queenstown by way of Killarney to Dublin, mentioning, apropos of something I have now forgotten, that Muckross Abbey was the most beautiful ruin I had seen in Ireland.

'Ah, you should see ——— ——— ———,' said a gay, joyous voice behind me, speaking of a famous Irish woman to whose beauty time has not been kind, and I turned to see coming toward me, eyes laughing, step quick, all smile and gaiety and good spirits, a very young middle-aged man – Oliver St. John Gogarty in the flesh. I knew at once I should like him much; in fact I already loved him for that entrance, with its flash of the precious power to perceive the hidden nearness of analogies seemingly distant until the imagination has discovered their essential closeness, a power that has given his friends many surprises and much pleasure. It was perfect, that entrance, well worth coming three thousand miles to see and hear.

We admired Gogarty's new Danish furniture purchased in Paris at the recent exhibition. Unlike Sir Thornley Stoker, Gogarty esteems the new, the fresh, the modern. President Cosgrave came in, a quiet, sober man who – unlike most Irishmen – did not want the centre of the stage. He talked little, and, I fear, I listened less. What were presidents to me? I sat finally in the presence of the man who had restored the snakes to Ireland; the author of the great limericks; the creator of that robustious company, Fresh Nelly, Mrs. Mack, Rosalie the Coal-Quay Whore, and the heroic and Rabelaisian Bryan O'Lynn; the cunning maker of the cleverest parody in English literature in which Gogarty flashes back to Keats, 'Silent, upon a peak in Darien,' 'Potent, behind a cart with Mary Ann' – certainly the most joyously witty man in all Europe.

And as if he sensed my three-thousand-mile expectancy, Dr. Gogarty talked brilliantly, telling story after story with the ejaculatory running comment and extemporaneous exegesis of anecdote and phrase which are his habit, as is his raised finger, shaken Puck-like close to the ear. I believe he is the only man in the world who can explain his own jokes and make them funnier thereby, I thought, studying him as he talked.

Youth is the first impression one gets from Gogarty in the flesh – all the Irish seem youthful, but Gogarty is particularly so; youth, and the responsiveness of mind and body that is its privilege. He is a man whose energy makes him restless, whose culture and information are rich and abundant, close to the tip of his tongue, ready for instant mobilization in the face of opening, invitation, or attack. His is a mind whose surfaces are intensely active, but whose depths are seldom stirred; a fluent, ready mind, flaring up easily into images and analogies, expressing itself from the surface, never pulling an idea up by its roots, never working against resistance; a mind that plays like a fine old violin, from which tone comes singingly.

At seven o'clock the next morning – this in a city where the shops do not open until ten – Gogarty was at the door of my hotel with a small car, and we drove out into the beautiful Dublin hills. The small roadster had no brakes, and we slithered down the steep wet hills around which the road curved in dangerous spirals. Driving under those circumstances would have absorbed all my attention, but not Gogarty's. For him it was only stimulation. All the while Gogarty gave me his memories of the poets, Greek, Latin, Scotch, English, and Irish, reciting whole ballads while we slid over the wet hills, ballads ranging from Robin Hood to an 18th century folk ballad picked up by Joyce in Mabbot Street. Through Powerscourt Demesne we tore, finally coming to a stop in a beautiful quiet glade surrounded by old trees and backed by a high cliff down which a waterfall fell in thin hairs of silver. There we got out. Were Gogarty's spirits quieted by the gentle genius of this place? Not at all. At his command we ran foot races to restore circulation, and Gogarty bested me by no mean margin in the standing broad jump, and he would have easily bested a better man than I. Then back to the car, I breathless, but Gogarty unwinded, and then a drive to the lodge of a house where I was to have luncheon. There he left me exhausted in mind and body, while he, with a gay wave of the hand, sped on his way back to Dublin, as fresh and unwearied as when we had set out five hours before.

The next morning at the same hour Gogarty was again at the door of my hotel; this time we were to go horseback riding. As we rode our

cobs slowly through the almost deserted Dublin streets on our way to
the Strand, we passed the house where Joyce used to lodge, and the sight
of it loosed Gogarty's memories of the author of *Ulysses*. He paid tribute
to Joyce's marvellous memory; he spoke of his beautiful tenor voice,
even more beautiful than McCormack's; and, of course, of *Ulysses*,
which he compared to 'an elbow of a broken statue which is the town of
Dublin.' I remembered that to George Moore Dublin was an old
second-hand clothes shop, and suggested that if we combined the two
images, clothing one with the other, we'd have a museum scarecrow, a
bit of foolish fancy that Gogarty generously rewarded with the high,
suspiratory 'Lovely!' which is the highest mark of his appreciation.

Soon we were on the Strand and off for a fine gallop around the
crescent-shaped beach which fringes the east of Dublin as the mountains
fence the west and south. The thunder of eight hoofs on wet sand was as
joyous as Gogarty's galloping wit, for unlike Joyce, whose wit depresses
and saddens, Gogarty is as exhilarating as a gay band playing spiritedly in
four-four time in the morning sunshine. Joyce believes in nothing
outside himself; consequently he can never rid self of self; he is devoured
by the swarm of his ideas, and yet he feeds on them, and on them alone,
and thus the heart-withering circle closes, shutting out the vistas that free
man from unhappiness. Gogarty believes in the magnificent adventure of
life which, like Taillefer, he charges with ardour, juggling his sword, a
feather in his cap, a song on his lips.

And then one week-end we set off to the West. To drive with
Gogarty in his small roadster had been a terrifying experience, but when
I saw before his door the shell-shaped Mercedes in which we were to
make our dash to the West, all yellow hood and mahogany trimmings,
shiningly sinister – when I imagined the potential power that now lay
quiet under that hood, I shuddered. The John McCormacks stopped in
unexpectedly for tea – the tenor, wife, and daughter – and that delayed
us, so it was after six when we started.

All my life I had lived in what we think of as a speed-crazed country. I
had seen my share of the speed that is born of gasoline and gin, but never
had I had such a ride. Gogarty had said, 'You'll see the country.' Well, I
did, in blurs. Getting out of Dublin, the motor coughed and spat. 'It
doesn't run well under fifty,' said Gogarty apologetically; 'I have to drive it
on the brake.' Driving on the brake consisted of seventy to eighty miles an
hour down the straightaways of the very narrow, very curving, but very
smooth Irish roads; at the curves, foot raised from accelerator, a consequent
checking of our terrific speed, an anxious peering around the bend and a
prayer that we might not find there in the road before us a peasant and a
herd of cows. Then the foot down again on the accelerator, and a resultant
surging forward of the long yellow hood into the next straightaway.

And how Gogarty loved it! Leaning his head over so that his mouth might be close to my ear, taking his hand off the wheel to shake his finger coyly past his ear, Gogarty talked.

He remembered his student days at Trinity College, Dublin, under that trio of extraordinary professors, Mahaffy, Tyrrell, and Dowden. He quoted the remark Tyrrell made after Mahaffy had been suspended from preaching in the college chapel for his attempt to exalt the Greek Gods over the Christian: 'Since Mahaffy gave up preaching in the chapel, I suffer from insomnia at the services,' his mimicry of Tyrrell's high, Oxford-accented voice making the remark much funnier than it is in cold print. He spoke of the many personalities with which Dublin bristled a generation ago, of Zozimus who, with a name like a Renaissance scholar in *us*, walked about Dublin in cricket costume, a strolling satire of the English game; who, although he knew Dublin like a book, insisted on finding his way home by compass. He told of the days when he and Joyce and Trench (Trench is Haines in *Ulysses*) lived together in the Martello tower that Gogarty rented for nine pounds a year. He told of how they objected to a British warship which was anchored off shore so as to interfere with their view, wrote a protest to the British Admiralty, and had the ship removed. And thus passed the lovely fragrant Midlands, Padraic Colum's country, and before I knew it, we drew up before the Spanish Gate in Galway town, our first stop.

From there on the country was lovely, Lough Corrib on our right and straight ahead the beautiful Maumturk Mountains in the closing hour of the long Irish twilight. In an unbelievably short time we drew up at the Leenane Hotel, two hundred-odd miles in little more than two hundred minutes, where I got out of the car feeling as if I had been shot across Ireland on a projectile.

The next day we drove from Leenane through Salruck to a point from which we could see the Mweelrea Mountains across Killary Harbour, where we talked to peasants who looked, as Gogarty said, 'not only Pre-Celtic but Pre-Anything.' Then back to Leenane and on to Letterfrack where we saw the ruins of Gogarty's old house, now re-risen Phoenix-like as the Renvyle House Hotel from the pile of ashes to which the Republicans reduced it during the Civil War. And if you stay at the Renvyle House Hotel to-day, someone is sure to tell you that it was the former home of a man who is in *Ulysses*. From Renvyle we went on to Loch Tully, where Gogarty has an island on which he was building a new summer place. Although the house was still under construction, Gogarty was already planning how he might alight near it in a seaplane from Dublin.

On our way back from the West we turned south at Galway to visit Kinvarra for a glimpse of the Norman castle Gogarty had bought there with the idea of later restoring it, and our visit surprised an Irish peasant who, to Gogarty's dismay, was stabling his horse in the tower built by the Normans four hundred years before Spenser lived in and absorbed the Irish landscape. When we got out to look inside the tower, Gogarty stopped before it and raised his right hand in the Indian-How-like gesture which he and all Dublin use to signify that what it is to follow is a quotation from William Butler Yeats himself. '"The Normans had form, Gogarty, the Normans had form," were Yeats's words when I showed him my tower,' said Gogarty. And then as we walked up the stairs of the tower, its four sides oriented to the four points of the compass, Gogarty spoke of Yeats.

Gogarty is delightful on the subject of Yeats, his attitude toward his famous fellow-townsman being compounded of reverence for his genius, delight in his foibles, gratitude for his kindness, and appreciation of the subtle mummer Yeats can be. Gogarty loves to peer into the folds of Yeats's mind, and he loves particularly to excite him into action. And Yeats, of course, plays up. 'I decided to take Yeats swimming,' said Gogarty, 'but in order to stir Yeats out of dream into action, I must appeal to his imagination. So I talked of the swimming match of Beowulf and Breca; of Swinburne's love of mixing with "the great sweet mother," "Clothed with the green and crowned with the foam", of Byron's fondness for bathing in the jasper sea. And his imagination thus excited, Yeats reluctantly agreed to go. We got into my car and set off, but as we approached the sea, Yeat's resolution began to weaken:

Yeats (after a mile or two, in a chant-like voice to the accompaniment of faint strains from a psaltery hidden under the hood of the car). Gogarty, I'm afraid I can't go in bathing: I've forgotten to bring a suit.

Gogarty. I thought you would; I have two.

Yeats (after another mile). Gogarty, I'm afraid I can't go bathing: I have forgotten to bring a towel.

Gogarty. I thought you would; I have two.

'When we got to the beach, I gave Yeats a suit and towel, put his pince-nez in my pocket, and we bathed in the jasper sea.'

But Gogarty was not so successful in getting Yeats on horseback. 'I knew,' said Gogarty, 'that if I could get Yeats on a horse I could put a new rhythm into English lyric verse.' And so he began to speak of the noble and benevolent Marcus Aurelius, who rides in bronze on the Capitoline Hill; of Chiron, wise tutor of Jason and Archilles; and of the Centaurs, who thundered headlong down the roadway of excess − surrounding horseback riding with the tradition that Yeats loves to see about the things he does and thinks of. Again Yeats succumbed, but this time Mrs. Yeats put her foot down. New rhythm or no, she was not going to allow her famous husband to get on a horse.

As we passed through Enfield or Kilcock, I forgot which, we were stopped by the sharp whistle of a policeman. We were doing fifty through the village square, but it wasn't for speeding that we had been stopped, primarily. Kevin O'Higgins, Minister of Justice, had been murdered that noon, and the police were questioning all cars. 'I am Senator Oliver Gogarty,' said Gogarty, mentally assuming the toga; 'can I be of help?' He couldn't, and we proceeded on to Dublin.

This past Spring – six years later – I saw him again. He was the same Gogarty, running down the steps of the Statler Hotel to greet me when I came to take him to his Harvard lecture, talking all the way to Cambridge in the automobile, overflowing with anecdote and comment on the life he had encountered in the lecture tour which had taken him from coast to coast, full of fresh thought and fresh enthusiasms. For Gogarty's intellectual capital is in rapid circulation, culture is for him an adventure – the discovery in an obscure Elizabethan poet of the wonderful line, 'He grasped at love and filled his arms with bays,' the epitome of the life of many a poet; the rescue of some fine ringing sentence with the sound of smitten bronze in it, from a medical treatise; the return to the world of a beautiful old Scotch song, hidden like a violet among the weeds of much that has been deservedly forgotten in an obsolete anthology; the perception in *Old Man River* of a microcosm of life concealed from most of us by the film of familiarity. Of course he had a new story about Yeats; baffled by Mrs. Yeats's watchfulness in his plan to put Yeats upon a horse, he had succeeded in taking him up in his plane, for Gogarty is now a licensed pilot and, the Mercedes garaged, he now wings his way to the West, singing, like the beautiful Swan-Children of Lir. He had taken up A. E., too, but that had necessitated a new safety strap – 'the ordinary strap was too small for the God.'

Gogarty was, as always, a delight to all who saw and heard him, his modesty endearing him to those who could only partially appreciate his wit, the heaven-sent modesty that goes hand in hand with the shyness with which in his poetry he broods on Beauty, fearful that someone may surprise him on his knees before Her shrine. Almost daily his poetry grows more gay and arch, more musical in its tune, swifter and surer in its choriambic dance, more beautiful in its expression of the delights Nature offers to the inviting eye. Sometimes in his verse that rare marriage of wit and beauty is so perfect as to make us regret all the more the occasions when the wit, laughing, banishes the beauty, bruising a rhythm and breaking a mood that have given us great joy. But gradually, and with all the sureness of Nature, the poet emerges from the chrysalis of the wit. By his poetry will the many of the future know the essence of a personality which, in the flesh, has been the wonder of the few.

(From *Selected Poems of Oliver St. John Gogarty*.)

# GENERAL INTRODUCTION

Oliver St. John Gogarty (1878–1957), unreasonably neglected after his death, is coming back into readers' attention now that his work, long out of print, often printed in small editions, and consequently hard to find in second-hand bookshops and in many libraries, is being reissued. For instance, new editions of *As I was going down Sackville Street* (1937) and *Tumbling in the Hay* (1939) appeared in 1994 and 1996 respectively, and new editions of *It isn't this Time of Year at All* (1954) and *I Follow Saint Patrick* (1938) are forthcoming. Ulick O'Connor's lively pioneering biography is also being republished.

In making his poems and plays available again in this edition it seemed to me I had to make a choice between three alternatives: first, simply to select the best of his poems (probably between at least forty and a hundred of them); or, second, to re-issue the *Collected Poems* (1951) and the published plays; or, third, to do this and add in the other published and hitherto unpublished poems, verse and drama.

It could be argued that the first option, of selection, would enhance the standing as a lyric, classical and satiric poet that Gogarty had gained in his lifetime by the inclusion of two of his poems in the *Oxford Book of English Verse* (1927) and seventeen in the *Oxford Book of Modern Verse* (1936) as well as more than two dozen poems in other anthologies. But since Gogarty's poems have not been available outside some anthologies, it seems unduly restrictive merely to make what would inevitably be a personal selection. Readers would thus be denied an opportunity of realising the quantity and range of poetry Gogarty wrote and of assessing its varying merits and qualities for themselves.

Merely to reprint the *Collected Poems* and the three published plays, the second and easiest option, would be to present readers with Gogarty's own selection of his poetic *oeuvre*. To do so would be to depend upon his judgement alone, and thus to deprive readers of some fine published poems, which, for various reasons, he did not include in

1

the *Collected Poems* as well as poems he wrote after the publication of that volume.

I have chosen the third option, because I should like to share with readers my enjoyment not only of the impressive, generally finished and polished work both of the *Collected Poems* and of the various single volumes, in addition to those poems – such as, for instance, the hastily written, heartfelt laments for his closest friend Arthur Griffith, for Michael Collins and for Arthur Russell – that appeared in journals or newspapers but also of the many unpublished poems, and the poems and a play attributed to Gogarty. Much of the unpublished poetry is, of course, of uneven merit, for it was intended for the immediate amusement of close friends, not for publication. In sending a poem to James Sullivan Starkey ('Seamus O'Sullivan', lyric poet, bibliophile and successful editor of the *Dublin Magazine*), in a letter of 19 April 1922, Gogarty wrote revealingly 'This is first shot . . . I suspect anything I didn't keep for years.' The manuscripts of published poems often indicate careful revision before publication, recasting of stanzas, for instance, as well as alterations of lines or words, and the printed versions of poems are sometimes altered in later publications.

This edition of Oliver St. John Gogarty's poems and plays is, then, divided into four parts. The first consists of the *Collected Poems* (1951). The second contains poems not included in the *Collected Poems* but found elsewhere, in separate volumes of Gogarty's poems. The third collects poems Gogarty intended to publish, poems privately printed, poems published in anthologies and in journals or newspapers, and poems contained in various MSS and TSS or in notebooks and letters to friends, as well as various poems and limericks attributed to him. The fourth contains the three plays, first published separately and pseudonymously in 1917 and 1919 respectively, and then together as *The Plays of Oliver St. John Gogarty* in 1971. The Appendices section includes, *inter alia*, an attributed play, a portion of another play, and 'The Ballad of Oliver Gogarty'. They are followed by Acknowledgements, a Chronology of Gogarty's Life, Notes and Notes on the Text. Holographs of some Gogarty poems are reproduced on the end-papers.

The reason for offering to contemporary readers these examples of Gogarty's unpublished poetry and poems attributed to him is that, apart from the intrinsic interest of this material, it gives unique insights into a Dublin that has almost vanished from personal knowledge, for it is now over a hundred years since Gogarty passed the First and failed the Second Arts examination of the Royal University of Ireland, attended lectures in University College, Dublin, and entered Trinity College, Dublin. This was the Dublin from which W. B. Yeats and Douglas Hyde had launched the Irish literary movement and the Gaelic League in the 1890s. It was then a city which resembled ancient Athens in its closely knit society: its authors and artists knew each other – and, as in a village, their family history and backgrounds. Many of them shared a desire to know the Irish past and to renew it in a way that would establish authentic Irish voices and attitudes in what seemed to many an increasingly standardised world.

This development of an Irish literary *milieu* was not a simple process. George Russell (AE) sapiently remarked to George Moore that a literary movement consisted of five or six people who live in one town and hate each other cordially. Perhaps the most significant of the differences between Irish civilisation (Gaelic and Anglo-Irish both) and that of the larger, neighbouring island was that Ireland possessed (and to a certain extent still possesses) an oral culture. This meant retentive memories in plenty and the quick transmission of speech which favoured the *bon mot*, the witty put-down, the scabrous aside, the high flown phrases of political rhetoric and their caustic antidotes, and the art and appreciation of story telling. New myths were built upon old foundations. Thanks to the writings of Standish O'Grady and Sir Samuel Ferguson, followed by those of Yeats and Lady Gregory, and of the later, more extremely nationalist generation of writers such as Daniel Corkery, Patrick Pearse, Thomas MacDonagh and their contemporaries, the Irish hero Cuchulain salmon-leaped with his fellows from saga material into twentieth century Irish ideology.

Within this oral conversational culture, obviously, lively speech mattered. In a non-industrial society where there was much poverty it was the cheapest, almost the only form of intellectual entertainment. At one level Synge captured its importance in his play *In the Shadow of the Glen* (1904) when Nora, the wife dissatisfied with her old husband, decides to leave him, not, however, with a young farmer but with a tramp, because of his 'fine bit of talk'. At a more intellectual level, witty, very often irreverent remarks went the rounds and Gogarty's more frequently than most. Quite early in his career he was recognised in the words of the formidable Robert Yelverton Tyrrell, Professor of Latin, then of Greek, then of Ancient History at Trinity College, Dublin, as 'the diner-out, the *diseur*, the man without whom no dinner party is complete'. He had learned the art of polite if forthright conversation from some of the Trinity dons, learned and ruthlessly outspoken, from Tyrrell, Henry Stewart Macran, the Professor of Moral Philosophy, and John Pentland Mahaffy, the Hellenist, whose pupil Oscar Wilde had been – until Mahaffy said to him 'Oscar, you are not clever enough for us here, you had better go to Oxford'. It was to Mahaffy, asking him at a college meeting 'Are you rising on a point of order?' that Gogarty replied 'No, on the spur of the moment'. His conversations, however, operated on levels other than the irrepressible. He was made welcome at the weekly 'nights' given by Dublin writers and artists which proved fine sounding boards for him, as did the Arts Club, a social centre founded in 1907, which provided a focus for a lively cross section of Dublin's artistic life. Gogarty had also developed a capacity for outrageous Rabelaisian remarks, for blasphemy and bawdy, among the students he met earlier in University College, Dublin, John Elwood ('Citizen' Elwood), Vincent Cosgrave, James Joyce and Simon Broderick as well as Francis Sheehy Skeffington and Tom Kettle. Later he used to meet friends – some of the nationalists such as Michael Cusack and Arthur Griffith he had met earlier at a shop called An Stad – in Davy Byrne's pub in Duke Street or in Fanning's pub in Lincoln Place, or in the Dolphin Hotel, or in a room set aside for them in the Bailey Restaurant, then a chop-house, also in Duke Street, where his appearances were greeted with eager expectancy of some quip, story, limerick or impromptu verse. Among this group of friends were George Redding, who worked in Guiness's brewery, and Neil Montgomery, a future film censor, both of whom wrote witty, largely unpublished poetry. The Bailey was a place where James Stephens has recorded that he heard for the first time poetry spoken of 'with the assured carelessness with which a carpenter talks of his planks and of the chairs and tables and oddments he will make of them'.

Exuberant wit could clothe most serious discussion: as a medical student Gogarty had adopted a jesting mask to confront the ugly realities of poverty, illness and death, and his wit later illuminated his hospital teaching. Verbal sallies could overflow into writing. The telephone system was not widespread nor was it used freely, but the post was surprisingly fast and reliable. (Letters posted before midday in a Dublin suburb would be delivered in the city or another suburb in the afternoon of the same day, or in London by the next morning's first delivery) and letter writing was a natural habit, a continuation of conversation. Some Dubliners went further than enclosing verses in their letters, they wrote entire letters to each other in verse. (As late as the nineteen-forties Sealy Jeffares, a sixth cousin of ours who was then nearing the end of his career as Secretary of the Royal Irish Academy of Music, used at times to invite my sister, then studying at the Academy, to a dinner or concert, the invitation usually cast in the form of a witty verse letter. My father would occasionally break into verse in a letter to my sister or myself. And many Dubliners in the Victorian and Edwardian period made up their own verses when asked to contribute to an autograph book.) Gogarty's are good examples of this genre, and some of them are included in the present edition. No matter that they can seem slapdash at times; they were unpremeditated, written down hastily, and unrevised; They reveal the writer's darting, mercurially associative flow of thought; they give us some idea of the lively exchange of ideas, the jesting, the typically Irish teasing (which is often a disguised expression of affection), the sheer enjoyment of literary allusion, of verbal dexterity; and they convey hints of what good Dublin conversation could be, before its practitioners aged and produced performances, economically repeated set piece jests and anecdotes. Gogarty's verse letters and casual *ad hominem* verses have a one-off energy; he was a very busy man with many interests outside his successful medical practice, and was not given to polishing up everything that exploded out of his inventive imagination. As a result, many of his early unpublished poems have a captivating spontaneity about them, notably those written in his medical student days, at what could be called the Martello tower period of his life when he had lived in the tower with its nine foot thick stone walls at Sandycove. Here he enjoyed swimming in the Forty Foot Hole, as several unpublished poems record, and he and his friends drank in the Arch, a pub kept by 'watery-eyed Murray'. An invitation to James Starkey conveys his desire to share the pleasures of Sandycove:

> To leave Rathmines and come down to the sea
> I would persuade thee, Starkey, with these lines,
> So that men won't forget me who got thee
> To leave Rathmines.
>
> Here green trees drink the sea-blue air, and we
> May look at rain or mountain when it shines,
> And it will shine for me, if thou'll agree
> To leave Rathmines.

A word is necessary here about Gogarty's friendship with Joyce who stayed briefly in the tower (which should be known as Gogarty's rather than Joyce's tower), who never forgave Gogarty for trying to help him and obviously seems to have resented Gogarty's later professional and financial success. Joyce's attitudes to Gogarty have been assumed by American critics – notably Richard Ellmann, who completely failed to do Gogarty justice not only in his life of Joyce but in his biased review of Ulick O'Connor's evocative, eminently readable pioneering biography, *Oliver St. John Gogarty: a Poet and his Times* (1964). These views have been given undue weight by subsequent critics who regard Gogarty as if he were merely Joyce's malicious literary construct in *Ulysses*, Buck Mulligan. Ellmann's inability to understand Gogarty and present him fairly has, however, been convincingly exposed by James Carens in his study of Gogarty's poetry and prose, *Surpassing Wit* (1979) and by J. B. Lyons in his admirable, discerning and detailed biography, *Oliver St. John Gogarty The Man of Many Talents* (1980).

What emerges from the fact of these pro-Joyce anti-Gogarty attitudes, so ably refuted by Carens and Lyons, is that it is difficult for those who have not grown up in or been on the fringe of Dublin's literary and artistic life (as it flourished between the 1890s and the First World War and continued, though much less vitally, in the early puritanical decades of the Irish Free State up to the Second World War), to understand not only Gogarty himself but the society in which he grew up and in which he became such a significant figure. Some critics have either not read him with unbiased attitudes, accepting Joyce's savage fictional portrait as a true one, or are lacking in independent critical appreciation, or, perhaps, may not even have read him at all. What is needed is an ability to understand the fundamental seriousness beneath the surface flippancy of Dublin conversation, to fathom Gogarty's own attitudes beneath the ironic jesting mask. His often savage wit, which portrayed directly, indignantly and convincingly his hatred of unnecessary suffering, of poverty, and of the endemic ill health created by the festering conditions of Dublin's overcrowded slums, disguised many kindnesses and generosities.

Just as the nature of Gogarty's complex character has been mis-represented by some critics to the detriment of his literary reputation, so his published poetry has been neglected by the explicators of the Ph.D. circus. He is perhaps not sufficiently solemn for them. He did not want to run the risk of boring anyone, and in 'The Forge' brought a cavalier insouciance into play:

> No wonder Pegasus cast a shoe
> When I succumbed to the English curse
> Of mixing philosophy up with verse.
> I can imagine a poet teaching;
> But who can imagine a poet preaching?

He lacks the complexities and ambiguities of modernism and so he doesn't lend himself to long footnotes. He writes not for an academic audience but for readers in general; he is not afraid of using capitals and exclamation marks liberally and mentioning, in a way unfashionable now, Death and Love. He wants an immediate impact; he is direct not oblique; as he puts it in 'The Forge':

> 'I know right well that a song should be
> Airy and light as the leaf of a tree'.

This is the blend of Herrick-like lyricist and Roman satirist in his poetic makeup. True, as Vivian Mercier remarked, he can use the clichés of classical poetry, but classical references, like Biblical or literary allusions, came naturally to him; they were a convenient shorthand for him and for those who shared his intellectual background.

They were more immediately effective than the symbolism that Yeats constructed out of the less well-known clichés of Blake, Swedenborg and Boehme as well as Irish mythology, for that symbolism made Yeats's poetry difficult for many of his contemporaries to understand. How well, how effectively, Gogarty deployed his classical echoes, notably in the stoicism of his poems on death which led James Stephens to praise him as the sole example of a classical poet writing anywhere. Stephens thought Gogarty would not be praised as he should be until about fifty years after his death.

Gogarty kept his private life private, permitting only very rarely indeed what we now realise are the barest of hints in a few poems about his married life and fatherhood. So, no need for the bucket excavators of biographical exegesis – though some water divining may be in order. Gogarty himself realised this, briefly annotating with a non-Irish audience in mind such matters as the Irish Academy of Letters, or Boss Croker or Glenasmole. What is The Ward, a reader may ask, or Ben Edair? And those not brought up in New Jersey may need to know the location of Brielle and Manasquan. The kind of annotation required is mainly factual and necessitated by the passage of time, or by a need to know some of the Irish or, particularly, Dublin references to people, places or events.

An image in an unpublished poem, for instance, refers (p. 399) to the elephant which was (and still is) an image projecting over the doorway of a shop at the corner of Dawson and Nassau streets. Beatrice Elvery, who appears in the poem, was a member of the Elvery family which owned the shop; she had been an art student (later, as Lady Glenavy, she became known as a distinguished painter) in Paris with her sister, with Estella Solomons, who married 'Seamus O'Sullivan', and with Cissie Beckett, who married one of the twin Sinclair brothers, William ('Boss' or 'The Beard' or 'Sink' in various poems). What of the teasing poems about the Sinclair brothers, who had an antique shop in Nassau Street? This needs some comment. It was Gogarty's apparent reference to them that prompted the libel action brought against him by Henry Morris (Harry) Sinclair in June 1937, his brother having died a few weeks earlier. Gogarty lost it (with Samuel Beckett giving evidence on behalf of Sinclair, his uncle by marriage) because of his quoting an allegedly anti-Semitic poem about the brothers in his autobiographical *As I Was Going Down Sackville Street* (1937), a poem not written by himself but by another Dublin wit, George Redding. All this needs probing, for there was obviously a habit among Gogarty's friends of making jokes at the brothers' expense. (Jocose unpublished poems about William are included in this edition). Was William Sinclair aware of this unkind jesting? It is likely, given the fact that Gogarty had earlier published such poems as 'To a Clever Little Lecher', 'To a Bearded Dealer in Old Objects of Art' and 'The Dandelion', and, given the tightly knit social life of Dublin, that he was, for before they left for Germany, where they lived between the two world wars, he and his wife kept a kind of permanent party going in their cottage on Howth Hill where poets and painters gathered 'and all the freaks and oddities as well'. He may even have enjoyed, or, at least, tolerated the badinage. F. R. Higgins, then a Director of the Abbey Theatre, said in evidence at the court case that he had heard Gogarty reciting the lines in question to the Sinclair brothers who had roared with laughter at them. But the lines included in *As I Was Going Down Sackville Street* had obviously gone too far, and William, when Gogarty recited Redding's lines to him in 1933, said he would sue if they were published. The friendship hardly argues anti-Semitism on Gogarty's part so much as careless disregard for the effect of the two caustic passages cited in the trial.

Gogarty's friendships are well revealed in his dashing letters and indeed particularly so in his verse epistles. A gregarious man, he liked being in the company of his friends. He wanted responses. He wanted a two-way traffic of communication (as, among others, his letters to Joyce reveal). He particularly valued friendships which stimulated his wit, his literary sensibility. For instance, his letters to G. K. A. Bell, a friend of his Oxford days, later Bishop of Chichester (see the limerick on p. 352) echo his then strong admiration for Swinburne, whose influence is clear in some of his early verse. He tailored the style of his letters to their recipients. His letters to the future bishop, for instance, are more discreet than those to, say, James Starkey, which are decidedly sprightly, Gogarty having no need to restrain his exuberant mockery and bawdiness when writing to him. His attitudes to his friends were genial, despite his irresistible ability to mock them. In 1920, for instance, when he removed Yeats's tonsils in the morning he discussed literature with the poet while he remained conscious, then came back six times at intervals between seeing patients in the afternoon, to suggest different versions of suitable dying speeches. He could not only parody Yeats's poems but laugh at his mannerisms and imitate them while revering him and being influenced by him into shedding outmoded poetic conventions: inversions, archaisms, which could be used as labour-saving devices, and 'hast', 'shalt', 'thou', 'thee', 'wert', etc. (Yeats, however, did not cure him of a habit of excessive capitalisation). Small wonder there are echoes between the work of the two poets in the 'twenties and 'thirties: there are many parallels in subject matter, form and imagery — as, for instance, in Yeats's 'Lullaby' and Gogarty's 'Good Luck', in their poems upon the myth of Leda and the Swan, in their employment of Europa and the Bull, and in their use of the coins from Syracuse and Sicily, not to mention their bawdy verses. In and after their senatorial days Gogarty frequently shared with Yeats the latest, often scabrous Dublin stories which could hardly be written down. Yeats complained in *On the Boiler* (1938) that neither he nor Gogarty, 'with our habit of outrageous conversation', could get near the Free State Ministers.

Some of Gogarty's own outrageous unpublished limericks are included in the present edition. They floated freely in the tides of Dublin conversation, and some of his obscene – and generally highly amusing – bawdy poems were recited, or sometimes sung, at medical students' parties largely. They remained in circulation for decades (I myself heard some of them recited in the nineteen-forties).

Only some few fragments of his 230 stanza-long Sindbad poem, a parody of Coleridge, now remain and are included here. 'Sindbad' recounted the adventures of Sindbad the sailor, so full of mercury as a result of his sexual excesses that it was inadvisable for him to stand near a fire since the mercury rose in his spine as if in a barometer, and having struck the base of his cerebral cortex rendered him unconscious. When on board ship his load of mercury affected the ship's compass, and he was thrown overboard, to be swallowed by a whale, on whom the mercury has adverse effects:

> And where that whale had defecated
> A continent is concentrated
> From all the food evacuated
> Which made no mean land
> And from its colour when located
> They called it Greenland.

Perhaps someone who heard the poem and is endowed with a long memory may yet regurgitate all of it, though the possibility of this happening lessens year by year. There may even be a full written version somewhere, for Gogarty seems to have contemplated its publication*. Its loss may be considerable for Gogarty's wit was often at its sharpest when deployed in Rabelaisian manner.

Enough about the unpublished material, then; what is to be said of the published work? It is worth remembering that in 1938 the *Times Literary Supplement* reviewer appreciated 'the pure and chiselled forms of his best poems' and that in 1932 Iain Hamilton praised Gogarty's ability 'to bring a vastness of passion under control, working from the surface of the rough

---

*In a letter of 14 June 1906 he referred to the 'American Edition' as being out, but this may have been a joke. It was in this letter that he announced the poem had reached 230 stanzas. In it a doctor from Aberdeen gives his informal views on life and belief (see L, p. 94).

matrix towards the potential perfection at the core'. I commend the introductory comments of AE appended to the *Selected Poems* (1933) and *Collected Poems* (1951) and Yeats's introduction to the latter volume, for they remain balanced and valid. Horace Reynolds' remarks in both volumes convey a valuable outsider's view of Gogarty's Renaissance personality as it was expressed in Ireland. He appreciated Gogarty's liking for fast driving; Gogarty had early realised the freedom conferred by a fast car, buying his vast house, Renvyle, in Connemara cheaply because of its apparent remoteness in 1917. His Mercedes and his butter coloured 40-50 hp Rolls Royce got him there from Dublin relatively quickly and easily. A companion vignette expands Reynolds' view of him; it is part of a letter from Ruth Pollexfen written during the First World War to John Butler Yeats describing Gogarty in his prime in the days when, as well as swimming and riding early in the mornings on Sandymount Strand, he could slip out of Dublin up the hills after doing his hospital rounds, to lunch in a pub, the Lamb Doyle, enjoying the fresh mountain air and the superb views of the city and the sea below. The letter describes a picnic in the Dublin mountains: three cars were loaded with the Gogartys' friends, among them Augustus John and the sculptor Albert Power (who came to blows at the end of the picnic) and Starkey, spotted walking in Rathmines en route and added to the party. Whiskey and champagne flowed, so did the rain, but after a severe shower Gogarty, 'who had been sitting still, jumped up calling out "now for the elevation of the Host" altho' he and most of the company were R.C. this profanity was greeted with roars of laughter'. And then encouraged by the applause he hit an officer (home from the Dardanelles) on the head with a loaf of bread saying 'there's the roll of honour for you'.

Gogarty was himself a brave man. Apart from the intrepidity needed to become a highly successful racing cyclist when he was a student – for it was a violent sport with heavy betting leading to aggression on the part of both competitors and spectators – he plunged fearlessly into the Liffey and into the sea on several occasions to rescue drowning men (in 1898 he was awarded the Bronze Medal of the Royal Humane Society for one of these rescues and subsequently received two vellum testimonials from the Society*), acts of which he never spoke. His conduct during the Easter Rising, the Anglo-Irish War and the Civil War (especially his own escape from death at the hands of the Republican gunmen who had taken him as a hostage, intending to kill him, by leaping into the Liffey, ice-cold in January, and swimming to safety); and his later attempts – vain because of his age – to join the forces in the Second World War

---

*cases 29461 (1898), 36350 (1899) and 31350 (1901).

indicate his contempt for danger. His bravery was of a stoic kind. It found expression in 'All the Pictures', the 'admiration, half amused' of how someone had received the news of imminent death:

> 'I have seen all the pictures' said
> My patient. 'And I do not care.'

An impressive feature of Gogarty's poetic technique was his ability to treat large issues, to reach out of personal thought or experience into general ideas in such poems as 'Sunt apud infernos tot milia formosarum' with its picture of the Underworld of 'Death's kind metamorphosis':

> Enlarged and free, the wings of Rhyme
> Cannot outreach its purple air;
> The generations of all Time
> And all the lovely Dead are there.

Gogarty's views on death explain the need for valour in facing it, as in 'To Death' or 'Marcus Curtius', though there is consolation to be found in the thought that 'Death may be very gentle'

> Death may be very gentle after all
> He turns his face away from arrogant knights
> Who fling themselves against him in their fights;
> But to the loveliest he loves to call.
> And he has with him those whose ways were mild
> And beautiful; and many a little child.

The age-old balance of Love and Death is economically stressed in 'And So On'

> This is nothing new at all:
> We have heard it all before:
> Beauty one side of the Wall,
> On the other side, the War.
> Love and Death; and no denying
> These things do not end by dying.

Facing the end of human life bravely is defensive perhaps, but clear-sighted in 'Palinode'. He is not, apparently, perturbed about what happens after death, as Yeats was in such a poem, say, as 'The Man and the Echo', nor does Gogarty ask himself the same kind of self-accusing questions. Instead he can look with some appreciative pleasure at his present achievement:

> I have been full of mirth;
> I have been full of wine;
> And I have trod the earth
> As if it all were mine;
> And laughed to bring to birth
> The lighter lyric line.

He sees this state, however, as lying under the shadow of age:

> A few years more to flow
> From miracle-working Time
> And surely I shall grow
> Incapable of rhyme.
> Sans Love and Song, and so
> An echo of a mime.

It is against Time that he, like the seventeenth century metaphysicals, sets Love. Behind the light-hearted poems, often Horatian in tone, to various Nindes, Lydias, Ethnes or Hermiones runs the wingèd chariot, treated with some whimsicality in 'Begone, Sweet Ghost'. Marvell may have exerted an influence on 'Fresh Fields', its sense of wonder matching his green thought in a green shade with its emphasis on 'green and gold' and 'gold and green', its simple translucency, its skilful alliteration emphasising the repetitions of 'gazing' and 'springing' and 'meadows', the 'wonderful and wordless thoughts' that give rise to brilliantly compressed elasticity.

The metaphysical element is less obviously present in early poems such as 'My Love is Dark' and 'Gaze on Me'; it moves to Herrick's more easy-going mood in 'To the Maids Not to Walk in the Wind':

> When the wind blows, walk not abroad,
> For, Maids, you may not know
> The mad, quaint thoughts which incommode
> Me when the winds do blow.
>
> What though the tresses of the treen
> In doubled beauty move,
> With silver added to their green,
> They were not made for Love.
>
> But when your clothes reveal your thighs
> And surge about your knees,
> Until from foam you seem to rise,
> As Venus from the seas . . .

> Though ye are fair, it is not fair!
> Unless you will be kind,
> Till I am dead, and changed to AIR,
> O walk not in the wind!

There are glimpses of another, darker vision where the contraries of sex and love meet in one, contrasted with all the violence of an apparently contradictory metaphysical paradox. Venus can rise from the seas in 'To the Maids not to Walk in the Wind'; but while in 'Perfection' her unattainable perfect beauty is still praised, the poet has found a lady 'than perfection perfecter'. And in 'To Aphrodite' the goddess gets her come-uppance

> Venus I called you when our love began:
> And I was right; and you Pandemian.

Though delicate *amo* poems are plentiful, a true *odi* poem, the savagely intense 'To Catullus', remained unpublished; this is one of the shorter versions of it:

> Until I felt, I never knew
> What fortune she had put you through
> Who held you on Love's rack,
> How could I sympathise before
> I loved just such a lovely whore
> A whore and nymphomaniac?

There are other kinds of poems of love, the fire perhaps tempered by time, by the memory irradiating 'Thinking Long', bidding the grand-mother to recall her bands of golden hair:

> And him who told you how the light
> Burst through them when you combed them low
> With sidelong head at fall of night:
> Before that vision fades away
> Just take this message from the Past:
> ''Tis love that counteracts decay
> And lights and makes all Beauty last.'
> And wonder if the love you spared
> To starve the light-heart man of rhyme
> Has left him low and you grey-haired,
> Though you are old, before your time.

It is possible that 'With a Coin from Syracuse', a poem echoing the
passion of some Yeatsian poems about Olivia Shakespear, may be written
about Gogarty's wife. No matter whether or not, it is an elegant poem
with a supreme consciousness of the beauty of line in the human body.
The subject of this poem is arguable; not so the well known, often
anthologised and sometimes misinterpreted 'Golden Stockings':

> Golden stockings you had on
> In the meadow where you ran;
> And your little knees together
> Bobbed like pippins in the weather,
> When the breezes rush and fight
> For those dimples of delight,
> And they dance from the pursuit,
> And the leaf looks like the fruit.
>
> I have many a sight in mind
> That would last if I were blind;
> Many verses I could write
> That would bring me many a sight.
> Now I only see but one,
> See you running in the sun,
> And the gold-dust coming up
> From the trampled buttercup.

Gogarty glossed the poem in 'Poets and Little Children', *Intimations*
(1950) and his comments show the way he wrote some of his poems:

> Here is a piece which sets a little girl running in a meadow golden
> with buttercups. She is made into the spirit and personification of
> the golden things in Nature, the gold of the meadows, the gold of
> the fruit, the gold of the leaf. And to give these things life she is
> made to run in the sunshine. And she is isolated by the simple
> device on the part of the poet of closing his eyes and seeing in the
> mind's eye only her. Thus is the stillness produced which the
> powder of the buttercups can dust with gold.

   His daughter's comment is more direct. She describes a summer
evening at Ticknock with her parents – Gogarty liked to drive up there
to see the sunlight on the granite and get the view of Dublin Bay from
the Dublin mountains, she explains, and goes on to tell how she was
wearing a pair of white sand-shoes 'and I was running in the long grass
and when I came back to my parents, my shoes were completely yellow,

which upset me a little. My father explained to me how it was the pollen off the buttercups that had covered my shoes; my mother said 'You can brush it off, and it was that that started the poem "Golden Stockings".'

'Back from the Country' is another poem with domestic origins, a good example of affectionate teasing:

> How I hid my laughter
> Fearing to offend you,
> Back from the country
> With your apple cheeks!

Other poems, too, have pleasing touches of domesticity, for while 'The Blackbird in the Town' celebrates the bird's mellifluous refrain, 'In a Backyard after Rain' bases itself upon an awareness of huddled houses and squalid gardens, and 'Just One Glimpse' conveys a sadness that the city streets can't be removed, with their houses between, their slums and stores, and instead the previous scenery of rocks and springs, oaks and roses be glimpsed just once. City life, as opposed to country, is sometimes found lacking. In 'Angels' for instance, the social conscience and desire for reform that prompted not only his plays but other practical activity emerges in his desire to

> Break down the tenement
> Walls that surround them;
> Lead out from festering
> Lane and back garden
> The heirs to the kingdom
> To sunlight, to highland,
> To winds blowing over
> Green fields.

He attacks in verse as well as in his plays

> The cynical largesse
> Of hospital-builders
> And all its bad conscience

The same dislike of the unnatural life of cities informs some of his American poems. While 'High Above Ohio' and 'Dawn in Vermont' praise the scenery, 'To a Friend in the Country' is based primarily on a desire to escape the intolerable din of New York. Gogarty, however, needed the stimulus of the city, and thought his ideal life would alternate between town and country (for him, the country included the seaside, as at Renvyle).

He could capture suburban atmosphere well. 'In the Garden', for instance, celebrates the momentary blossoms of spring, their momentariness reminding him of mortality. Unable to endure the tension of being aware of Beauty's implacable procession, he ends by striking an attitude: 'So I go where Beauty goes, I care not to return'. 'The Plum Tree by the House' is another garden poem which builds up to a contemplation of a moment of joy with a characteristically deflationary comment in the midst of it:

> There must be things which never shall
> Be matched or made symmetrical
> On Earth or in the Air;
> Branches that Chinese draughtsmen drew,
> Where none may find an equal to,
> Unless he enter there
> Where none may live – and more's the pity! –
> The Perfect, the Forbidden City
> That's built – Ah, God knows where!

Gogarty recorded his delight in spring in many poems which sketch in its blossoms, its colours, its scents and sounds before moving on to the reflections they prompt in him. 'Spring in Dublin' is an early poem on the subject, contained in *Secret Springs of Dublin Song*. Others are 'Suburban Spring' and 'The Eternal Recurrence'. 'The Apple Tree' praises creation with awed exuberance:

> What can we say but, 'Glory be!'
> When God breaks out in an apple tree.

'Sung in Spring', however, is more a poem of acceptance, bound up with Gogarty's delight in the concepts of sailing, movement, travel. This delight he expressed most memorably in the wonder of 'The Ship', a desire to get away from gloom and wet into a summer world elsewhere. But, after rejection of the idea of leaving, there succeeds the subsequent James Elroy Flecker-like romantic invocation of the ship's voyage back to Valparaiso, that 'white umbrageous city set beneath the Andes'.

> Over the golden pools of sleep
> She went long since with gilded spars;
> Into the night empurpled deep,
> And traced her legend on the stars.

The poet then hopes, optimistically, that he will have another chance.

(Kevin O'Shiel remarked that Gogarty had 'the Greek illusion about life going on forever and you're always young' and apropos his stay in America, he'd say, 'Oh, yes, I'm coming back, definitely.') The last line of the final stanza is typical of Gogarty's self-mockery, his realistic undercutting:

> But she will come for me once more
> And I shall see that city set,
> The mountainous, Pacific shore –
> By God, I half believe it yet!

Overflowing energy informs that exultantly impressive poem of praise 'Perennial', prompted by seeing an old cherry tree in an empty lot: unlike T. S. Eliot's paperstrewn lots this one is covered in April snow. And unlike Eliot's lugubrosities this poem's final lines reach an *O Altitudo* of joyousness at the miracle of creation

> I feel the soul within me sing:
> By God, I'm grateful for the Spring
> That makes all fading seem illusion,
> The foam, the fullness, the profusion;
> For every lovely thing misplaced;
> The bloom, the brightness and the waste!

A yearning for brightness and sunshine recurs in many poems, as in 'Send for the South'. 'If Sight were Sound' has a finely evocative use of alliteration and assonance in its richly textured lines describing

> the Summer silken tented,
> Drowsed by Paynim perfumes in its blue pavilion.

Like so many Irish writers Gogarty enjoyed writing about places, and those poems about Irish places, of which there are many, blend their visual imagery with the sounds of the place names, as in 'Glenasmole', the Gaelic for 'the Valley of the Thrushes', as in Bohernabreena, 'the Hostel by the wayside boher or road', evocative also of the past, the inland raids from the Lochlann galleys*. This linkage of places with their pasts, as in the medieval Irish *dinnshenchas* tradition, makes the poems

---

*His note refers to the Irish saga 'that tells how some Scandinavian marauders ambushed then burned a hostel, Bohernaabreena, on the River Dodder near Dublin in which sat a remnant of the super-human, half-magical race of Gaelic warriors which the old poets love to describe. The spear of the leader had to be kept cool in a cauldron, for it grew to a white heat at the approach of battle'.

more than descriptive pieces. 'New Bridge' prompts thoughts of those who built the Liffey's oldest bridge, while in 'Liffey Bridge' the poet moves from contemplation of the city's steeples vanishing into the dusk to condensed images of the time before the arrival of the Danes, back to the legendary Irish hero Finn. The effect of Norse and then Norman raiders is built into 'High Tide at Malahide' while an atmospheric poem, 'Fog Horns', shifts from present day fog horns in Dublin Bay to the war horns of those invading Danes who, according to the chronicles,

> Took a very great prey
> Of women from Howth
> They seem to imply
> That the women were shy,
> That the women were loath
> To be taken from Howth
> From bushy and thrushy sequestering Howth

The genetic effects of the mingling of races, he continues, can still be perceived in contemporary Dublin, his historical perspective ranging backward and forward about the Bay.

These poems of place are most effective when in compressed form. 'The Dublin-Galway Train' moves over-slowly across Ireland's central plain, whereas 'Connemara', a brief poem, seizes economically upon the real partition of Ireland, divided by the Shannon into East and West. 'Limestone and Water', akin to Yeats's 'Meditations in Time of Civil War', captures the brevity of hard won apparent peace:

> Wherever Life is made secure
> Beauty is gardened to become
> As lovely as its walls are sure.

The poem moves to a visual image, one virtually to be expected in this context in many places in Ireland (as in the case of Yeats's Thoor Ballylee):

> The castle by the shallow ford:
> In ruin but the upright line
> Above the tangle keeps its word:
> In death the unbroken discipline!
> And O, what great well-being went
> To build the enduring battlement!

Places can also be enriched by being associated with contemplative moods, as in 'The Mill at Naul', or, half seen, half imagined through closed eyes, can create a concentrated picture, as in 'The Waveless Bay'. 'Between Brielle and Manasquan', is the most effective of his recordings of American places (for he is not so successful with American scenes as with Irish). As the sand silted up the New England ports the poem fills up with the detailed belongings, the curiosities brought home by the now marooned old sea captains in their white painted houses, objects stored in some old store:

> Old compasses, chronometers,
> And here a sextant ornamented,
> A binnacle and carven wares,
> A captain's spy glass, rather dented,
> A keg that raxed a pirate's throttle,
> A schooner full rigged in a bottle:
>
> Weapons with silver horn inlaid;
> Blue glass the dealer says is Bristol's,
> Carved shells and bits of Chinese jade;
> Two old, brass-barrelled, flint-lock pistols,
> And, if these fail to take your fancy,
> A figurehead called *Spumy Nancy*.

This listing of objects is akin to the techniques employed by the Australian poet Kenneth Slessor, whose graphic 'Five Bells' has the same awareness

> Of the lapsing, unsoilable,
> Whispering sea

that brings Gogarty's 'Ringsend' to its superbly quiet closure.

'Ringsend', however, and, to a lesser degree, a less known sonnet, also given the title 'Ringsend', have a unique quality about them that stems from Gogarty's knowledge of the Dublin quayside and of Monto, or Nighttown, the red light area which used to lie between Gloucester Street and Montgomery Street. That knowledge came from his days as a medical student, for medical students abroad on their healing errands could get drink at all hours of the night in the back parlours of the Kips, the licensed brothels which ranged from the smart in Tyrone Street to the extremely sordid in Mabbot Street or Railway Street. Lines about Mrs Mack illustrate the relationship between medical students and the brothel keepers, and the status of the medical students, well aware of the dangers to their health upstairs:

> O there goes Mrs Mack;
> She keeps a house of imprudence,
> She keeps an old back parlour
> For us poxy medical students,
> To show, to show,
> That we are medical students.
> To show, to show,
> That we are medical students
> To show, to show,
> That we medical students don't give a damn.

In Cavendish Row was the Hay Hotel run by Maria, a former cook of the Gogartys married to Stephen, their former butler, after Gogarty's father had discovered them *in flagrante delicto* and they had been summarily dismissed. It was called the Hay Hotel because hay, kept in one of the windows, was available for cab horses while the cabbies and their fares were inside. An earlier poem 'When the Clearance was intended to the Kips' deals with the demolition of Tyrone Street, but 'The Hay Hotel', a ballade, prompted by the wiping out of the Kips in 1924, provides a larger, longer vista of Dublin's strange otherworld of vice. Here, then, are some of the Kips' characters memoralised: Fresh Nellie, the tough Mrs Mack, May Oblong, and Piano Mary. The last prompted a poem about faithfulness, supposedly by herself, written in 1936 in Yeats's Crazy Jane manner with echoes of Dowson's faithfulness to Cynara, in *his* fashion:

> He lay upon me head to tail
> And wriggled in his joy
> But it was all to no avail –
> I'm true to Billy Boy!
>
> He put me standing on my head
> More muscle to supply
> But little cared I what he did
> I'm true to Billy Boy!

A bookmaker, Dan Leahy, persuaded Gogarty to extend 'The Hay Hotel's' list, to include and celebrate Becky Cooper, and he obliged with an unpublished stanza:

> Shall Becky Cooper be forgot
> Have I forgotten Liverpool Kate
> And all the foam she used to frot

> Were she one night celebrate?
> I often tried to dam that spate
> When 'Fuck me like a horse!' she'd yell
> And who was I to remonstrate
> Before I sought the Hay Hotel.

The best of these poems is the hitherto unpublished 'The Old Pianist' (p. 456) another riotous ballade, about a supposed visit of the Prince of Wales to Mrs Mack's establishment. The madam is infuriated when Fresh Nellie transforms the Prince's visit from a social to a sexual occasion. The envoi addresses a ribald query to the 'Sweet Prince':

> Has Nellie put you back in splints;
> And will you tell the Jersey lily
> That Dublin can, at all events,
> Take London on and fuck it silly?

Rabelais was a strong influence and while hints of Dowson and Yeats may certainly be there in some of these poems there are also many echoes of other poets elsewhere in Gogarty's work and, particularly, many direct parodies, for Gogarty and his raffish student friends, Joyce and Elwood for instance, were constantly vying with each other in parodying. 'We quoted', he wrote expansively in *It Isn't This Time of Year at All* (1954), 'and parodied *all* the poets'. Swinburne's 'Atalanta in Calydon' was the basis for Gogarty's 'The Death of Diogenes, the Doctor's Dog' which good humouredly imitated Mahaffy's lisp as well as mocking his talk of his travels in Greece. The best known of Gogarty's parodies may be his use of Keats's sonnet 'On first looking into Chapman's Homer', with its evocative last line 'Silent, upon a peak in Darien', to create 'On first looking through Kraft-Ebing's *Psychopathia Sexualis*' with its echoing conclusion 'Potent, behind a cart, with Mary Ann'.

There are many instances of the solemn or excessively serious being overthrown. Here, for instance, is the first stanza of an impressive but very Victorian stanza of Arthur O'Shaughnessy's 'Ode'

> We are the music-makers,
> And we are the dreamers of dreams,
> Wandering by lone sea-breakers,
> And sitting by desolate streams;
> World–losers and world-forsakers,
> On whom the pale moon gleams
> Yet we are the movers and shakers
> Of the world for ever, it seems.

Gogarty seizes upon the opportunity for mockery:

> We are the masturbators
> We are the dreamers of dreams
> Spending in secretive places,
> Our totally purposeless streams
> And one with a mind at leisure
> Can roger an ancient Queen
> And make from a moment's pleasure
> A map on the damascene.

His parody of the last stanza of Richard Lovelace's 'To Althea from Prison'

> Stone walls do not a prison make
> Nor iron bars a cage;
> Minds innocent and quiet take
> That for an hermitage;
> If I have freedom in my love,
> And in my soul am free;
> Angels alone that soar above
> Enjoy such liberty

keeps closer to the original in order to invert it:

> Stone walls do not a prison make
> Nor iron bars a cage
> If in a tilt for sweet Love's sake
> The slavey will engage
> If I have freedom in my love
> Who in my love am free
> The connoisseur who rules above
> Knows no such liberty

The irreverence continues in the footnote glossing the connoisseur as 'Jehovah who collected foreskins'. It extended to Yeats's 'The Pity of Love' in a poem written in 1904 'from the Bard Gogarty to the Wandering Aengus' (Aengus was a character in Yeats's poems, the Gaelic God of Love, a name Gogarty sometimes applied to Joyce, in a letter to whom the parody was included):

### To Elwood Poxed

A pity beyond all telling
Is hid in the heart of love

As soon as you press it well in
As soon as you give it a shove,
In the house where the whores are dwelling
– Unless it is wrapped in a glove –
A little Hunterian swelling
Poxes the part that they love

Another parody of Yeats was contained in another letter to Joyce:

*'William Dara thinks of the sin
of his childhood and is sorrowful'*

If you wait till the mystic heron be flown
    With the one eye and three toes
I shall sit and sigh till the mouse-grey moss
    Obscures the old oak stump
For I a child by the market cross
    Thought of a rabbit's rump.

Gogarty's notes to this poem parody Yeats's style of annotation: 'The three toes represent Pain, Desire and Fear which figure in the poetry of the bird. The bird is Love resting in the above quotation. The one eye represents the retrospective view of life etc.'. Lady Gregory's Kiltartan style also lent itself to easy parody in various letters of the period.

Gogarty's attitude to classical themes was generally more respectful, though he could not resist poking fun at academe, tellingly contrasting art and academic comment in 'New Forms'. The praise in 'Virgil', however, sets the tone for his poems that use such images as Troy or Helen as in 'On Troy', 'Tell me now' or 'Thrush in Ash'. Homer has his praise in 'Anachronism', but thoughts of Virgil are linked with the Dublin scenery, for these are triggered off by seeing an ilex by the banks of the Dodder in 'Sub Ilice'. He achieves the same easy transition of thought in 'The Isles of Greece' which is light-heartedly hedonistic but firmly ironic:

Sappho's was, with all its Girton
Girls, the fairest isle of Greece

Deeper feeling pervades 'Good Luck', a neatly encapsulated poem. Gogarty's treatment of classical legend is, however, at its most pleasing in 'Leda and the Swan' where his fancy plays gently with the theme. Leda defies her mother's injunction not to go bathing, taking the opportunity, in a lonely place, of having a swim

> Lolling in the water,
> Lazily uplifting
> Limbs that on the surface
> Whitened into snow;
> Leaning on the water,
> Indolently drifting,
> Hardly any faster
> Than the foamy bubbles go

The encounter with the swan is handled with a delicate humour:

> What was it she called him:
> Goosey-goosey gander?
> For she knew no better
> Way to call a swan

The tone shifts as Leda tells her story:

> Of the tales that daughters
> Tell their poor old mothers,
> Which by all accounts are
> Often very odd;
> Leda's was a story
> Stranger than all others.
> What was there to say but:
> Glory be to God?

Then, however, with a masterly, easy and natural transition, comes the contemplation, of causes and effects, of the eggs:

> Who would dream there lay there
> All that Trojan brightness;
> Agamemnon murdered;
> And the mighty Twins?

Gogarty, of course, had reason for his particular interest in swans. 'To the Liffey with the Swans' which accompanied his releasing two swans on to the Liffey to record his gratitude for his escape from the gunmen parallels Yeats's 'Leda and the Swan'.* Gogarty's has a more exuberant, buoyant ending:

---

*The relationships between the two poets' Leda poems are explored well in Giorgio Melchiori, *The Whole Mystery of Art: Pattern into Poetry in the Work of W. B. Yeats* (1960), pp. 73–114 and in James Carens, *Surpassing Wit* (1979), pp. 97–99.

> Keep you these calm and lovely things,
> And float them on your clearest water;
> For one would not disgrace a King's
> Transformed, beloved and buoyant daughter.
>
> And with her goes this sprightly swan,
> A bird of more than royal feather,
> With alban beauty clothed upon:
> O keep them fair and well together!
>
> As fair as was that doubled Bird,
> By love of Leda so besotten,
> That she was all with wonder stirred,
> And the Twin Sportsmen were begotten!

In praising Gogarty's poem 'To Petronius Arbiter' Padraic Colum paid tribute to the fund of beauty from which Gogarty could quote: in praising his knowledge of Pindar he continued

> And then there were lots of people in Dublin at the time who had a tremendous verbal feeling for poetry, but Gogarty was distinguished by the fact that it was not only in English that he had this fund of poetry but in Latin, in Greek [he also knew Dante well and quoted him in Italian].

His classical reading no doubt made him aware of the pleasure of writing to and about friends – though he did not have a Ciceronian purpose, his was no studied correspondence written for future fame. The best known of his poems in this genre is probably his appreciation of Tyrrell, 'Aeternae Lucis Redditor', a threnody not only for his friend the classical scholar but for the Virgilian calm before the storm of the First World War, the ten line stanzas welded together with emphatic, stately rhyming. Very different but equally successful is his celebration of 'Farrell O'Reilly', his father's friend, seen through a boy's memories, the man's character sharply etched in anecdotal flashbacks. Sharp comment sometimes remained unpublished as in the lines on John Eglinton (the librarian, W. K. Magee) quoted on p. 359, and on various Dublin doctors, while George Moore was a butt in *Secret Springs of Dublin Song*. Some comments made in W. R. Rodgers, *Irish Literary Portraits* (1972) are germane, Brinsley MacNamara, for instance, describing Gogarty as apparently

> impelled by some devilish thing that was in him to say some harsh or bitter thing. But he never really meant it. There was no malice in them, none whatsoever.

He could make these remarks to people's faces; in Lady Hanson's phrase, 'he encouraged a reciprocal tongue'.

AE, however, evoked from Gogarty, as from so many of his contemporaries, an appreciative affection in the simplicity of 'To A Friend' and in the more complex layering of 'To A.E. going to America'. Poems to Augustus John, 'To my Portrait by Augustus John' and 'To Augustus John', reflect, in the first, the relationship of the poet to the painter who portrayed him, a little savagely perhaps,

> like Caesar late returned
> Exhausted from a long campaign

and, in the second, the host appreciative yet critical of his guest, his erratic driving, his moodiness, his sudden lapsing into profound gloom. These are direct poems, which remind us that John once flung a dish of nuts into Gogarty's face to stop him talking (whereas Gogarty, on getting Lord Dunsany to put up John, told the host John never drank and the guest that drink was forbidden in Dunsany Castle – and enjoyed the results).

The best of the poems to or about Yeats is very different: 'To the Poet W. B. Yeats winner of the Noble Prize 1924' is a straightforward celebratory poem (encapsulated in a later poem, 'Ars Longa') whereas one exhorting Yeats to 'Build a Fountain to commemorate his Victory' mingles with its praise a nice touch of friendly irony conveying the genuine nature of Gogarty's regard, something Mrs Yeats understood well. Someone, a typical Dubliner, attacking Gogarty, asked her if she realised that 'the man is sitting somewhere at this minute saying the most scandalous things about you?' To which she replied 'Don't you know that a man may do that and still be the most loyal friend you ever had?'

Despite the attractions of life in Dublin, Gogarty became disillusioned with the ethos of the new Ireland of the Irish Free State under de Valera's rule:

> We rose to get Ireland a Utopia
> And all we got was dev's myopia

He must also have been depressed by the way the jurors had voted in the libel action. J. B. Lyons records how it was said that a juryman had insisted 'Whatever about the Jewman, he must be made to pay for what he said about de Valera'. He left Ireland for the United States in 1939, at first thinking his stay would be temporary. His daughter later ascribed this voluntary self-exiling to his desire to see far more of the world before he died: 'He got restless and felt that time was running out for him'. Until then she thought him 'quite happy with his surgery', but 'he wanted to write'. To Austin Clarke, musing over Gogarty's decision to leave Ireland, he seemed driven by the compulsion of literary ambition.

At first he was very successful in America: and the United States did, as Denis Johnston remarked, 'provide him with a living in his last days'. While he felt perfectly free in America to write and talk as he liked, he missed the kind of company he had kept in Dublin; he lacked the stimulus that the repartee he expected there offered his often spontaneous, often reactive mercurial wit. True, he had good appreciative American friends, he liked many aspects of American life, but there had to be a lot of explaining – the common background of the intimate Dublin life was missing – and his poetic talent did not take altogether kindly to writing to suit the tastes of American editors and readers.

It was no doubt for the convenience of his readers everywhere that Gogarty grouped his poems under various headings as in the *Collected Poems*. I have followed his example in Part Three in the ordering of the unpublished poems and those attributed to him. The groupings he adopted were: Prelude; Odes and Addresses; Earth and Sea; Satires and Facetiae; Love and Beauty; Life and Death; Elegies. (It would perhaps have been more useful if he had reversed the position of Earth and Sea and Satires and Facetiae). It would also have been possible to arrange many of these poems chronologically, for Gogarty, obviously, changed and developed. But he was a poet of both varying moods and thoughts, as his own groupings suggest he realised: he was a poet who wrote in different genres. A strictly chronological arrangement, however, would not necessarily convey a sense of this versatility which makes the total impact of his work so impressive. Though Gogarty sought, perhaps paradoxically, his freedom of expression within conventional forms, he is not to be typecast; he is a recorder of the complexity which goes to being human. He told us that he had decided on having a good *and* merry life. As Denis Johnston pointed out percipiently, all his amusing conversational malice was principally conditioned 'by a desire to please his listeners not just for his own satisfaction which of course is the real distinction between a good companion and a bore'. Gogarty himself further remarked that 'One should have nothing to do with those to whom one will always seem bad'.

In his case this freedom had meant maintaining friendships with his bohemian friends while being a medical student in the tough traditions of Trinity College's medical school and the Dublin hospitals, which he recorded so well in *Tumbling in the Hay*, but at the same time becoming a friend of the classical dons Tyrrell and Mahaffy and of Macran the philosopher, not to mention becoming a successful racing cyclist. His mother's reactions to his cycling successes when she read of them in the *Irish Times* were typical of Victorian Dublin's respectable citizens. When she had enrolled him in Trinity College she had said to him 'Now that you are entered among gentlemen I hope you will never forget to behave like one'. ('A large order' remarked her son later, 'among the wild medics of those days'). Now she told him his professors would hardly find his cycling exploits a matter for congratulation. Cycling was not regarded as socially acceptable: she urged him to take up cricket or rowing. The cult of the gentleman was paramount; as John Butler Yeats remarked when his son turned down the chance of a job on a paper, despite one of the family's recurrent financial crises and despite his own inability to provide an income, 'a gentleman is not concerned with getting on'.

Gogarty had enough friends (and money) to pursue his medical studies in a leisurely way. He also had an early chameleon-like ability to fit into Dublin's very different social groups, while steadily becoming more himself, a man who later projected himself without much concern for the impression he was making. In short he became a Renaissance man whose physical fitness and energy matched his quicksilver mental processes. The prosperous ear, nose and throat surgeon was also a published poet, a recognised wit and raconteur. The Irish Free State senator was also an aviator, an archer, a hotelier. The autobiographer whose *As I Was Going Down Sackville Street* is a brilliant evocation of his Dublin life was also a novelist, and, continuously, a poet, lively, arresting and memorable. In Basil de Selincourt's phrase, 'poetry poured out of him, gallant and generous'.

Gogarty's poetry draws constantly upon an aesthetic appreciation of life's complexity and provides independent intellectual reactions to its contradictions. He blended the detachment he had learned in the classical discipline of his schooling and his subsequent delighted reading of classical authors with his medical studies and practice. He infused this often contradictory blend with the emotional impulses and instinct of his heart, timelessly lyrical in his appreciation of beauty. As an excellent raconteur he captured an audience's attention with economically strong opening lines, his cadences climaxing in effective epigrammatic endings. He held it with a flow of invention, with ideas given precise compression through imagery. He controlled through rhymes and rhythms a poem's progress to an unforgettable conclusion:

> Then do not shudder at the knife
> That Death's indifferent hand drives home,
> But with the strivers leave the strife
> Nor, after Caesar, skulk in Rome.

Read him, reader, you will enjoy him.

*A. Norman Jeffares, Fife Ness, 2001*

# Part 1

# COLLECTED POEMS
## (1951)

# PRELUDE

---

## *The Casting*

I pour in the mould of rhyme
   All that my heart would hold:
The transient light on the tower,
   The moat in its wintry gold,
Sunlight, and a passing shower,
   The gleam of your garments' fold
That baffles the eye as you pass,
Formless and lovely things
   Like speech that breaks in a laugh;
To leave them a shape with wings,
   And Time but a cenotaph.
I heat them with more than heat,
   Because they must glow in the cold;
I puddle the white-hot mass,
   And praying with words retold,
To temper Beauty from Time,
   I pour them into the mould.


## *Verse*

What should we know,
For better or worse,
Of the Long Ago,

Were it not for Verse:
What ships went down;
What walls were razed;
Who won the crown;
What lads were praised?
A fallen stone,
Or a waste of sands;
And all is known
Of Art-less lands.
But you need not delve
By the sea-side hills
Where the Muse herself
All Time fulfils,
Who cuts with his scythe
All things but hers;
All but the blithe
Hexameters.

# ODES AND ADDRESSES

---

## Ode

*Written at the request of the Irish
Government on the revival of the Tailltean
(Irish Olympic) Games*

Empyrean is the source
Of indomitable will.
God the runner to his course
Holds, and urges on until
Lips and face of blood are drained,
And the fainting limbs are numb:
Till the heart, by God sustained,
Bravely to the end is come.

By the Conflict is revealed
In a runner what is best;
By the struggle in the field,
By the speed which is the test,
By the speed that wears him down
Till the spirit alone can bear
Limbs that stagger for the crown
And the thunder in his ear.

Where are they who ran before
Under Tara's wide-eyed steep;
And the chariots that tore

Parallel the ridges deep?
Where are noble man and horse?
Ah, they both have lost the rein;
They have circled in a course
Tara shall not see again!

Aye, their hands are empty now,
And the green earth clothes their hill:
Gone the glory from the brow
And the sudden shout is still,
Blown upon the wind away
From the land that no man knows,
Folded in the earth are they,
And the grass as freshly grows.


HERALD:

Silence now and hear the King!


KING LEARY

We are, as our fathers were,
Lovers of the swift and strong,
Lovers of the open air,
Lovers of the horse and song
And the glories of the voice
In the deeds to be retold.
Therefore let us now rejoice
As the kings rejoiced of old.

Room enough for Peace is here
On the green and shaven swards.
For the pitching charioteer,
For the grave contending Bards,
For the young men in the race,
For the stately sport of dames,
For the maidens fair of face.
We have opened Tailltean Games.


HERALD:

The King of the South. Be listening!

THE KING OF THE SOUTH

King, we have come to this noble place
From the mountainous south of the narrow bays
Where, isled in grass, the short oaks grow,
Their low leaves wet by the tide below,
Where the golden sea-weed is lodged and low
Till the tide returns as smooth and bland
As the tremulous path to Fairyland;
And the moon at night renews the track
With a ladder of light on the waters, black:
A misty land that is poor in flocks,
Of tender valleys and heartless rocks,
Of stout lowlanders and, wild without fear,
The deep-breathed runner, the mountaineer.
King, we will try on your plain of Meath
Who may in the running be left to breathe,
As the circling race draws near to its close
And our men, reversing their way with foes,
Fly from each other along the track,
Who may for his running the prize bear back.
Our Bards will sing so the Dead may hear
In their green duns watching from year to year
The Summer come with its grasses tall
And, after a longer interval,
The sweet youth ripen to women and men
To love, to challenge, to glory; and then
The green earth laps them and, all too soon,
They join the watchers within the dun.
We are come, O King, where the games are sped,
To share life's crown with the still-foot Dead.


THE KING OF THE WEST

Where I come from, King, the skies
Are less coloured than the land;
And the wildest winds that rise
In their clouds are moist and bland.
If you climbed a mountain peak
When the sun has just gone down,
And the sea's without a break,
Heaven from sea could not be known.

Islands shimmer after dark
Floating in forgotten gold,
Islands reached by no man's barque,
Islands poets' eyes behold.
And I bring my bards to try
Who may conquer in the course
Where the wing's too slow to fly,
Where none may prevail by force.

## THE SONG OF THE BARDS

What should follow Sport but Song,
And the victor but renown?
Many men are brave and strong,
But if Courage strive unknown
And no poet make it sweet
With the words that rouse the deed,
Even better were defeat:
Who will men forgotten heed?

We can drive a host that wars
With the long embattled years:
Time gives ground when in the cars
Poets are the charioteers.
Beauty vanishing like Spring
We can rescue and respite,
Raise her from Earth's shadowing
Up into perennial light.

We can walk the reddened path
In the slippery wake of Conn,
Rouse the Hundred-Battled wrath,
Bid him stay or tarre him on.
We can tell of queenly joy
Underneath the trysting thorn,
And the anger of McRoy
When the wooden sword was worn.

We can sing the noble horse
And the wonder of his race,
Showing how the supernal Force
Turns to Courage, Speed and Grace:

For he sprang from soil and surf
Where the ocean weds the loam;
And he thunders on the turf,
And his speed gives back the foam.

While we hold the Shield of Song
Stands the lineage of Kings;
And our buckler against wrong
Louder than MacNessa's rings.
Loveliness we can renew
Unrestricted by its date,
And the brave man's death undo.
We can bend the neck of Fate.

Now from prairie, hill and bush
Which gigantic rivers drain,
Streams whose single-handed rush,
Like a Chief's, puts back the main,
Comes the old heroic race,
Men whose names are with us still,
And we hail them face to face
In the Games of Strength and Skill.

Where the blue eye beams with light,
Where there is the open hand,
Where the mood is dark and bright
There is also Ireland.
Welcome, Brothers, and well met
In the Land that bids you hail:
Far apart though we be set,
Gael does not forget the Gael.

## To the Moon

O born before our birth began!
Through all your blanched and listening vales,
Far from the echoing shores of man,
Aloof, may sing – what nightingales!

## To the Fixed Stars

Gazers at Earth who may not snatch
   A moment's rest, O Sentinels,
Who watch with none to change the watch,
   Is there a Rumour which foretells,

After long vigilance, relief;
   And timeless ease from ageless hours;
A respite from the blaze of Life,
   Deep in a shelter such as ours,

Where you may bathe your eyes in Night,
   Trusting in Death's long 'All is well'?
Ah, no! For what can give respite,
   And quench the light perpetual?

Our very shade which seems at rest,
   Spins at the apex of its cone;
The dark in which the stars shine best,
   Is by some solar radiance thrown.

Even the primordial Dark that once
   Engendered light, nor growth debars,
Is phosphorescent with dead suns,
   And pregnant with the dust of stars.

## Virgil

From Mantua's meadows to Imperial Rome
Came Virgil, with the wood-light in his eyes,
Browned by the suns that round his hillside home
Burned on the chestnuts and the ilices.
And these he left, and left the fallows where
The slow streams freshened many a bank of thyme,
To found a city in the Roman air,
And build the epic turrets in a rhyme.
But were the woodland deities forgot,
Pan, Sylvan, and the sister nymphs for whom
He poured his melody the fields along?
They gave him for his faith a happy lot:
The waving of the meadows in his song
And the spontaneous laurel at his tomb.

## To 'Aphrodite'

Venus I called you when our love began:
And I was right; and you Pandemian.

## To Lydia

What spirit was hoaxed
By your lily-white mesh
From its starry lagoon
On the edge of a cloud
Or the crook of the moon?
What lovely and airy
Capricious and proud
Princess out of faery
Was coaxed and endowed
By the sheath of your flesh
As the moon by a cloud?

As the wing thrills the hand
So your body is thrilled
By this thing from the air
That is held in your glance
And would leap out from there
But that your sweet presence,
So lithe and intense,
Restrains the wild essence
That longs to fly hence
And is but half spilled
To its stars by your glance.

## To Ninde

O young and lovely! Now I'm left
    With old ideals gone;
Bereft of power to praise, bereft
    Of high comparison.

When Helen first put up her hair,
    She may have looked like you;

Or Dian holding back a tear
  When her first fawn she slew.

There's not a limb in Melian land,
  Or veiled by Coan seas,
Which lissom chisel planed; or planned
  By rapt Praxiteles,

To match you from your folded feet
  To little lifted chin,
A line of perfect limbs which meet;
  And not a beam gets in!

But when there is not for the eye
  An equal in the heart,
The outer vision fades; so I,
  To find your counterpart,

Call back the loveliness to aid
  Which stars my world of song:
Ladies whom Time has lovelier made,
  And think of them when young.

But what are planets when the bright
  New crescent, tall and shy,
Tip-toes across the orchard light
  Which tinges half the sky?


## For a Birthday

When your Birthday comes, I say:
Happy be this holy day!
Happy may it be for you;
But for me it's blessed too
For the fact that I exist
While you live has made it blest.

Had I lived when Helen shone,
All my days would now be gone.
But I live while you are giving
Joy to all who see you living.
Since my happy lot did fall so,
Lady, 'tis my birthday also.

## To a Cock

Why do you strut and crow,
And thus all gaudy go
Through squalor, with a show
That tempts derision?
Do you a livery use,
Or dress you up in hues
You were not free to choose
Of your own vision?

Colours of dawn and joy
That with delight destroy;
Your body all a Troy
To house desire,
Your mien as proud and brave
As his who fought to save
The fatal Queen who gave
But gifts of fire.

Strange that a small brown hen
Should charm you thus! For men
Great Beauty shines, as when
The Argive valleys
Bore her limbs for whom Greece
For ten years knew no peace,
Or our own Western seas
Bore Grace O'Malley's.

Their birth no happy star
Attended; rigid war
Beleaguered towns, and far
Deep fields were bloody!
Demure is not the mien
Of Beauty, by her een
The insolent pale Queen
Who makes me ruddy.

What, if I could appear
As you do, and strike fear!
But would she fail to sneer
Who will not heed a
Lover? nor cry 'Absurd

You are, but as a bird ...!
Is it to be inferred
That I am Leda?'

Nor would it much avail
Were I to say 'The male
In beauty doth prevail
Largely in Nature,'
For she would but retort,
'Is man the only sort
Whose females must pay court,
My beauteous creature?'

Alas, befeathered bull!
My love's too pitiful,
Too pensive, kind, less full
Than that of bird or
Beast, overcharged with fate
And more compassionate
Than yours you satiate
Half linked to murder.

The more we rise above
The beast or even the dove
Sorrow distempers love;
But yours is gladdest,
Soon gathered and soon spent,
A fierce arbitrament;
And you do not repent
O perfect Sadist!

To Semele none came,
None to each Sabine dame,
Not Hercules aflame –
Not dawn to heaven,
Came with as great affright
As you do burning bright,
Not – for the poor hen's plight –
To Kathleen Kevin;

Further she cannot go,
She falters and lies low

Brought down by love, a throe
That throws us all;
Soon to be scaled and hacked
And, like a city, sacked
With nothing left intact
Within the wall.

When you have persevered
As did the dawn you cheered
When darkness disappeared,
Give not the strife up
Till by the Passion Play
Of Death for Life's relay,
The old authentic way
You conjure life up!

O trample her in dust
So that you slake your lust!
Pull back her neck and thrust
To kill the tempter.
Your peace how dare she fret
With feet demurely set?
Give her another yet
And don't exempt her!

Take vengeance for the sting
In love's elusive wing,
With beak and talon cling
In full refulgence.
O work for all your worth
To bring your spirit to birth;
For this kind goeth forth
By self-indulgence!

For when your spurs were gained
Passion was unrestrained.
Your hues were not obtained
From dust and ashes.
You did of old deride
His spirit who denied.
You are but gratified
By Life's fierce flashes.

Now indignation foams!
The purple of your combs
Is purpler than the plum's
Or purple heather's.
What though it must endure!
Break Beauty! O secure
Some respite from the lure
Of all the feathers!

## To My Friend the Rt. Hon. Lorcan Galeran (A Great Householder)

Meridian man, Enstomacher,
For whom the whole world's fruits are fare,
For whom all Life is but a Feast,
And all the world a future Guest!

Spread out the Board, dispense the cost,
There's not a moment to be lost
Until the Mystic Wine and Bread
Are guzzled and engulleted!

Others on canvas spend their soul,
You on the tablecloth and bowl;
And as you fill, proceed to quote
What Shakespeare and Sam Johnson wrote.

We take our seats at your commands,
Upon the fare stretch forth our hands;
And grow amazed, while grows the drinking,
To hear your hobby is clear thinking.

Your table, like a moon silvern,
Shows what a kitchen sun you burn,
An alternating sun that heats
The growing herbs and lowing meats.

O Tableland! O plain of Troy,
Whereon we wage the wars of joy!
You, Agamemnon to our force,
Big-bellied as the Trojan horse!

Well marshalled by your genial roar,
The servants massed in order pour
The blood some thirsty summer shed,
Now ten years rising from the dead.

Still from your cellars' costly glooms
Each bottle like an Orpheus comes,
And bends his golden neck till we
Can all but clasp Eurydice.

A Victory plunges through the air.
As well as Love, wine casts out fear!
The butler's Marathon goes round,
And still your friends orchestral sound.

The artists are in heart to join;
There's scholarship in each sirloin:
'Do you prefer it brown or red?
'What did you say that Shakespeare said?

'The book is somewhere on my shelves:
'Yes; God helps those who help themselves ...
'Don't mind, my Friend, it's only froth
'I like a dappled tablecloth!

'Wine should not make a man afeared.
'A chewing chin won't spoil your beard.
'Well, let your stomach fight it out,
'Starvation's no soft cure for gout,'

Thanks, thanks! For this (I won't refuse)
Opens the lips of every Muse,
Makes us expand, makes trouble cease
And brings the broad Tiberian peace.

Magee no longer thinks alone,
Clarke talks and rouses silent Hone,
While booming through the mist is heard,
Responsible, the clear-thought word.

I cannot move, I will not speak
Without Parnassus' second peak:

The Friend to whom you oft refer,
Your cousin dear and echoer.

Once you fill up the ravening Maw,
There's not a doubt about the Law.
Just cut that chicken through the girth,
I'm battling here for peace on Earth.

But there's a thirst I cannot slake
Till water-lilies drink a lake,
For I must get inside the cup
If I would drink what bears me up.

Once like your Body bulged the Earth,
Pear-shaped, before the Moon had birth.
O keep your tropic waistcoat tight,
Your Belly may fly off to-night!

And, mounted to the heavenly dome,
Another Moon would light us home,
Fair as the ocean shell that rose,
And harvest-full and grandiose!

Born of your bounty, take my Song
Redounding, like a dinner gong,
Translunary recorder pale
Of how your guests you can regale.

Till all the Earth's volcanic heat
Shall bear a better heart to beat,
Fame shall not fail you, generous man,
Magnificent meridian!


## To a Friend in the Country

*(Wyckoff, New Jersey)*

You like the country better than the town
And very willingly would dwell therein
Afar from the intolerable din
That makes New York a barbarous Babylon;
But far more willingly would I be gone

From all this mad bombardment of the brain
To fields where still and comely thoughts may reign
Deep in your stately mansion old and brown,
And coloured like a Springtime copper beech:
My God, I would give anything to reach
Your old house standing in the misty rain,
And turn my thoughts to things that do not pass,
While gazing through a window at the grass
And wet young oak leaves fingering the pane.


## To James Stephens

Where are you, Spirit, who could pass into our hearts and all
Hearts of little children, hearts of trees and hills, and elves?
Where is the pen that could, sweetly deep and whimsical,
Make old poets sing again far better than themselves?

You passed through all our past worst time, and proved yourself no caitiff.
America then listened to a voice too dear for wealth;
Then you went to London, where I fear you have 'gone native';
Too long in a metropolis will tax a poet's health:

It's not as if you had no wit, and cared for recognition;
A mind that lit the Liffey could emblazon all the Thames,
But we're not ourselves without you, and we long for coalition;
Oh, half of Erin's energy! What can have happened, James?


## To a Friend

If it be true that poets, as you say,
Envisage in their verse and populate,
By dreams that shall come true, the future state,
I must be careful whom I shall portray
Lest I sit down, forever and for aye,
With the strange characters I celebrate.
O awful thought: our Fancy is our Fate!
(Let me erase some writings while I may!)
But one thing I am sure of, dear A.E.:
I will confront the malcreated crew,
Victims or merely subjects of my song,

If I can reach the bourne where you shall be
Creating kindness as you always do,
And I may bring my fancy friends along.


## To the Lady —

In the most intimate years your gables grew
And stood by Oxford on their watery hill;
When all the days were spacious, they were still
A country home of music undisturbed.
You keep your life aloof from common things,
Lovely and strange in beauty of its own;
Like a tall Saint who clasps upon her breast
A Pindar hidden by a palimpsest,
And both ordain a life austere and curbed;
Fixed in the change, and timeless as a shrine
Upon the border of a Grecian town
Where there is calm beyond the reach of gold.
My mind seeks beauty and it dwells on you
Under the elms – and all the air was Spring's,
A leaven of silence in the misty dew
Leavening the light, the shadow leavening,
Your cloak and that tall feather, white under blue –
Walking beside a poet in the evening.


## To A.E. Going to America

Dublin transmits you, famous, to the West.
    America shall welcome you, and we,
    Reflected in that mighty glass, shall see,
In full proportion, power at which we guessed:
We live too near the eagle and the nest
    To know the pinion's wide supremacy:
    But yours, of all the wings that crossed the sea,
Carries the wisest heart and gentlest.
    It is not multitudes, but Man's idea
Makes a place famous. Though you now digress,

Remember to return as, back from Rome,
Du Bellay journeyed to his Lyrè home;
And Plutarch, willingly, to Chæronea
Returned, and stayed, lest the poor town be less.

## To W. B. Yeats Who Says that His Castle of Ballylee is His Monument

To stones trust not your monument
To make a living fame endure.
Who built Dun Angus battlement?
O'Flaherty is forgotten in Auchnanure.

And he who told how Troy was sacked
And what men clipt the lovely Burd,
Had seven Mayors to swear, in fact,
Their towns first heard his babbling word.

## To My Portrait, by Augustus John

'O infinite Virtue, comest thou through
The world's great snare uncaught?'

Image of me according to John
    Back from the world behind his brow,
Back from the boulevards of his brain,
    My painted wraith, what ails you now?
Whom have you met with or discerned;
    Where have you bivouacked or lain,
Who look like Caesar late returned
    Exhausted from a long campaign?
Where were the tropic fields you fought?
    What hostels heard your jibes and jests?
Alas! my wraith, you answer not;
    But on your face a pallor rests.
The opals of Elysian skies
    Such as he paints around his friends
Are not reflected in those eyes,
    In vain that coloured peace descends;

And never in the meadows where
   He sets his woman great with child,
And dew has calmed the atmosphere
   And all the willowy light is mild —
O never in his mind's Provence
   Did you come by that look of yours!
Some ecstasy of Love's mischance
   Undreamt of by the Troubadours,
Or message passionate or absurd,
   Has made you look as who should seek,
And yet lose, confidence in a word,
   And seem to think before you speak.
Is it a warning? And, to me,
   Your criticism upon Life?
If this be caused by Poetry?
   What should a Poet tell his wife?
Whate'er it is, howe'er it came,
   No matter by what devious track
My image journeyed, there is fame
   In that it has come surely back.


## To Augustus John

*These, though my tankard is*
   *Hung in the pantry*
*Up like Silenus's,*
   *And from the chauntry*
*Only dry memories*
   *Ring for the Muse:*
*From my indignities*
   *Take, and excuse.*


When you kept the gears in mesh
Driving on through Lettergesh,
And I kept not very far
Behind you in another car —
Not that I would cast a slur,
No; but accidents occur,
And your driving not your drawing
Was what there might be a flaw in —
Like a God a little cloud

Held you, as with speed endowed
You drove on through the divine
Light of day above the shine
Of the green and grapy sea,
Whose translucent greenery
Broke on crescent sands remote,
Goldener than Helen's throat.
For I never see a beach
Sloped within a galley's reach,
But I think of sands afar
And our Lady of the War,

Wondering how many spears
Kept Love faithful for ten years;
And you think me just a fool
Of the sentimental school,
You who revel in the quick
And are Beauty's Bolshevik;
For you know how to undress
And expose her loveliness.

You are right, but am I wrong
To love ladies named in song?
I who feel it like a duty
To love the rare and difficult Beauty
That danger never could forestall,
And towers round about it all.
What better than a far ideal
To help us with the near and real?

Well! you need not rail at me,
For you could not watch the sea,
Nor the purple mountains drawn
Like the neck of . . . . . . .;
Nor the Hawk of Achill strung
Like a cross-bow as he hung
Half invisible in blue;
All these things were lost to you.
For your eyes were strictly glued
On (a Yeatsian rhyme) the road,
And the lake vibrating bright
Just six inches to your right;
And the goats so slow to fly

Till they looked you in the eye;
And the dogs still missed at home
That you 'stood no nonsense from';
Geese that never more may tell
Who attempts their citadel –
Geese that fledged Augustus John
Till he seemed to be a swan,
Steering through the clear ozone
For a Leda of his own.
Or a Viking who has steered,
All blue eyes and yellow beard,
To some unawakened isle,
With a reassuring smile;
Or the lion-eyed Sordello
Mountain-met was just his fellow;
Or the gifted Robin Hood,
Driven from his sheltering wood.

Then we spread the things, Ah me!
You but tolerated tea,
And the shallow lucubration
Of a pic-nic conversation;
Till – I hope I don't presume –
Suddenly profoundest gloom
Wrapped you as you gazed apart,
And not one of us had heart
To inquire what was the matter.
So we kept our frantic chatter
Up, to save an awful pause,
Guessing what could be the cause
Of your sudden, silent mood,
What in daylight made you brood.
Could it be that vapour islands
Made an 'Evening in the Highlands'
With the mountains in array,
Or recalled 'The Stag at Bay'
And the gulf that is betwixt
Those who hunt and hang it fixed?

Did your thoughts' unwelcome pageant
Bring, perchance, your London agent?
With his face and forehead numb,

Eyes like an aquarium?
Not by trifles such as these
Was your heart deprived of ease.

Enough! There is no need to tell
How I broke the gloomy spell,
What I was inspired to give –
By bread alone doth no man live,
And water makes a man depressed:
Maybe silence had been best.

> *When my hawk's soul shall be*
> *With little talk in her,*
> *Trembling, about to flee,*
> *And Father Falconer*
> *Touches her off for me,*
> *And I am gone –*
> *All shall forgotten be*
> *Save for you, John!*

## To the Poet W.B. Yeats, Winner of the Nobel Prize 1924

*(To Build a Fountain to Commemorate his Victory)*

Now that a town of the North
    In which a discerning band
Has caused your name to go forth,
    And lifted on high your hand
Before all men on the Earth
    As a sign of a contest won;
What should you do with your wealth
    But spill it in water and stone;
With a Dolphin to scatter the spilth,
    To be for a sign when you're gone
That you in the town of your birth
    Laboured and hewed at a cup
To hold what the clear sky spills;
    Why should you not set it up

Under the granitic hills?
　What did the Roman of old,
After the Pyrrhic slaughter,
　But spend the hard-won gold
To bring in the Sabine water?
　Gracious and bountiful men,
Caesars and Cardinals,
　Laid hold of the mountain treasure, and then
Spilt it within the walls,
　For children to dabble and splash,
And break the bead at the brim;
　For sparrows to shudder and wash,
And the Dolphin's freshet unlimn
　The Dolphin under its wave
Till he seem to tumble and reel,
　For his back to a poet he gave,
And he follows at Venus' heel;
　He comes from the depths at a song:
O set him on high in his place;
　For he stands for what flows in the lovely and strong
And a sign of the Julian race!

# EARTH AND SEA

---

## *The Forge*

The forge is dark
The better to show
The birth of the spark
And the Iron's glow.
The forge is dark
That the smith may know
When to strike the blow
On the luminous arc
As he shapes the shoe.

The bellows blows on the dampened slack,
The coal now glows in the heart of the black.
The smith no longer his arm need raise
To the chain of the bellows that makes the blaze.
I see him search where the blue flames are
In the heart of the fire to find the bar,
With winking grooves from elbow to wrist
As he tightens the tongs in his bawdy fist,
As he hands the bar to his fidgety son
Who holds it well on the anvil down
Till he raises the hammer that stands on its head
And brings it down with a sound like lead,
For fire has muffled the iron's clamour
While his son beats time with a smaller hammer,

And the anvil rings like a pair of bells
In time to the beat that the spark expels,
And I am delighted such sounds are made,
For these are the technical sounds of a trade
Whose glad notes rang in the heavens above
Where a blacksmith slept with the Queen of Love.
The horse is looking without reproof
For the leathery lap that has hugged his hoof:
The patient horse that has cast a shoe;
The horse is looking; and I look too
Through the open door to the cindered pool
That a streamlet leaves where the wheels may cool.
I meditate in the forge light dim
On the will of God in the moving limb,
And I realise that the lift and fall
Of the sledge depends on the Mover of All.

O lend me your sledge for a minute or two,
O smith, I have something profound to do!
I swing it up in the half-lit dark,
And down it comes in a straightening arc
On the anvil now where there's nothing to glow.
What matter? No matter! A blow is a blow!
I swing it up in my bulging fists
To prove that the outside world exists;
That the world exists and is more than naught –
As the pale folk hold – but a form of thought.
You think me mad? but it does me good,
A blow is a measure of hardihood.
I lift the sledge, and I strike again
Bang! for the world inside the brain;
And if there's another of which you have heard
Give me the sledge and I'll strike for a third.

I have frightened the horse, though I meant it not:
(Which proves that he is not a form of my thought).
I shall frighten myself if I ramble on
With philosophy where there is room for none.
I was going to say that the blacksmith's blow –
If I were the Master of Those who Know –
Would give me a thesis to demonstrate
That Man may fashion but not create.
He melts the mountains. He turns their lode

Against themselves like a Titan god.
He challenges Time by recording thought,
Time stands; but yet he makes nothing from naught,
He bends Form back to the shapes it wore
Before the dawn of the days of yore;
He bends Form back to the primal state;
He changes all, but he cannot create;
And tamper he cannot with the ways of Fate.
Between ourselves it is just as well,
If Man ruled Fate he would make Life hell.

What have I done?
What shall I do?
　　　　　　No wonder Pegasus cast a shoe
When I succumbed to the English curse
Of mixing philosophy up with verse.
I can imagine a poet teaching;
But who can imagine a poet preaching?
Soon I shall hear the blacksmith's scoff:
'The ground is sticky, they can't take off!'
When I press with my thighs and begin to urge
The heavenly horse from the earthly forge.

I know right well that a song should be
Airy and light as the leaf of a tree,
Light as a leaf that lies on the wind,
Or a bird that sings as he sits on the linde,
And shakes the spray when he dives for flight
With bright drops sprinkling the morning light;
For song that is lovely is light and aloof,
As the sparks that fly up from the well-shod hoof.

## Sung in Spring

The gorse is on the granite,
　　The light is growing clear,
Our tilted, tacking planet
　　Has another course to steer:
Without a wind to fill her
　　She can hold upon the tack.
The Captain's lashed the tiller
　　So we dance upon the deck.

Some ships go by a motor,
    And some by sails and spars,
But our ship is a rotor
    And she rolls among the stars
And has no fear of crashing:
    Without a spyglass even
You can see the signals flashing
    From the light-houses of Heaven.

Our vessel in her sailing
    Just nods and bowls along,
And half her crew are ailing
    And half are growing strong;
And some make strange grimaces
    At us who dance and shout:
The news from outer spaces
    Depends on who looks out.

Some ships by island spices
    Are scented as they run
Or through ice precipices
    Behold the midnight sun;
And these go home to haven
    For they are trading ships,
But we are touring Heaven
    And we tour in an ellipse.

We do not fear commotions
    Or anything untoward
From rocks or winds or oceans,
    We have them all on board
With sea-room all prevailing
    For a never-ending trip;
Was there ever such a sailing?
    Was there ever such a ship?

We have not once been harboured
    Since first we left the slips;
We see to port and starboard
    Brave bright companion ships,
And they go with us roundly;
    But we in hammocks rocked
Shall be sleeping very soundly
    Before our ship is docked.

She leaves no wake behind her,
   No foam before her foot
Because the gods designed her
   A rainbow-rolling boat.
We only know she's rolling
   And all the more we sing
Because just now we're bowling
   And rolling into Spring.

No questions can prevail on
   The Master of the Ship;
He won't say why we sail on
   This never-ending trip:
Though young and old and ailing
   Hold contradictory views
I think that simply sailing
   Is the meaning of the cruise.


## The Dublin-Galway Train

Everything changes:
Time deranges
Men and women and mountain ranges
Why the Devil can't Time let Well enough alone?
He no longer stoops to set his '*Nil obstat*' on
Trusted, tried and comely things than he seeks to change,
Wither, age and alter them and the best derange.
This has happened just of late to the Galway train
That with passengers and freight crossed the central plain
Pulling out from Dublin town that Liffey's stream divides
West to old grey Galway town where Corrib meets the tides.
It strains at first, then settles down and smoothly rolls along
Past villages with Gaelic names that sweeten on the tongue:
Clonsilla, Lucan and Maynooth beside the long canal
Where yellow-centred lilies float and no one comes at all,
The long canal that idle lies from Dublin to Athlone,
To Luan's Ford: but no one knows who may have been Luan,
The Royal Canal that joins two towns and makes of him a dunce
Who holds that nothing can be found in two places at once:
A long clear lane of water clean by flags and rushes rimmed,
Where, crimson-striped, the roaches steer, and, by the lilies dimmed,

The greenish pikes suspended lurk with fins that hardly stir
Until the Galway train comes on and shakes each ambusher.
The lovely hills are left behind; but soon the rising sun
Will overtop the mountain range and make the shadows run.
The light that flushes the hills was low;
But now it gathers to overflow
And shadow each bush on the central plain
And gather the dews and catch the train.
And light the steam
In its morning beam
Making a fugitive rainbow gleam.
Past walled Maynooth
Where they reach the Truth
In the meadow called after Druidical Nooth.
Puff, puff!
That's the stuff
As if there weren't white clouds enough!

Like a charging knight with his plumes astream
The train comes on with its sunlit steam,
Past fields where cows are chewing the cud
To Mullingar where the Square Mill stood,
Where the cattle-dealers with rough red skins
And gaiters buttoned across their shins
Wait for another train; they wait
For cattle-drovers to load the freight
Of blunt-nosed cattle with tousled coats
Bound for the East and the English boats:
Cattle-dealers replete with knowledge
That is not taught in an English college.
It blows
And goes,
A whale that feels
The pistons stabbing its driving wheels.

It reaches Moate where a king lies still
Under the weight of a man-made hill.
On and on, until, quite soon,
It will come to the ford that was held by Luan,
Where, as in Spenser's pageantry,
The Shannon 'spreading like a sea'
Flows brightly on like a chain of lakes
Or linkèd shields that the morning takes:

The lordly stream that protected well,
When jar-nosed Cromwell sent 'to hell,'
The Irish nobles who stood to fight
That Bible-bellowing hypocrite.

From the bridge you can see the white boats moored,
And the strong, round castle that holds the ford.
Over the bridge it slowly comes,
The bridge held up on its strong white drums,
To enter Connaught. And now, Goodbye
To matters of fact and Reality.
Ballinasloe where the hostings were,
Ballinasloe of the great horse fair
That gathers in horses from Galway and Clare,
Wherever the fields of limestone are:
Mayo and Boyle and Coolavin
Between the miles of rushes and whin
And mountains high in a purple haze,
Streams and lakes and countless bays
Of Connemara where still live on
The seaside heirs of the Sons of Conn.
Then Athenry where the kings passed by
From whom was named the Ath-na-Righ.
It rests for a moment at Oranmore,
A square grey castle protects the shore.
The Great Shore, limit of Galway Bay;
And Galway is only six miles away!

The engine-driver can wipe the oil
From his forehead and hands,
For his well done toil
Is now over; and the engine stands
Only a foot from the buffer-stop
(He eased her down till he pulled her up).
Oh, see the children jump about
As doors are opened and friends come out
With paper parcels. What endless joys
Are hidden within those parcels of toys!
The county ladies in English tweeds,
With leathern faces fox-hunting breeds,
And shoes that give them a look of men,
Have come to the station 'just to look in.'
But never an officer home on leave

Is seen; instead, they only perceive
The rakel, card-playing boys debouch
And pay up their losses with search and grouch.
Oh, what a wonderful Noah's ark!
Lady Phillipa of Merlin Park,
Holding her parasol half up the handle,
Is back from Daly's of Dunsandle.
Where gold-headed Daly delights the gazers
As he leads the field of his Galway Blazers.
The Station Master opens a door
And clears a passage for Morty Mor,
For Morty Mor is known to own
The principal works of Galway town.
He is not one of the county set,
(Though he helps them out when they lose a bet)
His saw-mills hum and he sells cement,
Potash and lime to his heart's content.
The workers he sacks on Saturday night
Are back on Monday morn contrite;
In spite of his temper, deep at the core
The heart's all right in Morty Mor.
That little boy lost is found again;
He ran away to the end of the train,
For all he can taste in his youthful hour
Of splendour and terror and speed and power:
The harnessed hates of water and flame,
The engine brings with its seething steam.

The platform now is empty again;
And empty stands the Galway train.
(Strange that nobody came to call
On the lonely men in the urinal.)
Land that is loved in ballad and song,
Land where the twilight lingers long,
May you be crossed and crossed again,
Forgetting the bus and the aeroplane,
By nothing worse than the Galway train.
Who shall tell how, when I'm dead and gone,
Gaily the Galway train came on?
How it puffed with pride on a road of its own;
How it whistled, *Waeshael!* to each nearing town;
How brightly its brass and its copper shone?
It seemed to be painted to match the scene

Of boglands brown and the trees between
With its coaches brown and its engine green.
It brought the towns where it stopped good luck,
Goods, the result of a bargain struck;
And it never ran over a cow or a duck.

Now all is changed for an overplus
Of passengers packed in a reasty bus,
A crowd that stinks and the air befouls,
And children pewk as the full bus rolls:
(A popular government plays to the masses
And that's what they get who abolish the classes)
Lady Phillipa whose share of charity
Fails when it comes to familiarity,
Lady Phillipa, her feelings hurt
Because Democracy means such dirt,
Is sitting, a most disdainful rider,
With the man from her gate-lodge sitting beside her.
The Law of Change would be just a jest
Were we sure that all change were a change for the best.


## Just One Glimpse

It makes me sadder day by day
To think the streets won't pass away
And all the houses in between
Lift like a transformation scene
That would, for just one glimpse, disclose
The windy oak, the wilding rose,
Rocks, and the springs that gushed before
The streets connected slum and store.


## The Blackbird in the Town

*The music Finn loved was that which brought
joy to the heart and light to the countenance,
the music of the blackbird of Letter Lee*

Here behind the huddled houses
Which the squalid gardens break

Golden bill my heart arouses
With his golden gurgling beak;
Disregarding all the squalor
In a backyard after rain
Boldly lifts the Bird of Valour
His mellifluous refrain:
Lifts the fanfare heroes hearkened
When his singing shook the dew
In the dells by oak-leaves darkened
Eighteen hundred years ago,
Sings the song to which Finn listened
When he first was famed and named,
And the ruffian blue eyes glistened
For Finn loved the bird untamed.
I too hear the self-same whistle
Purling all round his nest
Singing to the eggs that nestle
Underneath a browner breast,
Hear the wordless notes transcendent
Over every human rhyme,
Careless, sweet and independent
Of all circumstance of Time;
And I think: though many wrongs ache
In my heart, what matters wrong,
If I sing but for the Song's sake,
If I reach as brave a song,
Filled with fight and self reliance
Warring with all evil chance,
Loudly whistling my defiance
In the slums of circumstance,
Or, above all, go one better
And, ignoring human wrong,
Bravely as the Bird of Letter
Fling on air a heartless song.


## In The Garden

Pink and white apple blossoms suddenly appearing
Making April lovely after a late Spring,
Constellating the air of morning with their beauty,

Crowding and populating empty invisible spaces
Long before the leaf, their coverlet of green:
Clarions of the world's unborn beautiful faces,
Reminders of the exquisite loveliness that has been.

Perfect beautiful momentary blossoms,
I who am momentary cannot long endure
The tension of your beauty, the knowledge that embraces
Beauty yet to come, Beauty gone before;
The uninterruptible implacable procession
Of Beauty moving onwards from the Fountain to the Bourne.
Therefore I take comfort and walk for a few paces:
So I go where Beauty goes, I care not to return.


## If Sight Were Sound

If sight were sound,
O the blazon of the gorse bush
Calling from the granite where the heavy air is scented,
Challenging the Summer with its golden clarion;
And how can Summer answer, the Summer silken tented,
Drowsed by Paynim perfumes in its blue pavilion?

If sight were sound, you could hear the blossoms tinkle
Tinkle on the tree tops popping into sight;
And, on the ground, you could hear the periwinkle
Ringing all its faery bells along the leafy light.

If sight were sound,
O the stillness of well-water
Waiting for the blessing of the crozier-holding fern!
The crystal, cold limpidity
Like silence in Eternity,
Like silence when the strings are hushed before the notes return.

If sight were sound,
O the northern Aurora,
Thrilling in the zenith like the song of all the stars!
Ah, could we hear, that song were unsustainable;
Sight is better soundless while the weighted spirit hears.

But sight and sound are mingled in the water's
Lovely lymph that wavers as it sings and rolls along
To form a pool wherein
Reflected lean the willows
Bending heads to listen to the sky's stilled song.

## The Crab Tree

Here is the crab tree,
Firm and erect,
In spite of the thin soil,
In spite of neglect.
The twisted root grapples
For sap with the rock,
And draws the hard juice
To the succulent top:
Here are wild apples,
Here's a tart crop!

No outlandish grafting
That ever grew soft
In a sweet air of Persia,
Or safe Roman croft;
Unsheltered by steading,
Rock-rooted and grown,
A great tree of Erin,
It stands up alone,
A forest tree spreading
Where forests are gone.

Of all who pass by it
How few in it see
A westering remnant
Of days when Lough Neagh
Flowed up the long dingles
Its blossom had lit,
Old days of glory
Time cannot repeat;
And therefore it mingles
The bitter and sweet.

It takes from the West Wind
The thrust of the main;
It makes from the tension
Of sky and of plain,
Of what clay enacted,
Of living alarm,
A vitalised symbol
Of earth and of storm,
Of Chaos contracted
To intricate form.

Unbreakable wrestler!
What sapling or herb
Has core of such sweetness
And fruit so acerb?
So grim a transmitter
Of life through mishap,
That one wonders whether
If that in the sap,
Is sweet or is bitter
Which makes it stand up.

## To the Liffey with the Swans

Keep you these calm and lovely things,
    And float them on your clearest water;
For one would not disgrace a King's
    Transformed, beloved and buoyant daughter.

And with her goes this sprightly swan,
    A bird of more than royal feather,
With alban beauty clothed upon:
    O keep them fair and well together!

As fair as was that doubled Bird,
    By love of Leda so besotten,
That she was all with wonder stirred,
    And the Twin Sportsmen were begotten!

## The Water Lily

Between two elements you float,
O white and golden melilote,
Emerging by a Cyprian birth
The loveliest flower assoiled of earth!
You float, becalming leaves between,
Like sunborn patines turned to green,
Where, by the lake's tree-sheltered shores,
Stem-anchored floats a fleet of flowers.
I fold the oars along the boat
To lean and, like you, dream and float.

The windy mountains, ledge on ledge,
Neighbour your lake by ocean's edge;
And breakers crash not far beyond,
Yet nothing moves the quiet pond
Whereon you float like some unheard,
Ineffable and perfect word,
As if the lake's still spirit drew
Out of the depths to bloom in you,
And gather all that depths may tell
Into one perfect syllable.

There is no sound. Your golden glow —
A sky above, a sky below —
Is now the centre of a sphere;
All else is waived nor enters here;
Nothing offends the fairest bud
That lifts from immemorial mud
Its parted lips as if to say:
'There is no dubious mystery,
No answer and no antidote:
Between two worlds I bloom and float.'

## The Dragon Fly

Oftentimes I wish that I
Were a glancing dragon fly:
That this bulk of bone and brawn

Instantly were off and gone
And I dancing on a beam
By a spring or little stream
Iridescent, shining bright
As if, by some blessed sleight,
Somebody had knotted light:
Swift and instantaneous
As if there were two of us
At the same time here and there,
Faster poised than piercing air;
Symbolising, as it were,
In instantaneity,
Slumbers an eternity.

For my colours I would use
All the rainbow's middle hues,
Stilled with speed or brightly flashing
Like a bubble; or a splashing
Dewdrop shaken from the trees
By a wing in Paradise;
While, below, the stream or spring
Kept the bright air shimmering:
Happy and ephemeral
With no Autumn touch at all:
Just a swift ephemeris
Fashioned to keep up with bliss,
Dancing off without decay:
A moment! And then, gone away!
Proof there lies, instinct in slime,
Time's swift triumph over Time.


## Liffey Bridge

I gazed along the waters at the West,
Watching the low sky colour into flame,
Until each narrowing steeple I could name
Grew dark as the far vapours, and my breast
With silence like a sorrow was possessed.
And men as moving shadows went and came.
The smoke that stained the sunset seemed like shame,
Or lust, or some great evil unexpressed.

Then with a longing for the taintless air,
I called that desolation back again,
Which reigned when Liffey's widening banks were bare:
Before Ben Edair gazed upon the Dane,
Before the Hurdle Ford, and long before
Finn drowned the young men by its meadowy shore.

## *The Plum Tree by the House*

In morning light my damson showed
Its airy branches oversnowed
On all their quickening fronds,
That tingled where the early sun
Was flowing soft as silence on
Palm trees by coral ponds.
Out of the dark of sleep I come
To find the clay break into bloom,
The black boughs all in white!
I said, I must stand still and watch
This glory, strive no more to match
With similes things fair.
I am not fit to conjure up
A bird that's white enough to hop
Unstained in such a tree;
Nor crest him with the bloom to come
In purple glory on the plum.
Leave me alone with my delight
To store up joy against the night,
This moment leave to me!
Why should a poet strain his head
To make his mind a marriage bed;
Shall Beauty cease to bear?
There must be things which never shall
Be matched or made symmetrical
On Earth or in the Air;
Branches that Chinese draughtsmen drew,
Which none may find an equal to,
Unless he enters there
Where none may live — and more's the pity! —

The Perfect, The Forbidden City,
That's built – Ah, God knows where!
Then leave me while I have the light
To fill my mind with growths of white,
Think of them longer than
Their budding hour, their springing day,
Until my mind is more than May;
And, maybe, I shall plan
To make them yet break out like this
And blossom where their image is,
More lasting and more deep
Than coral boughs in light inurned,
When they are to the earth returned;
And I am turned to sleep.


## The Eternal Recurrence

I thank the gods who gave to me
The yearly privilege to see,
Under the orchards' galaxy,
April reveal her new-drenched skin;
And for the timeless touch within
Whereby I recognise my kin.


## Suburban Spring

Now the delicious air
Persuades the lovely trees
To loose their golden hair
From old embroideries
And make an airy screen
Of gold that turns to green.

Delightful it is now
To see the crooked bough,

The crooked bough that dapples
The ground beneath the apples,
Look pink and fresh: as brave
As many a straighter stave
Or willow that, by sleight,
Makes drooping a delight.
Cherries in bloom spring up
As high as the house top.


And all the air is filled
With sprays suddenly stilled;
A soft, green, maple rain
Has paved the little lane,
The lane beside the rill
That runs down to the mill;
And every little gully
Gushes, replenished fully;
And in the fields beyond
The ducks upon the pond
Are dipping, scooting, ducking;
Foals, calves and lambs are sucking,
(A thing I would not mention
But for pastoral convention)
And Peggy's out, not caring
To ask how Dick is faring:
The Miller, where no breeze is
(It's dust or sinus) sneezes;
And men in sleeveless shirts
Are plying little squirts,
Or making rainbow mists
With a kind of hose that twists;
And all the world's agog
Like a seedsman's catalogue:
I know that Spring has come;
But not how, or wherefrom.
I would have been a fool
Had I not gone to school
To find out what brings on
This blithe phenomenon.
The teacher said, The sap
Is, once a year, on tap;
And, also, that we roll

Each day around the Pole;
And that these brave things come
Because it's out of plomb.


## Perennial

The other day I chanced to see
By an old lot a cherry tree,
An old wild cherry blooming brightly,
A sight of joy in the unsightly.
It sprayed the air with April snow
As merrily as long ago
When every little wind that blew
Could bend it, and with blossoms strew
The garden or the shaven lawn.
The lot was bare, the house was gone;
And yet the brave old tree bloomed on.

Bravo! I cried. You make me think
Of some old Roman soused in drink
His wreath awry upon his head,
For all that, primely chapleted;
Or that gowned man who loved to foster
My waking wits, *Tyrrellus noster*.
I like the rings upon your rind
Suggesting hoops. They bring to mind
Barrels and kilderkins enough
To stillion the Septembral stuff.
How do you keep your sap so young?
If I could only break in song
As you in bloom, and disregard
Ruin around this old back yard,
I'd raise such foison of sweet sound
That trees would jig it on the ground;
Kettles and garbage cans would swirl:
You'd think that Orpheus found his girl;
Or that this old daft heart of mine
Improved, as it grew old, like wine.
I feel the soul within me sing:
By God, I'm grateful for the Spring

That makes all fading seem illusion;
The foam, the fullness, the profusion;
For every lovely thing misplaced;
The bloom, the brightness and the waste!


## Thrush in Ash

Bare above the hedge, already
Thick with leaf, the leafless ash
Stands, resisting still the heady
Spring's excited sudden flash;
Like a deep reluctant lover
Whose still heart is slow to love,
But the more it takes to move her,
When she loves, the more she'll . . . Hush!
Coloured like his branchy cover,
Ash-eye speckled sits a thrush.
Lack of shelter little daunts him:
If the branches lack their green,
All the better may the mountains
Through the leafless boughs be seen.
You may count up five, or count tens
In between his fangled notes,
While the evening smooths the mountains
And on silence music floats:
Sweetly sudden knots in silence
Like the way a violet shows,
Interrupting green with sweetness,
Presently its purple glows
Like a drop of nectar taken
From the cup that Hebe spilt;
Dew fallen down from Ida, shaken
When great Hera kicked the quilt.
Lightly from the boughs ungreening
Floats the light and lyric cheer,
Just a voice that takes a meaning
From the place and those that hear.
And the silence feeds his whistling
As the evening lights the stars,
Or my ear my fancy, listening

To his interrupted bars.
O my fancy stop your straining
After subtle simile;
Listen to the curled flakes raining
From the song-bird in his tree;
Cease to taint with mortal dreaming
Such a liquid lovely song;
Now the evening air is creaming,
And the hills are smooth and long!
Like the mountains which the Magi
Seek beyond the starlit road
When the Tuscan mixes magic
On the painted oaken board,
And you see smooth light pervade all
Trees transfigured, leaves unstirred,
And the mountains to a cradle
Dwindle, cradling the Word.
Here the ash tree with a trellis
Of its young boughs yet unblurred
Screens the golden dusty valleys
Stilled to hear the singing bird.
Music: silence: silence aching,
Till the few notes twisted clear,
Lovely thoughtless music making,
Lancinate the inmost ear;
Exquisitely thin and sweeter
Than the high sharp sickle moon,
Perfect, being incompleter
Than a promise past and blown,
Sounds that cease before enticing
Thoughts and fetters of the word;
Here is Sound for Song sufficing,
Leafless ash and singing bird.


## The Oak Wood

You could not see a linnet's wing
Between the oaks that wait for Spring,
Because the air is green and dim
With mosses on each bole and limb.

But soon they'll tingle in the blue
And all their amber joy renew;
And transubstantiate to wood
The Spring's impalpable blue blood.

And they will drain, ere time be past,
From Beauty gall to make them last
To gaze on many a festive sight:
The wedded heir, the ruddy light.


## The Apple Tree

Let there be Light!
In pink and white
The apple tree blooms for our delight.
In pink and white,
Its shout unheard,
The Logos itself, the Creative Word,
Bursts from nothing; and all is stirred.
It blooms and blows and shrivels to fall
Down on the earth in a pink–white pall,
Withered? But look at each little green ball,
Crowned like a globe in the hand of God,
Each little globe on a shortening rod;
Soon to be rosy and well bestowed,
A cosmos now where the blossoms glowed
Constellated around the tree,
A cone that lifts to infinity.
Each rosy globe is as red as Mars;
And all the tree is a branch of stars.
What can we say but, 'Glory be!'
When God breaks out in an apple tree?


## Lullaby

Loll under pines where, faint and far,
The coast is like a scimitar,
So faint and so far down below
The blue in silence turns to snow.

Or call the spendthrift Summer up
When squandered is the buttercup,
And watch the purple pomp unrolled
On every acre's Cloth of Gold;
And hear again the drowsy hum
As drunken bees go barging home.

Or watch the pane that glimmers through,
When twilight makes the valley blue,
With yellow light to find its match
In one big star beyond the thatch,
And all the air's a mild alloy;
Of grief that's half akin to Joy.

If thoughts of Love be kept afar –
For Love can waken more than War,
Whose greatest captains could sleep sound
Before the fatal final round –

Sweet Sleep, the whole world's treasure trove,
The crown and only cure for Love,
Will come, and gently lead your soul,
So when it leaves the Will's control,
It may not on the fruitless coast
Of Waking Dreams be starved and lost.


## Angels

In an old court-yard,
Seen from a lane-way,
Down by the Liffey,
Somewhere in Dublin,
Whitened with stone-dust
Dwells an Italian;
And he makes angels.

There are too many
Makers of tomb-stones
Whitened and formally
Carven with crosses,

Dwelling among us:
But he makes angels
Down by the Liffey.

Now I remember
Pagan Pompeii
With its black frescoes
Brightened by Cupids,
Flying attendants,
Winged amorini,
Angels of Venus.

Aye; and I think of
Hermes the Angel,
After his flight from
Crystal Olympus,
Skimming and fanning
With his winged sandals
The violet water;
And in the four-fountained,
Wonderful island,
His thankless reception.

Backwards and forwards
To Middle Ages
Lightly my thought goes
Thinking of Dante
Drawing an angel;
And the tip-pointed
Wings of some airy
Angelic chorus.

What does the poor dusty,
Dublin Italian
Know of the grandeur
Of his great nation?
Grim civilisers,
Law-givers, road-makers,
Founders of cities,
Dreamers of angels,

Far from the sunlight,
Far from the citron,

White, with its branches
Over white tables
Lighted with red wine,
Under grape trellises,
Here in a lane-way,
True to his nature,
Making an angel?

O for ten thousand
Gifted Italians
Dwelling amongst us
Just to put angels
On the black fresco
Of this most dismal,
Reasty and sunless
Town where the meiny
Of Heaven's chief subjects,
The Christ-beloved children
Are housed in a horrible
Graveyard of houses!

I am a lover
Of Beauty and Splendour,
Lover of Swiftness,
Lover of Brightness,
Lover of sunlight
And the delightful
Movement of water,
Starving in Dublin
For Beauty and Brightness,
Starving for gladness:

God send an angel!
Not a mere figment
From childhood remembered,
God, but a far-flashing
Terrible creature,
An awful tomb-shattering
Burning Idea
Of Beauty and Splendour,
A winged Resurrector,
One with a message
To make the announcement:

Not in His Death,
But in Christ's resurrection
Lieth salvation.

Break down the tenement
Walls that surround them;
Lead out from festering
Lane and back garden
The Heirs to the Kingdom,
To sunlight, to highland,
To winds blowing over
Green fields; and restore to
The sons of a City,
By seafarers founded,
The sight of white clouds on
An open horizon.

Raise up a man —
What though he must shout from
The mountebank platform
To gain him a hearing —
With knowledge, with vision
And sense of the grandeur
Of human existence,
To plan out a city
As grand, if not grander,
Than Georgian Dublin,
With broadways and side-walks
And dwellings proportioned
To what in the nation
Is faithful and noble;
To save this old town
From the artisan artist,
The cottage replacing
The four-storey mansion,
The cynical largesse
Of hospital-builders;
And all its bad conscience.

Build up with gladness
The house individual
Set in its garden,
Detached and uncrowded;

So that the children
In health grow to greatness;
The family hold to
Its proper distinction;
So that the nation
Be saved from soul-slaughter,
The living damnation,
Which comes from the crowding
That leads to the Commune.

Build not in lanes
Where the thought of an angel
Is one with a tombstone;
But out where Raheny
Gives on to Howth Head
And the winds from Portmarnock;
Or build where Dundrum,
With its foot set in granite,
Begins the long climb
To the hill which O'Donnell
Crossed ages ago
In his flight from the city.
Why should the sons
Of the Gael and the Norseman
Be huddled and cramped
With broad acres about them
And lightning-foot cars
At their beck to transport them,
Which overcome space
Like the sandals of Hermes?

Nations are judged
By their capital cities;
And we by the way
That we fashion an angel.

## Song
## Made by Sir Dinadan for Sir Tristram
## That an Harper Might Play It
## Before King Mark

*Incipit citharista*

Two trees grew in a garden close.
    Cock a doodle doo! And who goes there?
These young leaves were fresher than those
    For those were withered and warped with care;
As the sap runs in the root of the wood
A tree doth wax in his lustihood
Till buds be thickened and leaves protrude;
    And sappy Spring is happy.

There was a nest in the elder tree.
    Cock a doodle doo! And who goes there?
A song bird's home in the leaves to be;
    But these were withered and warped with care.
A cuckoo sat in the leaves and trolled:
Cuckoo. Cuckoo. Look who look old.
Cuckoo, Cuckoo, Cuckoo, Cuckold!
    And sappy Spring is happy.

*Hic calcibus citharistam ejiciunt.*

## Dunsany Castle

The twin dunes rise before it, and beneath
Their tree-dark summits the Skene river flows,
An old divine earth exaltation glows
About it, though no longer battles breathe.
For Time puts all men's swords in his red sheath,
And softlier now the air from Tara glows;
Thus in the royalest ground that Ireland knows
Stands your sheer house in immemorial Meath.

It stands for actions done and days endured;
Old causes God, in guiding Time, espoused,
Who never brooks the undeserving long.
I found there pleasant chambers filled with song,
(And never were the Muses better housed)
Repose and dignity and Fame assured.


## Croker of Ballinagarde

Ballinagarde was a house to be sure
With windows that went from the ceiling to flure,
And fish in the river and hens in the yard
And Croker was master of Ballinagarde.

There were mares in the meadows: the grass was so good
That cows never tired of chewing the cud;
One mouthful sufficed all the sheep on the sward;
They forced them to fatten at Ballinagarde.

So close and convenient and wide were his grounds
He could hunt with the Tipps or the Waterford hounds;
And many's the cup and the Horse Show award
That shone on the sideboard in Ballinagarde.

He bought his own whiskey and brewed his own ale
That foamed up like beastings that thicken the pail.
No fiddler no more nor the man with his card
Was ever sent empty from Ballinagarde.

His daughter got married at sweet twenty-two:
To lose her was more than her father could do.
To give her away it had gone very hard,
You could tell that by Croker of Ballinagarde.

The wedding was over a week and a day
Before the last guest could be driven away;
For everyone's going he tried to retard:
'What ails ye?' said Croker of Ballinagarde.

One day when out hunting and going like fire
His horse was flung down – Oh, bad scrant to the wire!
And something in Croker was broken or marred,
So the parson was sent for to Ballinagarde.

The parson remarked as the grounds he druv through
'The land's in good heart. What a beautiful view!
It's but what I'm thinking 'twill go very hard
To comfort the owner of Ballinagarde.'

He tried to persuade him and make him resigned,
On Heavenly mansions to fasten his mind,
'There's a Land that is Fairer than this,' he declared.
'I doubt it!' said Croker of Ballinagarde.

## New Bridge

New bridge is the oldest bridge
   The Liffey passes through.
There must have been an older bridge
   When this new bridge was new.
But, new or old, the water flows
   In many a gleaming stage
As careless as a thing which goes
   And is exempt from age.

So pleasant is it on this bank,
   I often wonder why
They set the piers out rank on rank
   And raised the arches high.
They must, deluded by a dream,
   Have thought, as I have done:
The other side of any stream
   Is better than your own.

The water bends and thickens as
   It rushes at an arch.

The piers like soldiers in a pass
    Stand halted on the march.
The hissing stream escapes to fall
    In mocking undertones.
But would it be a stream at all,
    Without the bridge and stones?

They built as men built who believed
    In Life that lasts forever.
And hardly were those souls deceived
    Who bridged the clear black river?
The soul survived, as any dunce
    Can prove: for it is plain
That that which gets in trouble once,
    Shall troubled be again.

I'd rather hear these arches praised
    Than arches anywhere.
Not that the Eternal City raised
    To Settimo Severe;
Nor those that leave the walls therefrom
    To tap the Sabine ridge,
Can match these arches here at home
    In Liffey's oldest bridge.

The black bright water over there
    Is flaked beside the brink,
As if the stallions of Kildare
    Had bent their necks to drink.
And underneath an arch I see
    A long grey gleaming reach,
Half shadowed by a breeze, maybe,
    Or, maybe, by a beech.

The long grey lines of steel are gone
    Which crossed here long ago:
The colours, the caparison,
    All gone; and I would go
But that I fear I might repent
    My going, if I found
The side from which I willing went
    Looked better from beyond.

## Glenasmole

Do you remember that thrush in Glenasmole
In the high lane on the West side where I made the engine stop,
When he perched across the roadway like a fellow taking toll:
So well within his rights was he, he would not even hop?

That thrush is the owner of all Glenasmole,
From the mild bends of the river to the purple-stemmed rose bushes;
For the men who had the giving of such things when Life was whole
Called Glenasmole, as it is still, The Valley of the Thrushes.

There is not one of all the throng of giant men surviving,
The men who dwelt with magic, apple-cheeked and steady eyed;
But the thrush whose happy armour was their love of Song is living
And he sings the song unaltered that he sang before they died.

Strong is the delicate line of generations:
Two thousand songs unbroken of the thrushes in the Glen.
Two thousand years cannot restore the mighty exultations
Of men whose manhood now would be incredible to men.

Song under leaf by the water in the valley!
Bird's throat distended! For the men of old who died
Left a fame beyond all language in the music of their ally,
In the throbbing song outshaken of the bird with bosom pied.

There beyond the river and the ridge is Bohernabreena,
The Road House by the road that runs beside a vanished inn;
I can see it like a window opened clearly in the saga
Of an ancient battle ambush that no chivalry could win.

When the Lochlann galleys raided and consumed the kingly hostel
Where the chieftains sat in silence with their spears in water cooled,
What happened? O what happened? Can the soft notes of the throstle
Tell how the golden heroes in their chivalry were fooled?

Far though they are, forget not that the bushes,
The wild rose with its dull white thorns, the hedges and the stream
Are nearer to our longing in the Valley of the Thrushes
Than any glen in any hills that neighbour near to dream:

Wings that fly low for a moment in the twilight;
Kings undisturbed by the blaze and battle roll;
Bloom in the seed; the song in egg; the grey light
That holds so deep a glory in the Vale of Glenasmole!

## Limestone and Water

This is the rock whose colours range
   From bright to dark when wet with rain,
Clear as an eye whose colours change
   From smoke-grey blue to dark again:
This is the limestone base of earth
From which the best things come to birth.

And the stream shallows where it walls'
   Smooth steep, which ivy pennons coat,
Down from bare earth abruptly falls,
   And stands as if it stood in a moat;
Above, a sapling shows its root:
The wild stream darkens the cliff foot.

Out of this rock the stone was smashed
   That gave long beauty time to grow;
The hammers rang, the chisels flashed:
   It answered back with fire the blow;
And it gave gifts and guards enough
From limestone to the Parian stuff.

Water and rock by warriors wed
   Here with the landscape well accord.
They built beyond Time's ambuscade,
   Builders and wielders of chisel and sword.
So well they dealt with stone and stream
Eternity deals well with them.

And where the grey sky turns to white,
   Failing the limits of the land's
Far-shining girdle, dark, upright,
   The strong four-cornered tower stands;
And nearer, where the grey sky lowers,
The long green tunnels close on towers.

And here where Time has trampled down
   The white-thorn bush and blurred the track,
Up stands the steep unblunted stone
   And brings the lance-straight ladies back,
And lights again those eyes of theirs
As brave as glints from young men's spears.

For not a thing that ever grew
   To win Time's heart can Time forget:
With clouds he blends the lichens' hue;
   The mountains with the parapet;
And crowns that tower's denizen
Who had more than her share of men.

Wherever Life is made secure
   Beauty is gardened to become
As lovely as its walls are sure
   Foundations fit for Beauty's home.
And like long reaches, stilled by weirs,
So Loveliness wastes not with years.

The castle by the shallow ford:
   In ruin, but the upright line
Above the tangle keeps its word:
   In death the unbroken discipline!
And O, what great well-being went
To build the enduring battlement!


## Anachronism

Tall and great-bearded: black and white,
The deep-eyed beggar gazed about,
For all his weight of years, upright;
He woke the morning with a shout,
One shout, one note, one rolling word;
But in my dreaming ears I heard
The sea-filled rhythm roll again,
And saw long-vanished boys and men
With eager faces ranged around
A dark man in a market place,
Singing to men of his own race,

With long blithe ripples in the sound,
Of isles enchanted, love and wrath,
And of Achilles' deadly path;
The great ash spear he used to fling;
The bow one man alone could string;
Odysseus in the sea immersed
Who never heard of 'Safety First,'
Nor went to a Peace Conference:
For Homer was a man of sense,
And knew right well the only themes
Of Song, when men have time for dreams.
And then, indignant, down the lane
The great dark beggar roared again.


## Sub Ilice

Who will come with me to Italy in April?
Italy in April! The cherries on the hill!
The sudden gush of rivers where the valleys rib the mountains;
The blue green mists, the silence which the mountain valleys fill!

Is that Alba Longa? Yes; and there's Soracte.
Soracte? Yes; in Horace: don't you 'vides ut,' you fool?
No! She's not a model . . . you will have her husband on us. . . . !
Though her buttocks are far better than the Seven Hills of Rome!

Cherries ripe and mountains! Young wives with the gait of
Goddesses; and feelings which you try in vain to say
To the gay vivacious calculating native;
If you knew Italian you would give the show away.

What is the attraction? Why are we delighted
When we meet the natives of a race that's not our own?
Is that which we like in them our ignorance about them;
And we feel so much the better where we know we are not known?

Well, it does not matter. I am thinking of a stone-pine
Where an Empress had her villa on the great Flaminian Way;
And the blond Teutonic students who have come so far for knowledge,
And the fräuleins who come with them on a reading holiday.

If I met a tall fair student girl from Dresden,
Whiter than a cream cheese, credulous, and O
Earnest, and so grateful for the things that I might teach her,
And I took her touring, would she have the sense to go?

I would through a ringlet, whisper . . . 'This is Virgil's
Confiscated farmstead which his friend in Rome restored.
The Mastersinging races from the North came down here merging;
And your hair was heir to colour that great Titian preferred.

How my pulses leap up! I can hardly curb them,
Visiting the places which a poet loved . . . Ah, well!
Never fear the nightfall . . . Veniemus urbem!
My friend can take our taxi and go look for an hotel.'

Here between the last wave of the hills subsiding
And the river-beeches which are growing bald with age,
Gentle as the land's rise, lofty and abiding,
Rhythm's mountain ranges rose to sunshine from his page.

"'Is this Virgil's birthplace?'" Scholars are uncertain –
You cannot be a scholar if a thing is too well known –
There's the Idyll's ilex: if we use it for a curtain,
You can sit on half my raincoat and my half will be a throne.

Virgil was Menalcas: let me call you Phyllis.
Now look up the Idyll where they tried what each could do:
There! 'Vis ergo inter nos,' and 'turn about's,' 'vicissim';
My pipe though not waxed-jointed yet can play a tune or two.'


           *        *        *


Friends, you must forgive me for this utter nonsense.
To-day I saw an ilex where the Dodder streels along;
And that togaed exile made me so despondent
That I called the light and glory which it shadows into song.

Thwart in the world I control are many seasons,
Many climes and characters obedient to a spell;
I turn to human grandeur's most exalted voice for reasons,
And not the least, that Virgil led a soul estranged from Hell.

## Oughterard

Do ye know Oughterard with the stream running through it;
The bridge that falls down on one side like a hill;
The trees and the pleasant, respectable houses;
The white waterfall and the old ruinèd mill?

God be with the night when I drank there wid Sweeney
Till he brought the 'special' from under the floor
And dawn came in square through the bar-parlour window;
And 'Jaze us!' Sez Sweeney 'It's twenty past four!'

In old Oughterard I could get on quite nicely,
For there I know decent, remarkable men:
Jim Sweeney, the Sergeant and Fr. McNulty
Who took the first prize with his running dog 'Finn.'

Bad cess to the seas and bad cess to the causeways
That keep me from goin' back homeward once more
To lean on the bridge and gaze down at the goslings,
And get a 'Good morrow' from black Morty Mor.

## Connemara

West of the Shannon may be said
Whatever comes into your head;
But you can do, and chance your luck,
Whatever you like West of the Suck.

There's something sleeping in my breast
That wakens only in the West;
There's something in the core of me
That needs the West to set it free.

And I can see that river flow
Beside the town of Ballinasloe
To bound a country that is worth
The half of Heaven, the whole of Earth.

It opens out above the town
To make an island of its own;
And in between its sky-blue arms
The grass is green as any farm's.

As often as I take the road
Beyond the Suck, I wish to God
That it were but a one-way track
Which I might take and not come back.

The very light above the bay,
The mountains leaping far away,
Are hands that wave through homely air,
To make me shout 'I'll soon be there!'

It is not everyone gets on
Where dwell the Seaside Sons of Conn;
It is not everyone that's wanted
Where things are apt to be enchanted:

Where you may see if you look out
The hills and clouds tumbling about;
But suddenly the fun may stop
Until they find to what you're up.

You are supposed to understand
What brings the sea so far inland;
And why the water-lilies be
Close to the gold weed of the sea.

You must not ask what kind of light
Was in the valleys half the night,
Now that you are beyond Beyonds
Where night and day were tied by bonds.

And if you see with half an eye
Two lovers meet, O pass them by!
Remember that the Others do
As you have done by them to you.

And never ask the rights or wrongs
When mountains shake with battle-songs;
Because the Fight surpasses far
The things which merely lead to war.

The light is thronged as is the dark;
But here the wise make no remark:
For if it comes to comments on
The glory, then the prime is gone.

The lanes that end on hill or strand
Of this, the Many Coloured Land,
Are dearer than the burdened roads
That cross the Lands of Many Loads.

It's here that I get out to walk;
The Shannon's there for you that talk;
But I can only work my will
Where mountains leap and clouds lie still.


## Dawn in Vermont

The sun is rising mistily,
    The valley fills with gold.
I lie and wonder sleepily
    How many suns of old
Arose and filled the valleys
    And lit each tree from tree
Along the forest alleys
    And not a soul to see!


## High Above Ohio

Like a timeless god of old
With one glance I can behold
East and West and men between
On the pleasant mortal scene.

Looking at them from above
I can see them as they move,
I can tell where they will go,
Where they're coming from I know.

I who with a single glance
See them going and advance
Can perceive where they are winning,
See the End in the Beginning;

See alternate valleys gleam
Each one with its little stream,
And the undulant, immense,
Free, American expanse;

See the rivers on the plain
Break to catch the light again;
And the towns and villages
Islanded by fields and trees;

And I make a little prayer
As I see the people there,
For I have not quite forgot
That I share the mortal lot.

God, on Whom Time never bears
Disregard not mortal years,
For a year to men may be
Precious as eternity.

Look on men in thorpe and town
Walled between the Dawn and Down
And remember that their cares
Overbalance pleasant years.

Think, when looking through the clouds
At their little streams and woods,
Streams and woods to earthly eyes
May present a paradise.

Leave them happy on the earth,
Relative to death and birth
Till, in peace, their minds transcend
The Beginning and the End.

## Nymphis Et Fontibus

Soldier of Rome, well-trained and hard,
Who dwelt in Britain once and warred,
With no outlandish creed to mar
The stern salvation of the war.

Strong in yourself, you bore your care,
Your soul was like your camp, four-square;
And uncomplaining, iron-shod,
Marched with Rome's honour for your god.

No bigot! In barbarian lands,
Roman where Rome no longer stands,
This altar to your hard-won love:
Earth, and the Nymphs and Springs thereof.

## The Phoenix

Wakeful, I saw my window sashed
    With silver light before sunrise,
When, suddenly, the Phoenix flashed
    A rainbow streak across the skies;
And it was gone before I said:
    The Phoenix! In a book I read
The night before, I learnt to trace
That marvel to the happy place
It flies in, neither linde nor lawn
Of Earth, but in the Groves of Dawn.

There are so many things, the sight
    Goes clean through as it were X-ray:
The finer things that hide in light,
    Or in the heaven, that one might say,
Invisible, but we who know
How heedlessly the sight can go,
Employ the mind's eye but to find
That we are marvellously blind.

There are so many things that I
    Could see that now seem to be hid,
I feel that they would crowd the sky
    If I but lifted up a lid,
Or sang a song, or gave a shout,
That I would see them standing out;
But, as it is, what have I done
With all I've seen under the sun?

The Spring that comes before the Spring
    And waits while boughs are thin and bare,
A deepened light, a quickening,
    Annunciation in the air,
Delights me more, though cold and brief,
    Than buds abounding, and the leaf.

And then the silver isles out far
    On leaden edge of Eastern seas,
Beneath a dappled sky, which are
    Our daily lost Atlantides,
A moment seen, and they are gone,
Bright archipelagos of dawn,
Are more to me, and solider,
Than the near hills which never stir.

But would there be this seeking for,
    This wistful straining after things:
Islands surmised from lines of shore,
    Unless within me there were wings,
Wings that can fly in, and belong
Only to realms revealed by song,
That bring those realms about their nest,
Merging the Seeker and the Quest?

They beat in faintly purple air;
    Beneath them rise autumnal trees;
But Autumn's colours usher there
    A Spring which is Eternity's,

A Spring which overtakes the fruit,
Till blossoms crown the fond pursuit.
And there is neither Time nor Space
Within that paradisal place;
Nor separating length and breadth;

With Love identical is Death;
And no more fearful in that grove
Is Death to those who dwell than Love.

Not in our East then, but in verse,
    The far-seen flashing feather flies,
In Groves of Dawn whose wells immerse
    The star that lights and leads the Wise,
But rare's the book that holds the Word
That moves the uncompanioned Bird
To shake the air, and, in its flight,
Rain down the variegated light

That makes all timeless, and transforms
Unmagical and ageing norms;
And, when it falls upon, renews
The full blue eye, the twinkling thews,
And makes again the heart of man
Ageless and epinikian.


## Fresh Fields

I gaze and gaze when I behold
The meadows springing green and gold.
I gaze until my mind is naught
But wonderful and wordless thought!
Till, suddenly, surpassing wit,
Spontaneous meadows spring in it;
And I am but a glass between
Un-walked-in meadows, gold and green.


## High Tide at Malahide

*(To Lynn Doyle)*

The luminous air is wet
As if the moon came through
To hold as in a net
Such as the spiders set
By ditch and rivulet,

The grey unfallen dew.
The sun is not down yet;
As yet the eve is new.

The water is all a-quiver,
There scarce is room to stand
Beside the tidal river
So narrowed is the strand:
And, over there, the wood
Is standing in a flood,
Erect, and upside down;
And at its roots, a swan.

A silvern mist enhances,
By tangling half the light,
The glowing bay's expanses
Which else had been too bright;
For air is subject to
A tidal ebb and flow.

And all the weeds with sandy root
That in the sunshine on the beach
Crackled like ashes underfoot,
Are standing upright now to stretch,
All ambered from within, each frond
That sways revived in the great pond;
And every axon in my brain
And neuron takes the tide again,
Made all the fuller from the tide
That brims the sands of Malahide;
But what shall come into it now
I know not. I await the flow.
I must abide the cosmic main
Whose high tide floods the stranded brain;
For no such miracle is wrought
On earth like this by taking thought.

Oh, look at the ships
With their sails coming down
And the wonderful sweeps
That are steering them still
To the little grey town

On the green of the hill!
Are they Norman or Norse,
Or descendants of Conn
Returning in force
From a lost British town,
With women and loot now the Roman is gone?
They are Norse! For the bugles are wild in the woods,
Alarms to the farms to look after their goods:
To bury their cauldrons and hide all their herds.
They are Norse! I can tell by the length of their swords –
Oh, no; by their spears and the shape of their shields
They are Normans: the men who stand stiff in the fields
In hedges of battle that no man may turn;
The men who build castles that no one may burn;
The men who give laws to the chief and the kern.
Salt of the earth,
Salt of the sea,
Norman and Norse
And the wild man in me!
The founders of cities,
The takers of fields,
The heroes too proud to wear armour or shields,
Their blood is in you,
As it cannot but be,
O Townsmen of towns on an estuary!

O clear Swords River that now without noise
Meets in this marvellous equipoise,
O clear Swords River, O let me know
What is it you add to the undertow,
For sight and sound like a bubble tost
On the high tide no more than on ether is lost:
No sight or odour or country sound
Lately reflected or long ago drowned,
But rises again, and as beautiful
As the golden weed when the tide is full,
Or the clouds that floating becalmed, sublime,
Break out white sails for the halcyon time.
With what do you mingle your merchandise
Of hawthorns budding or Autumn skies;
The cackling flight of the golden nib
That rallies the leaf to protect the crib;
The moth gone mad in a zigzag flight

On the magical edge of the day and the night;
The flag leaves serried beside your fords,
Like bronze gone green in the ancient swords;
The shadowless light of the peace to be;
The scent of the rain when it dries on the lea?
White wings are all that endow the sea,
Except when it grates on its soundless bars;
Of diamonds shoaled from the fallen stars;
For all that you brought from the fields of home
Is saved, not lost, in the fields of foam,
And rises again, for it was not dead,
Here where the meadows and waters wed.
Remember that by no force terrene
Does the high tide rise till no sands are seen,
When silver limits the old green plain,
And the luminous mist floods into the brain
At will to replenish the Past again:
Such wonders cannot on earth be done
Till the moon join hands with the golden sun.


## The Isles of Greece

*Applied Poetry*
*(Lesbos)*

Marble was her lovely city
And so pleasant was its air
That the Romans had no pity
For a Roman banished there;
Lesbos was a singing island
And a happy home from home
With the pines about its highland
And its crescent faint with foam.
Lady make a nota bene
That Love's lyric fount of glee
Rose in marbled Mytilene
Channelled by the purple sea.
Sappho sang to her hetairai,
And each lovely lyricist
Sappho's singing emulated;
And this point must not be missed:
Women were emancipated

Long before the Christian era,
Long before the time of Christ.
Then not only were they equal
To their men folk but themselves;
And the lovely lyric sequel
Lives on all our learned shelves.
Yes: we may be fairly certain,
As results of this release,
Sappho's was, with all its Girton
Girls, the fairest Isle of Greece.


II

Ah, those Isles of Asia Minor!
Was there ever such a coast?
Dawned there any day diviner
On a blither singing host?
Do not give this thought an inning
Lest the critics take it wrong:
In proportion to the sinning
Is the excellence of song.
Sin had not yet been imported
In those days to the Levant,
So the singers loved and sported,
Raised the paean, rhymed the chant,
Until Hebrew fortune tellers
Terrorised the pleasant scene,
Hawking horrors as best-sellers,
Mixing bards and baths with sin.
Therefore pass no moral stricture
On that fairest of Earth's states;
And succumb not to the mixture
Of ideas up with dates.

We shall find as we go boating
(You are paying for the yacht),
That those isles on purple floating
Were the isles of guiltless thought,
Isles whereby a peacock's feather
Would, if cast into the bay,
In the green and purple weather
Be reduced to hodden gray.
Gloomy thoughts are just a failing

From which you must win release
If with me you would come sailing
Carefree through the Isles of Greece.
Therefore pass no surly sentence
From our time and towns fog-pent,
Much less ask for their repentance
Who had nothing to repent.


## The Waveless Bay

(*Kiltymon*)

I close my eyes to hold a better sight,
And all my mind is opened on a scene
Of oaks with leaves of amber in the green,
A mist of blue beneath them: to the right
A long cape fades beyond the azurite
Of one calm bay to which the pastures lean.
The rounded fields are warm, and in between
The yellow gorse is glaring stiff and bright.
It matters little what distraction drives,
Clouds through my mind and breaks the outer day.
For all I know that distant water strives
Against the land. I have it all my way:
Through budding oaks a steadfast sun survives:
Peace on the fading cape, the waveless bay.


## Fog Horns

The fog horns sound
With a note so prolonged
That the whole air is thronged,
And the sound is to me,
In spite of its crying,
The most satisfying,
The bravest of all the brave sounds of the sea.

From the fjords of the North
The fogs belly forth
Like sails of the long ships

That trouble the earth.
They stand with loose sail
In the fords of the Gael:
From Dark Pool to White Ford the surf-light is pale.

The chronicles say
That the Danes in their day
Took a very great prey
Of women from Howth.
They seem to imply
That the women were shy,
That the women were loath
To be taken from Howth.
From bushy and thrushy, sequestering Howth.
No mists of the Druid
Could halt or undo it
When long ships besetted
The warm sands wave-netted.
In vain might men pray
To be spared the invader
To that kind eye of gray,
To the Saint who regretted
Sea-purple Ben Edar.
They sailed to the town
That is sprung from the sea
Where the Liffey comes down
Down to roll on the Lea.

The fog horns sound
With the very same roar
That was sounded of yore
When they sounded for war.
As the war horns sounded
When men leapt ashore,
And raised up the stane
Where the long ships had grounded.
You hear them again
As they called to the Dane,
And the glens were astounded.
War horns sounded,
And strong men abounded
When Dublin was founded.

Whenever a woman of Moore Street complains
With hawser of hair
Where the golds and browns are,
And under her arm
A sieve or a dish
Full of flowers or of fish,
I think of that ancient forgotten alarm:
Of horror and grief
As she snatched at the leaf
In tunnels sea-ended that fall to the reef.

It was all Long Ago,
Only now to the slow
Groping in of the ships
In the sunlight's eclipse,
Are the fog horns sounded;
When war horns sounded
War ships could be grounded,
And dynasties founded.
But now they crawl in
With a far louder din
Than the old horns' could be;
And that's as it should be,
Because we put now
In the place of the prow
Of the dragon-head boats
A bowsprit of notes
With their loud, Safety First!
Where blue-eyed men burst,
And founded a city and founded a thirst!
And founded far more than to-day could be found:
The lesser the courage, the louder the sound!

But when the Dark Linn
Is aloud from the Rinn
I think of the women the sea-kings brought in:
The women of Dublin, the women who mother
A breed that the land and the sea cannot bother.
In flagons that ream
Like my own river's stream,
That gold of the granite
Gone black in the bogs,
I drink to our Race

That will go to the dogs,
Unless it can trace
And revive the old ways
Of the city when only
The bravest could man it,
Unless it can hold
To the virtues of old
When women resisted
And lovers were bold;
And steer through each upstart
Miasma that clogs
Its mind with the ravings
Of sly pedagogues;
And blow its own trumpet
To shatter the fogs.


## Between Brielle and Manasquan

The old sea captains, when their work
    Was done on the eternal sea,
Came each ashore and built a house
    And settled down reluctantly;
And in his front lawn each set up
A flagstaff and a telescope.

Each little house was painted white
    With shutters gay and pointed gables
From which the vines hung loose or tight
    Or twisted round like coiled-up cables;
And each green lawn was so well drest
It seemed a little sea at rest.

And some were stocky men with beards
    And some were tawny, blue-eyed men;
And, when they talked, you might have heard
    Surnames that end in '-ing' or '-sen';
All sensed, since they had left the scene,
A falling off in things marine.

You cannot find their houses now
    The place is so much built upon,

They lived – they say who ought to know –
    Between Brielle and Manasquan;
But you can find, in some old store,
The curious things they brought ashore:

Old compasses, chronometers,
    And here a sextant ornamented,
A binnacle and carven wares,
    A captain's spy glass, rather dented,
A keg that raxed a pirate's throttle,
A schooner full rigged in a bottle:

Weapons with silver work inlaid;
    Blue glass the dealer says is Bristol's,
Carved shells and bits of Chinese jade;
    Two old, brass-barrelled, flint-lock pistols,
And, if these fail to take your fancy,
A figurehead called *Spumy Nancy*.

These old seafarers in their day,
    If asked about impressions wrought
By isles of Ind or far Cathay
    Could give no record of their thought;
What wonder worker ever knows
The wonder of the things he does?

Aye; but the little children knew
    What deep lagoons they anchored in,
What reefs they took their vessels through,
    And of strange cargoes hard to win;
The Isles of Spice, typhoons and thunder,
The Yellow Sea, and all its wonder.

They came to think, as they grew old
    And found themselves with few compeers,
That things grow better when they're told,
    And they themselves improved with years;
They'd sail again, did it beseem
Experienced men to take to steam.

Meanwhile, the long deserted sea
    Resented them as one neglected;
She swished her tides resentfully

And tons and tons of sand collected
And silted up the narrow way
That leads to Barnagat's still Bay.

So that they lived as men marooned:
    They could not sail now if they hankered;
You'd think, to see their homes festooned,
    A fleet was in the Bay and anchored,
So gaily grew the creepers mounting,
So gaily flew the flagstaffs' bunting.


## Earth and Sea

It lifts the heart to see the ships
    Back safely from the deep sea main;
To see the slender mizzen tips,
And all the ropes that stood the strain;

To hear the old men shout 'Ahoy,'
    Glad-hearted at the journey's end,
And fix the favourite to the buoy,
    Who had the wind and sea to friend;

To meet, when sails are lashed to spars,
    The men for whom Earth's free from care,
And Heaven a clock with certain stars,
    And Hell a word with which to swear.


## The Ship

A ship from Valparaiso came
    And in the Bay her sails were furled;
She brought the wonder of her name,
    And tidings from a sunnier world.

O you must voyage far if you
    Would sail away from gloom and wet,
And see beneath the Andes blue
    Our white, umbrageous city set.

But I was young and would not go;
    For I believed when I was young
That somehow life in time would show
    All that was ever said or sung.

Over the golden pools of sleep
    She went long since with gilded spars;
Into the night-empurpled deep,
    And traced her legend on the stars.

But she will come for me once more,
    And I shall see that city set,
The mountainous, Pacific shore –
    By God, I half believe it yet!

## Off Sicily

Shells tilted up by Venus' heel
    Seen through the milk of morning air;
White Sicily confronts our keel
    With twin cliffs rising, each as fair
As that smooth-lined up-tilted boat
From which the Foam-Born Queen stept out.

But who can land where I am bound?
    In vain the natives tread their home.
They shall not find its holy ground,
    Who have not sought it in the tome
Whose letters twist like curls that deck
The nape of Venus' golden neck.

## Kingdoms

The sailor tells the children
    His stories of the sea,
Their eyes look over the water
    To where his wonders be:

The flowers as big as tea-cups,
    The great big butterflies,
The long unfooted beaches
    Where stored-up treasure lies.

More than a thousand islands
    Each curved around its pool:
All kingdoms filled with sunlight,
    Where no one goes to school;

The fish that leave the water
    In sudden bends of light
The birds as blue as china;
    The flies that gleam by night . . .

Till, slowly, I remember
    A wistful place; and then, –
The story of that Kingdom
    First told to longshoremen.

# SATIRES AND FACETIAE

## *O Boys! O Boys!*

O boys, the times I've seen!
The things I've done and known!
If you knew where I have been?
Or half the joys I've had,
You never would leave me alone;
But pester me to tell,
Swearing to keep it dark,
What . . . but I know quite well:
Every solicitor's clerk
Would break out and go mad;
And all the dogs would bark!

There was a young fellow of old
Who spoke of a wonderful town.
Built on a lake of gold,
With many a barge and raft
Afloat in the cooling sun,
And lutes upon the lake
Played by such courtesans . . .
The sight was enough to take
The reason out of a man's
Brain; and to leave him daft,
Babbling of lutes and fans.

The tale was right enough:
Willows and orioles,
And ladies skilled in love:
But they listened only to smirk,
For he spoke to incredulous fools,
And, maybe, was sorry he spoke;
For no one believes in joys,
And Peace on Earth is a joke,
Which, anyhow, telling destroys;
So better go on with your work:
But Boys! O Boys! O Boys!

## Ringsend

(After reading Tolstoi)

I will live in Ringsend
With a red-headed whore,
And the fan-light gone in
Where it lights the hall-door;
And listen each night
For her querulous shout,
As at last she streels in
And the pubs empty out.
To soothe that wild breast
With my old-fangled songs,
Till she feels it redressed
From inordinate wrongs,
Imagined, outrageous,
Preposterous wrongs,
Till peace at last comes,
Shall be all I will do,
Where the little lamp blooms
Like a rose in the stew;
And up the back-garden
The sound comes to me
Of the lapsing, unsoilable,
Whispering sea.

## After Galen

Only the Lion and the Cock,
As Galen says, withstand Love's shock.
So, Dearest, do not think me rude
If I yield now to lassitude,
But sympathise with me. I know
You would not have me roar, or crow.

## On Troy

I give more praise to Troy's redoubt
For Love kept in, than War kept out.

## To a Boon Companion

If medals were ordained for drinks,
Or soft communings with a minx,
Or being at your ease belated,
By Heavens, you'd be decorated.
And not Alcmena's chesty son
Have room to put your ribbands on!

## To An Old Tenor

Melfort Dalton, I knew you well
With your frozen eyes and your spastic stance.
Ah, but your voice was clear as a bell
When you tenored the ladies into a trance;
The finest tenor in town you were,
Finest; but those were the days of yore,
Oh, but weren't you arrogant then,
Weren't you arrogant, Chanticleer,
When you told each hostess to go to hell:
'I'll sing what I like and I'll read the score'?

Little they knew; but I knew what you meant:
Yourself you first had to magnify
Before your notes unto Heaven were sent –
(Peacocks and tenors and G.P.I.)
I knew it, and that is the reason why
I now am recording the wonderful tale
Of how you received an offer to come,
Though your eyes and your legs were beginning to fail,
And sing at St. Joseph's Old Maids' Home,
And all the honours you gained therefrom.

We sat in the nearest respectable bar
Waiting the message of how you fared;
And, though we wished it, we were not for
Success overwhelming quite prepared.
Sitting we waited and tippled the ale;
In came the scout with the wonderful word
Of how they tittered and how you scored:
'Called back four times.' And we roared, 'Waes-hael!
Melfort has done it again, good Lord!'
We were not allowed in the Old Maids' Home;
And rightly so, for they might be scared;
But 'Here, boy, here. Tell us all How Come?'
'He shuffled at first, then he came to a stand.
He did not bow as a fav'rite should
(He knew that his balance was none too good)
But he stared with a visage inane and bland.'
'But how did he merit such great applause?
Be more explicit, you poor recorder?'
'Once for singing, and thrice because
His dress revealed a quaint disorder.'

MORAL

(*Non Nobis*)

A moral lies in this occurrence:
Let those who have too much assurance
And think that public approbation
That comes from songs or an oration
Is due but to their own desert,
Remember Melfort Dalton's shirt.

## *To A Mushroom*

No one sang thee, little fielding,
　　Sang thy wondrous being and birth,
Till to mute attraction yielding
　　I first hymned thee here on earth.

Though I never saw thee start up,
　　I have seen thee when thou wert
Poised as with an hinder part up –
　　Oh my sudden quaint upstart!

In the short grass by the fount-head
　　Thou art found as free from rule
As a faun, and unaccounted
　　As a little boy from school.

Or a baby plump and ample,
　　Whose exuberance was led
By Silenus' bad example
　　Till the bowl fell o'er his head

Of all growing things the oddest;
　　Only of a sudden seen
Unexpected and immodest
　　As above a stocking, skin!

Soft, I must entreat thee gently;
　　For I can but do thee wrong,
And but think inconsequently
　　Who for daylight pitch my song.

Suns for thee must still illume an
　　Arid waste beneath the sky,
Wistful, cold and thwartly human
　　And Augustan – even as I.

Darkness only does not flout thee
　　When alone thou tak'st the light,
And the silence floats about thee,
　　Moon-loved dewy child of night.

Thine example shows quite clearly,
    That the things we think deranged
Would be most delightful merely,
    Merely if the scene were changed.


## To the Maids Not to Walk in the Wind

When the wind blows, walk not abroad,
For, Maids, you may not know
The mad, quaint thoughts which incommode
Me when the winds do blow.

What though the tresses of the treen
In doubled beauty move,
With silver added to their green,
They were not made for Love.

But when your clothes reveal your thighs
And surge around your knees,
Until from foam you seem to rise,
As Venus from the seas . . .

Though ye are fair, it is not fair!
Unless you will be kind,
Till I am dead, and changed to AIR,
O walk not in the wind!


## The Nettle

A very pleasant hillside falls among
Pines to the south, and in a greensward settles;
And while we loitered there my Love was stung,
My girl-Adonis on the thigh by nettles.
O what a bore! I must sit down, said she;
I cannot walk! . . . O darling, what's the matter?
A nettle stung me where you must not see,
Just where my stocking ends and thigh grows fatter.
But I will shut my eyes before it gets . . .
And you shall guide me so I shall not miss it –

Before the poison in your system sets,
I'll press my lips and very gently kiss it.
The little blister white upon the white
Of sudden snow where violets were peeping,
Was reddened by the cure which set it right.
Now if, years hence, you find they are not keeping
My grave with all the reverence that is due
To one whom Beauty's smile in Life elated,
O, Busybody, trouble not! Can you
Be sure the nettle waves to desecrate it?

## A Pithy Prayer Against Love

Gods, get me out of it!
Spirits of Laughter
Come to my aid now
And exorcise it!
O you, Priapus,
Stand till you're skyward,
Stand till you're all staff
And cannot rise it!
Let your preposterous
Pole fall upon her:
'That for her honour!'
Let not a thought now
Of comfort escape us:
Think what in boisterous,
Blowing Jack Falstaff,
Shakespeare made Love look.
Think how that cheerful
Chiel Hippocleides
Would this my fearful
Passion disparage;
Dancing incessantly,
Dancing indecently,
Danced, till he danced off
A cure for all heart-aches
(Dancing the cordax!),
Danced, till his carriage
Displeased the bride's father;
Dancing it further,

He danced off his marriage;
Danced to surmout his
Fate with: οὐ φροντίς!
Teach me his courage.

## New Forms

I gathered marble Venus in my arms,
Just as the rabble crowded on the stair.
I said, For her the sea gave up its storms;
And gently on her body breathed the air.
Alas, she fell, and broke to many pieces:
Discovered later by a Professor,
He cried, 'New forms, new forms!' And wrote a thesis.

## The Three

### FAITH

Brian O'Lynn as the legends aver
Was crossing a bridge with his wife and his cur.
The bridge it collapsed and the trio fell in:
'There's land at the bottom,' said Brian O'Lynn.

### HOPE

Let Surgeon MacCardle confirm you in Hope.
A jockey fell off and his neck it was broke.
He lifted him up like a fine, honest man;
And he said 'He is dead; but I'll do all I can.'

### CHARITY

Life would be less outrageous
If all the drinks were free;
And Health became contagious
And Old Age fit to see;
And, when we stretched our tether,
Instead of loitering,
All we went all together
Like blossoms in the Spring.

## Choric Song of the Ladies of Lemnos

(*The Lemnians having killed their husbands, faced with the necessity of defending the Island, resolve to press the crew of the* Argo *which carried Hercules into marriage.*)

Str. I.      Who will marry Hercules?
                  Tell me if you can.
             Who will catch his eye, and please
                  The strong silent man?

             Who will make a happy home,
                  For duty and desire:
             In Summer tend the honey-comb,
                  In Winter, tend the fire?

Antis. I.    What exactly is the sense,
                  And substance of your song?
             Is his strength in reticence;
                  Or is he silent, strong?

             Often strong and silent men,
                  With sorra much to say,
             Are with young and old women
                  Winsome in their way.

Epos. I.     'Tis the great Tirynthian groom,
                  A boyo hard to parry!
             Rather ask the question whom
                  Hercules will marry.

Str. II.     Thus to speak as if no choice
                  Were left, is to disparage
             Us, who surely have a voice,
                  And the half of marriage;

             To put the cart before the horse,
                  The groom before the bride.
             It is for the girl, of course,
                  Also to decide.

Antis. II.   O look at him with his club,
                  And his lion's fell!
             That's the lad who made the hub-
                  Bub below in Hell!

That which is the pirates' quest
   May be Hercules's:
To carry off the buxomest,
   And marry whom he pleases!

Epos. II.   Praise him for his shoulders' breadth,
Him who took the Town of Death,
Took the triple Dog therefrom,
And Alcestis to her home.

Praise him, for he carries through
All he sets himself to do;
No one ever saw him chuck
Anything he undertook;

Softly talk of marriage, he
Might embrace the colony;
And if he were duly roused
Who would then be unespoused?


## Europa and the Bull

(*To Arthur Train*)

'Where is little Wide Eyes?'
'Where but in the farmyard.'
'Have I never told you
To be careful of the child?'
'Well, you would not think that
There she would come harmward,
If you saw the stallion tremble
When she pats him, and grow mild.'

'Nurse, it's not of danger
From animals I'm thinking;
Rather of a fashion
Which of late has grown too rife:
Girls of county families,
Of men in my position,
With grooms are so familiar,
It's as bad as man and wife!

And then there is this Never-to-be-
Too-much-deprecated
Tendency towards bringing
Only daughters up as boys;
If the Queen were living,
She would never tolerate it. . . .
What's their masquerading
To the magic it destroys!'

'Well I know that queer things
Happen in the country:
Nothing could be queerer
Than a King to take his cue
From his subjects' families,
Or pardon their effrontery
Who dared to tell his daughter
Or her Nannie what to do.'

'I, not unobservant,
Nurse, have noticed anger
Often used by women
Who were not irascible,
Out of mere resentment
When they could no longer
Argue a position
Which had proved untenable.

If your speech is ended,
Listen, my good woman,
Nothing is achieved by
Incoherent talk:
Tell her that the country
Is an open farmyard,
Wide Eyes will go with you
And her maidens for a walk.

Any distance inland
Needs the stoutest buskin,
Sandals are more suited
To the firmly-sanded shore;
No matter where you go to,
Surely come by dusk in.

I trust we need not talk about
The farmyard any more.'

*    *    *

Dunes are here on this side,
There, that piny headland;
Midway, like a giant,
Is that landward-leaning tree,
Angry with the constant
Briny-blowing West Wind,
Poising up a shoulderstone
To cast it in the sea.

Do you see that wave there,
Where the crescent curves lift,
Transilluminating
For a second into green
Miles of crystal daylight,
Then, the hissing snowdrift:
Light so water-tangled
That its sightless self is seen – ?

That is how the daylight,
Barely vespertinal,
Save but for a feeling
That a moon was very near,
Looked above the headland
Of the sandy, sinal
Crescent, while it waited
For a crescent in the air.

Taller than the tallest
Of her young companions,
Wide Eyes never wilted
Where the broken ground begins:
That's the Archer Goddess,
With her bosom belted!
No; it is a tomboy
With the scratches on her shins!

Certainly unconscious
That she was a maiden
Who could fill with banners

Frontiers of Kings!
Once you saw her swinging
From her youthful haunches,
You would feel that manners
Were not all-important things.

'If I raced you up there,
Which of you could whistle?
Just you watch me running
When I get my second wind.'
Moulding in her short skirt
Limbs to jump the thistle,
A cry of wonder reached her
From the little group behind.

Gambolling and charging,
Low head shaken sideways,
Swerving as though guided
By his tassel rudder tail,
Snorting more than stamping
A ripple on the tideways,
A Bull, where nothing ever
Drew a furrow but a sail!

Eyes beneath a broad brow
Widen with amazement,
Not because the women
Who were with her ran away;
But because a bull used
Water for a pavement.
Down the fearless maiden went
To meet him at the Bay.

White as any Maytree
In the milky Maytime,
Clothed about her middle
With a dress as deep as haws,
On the beach she waited
In the silver of the daytime,
A blurred green moon above her
Like a May branch in the shaws.

Clear against the bright wall
Of the low horizon
On the bull came, prancing,
Lifting up his knees.
He came on as gaily
As a galley dancing
While its sail is being lowered
And the shouts are from the quays.

Like a man of Yorkshire
Grunting after Christmas,
When the curly foreheads
And the appetites convene,
White against the dark green
Pines along the isthmus;
He landed hardly wetted
By his gambols on the brine.

Beating Heart of Nature
What is it divorced us
From your mighty pulses
Throbbing into Sense!
Sorra much the Hermit,
Reason gives, who cursed us:
Even Love goes ebbing
From his deadly prescience!

Now he runs around her,
Now he stands before her,
Now his mighty breathings
Tighten up her clothes;
Now he runs around her,
Now he kneels before her,
Now she pulls her instep
From the spraying of his nose!

Who except a fool would
Think he knew the mental
Processes that act upon
A widow, wife or maid?
But the very sight of
Strength becoming gentle –
That is what they can't resist:
A married man has said.

Not the alabaster
Palaces of Minos
Ever held a better
Or a bull more quickly tamed:
Glancing coat half-ruffled
Like a pool amid the spinous
Dells of Ida's island
For a hundred cities famed.

From his dewlap only
Drops of water trickled,
For she felt his back warm,
Silky-soft and dry,
And no common bull's hide!
For it never tickled,
When she held the strong beast
Tight with either thigh.

Maybe, had she noticed,
When she first went near him,
That he had no halter
Nor the ring he should have worn,
She might have cast about her
For another way to steer him:
Bulls are ill-directed
When you take them by the horn.

Once he had her mounted,
Even had she willed it,
She could not have left him
While the sea was yet below,
But she held on lightly
To the garlands on the gilded
Horns, more blunt, but stronger
Than the horns of buffalo.

Some wondered was she laughing at
The bucketing and heaving
Bull who tried her courage
When he sent the waves aswirl;
Some wondered was she sorry for
The home that she was leaving:
All talk! They only wondered
What would happen to the girl!

Because the tales that suit me best
Are tales without a moral.
Like this – unless at Harmony
It hints in times afar,
Before with all creation
And ourselves we came to quarrel;
Before the animals found out
What animals we are.

Because I love the days in which
Such miracles were common,
Because I can suggest to you,
So sceptical of all,
(The mind provides the prodigy)
That many a horsey woman
Would welcome well such miracle
When riding for a fall – ;

Because the thoughts I dwell upon
Would never pass a teacher
Who maintains the Word was made
According to the word
Of men who separate Mankind
From Universal Nature –
For what eloping god to-day
Would turn into a Ford?

Because I hold an Age of Faith
Whose dogma is emphatic
Is happier than such as this
When, if there's faith about,
'Tis not in gods by girls transformed,
But Jewish mathematic,
I go for Truth to Beauty
Which is subject to less doubt.

So I see the white Bull
As the water yellowed
With the purple-vested
Girl upon his back,
Laughing when he dipt down,
Laughing when he bellowed,
Laughing when she dug her heels
To goad him on the track.

Peace instead of panic now
Where, long ago, erumpent
Through the trance of quiet
Of that farmstead with a roar –
Sand instead of cities since –
The Bull bore off triumphant
That sweet and self-made burden
From the blest Sidonian shore.

What about her father?
Formal proclamation
That it was her nurse's
Fault was no excuse
In the eyes of 'County,'
Nor a consolation;
But glory when the Church declared
His son-in-law was Zeus!

## *The Old Woman of Beare*

(From the Irish)

*(This to-day had been Fresh Nellie,*
*For she had as wild a belly;*
*Or a kind of Mrs. Mack,*
*For she had a bonnie back;*
*Or the Honourable Mrs. Lepple –*
*Nipple to a kingly nipple –*
*For she never took advantage*
*Of the favours of her frontage;*
*Therefore she was held in honour*
*By the warty boys who won her;*
*Therefore some old Abbey's shelf*
*Kept the record of herself,*
*Telling to men who disapprove*
*Of Love, the long regrets of Love.)*

Now my tide of youth is gone
And my ebb of age comes on;
Though the sonsie may be happy,
I'm no longer soft and sappy.

Age is causing all my woes:
I who had new underclothes
As I queened it every day,
Now have no one's castaway.

O the times that I had then!
You have money, I had men
Who could give their horse the reins
Yet not leave their own demesnes.

Of the men for whom I stript
None was weaker when we clipt,
But the fury of my flame
Magnified the man in him.

Now each bargain-driving clown
Wants two ups for one go down;
God, if I reciprocated,
They would think themselves castrated!

All my thoughts are of the years
When we drove the brazen cars:
Of the gold we used to fling; –
What was money to a king?

Now my arms are flat and dried
Which were round on every side,
Dearer once to kings than gems,
Dearer than their diadems.

Shameful now to lift them up
Round the hairless neck of youth;
Though my name may be a lure,
I am no boy's paramour.

See the careless lassies swing
As they walk the lane of Spring;
See the lassies go a–Maying
Safe awhile from Time's waylaying!

Once I never heard of stints
On my colours or my pints.
Particolours I could wear;
Now what colour is my hair?

I've no grudge against old age;
But what puts me in a rage
Is that women flaunt their gold
Heads before me when I'm old.

Kings are under Femen's stone;
Bregon holds their weathered throne;
The very stones are worse for wear,
And dappled grey is Bregan's Chair.

A wave stands up and shouts at sea:
It's Winter here for more than me!
I have no sheets; but, as I say,
McHugh will hardly call to-day.

The lads I loved are all aboard,
And strain through Alma's reedy ford;
No logs of oak will break and glow
To warm the beds where they are now!

There's not one left of all the band
That well could bring a boat to strand
Where I ran with little on
Who now am cloaked even in the sun.

Now whatever comes to me
Must be met with 'Glory be!'
Glory be to God at least
For each feat of old, and feast.

Glory be! I'm half content
Just to think of all I spent.
Passion never waned in me
For the want of . . . Glory be!

Every foot that moves must stop;
Every acorn has to drop;
For the blazing festive sconce
Darkness now, and prayer's response.

Cups of whey at night and morn
For the crescent drinking horn;
But the nuns and all their whey
Have not washed my rage away!

## Youth and Truth

When I was young the trees would bend
And shake their branches merrily;
As if they knew I was their friend
They stretched their little hands to me;
Grasses would run across the brake,
And little waves dance on the lake.
Then someone said, 'It is the wind.'
Oh, why should Truth be so unkind?

## Job's Healer

When the Comforters of Job
Had filled up each weary lobe
With suggestions, there appeared –
Goatee foot and goatee beard –
Most appropriately from mist,
Satan, the Psychiatrist.

He said, 'I've seen and overheard
How you look, and every word
You have uttered makes me guess
I can help you in distress.
First, let not your mind be bumptious:
Jonah, gulphed by his Subconscious,
Stands for fact. The parable
Is, of course, the whopping Whale.
Your Subconscious is your trouble
Which your Reason can but double.
Let us now proceed to state it;
Then we'll try to sublimate it.

Oh, your instinct was so right
When you cursed conception night,
For the source of all your bother
Is, of course, your lady Mother.
She craved, just before her wedding,
Highballs and a whole plum pudding;
And that ante-natal wish
Lands you in this kettle o' fish.

For, you know, too many Scotches
Make the skin come out in blotches:
Confluent furunculosis
Is the rest of your psychosis,
Which may represent the plums
In that pudding of your Mum's.

Things that on the land and sea go
Are projections of your Ego:
Leviathan and Behemoth –
You may add the Lord to both –
And we get three combinations
Of immense hallucinations.
God is merely a convention
That produces inward tension,
Or a goal man cannot match
Just to keep him up to scratch;
Else, he might be just as thievish
As you're itchy, old and peevish.

Sing this little song with me,
'Since there is no diety
What's the use of piety?
Or of goodness, or of badness?
Either way can lead to madness
As Responsibility
Leads to imbecility.
Long ago against Free Will
Mankind took a sleeping pill.
It is time he took another
Sleeping pill against his Mother.

Every man from woman came,
Only woman is to blame.
Every thing's hereditary
Therefore, eat, drink and be merry.'

Since your mind can now perceive
Only evil comes from Eve,
Borrow an ax,
With a couple of whacks
Kill your mother
And then,
RELAX!'

# LOVE AND BEAUTY

---

## Dedication

Tall unpopular men,
Slim proud women who move
As women walked in the islands when
Temples were built to Love,
I sing to you. With you
Beauty at best can live,
Beauty that dwells with the rare and few,
Cold and imperative.
He who had Cæsar's ear
Sang to the lonely and strong.
Virgil made an austere
Venus Muse of his song.

## Thinking Long

When children call you, Grandmamma;
And you with thin dark-veinèd hands
In silence stroke the heads that, Ah!
Recall the glorious smouldering bands
Of sullen gold that bound your brow,
And him who told you how the light

131

Burst through them when you combed them low
With sidelong head at fall of night:
Before that vision fades away
Just take this message from the Past:
''Tis love that counteracts decay
And lights and makes all Beauty last.'
And wonder if the love you spared
To starve the light-heart man of rhyme
Has left him low and you grey-haired,
Though you are old, before your time.

## Tell Me Now

### SHE

Tell me now is Love's day done?
Beauty as elect and rare
As when towns were trampled on
Lives to-day and takes the air.
Yet no amorous Triumvir
Throws the world and Rome away;
No one swims Abydos' bay;
Towns are not cast down, and none,
None begets the Moon and Sun.

### HE

Do not let him hear your taunt!
Love's as strong to-day as when
Walls could not endure his brunt,
And he broke the Trojan men.
He can do as much again;
Do not doubt him for an hour,
Tempt his pleasure, not his power;
Danger gives him no affront,
He is not cooled by Hellespont.

## Concerning Hermione

### I. THE CONQUEST

'Since the Conquest none of us
Has died young except in battle.'
I knew that hers was no mean house,
And that beneath her innocent prattle
There was likely hid in words
What could never anger Fame;
The glory of continuous swords,
The obligations of a name.
Had I grown incredulous,
Thinking for a little space:
Though she has the daring brows,
She has not the falcon face;
In the storm from days of old
It is hard to keep at poise,
And it is the over-bold,
Gallant-hearted, Fate destroys:
Could I doubt that her forbears
Kept their foot-hold on the sands,
Triumphed through eight hundred years,
From the hucksters kept their lands,
And still kept the conquering knack –
I who had myself gone down
Without waiting the attack
Of their youngest daughter's frown?

### II. EXORCISM

To banish your shape from my mind
    I thought of the dangerous wood
Where a man might wander and find,
    By a stream in the solitude,
The Queen it is death if one sees,
    Death by a merciless dart;
But how could that bring me release,
    Shot as I am to the heart?

Beauty will cure me, I cried;
    By Beauty is Beauty dislodged.
And I worked on a dream till I eyed
    The Queens whom the young man judged.

But the vision faded and slipt;
    And the cure was a cure of no worth;
For I said, when the Queens were stript,
    I have given the prize to a fourth.

Ugliness, Chaos and War
    I know, but I would not invoke;
They would feed you as darkness a star,
    And strengthen the beam of my yoke.
If Love be reborn in a song
    I with my fate will not quarrel,
But you, if you do him a wrong,
    May be changed to a reed or a laurel.


### III. EXCOMMUNICATION

Go to the fields of purple and gold;
    With lovers and young Queens remain,
Blossoms and battlements of old,
    Far in the background of my brain.
Rest with them there, but stand apart,
    Although you equal those who died;
For no one enters in my heart
    By Death or Love undeified.


### IV. SILENCE

The purple falls between the pines,
The sun that blanched Arundel walls,
Remembering them as he declines,
With purple fills his airy halls.
We drove all day; and all day long
Of Love and longing long we spoke;
And sang so often ballad and song,
The crescent moon cannot evoke
Another word; though Beauty calls
There is no word that can be said.
If Hesperus unhailed shines on,
O do not dream that Love is dead.
The hand I take is not withdrawn,
Between the pines the purple falls.

### V. A SOUND

She called me by my Christian name,
  Quite simply of her own accord,
And unexpectedly it came –
  O the exceeding great reward!
Where are the years of longing, years
  Of vigils and anxieties,
My perturbations now, my fears?
  Gone with the wind across the trees.
Enchanted now, I walk in peace,
  As one who walking on a sward
At twilight hears, or thinks he hears,
  A fanfare out of Joyous Gard.


## Release

*(To Calypso)*

Not fixed is worship as I thought
When first your pride I faced,
But by some wonder heaven-wrought
May be at once displaced.

The heart to one ideal tied
May be released one day;
One day the Messenger, espied
Above Pieria,

Shall stoop; and, as he skims and dips –
Each sandal's golden fin
Fanning the violet water tips
To rainbows as they spin –

Come with the order from above;
And, like Odysseus, free,
I for an human-hearted love
Again shall risk the sea!

## Melsungen

Love, let us go to the village of Melsungen,
Folded in the river which is flowing without noise:
Dark are the woods and the fields are green and golden,
Spreading to the ripple of the hills against the skies.

Hold down the car on the long road to Melsungen;
Hold the heart down that no speed can ever sate!
Through the noon already it has raced into the evening,
Raced, and reached the gables in the evening falling late.

Long have I gazed at your window in Melsungen,
Yellow in the lamp-light, while I watch the miles at noon,
Dreaming of peace as the arrow from the bow-string
Dreams, and gains in quiet from the speed which makes it swoon.

Love, let us lean from a dormer in Melsungen,
Giving on the valley where the light has found the stream,
Cool and becalmed, as the moonlight on the water,
Motionless and quiet as beyond our life a dream.

## Leave Taking

I pushed the leaves aside:
Upon a mountain lawn
I saw a little fawn
White-throated, vivid, pied.
'Her eyes are just as tender,
Her ankles just as slender,'
I said. With challenged grace,
It fled before my face,
Slim-ankled, velvet-eyed.

I watched a topmost spray
Of leaves that move and shimmer
In faintest airs of Summer
Before the trance of day.
I said, 'A curl can float
Breathless across her throat.'

The silver leaves stopt glistening
As if they had been listening
To what I had to say.

A bank of tangled briars
Sloped gently to the south,
Its leaves recalled her mouth
With their soft hidden fires.
'Her lips are bright as cherries
And sweet as wild strawberries,'
I said. Where leaves were spangled
The wild rose grew more tangled
With barbed and bending wires.

From some rush-hidden spring
A stream in little trebles
Tinkled from pools of pebbles
And gurgled, preluding
Each laughing, liquid note,
Coiled in a woman's throat.
I said, 'I hear her laughter';
And then, a moment after,
The stream began to sing.

The bank I rested on
Was gently curved and warm,
I dreamt about her form.
I said, 'She has withdrawn
Into herself delight
And joy from every sight.'
The wind that dusks the grasses
Tells when a spirit passes –
I felt that she was gone.


## Send from the South...

Send from the South warm thoughts to me
From alleys closed by Summer sea
Whence the great Gulf its Stream puts forth
Laden with Summers for the North;
And for the sun a purple throne
From which he may with joy look down,

Bending beyond his cloudy towers,
On main and islands fringed with flowers.
Send from the South warm thoughts to melt
The frost that all the more is felt
The farther off from you am I;
So that I may for solace sing
And to my heart your Summer bring;
For those whom distance parts too long
The only medicine is Song.


## Begone, Sweet Ghost

Begone, sweet Ghost, O get you gone!
Or haunt me with your body on;
And in that lovely terror stay
To haunt me happy night and day.
For when you come I miss it most,
Begone, sweet Ghost!

But do not clothe you in the dress
Whereby was young Actaeon killed;
He died because of loveliness,
And I will die from that withheld,
Unless you take on flesh, unless
In that you dress!


## Gaze on Me

Gaze on me, though you gaze in scorn;
O Lady, fix on me those eyes,
And then the darkness may be borne
When two such glorious lights arise;
For is there one, if stars shine bright,
Who will not praise the dark of night?

As gloaming brings the bending dew,
That flowers may faint not in the sun,
So, Lady, now your looks renew
My heart, although it droops adown;
And thus it may unwithered be,
When you shall deign to smile on me.

## Back From the Country

Back from the country
Ruddy as an apple,
Looking ripe and rural
As the maid a farmer seeks;
Fresh as an apple
Shining in the pantry,
Back you came to Dublin
Whom I had not seen for weeks:
How I hid my laughter
Fearing to offend you,
Back from the country
With your apple cheeks!

## Good Luck

Apples of gold the Hero dropt
  As he was in the race outstript;
And Atalanta, running, stopt,
  And all her lovely body dipt
A moment; but she lost her stride –
And had to go to bed a bride.

And was it not a cordial strong,
  By which the young Iseult was filled
With passion for a whole life long;
  For that the amorous juice instilled?
So he who kept the unwitting tryst
Was sure of love before he kissed.

But where can I get Western gold,
  Or posset of constraining fire? –
I who am fated to behold
  Beauty outdistancing desire?
Aye, and to falter wonder-struck;
There's no good love without good luck!

## *Applied Poetry*

All thoughts of you are joys
    And wistful fun!
My heart is like a boy's,
    What have you done?

For I can no more think
    Of pounds and pence
Just now, than I can think
    With commonsense.

The leaves of forest glades
    Where you are seen
Are still light yellow blades
    Before their green;

Each soaking meadow pool
    That's blurred with blue
To me, who am a fool,
    The eyes of you!

The glistening breezes spilt
    Through aspen tops
Where April kicks her quilt
    Of buttercups

And makes the meadow sway
    Its counterpane, —
As if Doll Tearsheet lay
    And leapt again,

Are surely hints enough
    That sweet and sure
Was he with: 'Youth's a stuff
    Will not endure.'

So let us find a bank. . . .
    What's this? You won't?
You think I mean to rank —
    Indeed I don't —

Doll Tearsheet with yourself,
   My Dear, you're dull!
How could a lanky elf
   Suggest a trull?

But she was meant to show,
   (If Will gave lessons)
That only women know
   The human essence,

And see beneath a part,
   Though clothed upon
By Evil, the rich heart
   Of gross Sir John;

Which no one else perceived.
   When he was sickly,
Who was it for him grieved
   But Doll and Quickly?

Significant and sad!
   But each descendant
Of Adam, good or bad,
   Is Eve's dependant.

We are a sorry race
   Whose horoscope,
Uncast by Woman's grace,
   Portends faint hope.

And now I find that he
   Who stole and cheated,
Compared with honest me
   Was kindlier treated. . . .

You used to love the Bard,
   Then more's the pity
That now you disregard
   What's blithe and witty!

And play the Grandmamma,
   Aloof, sedate:
'Our pleasant Willie, ah!
   Is dead in you of late!'

There! there! I don't suggest
　　You are not fit to live
Up to the very best
　　That life in Art can give.

See, there's a bank that's fenced,
　　Wherein, whereon
Joy may be lodged against
　　Oblivion;

And we hereafter, say
　　That we of yore,
One slanting sunny day
　　Could do no more

Than make this gentle bank
　　Joy's strong redoubt
Which years may not outflank,
　　Nor Memory flout.

'Well, to accomplish that
　　What must we do?'
'We must do something pat,
　　Something Come-to.'

Love can't be made by proxy,
　　Lest faith in Love should fail.
Heigh with the orthodoxy,
　　Come with me o'er the dale!

The only way to capture
　　What may not be expressed
Is turn it into rapture
　　Or turn it into jest.

So when you're old and fading,
　　A Christian Scientist,
Intent on self-persuading
　　That Evil can't exist

And I, for all my slimming,
　　Of somewhat stouter build, −
'To Rescue Fallen Women' −
　　Am Chairman of − The Guild. . . .

(My Dear, we can't eschew it,
  For Fate is farcical.
The mighty poet knew it:
  There's Falstaff in us all.)

When, after much persuasion,
  In public we appear
To grace a State occasion,
  Both you and I, my Dear,

Well honoured and respected,
  We meet our troops of friends:
Since on the Undetected,
  Respect so much depends,

I'll give you formal greeting
  And bow while whispering
This spell: 'My pretty sweeting!'
  To plunge our hearts in Spring;

For they, who hold together
  Half shares in Love's secret,
Can conjure Spring, and tether
  The years that bring regret.

## To Shadu 'L-Mulk

*(Delight of the Kingdom)*

from the Persian of Khalil Shah

My Loved One has another
  And a nameless paramour
Which causes me no bother,
  For she loves me all the more.

Thus, for the dam's rebellion,
  The ostlers often try her
With a jackass, till the stallion
  Strikes the cobbles into fire.

## *Leda and the Swan*

Though her Mother told her
   Not to go a-bathing,
Leda loved the river
   And she could not keep away:
Wading in its freshets
   When the noon was heavy;
Walking by the water
   At the close of day.

Where between its waterfalls,
   Underneath the beeches,
Gently flows a broader
   Hardly moving stream,
And the balanced trout lie
   In the quiet reaches;
Taking all her clothes off,
   Leda went to swim.

There was not a flag-leaf
   By the river's margin
That might be a shelter
   From a passer-by;
And a sudden whiteness
   In the quiet darkness,
Let alone the splashing,
   Was enough to catch an eye.

But the place was lonely,
   And her clothes were hidden;
Even cattle walking
   In the ford had gone away;
Every single farm-hand
   Sleeping after dinner, –
What's the use of talking?
   There was no one in the way.

In, without a stitch on,
   Peaty water yielded,
Till her head was lifted
   With its ropes of hair;

It was more surprising
　Than a lily gilded,
Just to see how golden
　Was her body there:

Lolling in the water,
　Lazily uplifting
Limbs that on the surface
　Whitened into snow;
Leaning on the water,
　Indolently drifting,
Hardly any faster
　Than the foamy bubbles go.

You would say to see her
　Swimming in the lonely
Pool, or after, dryer,
　Putting on her clothes:
'O but she is lovely,
　Not a soul to see her,
And how lovely only
　Leda's Mother knows!'

Under moving branches
　Leisurely she dresses,
And the leafy sunlight
　Made you wonder were
All its woven shadows
　But her golden tresses,
Or a smock of sunlight
　For her body bare.

When on earth great beauty
　Goes exempt from danger,
It will be endangered
　From a source on high;
When unearthly stillness
　Falls on leaves, the ranger,
In his wood-lore anxious,
　Gazes at the sky.

While her hair was drying,
　Came a gentle languor,

Whether from the bathing
  Or the breeze she didn't know.
Anyway she lay there,
  And her Mother's anger
(Worse if she had wet hair)
  Could not make her dress and go.

Whitest of all earthly
  Things, the white that's rarest,
Is the snow on mountains
  Standing in the sun;
Next the clouds above them,
  Then the down is fairest
On the breast and pinions
  Of a proudly sailing swan.

And she saw him sailing
  On the pool where lately
She had stretched unnoticed,
  As she thought, and swum;
And she never wondered
  Why, erect and stately,
Where no river weed was
  Such a bird had come.

What was it she called him:
  Goosey-goosey gander?
For she knew no better
  Way to call a swan;
And the bird responding
  Seemed to understand her,
For he left his sailing
  For the bank to waddle on.

Apple blossoms under
  Hills of Lacedaemon,
With the snow beyond them
  In the still blue air,
To the swan who hid them
  With his wings asunder,
Than the breasts of Leda,
  Were not lovelier!

Of the tales that daughters
   Tell their poor old mothers,
Which by all accounts are
   Often very odd;
Leda's was a story
   Stranger than all others.
What was there to say but:
   Glory be to God?

And she half-believed her,
   For she knew her daughter;
And she saw the swan-down
   Tangled in her hair.
Though she knew how deeply
   Runs the stillest water,
How could she protect her
   From the wingèd air?

Why is it effects are
   Greater than their causes?
Why should causes often
   Differ from effects?
Why should what is lovely
   Fill the world with harness?
And the most deceived be
   She who least suspects?

When the hyacinthine
   Eggs were in the basket,
Blue as at the whiteness
   Where a cloud begins;
Who would dream there lay there
   All that Trojan brightness;
Agamemnon murdered;
   And the mighty Twins?

## Faithful Even Unto Freud

Even judged by dreams which are
But phantasmal parodies
Of my life; and hollower

Than the glory of the skies
Which the seven maids maintain,
Heavenly sisters of the rain,

I am true. If you came in
To the Liberties of Sleep
Where, as proud as Saladin,
A preposterous state I keep;
Would you ever guess each bride
Was your own self multiplied?

Where, by water-lilies stilled,
Some forgotten old canal
Mirrors deep a window-silled
Maiden in a castle wall,
You again: but no disguise
Warms your willow-greenish eyes.

To a place where engineers
Coax a stream to climb a hill
And a marble reappears
Mountain-melted snowy still
Water, as before the Moor
Laid it on his rose-leaf floor,

I am banished beyond time,
To my faith an infidel;
Ruling in another clime
Devotees who serve me well,
Moving as they seek my love
Hips that like twin melons move.

With my boat's three-cornered sail
Shaped as is a rose's thorn,
While the morning yet is pale,
Gently filling, I am borne,
Where . . . it is not every man's
Luck to meet Corinthians.

Aphrodite's house is there;
She knows what you drove me to.
The most pleasant form of prayer
That a worshipper can do
Was enjoined. But nothing cures
Love the loved one still abjures.

## *Farewell to the Princess*

I who had your love,
Have now my pride;
And that is worthy of
All love denied.
Times change; but long ago
Men stood no suffering
That came from one alone.
I heard a poet sing;
And I make bold
To say 'Twould take a crowd
Of such as you
To bring me down,
I am so proud;
And if you multiply
New loves, so I.
He declared it took
Two fans in double yoke
To moider one,
Two fans, before his broke;
And three shy fans before
The man who studied war,
The Mandarin
Of T'sow gave in;
And twenty ladies to undo
The Duke of Ting,
The Lord of Lu.

## *Alas!*

I lost my Love,
I lost my Love
Because she came too rich to me.
How could I dream
Her need was of
A love as rich again from me?

And now her dear,
Dark eyes light up;

Her hands caress another's hair.
For me there is
Not any hope;
But thoughts that, O,
Enrich Despair!


## Women

Women are our subconscious selves,
Materialisations from our souls'
Regions where fairy queens and elves
Disport beyond Reason's controls.
Remember, if you call them fools
Who go, like dreams, by contraries,
That Spirits may scoff at earthly rules:
That you were born of one of these.
What else explains their vagaries
Unless this theory be truth,
That women are the Dryades
Of the lost orchards of our youth?


## I Wonder

I wonder when will women know the glories they suggest to us:
    If I were fit to sing to them of all that they inspire,
Their dalliance to open up the Kingdom of the Blest to us
    Would still be no less graced than hers who had a god to sire.

For queens they are, forgetful of the weight their brows has belted,
    No longer crowned above us all by aching diadems;
Some god put Lethe in the cup wherein the pearl was melted;
    And golden heads have still to hear that Troy went down in flames.

It surely cannot be that I, alone of men, remember
    The old mad grandeur and the days of glory gone to waste;
Because here Beauty gleams as fair as boughs rimed in December,
    And witless wears the ribbands for which helmets were unlaced?

And yet they look as though none heard what fortresses were
    wrecked for them.
  What armies squandered, for a smile, the sister of all Force;
What waters turned to wells of wine when battlements were decked
    for them:
  O why should I that Past recall which makes the Present worse?

It may be that our Present is for all the Past an Hades;
  A parody of Kings and Queens, and Beauty's paradigm;
It may be Time's Magnificat must name no living ladies;
  It may be that Forgetfulness excels a poet's rhyme.


## The Image-Maker

    Hard is the stone, but harder still
    The delicate preforming will
    That, guided by a dream alone,
    Subdues and moulds the hardest stone,
    Making the stubborn jade release
    The emblem of eternal peace.

    If but the will be firmly bent,
    No stuff resists the mind's intent;
    The adamant abets his skill
    And sternly aids the artist's will,
    To clothe in perdurable pride
    Beauty his transient eyes descried.


## With a Coin from Syracuse

    Where is the hand to trace
    The contour of her face:
    The nose so straight and fine
    Down from the forehead's line;

    The curved and curtal lip
    Full in companionship
    With the lip's overplus,
    Proud and most sumptuous,

Which draws its curve within,
Swelling the faultless chin?
What artist knows the tech-
nique of the Doric neck:

The line that keeps with all
The features vertical,
Crowned with the thickly rolled
And corrugated gold?

The curious hands are lost
On the sweet Asian coast,
That made the coins enwrought,
(Fairer than all they bought)

With emblems round the proud
Untroubled face of god
And goddess. Or they lie
At Syracuse hard by

The Fountain Arethuse.
Therefore from Syracuse
I send this face to her,
Whose face is lovelier.

Alas, and as remote
As hers around whose throat
The curving fishes swim,
As round a fountain's brim.

It shows on the reverse
Pherenikos the horse;
And that's as it should be:
Horses she loves, for she

Is come of the old stock,
Lords of the limestone rock,
And acres fit to breed
Many a likely steed,

Straight in the back and bone,
With head high like her own,
And blood that, tamed and mild,
Can suddenly go wild.

## Portrait

*(Diana Clothed)*

Who would have thought
That your mottled and your speckled,
Wavering and dappled,
Leaf-brown costume in the light,
Held at the shoulder
By an orchid's freckled anther,
Covering a bosom of an interrupted white,
Was but the pelt
That the Maiden, the Resistless,
Light of Heel, the Huntress,
Yes; the tall Toxophilite,
Skinned in the brakes
From a slowly dying panther,
Shot in the brakes
By her fatal arrow's flight? –
Nothing to do with a merciful mild amice; –
Too well I know, and it needs no second sight!
Ah, now I know;
I should long ago have guessed it,
From your way who wear it,
It is nothing more than this:
Cruelty clings to it –
It is nothing but the chlamys
Covering, and showing up
The breast of Artemis!


## Perfection

By Perfection fooled too long,
I will dream of that no longer!
Venus, you have done me wrong
By your unattainable beauty,
Till it seemed to be my duty
To belittle all the throng.
I have found attraction stronger;
I have found a lady younger
Who can make a hard heart stir;

Like an athlete, tall and slender,
With no more than human splendour;
Yet, for all the faults of her,
Than Perfection perfecter.

Though she guards it, grace breaks through
Every blithe and careless movement.
What shall I compare her to?
When she takes the ball left-handed,
Speed and sweetness are so blended
Nothing awkward she can do,
She, whose faults are an improvement!
If she only knew what Love meant
I would not be seeking now
To describe the curbed perfection
Of all loveliness in action.
Perfect she would be, I vow,
With the mole above the brow!

## Portrait with Background

Dervorgilla's supremely lovely daughter,
Recalling him, of all the Leinstermen Ri,
Him whose love and hate brought o'er the water,
    Strongbow and Henry;

Brought rigid law, the long spear and the horsemen
Riding in steel; and the rhymed, romantic, high line;
Built those square keeps on the forts of the Norsemen,
    Still on our sky-line.

I would have brought, if I saw a chance of losing
You, many more – we are living in War-rife time –
Knights of the air and the submarine men cruising,
    Trained through a life-time;

Brought the implacable hand with law-breakers,
Drilled the Too-many and broken their effrontery;
Broken the dream of the men of a few acres
    Ruling a country;

Brought the long day with its leisure and its duty,
Built once again the limestone lordly houses –
Founded on steel is the edifice of Beauty,
    All it avows is.

Here your long limbs and your golden hair affright men,
Slaves are their souls, and instinctively they hate them,
Knowing full well that such charms can but invite men,
    Heroes to mate them.

Eyes of the green of the woods that maddened Tristram!
Fair skin and smooth as the rosy-footed dove's wing!
Who would not fight, if he saw you, against this tram-
    melling of Love's wing?

Aye; and bow down, if he saw but half the vision,
I dare not call to the mind's eye, to adore you;
And be, if that great light shone with precision,
    Awe-struck before you.

## To Ethne

I saw a beautiful face,
    And ever since the seeing,
To pause for a moment's space
    Is to bring it again into being.

Over the splendour and gloom
    Of thoughts, like a misty star,
As a goddess out of a mist would come
    To the hard-prest sons of war.

Memory, enfold her and cling!
    And I will go forth against odds.
But heart, forget her and sing!
    This is no place for the Gods.

## *An Appeal from the Judgment of Paris*

Stateliness and elegance:
But a kindness in her glance
Gives a lover heart of grace
To appraise her lovely face.
Therefore, though she may not know it,
Sings her humblest, mildest poet
Whom the thought of her makes strong
Thus to challenge with a song,
Challenge Venus' whole entourage
By the virtue of the courage
That her gracefulness engenders,
Grace, the crown of beauty's splendours.


If that young Idalian lout,
When the apple went about
Only had the rare good luck
On her loveliness to look,
What a row there would have been
For, if he had only seen
All the ecstasies and loves
That her limbs make when she moves,
Venus had not had the pippin,
Nor would he have had the strippin'
Of young Leda's swan-white daughter;
Nor had Troy gone down in slaughter.


Paris lived too soon to see
All the sights that ravish me.
I am left alone to grapple
With my love without an apple:
So I sing by her inspired,
Her whose beauty when attired
By good taste can well outdo
All that nude Idalian crew
And still hide sweets; for more, I wis,
The body than the raiment is.

## Golden Stockings

Golden stockings you had on
In the meadow where you ran;
And your little knees together
Bobbed like pippins in the weather,
When the breezes rush and fight
For those dimples of delight,
And they dance from the pursuit,
And the leaf looks like the fruit.

I have many a sight in mind
That would last if I were blind;
Many verses I could write
That would bring me many a sight.
Now I only see but one,
See you running in the sun,
And the gold-dust coming up
From the trampled butter-cup.

## Praise

Why should I hold my praise
To wait for better days?
The best of times is now;
And this is good enough:
For Youth is at its best,
Youngest and loveliest,
Full of the sapling stuff;
And so are you.

We shall not in the flesh
Ever again be as fresh,
With courage quite so stout.
Never shall I surprise,
Never with more delight,
The little mist of light
As if your soul shone out
Before your eyes.

Roses and snow betoken
Your words before they're spoken;
Nothing can be more small,
Nothing more fair unless
The smile that makes them glisten . . .
O bear with me and listen!
The fact remains for all
Your humbleness!

The poplar never stoops,
The gentle willow droops,
Your walk holds both of these.
The movement of your hips
Has so much buoyance in it . . .
Be silent! Just a minute . . .
It makes me think of ships
Upon far seas.

Now let me have my say
In my own lyric way;
And then you may not frown.
My song is half a ruse
To praise myself in you,
Silence would never do,
It cost a man his Muse
When Rome went down.

Never shall it be said
Of me when I am dead:
He had too tardy sense
Of Beauty. Though your frowns
Are all my thanks, I tried
To sing of lovely pride;
There are no laurel crowns
For reticence!


## A Prayer For His Lady

If it be kindness, God, be kind
To her tall fragrant form and mind
And leave her in this world of ours

Unageing as she is in yours;
And let not Time's contagion blur
The image of your dream in her.

Little enough we have we know
Of love in Life to lead us through
And Loveliness is on the wing:
Leave the wild cherry with the Spring
In spangling showers to tremble away;
But of your grace preserve the clay.

## I Tremble To Think

I tremble to think that soon
Darkness shall close my sight,
And all that under the sun
I saw, and by moonlight:
Beautiful shadows and forms,
Colours, and, over the hill,
Clouds, like visible storms
At peace when the air is still;
The nameless, wonderful hues
That torture the eyes with joy
When the sea has a faint primrose,
On its blue and silver alloy –
All to be left untold,
The white and ethereal blue
That carries the chaos of gold
Dreams that I dreamt of you!
But these the years must spare,
Too transient far for time:
There is no age for the air,
Light is not of our clime.
But I whom the nets of the years
Surely at last shall enmesh
Before I can save in verse
The timeless traits of the flesh,
Shall have no peace till the cloud
Of thought takes definite shape,
And bodies you forth unbowed,
Tall, on a bare landscape,

Where earth the stone upthrusts —
Holding your exquisite frock
Against the morning gusts,
And light is on half the rock.

## To an Old Lady

Where are the eyes that remember your beauty?
Where is the lover whose lingering eyes
Remember the vision by which they were haunted,
Remember the one thing his whole being wanted,
When you took the Spring and his youth by surprise?

Why can we hardly imagine its blooming
When we consider a rose overblown?
Why should the mind with its outlook immortal
Join with those thoughts which dwell more on the portal
Less on the threshold of loveliness gone?

## And So On

Was there ever Beauty yet
    Time forgot to counteract?
If by Sorrow unbeset,
    Did her city go unsacked;
Nor some accident disguise
The Immortals' jealousies?

Beauty never comes on earth
    But an equal Grief is born;
Hidden, maybe, in the dearth
    Of the hours ere the morn;
Or that in her core are strife,
Gain of Love and loss of Life.

This is nothing new at all:
    We have heard it all before:
Beauty one side of the Wall,
    On the other side, the War.
Love and Death; and no denying
These things do not end by dying.

# LIFE AND DEATH

## The Airman's Breastplate

*(Part of the Lorica or breastplate of St. Patrick
turned into rhyme at the suggestion of an
Army Air Force Pilot)*

I arise above the clouds
Armoured in the strength of God's
Presence and omnipotence
That can drive all evil hence.

I arise in Heaven's might,
In the splendour and the sight
Of the Sun; and with the ire
Of Lightning and irresistible Fire.

Stabilised upon my road,
Held up by the might of God,
With God's wisdom for my light;
Eye of God for my foresight;
Ear of God to help my hearing;
Word of God to give a bearing.

Christ before me, Christ behind me,
Christ above me, Christ below me;
Christ to be my guard abounding

161

Against drowning, burning, wounding:
Christ in all I do and dare:
Christ in me to win His war.


## The Bubble

I saw a bubble on the water,
    A floating dome diffracting light
Into the colours of the rainbow
    Above the stones where waves were white.

I said, Too soon it must be broken
    And all its lovely world undone.
To my surprise it rose up rounded,
    A sphere of sunlight in the sun.

It may be dancing on the tree tops,
    It may be, by a light breeze, fanned
To where bright things cause little wonder:
    A meteor in Fairyland.

O wedding of the air and water,
    O child of two unstable things,
You just as well reflected sunlight
    As if you had immortal wings.

For Time itself may be unstable
    And in ourselves the fault may be
Disturbing all the sliding water,
    A rock of Immortality.


## Panurge

(*Emotional Humanity, the All-worker.*
*A note on Rabelais*)

Desire that drives where Lust obscures,
And Fear that wields a scourge,
These, as the Master dreamed, are yours,
                    Panurge.

Desire and Fear, the Masquers two,
Who act with us and urge
The Comedy we play with you,
                              Panurge.


Not since the most pellucid air
By the Illissus' verge
Heard the loud peals of laughter rare,
                              Panurge,


In lyric plenitude of joy,
Like Clouds whose rains asperge
The desiccations that destroy,
                              Panurge,


Such laughter-lore as this was taught
In which we mix and merge,
O profligate and polyglot
                              Panurge!


The meaning of the things we do:
Is Life a dance or dirge?
Depends upon the point of view,
                              Panurge!


How can we reach, though sail be bent
Beyond the horizon's verge,
Those isles of your astonishment,
                              Panurge?


Bring back the cannon's fearful crack;
Your fright and plight and purge;
The boar-cat Rodilardus, back
                              Panurge.


Bring back the fornicating Friar;
Let Sacred Strength resurge
And rehabilitate Desire,
                              Panurge!

## Time, Gentlemen, Time!

O would not Life be charming
    Could we get rid of clocks,
The still ones and alarming
    That break on sleep with shocks?

Then it would be respected
    And worthier far of Man
Than when by springs directed
    From gold or a tin can.

Why should Man's life be reckoned
    By anything so queer
As that which splits the second
    But cannot tell the year?

If we got rid of watches
    The trains would cease to run,
We could not fight a battle-ship
    Or aim a battle gun,

Nor tune the little engines
    Which fill the towns with fumes
And send men with a vengeance
    (Quite rightly) to their tombs.

If we got rid of watches
    And wanted to approach
The pallid peopled cities
    We'd have to hire a coach

And guard, who, to arouse us,
    So hardy in the morn,
Outside the licensed houses
    Would blow a long bright horn.

Our stars know naught of watches,
    There's not a wind that wists
Of mischief that Time hatches
    When handcuffed to our wrists.

No wonder stars are winking,
  No wonder heaven mocks
At men who cease from drinking
  Good booze because of clocks!

'Twould make a devil chortle
  To see how all the clean
Free souls God made immortal
  Must march to a machine.

It makes me wonder whether
  In this grim pantomime
Did fiend or man first blether:
  'Time, Gentlemen, Time!'

We must throw out the timing
  That turns men into gnomes,
Of piece-work and of miming
  That fills the mental homes.

We must get rid of errors,
  And tallies and time checks,
And all the slavish terrors
  That turn men into wrecks.

They have not squared the circle,
  They have not cubed the sphere,
Their calendars all work ill
  Corrected by 'leap' year.

But we should all be leaping
  As high as hollyhocks
Did we desist from keeping
  Our trysts with slaves of clocks.

How should we tell the seconds?
  The time a blackbird takes,
To screech across a lane-way,
  And dive into the brakes.

How should we tell the minutes?
    The time it takes to swipe
A lonely pint of Guinness,
    Or load a friendly pipe.

O make the heart Time's measure
    Because, the more it beats,
The more Life fills with pleasure,
    With songs or sturdy feats;

Our clocks our lives are cheating,
    They go, and ground we give;
The higher the heart's beating,
    The higher then we live.


## *Centaurs*

To get away from Reason seems
    To be the first thing one must do
To live in happiness; with dreams
    Some cloud the mind, and some bedew
The intellect with subtler juice,
    Till good Lyaeus sets them free;
Some use tobacco, some abuse
    The herbs of healing: suffer me
To live with leathery women and men
    Who give their whole mind up to horses;
Mount and dismount and mount again,
    And leave the stars to their own courses.
On through the morning air to go,
    To break the rainbow on the briar,
To hold the horse, to hear him blow
    The bellows of primaeval fire;
To feel life surging through the dark
    As waywardly as once it came
Before the filched unnatural spark
    Outshone the kindly natural flame.
Thus was the Ancient Wisdom found,
    A wisdom suited to my mind,
And taught by Chiron the renowned,
    The man and animal combined.

## *Anglers*

That pleasant Chinese poet Ching Chih Ho,
  Who spent his time in fishing with no bait,
Recalled at last from exile, would not go,
  Nor leave the stream where he could meditate
And foil all interrupters by his ruse,
  Sitting beside the water with his line;
Was it a wonder that he should refuse,
When he could catch his rhythms half asleep,
  Watching below the lilies fishes shine,
Or move not – it was all the same to him –
And river-mosses when he gazed more deep
And deeper, clouds across the azure swim?
  There's not a roof now on the courts whose schemes
Kept men awake and anxious all night long,
Distracted with their working out; but dreams
He made in idleness and turned to Song
  Can still delight his people. As for me,
I, who must daily at enactments look
  To make men happy by legality,
Envy the poet of that baitless hook.

## *The Old Goose*

The daylong rains are dried,
Cold is the mountain-side,
The evening light is pied,
  Not heaven's four quarters
Know if the moon be set,
But where green sods are wet
The white stream holds you yet,
  Lover of airs and waters!

Soon you will cross the loam,
And walk the pathway home
Before the faint stars come,
  And seek your stable.
Your old wild life exchanged

For comfort: all is changed;
For rime-white deserts ranged,
  A white-washed gable!

Oh, have you quite forgot,
The flights outbreasting thought
Before this homely lot
  Half tamed your pinions?
The mountains and the stars
Were once your only bars,
And where the north wind soars
  Were your dominions.

You know the depths of air,
You know the times of year,
To you all paths are clear
  And heights of heaven,
The fens and broken bays
Where never an hunter strays;
All cold inhuman ways
  To you are even.

And all those mirrors known
That turn the mountains down:
Your flight a moment shown
  In gloaming deeper
Than those high tranquil tides
Through which your courage rides
When some straight purpose guides
  Its wingèd keeper.

There's blue beyond the peak
Of Patrick's frozen Reek,
Oh take on breast and beak
  The night's dark onset,
Washed in the mauve twilight
O'er some far western bight,
Where islands rest in light
  Long after sunset!

Islands that gleam and float
Untouched by voyaging boat,
Withheld but not remote,

Where wave breaks slowly
Till all the beach is green,
Where the great lords are seen
Who fought and loved a Queen,
　Armed, amorous, and holy.

Easy to put life by
When friend and foe were nigh;
Easy for them to die
　Armed and elated!
And well they died in sooth,
Who found, in fighting, truth
Before old age had youth
　Repudiated.

Theirs was the exultant age,
Theirs the ecstatic rage;
And the embellished page
　Enshrined the slaying.
For, as old bards averred,
The song goes with the sword,
O wing that writ'st the Word,
　Write down this saying:

Love life and use it well:
That is the tale they tell,
Who broke it like a shell,
　And won great glory.
But you and I are both
Inglorious in sloth,
Unless our ranging youth
　Redeem our story.

For not preserved by fear
We fell on quiet here,
Our friends all dead and dear,
　A brave blithe army.
You have your grassy spring
And cloudy barrèd wing;
And I old dreams that sing,
　And memories stormy.

So that the egg be laid
For feathers unafraid,
What matter where is made,
    When strong winds tire,
The nest, if we can spend
Our age in peace, my friend?
After the journey's end
    The village spire!


## Non Blandula Illa

When that which bore my body up takes wings
At night-fall, and my limbs are thrown to rest,
I watch in wonder, as it makes its quest,
The place it chooses for its wanderings.
No easeful meadows nor delightful springs
Nor visionary islands lure it best,
But far-off on the margin of the West
A sea-grey house whereby the blackbird sings.
The waves come up like Berserks from the sea,
The crystal mountains yield a little sand,
Through level light the bird of valour calls.
Adventurous as a Viking must that be
Which will not rest when sleep on Nature falls
But hastens to the confines of the land.


## The Ho Ho Bird

My mind last night was gaily stirred
By wingings of the Ho Ho bird,
The Oriental bird that flies
Only (they say) in Paradise.
I watched its feathers trail and wing
Through air as soft as soundless Spring.
It left behind it as it came,
A path of amethystine flame;
Below, the willows slept, and bent
Their yellow heads and dreamed and leant;

A placid stream their tendrils showed;
Afar the turquoise mountains glowed
And pushed aside their mists to watch
The bird that has on earth no match.
Surely, I thought, it seems absurd
To see the landscape match the bird:
Mountains and trees and rocks and springs
Answer the waving of its wings:
When, suddenly, to my surprise,
My mind became a Paradise.


## The Emperor's Dream

When the internal dream gives out,
I let my eyes wander about
Amongst the gay and the grotesque
Ornaments upon my desk,

Where books are set on end and stacked,
By Plato and by Homer backed;
But, in the present mood preferred,
I see my Chinese crystal bird:

A Phoenix maybe, who can say?
That ship that, off Arabia,
Sighted the Phoenix flying East,
Its crew could tell about it best.

The did not need a second look;
They knew it by the course it took;
And who am I to disagree,
When China sends it back to me

To sit before me carven clear,
As if the very atmosphere
Of regions where but dreams abide,
Were seized on and solidified

To crystal that shall last as long
As Beauty gains from Art and Song,
From those who bend to carve or sing,
Their tribute to her flying wing?

Was ever artist more supreme
To catch, to hold, to mould a dream,
Year in, year out, day after day,
And never to let a line go astray

Till undistracted, undeterred,
He caught the seldom-flying bird;
From solid air he carved its crest;
And set it airy in its nest?

I send my thoughts across the skies
Of regions where the Phoenix flies,
Where Past and Present are as one,
To bow before the Emperor's throne;

And seek the artist in the court,
Where only such as he resort;
And from these barbarous times and ways
Offer my crude barbarian praise.

Before we meet, I shall be told
How one day in the days of old,
The Emperor hearing what he did
(For nothing's from the Emperor hid)

Commanded him to send a proof
Of what on wing or fin or hoof
He fashioned with such skill that, poor,
His name yet reached an Emperor;

And that, when he had seen the bird,
He paused, and solemnly averred:
The crystal wings without a flaw
Where those that in a dream he saw.

And how the artist with bowed head
And eyes cast down, replied and said:
That all that made for skill he owed
To Him from Whom perfection flowed.

For in the Emperor's mind were held
Art's emblems; and, if one excelled,
Of those who mould, or carve or limn,
His genius was due to him.

And that at this the Emperor laughed,
Praising the master of a craft
Which had so worthily enshrined
Things hidden in an Emperor's mind.

We need not meet, since this is so:
What every craftsman knows, we know:
Before our work stands up complete,
The Emperor must have dreamt of it.

And if we please the Emperor's whim,
And perfectly produce his dream,
Time can but turn the works of men
Into an Emperor's dream again.

## Lullaby

Wander no more, my Thoughts, but keep
Within the moated realm of Sleep;
Wander no more, nor farther than
The dusty wavering moth may span,
With wings that love the hearth-low light
With which the casement gilds the night;
                    Wander no more!

Content you there to rest and dream,
Nor watch the flickering armour gleam,
For nothing that the past has done
Need break your rest to ponder on,
Nor yet the future's lordlier scope:
Sleep is a sounder thing than Hope,
                    Content you there.

So yield to dream, and feel the sway
Of Earth upon the rainbow way;
And dream you feel it lift and take
A way you never felt awake;
For O, unless your dreams outdo
Your life, there is not much for you;
                    So yield to dream.

On darkness launched, now you go forth
Where there is neither South or North;
Nor now and then, nor here and there;
But something deeper than these are;
So may you, when you reach that bourne,
Be most reluctant to return,
                          On darkness launched.


## The Mill at Naul

I call to mind, to bring me sleep,
That ruin on the naming hill
Of Naul, with ivy on the keep
That looks down on a ruined mill.
Because my mind comes home and rests
On things which Time no more molests:
For keep above and mill below
There is no further way to go:
They have already gone so far
With Time, that as the hill they are,
Or as the mill-pond by the mill,
Which, though it flows, is standing still;
Or as the stream and broken range
That only know immortal change;
For Time gives here, in turn for peace,
Man's handiwork a timeless lease;
And makes and takes it to its own
As if it were a stream or stone.
And that is why I love to call
To mind the drowsy mill at Naul,
Because such old things flatter me
With warrants of Eternity,
When Time's close flag suspends the fray
With ivy green against the gray.

And I can leave my pride which raged
Too long, here, in the keep besieged;
And let my love descend to spread
Through lowly roofs the gift of bread;
And know that I need range no more
With Love and Pride accounted for.

I see the mill, as day is done,
In sunset of a tardy sun
That fills the valley to the East
With all the overflowing West;
Until the valley brims to hold
An airy pond of dusty gold
That shows, as if far down in dream,
The hill, the mill, the little stream.

The light is golden down below,
But, on the keep, the afterglow
Is cold as steel, and sideways flung
Where ivy leaves the walls unhung.

I saw it first through air so wet
With dew that falling leaves fell straight;
For woods, for all their brazen towers,
Withstand not Autumn's golden showers:
So where I stood the road was rich
With bronze and gold that filled the ditch;
And boughs and leaves dropped so much rain,
I said, The wheel may turn again,
And belt itself with drops anew,
And yet not beat these woods for dew.

And now I lie till, in my mind,
The mill is lit, the keep is lined
With men-at-arms on sentry-go
Who stand to watch the mill below.

I see the pond's potential power
Where might is stilled to conjure flour,
And, from the strength of rain pent up
From heaven, transform an earthly crop.
I catch the mill-wheel's homely sound,
The uncouth magic of its round
Splashing bright blessings, as it turns,
On twinkling tufts and dangling ferns,
Performing, with expansive girth,
The mingling rites of heaven and earth;
I see and hear it clear as day
Though Naul is eighteen miles away.

Don't think these are the only turns
The half-unconscious mind discerns.
I see far more than you can spy
Who are not half asleep as I;

I see the way, now half awake,
The protons and electrons take
To spin the world, and bring the grist
To wild dreams of the scientist,
Who knows, for all he hopes to know,
That round a myriad mill-wheels go
From some far pond, unplumbed and still,
Which breaks to power and moves the mill.

And now I dwindle till my stream
Is lost within the pond of dream,
The pond of dream which holds far more
Than any stream of earth can pour;
But, if I lie resigned and still,
The pond at length may rise and fill.

I do not wonder that none found
The roofless mill restored and sound,
Because the more the mind's alert
The more the inner eye is hurt,
An eye to which the light of day
Is rarely helpful, anyway.

Before I had a mind at all,
The mill was working well at Naul;
And, maybe, when I am resigned
To lose in sleep the wakeful mind,
The mill may start to work again
As once it stood to grind the grain;
And hum its song for many a season,
Where now it does not stand to reason.

It seems to me that far down there
The dusky light is dustier,
The dust is rising in the air;
And over every window square
There is an eyebrow dusty white;
And should that roof be half so bright
Unless with flour? It must be flour;
The mill is trembling into power!

And now I hear a distant drone,
The upper and the nether stone,
So far away it only comes
To fade away in waving hums,
That tell of work so sweet and strong
That all that holds it turns to song.

The mill beside the stream is lit
As if its walls were golden wheat;
And only in the upper streams
Of light a lonely sea-bird gleams
In one long arc . . . ah, let it go;
I want to watch the mill below.

The purple evening turns to dark,
I soon shall see the cobbles spark
Where unseen horses pull their load
Of sacks along a rising road.
I wonder if I dared look up
To see the hill, would all this stop?
And all the scenes that sleep has made,
To deeper sleep return to fade?
I wonder now, will this go on
When light, when light is quite withdrawn;
And if, when sleep is deeper still,
The mill without the Miller will?


## Palinode

Twenty years are gone
    Down the winding road,
Years in which it shone
    More often than it snowed;
And now old Time brings on,
    Brings on the Palinode.

I have been full of mirth;
    I have been full of wine;
And I have trod the earth
    As if it all were mine;

And laughed to bring to birth
    The lighter lyric line.

Before it was too late,
    One thing I learnt and saw:
Prophets anticipate
    What Time brings round by law;
Call age before its date
    To darken Youth with awe.

Why should you drink the rue?
    Or leave in righteous rage,
A world that will leave you
    Howe'er you walk the stage?
Time needs no help to do
    His miracle of age.

A few years more to flow
    From miracle-working Time,
And surely I shall grow
    Incapable of rhyme,
Sans Love and Song, and so
    An echo of a mime.

Yet if my stone set forth
    The merry Attic blade's
Remark, I shall have worth
    Achieved before Life fades:
'A gentle man on Earth
    And gentle 'mid the Shades.'


## Domi

This is the house where I lie down
At length to call the world my own;
And no one spies on what goes on.

This is the house that cannot yield:
Who built it knew well how to build.
None trespasses across my field;

Nor comes betimes because he thought
If late, I might be up and out;
Here I am safe from fools like that.

The light is not as, shall we say,
The diamond dome above the Bay
When light looks black at topmost day;

Nor such as, ere the sun is set,
Shines level where the boughs are wet,
And it is early April yet.

No, I acknowledge it is dim;
But all the more tempered for him
Who has seen all that life could limn.

Before I took this holiday,
I often heard companions say:
'I would that I were well away.'

And well away from all turmoil,
And well away from all the coil
Of anxious engaging toil.

Tiber and Nile and Thames of course,
Raise lordlier walls to men of force:
But this becomes a man of verse.

You must not judge by my retreat
That I found Life not wildly sweet,
Or that I turn my back to it.

'Twas pleasant as I saw it played.
But why should one whose looks grow staid
Hang on unto the harlequinade?

It needs no skill to be prepared
For the long solitude unshared:
Hither my old grandmother fared.

## Elbow Room

Astronomers describe a place,
Seen through a crack in the vault of Space
So dark, so absolute, so far,
No light wave from the oldest star
Nor even the thought of God can reach
And fainting fall on that far beach:
Abhorrent and inhuman this
Chineses call, 'The Great Abyss.'
But I am cheered, for now I know
There's somewhere left for a man to go –
(Always supposing one would care
When dead for going anywhere)
But what a place to make your goal
And lift your head and rouse your soul!
Oh! what a place to speak your mind
Without disquieting mankind!
There's where I would find elbow room
Alone beyond the crack of doom.

## All the Pictures

I told him he would soon be dead.
'I have seen all the pictures,' said
My patient. 'And I do not care.'
What could a doctor do but stare
In admiration half amused
Because the fearless fellow used
'The pictures' as a metaphor,
And was the first to use it for
Life which he could no longer feel
But only see it as a reel?
Was he not right to be resigned
To the sad wisdom of his mind?
Who wants to live when Life's a sight
Shut from the inner senses quite;
When listless heart and cynic mind
Are closed within a callous rind;
When April with its secret green

Is felt no more but only seen;
And Summer with its dusky meadows
Is no more than a play of shadows;
And Autumn's garish oriflamme
Fades like a flickering skiagram;
And all one's friends are gone, or seem
Shadows of dream beyond a dream?
And woman's love not any mo,
Oh, surely then 'tis time to go
And join the shades that make the Show!

## Sunt Apud Infernos Tot Milia Formosarum

I, as the Wise Ones held of old,
    Hold there's an Underworld to this;
And do not fear to be enrolled
    In Death's kind metamorphosis.

More wonderful than China's halls
    To Polo; more than all the West
That shone through the confining walls
    When great Magellan made the quest.

Enlarged and free, the wings of Rhyme
    Cannot outreach its purple air;
The generations of all Time
    And all the lovely Dead are there.

## To Death

But for your Terror
Where would be Valour?
What is Love for
    But to stand in your way?
Taker and Giver,
For all your endeavour
You leave us with more
    Than you touch with decay!

## Per Iter Tenebricosum

Enough! Why should a man bemoan
A Fate that leads the natural way?
Or think himself a worthier one
Than those who braved it in their day?
If only gladiators died,
Or Heroes, Death would be his pride;
But have not little maidens gone,
And Lesbia's sparrow – all alone?

## Marcus Curtius

*In response to an oracle which declared that a gulf
recently opened in the Forum could only be closed by
casting into it that which Rome held most dear,
Marcus Curtius, fully armed, mounted his war-horse
and plunged, for that which Rome held dearest was
her chivalry.*

'Tis not by brooding on delight
That men take heart of pride, and force
To pull the saddle-girthings tight
And close the gulf on staring horse.

From softness only softness comes;
Urged by a bitterer shout within,
Men of the trumpets and the drums
Seek, with appropriate discipline,

That Glory past the pit or wall
Which contradicts and stops the breath,
And with immortalising gall
Builds the most stubborn things on death

## Non Dolet

Our friends go with us as we go
    Down the long path where Beauty wends,
Where all we love forgathers, so
    Why should we fear to join our friends?

Who would survive them to outlast
   His children; to outwear his fame –
Left when the Triumph has gone past –
   To win from Age, not Time, a name?

Then do not shudder at the knife
   That Death's indifferent hand drives home,
But with the Strivers leave the Strife,
   Nor, after Caesar, skulk in Rome.


## Death May Be Very Gentle

Death may be very gentle after all:
He turns his face away from arrogant knights
Who fling themselves against him in their fights;
But to the loveliest he loves to call.
And he has with him those whose ways were mild
And beautiful; and many a little child.

# ELEGIES

## To Petronius Arbiter

Proconsul of Bithynia,
Who loved to turn the night to day,
Yet for your ease had more to show
Than others for their push and go.
Teach us to save the Spirit's expense,
And win to Fame through indolence.

## Bill Baveler

Bill Baveler kept the Brown Stone Inn
    To serve the township and the traveller;
And many a time I would drop in,
    When noons were hot, to 'see' Bill Baveler.

Somewhat below the middle size,
    Though he was short, he was not bossy;
He had large, candid, dark blue eyes
    Like his linoleum, clean and glossy.

He was too old to go to war,
    His heart was bad, he could not march hard,
He hoped he was not 'steering for' –
    He'd look churchwards – 'the marble orchard.'

His rustic mind would entertain
   His simple guests whose minds were simple.
It took no zephyr from the brain
   To make their round cheeks 'cream and dimple.'

'What are those great big things with guns
   That on the enemy like hell come,
Like great big trucks, big iron ones?'
   If you said 'Tanks,' he'd say 'You're welcome!'

His soul was sound and free from harm:
   A gentleman whose ways were gentle.
He'd take me gently by the arm
   At dawn when I was growing mental;

And guide me down the village street,
   (Because the moon was full of malice,
And each house looked the same in it)
   And say, 'There is your fairy palace.'

Ah, Death, you always take the best
   And Time alone makes you the leveller.
You might have taken any guest –
   You might have spared the good Bill Baveler.

When next you raid that little town
   Your victory can be but cheaper,
There's no one better left to down
   Than was The Brown Stone Tavern keeper.


## Farrell O'Reilly

You, Farrell O'Reilly, I feared as a boy
With your thin riding legs and your turned-in toes;
I feared the sharp, gimlet-like look in your eye,
Your rumbling brown beard and your pocketed nose.
Old friend of my Father what brings you back now?
You died fifty-nine years or sixty ago.

They say, when a man is about to be drowned,
His youth flashes back and he sees his life clear;

So, maybe, because I am nearing the ground
The days of my youth and my childhood are here.
If so, they are welcome if they compensate
For days that are yearly increasing in weight.

My Father no sooner would talk of Kilbeg
And carefully measure the charge for each cartridge,
Than I saw myself strutting behind with the bag
And heard the men talk as they walked up the partridge.
The coveys were scarce, and the cause of the trouble
Was 'Farrell O'Reilly's too proud to have stubble.'

O thick-sodded fields that have fattened the herds
From the days of the kings in the dawn of our time,
O fields of Moynalty, The Plain of the Birds,
None ever drew plough through your land on the lime!
King Leary of Tara just over the way
Knew more about Meath than the men of to-day.

My young eyes were good and rejoiced at the sight
Of a drake with the sun all a blaze on his green
That flew on a sudden from left to the right:
What banging! But only a feather was seen.
When each man exclaimed to the other, 'Bad luck!'
I could not help thinking 'twas good for the duck.

Remote as the days in an old mezzotint
When Farrell O'Reilly would lean to his gun
Top-hatted; and aim with a vigilant squint,
(If he missed, it was due to the wind or the sun)
My Father stands clear; but I see clearer Farrell
His left eye shut tight and his hand up the barrel.

In spite of their failure, I gaped at the men,
Their failures were feats to me looking for wonder.
How little I doubted Authority then!
Authority added distinction to blunder.
They could not do wrong, though they played ducks and drakes,
For great men can lend a prestige to mistakes.

'Now hand me that bag, for you can't lift a leg.'
I said, 'It's so light I can carry it farther' –
A thousand wide acres surrounded Kilbeg –

And Farrell said nothing, but looked at my Father;
Then carried me home; and I found, for a truth,
There's sometimes great kindness behind the uncouth.

The little pine wood with its floor of dense laurels;
The river slow-moving with bulrushes rimmed;
The well-house, the lis – all the things that were Farrell's,
Though half were forbidden, are shining undimmed:
The harness room filled with bits, saddles and bridles,
A room where the dairy maid gossips and idles.

I feel the lull now that came over the men,
And I see the groom wafting his smoke with his hand,
Intent as his polishing started again;
'The Master!' A hint that they all understand;
The dairy maid holding her blouse at her throat,
As he enters the yard in his cut-away coat.

Like everyone else who was in his employ,
Alert, lest, surprised, I be taken in error,
In spite of foreboding, I snatched at my joy,
For joy is a pleasance surrounded by terror.
Wood, river and well – to maid and to man
Sharp Farrell O'Reilly appeared as god Pan.

Wood, river and well – the wild things of the fields;
The lis with its lonely and wind-twisted thorn,
Enchanted me early; now everything yields
To the breath I drew first from the winds of my morn:
So, Farrell O'Reilly, in token from me,
Accept this wild leaf from your own twisted tree.


## 'Aeternae Lucis Redditor'

*(To Robert Yelverton Tyrrell,*
*Professor of Classics, T.C.D.)*

Old friend, long dead, who yet can thrive
More in my heart than men alive
Because in you the flame lived more

Than ever since the days of yore
When, everywhere that Rome was known,
The post-triumphal silence shone,
And in the vespertinal hush
The trumpet yielded to the thrush:
Because those days you could restore:
Aeternae lucis Redditor.

You shared with us the mood serene
That ruled the universal scene
When Peace was guardian of the poor,
And only rusty was the door
Of Janus, and the pillared shade
Revealed the studious colonnade:
The toga with the purple hem,
The temple that with quiet flame
Acclaimed the distant Emperor,
Aeternae lucis Redditor.

Too seldom on this world of ours
Unwrackt the eternal radiance pours.
Again we shall not see it pour
As in the days and nights before
We lost the wide Virgilian calm;
Days when we sought to earn the palm –
Through the endowment of a wit
Which made us eligible for it –
From you who were Wit's arbiter,
Aeternae lucis Redditor.

'Twixt you and me and me and those
Irremeable the River flows
Since we beheld with joy and awe
The light by which blind Homer saw.
And not again in this our time
Shall sound magnanimous the rhyme;
The wolves have torn our pleasant folds,
And the Great Wall no longer holds.
But Love can bridge the Stygian shore,
Aeternae lucis Redditor.

## Elegy on the Archpoet
## William Butler Yeats
## Lately Dead

Now that you are a Song
And your life has come to an end
And you wholly belong
To the world of Art, my friend,
Take, for well it is due,
This tribute of my rhymes
With mind unswerved from you
In these enormous times;
Not that I wish to intrude
To mix with mine your leaf,
But that I would entwine
In your magnificent sheaf,
After sad interlude,
A spray cut from that fine
And rare plant, Gratitude.
For anything I owe
In the art of making songs
Largely to you is due,
To you the credit belongs
Who never stinted or spared
Yourself in the difficult feat
Of getting a man prepared
To sing in his own conceit.
None may carry a stone
To your high tower of thought
But surely I can own
Whose was the influence caught
Me in wild wear disguised
And undistinguished found me,
Encouraged, authorised
And with the laurel crowned me;[1]
And make it lovingly clear
While memory is fresh
What manner of man you were
While here clothed on with flesh.
The world knows well your rhymes,
But I would depict you to please

The men in coming times
By a picture of you in these
And make them as grateful to me
As I would be could I find,
Searching past history,
Troubled Euripides
Or unvexed Sophocles,
By some contemporary mind.

II

The noble head held high,
The nose with an eagle's gaze,
The sharp appraising eye,
The brown unageing face,
The beautiful elegant hands
As white as the breasts of the love
Of Ossian in faerylands:
Among us but ever aloof,
He never hurried or ran,
With eyes on a lordly track
A tall upstanding man
You dared not slap on the back.
He moved in a diffident way
As if a new-comer to earth
Wrapped in a magical day
Older than death or than birth:
A man come down from the men
Who walked in the morning dew
Of dark Ferdia's strain
With lips like berries of yew:
A race that hosts in the hills,
A race few eyes can see,
A race that our day fills
With perverse, mischievous glee:
A head never turned by fame,
An eerie spirit that takes
Its preternatural calm
From sloe-black mountain lakes.
You heard the sound of his soul
Through words in their equipoise;
The sound of his soul was beautiful:

He had a most beautiful voice.

### III

O brain that never lacked full power,
O spirit always of the tower[2]
That never stooped to earthly lure
But at your height were self-secure:
With wistful child's benignity,
With Man's most noble dignity
You never compromised with fear
You brought the Brave among us here,
And high above the tinsel scene
Strode with the old heroic mien,
And equalled to your intellect
The grandeur of your self-respect.

### IV

O happy were your days on earth
When we sat by the household hearth
And, as the Autumn glow went out,
Bandied the whole bright world about,
Making Reality betray
The edges of sincerer day;
Or in that orchard house of mine, –
The firelight glancing in the wine
Or on your ring that Dulac made –
How merrily your fancy played
With the lost egg that Leda laid,
The lost, third egg, Herodotos
In Sparta said he came across;
Or broached a problem more absurd:
In the Beginning was the Word,
Since there was none to hear, unheard?
Or linking stranger mysteries,
The Spring with dates of the decease
Of Caesar, Christ and Socrates,
You let imagination range
Into the fabulous and strange
Realms of the mind where, at its source,
Life is exultant and perverse.

Then presently you would recite
The verses you made overnight,
Affirming that a song should be
Bone-bare in its simplicity.
Exemplifying this, you chose
Before the Adonais, those
Straight lines of Burns on Captain Grose
'No, no! on Henderson, not Grose':
'For Matthew was a queer man';
Preferring the heartfelt, sincere,
Artless humanity of 'queer'
To Shelley's cosmic sermon.
Sometimes you brought invective down
Upon the 'blind and ignorant town'
Which I would half disclaim;
For in my laughing heart I knew
Its scheming and demeaning crew
Was useful as the opposite to
The mood that leads to fame;
For very helpful is the town
Where we by contradicting come
Much nearer to our native home;
But yet it made me grieve
To think its mounted-beggar race
Makes Dublin the most famous place
For famous men to leave:
Where City Fathers staged a farce
And honoured one who owned a horse;[3]
They win right well our sneers
Who of their son took no account
Though he had Pegasus to mount
And rode two hemispheres.
Return Dean Swift, and elevate
Our townsmen to the equine state!


V

Now you are gone beyond the glow
As muted as a world of snow;
And I am left amid the scene
Where April comes new-drenched in green,
To watch the budding trees that grow
And cast, where quiet waters flow,

Their hueless patterns below;
And think upon the clear bright rill
That lulled your garden on the hill;
And wonder when shall I be made
Like you, beyond the stream, a shade.

### VI

We might as well just save our breath,
There's not a good word to be said for Death
Except for the great change it brings:
For who could bear the loveliest Springs
Touched by the thought that he must keep
A watch eternal without sleep?
But yet within the ends
Of human, not eternal things,
We all resent the change it brings:
Chiefly the loss of friends:
Tyrrell, Mahaffy and Macran,
The last the gentlest gentleman,
And golden Russell – all were gone,
Still I could turn to you alone.
Now you have turned away
Into the land of sleep or dreams
(If dreams you rule them yet meseems).
With clowns in tragedy,
Here solitary, I, bereft
Of all impulse of praise, am left
Without authority or deft
Example in a rhyme.
There never was a poet yet
Could put another more in debt.
England's great-hearted Laureate[4]
Is here to testify to that
As, more indebted, I
Whose hand you held, whose line you filled,
Whose mind with reverence instilled
For the most noble and august
Art that can shake men more than lust.
Here I must bide my time
And, through my loss, grow more content
To go the way the Master went
And follow on a friend

Praising the life by art imbued,
The Apollonian attitude
And lips that murmured metre till the end.[5]


GOGARTY'S NOTES TO THE ELEGY ON WILLIAM BUTLER YEATS

1. The Irish Academy of Letters, founded by W. B. Yeats and G. B. Shaw, crowned the author's book, WILD APPLES, some years ago.
2. 'Of the tower' is a term derived from falconry. It meant a hawk at the top of his flight and ready to stoop.
3. Boss Croker, after his Tammany career, resided in Ireland and won the Derby with a horse bred in Ireland called *Orby*. The City Fathers gave Boss Croker the *Freedom of the City* but refused the author's suggestion that they give a similar honour to Yeats.
4. In a memoir written shortly after Yeats's death, John Masefield, the English Poet Laureate, referred to him as: 'him to whom I owe all.'
5. Lady Dorothy Wellesley in her book, *Letters on Poetry from W. B. Yeats to Dorothy Wellesley*, tells how when unconscious, dying, his lips still murmured rhyme.

Part 2


POEMS FROM
OTHER COLLECTIONS

FROM
# *HYPERTHULEANA* (1916)

---

## *To the Muse*

What would my mother say,
Muse, if she met you?
Ask me, in great dismay,
Where did I get you?
And, with a text at me,
Say: 'Have a care!
Show me your company
I'll tell you who you are.'

Should I exalt with pride
You o'er another –
Where is the son could hide
Love from a mother?
Then, for she loved me much,
She'd say: 'My child,
Pitch one may not touch
Without being defiled.'

'Mother, must Virtue be
Always dejected?
Is it a sin for me
To live unaffected,

Taking the Muse's part?'
'Son, for a surety
Two things harden the heart,
Drink and impurity.'

Flushed is your bonnie face,
Cambered your belly
Muse, like the straying Grace
In Botticelli.
Wild with the fruit and blooms'
Mystical birth
Which the dark wood illumes,
Drunken with mirth.

Dublin and Dublin's lanes'
Typical daughter.
Fair, for the blood of Danes
Moistened the mortar;
As that rose-scattering
Queen, the Italian's,
Tall, though your shawl may bring
Rhubarb and scallions.

Why, my ill-tempered lass,
Fond though abusive,
Is the short time you pass
Here so elusive?
How can you come and think
You are delightful
Who are till primed with drink
Grudging and spiteful?

Vain, but your vanity
Makes its own mirth-place;
Profane, profanity
Church Street for birth-place
Claims — where your mother lives —
And the Hereafter
Only a flavour gives,
Muse, to your laughter.

I, when I think of where
Your love has led me,

Could not the memory bear
If you betrayed me.
Hear me as in the days,
Heedless of rumour,
I overlooked your ways
For your good humour,

What though they disapprove
In town and country,
Calling our way of love
Brazen effrontery.
Let them, my Lady brave,
All go to blazes;
When can they say we have
Cared for their praises?

But to the few robust
Friends who desire us
Sing with the careless lust
Song can inspire us;
Then they will plainly tell,
Reading it rightly,
You, though I loved you well,
Loved me but lightly.

## The Feast

To My Right Honourable Friend
William McElroy (A Great Householder)

Meridian Man, Enstomacher,
For whom the whole world's fruits are fare;
For whom all Life is but a feast's
And all the world is filled with guests!

Spread out the Board, dispense the cost,
There's not a moment to be lost
Until the mystic Wine and Bread
Are guzzled and engulletted!

The Summit's reached! The glasses chime,
This is the Kairos, the High Time.
We banquet, and beyond the doors
We'll hear the snarling carnivores.

Your table like a moon silvern,
Shows what a kitchen sun you burn,
An alternating sun that heats
The growing herbs and lowing meats.

O, tableland! O, plain of Troy,
Whereon we wage the wars of joy!
You Agamemnon to our force,
Big-bellied as the Trojan horse!

Well marshalled by your genial roar,
The servants massed in order pour
The blood some thirsty summer shed,
Now ten years rising from the dead.

Still from your cellar's costly glooms
Each bottle like an Orpheus comes,
And bends his golden neck till we
Can all but clasp Eurydice.

A Victory plunges through the air!
As well as Love, Wine casts out fear!
The butler's Marathon goes round
And still your friends orchestral sound.

The artist poor is heartened to join,
There's scholarship in each sirloin.
Do you prefer it brown or red?
What did you say that Shakespeare said?

The book is somewhere on my shelves.
Yes, God helps those who help themselves.
Don't mind, my friend, it's only froth:
I like a dappled tablecloth!

Wine should not make a man afeard;
A chewing chin won't spoil your beard.
Well, let your stomach fight it out —
Starvation's no soft cure for gout.

Thanks, thanks! For this I won't refuse
Opens the lips of every Muse,
Makes us expand, makes trouble cease
And brings the broad Tiberian peace.

Magee no longer thinks alone,
Clarke talks and rouses silent Hone:
While booming through the mist is heard
Responsible the clear-thought word.

I cannot move, I will not speak
Without Parnassus' second peak:
The Friend to whom you oft refer
Your cousin dear and echoer.

Once you fill up the ravening Maw
There's not a doubt about the Law;
Just cut that chicken through the girth,
I'm battling here for peace on Earth.

When water-lilies drink a lake
I'll dare your health and bounty slake.
Justly to drink what bears me up
I needs must get inside the cup!

Once like your Body bulged the Earth,
Pear-shaped before the Moon had birth.
O keep your tropic waistcoat tight,
Your Belly may fly off to-night!

Then past your chimneys in the dome
Another moon would light us home,
Fair as the ocean shell that rose,
And harvest-full and grandiose.

Born of your bounty take my Song,
Redounding like a dinner gong,
Translunary recorder pale
Of how your guests you can regale.

Till all the Earth's volcanic heat
Shall bear a better heart to beat,
Fame shall not fail you, generous man,
Magnificent, Meridian!

## To George Russell

This is my book: I hasten to bestow its
Freedom on you maker of poems and poets.

## To a Mushroom

No one sang thee, little fielding,
  Sang thy wondrous being and birth,
Till to mute attraction yielding
  I first hymned thee here on earth.

Though I never saw thee start up
  I have seen thee when thou wert,
Poised as with an hinder part up –
  O my sudden quaint upstart!

In the short grass by the fount-head
  Thou art found as free from rule
As a faun, and unaccounted
  As a little boy from school.

Like a baby plump and ample,
  Whose exuberance was led
By Silenus' bad example
  Till the bowl fell o'er his head.

Of all growing things the oddest:
  Only on a sudden seen,
Unexpected and immodest,
  As above a stocking – skin!

But that's white and thou art yellow,
  With a greyness in the hue,
Which makes all attempts to fellow,
  It no easy thing to do.

I have seen a dead pig scalded,
  And the pallor that persists
While the puffing cook makes bald it
  And the stable-boy assists;

I have seen the caves of Cheddar
    Pastel, intestinal, blurred;
But thy whiteness is far deader,
    In thee light is sepulchred.

I have seen the colon-coloured
    Faces of the curates' wives –
Not to know would mark the dullard,
    'Tis their sedentary lives –

What a symbol of that dismal
    Sect who preach on Dead Sea fruit,
Petty, pale, and priapismal!
    Yet suggest no substitute.

Soft, I must entreat thee gently;
    And I can but do thee wrong,
And but think inconsequently
    Who for daylight pitch my song.

Suns for thee must still illume an
    Arid waste beneath the sky,
Wistful, cold, and thwartly human
    And Augustan – even as I.

Thine example shows quite clearly
    That the things we think deranged
Would be most delightful merely,
    Merely if the scene were changed.

Darkness only does not flout thee
    When alone thou tak'st the light,
And the silence floats about thee,
    Moon-loved, dewy child of night.

Wastes of evening silvered, cooling,
    Morn that yields her gentle reign,
Only know the white moon's ruling
    In the daylight melt again.

Daylight comes: thou hast not vanished;
    Now the sun must be endured
By thy flesh outcast and banished
    Into day and uninured.

Thus beyond thine own world's mearing
  Thou art left to mark the track
Where a Centaur I, careering,
  Into darkness galloped back.

To Francis Ledwidge

## To His Friend the Apothecary Poet

*(To make something up for him)*

When you compound a verse or song
Make it translucent, not too strong;
Pour the full measure gauged right,
That it have body, yet be light;
And ever let the essence be
An undefined entity.

Send me some vitalising dose
Such as your own, with such a close
As makes me wish it well were mine –
That 'brave dead singer of the Vine',
Or some shy sonnet, untransgressing,
But bubbling up and effervescing.

Nothing like Herbert's send me home
(Or with it send some laudanum),
No thought of Newman's send me back
(Or send an aphrodisiac),
Nor brusque and Browningish offence
Of poesy and commonsense.

Send me the brew that Shakespeare knew,
And Ben, and all the Mermaid crew,
That made both soul and body well
Ere these grew incompatible,
Something that we may quaff, and laugh,
Nor fear it for an epitaph.

Send me a Syrup to give me
Content but not complacency,
Something to lift the mind with Art

And yet to satiate the heart
Without reaction as the Vine;
Send me a song, send me a line!

## The Isles of Greece

[*In* Collected Poems *a different poem is given
the title 'The Isles of Greece', p. 100.
A different version of this poem entitled
'To a Sailor' is included, p. 402*]

Silent Sailor man attend,
Ere you voyage from Ringsend!
By your walk and wad I ween
You have in the Navy been.
Jones, whose Christian name is Davy,
Spare you long to grace the Navy!

Navy – nay, I'm quite erratic,
I meant to say the Adriatic.
Tell me have you seen the sea grow
Darker down by Montenegro?
And were you the sailor man to
Sail the waters of Lepanto?

Did they rise, or were they murky
Over all those men from Turkey?
For, you know, 'twas very pleasant
That the Cross should swamp the Crescent:
Thus both you and I and others
Kept the faith that keeps us brothers.

Well, we'll leave them there in peace.
Tell me of the Isles of Greece.
Grow they olive, vine, and palm?
Was it boisterous or calm?
Did you make a *nota bene*
As you sailed by Mytelene?

Are there really now in loads
Rhododendrons grown in Rhodes?

Say what isle would strike a roamer
As a birth-place fit for Homer?
Did you see the isle Calypso
Lived in when she got the slip so?

What would Ajax find amiss
Now in twice-washed Salamis?
Did you, in effusive joy,
Point and mutter: 'There was Troy'?
Did you not with grief and woe
View the Archipelago?

But the sailor turned to me
With an aspect like the sea,
When against some rocky strait
It must needs expectorate,
With, 'I don't give' (pardon, please)
'A damn for all your Isles of Greece.'

Then I shouted: 'Let me greet you,
Sailor, I am glad to meet you!
I have longed for one of these
Health-restoring heresies.
I am sick of affectation,
Thank you for emancipation!'

'Yes,' he said, 'it's rather funny
Why the people waste their money
Seeking Homer, Paul or Pilate
In each ordinary islet:
Searching for heroic spooks
On excursions run by Cook's.'

Ah, his eyes were bluer than
The Mediterranean,
And he looked on Life, a bowl,
Steadily, and drank it whole,
And cared not, with his mind at ease;
'A damn for all the Isles of Greece'!

Sailor, but a landsman speaks,
You are Greeker than the Greeks.
It is we are out of joint,
From our feverish touch aroint!

Our indecent souls' exposure
Shrinks before your self-composure.

Hero-lovers, we'd insist
That Plato was a Methodist,
And our 'Greece the beautiful'
But an ancient Sunday-school –
Oh, your talk is vitalising
After years of Arnoldizing!

We brood ever on the Past,
But you sail before the mast;
Time but serves to enervate
Us, but you are up-to-date,
And you thus lay bare of myths
Ionian thalattaliths.

          To W. K. Magee


## To an Aviator

O in the Lightning's path
Trespassing undaunted,
Over the pineless air
Stamping on ether,
White-lipped, confronting God,
Pallid with insistence,
Falling, you rise again,
Raping the distance!

Lost in the neutral blue
The superhuman spaces,
Through the old silences
Echolessly dancing.
O dizzy Bacchanal,
Shaking your thyrsus,
Death put behind you like
A mendicant's curses.

Say, was that ground your home
Where Everest is tented?

What stuff was in your wove
That finds the air substantial?
Whose the heroic breast
That suckled you, a lisper,
To whom now Niagara
Is less than a whisper?

## To an Art Critic

With your regrets don't move my mirth
That Beauty walks no more on earth,
For you would be revealed at once
In your true colours as her ponce.

## To M.—

If soul is Form, your shape so great to us
Might make us think you were magnanimous;
But, petty giant, shall we doubt the soul
When one so little wields so great a whole?

## Westward

When we drove out from Care released
    How well we met that parish priest,
Full in the form, full in the face,
    A man well built for saying grace!

When aptitude becomes a fault
    Then blame the gift we had for malt:
Or let him be enrolled with such
    As sin through loving overmuch.

We felt, when seated in the gloom,
    His presence permeate the room,
And, drinking, he would gently sigh,
    For tristful is mortality.

Because the artist is at best
  A bird that may not find his nest,
It does him good awhile to perch
  Beside a gargoyle of the Church,

And from the dream that's fixed in stone
  Survey and grasp and mould his own.
So when we next drive out to feast
  We'll call upon that parish priest!

              To Francis Macnamara


## *To His Friend to Try Another Tavern*

They tell me, friend, no transient fit
Has held and holds you where
The muddled mirth and hogshead wit
Pervade the smoke-filled air;
But that you sit amid largesse
Insisting on punctiliousness.

Pandemian joys should be confined
To those whose bodies lack the mind
That darkens through your eyes.
The time for strenuous things is ripe!
Leave Davus to his greasy tripe
And consequent supplies,
Till Euphumistic calls of 'Time'
Cut short the lingering pantomime.

Goodbye to the loose thought that blunts
The insight, and corrodes the soul.
Goodbye to the too frequent bowl:
A long goodbye to Delahunt's.

I know a pub beneath a hill:
Nine barmaids keep its bar select;
And keep your corner dusted still.
Its chucker-out demands respect:
Of those he chucks out everyone
Is locked up by Oblivion.

You've travelled further, friend, than I,
You're to the Muses better known.
Go confidently in and try
If they'll serve both or you alone.
I'll talk to him who peeps outside. He
Will tell me if I'm bona-fide.

The Past is ours: but — what's far more —
The Future can be catered for,
It's Spirit's in the Still.
Give it some rare ethereal taste
So men may, when we're gone to waste,
Exclaim: He mixed it well!

## Urbs Intacta

I wrote a poem lately which no praise did
    Evoke, cajole or wrest; I did not frown
For Dublin, when I think how other lays did,
    I rather dread the culture of your town.

## To Kasimir Dunin Markievicz

Kasimir, a name that clashes like a sword
Through skulls of dullards and brings back old joy!
Kasimir, the great eternal-hearted boy!
A Centaur laughing on his mountain sward
Could just as little with our life accord
As you can with the little peoples here,
A thing of brain and beauty, stallion and seer,
Like him who taught proud Hector's overlord.
We whinge in art and ethics, you're above
Our best in painting, poetry and love
As these faint-hearted by their envy prove;
Thus: Dublin getting as they all aver
More than a Roland for its Oliver
When you came out of Poland, Kasimir.

## Spirat Adhuc Amor

Long before Merlin slumbered in the wood
The grand enchantment lured, in spite of teen,
Both men and maids and bound them, as the queen,
Who left but ashes where a city stood,
And him whose death was in Abydos flood
And him who clasps his love in nether scene.
And though there comes 'twixt Troy and Stephen's Green
A long, inevitable interlude,
Yet who shall say our housemaid's evenings out
Hold less of the romantic, though she hear
Nor stricken steeds nor armed Ajax shout,
Nor see the tranced forest dimly lit?
The cabmen and the soldiers still are here –
She's twenty-one, and that makes up for it!

## On First Looking into Kraft-Ebing's Psychopathia Sexualis

Much have I travelled in those realms of old
Where many a whore in hall-doors could be seen
Of many a bonnie brothel and shebeen
Which bawds, connived at by policemen, hold.
I, too, have listened while the Quay was coaled,
But never did I taste the pure obscene
Much less imagine that my past was lean,
Till this Kraft-Ebing out his story told.
Then felt I rather taken by surprise
As on the morning when I met Macran;
And retrospective thoughts with doubts arise:
Was I quite normal when my life began
Of Love that tends to rural sympathies
Potent behind a cart with Mary Anne?

## Sonnet

*(When the Clearance was intended to the City)*

Sergeant with manners like an inspector's,
Whose chance upon these defenceless doors may seize,
If nights upon us did you ever please
Spare us, and we will stand you free encores.
Against lust rampant most our business scores,
We bring the hardest roues to their knees,
And those temptations that by no means cease
Are cured by yielding kindly to the whores.
Lift not your baton 'gainst our bawdy bower!
Has Hercules not laboured once till day?
And Jove come – Capital! – a golden shower
(Damn the expense!) to spend on Danæ?
If gods found comfort in a paramour
We, too can take the perilous stuff away

## 'Memento Homo Quia Pulvis Es'

(At La Trappe)

The strong sound of the deep bell burns
The darkness, and my soul resumes
Its meditation now, and turns
To think exclusively of tombs:
No, no! Those Greek funereal urns
Were not intended – I've been told –
Merely to meditate on mould.

I meditated: Man is Dust,
And into dust he shall return,
Until I wondered why God thrust
His breath into the dust to burn.
He gave it life; who gave it lust?
And who's to blame? If Dust is man
The trouble in God's breath began.

God damns his breath, which is man's soul
For misbehaviour of the clay –
His breath must be beyond control
To leave man Freewill, anyway;
And then his breath must be most foul
That thereby it should damn a soul.

Freewill to do or leave undone
Means, first, repudiating laws
Lest they have influence thereon;
And then, effect without a cause:
For that Freewill should have effect,
All causal things it must neglect.

And when I think of all the work
And time they spent in teaching me,
A little doubt begins to lurk
Of even the power of thinking free.
For what must I all danger shirk,
The value of a Saint's vocation
Varies directly as temptation?

A slight distraction unawares
Beset me in a twofold way:
I saw the legs of one who chars
And cleans the chapel out each day,
As she was washing down the stairs,
And I was bending down to pray,
I said: 'If hers are not so trim
Her daughter's might be tight and slim'.

And then I prayed a little space:
'O, Thou Lord God, what is this thing
Besets me in Thine Holy Place?
Why must Thy washerwoman fling
Her petticoats before my face
And set me wild with wantoning?
O, cool me with Thine Holy Water
That I may think not on her daughter!'

To James Stephens

## To the Rev. George O'Neill

*(Who resigned from the Feis because of a Kissing Song)*

Austere, revered and reverend O'Neill
Who, scanning history with affected eye,
Saw Love lead men and many a state to die
Betraying with a kiss the commonweal,
Was it his sin whom no one could anneal,
The Horsel and Wagnerian melody
Or Youth's reiterated 'Pudding and Pie'
That made you strongly hating, strongly feel?

Pray that we spring from eggs like Leda's brood
(Erin an incubator gently warmed)
So shall our loveless children make for good
Songless, in silence, but by Love unharmed;
So shall our green land daily grow more green
Where sex is sin and virtue epicene.

## The Two Despairs

Hell's river nine times folded carried down
Hope's wreckage: – apple blossoms mixed with mire
And loudly from the apathetic choir
Wailing arose remembering renown.
Those who on earth had worn the parsley crown
Cried out again in anguish; each could see
The drown'd white limbs of his soul's effigy –
Thus tortures thought when life is overthrown.

Next morn I sought a doctor: 'Tis the age
(Reluctantly I make the sad avowal)
When men think less of Beauty than the Bowel.
And I had scarcely questioned when the sage
Said: 'Take these little tabloids for the packed
Condition of your intestinal tract.'

## To a Clever Little Lecher

Willy's deep as stillest waters,
   Yet unlike them is not still,
For the race of Adam's daughters
   Gives no peace to Wily Will.

Wily Willy's not a dreamer,
   Yet the vision, it would seem,
That has changed him to a schemer
   Is far stronger than a dream.

It can warp him, it can twist him,
   It can make his virtue fret;
Love on the instalment system
   Keeps him neck and ears in debt.

Until he is not a dwarf and
   Until sex and scheming cease,
Wily Willie will be orphaned
   From the parentage of Peace.

## Conscription

'The pen is mightier than the sword':
   But in the battle's rush
The painter, though in peace he scored,
   May, fox–like, lose his brush.

                To W. O.

## To an Amphisbænic Friend

*(The Begetter of Only the Ensuing Satire
and a Few Female Children)*

That Greek whom Juvenal despised,
Esurient and undersized,
Had scarcely left him words to speak

Had he met you, had Greek met Greek.
Disgust and consternation, too,
Had failed, had he included you.

Long-faced, squat backed, the shoulders high,
The lashes gone from wet blue eye,
The lip protrudes, the chin does not,
The huddled teeth are undershot,
Scant chestnut hair, King Billy's nose,
Long legs and silken underclothes.

You would be thought, though sick with lust,
Clean, and though undersized, robust;
And brave! you who have puked with fear;
And yet, though whiskey-soaked, austere!
Must all that's cold and noble be
A toadstool to your vanity?

## To a Bearded Dealer in Old Objects of Art

You live to sell the beautiful and rare.
I often wonder how your friends must fare,
Except that Fate ordains to make amends,
Your goods should not be rarer than your friends.

### ANOTHER TO THE SAME

To things of Beauty and of olden culture,
Your shop gives an exhumable sepulture:
But why the beard of prophet or of fakir,
You who are merely Beauty's undertaker?

## The Dandelion

I saw a Dandelion gray in Spring,
The blossom of the ash-pit of the town;
Its thatch, like little thoughts, each puff did fling
Until it bent it half baldheaded down.
But deeply-rooted in the acrid earth

Amongst discarded things it safely grew:
To smite it had but multiplied its birth –
Therefore I left it as I now leave you.

                                    To W. S.


## Helen's Lamp

A little lamp, but the great sun
Sees not half I gaze upon.
These verses Paris round me traced
For Helen by my light looks best.


## A Line from Rabelais

*'Faire and Softly Passeth Lent'*

From Christmas and from Carnival
Repletion on the sense remains,
Therefore it needeth Interval
To ease the weary body and brains;
So Holy Mother Church ordains
The Monk should rest on diet thin
And grumble not but be content;
Thus is the body purged from sin:
*Faire and Softly passeth Lent.*

Unversed in disputatious lore,
I love all pure and holy things:
The quiet thoughts that shine and soar
Like gulls that hardly move their wings;
I love the calm that evening brings,
The dewfall and the sun's descent,
The bird that in the darkness sings:
*Faire and Softly passeth Lent.*

Here in the old cathedral close
I walk about and meditate;
Or, if the sun is shining, doze;
Or watch the people pass the gate;

Or with the idlers remonstrate;
Or help the Brothers feed the birds;
Or, gazing over byre and bent,
Survey and count the Convent herds:
*Faire and Softly passeth Lent.*

How pleasant is the Chancel dim
When clouds of incense lull the air,
The Choir murmuring hymn on hymn,
And all the monotone of prayer!
Long evenings in the twilight there
I sit and counsel and anneal
Each plain or pretty Penitent,
And stoutly curb the thoughts I feel:
*Faire and Softly passeth Lent.*

God is displeased with Koska's wife –
She's yielded to that man again:
A worthier villain on my life
Ne'er merited the Extreme Pain!
But my good Joan the Chatelaine,
She calls my penance mere restraint
And swears, ere April buds be sprent,
To find a way to vex a saint:
*Faire and Softly passeth Lent.*

By murmurs 'gainst our Holy Church
They say their husbands most have sinned;
But they who dare God's name besmirch
Shall surely, even in this Life, find
The evil thought is soon divined
And punished: Master Rabelais,
And he was always malcontent,
Has lost salvation for his say:
*Faire and Softly passeth Lent.*

Lord let me find while Time wears on,
While my days here are being spent,
Before the Resurrection
*Faire and Softly passeth Lent.*

To George Moore

## *Epitaph*

If it's worth while to talk about my end,
Say: about Fame he did not greatly bother,
Because he found himself the Poets' friend,
And that's more than they are to one another.


## *Epilogue*

*To the People of Ireland in the coming times*

Inheritors of this our Song!
Inhabitants of larger day!
If you sometimes look back and long
That you had met us, hear me say:
You're happy, though you may not know it,
To have the Verse and not the Poet.

# SECRET SPRINGS OF DUBLIN SONG (1918)

## *Spring in Dublin*

When East wind's roll of ruin blows,
And tenements hang out more clothes,
And old men go on frozen feet,
And spits lie spattered on the street,
And hazards held at sinecure,
Fill all the air with dry manure;

When Dublin sends by dirt and rheum
Brigades of babies to the tomb,
And on the side-cars, holding seven,
The pic-nic parties seek Glasnevin,
And back-yards like a play by Synge
In gloom and squalor hail the Spring.

Then she comes tripping down the street,
And not a Bobbie on his beat
Can hold her up, or stop the Spring
From shamelessly soliciting –
Even the Vigilance Committee
Can't keep the Spring from Dublin City.

Her motion may not be adjourned,
She is perennially returned.
She pays no rates, she does not care
Who schemes to be the next Lord Mayor.
Sweet fosterer of bud and graft,
She leaves Cork Hill unepitaphed!

Now dogs at every corner range,
New Limericks fill the Stock Exchange,
The ducks now splash in Stephen's Green,
Where cripples on the benches lean,
And merrily the children race
Round noseless men with half a face.

She strews fresh sawdust in the pubs,
Fresh laurels in the area tubs.
Rathfarnham's lanes with song she fills,
And lovers' monosyllables:
On what does Spring not ope the door
When off to Paris sails George Moore?


## A Double Ballad of Dublin

Dublin Town was a town before
You were a man or your grandfather.
The Danes are buried at Inchicore
Who walled it in where the hurdles were.
The ridge of the Hazels was ringed with care
And taught in its turrets of stone to frown:
At mountain and marsh would the watchman stare
And winding Liffey by Dublin Town.

Thus it was in the days of yore.
Where will you find the like of it? Where?
London's fog-coloured faces? More
Numerous – yes – but they are not rare;
A city that people of all kinds share –
Keep to blue eyes and tresses of brown –
Aberdeen? Well, you have me there!
But winding Liffey in Dublin Town.

Dwelling and office and store on store,
Merchants and money to change for ware,
Ships in the harbour, goods on the shore,
Will not make a town if the soul be bare.
Here is a dream and tradition to spare,
Memoried sorrow and old renown;
Hearts quick to soften and ready to flare
And winding Liffey in Dublin Town.

Though in the houses of ancient lore
Bishops divide the Episcopal chair,
Many there are when the weather is frore
Sights and sounds goodly to see and to hear:
The tower of Christ Church tall and square
When the high Christmas stars look down;
Bells intermingling sounds in the air,
And winding Liffey in Dublin Town.

City where magical twilights pour
Drawing the beautiful hills anear,
Town where the citizens out of door
Longing to talk, to the streets repair, –
Gossips obstructing the thoroughfare –
To gaze where the reek is northward blown
Melting to bronze in the sunset glare
And winding Liffey in Dublin Town.

But to acknowledge the truth, Asthore,
In spite of what happens to those who dare,
Here there is something corrupt at the core
A city unclean with a paid Lord Mayor,
Pestilence, sorrow and poverty's lair,
Pride's in a grandeur overthrown,
Bawdy and faithful, squalid and fair –
And winding Liffey in Dublin Town.


## *To Citizen Elwood in South America*

Ah, John
Since you are gone
We've proved you what we knew before

The One and Only
You left us lonely
When to that Southern land you bore
Our mighty loss and sadder sequel
Because we cannot find your equal.

The gloom remains,
And things are formal.
The gloom, alas! with us is normal
And nothing lights it or destrains.
Oh, send us of your wisdom keen
Something to act as formaline
Acts on the effluence of drains;
Something to fumigate like sulphur
And ruffle all the black rats' dull fur
That spoils the colour in our brains.

Oh, merge us in a cloud of wit
Until we 'gin to lift with it
And lose ourselves as it enshrouds!
Oh, send to bring the Springtime back
Your basic old subliming knack –
The gods are hidden in the clouds!


## Rondeau

O Moore, when first with fire and sword
Your ancestors sacked Baltimore,
The townsmen cried with one accord:
        'O Moor!'

Transmuting Time your race abhorred
Transmuted and on Irish shore
Beheld 'The' at a chieftain's board,
        O'More.

But now from bois and boulevard
Your risky storiettes you store
And wonder why you're not encored
        Oh, Moore!

## The Poet to the Physician

[by Seamus O'Sullivan]

If Fortune ever seem to send
Fame to my verse before my end,
Come with your healing arts and save
From early fame by early grave.


## The Physician Replies

If Fortune ever seem to send
Fame to your verse and not an end,
Then with your verses must endure
My failure to effect a cure.


## To Carson, Swimmer of Sandycove

Where hast thou been since salt to Sandycove
    Thrice three Springtides have ebbed and flowed again,
Aye, sighing ebbed because thou wert not 'in'?
    Why on the banks of granite dost thou rove
As, in old time, on Sundays thou wert seen
    In suit of serge dressed like the sailor-men,
What time their long precarious voyage they make
    To Murray's haven and the inside bar?
Thou seemest strange; we don't know where we are
    For Carson out of water takes the cake!

Or didst thou seek some mild Antartic isle
    Where by thy side the snoring walrus swam,
Whose second teeth come, when they come, to stay?
    Where thou could'st meet the icebergs with a smile,
Nor for the Polar Bruin care a damn,
    If he, perchance, pursued thee on thy way?
For what dost thou, O Carson, care for cold,
    Thou that wast far below our Zero born!
Need I repeat that 'Winter's Tale' so old:
    The Bobbie weakened by thy rathe lanthorn?

No, thou art Carson and none other one!
    It was for thee that lame McCurdy lied,
And Griffith's towel was untimely wet;
    It was for thee revering Starkey tried
With daily toil until that stroke he won
    Which thou employest to the land to get.
Aye even here the glory of thy hide
    Where all are over-famous faintly burns
While Ireland, like Buda Pesth, returns
    To be like thee who never missed a tide.

Where hast thou been? For surely thou hast strayed
    Within some evil influence malign,
Or in the Adelaide was aye delayed
    And, for the ocean, swam'st in 'normal saline.'
Ay! Gordon loosed for thee that Gordian knot
    That is thy umbilicus well-renowned,
And Starkey mingled, though he knew it not,
    Black draughts for thee, and for thee did compound!
Alas, O Golden Carson, thou hast quaffed
    From lover's hands an ebb-compelling draught!

Ah, horrid dream of fact be thou factitious!
    Glide hither every nymph, each Nereid glide,
Now undistinguished from your native foam!
    Old Nereus and old Proteus be propitious,
And buoy my keel of song with flowing tide
    Until unto those hidden isles I come –
Far hidden in the distance of blue seas, –
    Where Carson breasts the waters let me sail;
And if it chance that I discover these,
    To float my leaky vessel I'll go bail!

Loosen the sail and please support my ship so
    That I may sail where only Carson swam.
None else save Carson and the grave Ulysses,
    Laertes' son that left the quaint Calypso.
(He couldn't for her bosom care a damn
    If, like thee, Carson, he preferred then this sea's)
There didst thou swim and round thee Dolphins sported,
    There nymphs bespoke thee, as thy side they won.
Thou thankd'st them, 'trudging,' and most kindly snorted
    In articulate communion!

Perchance there fishers fishing for the tunny,
    Which first they catch, and then proceed to spear,
(And, Kirke-like, later, bleed the purchaser)
    Beholding thee grew suddenly less funny
And each one whispered in the other's ear –
    Sitting with eyes shut fast, afeard to stir –
'O leave the sea, 'tis not to be relied on!
    I saw by accident, and in the rear,
(I fear a tempest must be very near),
    The bottom of the body of Poseidon!'

But thou, swim on! and when thou comest to fare on
    The seaward tide that shoreward will not turn,
But meets the dim unnavigable sea,
    Though we must die, thou needst not go with Charon,
Nor obol in thy mouth will mourners lay;
    And he will mourn in vain, if any mourn,
For thou wilt, slowly, where the Styx is wound
    Unwind thy vain, unmeaning cerements
And take – the temperature, at all events,
    Back with thee swimming to regain the ground!

## From 'The Queen's Threshold'

### Act I (interrupted)

### I.

What was it Queen Mary said
    As he climbed the stagey stair?
Comes a-singing in my head,
    Can you say who put it there?

Plays of China and Japan,
    Plays of most reluctant Greece,
Plays – for God's sake stop the man!
    Will his lecture never cease?

And she twitched her garment's hem,
    But his silence had been wise;
What were all his plays to them
    On the stage with the Allies?

II.

But her poet answered her,
    This the aim of Fame would baulk.
What's fame for, if not to air
    A gift for most immoderate talk?

Peeresses a shining ring
    Yearn about me as I walk;
If a poet cannot sing
    He must talk, he must talk.


## The Old Man Refreshing Himself in the Morning

I heard the old, old man say:
    'Mineral Waters,
The doctor ordered me lithia.'
His face was like the face one sees
In Galway county families
    By the halters
Of flapper meetings led astray,
Where tide is low and bookies' pay
    Mostly falters.
I heard the old, old man say:
'What do you think will win to-day
    By the waters?'


## On the Death of His Aunt

(*To the Gravediggers to inter her gently*)

O ye, who disinterested plant
This mortal remnant of my Aunt,
    And, planting her, grow dry,
Suspend your vacant pensiveness,
And turn those thoughts to my distress
    Which pints preoccupy.

She was, as ye'd know if ye knew her,
The widow of a worthy brewer,
    A brewer's worthy widow.
And though some called her sentimental,
I found her generous and gentle,
    Not minding what I did owe.

Between us Love was so prevailing
That when she ailed I too was aleing,
    And on her husband's ale.
(For though the evil that men do
Lives after them, if men will brew
    The good will then prevail).

She loved him – oh, and I did strive
For years to keep that name alive,
    Though it was on the bier.
But since he's gone where all the best did,
And she's by 'Sergeant Death' arrested,
    And I'm remaining here,

To mourn them both I'll wet my throttle
With dark drinks from a sable bottle
    With two Saint Andrew's crosses:
And yours, and rest; for well I know
My grief will thus not cease to flow
    In mourning o'er my losses.

## Praise and Friendship

### THE QUESTION

I.

Why should you, when I praise your verse,
My praise with leniency asperse,
And put the cart before the horse,
    When Verse's kinship,
Your gift direct and mine perverse,
    Makes up our friendship?

THE REPLY

[by Seamus O'Sullivan]

II.

When last you did a 'verse rehearse'
You said in lines, like Redding's, terse:
'Your gift direct and mine perverse'
    Ah, too correct!
You will attain your fame per verse,
    And I die wrecked!


## *Threnody on the Death of Diogenes, the Doctor's Dog*

VETERINARY SURGEON:

Take muzzle from mouth
    And the can from his tail,
He's as dead from the drought
    As the deadly door-nail.
I fear he has found hydrophobia, not even Pasteur
    may avail.

DOCTOR:

When I wambled awound
    In the gwound that was Greece
I was given that hound
    By the King's little niece,
And had rather be fined e'er I found him to gaze on
    his saddest surcease.

CHORUS (SCHOLARS OF THE HOUSE):

He was given that hound
    By the seed of a King
For the wisdom profound
    Of his wide wandering.
But was it the owner, or donor, or dog that was led
    by a string?

VETERINARY SURGEON:

I can sell you a dog
    That will growl at the dons
And bark without brogue;
    And if ever he cons
The brazen-faced bust of his master, will waggle his
    tail at the bronze.

DOCTOR:

ὦ χαῖρε, ὦ κύον!
    No new one for me,
For never a new one
    Again shall I see
Like thee that art gone to the dogs in the home of
    Persephone.

CHORUS:

For the dead dog no home is,
    Unless that it be
Where the cats' hecatomb is
    Of pork butchery,
When spaniels are sundered for sausage, fulfilled of
    catastrophe.

DOCTOR (MEDITATING):

The eagle is Zeus'
    A bird there may be –
The owl too obtuse is
    The turtle too free
To suitably serve as a symbol, a sign and a signal of
    me.

CHORUS:

Leave Venus her turtles;
    Mock turtle for thee,
Who not among myrtles
    But rather woulds't be
Among the élite at a banquet, in the shade of a
    family tree.

DOCTOR:

What bird shall I get me
　　That monarchs may know,
And ladies beset me
　　Wherever I go,
All converts to my 'Conversation' which only on
　　these I bestow?

CHORUS:

Get hence to the land
　　Whereof Bion did sing,
When he wept on the strand
　　And there swept on the wing
A bird that is called the Kingfisher, and catch it to
　　capture the King.


## The Pilgrimage to Plunkett House

I saw, Piers Plowman-like, a plain of men
Who looked like people who look after cows,
And to my query: 'Ho, what do ye then?'
'We make the pilgrimage to Plunkett House.'

From every pasture, mountain, dale, and fen
They issued gaily waving flags and boughs,
And with one voice they chanted the refrain,
'We make the pilgrimage to Plunkett House.'

'Tell me,' I shouted, 'if a clucking hen
Can't rear a pheasant, can she rear a grouse?'
But with one voice they chanted the refrain,
'We make the pilgrimage to Plunkett House.'

'Poets precede us and we common men
With lukewarm fervour many a cause espouse:
So that we catch the Golden Crop again
We make the pilgrimage to Plunkett House.'

'Mecca is under sand, Jerusalem
Is in Chicago with an Oil King's spouse,

Is there a prophet left us?' And from them,
'We make the pilgrimage to Plunkett House.'

Some say he was a man of beard and brawn,
And that to such we should not pay our vows,
But we know well that he is Mananaun
Who make the pilgrimage to Plunkett House.

The sand-stone pillars rise, the plated door
Swings as the handle, sun-wise turned, allows;
The hosts are kneeling on the stairs and floor,
Who make the pilgrimage to Plunkett House.

This is the place: the sacred air is thick,
Each herd of the believers gently lows;
This is the shrine: the wall with gods is quick:
We make the pilgrimage to Plunkett House.

Here is the seat where every morn at ten
The kind god chaunted and the crops arose,
There is the dungeon for the gombeen men
Who make no pilgrimage to Plunkett House.

'What offerings bring ye, ye that come from far
O'er valleys and the gloom of mountain brows,
What offering to the High-Priest-Registrar
Who reads the omens in the Plunkett House?'

'We offer at this shrine of Mananaun's
Potatoes that were Champions in their youth,
So may the grass grow lushly on the lawns
Of all the Pilgrims to the House of Truth.'

*(Poets of the Plunkett House chaunting: − )*

E'er out of Dana Banba came,
Man kept himself with milk and corn;
Death after life was much the same,
And Life − result of being born.
But Dana cast on men a dream,
She knew the songsters and their ilk:
To poets first she gave the cream,
To others separated milk.

Therefore to Dana let us pray,
To Dana and to Mananaun,
That, having hearkened us, she may
Persuade him bless each loft and lawn.
Oh, Goddess hearken to the lot
Of these thy pilgrims come from far,
The sacred carrot faileth not,
And thunder rumbles round Rathgar.

## A Lament for George Moore

Lonely, O Moore, your old friends are;
    We miss you; and, forgive the banter,
We miss the generous cigar,
    The coy decanter.

We miss the nights when you were here –
    All Ely Place a catacomb,
Where we sat solemn and severe
    Denouncing Rome.

We were the Stellar Zodiac
    You took your part in:
Virgo Magee, Leo Æ.
    And Edward Martyn.

Who hailed your firstlings as they grew
    Chapter by chapter;
And when we showed our Muse to you
    You did adapt her!

Guidance from thoughts thus crowding thick
    Was what you needed.
You were the grandest Catholic
    That e'er seceded.

Thus through a window shines your ray
    All polychrome,
For 'still the light that led astray
    Was light from' Rome.

We miss Les Dames aux Temps jadis,
    And all whose Christian names would fall so
Ingenuously of living ladies –
    We miss them also.

Now Yeats suggests (with Goethe) here
    The likeliest measure of a mind
Is – what we can't find anywhere –
    The girls it leaves behind.

O bad gray head good women knew,
    There comes a thought unmixed with sadness,
In that the worst that you could do
    Was hardly badness!

O hazardous and harmless lover,
    Come back to Ireland, come back and bring
(What though your writings are all passed over)
    In your person a Playboy unguessed at by Synge!


## To George Moore on the Occasion of his Wedding

*('Inexpressive Nuptial Song')*

### BALLADE

★★★ ★★★ ★★★★, ★★ ★★★★ ★★★★★,
★★★★★★, ★ ★★★★★★, ★★★★★★★★ ★★★★,
★★★★ ★★★★★★ ★★★ ★★★★ ★★★★★★ ★★★★,
★★★ ★★★★ ★★★ ★★★★★ ★★★★ ★★★ ★★,
★★★ ★★★★★★★ ★★ ★★★★★ ★★★★★,
★★★ ★★★★★ ★★★★★ ★★★ ★★★★ ★★★★★★
★ ★★★★★ ★★★★★★★ ★★★★★★,
★★★★★★★★★★, ★★★★★★★, ★★★★★★, ★★★★.

★★★ ★★★★★ ★★ ★★★ ★★★★ ★★★★ ★★★,
★★★ ★★★★ ★★★★★★★ ★★★★ ★★★ ★★★★★★,
★★★ ★★★★, ★★★ ★★★★★★★★★ ★★★★★★,
★★★★ ★★★★★★ ★★★★★★ ★★ ★★★★★★★
★★★★ ★★★ ★★★★★★, ★★★★★★ ★★★★★

*** ** ** ***, *** **** ** *****
*** **** *** **** **** ****** ******,
**********, *******, ******, ****.

**** *** *** *************, ****
*** ***** **** **** ***** *******' ****,
*** **** ***** **** ** *** **** ***,
****** *** **** *** *** ******,
*** **** ** *** ********,
*** ******* *** **** ******* *****,
***** ****** *** ******* *****-*******,
**********, *******, ******, ****.

### ENVOI

******, ***** *** ****** ** *** ****** –
*** ****** ****, ********* ****.
***** **** ****, ******* * ****,
**********, *******, ******, ****.

# *The Ship and Other Poems* (1918)

---

## *The Centaurs*

Because the Centaurs know the hills
And know the hollows of the plain,
And all the clefts their laughter fills,
They stamp the ground and laugh again.

Galloping fast with dizzy leaps
They rear and plunge beneath the plain;
And there is laughter on the steeps
And laughter in the deeps again.

## *Castle Corrib*

Of old the rigid deed was done,
And kine were snatched and castles won,
And many an acre occupied,
And then the iron statesmen died.

And though there comes a softer crew
Enriched by all they gain or brew,
And fields are stocked and keeps are stored
The men around regret the sword.

FROM
# *AN OFFERING OF SWANS* (1923)

---

To William McElroy

# PREFACE

Oliver Gogarty telephoned to me at the Savile Club a few months ago to know where he could buy two swans. Up to his neck in its ice cold water he had promised two swans to the Liffey if permitted to land in safety. I made inquiries and was able to report in a couple of days that there were certainly swans for sale at a well-known English country house and probably at the Zoological Gardens. He had been kidnapped by armed men from his house in Dublin between seven and eight in the evening, hurried into a motor, and driven to a deserted house on the banks of the Liffey near Chapelizod. As he was not blindfolded it seemed unlikely that he would return. 'Death by shooting is a very good death' said one of the armed men. 'Isn't it a fine thing to die to a flash' said another armed man. 'Have we any chance of a Republic, Senator?' said a third. They sent a man to report on their success and while waiting his return Oliver Gogarty played bodily feebleness that they might relax their care, and the restless movements of terror that they, alarmed lest his clatter reached the road, might bid him take off his boots. He saw his moment, plunged into the river and escaped in the darkness, not hearing in the roar of flooded water the shots fired at random. Forced for his safety to leave Ireland for a time, he practised his profession in London and

237

I wonder if it was the excitement of escape, or the new surroundings, his occasional visits to old English country houses, that brought a new sense of English lyric tradition and changed a wit into a poet. The witty sayings that we all repeated, the Rabelasian verse that we all copied rose out of so great a confused exuberance that I at any rate might have forseen the miracle. Yet no, for a miracle is self-begotten and, though afterwards we may offer swans to Helicon, by its very nature something we cannot forsee or premeditate. Its only rule is that it follows, more often than otherwise, the discovery of a region or a rhythm where a man may escape out of himself. Oliver Gogarty has discovered the rhythm of Herrick and of Fletcher, something different from himself and yet akin to himself; and I have been murmuring his 'Non Dolet,' his 'Begone Sweet Ghost' and his 'Good Luck'. Here are but a few pages, that a few months have made, and there are careless lines now and again, traces of the old confused exuberance. He never stops long at his best, but how beautiful that best is, how noble, how joyous.

W. B. Yeats.
30th August 1923.

## My Love is Dark

My love is dark, but she is fair;
As dark as damask roses are,
As dark as wood-land lake-water,
That mirrors every star.

For like the Moon who shines by night
She wins the darker air
To blend its beauty with her light –
Till dark is doubly fair.

## When the Sun Shines

When the sun shines on Mary's hair,
The splendour seems to own
That solid beams of sunlight there
Are blended with the brown;
And in the golden coils of it
A thousand little rainbows sit.

Then do not wonder that my sight
By her is ravished
When she can take the heavens' light
To bind about her head;
Or that I praise her more than all
Who holds the rainbows in her thrall.


## 'Please Drive Slowly Through Little Waltham'

A young man leaning on the bridge,
The gable timbers gray,
The willow fields, the vicarage
And the light yellow hay –

You cannot see them once you climb
The gently rising hill,
For curving road and elm and lime
The eyes with frondage fill.

But Little Waltham's winding street
Has houses that have reared
Names that the churchyard can repeat,
Names to their own endeared.

Here Time has bent a back that stood
Full stiff at Waterloo;
Here eyes have closed that Robin Hood
Has surely gazed into.

The poplars rise, the roses blow,
The builder oaks expand,
The streams with just reflection flow
And all the air is bland.

Aye, very pleasant is the spot
Within the vale's expanse,
Untouched by Fame, if Fame were not
The land's inheritance.

Here Spring is mild as Autumn is,
And Autumn blithe as Spring;
From blossoms to the blackberries
Time moves here in a ring.

Delirious Youth once fiercely caught
Me, and so strongly filled,
That bonds I tolerated not
Till half my life was chilled.

But now I will not hasten through, −
O young man on the bridge −
For soon enough all fades from view
Beyond the valley's ridge!


## Amor

The northern-browed, eternal hills
Hold valleys full of yellow light;
And hollies which the black-bird fills,
But no one hears that long delight.

There's many a scarred sea-faring man
Makes peace beside the lamp at home.
And is it not the wildest glen
That flavours best the honey-comb?

So when you next denounce the ways
And times and town where Cæsar dwelt,
Before disparaging those days
Recall what Rome spelt backwards spelt.


## The History Examination

I know how Love maltreated Troy;
(I know how Love besets us all)
The Eagle, the Idaean boy. . . .
− But that's not History at all.

How Fergus won the wooden sword;
And what gave Lancelot his scar:
For all that History can record,
There's little left but Love and War.

Where Liffey's last, sweet reach is long,
I know how little Iseult grew:
When things are themes for mighty song
What matter if all History's true?

You ask for facts? Well, I remember –
To show you I can be exact –
Poppaea's hair was golden amber:
Historian, is not that a fact?


## Folia Caduca

Autumn, autumn, the leaves are falling;
Earth who has given them gladly receives.
Through that stilled air they come at her calling:
The generations of golden leaves.

The generations descend and wither;
Winter from withering who can withold?
Deathward he calls them and they go thither;
Leaves like men change Earth into gold.

I look upon men like leaves, and I ponder
On a golden death that no longer grieves.
Where is the leaf that would carry beyond her
The spendthrift gold of the fallen leaves?

# AN OFFERING OF SWANS
# AND OTHER POEMS (1924)

---

## To Edward Moreton Drax,
## 18th Baron Dunsany

*To ward off Time's abuses*
*The name is set above,*
*By one who loves the Muses,*
*Of one the Muses love.*

## Slanting Light

I love to fill my eyes with light
   In gazing o'er broad meadow-land,
When all the grass is tipped with white,
   And trees on one side lighted stand
As bare as Danae did of old,
Untrammelled in the stream of gold.

Can barrenness give birth to joy?
   What is it makes me wish to sing?
O undeceived by Death's decoy,

No grave is deep enough for Spring:
And soon the frozen boughs will thaw
And throw broad pieces down the shaw!


FROM

## Seven Concerning Hermione

[These two sections of the poem were
omitted in *Collected Poems,* see p.135]

### VI. A PRIVILEGE

Only along the thin white ridge
That marks her head where hairs divide,
Have I a lover's privilege
To kiss the sources of a tide,
That if unkempt, uncoiled, unloosed,
Would run away like streams unsluiced –
Streams that can gather force and spread
Till on their banks be founded towers.
Towns are not dearer than her head.
London and Poictiers, nor the dowers
Of Queens by strong men coveted,
Nor all the treasure spent on pride,
Could buy what would be islanded,
If she but left her hair untied.

### VII. A MIRACLE

Pygmalion made of ivory
The loveliest woman that could be;
And Venus made her blonde and warm,
A quick chryselephantine form
To soothe Pygmalion's amorous heart;
And he was wedded to his Art.
If that's not miracle enough
To make you dread the power of Love.
Will you who disbelieve my rhymes
About Love's power, believe in Time's?
Time that can tarnish golden hair,
And make the sloping shoulders square,

And loveliest miracles reverse.
How will you deal with that slow curse,
Who hide more beauty from the view
Than sculptor's chisel ever knew?


## Early Morning – Germany

The wayside trees are red and ripe,
    The timber turns to food,
Delicious as its prototype
    When Mother Eve was wooed.

And through the unawakened air
    That stirs not with the rill,
The smoke is rising here and there
    Between me and the hill.

Now sleeps a golden head of mine,
    By never-frozen wells
Far in an island rich in kine
    Where blue-eyed Brenda dwells.


## To a Trout

Into the brilliant air you leap,
    Leaving your dim immortal home,
Quick as a thought out of the deep
    Into a living word may come.
Why do you leave the lovely gloom
    Whose floors are paved, when waves are sunny,
With golden patines on the brown
    All pleasanter than last year's honey?

Not where the winds and waters make
    A miracle of purple wine,
Nor where the margin of the brake
    Is sanded to a crescent line,
And hollies for a moment shine,
    Like Thyades when they're undressing;

But where the floating lily isles
   Have kept the ripples from transgressing.

None knows what makes you spring in air;
   And no one knows what sets me silly,
Why with a hookless bait I fare,
   A hookless fly and a dumb gillie,
To cast for Beauty on the wind,
   While tempting Fate's your like employment;
Then why should Life bewail its end,
   If Death's the salt of all enjoyment?


## To The Lady —

(Who acted Queen Elizabeth for the screen)

Strange that you should have acted Gloriana
Who rule us in more spacious days, Diana!
She was the imperfect morning in which you
To the perfection of this full day grew,
So moted with your glory that we are
The lit companions of your blazing star
That makes our NOW the noon-day of all time,
And puts sweet flesh upon the limbs of rhyme
To sing the harvest of Creation home.
To what enchanted margin have we come?
Why is your spell not fragile? Can it last?
Beauty was all too brittle in the past;
And long in one place Joy has never been;
Nor without danger Artemis was seen.

I flap my wings and poise in the blue air,
(Little the dangerous for danger care),
With sharpened beak and eyes that never blink,
To pounce on Beauty on Destruction's brink.
Where do you lead? And what unguessed at coast
Will echo with your fame when we are gone?
What lands will dream of Beauty modelled on
That which we gaze at till our eyes grow dim?
I cannot see your equal, much less limn
Her features who will dare to evening lands

Bring back your crescent lids, your lips, your hands,
And distillation of distinguished words
Which drop as slow as honey out of gourds:
'It was no dream': I heard them; well they might
Assure me no enchantment lured the sight!

But lest one think to feel your very breath
When we are lying in the gap of Death,
I sing and say to all who then may be:
What they behold is but your effigy,
An aberration out of Beauty's path,
Pretender in Perfection's aftermath!
Where are the regal tresses of dull gold,
The strange vert eyes so steady and so cold,
The body carried to an inward tune
As if the Graces had become triune?
Nor would we rise, nor have a voice recall
Us who in brave days loved the original.

## Pankration

The Hero still contends,
    He strives to break the hold,
Cheered by his town and friends,
    And the great names of old.

O breach the City wall,
    The City of his birth!
For him the untaken town must fall
    That sent such valour forth.

## And Now

Good Sir, it's time to go from this
    Down to a public house I know,
Where half a mile of River is,
    And half a dozen poplars grow!

There's nothing wrong there with the ale;
   And we will feel as free from wrong,
If we let industry prevail,
   That maybe you'll break into song;

Or I will sing that song of mine,
   Of him who on a publican's daughter,
Begat the Dacian Constantine;
   And he was king beyond the water.

## Lambay

Hush, my Heart, you must not say:
It is lovelier in Lambay,
When that island meets the eye
Somewhat bluer than the sky.

Lawns it has and pleasant streams
Calm and flowing in your dreams.
Ah, but if your dreams came true,
What would happen, Heart, to you?

With your dreams you must not part;
Hold them in; and then, my Heart,
You and I will be instead
Calm and free and islanded.

## Relativity

(To Einstein)

Who am I to wonder at starlight bending,
Time a co-relative, parallels that swerve;
When a name like Eleanor, Margery or Alison
Takes the mind that ponders it and bends it on a curve?

## Meeting Kim

Like a bough when it plays
    In its joy of the wind,
As a poplar tree sways,
    As a boat is inclined,
So she moves, so she comes;
    Till to me the long street
Is a meadow that blooms,
    Or the waves at her feet.


Could we lie till the beams
    Of the sun came to pass
Through the succulent stems
    Of the new springing grass;
Could we walk by the edge
    Of the desolate sea,
With the dunes for a hedge,
    How bad it would be!


## Medicus Poetæ

You keep a watch for Beauty steady-eyed
By wood and grove, by wells and meadow streams,
And by the crescent sea-shore, for it seems
That there the goddess likeliest may be spied;
And then your vision in your verse you hide,
Or in some mouldy book or manuscript
Read what the poets said who saw her stript,
And kept themselves in glory till they died.
But I by bed and in the lazar-house
Where misery the Feast of Life derides
And Death confuses Autumn with the Spring,
Can sometimes, though I see not Beauty's brows,
Catch the uncertain syllable that bids
The blackbird leap from his dark hedge and sing.

## *To Tancred*

Tancred, you have much energy and nerve
And courage, and are still so undismayed,
Though you so long in fairy-land have strayed,
And of the Muses did so well deserve,
That little in Reality can serve
To recompense you for the price you paid –
Well jousted, and well ridden! O well played!
Who from the straightest course did never swerve!

In porphyry and grandeur sleep the kings
To whom your name and lineage cast true.
A thousand years in vain have worked their will,
For I think of them when I think of you,
Dismounted in these days of level things,
Moving as if the steel encased you still.

## *WILD APPLES* (1928)

---

### *Portrait*

Lights on her gaudy hair,
How she advances
Joyous and debonair!
And her eyes' glances,
Though the sun shines on her,
Are not made duller:
Joyous and debonair
Motion and colour!

Can there be anywhere
In all creation
Any sight lovelier?
Did the Greek nation
See in its columnar
Towns, or its isles,
Any sight lovelier?
Wait till she smiles.

### *Portrait*

You in your apple-tree
In your sun bonnet

(Ribbands upon it),
Dimples that laugh at me!
Thus you came into view
Over our hedge,
Blithe as the light on you
At the lips' edge!

How many years ago?
What does it matter?
Years cannot scatter
All I beheld in you.
Sleep brought it back again
In its old sweetness:
Time can but steal in vain
From the rich darkness.

## Portrait

*Jane W. . . .*

She does not seem to care,
She does not know her hair
Is golden with an hint
Of Trojan ashes in't.
She does not seem to know
How rarely dark her eyes go
With honey-coloured hairs
Drowning the coral ears.

She does not know her worth,
She thinks that Love is mirth,
And laughs; I never saw
Beauty more free from awe.
Yet if the Queen of Love
Descended from above,
What could she do but choose
Her body young and loose,
Her calm and easy ways
And that wide level gaze?
And maybe in that dress
Add to her loveliness.

The Past was mine – but O
With this unmelted snow
America has caught
The eye of all my thought:
Helen, your foster town
Once and for all is down,
And now Grand Rapids race
To take Scamander's place,
Araby the Blest
Loses the Phœnix' nest!

And now, and now
My song shall tell – but how?
Can poetry compose
The budding of a rose,
Or prosody out-do
The throstle in the yew,
Or memory make up
For life and love and hope?
Before her living word
My singing is absurd:
'You have my hand,' she said,
'Where shall I put my head?'

## To George Redding

George, when I look at the illustrated papers,
The kind that, nowadays, nearly everyone reads
Tingling I think of the women and their capers:
    Helens by hundreds!

Never before were there half so many lime-white
Ladies, the times past retarded their emergence.
Now every pastime brings them into limelight,
    Matrons and virgins.

Say in what time, in what city there has been a
Beauty to compare – O not in Rome or Paris! –
With Helen Wills, or with the lovely Senor-
    ita d'Alvarez.

Why can't we sing as the men of old? The simple
Reason is this that our cup of joy too full is.
Countess Bezzi Scali had with but a dimple
    Silenced Catullus.


## Bacchanalian

### I.

To-night, for poems, white and red wine drink;
For gold and purple is the poet's ink.

### II.

With you night's more than daytime! Could our breath
Mingle, I'd welcome the long tryst with Death.


## To Some Spiteful Persons

Your Envy pleases me and serves
My fame by all your muttering talk,
Just as the starling flock that swerves
With shrieks aside, and shows the hawk.

Men will lift up the head to stare,
Although it never stoop to strike,
At that still pinion stretched on air,
When all such chattering fills the dyke.


## The Yacht

Her ruddy pines stand straight up in the day
And scribble in the water: all is well.
My thoughts break out in canvas to the swell
Beyond our little harbour in the Bay,
To other isles and mountains far away
Where those who go in white and purple dwell.
But of the long adventure who may tell
Who steer for Beauty, if the Dream betray?

That was a puff from Pindus: now she heels!
The snow-born breezes bosom all her snows,
O hold her down on rock-bred Homer's isle!
No; it were better done to turn her keel's
Green blade back homewards while our own sea flows,
And the unaging Wind is blowing still.


## Song

Dreams, bring her back!
For, Dream-like, she
Is lovelier than Reality!
And only You can wander where
Dead wonders and the times past are:
For You those suns are shining yet
Which are, for me, forever set.

Dreams bring her back!
That I may have
A proof that You can pass the grave.
For, Dreams, if You have naught to give
Of exaltation while I live,
What hope shall be when I am gone
Where traffic is with shades alone?


## To Reformers

Tell me you who would design a
Perfect Paradise for man,
Could it better be than China
In the days of Kubla Khan?


## The Crowing of a Cock

The knowledgeable Spengler says,
'Twere better far for you and me
To turn to take mechanics up

Than forge a lyric nowadays,
For Culture is a fading tree
That, broadening, withers at the top.
Where Spengler lives that well may be
But Culture is of small account
Where men are governed by a clock,
Nor hold the Muses paramount,
Nor hear the crowing of a cock.

# *WILD APPLES* (1929)

---

## INTRODUCTION

It is not often that a friend of many years enchants us by the revelation of unexpected beauty. Oliver Gogarty had for two decades delighted his intimates by a wit from which nothing was immune, neither the illustrious in the heavenly city or his own, or perhaps, I should say, the imaginations some had of heaven or of themselves. There were most brilliant grotesques in verse, sometimes as intricate in pattern as the ornament on the Book of Kells, but by their nature much of that early verse was esoteric, we would lament that so original a talent ran like Alph, the sacred stream, in a subterranean brilliancy. We might, we would say, have had from Oliver comedies as witty as Wilde's, or a narrative of personalities more diverting than the *Ave Salve Vale* of his friend, George Moore. We were hopeful that the art which bedazzled us would sometime incarnate in a form where we could share our laughter with the world. I thought anything was possible, novel or drama; but I did not expect beautiful poetry. A prodigal wit rarely appears the chrysalis out of which we expect the winged lovely creature Poetry to be born. Then he began shyly to show us verses of a different character, and one by one these lyrics entered into memory and created in us a new imagination of our friend. The new verses had lost some of the substance of the earlier but not any firmness of outline. They grew to be precise and delicate as if cloud or air or light could be carven or counterfeited in

256

words; a luminous quality we can see to perfection in his *Plum Tree by the House*. If the later Oliver writes of girl or woman he suggests in them an airy distinction as if he saw the psyche fluttering within the flesh. Though he may speak only of a physical grace he makes us think rather of mind than body. The verses get more and more airy in character. When he has become at home in this new mood I have hopes that the wit which animated the earlier verses will return without frightening away the beauty, and we may have in him the same rare union of wit and beauty which enchants us in the lyrics of Heine.

I take great delight in the poetry of my friend and I write this in the hope that some who know me may be led to take in it the same pleasure as I do.

A. E.

## Galway

A grey town in a country bare,
The leaden seas between,
When light falls on the hills of Clare
And shows their valleys green,
Take in my heart your place again
Between your lake and sea,
O City of the watery plain
That means so much to me!

Your cut-stone houses row on row,
Your streams too deep to sing,
Whose waters shine with green as though
They had dissolved the Spring:
Your streets that still bring into view
The harbour and its spars;
The chimneys with the turf-smoke blue
That never hides the stars!

It is not very long since you,
For Memory is long,
Saw her I owe my being to,
And heart that takes to song,
Walk with a row of laughing girls

To Salthill from Eyre Square,
Light from the water on their curls
That never lit more fair.

Again may come your glorious days,
Your ships come back to port,
And to your city's shining ways
The Spanish dames resort!
And ere the tidal water falls
Your ships put out to sea . . .
Like crimson roses on grey walls,
Your memories to me!

## Upon Horan

Your bastards, through some failure in your force,
Were prematurely born or early buried;
So you, with small disgrace and no divorce,
Failed into Virtue; but she too miscarried.

## When it is Too Late

When your looking-glass no longer
Throws enchantment back again,
That enchantment which was stronger
Than you guessed, on lives of men,
Take my book to find reflected,
Safe from ravage of the years,
All the pride by time rejected:
Only then, break into tears.

## To Berkeley

I too, could prove from my eye which is susceptible
Sadly of deception that things are not what they seem:
Saw you my example, you would say that I had chosen well:
Julia when she dresses is more and more a dream!

## This Kip

*(Ce bourdel où tenons nostre estat. – Villon)*

Whore-master of the Body, O my Soul,
Hard is his lot who seeks a harlot's love!
Yet, though in loathsome ways constrained to move
With honour lost, treasure and self-control,
Contemptuous scowl while adding up the toll
Of sumptuous hours, and, even as you shove
Coins in your pouch, be stern and disapprove;
Remembering that, capricious, from her rôle
Of revel in the raucous, flaring kip,
She'll turn to you for solace from its rows;
For reminiscent sweet companionship,
To reach again to days, ere all was changed,
When there were fields to walk in unestranged,
And morning sun, and quiet in the house.


## The Weathercock

By pointing to that golden bird,
You mock me laughing, There you are!
But I see in him bravely reared
Above the pebbled tower and Square,
A guard against the lightning's stroke,
A sign to bring the church good luck.

Point him again! I would become
The bird which you point out to mock,
With long brown tendons on your thumb,
I would become the weathercock:
Neither inconstant nor unkind
Were I the cock and you the wind.

For I would, in those fields of air
Love you as in these fields of grass
And meet your moods and seem to veer,
Swinging around to let you pass;
Until the verger at the vane
Would look and say, There will be rain.

O what a mascot I should make
For lovers as the eve advances;
Wishing the sun down for their sake
Whose shadows run to leap the fences;
Watching the big star bless their hour,
Lonely in light above the tower!

But would you have the heart to leave
Me long there in suspense above
The little garden of the grave
To gaze on other lovers' love;
To be forever left in the lurch
While wedding parties entered church?

The church to which Love hopes to urge
You doubting where his lamp is fixed,
The church to which the paths converge,
The church where NOW and THEN are mixed,
The church which gathers things divine,
And tops them with its lucky sign.


## Petersen Lane

The masts at the bottom of Petersen Lane
Are red in the glow which a level sun casts;
And if you look close, you can see the long grain
Of the great pines of Norway which make up the masts.

The tall poplar neighbours that knew the long day,
And gazed out at azure-bright pinnacled forms;
The resinous timbers immuned from decay
By thunders ancestral and morningless storms.

The pub at the corner abuts on the Quay,
And there go the dockers, there everyone goes
Who likes to be drinking with men from the sea;
And mothers prolific and impudent pros.

The third-story skylarks are singing again;
The children are dancing. O when may their feet
Escape from the alley called after the Dane?
There's hope in the masts at the end of the street.

## The Ship

There goes the Ship! The plunging prow
Cannot be seen so far from home;
But you can in the mind's eye now
Behold the clear green cleft to foam.

Her sails in air are tautly bent,
The sunlight sets her spars on fire;
Of element for element
What lovelier outcome of desire?

Clipt by the wind, the wave leapt up;
And now their ambient child comes on,
The surge spreads out behind her poop;
And air and water blend in one

And she can hold her stately head
Up where the white bird hardly stirs,
And on the yielding crystal tread,
Proud of that lineage of hers.

But where's she bound for? Who can tell?
For what one does not know, who cares?
I only know she looks right well,
And bravely on the deep she fares.

## Hertes Hele

I love the beauty of this Autumn day,
And grieve to think that sombre-coloured night
Must cling about it as a cloak, and lay
A chilly hand on all that shows so bright.
The gaudy trees that now their flags display
Shall lose the pleasant flourish of their plight;
And the small bird, for all his merry say,
Hopping without a sound be lost to sight.
Let us enjoy the beauty while we may,
Filling our eyes, for brittle is the light;
Then with the foison grandly go away,
And furl our dreams, and let our songs take flight,
Because Love too that made a little stay
Came with the blossoms that outlived a blight.

FROM

# *WILD APPLES* (1930)

---

## PREFACE

### I

Some years ago I made a selection from Oliver Gogarty's poetry for the Cuala Press; and now I make another from what he has published between that and now. Oliver Gogarty is a careless writer, often writing first drafts of poems rather than poems but often with animation and beauty. He is much like that in his conversation; except that his conversation is wittier and profounder when public events excite him, whereas public events – some incursion of Augustus John, perhaps, benumb his poetry.

Why am I content to search through so many careless verses for what is excellent? I do not think that it is merely because they are excellent, I think I am not so disinterested; but because he gives me something that I need and at this moment of time. The other day I was reading Lawrence's description in his 'Revolt of the Desert' of his bodyguard of young Arabs: 'men proud of themselves, and without families . . . dressed like a bed of tulips;' and because brought up in that soft twilight – 'magic casements'; 'syren there' – come down from the great Liberal Romantics, I recognised my opposite, and was startled and excited. The great Romantics had a sense of duty and could hymn duty upon occasion, but little sense of a hardship borne and chosen out of pride and joy. Some Elizabethans had that indeed, though Chapman

262

alone constantly, and after that nobody – until Landor; and after that nobody except when some great Romantic forgot, perhaps under the influence of the Classics, his self-forgetting emotion, and wrote out of character. But certainly nobody craved for it as we do, who sometimes feel as if no other theme touched us. I find it in every poem of Oliver Gogarty that delights me, in the whole poem, or in some astringent adjective. It is in his description of his own verses when he compares them to apples and calls them 'a tart crop', often in his praise of women: –

> She does not know her hair
> Is golden with an hint
> Of Trojan ashes in't.

and almost too deliberately there when he longs to have brought for some lovely daughter of Devorguilla's sake: –

> Knights of the air and the submarine men cruising
>     Trained through a lifetime.
>
> Brought the implacable hand with law-breakers,
> Drilled the Too-many and broken their affrontery,
> Broken the dream of the men of a few acres
>     Ruling a country;
>
> Brought the long day with its leisure and its duty,
> Built once again the limestone lordly houses:
> Founded on steel is the edifice of Beauty,
>     Steel it arouses.

## II

The other day I was asked why a certain man did not live at Boar's Hill, that pleasant neighbourhood where so many writers live, and replied 'We Anglo-Irish hate to surrender the solitude we have inherited', and then began to wonder what I meant. I ran over the lives of my friends, of Swift and Berkeley, and saw that all, as befits scattered men in an ignorant country, were solitaries. Even Shaw, who has toiled at public meetings and committee meetings that he might grow into an effective superficial man of the streets, has made the wastrels of 'Heartbreak House' cry when they hear the whirr of a Zeppelin overhead 'Turn on all the lights.' Unlike those Fabian friends of his he desires and doubtless dreads inexplicable useless adventure. And Synge sang of himself as 'Almost forgetting human words', and it was his solitude that got him into trouble; and heaven knows into what foul weather Oliver Gogarty's Anglo-Irish muse has launched the gayest of its butterflies. Yet I recommend Irish Anthologists to select 'Aphorism' which being clear and inexplicable, will be most misjudged. I would be certain of its immortality had it a more learned rhythm and, as it is I have not been able to forget these two years, that Ringsend whore's drunken complaint, that little red lamp before some holy picture, that music at the end

'And up the back-garden
The sound comes to me
Of the lapsing, unsoilable
Whispering sea.'


III


Oliver Gogarty may console himself for he keeps good company. An Arab king sent a man to Lawrence, saying that as he had just given him a hundred lashes for excess of individuality – he had killed an enemy in court under the eye of the judge – he was exactly the man Lawrence wanted for his bodyguard. Yes, we shall be forgiven our butterflies.

W. B. Yeats


## Sandymount

The wide blue dome of day
Spreads from the Golden Spears,
And, arching to Lambay,
Rests on its purple piers.
A faint blue mist on high,
Hiding the cirrus veils;
And out far on the Bay,
Beyond clear Howth, white sails.
The children cease from play,
They call and point and look;
The mail boat has come in

Under its cloud of smoke;
And on a bank of sand
The sea-gulls on their breast
Take the declining West.
The Earth, the Air, the Sea,
The votive poplar trees,
The light without a glare,
Are tranced in happy peace.
But would I hold in song
The sun; and leave immersed
The sweet day in one long
Perpetual Amen?
I should stop thinking first,
Stop thinking and . . . what then?


## To Moorhead, Blind

It takes us all our time with all our eyes
To learn, to know, since knowledge comes from sight;
And long before we give light back for light,
The hour of sunset strikes and daylight flies:
But you had swifter thought, your faculties
Gathered more quickly, so the mind is bright
That met, before the dial struck, the night;
And that black darkness bids me moralize.

When we old friends, old pupils have been sent
Out of the brittle brightness of the air,
If succour follow in such banishment,
Gleams of your fortitude shall find us there
Amidst the sudden vague beleaguerment
Of that great darkness where you, living, are.

# *SELECTED POEMS* (1933)

---

## *Colophon*

While  the Tragedy's afoot,
Let us play in the high boot;
Once the trumpets' notes are gone,
Off, before the Fool comes on!

# OTHERS TO ADORN (1938)

## Reflection

Sun, and not a breeze at all
On the willow-lined canal
Where the nodding horses tow
An old boat with painted prow
Dark and heavy, gliding on,
While its new paint in the sun
Circles out an eye to watch
Every little roof of thatch;
Trees and bridges; grassy border;
Plumey trains; and, set in order,
Posts to bring the telephone
To each little country town,
Where the gombeen man rings up
His stock-broker's bucket shop;
But the wire holds the birds
Quite unconscious of his words;
As each tiny singing throat
Twitters welcome to the boat:
And the steersman knows how far
It is still to Mullingar.

Would there be so much to lose
If I changed into his shoes,

267

With my buttocks on the rudder,
Cleared from Ringsend on the Dodder,
With no care except to wipe
On my sleeve my old clay pipe?
He would make the change with pleasure,
For he envies me my leisure;
But the boat that I would steer
Is the boat reflected where
Sunlight first must shine to show it,
And no earthly horse can tow it;
And no ripple must disturb
Garden wall and grassy kerb.
But with these on the canal,
Is there need to change at all?

At Gibney's, from the
IXth Lock, Clondalkin.

*April 1937.*

FROM

## *ELBOW ROOM* (1939)

---

## *Applied Poetry*

(*Lecture I. Sappho*)

For extracting all the essence
Of the lords of lofty Rhyme
In the Summer I give lessons
To one pupil at a time.
If I took more than one pupil
As we walk or talk or ride,
I would feel a kind of scruple
Lest attention should divide.
Private then is my prefecture
And most pleasant in its way
When the modern Aspasia
Hears me lecture day by day,
Hears me on the poets lecture
Who were living far away
On the Island edge of Asia
And light-hearted Attica.

## *PERENNIAL* (1944)

---

### *Dedication*

To James Augustine Healy

Dear James, Book-lover, when you see this book,
(The title page is all right I assure you)
Although it be 'unopened' take a look
Between the leaves, I hope they will not bore you;
There, if you read, you may find lines that tell
Since you love books, my verses love you well.

As well they should, for you for such verse-makers
Have done far more than those who just applaud
And leave the poet to the undertakers
Or to post-mortem praisers, or to God
Or ladies who, pen-pecking. mollie coddle
The Muse with mash from a bemused noddle.

Therefore to you this book is dedicated
By me who know that, but for men like you,
Shakespeare had never writ nor Yeats abated
The cares old age and loss had brought him to.
Take with a heart and a half this book, Book-lover,
But cut no pages for you are their cover!

## Remembering Albert Spickers

Had I the proud Pindaric tongue
To praise men who strove well when young,
Calling their parents and forebears
To combat the oblivious years,
I might place Albert well among
The Delphic or Olympic throng,
Unless the theme outdid the song.

For he was young and cleanly limbed,
As resolute as those who climbed
Through arduous days and free from blame
From the unpitying dust to Fame,
Whom the old hero-maker hymned,
Lifting his heart up as he rhymed,
To keep their leafy heads undimmed.

Albert was dutiful, a son
In whom his parents met as one:
His Father's stature, skill and face,
His Mother's kind and learned grace;
Bright as an off-spring of the sun
Golden his hair and body shone –
Before his fame his day is done.

Art's devotee, we saw him quite
Relinquish Art to arm for fight;
Ready to give what he has given
To keep Life chainless under Heaven,
Bending his mind to learn the sleight
And airy lore that masters flight,
In jeopardy was his delight.

Stronger than all who went before
His had to be the nerves for war,
For never since the world began
Have strains like these been put on Man.
Skilful and calm, of those who dare,
Young Coeurs des Lions of the air,
He was a comrade and a peer.

He has gone back to that great Love
Which sent him shining from above.
Let us not think the leagues are dim,
Dark or companionless for him,
He will meet many who improve
The Light that they were shadows of,
And with them as a comrade move.

You cannot call a great soul spent:
Nothing from life is lost or rent,
Conserved and hidden though it be
In the Eternal Energy.
Besieged in Life's beleaguerment
It breaks from that which held it pent:
With Life's great sortie Albert went.

Fated before his fame to die,
He outsoared mediocrity.
He died so young that his forebears,
Brothers and sister are his heirs,
Heirs to his name for courage high,
Heirs to the candour of his eye,
Heirs to his young, bright memory.

## To Major Eugene F. Kinkead

*Sometime Sheriff of Hudson County, New Jersey*

Major, who steadily upheld the Law,
    Not by strong armor but the greater might
    Of human kindness and the sense of right
Which those in insurrection felt and saw;
And, though they had not given in to Awe,
    Trusted a man so fearless and upright
    And rich in understanding, with their plight;
And gained a vindication without flaw.

Man's doom is doubtful; but one thing is clear:
    That Good beats Evil down in spite of skaith;
And when I come across a man like you
    Serene amid the discord and sincere,
    Belief in human nature cheers anew
By re-confirming, when it flags, my faith.

FROM
# PERENNIAL (1946)

---

## Improvements

Life would be less outrageous
If all the drinks were free;
And Health became contagious;
And Old Age fit to see;
And, when we stretched the tether,
Instead of loitering,
All we went together
Like blossoms in the Spring.

# *UNSELECTED POEMS* (1954)

## *Adam and Eve*

In an unlocated Garden
Our First Parents used to roam
While a most assertive Warden
Ran their happy, houseless home.
They had vegetarian menus,
Nothing then was poisonous,
No one thought of cooking sinews
For they hadn't got a house;
And they wore not even sporrans,
For they hadn't got a kilt;
Our First Parents lived like morons
Or like nudists – in their pelt:
Never answered a reveille,
They could always take their ease;
They were happy as two jelly
Fishes floating in warm seas.
Happiness might have been boring
Had they not been kept in awe
By a cross 'tween Hermann Goering
And falutin' Bernard Shaw.
'On one tree is one restriction –
(No; it's not the prickly pear) –
If you do not want eviction

You must leave the apple there.
It is called, The Tree of Knowledge
If you taste it, out you go;
And your kids must go to college
Where the racket is, to know.'

All went well till over-idle
Eve who hadn't much to do,
One day left the path to sidle
In the forest out of view
Where she said 'I think a nap'll
Hardly fail to do me good.'
So she dozed beneath the apple
In the centre of the wood.
Coiled about its bole and branches
Was an elongated thing;
Though it hadn't any haunches,
Yet it had an awful sting;
Its divided tongue was double
As its meaning when it spoke:
Words can cause a lot of trouble,
Words were then the Devil's joke.
Fourteen coils its length attested;
*Spironema pallidum*
Never Man as much molested
As that snake-head pendulum.
'Eve' it said. The poor fool listened;
Oh, the Serpent was astute,
And its coils with pleasure glistened
When its words were bearing fruit;
'Everything within the Garden
Is lovely, lovely. Only you
Are unconscious that you starred in
God's great movie, yes, you two.
Now I feel it is my duty
To point out your loveliness,
You will not perceive your beauty.
Till you take a bite of this.
You are like the apple blossom
Pink and white; there's no alarm –
Take your hand from off your bosom –
Pink and white can't do you harm.'
And it pointed out the pippin;

Eve reached for it and did eat.
Adam found her gently nippin'
'Here,' she said, 'it's very sweet.'


Wham! The welkin roared in anger;
And the Voice of God was heard
High above the awful clangour,
'Ye have disobeyed my Word.
Get ye gone! Get out of Eden;
Never hope to come therein.'
Eve went out with Adam leadin',
Though she led him into sin.
Yes; the welkin roared damnation
With the anger of the Lord;
And an angel took his station
By the Gate with flaming sword.
By the Voice exasperated –
This is roughly what it said –
Adam was the first berated:
'In your brow's sweat earn your bread.'
Then to Eve . . . I've no intention
Of repeating what it spoke
Save to say it did not mention
Anything to ease her yoke:
Quite sadistic and frenetic,
For it mentioned no such thing
As a caudal anaesthetic
To relieve her child-bearing.
Adam thought, 'This can but serve her
Right who ate forbidden fruit.'
Angel held his *flammen werfer*
Mockingly at the salute.


'Well, that's that!' said Eve to Adam.
'Now since we are on our own,
Don't you dare to call me "Madam"
Till we're married. Put this on.'
And she handed him a fig-leaf
Which he donned; and one presumes
For herself she kept a big leaf
All bedecked with peacock plumes.

Now the angel with the flaming
Sword who stood beside the Gate
Finding Adam not worth blaming,
Dropped his weapon from the straight
Pointing earthward, where it roasted
One fat Paradisal duck;
Yes, it roasted and it toasted,
For the bird was out of luck.
Eve dived for it. Oh, she hastened
To retrieve the roasted bird
For she now was strictly rationed
By the edict of the Lord.
Adam smelt it; he was fasting
Since they Eden both forsook;
And the bird was well worth tasting
For an angel was the cook.
But he could not be too hasty,
Sprinting he could not achieve
Since his mild thoracoplasty
Suffered at the birth of Eve.

Oh, they did enjoy that dinner,
Though they hadn't got a plate,
It was such a welcome winner
O'er their vegetable state.
Anything it lacked in flavour
Passed unnoticed for, of course,
Diplomatic Adam never,
Never mentioned apple sauce.
From that day he called her, 'Duckie,'
'Duckie, kindly pass the duck.'
Later on, he thought her lucky
When to motherhood she took
And she bore a pair of sprightly
Boys; but on the brow of Cain
Grew a mark that looked unsightly
For he did his brother in.
This is how the sad thing happened:
Cain, the elder of the two,
Could not take a wordy rap and
Abel with a spade he slew.
Abe had said, 'Cain, stop your struttin';
And don't think because you've had

Since your birth a belly-button,
You're a better man than Dad.'

This, I hoped, were all a fable
For, with much reluctance, I
Wondered oft how Cain was able
To increase and multiply.
Maybe, Adam's first wife, Lilith,
Pre-step mother, was his mate.
(The Mills of God are, when God milleth,
Disinclined to festinate.)
If old Freud to-day were living
Who was so obsessed by sex,
He would point without misgiving
To an Œdipus complex.
Incest, murder, disobedience
To the dictates of our God,
These are all Mankind's ingredients,
Can you wonder we are odd?

Ask me not for a solution
Of this parable of Eve.
Perhaps, it means that Evolution
Starts when we begin to grieve;
Perhaps, it means inconoclasm,
Putting Dresden after delph —
Eve is Adam's ectoplasm:
Blaming her, he blames himself.

Maybe, Eden Eton is, —
Here, I pray you damp surprise —
A school 'where ignorance is bliss
'Tis folly to be wise.'


## Noah's Ark

Noah should have left to drown
Or most rigidly alone
All the microbes of disease,
To wit, the one that makes you sneeze
And that of dental caries;

But old Noah did not bungle
With his inmates of the jungle;
Did not have to give them physic,
For the Lord had made them seasick;
So, instead of roar and riot,
Everything was rather quiet.
Thus the sympathetic cat
Vomited beside the rat;
And the lion and the lamb
Jerked a friendly diaphragm;
For the lion, far offshore,
Could not be a carnivore;
And the lamb, while the Ark wallowed,
Did not care if he were swallowed.
(Twas the equinox of autumn,
And the Ark had a flat bottom)
So peace reigned instead of ructions
In spite of close-up introductions.

Noah had to make excuses
To the two hippopotamuses
When they bellowed, 'As for us
We are both amphibious,
And a gambol in your Flood
Cannot help but do us good.
So we want to disembark
From your dessicated Ark.'

Noah answered softly, 'Whist!
Do you want to make her list?
All the earth is swallowed up
There is nothing left to crop,
And the gathering miasma
Is enough to give you asthma.'
Then he touched each orbed buttock
With his presentation boat hook,
And he said, 'Until we're harbored,
You will stay to port and starboard
Just to stabilize the boat.'
This is where we end the quote.

Next he shouted, 'That will do!'
To the sprightly kangaroo.
'Must I always tell you, "Stop it!

Find some other place to hop it"?
Looping through the Giant Sloth
Shows how foolish you are both.'
Then he put a whorled snail
At the junction of her tail
Just to inculcate the notion
That there's something in slow motion.

While all this was going on,
The Queen bee murmured to the drone,
'Though you've got me where you wanted,
Don't you take too much for granted.
I had lovers once in swarms
Mad to take me in their arms,
Thousands who would call me "Honey."
Here I think it far from funny
That from them I should be thus banned
With a fraction of a husband.'
All the drone could say was, 'Hum.'
While the Queen said, 'Bumble, bum!'

'Land ahoy?' asked Noah. 'Nope!'
Said the dappled periscope
Noah used, for the giraffe
(Making the hyena laugh)
Was his lookout since no necking
Was allowed between the decking.
'Never,' said he, 'have my orbits
Seen so many floating carpets.'
Noah yelled, 'Hurray, hurrah!
We are off Armenia.
And that loud "rat-tat-a-tat"
Means we're stuck on Ararat.'
Then, on summits snows had blanched,
Beached a bark was never launched.

Oh, the joy and the elation
Of the Great Disembarkation!
The enlargement and relief!
They were almost past belief.
Oh, the clawing, pawing, stretching
Of the muscles stiff from retching.
How they looped and rolled and grunted
For their free style had been stunted

So much that the careful Noah,
Like a pole, paid out the Boa.
Joy! They saw before their eyes
The rivers five of Paradise.

Who could tell to them what land meant?
Suddenly, the Lord's commandment
To get rid of inhibitions
Brought on by the Ark's conditions,
And repopulate terrain
Emptied by the recent rain,
Was remembered, and seemed good.
Anyhow, a lively mood
Filled the creatures with a fire
Which the poets call 'Desire.'

You could hear the bull moose calling,
And the tigers' caterwauling,
While the duck-billed platypus
Laid mammalian eggs for us.
Everywhere the earth was humming,
Everything was so becoming,
'Becoming Childers everywhere':
Pairs repairing off to pair,
Till the universal flame
Caught old Noah, who became
Skittish and inclined to sing.
First, he danced a Highland Fling;
Then he sang, 'Let's have a mirthday
It is my six-hundredth birthday.
No; it's my six hundred and first;
And I'm perishing from thirst.'
Then he piped: up came a pipe,
Wine whose grapes were overripe;
But the little fermentation
Added to their delectation
(Often yellow effervescence
Has abetted convalescence)
And the pipe escaped bilge waters,
So he shared it with his daughters,
Till the dawn of morning saw
Noah his own son-in-law!

## *Ars Longa*

(To W. B. Yeats)

I celebrate that old Coan
Who taught beside his purple seas
The noble art of healing man,
I celebrate Hippocrates.
I too have combated disease
And though there is a lengthy span
Between us of the centuries,
I go back where the lore began:
I see the water shadows flow
Above him; and the silent throng
Around him in his portico.
I listen, while the sunlight streams,
To words that ease our mortal wrong.
I listen to his apothegms
And for disease prescribe a song,
For 'Life is short and art is long'
Aye; and the craft so long to learn;
The chance is sharp and off it's gone;
And the mind finds it hard to discern;
For life is short and art is long –
O take it twenty times a day,
The very thought should make you strong.
For what can wear your art away?


## *One World*

I asked a fish to wed a duck
    And close the gap 'twixt fowls and fishes.
I thought his answer rather truc–
    ulent, 'You keep your madhouse wishes.'
I said, 'You'd get, had I my wish,
A scaly bird, a feathered fish.'

I heard a big bee barging go
    Across the fields where grass was sunny.
I said, 'if you will cover that cow,
    The land will flow with milk and honey.'

He must have tried it all too soon
Because the cow jumped over the moon.

Nevertheless, from mental strife
   I will not cease till dawns a blue moon,
And I have merged all kinds of life
   Into one great and glorious Commune.
Expunged what differentiates:
Where all are equal, all are mates.

Think of the inexpressible joy
   If we could only close the chasm
That separates all life. Oh, Boy!
   If all went back to protoplasm
And brought a peaceful, plastic stage
Like some moon-glimmering Glacial Age.

## Dispute Between the Head and Heart of the Poet

HEAD

What is it now my heart?
I hear you paeaning;
Surely you would not start
More Hymenaening?
Have we not been in love
Head, heart and soul full
Have you not had enough?
None like an old fool!
Many a wild goose chase
Have I attended
Only to save your face
When the hunt ended:
Quests of the Beautiful,
The Rare, the Ideal,
When the pursuit, if full
Of fancies, was real.
Now for this latest fad,
Let me assert
You'll go alone, me lad –
Headless, an heart.

HEART

Oh, she's a beautiful
Marvellous being!
None but a surly fool
Judges unseeing.
She is a wilding rose,
Rock-pent and lonely,
As for the others, those,
Harbingers only.

HEAD

All this before I've heard,
This, and much more.
Save with 'the Best' when had
You an amour?
Let me repeat to you
Names you confessed;
I'll name but a few,
All of them 'best':
Constance, the lovely-lipped,
Truthful and pretty;
Kathleen, the trimly-hipped,
Thoughtful and witty;
Quaint thoughts that trammel a
Dream of Denise;
Shame-faced young Pamela
In her chemise.

HEART

Thick is her golden hair
Filling its band full;
And if you felt her bare
Breast, but a handful!
All her soft curves unfold
Beauty as terse as
That the curved letters hold
In the Greek verses.
All you've seen hitherto
And, as a sequel,
Opposed your blethers to,
Are not her equal.

All merely movie tones
Seen in the dark.
She is Life's blood and bones,
And the day's spark.

HEAD

Heart, but I am too old
Now for this questing.
Time is not backward rolled
At your suggesting;
Nor were I young again
Would I compete.
You are not only vain
But indiscreet.

HEART

Old! were you ever young
Blithe and uncautious?
Now your sarcastic tongue
Sounds to me nauseous.
Filling each gusty day
In with your zeros
Is not the lover's way,
No, nor the hero's.
Let me ask once for all
Where but for me,
Reckless, emotional,
Where would you be?


## The Phoenix and the Unicorn

The Phoenix and the Unicorn
    Are in the hills again,
Two messengers of God to warn
    Our scientific men
That, though they scale and scan it
    With, 'Thus far and no more,'
There're things upon our planet
    There's no accounting for.

The Phoenix and the Unicorn
  Are here, for it is odd
That men who by God's grace are born
  Should dare to limit God
And squeeze His works their minds within
  By man-made laws at most
Who made, 'Impossible' the sin
  Against the Holy Ghost.

Of late I met a traveller
  Who said these words to me,
'The way is high and very far
  And what you hope to see,
Abide steadfastly by this rule,
  You may to no man tell;
For men would take you for a fool,
  Your quest, impossible.'

So urgent is each image
  I feel I must go soon
To seek on lonely pilgrimage
  The Mountains of the Moon,
Because these faithful eyes of mine
  Would see, ere I expire,
The Unicorn's anfractuous tine,
  The Phoenix fledged with fire.


## Without Venus

Cupid's dodges manifold
Far too often have been told;
And his Mother, Venus' capers
Overflow the daily papers:
So I choose to sing the huddle
Love can make in pool and puddle
Where the goddess is unknown
And her pestilential son.

There the little protozoa
In their loves out-Noah Noah
For they simply break in two

Then each half says, 'I am you';
And before their love is done
Every father is his son,
And (what fills me more with awe)
Grandpapa and son-in-law.

There they feel not Cupid's dart
For they haven't got a heart:
What would be a heart with us
With them is a nucleus.
False steps set them not at odds;
They are simply pseudopods
Into which they slip and bulge
When in love they would indulge;
This is why the Queen of Sheba
Can't compare with an amoeba.

When I ponder on a puddle
And I think of all the muddle
Cupid makes, I wonder, here
If they have not something there;
For they split themselves in two
Ere a lover comes to woo,
Yet increase and multiply
In the twinkling of an eye.

In their petty, pristine state
None is illegitimate,
None unfaithful, none neglected:
Everyone is self-respected;
None maltreated, none coerced,
None deserted, none divorced –
All through doing hari kari
When they are disposed to marry.


# A Report on the Sexless Behaviour
# of Certain Microscopic Immortals

Life would not be so complex
Were there no such thing as Sex;
And what's more and worth broadcasting,
Life would then be everlasting;

For with differentiation
In the cell came Copulation;
And with Copulation, Death.
That's what Sex contributeth.
They have adumbrated this
In the Book of Genesis.

But the Paramecium
Never thinks of Kingdom Come.
His is life without perdition
For he multiplies by fission;
And while busy multiplying
Simply has no time for dying,
Nothing left with which to die:
All he does is multiply,
Turn himself into a tenth;
And so on unto the nth.
'Tis the same with the bacillus:

Sex alone is what can kill us.
Could we hear those birds bacillar
Sitting on a sightless tree,
What they sing would be a thriller,
But we cannot hear them sing,
'Grave, where is thy victory,
Sex, where is thy sting?'

FROM

# PENULTIMATE POEMS

*(A volume planned by Gogarty before his death)*

---

## To a Moth

Daft, heavy-winged, wavering sprite,
Banging your head against the light,
You make me think how like I am
To you who love the core of flame –
Questing forever, still possessed
By one small spark that imps the quest;
The more you seek the parent spark,
The more it casts you back to dark.
Now, if you were not quite so daft,
Instead of waving fore and aft,
You might, like some less wandering lover,
Give one straight plunge and get it over.
You are braver far than I –
Into the flame I watch you fly
And singe yourself, then off again
So that the dark may heal your brain.
Dim butterfly from fields of Dis,
You may be all I have, I wis,
To call to mind, when I go down,
The light I loved and blinding noon.
Therefore, in pity and to spare

289

Your life, I thus reduce the glare
And sit within the shadowy room
To share with you the sheltering gloom,
Where I sit thinking long and loath
To let this thought cocoon us both,
And yet tis true. For, by my troth,
The light must fade to save the moth!


## Free Will

The blackbird singing in the rain
While yet the dawn is shadowless
Cannot relieve the long duress
That lulls and moistens his refrain.
Until the Spring comes around again
And with all that loveliness,
Autumn his singing silences,
And Winter makes it all in vain.
Aye; but the blackbird in the heart!
No rain can damp or darkness tether
The song that tears dull days apart
And merrier sings the worse the weather,
And merges all bright times together,
And knows not seasons for his art.


## The Village of Plandome

When at long last I cease to roam
And all my wandering days are stilled
In Memory, one thing therefrom
Shall shine with light and fondness filled,
And I shall see each white, bright home
That makes the village of Plandome:

The painted walls, and, built of stone,
The chimneys at the gable ends;
The shutters gay that open on
Lawns that the owner gladly tends;
The slabs of green and purple tone
That lead across each open lawn;

And all the lively wives that wear
Upon their heads bright handkerchiefs;
The children racing here and there;
The gardeners without any sleeves;
And, coming from the greengrocer,
The dawdling whistling messenger;

The village street so gay with stores;
The stores so filled with shining fruits,
Apples and plums and cucumbers
And all the far less coloured roots;
The girls that walk by threes and fours;
The bridge where the white stream up-pours.

The bustle when the train pulls in
And each important man appears:
The children raise a merry din;
And, later on, each gossip steers
To him who keeps the village inn,
Retired, sea-faring Stephansen.

I shall recall the Plandome mill
That stands between the fresh and salt,
The wheel's gone long ago, but still
That hardly is the miller's fault:
He's dead two hundred years. The rill
Sings on beneath the window sill.

When I was young had one foretold
That stream and street and lawn and house
Would one day like a dream unfold
I would have been incredulous.
I know it now: when we grow old
Our youth becomes our Age of Gold.

## Sodom and Gomorrah

In quaint Gomorrah's Latin Quarter
They played all things they hadn't oughter;
And the adjoining city, Sodom,
Had no employment for a Modom.

The justest man of all was Lot,
A drunken, old, lacivious sot,
Awoke one morning and he saw
Himself as his own son-in-law.

I often wondered whose the fault
Turned Mrs Lot to a pillar of salt,
Until I realised Jehovah,
(Once he had really taken ovah)
Strongly objected to dissenters
While he was bombing civic centers.

## Before Psychiatry

In the days of the knight errants
Adults did not blame their parents.

## Perfection

The rule of Life: Perfection won through Pain;
And they who win Perfection cease from strife;
They cease, alas, from striving which is life,
For what is life but one perpetual strain?
They need not enter in the lists again;
Their prowess there forever brings relief;
Exempt, alike, from victory and grief,
So, sweatless, now forever they remain.

Therefore, I see in all unseemly things:
The halt, the maimed, the deaf, the dumb, the blind;
The raucous voice that, although tuneless, sings;
And they who find it hard to draw their breath; —
Well they call upon us to be kind —
But resting places on the road to death.

## A Whodunit Who Didn't

If I could find a Whodunit who didn't
Have all its cops stupid and all overweight;
Its private detectives by alcohol riddled
And all its blondes lovely and – well – passionate;
If I could find a Whodunit who didn't
Have pages where telephones went ting-a-ling,
If I could find a Whodunit who didn't:
Do you think for a moment I'd read the damn thing?

## Supersonic?

Life would be quite a tonic
If in the pubs were found
Juke boxes supersonic,
Past the barrier of sound;
Then you, instead of noises
Of blare and blare and squawk,
With unraised, pleasant voices
Could hear each other talk.

## Make us Aware

Make us aware without a war
Of what we have and what we are;
Without the prison camp and the whip
Make us esteem our guardianship
Of dignity and happiness:
Make us aware what Freedom is.

Abundant life, abundant food,
Abundant things that make for good:
Freedom that all men may enjoy;
And work lest these good things should cloy.
From us the contrast keep afar
Of slaves that groan, dragooned for war.

Freedom at night in peace to rest;
No carbine at the woman's breast;
No fearful knocking at the gate;
No wrack, no drug, no slavish state;
Freedom to live beneath the Law
And hold not man but God in awe.


## Full Circle

Ghengis is dead in Karakoram;
    All his victorious hordes stand still
That like wild water o'er dam
    Flooded the lands that had no will;
Wave upon wave they rushed unsated
While squabbling nations lay prostrated.

Full circle now the history swings:
    The hordes are here, the damaged wall;
Dazed and confused while danger rings,
    Nations to weakened nations call.
Of Life shout loud with fiery breath
While broken Europe flirts with death.


## Misgivings

Of late I am beginning to have misgivings about my soul:
If it can't keep body and bones together,
And protect them from exigencies of the weather,
Blowing from the Tropics or down from the North Pole –
Not to mention the dismemberment by death
Of the poor limbs that worked so hard to save it –
What are the chances that the soul itself will brave it,
And prove itself immortal when I draw my latest breath?


## When

When shall war bring peace and solace
And put an end to all dissentations?
When China's paved with Coca Colas,
And we are floored by good intentions.

## A Wish

I wish that I were far away
   In some unfound and happy place
Where I could walk and watch the bay,
    Or, through the trees the mountains trace;
There I would lounge and take my ease
   From pleasures and anxieties.


## The Eternal Feminine

The lake light in your laughing eyes,
Your bows and frills and golden bangles
That make half-heard, sweet harmonies,
Convince me, girls, that you are angels
Come down to bind our mortal line
With loveliest links to the Divine.

This was the path my father found
In days when he met such another
As one of you; and I am bound
In his belief who knew my Mother:
This is my joy on earth, and even
My sole securest hope of Heaven.


## Psychoanalysis

### [I]

Said my psychiatrist,
'Nobody's normal.
You're a Narcissist
With a brain storm all
Swirling with many a twist
Through half your brain;
An exhibitionist
And schizophrene.

You are too early weaned
And bottle fed;

You felt yourself demeaned
When sent to bed:
Hence, it's late hours for you:
And your cheek's mottle
Proves your addiction to
Pulls at the bottle.

You stamped your baby foot,
In days of yore,
Where your Papa had put
Tacks on the floor.
That's still affecting you,
Naught will avail
Until your lifted shoe
Rests on a rail.

As for the dreams you dreamt
Of diving bells;
Mermaids with hair unkempt,
Codfish and eels:
These I will not explore,
Lest there be fallacies,
Till we have done far more
Psychoanalysis.


## Psychoanalysis

### [II]

Thanks for the check. Ah, well!
Let us resume.
What was that diving bell?
Your Mother's womb.
Eels? Yes; those eels were just
Spermatazoa
Storming the ark of lust,
Incestuous Noah.
'Mermaids with hair unkempt'
Should not surprise
You as a foetal fish
Whose baby eyes
Saw amniotically

Things that are seen,
All embryotically,
As submarine.
They meant your Mother's hair
Wanted a comb,
Towsled, while still you were
Held in her womb.
And the codfish you saw
Or dreamt of, rather,
Shows you resented her
Love for your Father.
But, when she suckled you,
Worse was to come:
What broke and buckled you,
Made you so glum,
Was her passion of
You as a child
Broken by Mother's love,
Torqued and defiled,
To get the benefit
Of this analysis
You have to learn yet
Nipples and phalluses;
And that the cause of all
Spiritual bother
Is not yourself at all.
No, It's your Mother.
When you have learned that,
On realising,
You must do something pat,
Something surprising,
Something that, once for all,
Strikes at the source,
Something unfilial
To end the curse.
Deed such as Nero did
Who tried to kill,
'The Mother who bore me,
And bores me still.'
Borrow an ax
With a couple of whacks
Kill your Mother and then
Relax.

## The Changeling

### [I]

*(A spray of mountain ash over the door would*
*have saved the human child from the fairies)*

All for the want of the crimson berries
  Of the mountain ash on the chamber door
The child is off with the mountain fairies,
  And back to his parents shall come no more.

His father was talking about his prize setters,
  His mother preparing his baptismal feast,
When a fairy stole in and undid the soft fetters
  That bound him to father and mother and priest.

In the hills he is hidden away from the sunlight,
  In the hills that are marked by the old twisted thorn;
The light of the day is exchanged for the moonlight,
  And life that was certain for living forlorn.

The firelight gleams; and the gossip is nursing
  The strange twisted thing that was left in his stead;
His father knows all, and is silently cursing
  The fool for forgetting to safeguard the bed.

But he on a steed where the tree-guarded liss* is
  Will follow the pass on the winds of the night;
Or dance on the sands where the long water hisses
  And throws down a yellow and vanishing light.

The changeling, the restless, the withered replacement
  Can feel that the fairies are riding the air
When the moon gives no light, and the dark of the casement
  Is filled with Arcturus and claws of the Bear.

*Liss, a fairy fort.

## The Changeling

[II]

They ought to have guarded my cradle better
In number five Rutland Square East;
In Dublin they thought that it need not be done;
My father was talking about his prize setter,
My Mother preparing my baptismal feast,
When who should slip in but a fairy from Letter,
(My nurse saw him dodging that day through the town)
Who softly undid each invisible fetter
That bound me to monarch, to lawyer, to priest,
To Father and Mother and kin of my own.
I cannot be sure I have fared any better
By being forever the Good Peoples' guest,
And from my own kindred forever foregone.

Alas, I am now made immoral, immortal
And so to mortality must be averse;
They shriveled me early who never were young;
My parents have passed through the ultimate portal;
A shade is the gossip who once was my nurse;
Alike to me now are the yew as the myrtle,
For youth that was bended is long since unstrung;
And gone are the days that to youth were so curtal:
For lovers, all days are too fleeting and scarce;
But I am unmoved as the mountains upflung,
A lover of gloaming and dells where the whortle
Drops berries in water that gleams by the gorse:
My sole recompense but a rivulet's song!

Ah, no; there are others: the moon on the water;
The stillness of eve in the long primrose light,
Ineffable stillness, Eternity's self!
The sharp lunar crescent so clear in its quarter;
The dim plenilune in the Septembral night;
The silence when air is weighed down as a porter
Of sweetness too heavy to burden an elf;
The gold of the gorse that no Autumn can alter,
Though harvests are gathered, it still remains bright
As heather that glows on the bare mountain shelf;
All these are the treasures that make me a martyr

To Beauty eternal I hold as a right,
Intangible Beauty, unhoardable pelf.

I dwell in a gloaming where night and day mingle,
A gloom that owes nothing to night or day,
Unmoved by the motion of all that is made.
I gaze on men living, but cannot commingle
Or take any part in their kind human way:
No laughter, no work and no seat by the ingle,
No hope to be nedded at last by the spade,
I, changed and transported to lake, bog and dingle
By Letter's wild highland, inhumanly gay
For all that within me are moods that are staid,
Excpet in the dances when tide from the shingle
Flows back and sands glisten beneath the moon's ray,
And floors on the whispering silver are laid.

But what of my double the wizened replacement
They laid in my cradle one night long ago?
I find myself wondering how he did fare
Amid that kind household who loved to effacement
Of all their own feelings that bringer of woe.
And his? I can tell of the utter amazement,
To judge him by measures that cannot comapre
With theirs who knew not what the nights and the days meant
To one of the Faery who dimly must know
His siblings are mounting to ride through the air,
His siblings are mounting to ride when the casement,
That gives on the darkness of night's purple glow,
Is filled with Arcturus and claws of the Bear.

Our joy is by night, your work is diurnal,
A sequence insipid of days upon days;
Delight is your drama with Death for a mime,
For Death has endeared to you pomps that are vernal
And made you too wistful while Autumn delays;
But I by some sleight am a critic supernal,
Though blood of your blood but a poor paradigm,
A changeling as if by some edict infernal
Condemned to love solitude more than your ways,
Removed beyond even the phrensy of rhyme,
Constrained to look down from a standpoint eternal –
A judging spectator who grudges his praise –
And dances while Eternity corrugates Time.

# Part 3

# POEMS PUBLISHED IN JOURNALS AND UNPUBLISHED POEMS

# THE EDITOR'S PRELUDE

Part Three consists of poems not included either in Gogarty's *Collected Poems* or in any separate volumes of his published poetry. Some of them have been published in various journals and newspapers, but many have not been published before. They are uneven in quality: a few are incomplete, a few are fragments which show how Gogarty's mind was working. These hitherto unpublished poems and verses come from letters and from various manuscripts and typescripts held in libraries and private collections. The Editor is deeply indebted to individuals and librarians for permission to include them in this edition; they are separately thanked in Acknowledgements.

Obviously, some of the poems in Part Three could not have been published in Gogarty's lifetime. Their bawdy or obscene or blasphemous or libellous content would have caused considerable offence. What Irish publisher would have risked publishing them? What Irish printer would have been found to print some of them? And if they had appeared what harm could they not have caused to Gogarty's medical career? For a surgeon to be known as a poet was risky enough for his reputation, but to have Rabelaisian parodies or blasphemous verses, however humorous, published under his own name would have been more than detrimental, it probably would have been disastrous. Besides, Gogarty did not want to be taken merely as a 'smutster and funster' (a phrase he used as early as 1904 in a letter to G. K. A. Bell). He saw himself as a poet, but, as he told his friend Seumas O'Sullivan in a letter at the outset of his career as a surgeon, he felt he was about to lose his liberty before a lifetime of respectability – which would inevitably mean insufficient time for poetry. In later life he did not want to risk his family being embarrassed by his being associated with the publication of such outspoken work. It would never do, he had argued in a letter of 24 November 1953 to Horace Reynolds, to have the proposed *Merry Muses of Hibernia* cast up before his daughter, for instance in later life 'when they both were gathered etc.'.

And the effect of losing the libel action over *As I Was Going Down Sackville Street* must have made him somewhat cautious about what he committed to print, though much of his conversation continued in the ebulliently outspoken vein that he had begun to explore as a young medical student with his equally uninhibited chosen companions.

There were reasons enough for the Rabelaisian tone of some of the poems: they were one means of coping with the stresses and strains of medical life, as a passage in the seventh chapter of *It Isn't This Time of Year At All* makes clear, when Gogarty is considering the occasionally wild behaviour and often outrageous language of the medical students of his day: these would now be called the result, he wrote, of 'occupational neurosis':

> The young nurses, finding themselves confronted daily by dirt, disease and death, grew tough. The medical students went wild as a reaction. Youth betimes confronted with Death: the outcome of this unnatural juxtaposition was outbreaks of wild licence among the men, and callousness among the young nurses, most of whom were in their early twenties or younger.

There are now, however, compelling reasons for making as many as possible of Gogarty's unpublished poems and verses available, not only to extend knowledge of his poetry but also to convey something of the varied social *milieux* in which he moved. Despite the uneven achievement of individual poems, many are excellent and will be enjoyed by readers.

Some of these poems, of course, Gogarty intended to publish in his lifetime, such as those of *Penultimate Poems* which are included in Part Two, for this was a volume he was planning before his death, and for which he had a publisher, though the volume did not reach print. There was also the prospect of a volume which Gogarty thought should be entitled *Levia Carmina*, but which his American academic friend Horace Reynolds thought should echo *The Merry Muses of Caledonia* (a collection of bawdy poems and songs made by Robert Burns, extolling erotic love and laughing at the human condition) with the title of *The Merry Muses of Hibernia*. Some of its poems are included here in Part Three. The idea of the collection was mooted by Reynolds, and, as J.B. Lyons has put it in his biography, Gogarty waxed warm and cold in turn over the project. Various names (echoing the dactylic 'Gideon Ouseley' that echoed 'Oliver Gogarty') had been assumed in *Tumbling in the Hay* and were now considered for the author: Malachi Mulligan, Hercules Mulligan and Farrell O'Reilly; but the final typescript version bore the name Oliver Gogarty. The subtitle 'A Small Gathering of Quaint Songs' was followed by 'made and absorbed', the last version's 'remembered by Oliver Gogarty' covering 'As I was going down Sackville Street' (see p. 601). American versions of this ballad were collected by Reynolds, spurred on by realising how both Joyce and Gogarty recreated very differently the version heard in Dublin.

Gogarty had written out some of the poems by hand for Reynolds, whose final typewritten version had 'Boston, Massachusetts 1954' at the foot of the title page, suggesting a likely private printing of the book. Caution seems to have triumphed, however, and the book did not reach publication. It included the following poems: 'The Hay Hotel', 'As I was going down Sackville Street', 'The Old Pianist', and 'The Getting of Gargantua' as well as twelve parodies and limericks. As some of the contents had been published before and Gogarty and Reynolds had argued over the inclusion of the limericks (Reynolds found 'the more scatological the more tiresome' in a letter of 9 August 1954) not all the poems included in the projected volume are included under its title here, 'The Hay Hotel' and 'The Old Pianist' being placed in the 'Monto poems' section while the parody of Keats's 'On first looking into Chapman's Homer', 'On first looking into Kraft-Ebing's Psychopathia Sexualis', is included in Part Two's *Hyperthuleana* (1916) where it first appeared. The other eleven poems are placed in Part Three, in the sections headed 'Parodies' and 'Limericks'. Gogarty's 'Foreword for a proposed volume, *Ditties of No Tone*' (p. 405) might well serve as an afterword, to remind us of the traditions within which he wrote his own bawdy poetry:

> Culture in the height of Greece
> Gave us Aristophanes,
> Martial in the Roman day,
> And Religion Rabelais . . .

The various sections of Part Three are set within the six groupings which correspond with those that Gogarty used in his *Collected Poems* (with the exception of this Prelude). The poems and verses within these groupings and the sections in *Satires and Facetiae* and *Life and Death* are generally arranged in approximate chronological order, approximate as it is occasionally impossible to determine the date of a poem's composition. In consequence, the poems within a section may range from youthful badinage to assured poems of middle age and poems written during Gogarty's later years in the United States.

What is revealed here is not only the range of Gogarty's verse but his capacity to blend originality with classical convention. His classicism was natural, inbuilt; his originality exuberant, inventive. He had an instinctive, irrepressible sense of humour that is highly infective, a capacity for mockery as well as a geniality, a desire for reciprocal friendship. Thus the early jesting poems to Seumas O'Sullivan, like other poems of his Martello tower period, arise out of his being part of a lively, literary ambience. Significantly, the writing of verse letters was part of it. Gogarty and his friends found it easy and entertaining to channel their overflowing energy into words that shared with friends anecdote or idea, wit or epigram. Since Dublin's was an oral as well as a written culture, the words were often extempore, for poetry in Dublin, at least in the first quarter of the twentieth century, though often technically accomplished, was primarily social, natural, uncontrived.

Many of Gogarty's poems, then, achieve an enviable air of spontaneity. As a busy surgeon, he did not have the time – the liberty, the loss of which to his medical career that he had lamented to Seumas O'Sullivan – for the seemingly endless revision that underpinned Yeats's perfection of the work, so the spontaneity was not, in many cases, the result of careful art but of the circumstances in which he wrote: he might write a poem, his daughter said, 'between an antrum and a tonsil.' ('He never stops long enough at his best,' Yeats remarked, 'but how beautiful that best is, how noble, how joyous.') He did, however, alter and rewrite published poems, as some of the textual notes demonstrate. (See, for instance, how much more effective than the whole forty-one line poem 'To Catullus' is a briefer alternative version of the opening lines, quoted on p. 13.) He did change aspects of his style, too, mainly under Yeats's influence, something well recorded in the appreciative memoir he wrote about his friend that was published by Liam Miller of the Dolmen Press in 1963. It should be emphasised that many of the hitherto unpublished poems or fragments of poems included here were often written to amuse fellow students and can be jejune (as in the case of 'Sinbad'); others, however, were often dashed down in moments stolen from a crowded, successful life: they were occasional verses, not worked over nor intended for publication.

Some readers may find some of the language in the unpublished poems coarse: that tends to happen when flippant verses written in the vernacular are read, not heard. The speaking voice can carry an audience with it, delivering the unexpected with a flourish, a sudden impact that vanquishes the vulgarity while using its forthrightness to the full. Gogarty's poems and verses record very effectively quick, spontaneous, compressed responses to a variety of things: his intense appreciation of natural beauty, his reactions to topical occurrences, his highly emotional yet tempered regrets for the deaths of his friends, his admiration for aspects of human character and behaviour, his displeasure at meanness of spirit (not least in reviewers), his pleasure in parody, his delight in drinking, his love of the limerick, his enjoyment of bawdry, in short his sharp conveyance of his reactions to the many aspects of human life that seized his often ironic, often awed attention: above all experiences and reactions he wanted to share with his friends.

A.N.J.

# ODES AND ADDRESSES

---

## Ode of Welcome

The Gallant Irish yeoman
   Home from the war has come,
Each victory gained oe'r foeman,
   Why should our bards be dumb?

How shall we sing their praises
   Or glory in their deeds,
Renowned their worth amazes,
   Empire their prowess needs.

So to Old Ireland's hearts and homes
   We welcome now our own brave boys
In cot and hall; 'neath lordly domes
   Love's heroes share once more our joys.

Love is the Lord of all just now,
   Be he the husband, lover, son,
Each dauntless soul recalls the vow
   By which not fame, but love was won.

United now in fond embrace
   Salute with joy each well-loved face.
Yeoman, in women's hearts you hold the place.

## *In Memoriam: Robert Louis Stevenson*

*Under the wide and starry sky,*
*Dig the grave and let me lie:*
*Glad did I live and gladly die.*
    *And I laid me down with a will.*

*And this be the verse you grave for me —*
*'Here he lies where he longed to be:*
*'Home is the sailor, home from the sea:*
    *'And the hunter is home from the hill.'*
                ROBERT LOUIS STEVENSON

Beneath a well two jets of silver sand
    Forever wave, like little elfin plumes
Shaken for glee, down in the fairyland,
    Whence springs the stream that liquidly illumes
A teeming valley. Whilome to its strand
    Came jocund Chaucer, and he stooped to quaff,
Raising the waters in his curvéd hand;
    Then fenced the well round working with a laugh.

Freshly to-day the boughs are blossoming.
    Which long ago he wove about the well;
The air is blithesome with eternal spring,
    And roses ever heart-shaped scent the dell
Wherein the tender linnets sweetly sing,
    Green as a mossy branch in apple time:
The thrush pours out a soul in carolling,
    And bees still pay for pollen with a rhyme.

Each passing poet while he sang, designed
    A garland in this garden; many there
Immortal wreaths of wondrous hues have twined,
    Which aye portray in blossoms meet and rare
The floral thoughts that budded in their mind.
    Fair, 'midst the fairest, shone the rare design
Of him who culled and gave his life to bind,
    And binding bled, pierced by the eglantine.

By him were all the choicest blooms that sprung
    In Chaucer's garden, woven into words;
Dark purple pansies aptly set among

The earliest snowdrops, winter's frost affords
As hansel to the spring. He fondly strung
    The daisy chains that children love, whereby
To draw us back to days when we were young;
    And simple plays had power to satisfy.


We see again a mother's smiling face,
    We feel again her hand upon our hair;
Old thoughts come back – The happy dwelling place
    And those bright days when resting was a care.
The butterfly, she would not let us chase.
    How can the heart he softens thus refrain
From overflowing? For a golden space
    We have our holy childhood back again.


Ah! tears are welling in the sternest eyes
    For all the sunny heads of long ago;
Old friends, old playmates, who no more may rise
    To join the merry games we used to know.
And now our latest comrade with them lies;
    Who can recall the dear days that are fled,
And make us young again in memories?
    No man but Stevenson – and he is dead.


But tears are not for him; no wish had he
    For our regret who did so gladly die;
Round his Samoan grave the lonely sea
    Heaves a great heart, but utters not a sigh;
Shoreward, the waters croon a lullaby.
    His virtues with a light that shall not fade,
Shone, as those tropic blooms glow 'neath the tree
    That bends to hug the earth where he is laid.


No tears for him, for he has persevered
    'Gainst adverse storms; no tears, for he has won,
Though weak and wearied, and become endeared
    With Goldsmith and with Scotland's darling son
To mankind's common heart. Safely he is steered
    To 'Treasure Island,' in whose blue lagoon
Shining far brighter that she e'er appeared
    To us, floats holily the pure faced moon.

Rest! Friend of children and the Poets' friend.
    And all whose hearts are one with Nature still:
Thy island chieftain if he chance to wend
    When hunting, will not fire hard by the hill
Where sleeps his 'Tusitala,' he who penned
    And told enchanting stories. Through his life
He went with kind faced laughter to the end.
    And won with boyish heart a Titan's strife.

The king beneath his ponderous pyramid
    Has not as grand a sepulchre as thine:
A coral island rising sheer amid
    A realm no earthly monarch may confine.
Nor were the works of this great king who bid
    His myraids raise a puny mountain high,
As great as thine in living blossoms hid,
    And which as long as hearts beat shall not die.


## To his Extraordinary Friend
## George Kennedy Allen Bell

*About to go to Switzerland*

Before you say a long farewell
Or sound for me a parting Bell,
    From London's crowded town
I pray you tell what things are done
Within the blooming 'Rose and Crown'
    Of wayward Wimbledon.
And tell me all you left unsaid
About the Bard with nose as red
As cochineal enclareted:
For you must make him doff his hat
With meteoric sashes that
Are fashioned like a great cravat
(As pendant and preposterous
As his would be could Aeschylus
Rise from his grave by Gela lent,
Where Aitna stands a monument,
To advertise in Rotten Row
Himself with poet-Yeats-like bow

If we've agreed about the bow, it
Reveals the greatness of the poet.)
And shows the hair 'to ashes turned'
The hair that Balliol almost burned
For knowing naught of Genesis
And, ah, too much of Guinnesses.
A head within so strange a hat
Must surely be worth looking at.
You know the beverage each bard chooses
Bespeaks his favour with the Muses.
Homer, as Horace presupposes,
Arguitur laudibus vinosus –
And wine-dark was his song:
As wine-dark as those isles that be
Amid the sunned space of the sea
When summer clouds do throng.
Whatever Pindar's barmaid brewed her
We know it mixed ἄριστον ὕδωρ
So it was, therefore, strong.
One need not read too far in Burns
Before one certainly discerns
The beverage for him.
And Keats, although we can't compare it,
Full often over pints of claret
Was 'winking at the brim';
And you, O Bell, with claret-cup
Made all the Muses give me up
Either to sink or swim;
Though I shall sail on pints of 'plain'
To storm their sling-y mount again
And swear that I'll bedim
The glabrous leaf of Phoebus' bays,
And with spiked chestnuts strew their ways,
If from me they withhold
The drink that may intoxicate
And leave me like a straw to Fate.
And yet, as swinked gold
However got, is good for all,
So, though to drink it makes me fall,
Yet others shall uphold.

While I write thus, entrenched with Trench
You, maybe, sitting with a wench,

Upon a 'weeded stone',
Between the half light and the dark.
In Wimbledon or Richmond Park
Peruse Hyperion!
Where'er you be, whene'er an hour
Is left you, write me at 'The Tower'
Where, oftentimes, alone,
As I shall afterwards recount,
Gazing from out my guarded mount,
Out to Hamancos? No,
But northwards, and o'er Dublin Bay
To Howth (whereon in holiday
Professor Dowden's now)
I mark the ever-changing sea
Whose wonder drowns the thought in me
Obey the unseen moon
With ebb and flow, as man obeys
With good and evil all the ways
Of that which does commune
So rarely that he cannot mete
Its notions all, nor make complete
Ascent to plenilune.

And that's how God's dichotomised
By some, by others minimised
Or totally eclipsed.
But, lest you think it odd
That I should dare to talk of God
While man remains uncared
I shall for just this once curtail
My letters to you – do not fail
As I hold you a Bard,
To let me know some more of Swinburne
Whether by river broad or thin burn
He wanders – don't discard!

Also record, O passing Bell,
– Surpassing too as I can tell –
O you whose lips drop hydromel!
Whatever mountain peaks shall rise,
And glistening pierce the thick blue skies,
When you are bound from merry England
To many-mountained Switzerland;

But most those peaks of thought that be
Raised through your mind's transparency:
Those heights of song that heights of snow,
Seen when they all translucent glow
And the West flames, may symbolise
To men who see with outward eyes
And should to me, could mountains move
And the sun shining sing of love.
I too, who am inturreted
Some hundred feet above the bed
Of Ocean, shall make answer brave
As may be to you o'er the wave
Four thousand feet, which marks, ah me,
Or hints at a disparity.
I then shall tell of visions seen
Deep in the moonlight-coloured green
Of sunlit depths what time I rove
The wayless ways of Sandycove.

When buoyed on airy waves, I ween
I fly a bird through ways of green,
Or on rolled clouds embosomed lie
While the young sunlight floods the sky.
I long for you to wend with me
The soft green ways of the sleepful sea
And make this old Silenus' den
(I send the photo of it early
I know you'll like its aspect rarely)
A cave remote from boys and men
And the nymphs even, your abode
Ere next term leads you to the road
That winds along to Oxford town
And the dull usage of the gown.

## [Beginning of a poem to G.K.A. Bell]

Here from the side of the sea, green water
    That a cloven rock to its dear deep hems,
I write to one whom the Sky King's daughter,
    The Muse, beloves by the willow green Thames.

## Foreword

[*to* Ireland]

All things of any weight or worth
From East to West, from North to South
   The month revolving sees:
From East, where mountained Wicklow rears
Against the dawn the Golden Spears;
And Dublin by the Bay appears,
   And rich Moynalty's leas;
Out to that limit of the lands
Where thunder-footed Moher stands
Whose granite-guarded breast expands
   And breaks the pouring seas;
And from the North, whose forests rang
With birds that for the exile sang
   Remembered memories;
Down to those hanging gardens where
The moist sweet winds and odours are,
And sunlight to the lake-water
   Comes globéd thro' the trees –
All that our Isle holds loveliest
The Isle that morning loves the best –
   Find place and praise herein:
Old Erin in its shade and light,
Her daughters and their beauty bright,
Her sons and all their mirth and might,
   And shades that intervene,
For Horace tells, and all we know it
How they who lacked a sacred poet
   Died nameless and unseen;
And can it, therefore, be denied
That if men songless, noteless died
To keep a nation in her pride
   Requires a magazine?
The generations come and pass
Like cloud shadows on the grass
   And not a trace we see,
But here we hold up to our land
The mirror in an Irish hand
That all our actions may be scanned
   In their eternity.

## Ireland's Welcome to the Fleet

All ye whom Love brings hither
A welcome take from me,
All ye who ride at anchor
On waves that lisp no rancour
But, hailing altogether
As masters of the sea
All ye whom Love brings hither
A welcome take from me.

The floating walls of England
Are builded round the world,
On seas both far and soundless
Their turrets are not groundless
Than where a day may bring land,
Or favouring flags unfurled;
The floating walls of England
Are builded round the world.

But now in no strange waters
Ye break an alien foam;
I know the hand that steers you,
The heart that lifts and cheers you,
And all my sons and daughters
Shall hail him to his home,
For now on no strange waters
Ye break an alien foam.

As warm green hills that border
Our Eastern sea-board,
He grew, whose rule is grander
Than any land commander,
Ennobling his order
And the lords of Waterford
In warm green hills that border
Our Eastern sea-board

The mountains that embrace him,
The bosom of the bay,
Where his great fleet lies sleeping
Depend upon his keeping,
Though all the world should face him

To ward and watch alway
The mountains that embrace him
The bosom of the Bay

To guard and find for ever
The island of his birth:
If West and East be shaken,
His lightning shall awaken
Lest foemen should dissever
The land that knows his worth
To guard and find for ever
The island of his birth


## *Cervantes: Tercentenary of* Don Quixote

Three hundred years since first your rare Knight started
     Are passed, since first on his adventurous quest
He rode in hope with Sancho simple-hearted
     To wound wrong-doers and to heal distressed;

To raise his Lady's name beyond all others
     To fight for her and guard her from disgrace
To set men free imprisoned men his brothers,
     That each one might behold her heavenly face.

Three hundred years adown the ages ringing
     With loud and careless laughter, he rides on
By sun-pierced glade and greenwood ever-singing
     By hamlet, glebe and thorpe and tower and town.

Under the light of skies that never darken:
     Those clear and sunniest regions of the mind
Most merriest found of all that bent to hearken
     And tell the twofold secret of mankind:

That showed in light serene and ever-sunny
     The Rueful Knight his steadfast purpose keep:
And told the saddest tale with mouth of honey
     That whoso hears knows not to laugh or weep:

That who hear it now incline to wonder,
     Finding the mirth more deep than when a boy

I listened to the 'Knight and Squire,' and ponder
　　On all the wisdom mingled in your joy,

Your joy that fills three hundred years with laughter
　　And makes men, out of lands that beat back Spain
And from far lands Columbus ne'er sought after,
　　Cervantes, call and welcome you to reign;

To reign as King in children's hearts and sages' –
　　O happiest heart and lips by scorn uncurled
Since his that shook the broad Athenian stages
　　And sent Old Wisdom laughing down the world!

That to the children you may show the splendour.
　　Tempered and trued, that lightens old Romance,
And to the wise your wisdom and the tender
　　Calm smile and secret of your sufferance.

For though in hearts that yet are unbegotten
　　Your Knight may waken only laughing tears,
As he has done in hearts long since forgotten
　　That throbbed and ceased throughout three hundred years;

And though I hear three laughter-ringing ages,
　　I know not as I lift my praise to you
For all that southern sunlight in your pages
　　If there the shadow is not deepest too.

Therefore I send my thought out like a swallow,
　　Over the waves that ebb not as they flow
Dividing all but thought from thought, to follow
　　And find you in your sunshine long ago,

Searching your summer for a cloud of sadness
　　To see the brave Knight cast so rudely down,
Seeking for sorrow hidden in your gladness
　　And pity for the dulness of the clown.

I see the Knight battling forever vainly
　　Whelmed in the casual coil of human things,
I see the Squire still following on ungainly
　　Lured on by Hope through all his wayfarings.

The inn, the mill that to the knightly vision
　　Appear transfigured, and I mark each blow

He strikes, I hear the insults and derision
    That hail him and proclaim his overthrow.

And it is clear: the Fighting and the Failing,
    The Faith that leads, the Fear that needs be led,
The Star that grows more dim and less prevailing
    The nearer earth, the more its rays are spread.

These things I see, but you who saw them nearer
    You whom I seek for, you I do not see,
But only hear more loudly ring and clearer
    The long perennial gospel of your glee.

You saw when roseleaves blow the Rose is broken,
    The Star that touches Earth is quenched and dead,
The Thought transferred is fettered by the Token,
    You saw the rapt Knight bruised and buffeted.

Yet no cloud stains the brightness of the one light
    That hides you, and our human vision bars,
As his whole robe of darkness and of sunlight
    Hides Shakespeare: darkness giving birth to stars,

And light, like yours, alive with exaltation
    O Eagle pinions, could we lift afar
Striding the stellar heights of inspiration
    The gloomy Earth might glisten as a star!

And we, too, see the sunlight all-surrounding
    Who, seeing shadows by our earthly light,
Draw comfort only from the joy abounding
    In you – for light, in him – despite the night:

Despite the dark with which our life is rounded,
    Despite the light to which that life lies bare,
Sweet as a hanging blossom mirth resounded
    Sung in the Northern as the Southern air.

Heard like a song in interstellar spaces,
    Proclaiming him whose name with your's I wreathe –
Since ye together deathward turned your faces
    Tuned sweetly to the ways of life beneath.

Let be: I will not seek beyond the curtain
    And thin veil of the daylight softly spun

What the night holds must ever be uncertain
   To eyes whose light is borrowed by the sun.

You, while the Southern day endured above you
   Gave of your life a portion and the grave
Gains not those years that make the whole world love you
   Years wherefrom all that sweetens life you gave:

Sun, and soft breezes through the cork trees blowing
   And wisdom imped with laughter in a peal,
Clear as the stream down from Parnassus flowing,
   Of old Castalian laughter from Castile,

Blend here – a book for all the lost Romances,
   As noble and more marvellous than they,
And Time your sunlight gilded thus, enhances
   Your name, and, having borne it on to-day,

Three hundred years adown the long unending
   Alternate change of seasons: – hopes with fears,
Springs with the Winters, leaves it time-transcending,
   Cervantes, as it shines three hundred years.


## The Horse Show

Daughter of the ocean, dwelling in his garden,
Where the morning lingers and longest leaves the dew;
All his strongest seas are set to be your warden,
And the mountains lifted up to wall the storms from you!

Could a gift be fairer for the fairest of his daughters,
For the isle that shares her couch with the Star of Eve;
What of all the wonders in his kingdom of the waters,
Greater than his gift of old to Hellas could he give?

So throughout your fields of green as o'er the green sea courses,
Waving manes and flanks afoam of limbs that flash and flee;
Stamp and wheel and thunder on your world-outspeeding horses,
Ocean's gift to Erin in her garden of the sea

Now that August brings the year the first of Autumn's favours,
Giving hills the purple and the woods their youngest gold;

Now that ocean breathes ashore his submerged forest savours,
And the year holds festival, your festival we hold

Steeds from north and steeds from east, from Meath's imperial
    pastures,
Steeds from southern inland rills, or foaled beside the foam;
Meet, unmatched for grace and speed, in numbers that surpassed
    yours,
Hellas when your charioteers tore up the Olympian loam.

And now, Erin, give again your welcome to the stranger,
Let your dark, sad eyes again be lighted with a smile;
Be forgetful to lament time's overpast or danger
Now that beauty, grace and strength are meeting in your isle.

Time is past that shone as gold and yet was not more glorious,
Time is like the eagle that grows golden as he flees;
No time half as fair as now, when o'er the world victorious,
Erin folds her horses in her garden of the sea.


## Ode on the Bicentenary

### I

Old Fortress, built to form and give
Guard to the Soul's prerogative,
    Twice in the neighbouring hills,
That take our dawns and days to breast,
Have centuries passed and come to rest,
    And Time once more fulfils
Each gray old court and thoughtful close,
Where hawthorns blossom out the rose,
    And green makes young the gray,
With many a mind for learning framed,
And many a name by all men named,
    That, gathering here to-day,
Welcome receive for all our sake
And honour give, and honour take;
And with memorial Time look back
To view what cities mark his track;
    What thought-built towers and towns,
Since here our School was housed and freed

From that once dominating creed,
  That now no longer frowns,
Lost to its human high emprise,
Nor binds the hand nor blinds the eyes
  Nor views the Quest with awe
Of Truth, whose growth is unconfined
Through surgence of the forms of mind,
  That shadow forth the law
Unalterable: Stress and Strife
Inherent in the flame of life,
  That must consume to glow,
Yet, ere its life die down can serve
To show what laws that life preserve:
  And he who planned to learn
These, and our School built here for this, –
Two hundred years that name of his
  Hear honoured now,
  John Stearne!

II

Sweet is the placid life of herbs,
  And sweet the thought that ours,
In that they heal what health disturbs,
  Is kindred to the flowers;
And through the seeming lifeless things
  Whose faint proportion mars
Or fills its source with lustier springs,
  Is kindred to the stars.

III

It was not theirs too close to scan
Here in the homely days of Anne
  The nice relations set
By Nature, nor the laws remote
Of malady and antidote
  Not all revealed: but yet
'Able Physician' each could be
Through his broad human sympathy,
  Benevolent and wise;
Like Nicholson who could divine
What smallest wort or seaward pine
  Of healthful balm supplies;

Helsham whose book beyond its peers
Taught science for an hundred years;
   And Molyneux who earned
Two fames that leave him unforgot,
A scholar and a patriot
   Whose book the hangman burned.
And Hoyle, the old anatomist,
   The heir of many a famous name,
Precursor to our Cunningham,
   And Griffith, alchemist,
And all our time shows hardly one,
To equal old Sir Patrick Dun;
Who left a School with fame to ring
Where Goldsmith stooped ere conquering.
They could not analyse or weigh
   Exactly, or enlist
In many a scheduled history
The misery and the mystery
Of human maladies: but they
Were richer in the days of yore
In that full, unrecorded lore
   Clear-sighted Kindness gains
From long Experience, when the heart
Is not aloof or kept apart
   From working with the brains:
Thus each was so much more the man
In those old courteous days of Anne.

IV

But who can vanished Time rebuild?
   When dreaming in the gloom
Sometimes at eve, when noise is stilled,
And all the middle air is filled
   With moted light and bloom,
The rose-red Georgian houses seem
To catch a glory and to gleam
   As when their lights of old
Shone out, with many a taper's blaze
On Dublin of the bounteous days.
   Built by the liberal and the bold
In spacious street and square.
   What memories are theirs to hold

Of gallant and of fair:
Each room a house, each house a town,
   Each hall a thoroughfare!
Where feast was set and dancers swirled,
   Where bravery was seen
With beauty powdered and be-pearled,
   Where talked the lucid Dean –
A Naples of the western world
   As fair a water's Queen!
And they who dwelt so richly blest
   Did not then overprize
Life: but the ways of life possest
   More honour in their eyes:
And so their daily round was graced
By costumes bright and deeply-laced,
And they had weapons richly-chased
   And passions quick to rise.

So there are those who in this time
   Can see but Honour strained:
A fear of meanness grown sublime
   In all the bumpers drained,
In all they did when gambling hard,
Staking a county on a card;
Or set to feast as heretofore
When boots were placed outside the door,
   Or ever round the drink went
And tacks were strewn upon the floor
   To punish each delinquent.
They were indeed a fearless nation
Whose only sign of hesitation
At Death was Cheyne-Stokes's respiration.

Thus lived they fighting, gaming, supping
And never people needed cupping
   So much – And Oh! they were not spared!
Their lives were full, their deeds were doughty,
And God, who made all things gouty,
   Did not withhold their lives' reward,
Except from those who, once too sporty,
With dropped wrist died from lead at forty,
   But died in times that did not reach
To atheroma or retention

Which Metchnikoff and Osler mention,
   Who do not practise what they preach:
A fact for us so much the better
Who do not need the old blood-letter
   Whose treatment aptly dealt with each
Flushed face and duplicated gorge,
In those old crusted days of George,
Before this public rape began,
And Peasant grew to Overman.

v

Built in a Queenly reign, a Queen
Your past best times has ever seen
   Since that old doctor, when
He ruled as mayor beside his town,
Your strong foundation fastened down,
   That sinks not in the fen.

Anne saw the School's foundation come,
Victoria what arose therefrom,
   And we who breathe the air,
As this will-driven car of Time's
In ever broadening circle climbs
   The mystic spiral stair,
Grow proud to think there must succeed,
Evolving from your ancient breed,
   In some yet dateless term,
A mightier race that is to come
And seize the future in the home
   Of Stokes who stood so firm,
And of that Stokes who taught so well,
What Graves made so discernible;
   And Hamilton who kenned,
And made a mirror for the mind
In which but few have since divined,
   And who called Wordsworth friend.

His home who into billows hurled
The baseless fabric of the world,
   Till, prophet-like, he heard
The faint, mute, translantic cry
Of floating cities doomed to die.

The permeating Word
Never informed a spirit more clear
Or kindlier than Fitzgerald's here . . .
    What Wilbur Wright achieved
His mind original foresaw;
    He planned to climb the blue
Like Icarus, as free from awe,
    As early dying too.

But has it lessened at its source
Their Spirit? the sustaining Force
    And glorious Way they went,
That grand old spirit grows not less,
But strengthens in the old largesse,
And calm, magnanimous intent
Of Iveagh the Munificent,
    The open heart and hand
Ready to pity and relieve,
The wisdom ripened to perceive
    The cause of things, who planned
To make cure needless and prevent
Disease, who cleared the tenement,
The tomb of life, and fanned
    With sunsoft breezes small wan cheeks
    That stifle where the city reeks —
These are the names of these our men, —
In these we welcome you again.

When years yet speechless shall have wrought
Upon their web, a growth of thought
    Let science leave as theirs;
Let Love and Lore with golden sleeve
In fresher hues your story weave,
    Old School, for future years!

## The Injection: To Lord Dunsany

If fighting were the worst of War
For you I'd have no fear,
For there is Honour in a scar
And Glory on the bier;
And since Disease has killed far more
Than all the Dreams that lead to War,

I send this transport out to you,
A millioned mighty arm,
Against a foe that skulks from view;
And know that, saved from harm,
You will, with this within your veins,
Win inconceivable campaigns!

Tell me what Hero ever brought
To war a battlefield.
You know how Alexander fought,
You know what made him yield.
By you that foe may be withstood
For you have Victory in your Blood!

To you who made lines live once more
The fates be not unkind!
For few have ever gone to War
Who leave so much behind;
And if his death you may not share
Be you like him unscathed in war.

For me when Glory walks abroad
Where I may not endure,
It is a rigid thing, My Lord,
To will to live obscure;
When every man strikes for the State
To bear the brunt of 'stand and wait'.

But if by any means of mine
Your life may be preserved
To this my lot I will resign —
I shall have also served,
And kept — I have not far presumed
A mind like yours from being fumed.

If you do this I'll ask you down
To rest till Sunday morn,
With leave to hang your hat upon
My great rhinoceros horn
Who have for style and line and gloss
'A nose like a rhinoceros'.

## *To Her Most Gracious Majesty*

God guard your head from Time's assaults
As He has kept your Fame from faults,
　　Till Time shall turn and grow
Less grimly on destruction bent,
To Loveliness more lenient,
　　To Worth more kind than now.
May he make happy and secure,
(As in this House in Miniature),
　　Homes for your Love to keep:
Towns on the skyline of the lea,
Orchards that foam from sea to sea,
　　And the main, fruitful deep:
Filling with courtliness and grace
The low-roofed and the lofty place,
　　The quiet gardens filling,
With Peace so deep, assured, serene,
So unmistable of mien,
　　High-Natured and good-willing;
That in its precinct everyone
May feel descended from the Throne.

## *To Maurice Baring*

To judge you by the things you love and praise,
You who praise honour, bravery and love
Were, well-assured, to set you far above
The louder voices of these boisterous days:
But when enlightened by the dream you raise
Of her who on the lawn was seen to move,
All loveliness for background, I would prove
Led by your vision, in a schoolman's phrase,
That, as none can desire beyond his bent,
Nor paint that which his soul has never kenned,
Therefore no poems have been better penned
Than yours which hold this splendour for content,
And are like to hold out to the end
While Beauty bears the year's beleaguerment.

## *To Stuart Benson*

Outlasting bronze was classic verse
Until you came, dear Benson,
And put the whole thing in reverse
With bronze outlasting men's song.

## *To Madame Chiang Kai-Shek*

Madame, three thousand years ago –
A little space in China's story –
Men for a lady went to war,
By our great fight transcended far,
And Homer heard of it, and so
All Europe rang with Helen's glory.
He told how countless spears were hurled
For the first lady of the world.

Madame, today that lady's place
Is yours, the world's outstanding lady,
With roles reversed: you ask for peace
And aids from war to win release,
Beauty transcending by your grace
And making all men charmed and ready
To save a culture and a pride
In your sweet self personified.

To save from grim barbarian lords
The delicate and gracious things:
Wisdom and truth and forms of thought
The immemorial ages wrought,
From vulpine and foresworn war lords
Who still, for all their vaunting brings,
Are savages in heart and brain
Who mix with chivalry chicane;

And to bring back the fragrant days
And lovely moments to our time
And make them worthy; and make us,

O lady most illustrious,
Worthy of you to whom our praise
Is tendered in this reverent rhyme.
Our own great pride, in days to come,
Will be that here you were at home.


## To the Grand Daughter of Lord Dunsany, aged two, in the garden of Dunsany Castle

Dainty little lady
With your Mother's eyes;
Where the brooks are shady
Such light in them lies;
Flecked as is the water
In the sheltered brooks,
Randall Plunkett's daughter
With your Mother's looks.

I have seen the garden
Pink and white in Spring,
And its grey walls warden
Peaches ripening:
Pink and white to peaches,
What one year can do
In the garden's reaches:
But your years are two.

Gael and Welsh and Norman
Its old walls have heard;
And the shouts of war men;
Yet they stood unstirred.
Fruit of blood and battle,
O so sweet and young
With your childish prattle
In the English tongue!

# EARTH AND SEA

## *[Poem from Oxford]*

I left the Trout at Godstow Bridge
A whore stood under the garden wall
Time grants Lovers a privilege
And the whores increase tho' the hours grow small

Down in a punt with a pint of ale
I'm the pint and the pint in me;
I lay and listened [to] the nightingale
As he sang from his unobtrusive tree

For this was the plot that I quietly planned:
To float above and below the moon:
While the world receded on either hand
To lie in an interlunary swoon

To lie until buoyed on the misty song
That pulsed in the trees like a limpid star
I found myself floating forever among
The isles where the [?losses] of the senses are

But whether the sky was too sweetly sung
And pleasure thus fraught with the greater pain
Or the mists too dense that around me hung
Somehow I failed to enjoy the refrain

I thought of John Keats, I thought of the shore
And the fines unless that I landed soon;
And I thought or I felt that for want of a whore
Somehow I failed to enjoy the moon.

## Ringsend

At midnight where the coal-dust on the Quay
Darkens their sea-spun raiment, and the air
Burns without colour in the torches' flare
They cast the fish, no longer fleet and free,
The fish whose breath of life is liberty,
On shores confined and ruinorous and bare,
And leave them lying in the darkness there,
Dragged from the great republic of the sea.

And yet the fins that here lie heaped and hurled,
Winnowed the water in Corinthian bays,
Tasting the forest freshets in the blue;
They felt the wavering sunlight, and they knew
The ever-during quiet in deep ways,
Made green with all the verdure of the world.

## Ringsend

*[Earlier version]*

At midnight when the coal dust on the Quay
Blackens their sea-spun raiment, and the air
Thick with the blustering torchlights' echoing flare
Is withering up their brightness, noisily
The fish are cast ashore and left to be
Hurled into many a cart with careless care
That shall in crushed glory landward bear
The tribesman of the chainless realm of sea.

And yet the fires that here lie heaped and hurled,
Winnowed the waters in Corinthian bays,
Tasting the forest freshets in the blue –

They fret the wavering sunshine, and they knew
The ever-during quiet of the ways
Made green with all the verdure of the world!


## Clouds

Between two sycamores the lake
Is darkly blue, a moving pond,
And fields, bent up above it, make
A bulging curtain and beyond
That curtain's green of cooling shroud
Which saves the eye from glare, the view
Is dark beneath a lighter blue,
A blue where I can gaze on slow
White bending galleons which go
From West to East, and God knows where;
I only rest my eyes and stare;
I rest my brain without a care,
In gratitude, since God endowed
The soundless sky with cloud on cloud.


## The Little Dark Wood

I dwelt by the Lake of the Little Dark Wood
  That lies by the edge of the neighbouring sea,
The lake wherein mountains invertedly stood
  When mists of the morning the water let be:
Plum blue in the water the mountains reflected
  Were clearer than ever they looked in the day
Where flat water lilies were floating collected,
  And black sallies sheltered their little still bay.
All through the long noon in the wood by the water
  I lingered and found that the better my mood,
The better the lake looked though less than a quarter
  Was lulled by the lilies to mirror the wood.
At evening, the gentle wind losing its motion
  Would leave the lake levelled to double the sun
That set in an oval ball over the ocean
  Until the bare mountains were purpling alone.

Sometimes the sun set in a revel of silver
   All squandered except what the lake water saves
To roof the dim haunt of the trout, eel and elver;
   And that spilth of silver far out on the waves.
I left the dark dell by the lake water-wooded
   Because so much beauty was sibling to pain,
Besides, with its magic my mind was so flooded
   I need but closed eyelids to bring it again.


## [Out of Dublin]

Follow the road along with me,
Mulhuddart first, and then Clonee,
Meath of the pleasant watercourses,
And Rogers rude who deals in horses.


## [With the Coming-in of Spring]

Now with the coming-in of Spring the days will stretch a bit,
And after the Feast of Brigid I shall hoist my flag and go,
For since the thought got into my head I can neither stand or sit
Until I find myself in the middle of the County of Mayo.

In Claremorris I would stop a night and sleep with decent men
And then go on to Balla just beyond and drink galore,
And next to Kiltimagh for a visit of about a month, and then
I would only be a couple of miles away from Ballinamore.

I say and swear my heart lifts up like the lifting of a tide,
Rising up like the rising wind till fog and mist must go
When I remember Carra and Gallen close beside
And the gap of the Two Bushes and the wide plains of Mayo

To Killaden then, to the place where everything grows that is best,
There are raspberries there and strawberries there and all that is
   good for men;
And if I were only there in the middle of my folk my heart could rest
For age itself would leave me there and I'd be young again.

## Lullaby

Baby come out of the garden
Mother is calling you: come,
Evening is falling, Mother is calling
Mother is calling you home.

Baby come out of the garden
Mother would rock you to rest
Now that the daytime has ended your playtime
And put you to sleep on her breast.

Hush, Baby, hush for the garden
Mother would not see you weep:
Mother that plays with you, Baby, and stayed with you
Mother that rocks you to sleep.

Dream Baby, dream of the garden
Dream if you're longing to roam
Out where the hours are closing the flowers,
Baby, away from your home.

## [April]

Ah, but April
Drenched, and flushing crimson
When she puts her robe on
Lest her stripling form was seen;
Often have I watched her
Where the river brims on
Grasses freshly flattened;
And the light is misty green.

Yes, I saw her early
Lovely, laughing April
As she ran for shelter
Sprinkled with the rain

## [Spring]

If the only life we know
Comes from darkness into Spring
Till the Winter lays it low
Does that end its – blossoming?
Say, what Season overbears
That which holds the seed of years.

## Chestnut Time

From amber boughs
Plump chestnuts plop
And, breaking course,
Out brown fruits pop.

Winds, each with each,
Fierce forces join
To rob the beech
Of his red coin;

To ruff the gown
Of wood and wold,
And to bring down
The orchard's gold

While over these
A surging sky
Fashions a frieze
Where galleons ply.

## Magical Frost

I saw the trees against the stars
All lit as if with frozen light
That made with their transparent bars
A fairyland of all the night;
And made me wish that I dwelt there
Without a body, but aware.

## Tradition

I heard the drovers crying out to keep
The sheep from straying as they drove them by,
And thinking of that, inarticulate cry
Heard on the hills before men learnt to reap,
I wondered at the changeless years that creep
Down from the vales of green antiquity,
To leave us with the self-same history:
Sheep and drovers' cries, drovers and sheep
The driven sheep, the drovers and their call!
When one regards their fate, and thinks it over,
So little left to choose, O Inis Fail,
I am – and thus I prove myself your lover,
Because the one tradition levels all –
Uncertain whether to be sheep or drover.

## To Nature

I have seen almost all your vagaries:
Tantrums of your thunder;
Hurricanes of awe.
Though I never said it, I
Thought you were hysterical
When your arid barreness
Frightened all the fairies,
Stamped out all the shady
Leaves and drove the lyrical
Rivulets awa'.
There were times you won me
(Is it any wonder?)
With your soft susurrus
And the velvet on your paw.
There were times you won me
When you whispered like a lady
And the small birds made a chorus
And I thought of running water
When the wind was in the poplars,
Or the moon was on the shaw,
If I say but one thing,
Don't forever shun me –
People will dispute it

Till the cows come to the sta',
You must give me credit, I,
Seeing all your stunting
Never once imputed
To you a moral law.

## Spring in the Desert (Arizona)

A mighty change of heart and mind
Is needed here before you find
The vision and the skill to trace
The beauty of this arid place;
But to the eye that's well endowed
There's beauty in all works of God:
And there must needs be loveliness
In miles of sandy aridness,
Although no cactus waves to Spring's
Fresh gusts and sudden flusterings,
Or lends a dewy, green resort
To birds who sing while they pay court;
But, rather, resurrected stands
A skeleton with praying hands,
Or seaweed reaching for the flow
Of seas receded long ago.
Yet each maintains successful strife
With wastes inimical to life
And, standing in his own right, gives
A proof of life where no man lives,
All braced against the burning hours
In armour buttoned on with flowers,
And brings by contrast back to me
Through apples in blossom, a glimpse of the sea.

## Evening Star

The light begins to die,
A long low cloud has blackt
The West with one thin bar;
But only lift the eye,
And, halfway up the sky,
Lonely, the Evening Star
Shines in its azure tract.

## Wind

Wind, the old sower came over the hill
And scattered invisible pollen until
He fruited the forests and stippled the fields
And blessed all the orchards with bountiful yields;
And then as he gazed on his work complete
Where meadows were mingled with wild meadowsweet:
You'd never have guessed, for he hardly moved,
That it was the golden pomp he loved.

## By a Stream in Bergen County

Wherever water wanders
   From some high mountain brake
To find, through granite boulders,
   Its way into a lake,
I need but look and listen
   To little pools afoam
Where sunbeams, netted, glisten
   To find myself at home.

The water knows no troubles,
   But, while it wanders, sings,
Alight with wayward bubbles,
   That burst in treble rings;
And bring to mind the airy,
   Faint music heard afar
From fairy rings and fairy –
   Dim pools that dance a star.

The lakes of Bergen County
   Are coloured like its skies,
Its orchards full of bounty,
   Its people kind and wise;
And I could dwell forever
   This little stream beside
Brought home by waves that sever
   And waters that divide.

## *Florida*

The tide's on the turn. My thoughts too are turning
To where the palms lean by the edge of warm seas.
The tide's on the turn: my whole frame is yearning
To bathe in the water beneath the slant trees.

Or watch the Gulf Stream where its waves in the sun dance
That fill Europe's else icy islands with flowers;
Or dally and dream in the blessed abundance,
The warm floral land of the sun-certain hours.


## *The Stream*

I dawdled along
By my own little brook
That leaps with a song
From its own little nook,
And I looked at its fall
And I thought, To a minnow
That water is all
He can live in and winnow:
Poised in the calms
In the currents more tense
And dazed by the little fall's
Turbulence,
With never a thought
That its watery state
Could possibly shrink
And evaporate.
Then I mused, What if I
Found my element gone,
And the earth, sea and sky
Were rolled into one
With lightnings and storms,
Volcanos and geysers
With wars and alarms
And their substitute Caesars;
The pouring stampedes
From the various states;

The millions in need
And the potentates;
The blustering shouts,
The churches in flames
And God listening in
To the pious war aims
Of lawyers and lords
And ladies that swish
Their skirts like the tail
Of a tremulous fish; —
Were all gathered up,
Then the whole thing would stop
And Creation come down
With a hell of a flop
(As it will some fine day)
Creation come down,
An unpopular play,
With a hell of a flop.
An end, I confess,
I might heartily wish
If it were not to me
As the stream to a fish.

## [The Green Glint]

Lucky is he
Who chances to see
By night the Green Glint over the sea.
I saw it once
And an old man said
'You are made up now
Till the day you are dead.'

## Flyer in Manhattan

Though grounded his love remembers
Texas, and Mt Rainier
Rises behind the question
In his glance, waits there.

Heroic through Utah, Nevada,
All his dreams pass,
In his mirror wide rivers
And forests frame his face.


## Conflagration

Who sets the Autumn woods on fire
    With yellow and green and crimson flames,
Until each tree reveals a pyre
    Of leafless, gaunt and blackened stems?

Cherish no hope to catch the thief;
    These marvels are divinely planned:
The boles themselves shall break in leaf
    When Spring's soft flame delights the land.


## To Girls to go Harvesting

Never before, since trees were planted
Was so much waste and so much wanted;
Or more abundance with more fear
Of many a lean, uncertain year;
And never, as each farmer swears,
Was such a lack of harvesters.

Therefore, ladies, lend a hand
To save the foison of the land;
To pick the apple, peach, tomato,
Or dig the homelier potato,
Cut with a tractor corn and hay
Or save it in the old world way;
Batter the butter, cans in boilers
Sterilise; and feed the broilers;
Jerk the cows with bee-like noses,
Against all cow tuberculosis,
And though you do it right or wrong
Be sure to raise a harvest song.
What though you work with rake or scythe

Or dairy pails, Oh, Girls, be blithe!
There is no pastie, pie or little tart
Can lighten labor like a light heart:
It sweetens cream and makes it thicker
(And that's what brings the butter quicker)
So gaily sing while driving, churning,
Or from the harvest home returning.
And in the orchard when you do't
Gather the constellated fruit
That makes each tree, when it's not scarce,
Shine like a rosy universe.
Basket the apples by the score,
They never may be wanted more
Against next year when all must band
To save, and every wife must husband.

Slacks should be worn by girls when climbing
(Advice not given for the rhyming)
As far as I can see, I'm sure,
When climbing trees they're de rigeur;
And gloves will save you from the oil
The glowing tractor spends on toil,
Or let the plump tomato's wine
Your oval nails encarnadine;
But, oh, if you would save your skin
Be sure to get the harvest in.

## Fishing in Panther Creek

Wandering water found and grooved the Catskills
Cast down from the heavens to a plateau upon Earth,
Singing and undaunted, so the wise ones tell us,
Water wrote on stones the tale of hill and vallies' birth

'You'd think today was just the day
The day for the White Coachman.
The fish are off their food to-day
And sitting pretty still.
The wind (and not to speak of) the willows was against us.
It may die down before midnight; so set them up now, Bill.'

Eon after eon in the years' procession
Pliant, pure and sprightly, the water worked unseen;
Boulder called to boulder and the bare walls echoed;
The gold sun touched the valleys with his wand and all was green.

'There's too much sunshine out to-day,
Besides no trout are rising;
The river's rather full to-day
It made my waders fill.
The waiter has our orders for something appetising.
We'll have to wait till after six, so set them up now, Bill.'

Gushing dashing water dances on a pavement
Paved with years of patience till a plateau of its own
Clear and clean from shale or clay is filled with waves translucent:
Mad merrimen that leap and sing and tumble up and down.

'There is not mud enough to-day
In spite of last night's raining;
The water's rather low to-day
You can't expect to kill
A fish; no, not with dynamite. Don't take me as complaining,
You should have seen my last year's catch, so set them up now, Bill.'

The heavens break: a cloud has burst. Oh, see! the waves remember
With indignation thunderous the old and primal wrong
Before they build their paradise wherein to sing and wander.
They roar and climb the heavens to-day and choke in foam their song.

'What can you expect to-day
When every bridge is broken?
No fish could see a bait to-day
With mud in eye and gill.
Don't take me as complaining; but, by that selfsame token,
We'll have to wait till comes a drought; so set them up now, Bill.'

Bill the barman said to me, 'I've heard of their tuxedos
When men dress up for eating; but do you know what I think
When I see all them fishermen that's so dressed up for sportin',
You'd swear they put on waders just for wading into drink.'

## Fishing in the Catskills

Wandering water found and grooved the Catskills
Cast down from the heavens to a plateau upon Earth,
Singing and undaunted, so the wise ones tell us,
Water wrote on stones the tale of hill and valleys, birth,

— *There's too much sunshine out to-day,*
*Besides, no trout are rising;*
*The river's rather full to-day,*
*It made my waders fill.*
*The waiter has our orders for something appetising.*
*We'll have to wait till after six, so set them up now, Bill.*

Eon after eon in the years' procession
Pliant, pure, and sprightly, water worked unseen:
Boulder called to boulder, and the bare walls echoed:
The gold sun touched the valleys with his wand, and all was green.

— *The wind the way it blew about us*
*The willows was against us —*
*The trout are off their feed today*
*And setting pretty still,*
*If not they could not fail to rise and snap up the White Coachman.*
*Well things may change before the night, so set them up now, Bill.*

Crushing water dashing dances on a pavement
Paved with years of patience till a plateau of its own,
Clean and free from shale or clay and bright with waves translucent
Mad merriment that leaps and sings and tumbles up and down.

— *There is not mud enough to-day*
*In spite of last night's raining;*
*The water's rather low to-day*
*You can't expect to kill*
*A fish, no, not with dynamite; don't take me as complaining.*
*You should have seen my last year's catch. So set them up now, Bill.*

The heavens break. A cloud has burst. Oh, see! The waves remember
With indignation the old and primal wrong,
Before they built this paradise wherein to sing and wander
They roar and climb the heavens to-day and choke in foam their song.

*– What can you expect to-day*
*When every bridge is broken?*
*No fish could see a bait to-day*
*With mud in eye and gill:*
*There's mud in eye, of course there is; and by that selfsame token*
*I do not feel to bright myself, so set them up now, Bill.*

Bill, the barman, told his wife 'I've heard of their tuxedos
When men dress up for eating. Do you know what I think
When I see all them fishermen with rods and reels and baskets?
I'd swear they put on waders just for wading into drink.

## The Hermit Thrush

*(The incomparable one, the hermit thrush in the*
*swamp cedars singing.'* WHITMAN)

From cedar tree to cedar tree
   He flies; and now he sits and sings
An intermittent song that he
   Through all his change of sweetness rings:
Swift joy, and then of flowery pomp
He sings above the dismal swamp.

As swift as fountains seen through leaves
   His notes leap up and break on air
Until the listening mind perceives
   In song a symbol hidden there:
Swift, swift the notes and sharp and sweet;
And so is joy the more 'tis fleet.

He stops. All silence. Then a low,
   Soft whistle exquisitely poured
That lulls the mind from any woe
   That might within it have been stored.
It tells of men who lie at ease,
The harvest moon beyond the trees.

With folded wings he conjures up
   The endless, blest Elysian Fields;
And I who hear am filled with hope

To which all thought of squalor yields
And all conflicting things which throng
The dismal swamp. O what a song!

## And No Farther

Millions of Americans
Sitting in their living rooms
Talking frantic politics or simply chewing gum;
Millions of Americans
Waiting for the millenniums
Just around the corner, and as far as they can come.

## And No Farther

*(an unpublished version)*

Millions of Americans sitting in their living rooms
　　Talking vital politics or merely chewing gum;
Millions of Americans waiting for millenniums
　　Just around the corner and as far as they can come.

Millions of Americans growling at the Government
　　Studying the columnists who write to make them swear
Millions of Americans wondering if Hoover meant
　　That to help a neighbour you must leave your larder bare.

Millions of Americans missing all the wonderment
　　Electric-lighted palaces pavilioned on the air
The evening star all liquescant in the azure of the firmament
　　The tumbling moon that's looking for the men who put
　　　them there.

## Fellow Victims

Don't drown me, madcap tides, I prayed;
For, if your floods should drag me down,
A kinsman you shall have betrayed:
I too am moidered by the Moon.

## [Before Building]

That would just for one glimpse disclose
The rooted oak, the wilding rose;
Rocks, and the springs that gushed before
Paved poetry connected slum and store


## Air Land and Sea

Air, land and sea
Attest our skill;
Air, land and sea
Shall merge until
As one in three,
Air, land and sea
Confirm our will
To live forever free.

Free as the air, and chainless
As all the winds that blow;
Firm as the air, and chainless
As all the winds that blow;
Firm as the land, and stainless
As mountains robed in snow;
Wide as the sea, and reinless
As all the waves that flow.

To all as unoppressing
As we live unoppressed;
To lend a hand redressing
The ills of East and West;
Thrice armed for right, confessing
Allegiance to our own
Air, land and sea, possessing
The might of Three in One.

# SATIRES AND FACETIAE

---

## DISLIKES AND DISAPPROBATIONS

### [Epigram on Connolly]

Don't pass Connolly, Death!
That putrescence is his breath.

### [A Lock-In]

You talk of Griffith and his fleas
Remember for you ought
That you were also with the 'flees'
When Ireland rose and fought.
When Dublin's streets ran red with blood
With your embattled brother
You were with the also rans
Assisted by your mother.

### [On his Mother's dishonest Solicitor, run over by a car, reputedly a Rolls-Royce]

Struck off the Rolls
Reinstated
He broke his head
And now dishonestly lies dead.

## [On the Charges of his American Agent for Lecture Tours]

They named Clarke Getts, my agent, well.
For all for which his client sweats
On lecture tours with long travail
Clarke Gets.

## To a Lady Reviewer

Maulie Colum
Won't extol 'em
No matter what men may
Put into a volum.
Why is Molly
So unjolly:
Mary Colum
Sour and solemn?
She knows she may maul
But she never can *moll* 'em.

## Coming from the Movies

The palm-ringed shores in high relief,
Below them, shadows green and dim;
The long white thunder on the reef;
The pool where rainbow fishes swim:
And then the reasty, raucous street,
The noise that throngs and shakes the air;
The chewing gum beneath the feet;
The colored taxis everywhere.

## [Anger]

For a fire is kindled in mine anger
And shall burn into the lowest hell
And shall consume the earth and her increase
And set on fire the four [ ? ] of the mountains.

## *[Copywriters]*

They knew all the tricks to make men impute
A cause to what's really an attribute;
And words such as these you might be sure
To read in the cod-piece literature:
  'Men like gods!
  If you cherish your cods,
   Zocks will take care of the cods and odds'
The air would fill with a lovely
       chant:
  'Zocks supporters with slits
       aslant
  Men, why live in suspense,
      suspend.
  All call Al Wasserman Zocks
      your friend.'


## *A Wish*

I wish I had within my grip
The inventor of the pneumatic drill;
I'd take good care it did not slip
Till I had shoved it up, until
It reached a spot under his hat
And drowned his screams with its RAT TAT.

## LIMERICKS

### *The Virginal Kip-ranger*

There is a young fellow named Joyce
Who possesseth a sweet tenor voice,
He goes to the Kips
With a psalm on his lips
And biddeth the harlots rejoice.

### *On James Joyce*

There is a weird spectre called Joyce
Re-arisen from Monasterboice,
His whole occupation
A walking negation
Of all his acquaintance's choice.

### *On James Joyce's brother, Stanislaus*

Poet Kinch has a brother called Thug,
His imitator, and jackal, and mug.
His stride like a lord's is
His pretension absurd is
In fact he's an awful thick lug.

### *On Parker, the Grinder*

There once was a solar eclipse
Which could only be seen from the Kips.
As the daylight grew darker
I thought I saw Parker
Astride on a . . .

## On Ryan, a Fellow Student

If in Richmond Asylum we probe,
We find, clad in fantastic robe,
Ryan tracing ellipses
And making eclipses,
While he murmurs, 'That bloody ould globe!'

## The Young Man from St John's

There was a young man from St John's
Who wanted to roger the swans
'Oh no!' said the porter,
'Oblige with my daughter,
But the birds are reserved for the dons.'

## [Rewritten Classic]

Then out spoke the King of Siam,
'For women I don't give a damn.
You may think it odd of me;
I prefer Sodomy.
They say I'm a bugger, I am.'

## On Miss Horniman

What a pity it is that Miss Horniman
When she wants to secure or suborn a man
Should choose Willie Yeats
Who still masturbates
And at any rate isn't a horny man.

## The Young Lady of Chichester

There was a young lady of Chichester,
Whose curves made the Saints in their niches stir;
Each morning at matins
The swish of her satins
Made the Bishop of Chichester's breeches stir.

## On being elected to the Irish Academy of Letters

There was a kind poet called Yeats
Who put me with those whom he rates –
   Don't think it bad of me –
   In his Academy;
Off which of our heads are the slates?


## On a Fallen Electrician

Here's my tribute to 'lectrician Joe,
Who fell to his death through the O in Oxo.
He's gone to a land which is far far better
And he went, as he came, through a hole in a letter.


## A Lesbian Maid

A Lesbian maid of Khartoum
Took a nancy boy up to her room,
As they turned off the light,
She said 'Let's get this right,
Who does what and with which and to whom?'


## A Talented Student

A talented student of Trinity
Scuttled his sister's virginity;
He buggered his brother;
He had twins by his mother;
Then he took a First Class in Divinity.


## Ghostly Feeling

Last year when I dwelt on the Coast
I had an affair with a ghost.
In the midst of the spasm
The poor ectoplasm
Exclaimed, 'I can feel it – almost!'

## The Fussy Boys

Have you heard of the Fussy Boys, Ferrar and Strauss
Who ran an hysterical publishing house?
The error of Ferrar
The terror of Strauss
Made authors as poor as the famous church mouse.

## That Exquisite Fellow called Coward

That exquisite fellow called Coward
Was paid to feel strongly empowered
To fight in England,
Having previously planned
To leave the old sod unendowered.

## Sing a Song of Sexpence

The King was in his counting house
Counting up his pelf;
The Queen was in her parlour
Playing with herself;
The Maid was in the garden
Trying to show the Groom
The vagina not the rectum
Is the entrance to the womb.

## The Young Maid of Madras

There was a young maid of Madras
Who had a most beautiful ass.
It was not round and pink,
As you bastards might think:
It was grey with long ears and ate grass.

## Of Daniel O'Connell, who, it is rumoured, begot many bastards

They sent his heart embalmed to Rome
But left his testicles at home,
And thus from this we plainly see
The phallus is no fallacy.

## Brian O'Lynn

Brian O'Lynn had the pox and the gleet,
And he stunk like a privy in Mecklenburg Street;
Great globules of mercury dropped from his chin.
'Be Jasus, I'm rotten,' said Brian O'Lynn.

## The Young Lady from Louth

There was a young lady from Louth
Who went for a trip to the South.
Her father said, 'Nelly,
There's more in your belly
Than ever went in at your mouth.'

## The Young Fellow at Bray

There was a young fellow at Bray
Thought syphilis might pass away,
So now he has tabes
And two-headed babies
And thinks he is Queen of the May.

## The Young Girl of Antigua

There was a young girl of Antigua
Whose mother said, 'Nellie, how big you are!'
But Nellie said, 'What?
Do you speak of my twat,
My bubs, belly, bum or my figua?'

## A Professor of Trinity Hall

A professor of Trinity Hall
Possessed an octagonal ball
The cube of whose weight
Plus penis, plus eight
Was four-fifths of nine-tenths of Fuck All.

## [The End of the World]

There was a young man who said 'Run,
For the end of the world has begun.
The thing I dread most
Is that damn Holy Ghost,
I can deal with the Father and Son.'

PARODIES

## [Parody of Swinburne's 'Itylus']

Thy heart is as light as a leaf of a tree
But mine goeth forth amongst sea-gulls hollow
To the place of the slaying of Itylus,
Thou art classic, romantic is Gogarty.

## Hymn of Brahma

Soon your old land will be free once again.
The Indian soothsayers are rousing the people
with a stimulating, that is a rousing diet.
This is a poem an Indian poet made:

The d–i–amond stars in the mystic gloom
    Were twinkling as in p–a–in
While the **Mighty Mother's Voice** said 'OM'
    And sang this sad refrain
'I am the Pot and the Potter
(I am the Penis and the Quent)
I am the Son and the Daughter
I am the Straight and the Bent
I am the Smiter and Smitten
(And also the place that is smote)
I am the Bite and the Bitten
(I am your Breeches and Coat)
I am the Debt and the Debtor
(Tho' Tailors may never think thus)
I am the Begot and Begetter(!)
(The Doctor the Child and the Nuss')

*Interruptions in brackets:*
*From this you may know that your old island is still*
*the nest of song that it was before Colum was killed*
*and bids fair to become again the Isle of Saints.*
*This ends the Kiltartan English.*

## William Dara thinks of the Sin of his Childhood and is sorrowful

If you wait till the winds be blown and blown
    And the last grey clouds unclose
If you wait till the mystic heron be flown
    With the one eye and the three toes

I shall sit and sigh till the mouse-grey moss
    Obscures the old oak stump
For I a child by the market cross,
    Thought of a rabbit's rump.

*Gogarty's Note:*
*The three toes represent Pain, Desire and Fear which*
*figure in the poetry of the bird. The bird is Love resting*
*in the above emotions. The one eye represents the*
*retrospective view of life, etc.*

## To Elwood Poxed

A pity beyond all telling
Is hid in the heart of love
As soon as you press it well in,
As soon as you give it a shove,
In the house where whores are dwelling
– Unless it is wrapped in a glove –
A little Hunterian swelling
Poxes the part that they love

## [Parody of 'To Althea from Prison']

Stone walls do not a prison make
Nor iron bars a cage
If in a tilt for sweet Love's sake
The slavey will engage.
If I have freedom in my love
Who in my love am free
The Connoisseur* who rules above
Knows no such liberty.

*\*Jehovah who collected foreskins [Gogarty's Note]*

## The Policeman is bathing – to Girls to have no Fear but Caution

Steal to his clothes – he beats the sea
    That used to beat the shore;
And one by one peep quickly, girls,
    But see ye do not more
For though he swims in chilling waves
    And waves surround the Pole –
The cold that the leviathan laves
    By no means may control
His anger or his eagerness; – if he but turned his head
I fear you'd know the folly, Girls of being comforted.

## [Lack of Knowledge]

John Eglinton my jo, John
Since when had you a quent?
I think ye canna go, John
Although ye are na spent
I fear yese gin to geld, John
And canna make it flow,
For even if it swelled, John,
The lassies wouldna know.

John Eglinton my jo, John
Gang solder them tegither
And hang them round your neck John
In a little pouch o' leather
The folly of your youth, John
Has weakened you to go
Your virtue is a farce, John
Because ye dinna know.

*This is most ecclesiastical. The schoolmen equate knowledge for temptation, etc. [Gogarty's Note]*

## [Languorous Lotus-Land]

Tell me, is O'Leary harboured
In the town that drifts to starboard,

With his pallid features barbered
   And his pointed pleasant chin?
Looking like the ghost of Huysmans
Has he just contrived to squeeze mong
Cavaliers, his divertissement
   Really counting as a sin?
Surely there could be no quorum
Formed of those who take a jorum
Surely, O si quis piorum
   Curtis in the turquoise day. . . .
He owes his reputation
To the single occupation
Of a timely resignation
Gentle, he did not disdain us,
Gentle as a ring-dove's anus,
Gently there *tendebat manus*
   In the same old earthly way
Singing though he feels but so so,
Singing as you might suppose so
Much less bard than virtuoso
   Singing in the waveless Bay
Of the dear old days laudator,
Little things from Walter Pater,
Of his drink a contemplator
   While the waiter waves the tray
Leave him not, Episcopalian!
Leave O'Leary not an alien
To that City Asphodelian
   Courteous in the hidden way
There they live — and more's the pity!
Like an indolent committee
In the Syphilitic City
   Built above the River Goh.
All their days are long and listless
They are minded to insist less
For the will might make the bliss less
   Since a dream-shaft pierced it through,
And their minds are filled with plenty
In that dolce far niente,
O come kiss me sweet and twenty,
   Tell me what I'd like to do.
All the nights are calm and star-lit
As when green succeeds to scarlet:

Who would have the harbour harlot
   Dimmer than the Evening Star?
They can watch the river lapsing
And the swallows round the apse in
Upward flight as they were perhaps in
   Other days that are no more.
Here where life is all but langour
No one dares indulge in anger
Lest an aneurysmal pang or
   Paralytic stroke encore
Earlier warnings half unheeded.
We who do not live as they did
Kindly leave them unupbraided
   Rather we could hear them sing
Curious these Cherubim in
Chorus singing Yo, Yohimbim
Yo, yo ho, Yo ho Yohimbim
   Like the bird of loudest lay,
But the sole Leone tree
Spreads, its bark beyond their reaches
On West Africa's lonely beaches
   Yo, yo ho is all we'll say.


## [Five Parodies]

### I

Over the daffodils, upon the hill,
Swing-swing singing, the Convent girls
Play, play on laughing with merry goodwill
Glad of the giddy young wind in their curls;
Under the hillside dusk grasses sway:
What is the little wind coming to say?

What does it tell to the willows that dream
With old heads bowed to the wind's light word:
The willows that age by the ageless stream
Have leaves grown grayer, the leaves demurred
What is the stream? but the stream grows bright
And the willow-tree leaves are erased from sight.

And now where they shine with six golden rays
The daffodils (rays like the Evening Star's
When its beauty is mildest through Earth's sweet haze)
The daffodils' beauty the little wind mars:
Tut, Tut, Tut, had their drawers no frills
But you must play flick with the dear daffodils!

II

TO S Mc————

Tie-gear! Tie-gear burning bright
Thro the coolness of the night!
What abortive hand or eye
Framed thy fierce asymmetry?

Whose the hand and whose the art
Took the crimson from the heart?
O'er whose vest did'st thou protrude
Like a ploughshare soaked in blood?

Tell me, are there ties like these
In the 'Garden of the Bees'?
Then the bees must all be known
By the red behind their zone

These when they were overwarmed
Underneath thy nose they swarmed
Seeking there to give relief
Which escaped thy handkerchief

Bees, Bees! beneath his nose is
All the Helicon he uses!
And he hopes to change thro you
This thing into honeydew!

Tie-gear, Tie-gear burning bright! . . .
Out, out, out, put out the light!
Or, if it be possible
Let that necktie pass – to hell

All the bees could not win pardon
For this outrage in the Garden.
Surely 'twas thy hand that planned it
Planned the Book of Verse and – scanned it!

III

BROWNING

A Danger Signal on the Quay?
A man-with-haemorhoid 'shirt tail?
The Garden of Gethsemane?
A Bookie's face who would not pay?
Can't guess? Or try-and-fail!

I could propound another poser:
I ought, you think then, to propound it?
Say what's behind – A face, or no, Sir?
A lobster-boiled Metempsychoser?
Be sure you don't confound it.

The hinder part of Marsyas
When Phoebus rubbed well with spice?
Is't coming here along the grass
If you're afraid to turn your –
Shut eyes is my advice!

IV

Of noses and their worth
I must make bold to sing
And labour till I bring
A nasal ballad forth
Wherein I'll try and track
And show how rich and rare is
The [?mover] at the back
And the anterior navis

Begin, my Muse, begin
In varied strains and valid
To modulate the ballad
With accents from within
Begin, though it outstrips
The Truth – yet I suppose
No lie can pass your lips
If you talk through your nose

Sing first the holy nose
The righteous and the narrow
That's pointed like an arrow

The way that all flesh goes!
And since that one is past
Lets sing a counterblast
Upon another nose
One subject took to
or ——————— abuses
Some turgid [? tribulatory]
To growing polypusses

To spifficate God's foes:
All latitude His Grace
For those he loves avoids
And hence it shows a face
That's straight with adenoids
Ah no, the primrose path,
The broad way and the green
The mo[?] and obscene
That brings the aftermath!
This nose walks after truth
And holds itself on high
But narrows both the mouth
And basis cranii
Which burgeon out and bulge
So altruistically
They cannot neutralise 'Me'
Unless they would divulge
The secret of their leaven,
And from this one concludes
They either go to Heaven
Or down to Dr Wood[s]

V

No counterblasting nose
That hasn't got a bridge
Nor any privilege
To lead one to suppose
Its owner
    Although
No way that all flesh goes!
And now since that is best
Let's blow a counterblast
Upon another nose

## Pax Britannica

This war is too much with us: our platoon
  Are growing weary. We lay waste no Powers
  Except the group which is accounted ours,
The Serbs, and our near neighbours the Walloons.
Dublin bears witness with its armed gossoons,
  And that wee race where Montenegro lowers.
  Our navy has conveyed to watery bowers
The great Earl Kitchener of the Cartoons.
If things go on at this rate, there can be
  Only one way to make our foes forlorn:
Make them our Allies: Peace hath Victory!
  And in the sharing they will be outworn,
For by the force of our morality
  When not by arms nations are overborne.

## [Parody of Arthur O'Shaughnessy's 'Ode']

We are the masturbators,
We are the dreamers of dreams,
Spending in secretive places,
Our totally purposeless streams;
And one with a mind at leisure
Can roger an ancient Queen
And make from a moment's pleasure
A map on the damascene.

## A Scotsman speaks to William Shakespeare

Cum into the open, Wullie,
  Nor fear to speak your mind;
Cum into the open, Wullie,
  Wi' the flaucht o' human kind.

Must all we dance like marionettes
  What time you're sittin' tight,
So nane of us your fellings gets?
  Weel, maybe you are richt.

LIGHT-HEARTED VERSES

## [To William Dawson]

No need to boast yourself well-read.
The gift's hereditary rather.
'I read before I go to bed,
Chapters of Sappho': thus your father.

## [Note to a Friend]

But Bob old cock, get here by four.
The second room above the door
Is where I sit and idly pore
O'er books and papers.
I want to send you where need is sore,
I do be japers.

## [Idea for the Ending of a Poem]

. . . scalded when he pissed
– And now he prays to Mercury
Who was an atheist

## [To the Wandering Aengus]

I thought, beloved, to have brought to you
A gift of quietness, and ten and six;
Cooling your brow – and your landlady too,
With ready spondulicks,

Homeward I go not yet, because of those
Who will not let me leave lest they repine:
For from the Bank the 'stream of quiet' flows
Through hands that are not mine.

But, O my Knight! I send to you the stars
That light my very creditable gains.
And out of Oxenford – though 'on my arse' –
My scorn of all its praise.


## At Burford

See the garden wall,
What a sight it is;
And above it all
See the little knoll
For the girls to fall, –
That is Ma[c]kenzie's:
See the garden wall
What a sight it is!


## [The Spud]

(To George Redding)

Have I told you that the Spud
Cannot float his Mayo mud,
Cannot help it going dud
            Any day,
[And you would not have it marred]
If he is too long debarred
From a Paris boulevard?
            China clay!
Far too long untouched has lain
Tripping past his busy brain:
Dainty rogues in porcelain
            Stout or thin
Only want his cunning hand
Until we may see them stand
Modelled (as their Maker planned)
            Kaolin?
Kaolin that can't get out
Till the Spud has stared about
And selected from the rout
            One or two

Dainty demoiselles and hired
Till he finds himself inspired
That is all that is required,
                And then home
Unless something rare and riche
Coming up from the 'Boul' Mich'
Makes her silken leggins swish
                Past be Dour . . .
"Business, BUSINESS can't be done
Damn it on a telephone"
When I say I might have known
                There I leave you!

## [George Redding's Reply: The Mayo Spud in Paris]

Oh you are right
There is no doubt
No balance sheet
Will be made out;
A call, maybe
On you and me
We shall not see
A company
At God knows where
In far Mayo
But should the Spud
To Paris go
There will be
*The* company
Of Heart's desire
That stings like fire
Of sweet young things
In silken hose
And others without
Any clothes,
When shapely limbs
Are twirled in the air
He will not know
He will not care

They will not run
Before him there
When he goes down
A fervid man
To plump Louise
Or swift Suzanne
He will not know
Or care a pin
If China clay
Or Kaolin
Be white as snow
Or black as sin!

## [McGurk]

I had a vision as the last
Guests rose and half subsided home,
A vision of days gone past
And days to come

And I beheld in mingled dream
Two roads converge towards a Janus;
Up this, down that did pageants stream,
As food between your mouth and anus,

And I beheld the one McGurk
Unmoralised, unmarital,
Then young and grave with thoughts of work
That now does none at all

The one McGurk then young and grave,
Then grave and young, now old and gay,
Walk up the gradual architrave
That rises, and then slopes away.

And with him went in hoary beard,
Like to the image of the Sire,
Who on the staircase erst appeared
And out his friend did fire.

Old Truth, with palsied steps and slow,
In sombre garb and beard all hoary
With whom whoever cares to go
Gets bored, but crowned with glory.

And these approached to T.C.D.;
The younger gained a Fellowship
And finding they could not agree
He gave old Truth the slip,

(Oh, what a slip, oh, what a fall
Was there! Then you and I fell down;
And Mrs Mac began to call
And chase us round the town!)

And I was filled with great regret
For those best days ere I did waken,
Regret for what – well, I forget –
And chances never taken

For ere McGurk gave way to joy,
And gave himself to moralising;
I had no need of dear employ
And chances quite surprising

And those are gone, and he is old;
And am I loaded down with scruples,
Since Mrs Mac began to scold
And guard his lady pupils!

Dear things with philosophic brains!
And tastes – like a philosopher's!
Perhaps one, lingering, now remains
And with McGurk confers!

I doubt it – for she watches them,
Who watches too well all of us!
Although I from his window came,
I am his incubus.

# *[That City]*

As a refuge against sense is
Welcome when it recompenses
Poets from their brain expenses
    So that City seems to me.
Faint and founded on a ditty
Is that city, is that city
Which you think a trifle spitty
    But how could it fail to be?
Built above the nameless river
Lapsing like the Guadelquiver,
'Little breezes dusk and shiver'
    Where that river takes the sea
By the cenotaph of Keelin
Where the widowed wife is kneelin;
There the friends of Nolan Wheelan
    Wheel on seeing Nolan see.
But he follows Nolens volens:
'Talking without semi-colons,
Maurice Joy who dealt in whole uns
    Connotating Connolly
Could not as an aftermath chair
Such a speaker. May the bath-chair
Be his fate and not the lath-chair
    Of the rickshaw bring him nigh.
Make him Lord Mayor, make him grama –
Phone his life away in drama
Make him a Thibetan llama –
    But the mist blows in again!
Very likely 'twill be raining
Till the cloud dissolves again in
Drops of water on the brain, in
    Any case it's only rain.
Is there no way to assign him
As a clerk to Richard Lynam?
Can we? Can they not confine him?
    In a land where no man steers?
Thank me that I do not *mention*
Once that cursed Socratic *question*!
Helen with her old age *pension*
    Closes both her eyes and ears.
From the main sea deep sea Sinbad

Signals now, and by a wind bad
I'm borne darkly. I have been bad,
   I've been fearfully afar!'
Thank you for your restful ditty.
We who drift towards that City
Often want some little miti –
   Gation of our living pain –
Who have drunk a lighter Lethe
Like to ether, like to methy –
Lated spirits. 'Who will feed thee'
   Sang to Bard who sings again
Of that City quite uncarnalled
Where the weedy streets are tarnelled
And the face of Matthew Arnold
   Turns averse, and round again.


## [Fragmentary Question]

Panurge, in Grecian time if you
Had met my friend Macran
To further lust would not you too
   Urge Pan


## Ad Priapum

God send his grace to me and you
Nor suffer us to share the plight
Of him who took all night to do
That which he once could do all night


## To One who chews the Cud
## of Wildish Corn

Things that the future hides from view
We still may think we yet may do.
But what of our friend who thinks he did
Things a transparent Past keeps hid?

## A Trinity Boat Song

Verse pattern

### I

There's a voice that is all-compelling,
Calling to you and me:
'Come ye forth from your inland dwelling,
Come ye forth and be free!'
Let us go where the river is calling,
Where the ripples make revelry,
In the spell of enchantment enthralling,
On the silver road to the sea.

### II

Leave the path to the grass and daisies,
Leave the squares and the street,
Seek the stretch of the wider spaces,
Where the heart has freedom of beat

### III

Sigh no more for a springtime maying,
Hawthorn and lilac sweet,
And the beckoning paths where you once went straying,
When the heart first learnt to beat.
Days that have fallen in darkness,
Never recaptured shall be,
Leave your sorrows behind you
On the silver road to the sea.

Chorus pattern

Gently-flowing river,
Sing me your renown,
May you flow for ever,
River of Dublin town
For the joys you brought us,
For the songs you sung,
For the truth you taught us,
When the world was young.

Alternative

River, immemorial river,
River, of enduring renown,
May you flow untroubled for ever,
River of Dublin town.
Sunlight and ripple and laughter, etc.


## T. W. Wilson on Homophony

How better 'Bellson'
Would sound than 'Wilson'
And give your father a lacked surname!
Were Bell your father,
You would not bother
About sweet discords
That fail to rhyme;
But, sound-engendered,
That Shakespeare jingled with 'note' and 'pot'
'Plenty,' 'empty, farthest,' and 'Harvest,'
Sedley did likewise and then did not
Rossetti make 'German' to rhyme with 'woman'?
Song's great masters who grazed the goal! –
On their steeds thundered
Where you would have blundered,
Upsetting the song-cart and playing the fool.
More I could teach you
Could sweet sound reach you,
Who call for music and like it square;
But, filled with scruple,
I doubt my pupil.
Besides, I don't quite know who you are.


## [A Rejoinder to George Redding's 'The Quiver']

Oh, Marie Stopes, I never knew how far it
Was wise to mingle Love and Faith until
I saw the holy brother of Boyd Barrett

Aim his full quiver on Killiney Hill.
Ah, George you never knew or felt
The reason why your hero knelt
Before his wife half through the night,
By day, behind the acolyte.


## [Comment on Thomas Bodkin]

Of all the Muse's mixed and odd kin
Surely the most absurd is Bodkin


## Tom Greene of Gort an Tochain

Ever and aye in my hero's house
Is a bright and carefree company
And in peace and comfort the priests of Christ
Sit at the table's edge
Salmon from the pool and sheep and fowl
The freshest flesh of beeves
Hearty [?healing] spirits and ale that come
Over the [?edge]] of the sea
Drinking gambling [?reeling]
A crowd uproariously drunk
And a band eager for amusement.


## [Impromptu Lines on driving past
a Country Wedding]

The desire of the cow for the bull,
Of the mare for the stallion,
The ache of the maid-of-all-work
For the private of any battalion.

## *In the Stud-Farm*

Here's a fine mare for you!
Aye; take a good look;
Bred from the best of them
All in the stud book!
Here, where she will not slip,
Far from the cobbles,
O but it's she's the rip,
Where are the hobbles?
Aisy, my beauty, O,
Aisy, go aisy,
Don't let the teaser now,
Drive her half crazy,
Take the brute off, will you,
You young rapscallion!
Here comes the blood-horse, Whoa!
Give her the stallion!

## *Talk (at all levels)*

They talked and talked at Nineveh,
Memphis and Babylon;
And, when the men had had their say,
The women then came on
And talked and talked and talked away;
And what they talked of in their day
It matters little now, for they
And all their towers are gone.

## *[Diary Entry]*

Trip no further pretty sweeting
Girdles end in lovers' meeting
Every old maid's son doth know.

## [Part of an early Love Poem]

The girl by whom I am beguiled
Must have high cheekbones and a child


## Logical and Zoological

How they differ from the Image and each other!
How they jabber on the seats in Central Park!
If it's true in Eve they had a common mother
She must have met more Adams after dark.
I will go and see the mighty graminivora,
The water horses that are really hogs,
Because those pig boats do not seem to differ a
Whit from one another or great logs.
And though their bulk may be a bit monotonous
There is comfort in this thought at any rate:
There cannot be an ugly hippopotamus
Because from form it does not deviate.


## To Mora

Deare, what a brain you've got!
But – wait a minute!
Likely it is as not
That I put in it
Thoughts that I think of you:
If so, 'tis plain
That what I said was true
Deare, 'what a brain!'


## The Buck

'Whom did I meet but Tiger Roche
As I came into town?'
He stood in the path of my approach

And looked me up and down.
He stood in the path of my approach
And slapped his silver sword.
Then up and off, and away in his coach;
And never said a word!

## First Edition

I listened to the brooklet
With its rain-fed swell.
The water tried to tell me,
It was a cheery message,
And I cried, 'Gadzooks,
We should have no gloomy presage
If our books were brooks.'

## [Noise]

If screaming noise could quench a fire
The Fire Department might retire,
And as for the insurance brokers
They'd not be grim but all be jokers.

## [Stop!]

O busmen, driving to and fro,
Both you and I know where to go
But at the bus stops please slow up,
And when I give the signal stop.

## The Subway – Rush Hour

To reach the doors was such a strain
Against the people landing.
It was a very crowded train:
Even men were standing.

## Take my seat please

He rose within the crowded bus;
A gentleman she ranked him.
She fainted to be treated thus;
He fainted when she thanked him.

## Aeronautic Sport

The wind was wild
Fresh from the sea
A playful child
High over me.

An eagle beat
Against the air,
No defeat
Acknowledged there.

The pulsing wings,
A wordless song –
Great graceful things
Immense and strong!

At length the bird
Half circled, sped
Into the curd
Of cloud ahead.

Joyous and wild,
It rose to glide –
As a gleeful child
On a playground slide.

## A Contretemp

I could not well ask him his name;
His face was quite unknown.
I thought, 'Ah, well, I'm not to blame;

I can't remember everyone
I'm pointed out to. Such is fame!'
And then he asked, 'What is *your* name?'


## Barberism

Do you know what we are heir to
Do you know what kind of hair-do
We should wear?

A Fakir thinks that he should never
Cut or trim or else disfigure
God-given hair.

For maids a glory to enjoy
For Nuns, a pride and to destroy,
Depends who wears it.

Would you wear a cut as crews do
Or prefer an Indian scalp you?
Could you bear it?

A poet just to make you think
Lets his hair fall in the ink
So you will know.

A Monk a Tonsure wears with pride
Yet with a scull cap doth it hide
So it won't show.

All the hairy beast[s] we know of
Use hair for cover and not show off.
Unless they're tame.

Poor poodles are domesticated
Tasselled legs and waists truncated.
They show their shame.

Poor man though cares have shown his tresses
Still delights in Maiden's dresses
Till death called.

No matter what you think of him
Though he knows his hair is then [?thin],
He's still two-balled.*

* or 'Bald' [Gogarty's note]


## [A Poem by Simon Swishback]

To lash our buttocks for a while
Will warm your heart and mine.
My lash is all stout leather,
Yours a pennyworth of twine

But half a dozen strokes or so
May do the trick for me
Then I like any man of sense
Can beat my walnut tree.


## To a Critic

You ask me why my simple fife
Is not tuned seriously to Life.
What bird has ever gloomed his note
For fear of days when he'll be not?
What salmon for its roaring wall
Has ever feared the waterfall?

## SOME MARTELLO TOWER POEMS

### [Murray]

Standing between me and the sea
Our Murray stood and spoke to me
'A sign of summer that you're here'
I answered gazing at the clear
And sea-blue eyes I just came down
To get a breath of air from town
Then added in an undertone
'Won't you have something of your own?

### Carmen Carsonii

Down the Western Avenue,
Leaving Murray's on the right
After Murray's leaves the view,
Castle Carson comes in sight
And on the steps
The master, perhaps
May be seen – of No 2

In the tavern in their beer
First the local fisherfolk,
Navigating without fear
Foaming waves in staves of oak;
Only he
Prefers the sea,
And that salty life austere!

In the tavern peal on peal
Rumble loud the fisherfolk;
They may sit there till they reel
And till Murray's fills with smoke:
But he swims
With waving limbs
And a re-appearing head.

True, his strokes are not divine,
Are not strokes of such high art
As – say, Starkey, yours or mine,
In regattas taking part:
But his skin
And his time in, –
The thermometer and twine!!

Gainst the cruel penile laws
Bidding: veil your yellow hair,
Who but Carson gained applause
For he left his body bare;
To him stript
(And sacred script)
The body more than raiment was.

Yellow in the harvest moon;
Yellow as September corn;
As an ivory handled spoon
(where the ivory is horn);
As a yolk, or
Lump of ocre
Is his perfect plenilune

Ah his brain is now befogged
Since that drowning of his wife!
All his 'λογοι' waterlogged;
Gone is half his naval life;
On the jetty
Now Rossetti
Is not seen in 'glasses' clogged

Never feeling of unrest
Broke the pleasant dream he dreamt,
Only made to be undressed
All his yellow body seemed,
No desire
Of more allure
Stirred or fluttered in his breast

Carson, or for shorter, 'Cars'
Shall thy name be oblivious?
Nay, nay, the sea itself debars,
And the colour of its stones:

The sea with mystic
Change, and cystic
Stones that did invade thine – !

As old Neptune will arrange –
'No part of him that doth fade'
He will suffer a sea change
As the seaside stout purveyed
'Up' in Murray's
Where none hurries
And the tales are rich and strange.


## Carson

He comes down to the sea
With his thermometer in the morning
He undresses slowly, there is no haste,
For all his movements partake of
That leisure which is the tides
We heard that your eyelids are a little [?yellow]
He is browner than the rocks
On which he sits; he has been
A diver in deep seas; he has
Journeyed on through many far waters
He has touched the Muglins


## [McCreedy]

McCreedy sat by the Tower window
At midnight, eating a herring.
And he looked and he saw
the finest pair
Of pants of a man seafaring

'O where are you going you sailor man'
Willie pants like a gas balloon?
I'm going to dampen the hole of my . . . ,
By swimming out under the 'mune'

McCreedy swore and McCreedy swore
Till his swears swore his words to a sword
'And by Merry St George and whole Key Quhair
[?There's not] a hair of it heard' Absurd!

## [McCurdy]

'Methought I saw McCurdy with his sword
Oh! Not the woman! Not the woman, Lord!

SEUMAS O'SULLIVAN
[JAMES SULLIVAN STARKEY]
POEMS

## *[Sandycove Lines]*

O ye who dig for treasure trove
   Amid the rocks of Sandycove,
What rapture could you seize
   One phallic fragment, or unroll
One tender, twilight-litten scroll
   Of Starkey's hazel-trees.

## *Advice to Seumas O'Sullivan*

In dungeons of dark desolation
I, prisoned, peer out from the bars
To thank thee for kind consolation
O thou who add'st light to the stars!
Although I have studied and striven
And fearfully fuddled my brain
But damn little marks was I given
They've stuck me again.

The Fellows of Trinity College
Are painfully matter of fact,
They value not wisdom not [?but] knowledge,
Exacting to have it exact;
And their soul can be but a sparse soul
And sadly constrained their view
Who gaze on the earth through an arsehole
And think they see true

They stick me who stuck me relentless
On many occasions before,
When spirit and body had spent less
And needed less *hydrog Psichon*

Employing the dose as a tonic
And not as specific – but can'st
Thou minister that to a Chronic
We'll make him advanced?

When top of the poplar trees tall [?]
By night o'er the grave of Medea
In poisonous pastures of Colchis
Pursuing the Pharmacopea,
We wandered and squandered in searching
Time precious and found out the root
And who I found then but a birching
Am still in pursuit

Ah, God knows where the stalk is!
It springs not nor buds on the brere
And not where the wanderer's walk is
Who goes by the Mareotic mere:
The stalk of the herb that one uses
To change all the thoughts of the minds
Of those who are 'wooing the Muses'
To medical grinds

I said 'If I may not invite you
To pass whom often you past
Your hearts must be hardened 'in situ'
You know not the first shall be last
If experientia docet
And experientia did'
'How often?' Well, only God knew it
I tried and was chid.'

## *To Stark to leave Rathmines*

To leave Rathmines and come down to the sea
 I would persuade thee, Starke[y], with these lines
So that men won't forget me who got thee
To leave Rathmines
That 'strong ones are gone over it' confines
Thee also if thou would'st consistent be,
To leave the quiet grasses of Rathmines
Here green trees drink the sea-blue air and we

May look on main or mountain when it shines
And it will shine for us if thou'lt agree
To leave Rathmines.


## To Starkey for the Second Coming

When these heavy days are over,
Take a ticket for the train
To where Bank-clerks are in clover
By the soft, seductive Seine.

I can see the footsteps even,
See the skirts to ankles cling;
And above – the heights of Heaven:
Fold on fold and string on string!


## [Invitation to my dear Stark]

He left the lanes of Duke Street with its shawls
And sought Rathfarnham where, through sheets of foam,
Shy traffickers, the laundry lassies come –
And in his breeks undid his corded balls.


## In Loco

When Kochler called a sight it were
For Gods or Yeats had Yeats been there,
Though blind, he would have been appalled
    When Kochler called

We were na fou – with room to spare
We sat like Cardinals installed
But Famine flooded out the 'Qhuair'
    When Kochler called

Old Homer, blind to outward air
Anacreon, both blind and bald
With standing hair had raised a prayer
To their fame forestalled
And Starkey, standing stocious, stare
     When Kochler called


## To Starkey by 'John Eglinton'

Standing aloof in giant droughtiness
Of you I hear, and of your large whiskies
As one whose heart inclines to wantoness
Yet cannot summon courage for the Quays
So you get blind! but then the ale is blent . . .
And Byrne unbottles more than he can give:
Thus sea-born Carson holds your heart content,
McCurdy makes you[?r] smooth-paced verse contrive
So in the books of Lyster there is light;
And more than but *one* use for Vaseline;
When heaven is filled with darkness stars grow bright,
You get the rhythm right from blindness keen
Such singing have you as it once befell
To Orpheus, but he ended up – ah, well!


## [A Letter to Starkey from Dresden]

O you who in the lines we love
Make Sirmio of Sandycove!
Take safely to that dear resort
This freight of verse; and bring to port
My pinnace stuffed, as I opine,
Far down beneath the waterline
With ballast trembling consigned
To beat against your Western Wind
That brings you poesies precise
But pungent with the ancient spice
Which mocks an ear you think rebels
'Gainst your hendecasyllables
And moor it neath St Carson's Mount
Its cargo will discharge account,

You'll find your fillet on the bows —
When you're in Murray's Custom House.

First, from beneath its leaky planks,
Accept, unwaterlogged, my thanks
For song, that could it burst its traces
Had impregnated all the Graces
And made them fain to grace your seaside
And rival Carson — on the leeside

Had you not sung, my song had moved
Reluctantly north as those men hooved
(How aptly headed by McCurdy,
If only were the war more wordy!)
Who, erst, reluctant struck aghast
When ordered up to strike Belfast;
Or as those 'sticky' waves that bear on
The more-than-seasick crew of Charon,
To your fair Isle whose few are manly
And it still rains quotidianly;
Save you and [?*Sinn*] and Starkey,
There [?are] very few now left there larkey
But most would give my lines a welcome
As they had fiercely out of hell come.

Tell me the latest from the Lan'
Who's gone, and who's the coming man
Where a Reviewer Colum calls
The Irish Burns (without the balls)
Where Kettle 'thinks' inside the Church
Lest its priests leave him in the lurch:
But tells outside it many a story
Because he's self-contradictory(!)
Is t' *Pledge-bound Party* speechless, dumb?
Or plays it still the Kettledrum?
And have they left the hazel down
Who erst exploited Hazleton?

Send me a word from that isle spent
In still delightful merriment
As one who nods between the drinks
Half sad to think that still he thinks
Vowing to higher things to climb

Before the sudden: 'Gentlemen, Time!'
Tell me if Maurice Joy's now well
Who brought the cold to Newcastle;
And does he in his bardic feats
Still emulate the end of Keats
(Who, Marvellous!, the Muses sung
Although he hadn't got a lung)
Or seeks he now the loves of Herrick
Adown the docks, behind a derrick;
Or – what the devil does he do?
From him I heard not – scarce from you.

I know that Starkey, lately, squiffy
Rolled down the lea, over the Liffey,
And, wrapped up in his mantle green
(As the translucent Vaseline),
Sent a great Idyll here to me
Reverberate with Kelly's Quay;
And sang a Sailor loud in prose
Who not to sea but Mooney's goes
Where with a jackknife tinct with pitch
He carved a marvellous sandwitch
And proved with pints again, again
The tide in the affairs of men
Which, if one's friend's not inopportune
As surely leads on to: 'Fortune!'
Whereby my soul was so much cheered
That my dear heart said I was beered
Was it not true? Well – I think – barely
The Spirit of Delight comes rarely!

Thank you, my friend, for the delight
Caused by accounts of Christmas Night
When you all let Soracte go –
To Hell! – in altitudes of snow;
And warmed, for many a crackling hour,
The quaint recesses of the Tower
Where not Childe Roland ever came,
But chilvalrous McCurdy lame
Who wore the buskin, not the sock
Of old when he demanded hock;
And lifted from his dismal state
That Oxford man disconsolate.

Write me again, ere time is called,
Some letters to the Weiner Wald
And hear me still apologise
In that I did materialize
And write the raucous rhyme at last
That should have been in days now past
Ported and stamped and sent to sea,
Save for my irregularity!
In many ways I could excuse
These aberrations of the Muse
But now the Porter, beer-bereft,
Mumbles I've but ten minutes left.
You'll see me in a Neptune's day
(If Kepler spells it in that way!)
By which I only 'try to mean'
That in a month I will be seen
And show you: 'Hell – A 'Miracle Play'
By Oliver St. John Gogarty.

## [At Woodenbridge]

I went through woods that glister
Where road with river turns
To find the Tramp's brown Sister
The Baby and the Ferns

## [Your Father's Hat]

Your Father's hat? – Your throat was sair
And when to ease you both of that
I took, descending from the stair,
    Your Father's hat

I meant to purge his mind from care –
You know of course how Rubringat –
And let him get a debonair
    Grandfather's hat.

The weather you'll admit was rare
How soon you healed when I stole that
Sunlight absorber from the air
    Your Father's hat!


## Limited Edition

Thanks for your book of verse which ends
In verse where your wit offends –
For what man has *one hundred* friends?

POEMS CONCERNING DERMOT FREYER

## [Verse Letter to Dermot Freyer
## From Nürnberg]

Dear Freyer, scythed Time has, hang him,
Borne me afar, since at the Langham
Both you, and he whose new-found verse
Is rich, Catullus-like and terse,
And sings in strains each gay lady
Of Les Belles Dames du temps jadis
As did their poet erst in France,
But with more tired elegance. Ah me, a tear
Unborn of Nurnburger beer,
Mantles of eyne as, mantling yours,
That darkened glass your gaze obscures
And makes one waiver in his faith
To think no lady caused the scaith
To eyes that, one night could not choose
But wander from a lady's shoes
To – where no married man should go:
But Lord Christ save us all from woe!
Write me anon a line of grace
From that your proud prostatic place,
A word about yourself and Tancred
Who sang for sons of fathers chancred.
Write to Vienna, be not lax:
This leaves the city of Hans Sachs.

## [A Villanelle of Thanks]

I got a book of verse
In lighter vein from Freyer,
(It wasn't very de-ar,
I didn't disemburse);
A friend can oft amerce
The price of papi-er:
I got a book of verse
In lighter vein from Freyer.

I got a book of verse
He wrote with half an eye,
The other – Misey Die!
He couldn't get it worse!
I don't want to asperse
His spotless Characteer
(Iritis is a curse;
Rheumatic? – very queer).
I got a book of verse
Writ well by Dermot Freyer.
Well, Thamyris was blind
Likewise Maeonides.
One very rarely sees
A poet's eye defined
With all those 'fine frenzies',
(And other little sprees
That one could call to mind:)
Well, Thamyris was blind
Likewise Maeonides!

I got a book of verse
And I was much élate:
But not at that hard fate;
Boys will be – dissipate!
I'd like to ask the nurse.
My fancy dares to scarce,
Though free, emancipate,
To whisper – lips won't purse – !
'How deli – delicate!'


## A Line from Corrymore:
## Cautionary Tale for Casual Guests

When you enter Corrymore
Leave behind you at the door
Any hope that you will find
Much that you have in mind.
Though it calls itself an inn,
This disguise is very thin –
Very thin and quaint and crude;
If you're in a cautious mood

*Don't* be tempted here to stay,
Start your car and speed away;
Many things are very queer
In the house of Dermot Freyer.

First the greeting that you'll get
Ere a timid foot you set
Into lounge to look about you:
Clearly they could do without you;
As indeed they will if you
To the questing eye 'won't do',
Earning some sub-acid stricture –
*Item, THIS* would blot the picture!
O ill-favoured! O uncomely! . . .
Cocktail crazed . . . No, quite *too* 'homely'. . . . .
Loud – and rich beyond belief. . . .
Plaintively too fond of beef. . . .

Such be some that court disfavour:
Yet if you're prepared to brave or
Brush aside odd inquisition,
Seeking *still* to gain admission,
Even so your path to bar,
'Mallaranny isn't far,
There's a fine hotel there: one' –
Pensively persuasive – 'run
Much more capably than this;
It's a chance you shouldn't miss. . . .
You prefer this? . . . Really. . . . Oh,
Well: . . . I wanted you to know . . . '

In the dining-room, at meals,
Sadly scant, our staff reveals
Not one raw-boned lanky lad,
Greasy-dinner-jacket-clad,
Handy Andy, thumb in dish,
Spilling gravy, soup, or fish
Down your neck or in your lap,
As the casual chance may hap.
Girls – *young* girls – here wait and lay
Tables – horror! – bright and gay,
Scorning sombre greys and blacks:
Sometimes . . . *sporting 'shorts' or 'slacks'*!

In the morning when you wake
Cheerily your tub to take,
No neat maid will knock and purr
Softly, 'Your bath's ready, sir':
Unattended you must learn
Gleaming H. and C. to turn,
Humbly bend while your own chaste
Finger-tips plug in the 'Waste'.
(Maybe when you feel the flow
You'll forgive this; these are no
Taps that say that which is not –
'Strange! . . . the hot water here is HOT!'

If in this context, further, note
If by any chance you ask to quote,
'Are baths extra?' one will say
With a smile of mild dismay,
'Holding more enlightened views,
Corrymore would rather choose
Only, only those who *won't*,
Or by daily custom *don't*
Take baths regularly should
For their own and others' good,
Pay *much* more, in that they be
Such unsavoury company.

Unabashed we give you warning –
Heed it well! – if, night or morning,
Drowsily your hand should grope
Under bed, in urgent hope . . .
You'll not find it there! No, no:
Out in the passage you must go:
Here's no bedside cupboard shelf
Harbouring Victorian delph –
Hateful custom! – while at hand
Stares at you your need's demand,
Purposefully obviating
Loathsome task of pot-vacating.

Yet being kind and wordly wise,
Tactfully we recognise
Under certain circumstances
As, e.g., when age advances –

There's the rub, the shining truth!
No excuse, observe, for youth –
Such may be too harsh a test
Sometimes, for a harrassed guest.
So, if cause and plea be stated
Frankly and substantiated,
Special permit's issued: then
Guest (with trophy) smiles again!

## JESTING ABOUT THE SINCLAIR BROTHERS

### To W.A.S.

Your dream of Beatrice Elvery
Your business in old ivory,
Your pachyderm; your spouse
Who trumpets your sagacity –
Thus Nassau Street has come to see
A second Elephant House!

### [Lines addressed to William A. Sinclair]

Oftentimes of you I think
  Sink!
And your vision has appeared,
  Beard!

### Gretta

[?Sink] with his whiskers was
Gazing out through the glass
Through his shop window glass –
  Say what he sees!
Ladies in Nassau Street
  Striving to hide their feet
'Spite of the dirty road
  'Spite of the breeze;
Nurses who wheel a pram: –
Marvel – the Dalkey tram,
Bright as the orient
  Seen through a song
O there is hardly time!
Mark how the beauties climb
Now the whole heaven moves
  Gong upon gong!
How can he seize the whole?
  How can he sate his soul?

No one has ever yet
     Rogered a tram
No; but a drunken drab
     Clipped in a taxi cab –
Harry bemoans the cost?
     Who cares a damn!
Gretta, each syllable,
Soft as a chance [?chancre] fell,
Gretta he whispered,
     And grew unafraid,
Now for a bargain sale
Armour and coat of mail
Selling at half the cost
     Jewel or Jade
What though his balls be hung –
     Has he not heard the gong
     Now is the time to live
     Grasping the spoils
First to the Bailey for
Fodder to feed the whore
Then the Pine Forest or
     Maybe Lamb Doyle's
'Ah, had your prick a price
Then you could make it rise
Well, you can feel my thighs
Will o' the wisp
Late in a taxi both
Grope the way home to Howth

Picture the lewd delight
Out on the hill tonight.


## Nocturne 7.15 pm

He passes from Bailey to Bailey
To Fear from the place he is feared
He dreams of Delight dying daily
And mumbles the fringe of his beard
His eyeballs roll under his glasses:
Ruminant randy and cross
Like a beehive in summer there passes
The bossed but the Boss!

## [On William Sinclair]

Tell me all about the Feast
Given by the one-backed Beast
Was it as he had designed
Fun for him, for you 'a blind'?
Was each guest an entertainer
You were gay but he was gainer.
Did the players bring the plays
Free to him whoever pays?
That's what I imagine you
Found when supping with the Jew
Was the moon a frightful sight
Shining on Argenti Nit?
Did the man that's strong and terse
Grip the meeting in a verse?
Strange it is; but really you
Must give credit to the Jew.
Was there ever yet an elf
Took such interest in himself?
Business done, he drains a bowl
Starts stock-taking in his soul,
Which indecentist exposure
Rather helps his self-composure
And in viciousness and vanity
Bears the lusts of all humanity.
Still with me I'm sure you'll think
There are people worse than Finck
Have you written any verse yet?
Are you on your —— yet?

CLASSICAL THEMES

## *Beyond Hydaspes*

I must be some old hero's Purgatory:
My pulses race and hammer in my arms;
I have a merry courage in alarms,
And, tip-toe, tremble with forgotten glory;
And backs are brittle, and the days are sorry
When men stampede before a woman's charms,
And I sit here, lest local gossip harms
The deathless and the fearless Spirit's story.

Do you think Alexander cared a damn
If men beyond Hydaspes took affront?
With him detracting nations did not count;
But I, when I remember where I am,
It makes me want to take the topless tram
And peuk across the wall at Sandymount.

## *To a Sailor*

Silent Sailor Man, I say!
From the arms of Austria
Shining on your hat I ween
You have in the navy been
Though it makes but few cry 'Cave',
Tell me of the Austrian navy.

Navy – nay! I'm quite erratic –
I meant to say the Adriatic.
Tell me, have you seen the sea grow
Darker down by Monte Negro?
Or have you – to fill the canto –
Sailed the waters of Lepanto?

Did they rise? or were they murkey
Over all the men from Turkey?
For you know 'twas very pleasant

That the Cross should swamp the Crescent:
Thus both you and I and others
Kept the Faith that keeps us brothers.

Well, we'll leave them there in peace
Tell me of the Isles of Greece:
Grow they olive, vine and palm?
Was it boisterous or calm?
Did they make a 'nota bene'
As you passed by Mitylene?

Are there really now in loads
Rhododendrons grown in Rhodes?
Say, which isle would strike a roamer
As the birthplace fit for Homer?
Did you see the isle Calypso
Lived in when she got the slip so?

What would Ajax find amiss
Now in twice-washed Salamis?
Did you in effusive joy
Point and mutter 'there was Troy'?
Did you not with grief and woe
View that archipelago?

But the Sailor turned to me
With a murmur like the sea
When against some rocky straight
It must needs expectorate,
With – 'I don't give' (pardon please)
'A damn for all the Isles of Greece'!

Then I shouted 'let me greet you!
Sailor, I am glad to meet you!
I have longed for one of these
Health-restoring heresies.
I am sick of affectation,
Thank you for emancipation'.

'Yes' he said, 'its rather funny
Why the people waste their money
Seeking Homer, Paul or Pilate
In each ordinary islet –

Looking for heroic spooks
On excursions run by Cook's!'

Ah, his eyes were bluer than
The Mediterranean;
And he looked on Life, a bowl,
Steadily, and drank its whole;
And cared not with his mind at ease,
'A damn for all the Isles of Greece'.

Sailor – but a landsman speaks, –
You are Greeker than the Greeks
It is we are out of joint;
From our fevered touch aroint!
Our indecent souls' exposure
Shrinks before your self-composure.

We brood ever on the Past,
But you sail before the mast;
Time but serves to antiquate
Us, but you are up to date –
And you do not give a damn.
Would you care to leave the tram?

## [Opening lines of Oedipus Rex]

Thebans, my children too, and lateliest born
Of all those generations which date back
To Cadmus in the old time King of Thebes.

## George Moore's Garden Shrine

But do thou take corn
    And a little wine
Going forth adorn
    Quaint Priapus' shrine.
Crown the Lampsascene
    Whose Kingdom (come to us)
Shall be as it has been
    In fervent Lampsacus.

## In Haven

No longer now the Spirit of wonder stirs
Unnoticed now they furl the sails that shine
Over the untold laughter of the brine
And how they fare and where from none avers.
And no one questions now the mariners.
Is that which metes the world found undivine,
An eve without the glories vespertine
A dull grey heaven which no light diapers?

Oh for a word from Colchis promontory!
Some hopeful rumour of a wide renown
Borne to an isle at eve on drooping sail:
The long-lost faces eager with their story.
One little temple decked to bid them hail,
And all the folk to meet them, hastening down.


## [Foreword for a proposed volume, Ditties of No Tone]

Reader, lest you read amiss
Prithee to remember this,
Culture in the height of Greece
Gave us Aristophanes,
Martial in the Roman day,
And Religion Rabelais.
Then pleased if you will not be
Blame your day for our degree,
Your small religion and less culture
And these lesser Times' sepulture.


## [Talassio]

No one knows the Fate that filled it;
Something in their past distilled it,
And the town is called God Willed It
     Where it is not Goodness knows

Seagulls lift on pinions flappy,
And the old men cry Talappy
One might be unduly happy
　　Gone as far as pleasure goes.

'Do not take too much for granted'
Is the song the Mermaids chanted:
But we waded in undaunted
　　Where the best part only shows

'Talassio' was the cry of Congratulation
To the bride in the time of Romulus.
It does not require a great deal of
　　Paralysis to impede the 's'

## [Four Lines of Sappho's Greek]

O Hesperus, that shepherd's back again
All that went straying in the brightening dawn
You bring the sheep, you bring the goats again
Again the mother gathers up her son.

## Good Luck

Nobody knows from whence it comes;
But all men know that it's impartial.
Men of the trumpets and the drums,
Arrows and shot and all things martial,
Because they once men's lives controlled
Are chosen first, like Alexander,
Caesar and Ghengis who enrolled
Embattled ranks and war's grim splendour;
These were Good Luck's embodiment,
Despite the fact that Good Luck left them
Before their end, as if 'twere meant
To mock them ere it had bereft them.
Give me, though far from famous, men
Who, though not necessarily, were plucky
Or even rich, I'll give you then:
'It's better to be born lucky.'

## [Happy and Glorious]

Pindarus said, as I surmise
Twenty five hundred years ago,
'Happiness is the chiefest prize,
Glory, the second of the two.
He who has lighted upon both
And taken both to be his own
Has missed no meed in life. In truth
He has attained the Supreme Crown'

## The Supreme Crown

The mightiest lyrist of them all,
Pindar, declared in his own day
In accents wise and musical –
Keeping the Games before his eyes –
'Happiness is the chiefest prize;
Glory the next; but if one may
Win both of them and hold them down,
He hath achieved the Supreme Crown'.

## [Dialogue]

'My Lord,' said the Singer of Slane,
'I fear I'm becoming inane,
    For ladies vampiric
    Attend on each lyric
And banish the sleep from my brain.'

'Rejoice O you wakeful of brain,
So few to a frenzy attain!
    Now sentiments, Ledwidge,
    Will come to your head which
Could hardly have come to you sane.'

'But what of the maidens severe
Who out of the plaster appear?
   And an eye I discern,
   Wherever I turn,
That drives me to madness with fear?'

'Now really your fancy obtuse is –
The manifold maidens are Muses,
   And the Eye don't you follow
   Belongs to Apollo
Who searches the soul and accuses,
Whom lethargy always accuses.'


## 'Hesperus, Thou Bringer of Good Things'

—Sappho

Now twilight comes and with it blooms,
   Where no cloud moves and heaven is still
And all its wider realm resumes,
   A yellow, starry daffodil,
That star whose whispering name to us
Is lonely, lovely Hesperus.

More than two thousand years ago
   'Twas called the Bringer of Good Things
By one who surely ought to know
   Whose voice of love forever sings;
It brought the sheep back to the fold
And led them with its leaves of gold.

And now a dearer eye than hers
   Who sang of love in Mitylene,
Looks where that love lamp never stirs,
   And all the west is apple green;
And thinks – Oh, if she thinks of me
A Bounty Bringer it will be!

For she can sing, though not with words
   Or longings from the pent-up lyre:
Her whole sweet shape with grace accords
   Like Hesperus made one with fire:

Eyes, lips and hands; but that's not all,
Her very limbs are lyrical.

Asleep is the all-seeing sun,
    And on comes now the ambrosial night;
O Hesperus, make two hearts one
    Whose eyes in your soft beams unite,
My Star of Hope, because you are
The Evening and the Morning star!


## An Epical Tale

Here is an epical tale
Here are fabulous things
Brought within reach to hail
Out of the old, remote,
Heroic, perilous pale,
And mythological springs;
Leaving no room for doubt,
Telling the same old story,
How with adventurous heart
The resolute, lonely-souled,
Confident human creature,
Combated and controlled,
Recoiled, defied, out-fought
The chainless forces of Nature;
And lawless things were tamed.
Fame is approval of human good
Totally or finely understood
Therefore of these men here
Millions have praised the merit
Because they have brought them near
To naked God in the spirit:
What is it, spirit or will,
That moves the limbs of us men
For a little while; and then
Leaves; and the limbs are still?
The strange self-moving thing,
Master of things that move,
That leaps from a timeless Spring
And beats with a heart of love.

## *To Catullus*

You must not think none ever knew
The torture that she meant to you
Who held you on Love's wrack.
How could one sympathise before
He met just such a lady whore
And nymphomaniac?
How can the sheets of silk excite
A lover of the dangerous night?
How can she be content
When to the murderous lanes and streets
Where she unprivileged competes,
She knows the dark descent?
What are your songs to oaths she's known,
Released at length, when trunks are down?

The muttering navvy staggers home,
She reads her praise in curses.
What is your hair pomaded then
To maddening breaths of reasty men?
What to the low and settling grunts
She hears and shivers yet confronts,
Are all your trickling verses?
Where are the floors and rugs to beat
The cobbles of Fishamble Street,
Or lawns, Fumbally Lane?
Can ritual of coaxed-up fire
Match Manhood's earthquake of desire?
A mannikin match men?
Where can she look for such content
As that she finds, when bruised and spent,
She tells herself her life is bent
To help the unspoiled poor?
Where is the powder or cold cream
To match the two days growth of him
Whose chin her soft cheek tore?

Oh, face the knowledge now nor fret;
'Tis nothing to the long regret
By which attempts will be beset
To change in middle age

A woman when, with one excuse
For good, she lets herself run loose
And makes the town her stage.


## Locusts

The obscene insects throng the air,
Their swarms put out the eye of day;
Parnassus Hill they first waylay,
Stripping its groves till all is bare.
The spirits of old who wander there,
Unarmed against such swift decay,
Trust that the two Peaked Hill will stay
When all is done that locusts dare.
The legions of these pests beslime
All that they touch, but hear them screech!
They would transmit their locust speech,
The squawk that rhythm lacks and rhyme,
And brings within the common  reach
The Hill that very few can climb.

RELIGIOUS THOUGHTS

## Samain

*(The thirty first of October to the first
of November: the Eve of the
Celtic New Year)*

This is the night of all the year
That we may harry Faeryland;
But if its chiefs do not appear
To guard its gates and take command,
Don't think they are not well aware
Of all attacks we may have planned.
We must not be deceived, for they
Defend it in a different way.

A way more subtle than the dawn
That fades and fades, and all is light!
Or as soft weather acts upon
The mind that is all set for fight:
A dewfall of the will. Anon
It's all around us in our plight;
For Faeryland is guarded well
By magic and by many a spell.
And Faeryland has a time of its own
That makes immortal denizens:
Nothing therein is overblown;
And even space itself extends
So that its hosts can muster down
In hollow hills; and yet it lends
Scope that they fill, and guardians be
Of the Great Land Beneath the sea.

For long ago Amairgin gave
To us the surface of the earth;
The Danaans that Beneath the Wave
Where all delights have being and birth;
But woe betide one if he crave
To go back from the Land of Mirth
Because he does not understand
Time has no hold on Faeryland.

## [Idea for the Beginning of a Hymn]

The occidental ocean of the sky
Flames, and the west is all a wake of fire.
Against the purple isles inaudible
In golden foam the light breaks –


## The Song of the Cheerful
## (but slightly sarcastic) Jaysus

I'm the queerest young fellow that was ever heard
My mother's a Jew; my Father's a Bird
With Joseph the Joiner I cannot agree
So 'Here's to Disciples and Calvary.

If any one thinks that I amn't divine,
He gets no free drinks when I'm making the wine
But have to drink water and wish it were plain
That I make when the wine becomes water again.

My methods are new and are causing surprise:
To make the blind see I throw dust in their eyes
To signify merely there must be a cod
If the Commons will enter the Kingdom of God

Now you know I don't swim and you know I don't skate
I came down to the ferry one day & was late.
So I walked on the water & all cried, in faith!
For a Jewman it's better than having to bathe.

Whenever I enter in triumph & pass
You will find that my triumph is due to an ass
(And public support is a grand sinecure
When once you get the public to pity the poor.)

Then give up your cabin & ask them for bread
And they'll give you a stone habitation instead
With fine grounds to walk in & raincoat to wear
And the sheep will be naked before you'll go bare.

The more men are wretched the more you will rule
But thunder out 'Sinner' to each bloody fool;
For the Kingdom of God (that's within you) begins
When you once make a fellow acknowledge he sins.

Rebellion anticipate timely by 'Hope,'
And stories of Judas and Peter the Pope
And you'll find that you'll never be left in the lurch
By children of Sorrows and Mother the Church.

Goodbye, now, goodbye, you are sure to be fed
You will come on My Grave when I rise from the Dead
What's bred in the bone cannot fail me to fly
And Olivet's breezy – Goodbye now Goodbye.


## [To Rabelais, the fornicating Friar]

How can we reach though sail be bent
Beyond the horizon's verge
Those isles of your astonishment, Panurge?


## [Celibacy]

Sex-scorners and self-appeasers
Of whom no maiden dreams;
The gray, gelatinous geysers
Of monks in their gay Thelemes.


## [Taking the Name]

The plainer Dubliners amaze us
By their so frequent use of 'Jayshus!'
Which makes me entertain the notion
It is not always from devotion.

## Why

I watched the constellated towers
　　Tier upon tier in azure hung;
Below where windows filled with flowers,
　　And streets bemerded by dogs' dung.

Why should the minds that build in air
　　Broad and unbounded as the skies,
Condemn the straining dogs to bear
　　A life that turns the streets to sties?


## Christ and the Money-Changers

*(On seeing the Church on Fifth Avenue at
48th Street sold for commenial purposes)*

To set mankind a clean example
Christ scourged the cashiers from the fane
But their revenge was sly and simple:
The money-changers bought the Temple
The hard bright eyes are back again.


## Jonah and the Whale

Doubt would oftentimes assail
Me, a youth, about the Whale,
When I feared I had no *bona*
*Fides* in the Whale and Jonah

There are very many species
On the Ocean's superficies
Of those large, marine mammalia
Called Cetacea or Whalia,
Which could give an exhibition
Of extremes of deglutition.
Yes; a whale a man could swallow
And eject him from the hollow

Of his tummy if ingestion
Interfered with his digestion.
Jonah's Whale, it seems, was loath;
But I've got to swallow both.

So my youthful faith was shaken
Until I was duly taken,
To undo this mental twist,
To an old Psychiatrist,
To a man with mind so supple
That my little boyish scruple
Touching Jonah and the Whale
Could no more my faith assail.

'First,' he said, 'our callow youth
Is too anxious for truth.
"What is truth?" asked jesting Pontius.
What's the Whale but the Subconscious
Of poor Jonah? And the "Whale"
Is what will engulf us all
If we cannot sublimate it.
Jonah managed to abate it.
When he spent that lost week-end
In his Whale. You see, my friend,
In the reign of Jeroboam
There were queer things in the foam.'

I wished my shaky faith remained:
Some things are better unexplained.


## [Strong Men]

Strong men are they who guide their ships
Through darkness by the steadfast stars;
Words come not easily to the lips
Of such stout deep-sea mariners;
But these who bridge the sea-cleft lands
Do praise the Lord by work of hands.

He gives them courage for the deep
And Faith to bear them bravely on;
They do not let that talent sleep

But watch until the harbour's won.
His thunders are their organ stave,
His lightnings light their awful nave.

They praise the Lord who made a path
For them who go down to the sea:
To save them from the After-wrath
He takes hard work for piety;
Nor scorns to stoop to soothe the cares
Of men whose hands and hearts are prayers.


## For As Much As

*('For as much as the pearl is a product which
from an inward trouble and from a fault
produces purity and perfection, it is preferred, for
in nothing does God so much delight as in
tenderness and in luster born of trouble and
repentance'. From the Persian.)*

Blame not the inward restlessness,
The doubt or even the despair,
Those portions of divine distress
That every spirit elect must bear;
That is the way Perfection grows:
An irritation in the shell,
And, lo, the luminous pearl glows.
This law is inescapable:
Before the luster comes the goad.
Take comfort, for the truth is plain,
For every being the road
That rounds Perfection winds through pain.


## Then and Now

The gods have left Olympus Hill,
    The gods who walked with men of old,
Encouraged those of right good will,
    Punished the proud and the overbold;
    The nymphs from oaks and streams are fled
Since the Voice shouted, 'Pan is dead!'

When Europe lay enslaved and prone
  Under the legions' conquering boot,
A Babe was born, not by a throne,
  But starlit in a herdsman's hut;
And every slave rose from the sod
Filled with the hope of seeing God.

Now slaves are born without a soul,
  The individual is 'purged,'
Men only live as one great whole,
  Free Will is in a monster merged,
Men may no more be free or great,
The only great thing is the State.

And with this automatic man
  Goes the sly sophists' subtile creed
That puts restraint beneath a ban,
  And dignity of word and deed;
And not divinity but sex
Informs this animal reflex.

Better the dryads in the wood,
  Better the naiads in the stream,
The gods of old, who helped the good,
  Than this new godless, hopeless theme
Of bestial tenets which disgrace,
Degrade, and bind the human race.

POLITICAL POEMS

## *Wie Geht es Gagenhofer?*

King of the Iron men
In shining armour dight
Where did your heart look when
Whelmed in the roaring night,
The travail of things transferred
Storms of the splendidest springs?
Whom did you seek full armed
Whom but the men who could sing?
Child of the land of laws
Son of the lyric land –
In the mid battle a pause
A grasp of the straining hand;
What have the fates to offer
How goes it Gagenhofer?


The bard is of the heights
He sees when all is blind
The heart of passion lights
The prophesying mind,
The sea heaves up, the land
With ruinous guns is rocked,
What in the dark is scanned,
What in the future locked?
What have the fates to offer


How goes it Gagenhofer?
To banded nations rage
In Earth and land and sky
Death is the equipage
Lovers of women die.
A blood-red bird careens
Through chaos unperturbed
Suns in his plumes he screens
When shall his flight be curbed?
What have the fates to offer
How goes it Gagenhofer?

To wonderful goals impelled
The legions bleeding strain
Is Energy dispelled
Can Life flow forth in vain?
What have the fates to offer
How goes it Gagenhofer?

Of old the legend ran
The soldier far renowned
That Macedonian man
When for the battle bound
Brought with him for the song who sang
Of Thetis' child the wrath
And how the archer rang
And none withheld his path;
Who shall against you bring
A word time disabuses?
An Apollonian King
Who counsels with the muses
What have the fates to offer
How goes it Gagenhofer?

By rhythm the gods are bound
The fates in the skein are noosed
The soul is kin to sound
And first by sound was loosed.
Four million march in time
To the sound of the guardian song
Who breaks or binds the Rhyme
A Nation's soul keeps strong
What have the fates to offer
How goes it Gagenhofer?

May no Tiresian word
Plower who plows for Peace
Whose Ploughshare is the sword
Whose terrible gifts are these:
Courage the first of things
Logic the word of god
Law like a song that sings
Equal and just, unaw'd, –
With doubt your hope forbode
Doom with ambiguous breath

The breakers of the road
That leads to life past death –
What have the fates to offer
How goes it Gagenhofer?

Remote in the west we dream
Aloof from springs newborn
What in your East shall gleam?
What stars rise with your morn?
What has your warsong roused?
Send of your heart housed speech
A word we may keep heart housed
Here till the end's in reach.
Poet our land is fair;
Rich fields with beauty mated
The fairest fields that e'er
Injustice devastated.
What have the fates to offer
How goes it for Gagenhofer?

## [To Lord Dunsany]

While [?] dangers you have faced before
When you took ship and sailed afar
And fixed your bayonet in war
And stood to charge against the Boer!
Have you not heard the lion's roar
That shook your ground when all your care
Was but for light to strike him fair?
And Plugstreet Wood: your point-blank scar:
When Law degrades itself by law
That all the humble country scorns
And by misuse of force suborns
You to behold the Farce of Awe,
Remember that your lightest page
Had filled a far more tragic stage.

## [To a German complaining of the Occupation of the Rhineland after 1918]

To have the black troops on the Rhine
Is bad enough; but Hans
If you were ruled by 'English swine'
You'd have the Black and Tans.


## [To Erskine Childers]

That dear, old, chivalrous, lean, Spanish Knight
Who armed in peace-time tilted at a mill
Had Sancho stout, who wondered how his fill
Could be obtained from such fantastic fight,
Behind him as a servant to requite
For staunch obedience to his Master's will
But you reverse relation, Erskine chil
And urge your leader on in woeful plight!
Drive him no more! The rueful countenance
Is out of fashion with the times for that.
Try to be loyal to one land at least;
And let him rest his bravely wielded lance
Let me have men about me who are fat
Now that the time comes to spread out the feast!


## Don't hang Hitler

Don't hang Hitler; he'll be hanging
When the bombs shall cease from banging
And the reconstructions start:
Goering, too shall do his part,
(Less obscene about the waist),
Mixing tons and tons of paste;
On a scaffold then shall caper
Hitler, and be hanging – paper!

## To Ireland Befooled

Land of the low green, rounded hills, land of the streaming plains,
Has Freedom brought you graver ills than bondage brought you pains?
If you have lost your ancient joy and pride in being proud
What matters who mints the alloy that circles with the crowd?
If you have lost the glance of those who lived so madly grand:
The quick intolerance of foes, to friends the flinging hand,
Then more is lost than gained for you and freedom brings but in
Leave to hob nob Fildy Rue and mendicant O'Lynn.

Great kings once lived beyond the Boyne and bards belonged to kings
Who heard the Hundred Battle join and told it to the strings;
How Niall brought the captives home and what far lands were flamed
When back the legions reeled on Rome; are those men's spirits tamed?
And nothing left us now but laws for equal lots all round
Enthroning Mediocrity which moves without a sound?
If for the Gael nobility has now become a slur,
God send the Great Earl back again who waits beneath Lough Gur.

## Freedom

Dublin was a goodly town,
And, O, but she was great
When Harry pushed the pedals down,
And Dinny threw the weight;
She had a gallus group of sons
As good as, man and boy,
The hardy lads that Helen saw
From the West tower of Troy.

But now I see a chestless crowd
With cigarette on lip,
Assemble where the shouts are loud
To buy a betting slip;
They never wore a boxing glove,
Or buffeted the sea.
Why should they? Is it not enough
That Ireland is free?

Now Dublin's full of cinemas,
The property of Jews,
Depicting Yankee 'Sugar Das'
Or heroes of the stews,
With moral made to show that 'Love'
Exempts from honesty.
What matter, is it not enough
That Ireland is free?

Ah, free to go to College Green
To hear the demagogues;
To go to cinemas obscene:
At evening to the dogs;
But is it free to claim again
Its ancient dignity?
A Dago's at the head of things;
But Ireland is free.


## A Reply to Crazy Jane

Where are the myriad hosts who bowed
Before the kings of little sense,
The madmen quarrelsome or proud,
Obeyed with Death for recompense?
Our king's a modern king, and hence
If but a lewd Catullus sing,
He does it at his own expense!
To save us all, God save the King.

The kings of other days were wise
And sorted queens behind a fence:
King Solomon kept large supplies;
And Kubla parked them round in tents;
But envy frowns, and frenzy glints,
And, had our Monarch half a fling,
Would print it in the daily prints;
To save us all, God save the King.

The hosts remain; but past the bourne
Where none pays cesses, tithes, or rents,
The kings are gone, save one at Doorn,

Who is a king at all events!
But now the ranters all are gents,
The shoe-blacks turn from shoe-blacking,
And their black looks are common sense.
To save us all, God save the King!

Now none dare spend a soul in war;
So Chivalry is past its tense,
Where all elaborate manners are
And the mailed hand's extravagance;
Gone is the proud and dissolute glance,
The marbled lawn and money string;
A contrite heart's a great advance;
To save us all, God save the King!

Remove the king and what remains
But all the weary competence
Of Kiplings, Jews and common men's
Utopias and Presidents;
And 'Safety First' and 'cent per cents',
For, if you bring the mob, you bring
In Glory's disestablishments:
To save us all, God save the King!

ON DRINKING

## *[Changing Beer]*

Goodbye to Murray mild, my cheer
Is changed to Nürenberger beer!

## *Sounds*

There are some sounds that do me good
And bring brave sights to me,
And like a merry interlude
Sustain a tragedy.
One sound is from the water borne,
Another from the plain:
The long blare of a deep-sea horn,
The bright shout of a train;
Small birds that practice in the glens
Before the light wins through;
The brave cock bragging to his hens
With 'Cock a doodle do!'
The coulter's clink before the team
And, when I climb the hills,
The tinkle of a two foot stream
That sounds like little bells;
The cooper singing as he thrums
His barrels to the tune –
As if they all were kettle drums –
'There'll be good drinking soon.'
And when they are too full for sound
The next note that I praise
Is when a friend puts up his round
And murmurs, 'Happy Days!'

## *Sounds*

*[an earlier version]*

There are some sounds that do me good
And certain sights to me

Are like a merry interlude
In some dull tragedy
One sound is from a distance borne,
Another from the plain;
The loud blare of a long sea-horn,
The bright shout of a train;
The small birds practise in the glens
Before the light wins through;
The brave cock bragging to his hens
With Cock-a-doodle-doo!
The coulter's clank behind the team;
And when I climb the hills
The tinkle of a two-foot stream
That sounds like fairy bells.
The singing cooper as he thrums
And belts his staves as if
His barrels were all kettle drums
And all the sounds they give.
And when too full for further noise,
I do not fail to mark
The little squeak a bottle gives
When Fanning pulls the cork.
But p'raps the pleasantest of sounds
Before Life's shining shelf,
Is all the talk between the rounds
That interrupts itself.


## [Driving to the Ward]

When you and I drove to the Ward
O but the air was bonnie!
Outspread the undulating sward
The clouds hung large and sunny

Those gorgeous galleons rode still
All in the deep blue glory
Whose [?wreckage] brings the daffodils
And Spring's delightful story

We had a thought between us blent
Our aim a destination

And that is why the motor went
With such a festivation

The eye with seeing is not filled
The heart's not filled with thinking
The only thing we could be stilled
And that was done by drinking.


## [What might have been —]

These were the drinks we might have had,
The [indecipherable]
These were the nights — and all too sad
The Doctor might have called.

It would have been the same thing now
Methought, but with this gain to me
You cannot milk a buried cow
But might have milked her, see!

Or, in the words of that pure ghost
Who sang of Arthur impotent —
It's better to have loved and lost
Than never to have spent

So, since it's past, and I am not
(The Time is always out of joint
For when you feel you'd like a pot
You cannot get a pint!)


## A Large One deep in the Lamb Doyle

'O Father I hear the sound of guns.
O say what that may be?'
'Tis a cabbage, my boy, I had for lunch,'
And he steered for the WC.

## The One Before Breakfast

*(Spoken extempore in the bar of the*
*Shelbourne Hotel)*

The One before Breakfast
Alone in the Bar,
Will slide down your neck fast,
And ease the catarrh
Your glass with its end up
Will scarce leave your jaws,
When your belly will send up
A round of applause.

If Dawn is distressful,
The Morning's far worse
When they who were less full
Call drinking a curse
And ask you to chuck it.
You certainly shall
When you kick the bucket.
'A large Catch-me-Pal!'

## In the Snug

I drank with George; & called
                            The men
Of old, the Bards who could
                            importune
The Muses, to repair again
With words, the outrages
                            of Fortune.

## [A Whiskey Below Par]

Old Anacreon
  Was the wine's best poet;
Had he Inisowen,
  How his verse would show it!

*Gogarty's note: Inisowen, of course, is Irish Whiskey*

## [Bona Fides]

Long ago we had ambitions
– None of them Academicians' –
Such as suit a simple mind:
Leap a stream or drink a pint;
And our friends had hopes in keeping,
(Ah, 'by brooks too broad for leaping')
That our names would bring no scorn
To the town where we were born;
That, at last, we might be buried
Where we both were born and married,
When we shuffled off our coils,
Aided by the Lamb (of Doyle's).
Thus we made each wilding lyric
Somewhat sweeter than satiric;
Spending spirit on the air:
Carefully only not to care,
Now that spirit has preserved us,
For, since Wiley Yeats observed us,
Death has closed his Seven Day Portals . . .
Are we bona fide Immortals?

No one put in our old bans,
Cocktails on the list of wines.


## [Drink]

What ran to headward when I fell;
What gave me points unanswerable;
What shot me from the Grand Hotel?
                                'Another!'


## Hiking

I

At 'The One-eyed Man's'

Drink to me with thine only eye
While it is wholly thine;

Or leave the glass within the cup
And I'll not ask for wine.

The thirst that from the bowl doth rise
To some brings second sight;
But only those with single eyes
Have bodies filled with light.

II

Here we are at Pubis Regis
Where King Stephen doffed his breeches
Saying as he took them down:
'This is worth more than a crown.'

III

Dearest, do not read the signboard
Of this pleasant public-house;
Rather gaze at the half timbered
Gabled stories roofed with moss.
Here the King and Tanner parted: –
Manners in those days were slack –
Hence, the banner retroverted;
Hence, the 'Ill Wind Inn,' this shack!

III

*[Another Version]*

## *The Ill Wind Inn*

See if you can read the signboard
Of this ruined public house;
And then gaze at the half timbered,
Gabled stories roofed in moss:
Here the King and Tanner parted –
Manners in those days were slack –
Hence, his banner retroverted;
Hence. THE ILL WIND INN this shack.
(Nor trust those ages that do coarsely sing
The farting tanner and familiar King.)

Herrick

### IV

Is this the way to Melbury Bub?
Is there such a place at all?
I don't know — and here's a rub;
If we wakened at a pub;
Not to mention miles to trudge —
Would there be a maid to call
Us, or would I get a nudge
From you lying 'neist the wall?

### V

Look! my Dear, it's Steeple Bumford!
What is it that makes you blush?
Hiking would be all discomfort
If we took it with a rush.
Sit, lest dusty roadways tire . . .
Sit in shade to hear the thrush:
Since it keeps my knees much drier
Sit down on your makintosh.

### VI

Waiter, if I call for sodas
Say you've only lemonade:
Ere you bring it first unload as
Stiff a whiskey as they made;
Here's a pound to pay the piper:
Don't forget me: watch your steps,
While the lady sees her hiker
Rise to higher things on Schweppes.


## The Wondrous Ties of Bartenders

The wonderous ties of bartenders
Can take you fast and far
From where the folk of both genders
Sit hunched about the bar;
And you can sail on greenish seas

In yachts with purple sails
Where all beyond the slanting trees
Is innocent of gales.
But, oh, what tropic storms arise
When all the sea awakes
And lifts in foam and multiplies
If one a cocktail shakes!
Then waves arise and swirl around
And every palm tree dips,
While, forced to fly each puffing sound,
The sea is cleared of ships.
Then there are geometric ties
With lozenges and squares;
And ties with birds and butterflies;
But none of these compares
With ties by the Abstractionists,
For, if you gaze therein,
They will abstract with subtile twists
The alcohol from gin;
And you must say, 'The Same Again'
And say it o'er and o'er
Until you leave all upright men
And sink upon the floor.
Pink, yellow, blue and greenery –
Oh, Silver-shaking guys,
If you would stick to scenery,
I'd praise you for your ties.


## The Triumph of 'Time!'

I rode in triumph through New Mexico
At sundown when the purple deserts glow.
Indignantly the dusky beauties scorned
The eye that looked straight on and never turned.
I would be ruling still that glorious clime
But for – and suddenly – 'Time, Gentlemen, Time!'

## [Joyful Bondage]

House me with books on which to pore
Beside an old gray bonded store
Whose walls are so familiar grown
That they to nobody are known
Whose windows dark and deeply set
Suggest a monk-house in Thibet
And passers-by are unaware
Of all the joy that's bonded there.

MEDICAL MEDITATIONS

## [An Invitation]

Oh, leave the prostate in its press,
The Peter in his study,
And seek this Isle of green access,
Where everything is ruddy.

## Song
## [Medical Dick and Medical Davy]

The first was Medical Dick
   The Second was Medical Davy
The First had a Bloody Big Prick
   The Second had Buckets of Gravy
To show – To show – to show what medicals are.

II

Then out spoke Medical Dick
   To his colleague Medical Davy
'I'd swap my bloody big Prick
   For you with your buckets of gravy
To show etc

III

'Steady Medical Dick'
   Said Sturdy Medical Davy
'There's very little value in a prick
   When you haven't got the passage of the gravy
To show etc

IV

'Every bullock were a bull
   But for the little matter of a ballocks
If your prick can keep the women full
   You'll find they'll never grumble at its small looks
To show etc

## *Aide-memoire for Anatomy*

'I'm going to swerve,'
Said the lingual nerve.
'Well be sure you avoid,'
Said the pterygoid,
'Myself and the ramus
When passing between us.'
'Oh, you'll be bucked,'
Said Wharton's duct,
'When you land in the kip
At the tongue's top tip.'

## *[Desirable Diet]*

Fluid, farinaceous, fish;
Then a chicken in a dish;
Then to mutton, then to beef;
Then from all rules there is relief!'

## *Sindbad*

On 14 June 1906 Gogarty wrote to James Joyce, saying that the American edition of *Sindbad* was out. It ran to 230 stanzas. He quoted one of the stanzas (it appears in somewhat altered form in the NLI version, p. 441). As most of this long poem has been lost – it was not published, as far as is known; the letter may have been a leg-pull – it has seemed apposite to quote relevant passages from Gogarty's *Tumbling in the Hay* (1939). These open with the Dublin surgeon Sir Thomas Myles patrolling the wards in his white coat with his students in tow. A manuscript version of fourteen stanzas, 'The Voyage of the Morbid Mariner', not in Gogarty's hand, is also included here, from the Harry Ransome Research Center's holdings. VI is a version sent by Gogarty in a letter of 6 November 1923 to Lady Lavery, from the collection of Guy St. John Williams.

I

[IN SITU]

We in our white coats followed, one on each side, like two acolytes. At the last bed near the window at the end of the ward he paused, and, taking down the patient's chart which we had written up, read aloud the following notes to his class, which consisted of about twenty medicals and a strange, gigantic doctor from Cripple Creek in a dickey, and top boots under his trousers, who was over here in order to do some post-graduate work:

| | |
|---|---|
| *Name* | Sam Simmons. |
| *Age* | Fifty-two. |
| *Occupation* | Sailor. |
| *Address* | Whaling ship *Spitzbergen*. |
| *Diagnosis* | Tertiary syphilis: aneurysm right popliteal space; gumma of nasal septum. |

This unfortunate mariner in the last bed by the window was the butt of the cruel wit of Dublin. Patients take a pleasure in chaffing each other, but the chaff can be deadly on occasion. It was our duty to stop it, but unless one slept in the patients' ward there was no way of putting an end to it. And we were uncomfortable enough housed where we were without sleeping with the diseased. Thoughtlessness can give rise to cowardly and cruel jokes. One morning when I came in unexpectedly I heard a muffled shout from under the bedclothes:

'Eh, Sindbad,
Was the last hatch you were in bad?'

Gross guffaws hailed the sally with delight.

I spoke out. 'If this goes on I will read out aloud the diseases from which every man in this ward is suffering and we shall see who will be much better or worse than the sailor.' It would have availed little to ask the sailor who were his persecutors. The sailor with false loyalty to blackguardism would not give them away.

Sir Thomas was beginning:

'We have here a distinguished citizen who went down to the sea in ships and faced the watery wastes in pursuit of his business, which was the pursuit of whales. Many of us have pursued game of one kind or another, but who of us can say that he has hunted a larger or more dangerous quarry? And yet, gentlemen, this man here before us has faced the roaring seas and the biting blast. He has heard the thunder of the breaking ice and he has braved the terrors of the Arctic night. Perched aloft in his cockpit, those eyes have scanned vaster horizons than we have scanned, while he described an arc with his body as the heaving waters swung the ship with him in his precarious position. Picture him to yourselves, gentlemen, as he watched and waited until at last the monster, the physeter, Nature's largest living thing, appeared. He has seen the great whale shouldering off the seas as he comes to the surface; and regardless of the inappropriatness, perhaps, of the epithet to the gentler sex, he shouts, 'Thar she blows!'

'Is not that right, Sam?' Sir Thomas inquired not unkindly of the fascinated able-bodied seaman, who was cheered to find himself the object of so much interest and to see his profession placed in such romantic light.

'All hands on deck! And then, gentlemen, Samuel comes sliding down from the cockpit in his haste to stand to the great sea-beast. Ah, but, gentlemen, the shore has its dangers as great as, if not greater than, the deep. Deadly are the ways of the deep, but the ways of women can be deadlier than the sea: some visit to the docks of a coastwise city, some dalliance, some little sport with Amaryllis in the shade, some entanglement with Neæra's hair, and the harm was done, and the lurking principle entered in then that appears on the surface twenty years later. Show us that right knee of yours, laddie!' Turning him on his face, Sir Thomas delicately felt the aneurysm. '"Thar she blows!"' He made a warning grimace. The case was beyond hope. 'Sliding down a rope, gentlemen, or climbing up one will, when the sheaths of the blood-vessel are atheromatous – you perceive what atheroma means, doctor?' he asked amid much laughter, turning to the enormous man from Cripple Creek, – 'cause this distension and the thinning of the arterial wall which we call an aneurysm.' The sunny-headed, dusty giant blushed, nodded his head, and drove his dickey out over his low waistcoat. More laughter. So much for that. But we didn't laugh long. At least Birrell [a fellow medical student] didn't. 'The history of this case is perhaps best expressed as my distinguished clinical clerk has expressed it, in lofty rhyme.' Sir Thomas produced – where he got them from no one could tell, but they were undoubtedly Birrell's – a piece of paper with these verses:

'O what a wondrous paradox!
A sailor who escaped the rocks
Was wrecked by going down the docks
    When safe ashore;
And brought to light a hidden pox
    And Hunter's sore.

'Ah, did he, when he weighed his anchor,
Weigh all the consequence of chancre?
For if he did he would not hanker . . .
   . . .'

'You gave him those verses,' Birrell growled at me.
'I did not, I assure you,' I whispered back.

'The diagnosis here is not in doubt, nor the ætiology, as it might have been in Falstaff's case, when he invoked "A gout on this pox, or a pox on this gout." We may exclude the gout. Now the question is, what to do for this poor fellow who has got what is known in Dublin as "the bad disorder." He makes no bones about telling us that he got it. He cannot remember where. "A little unremembered act of kindness and of love." [from Wordsworth, 'Lines composed a few miles above Tintern Abbey':

> . . . that best portion of a good man's life
> His little, nameless, unremembered acts
> Of kindness and of love]

He is more straightforward than the clerical gentleman who asked me, "Could you get this in a water-closet?" "You could, my friend, but it's a damn dirty place to take a lady."
'It is astonishing how accurately Shakespeare enumerated the signs and symptoms – there is a difference between signs and symptoms – of syphilis. You remember in *Timon of Athens*, when Timon is addressing those two pieces of light flesh, Phrynia and Timandra, his direction to them,

> 'Consumption sow
> In hollow bones of men; strike their sharp shins
> And mar men's spurring. Crack the lawyer's voice,
> That he may never more false titles plead,
> Nor sound his quillets shrilly: hoar the flamen,
> That scolds against the quality of flesh
> And not believes himself: down with the nose,
> Down with it flat; take the bridge quite away
> Of him that, his particular to foresee,
> Smells from the general weal: make curl'd-pate ruffians bald;
> And let the unscarred braggarts of the war
> Derive some pain from you: plague all;
> That your activity may defeat and quell
> The source of all erections.'

Strike their sharp shins. Shakespeare must have known that the nodes on the front of the shins are a tertiary phenomenon. They say that he had it himself and that he was fumigated for it in London. It might explain his early death at fifty-two, and the hemiplegic handwriting of his signatures.'
To some whose faces looked shocked, he said: 'There was never a good man yet who hadn't a touch of the pox or of tuberculosis. There's damn little harm in an old Dublin pox.' The effect of this on the patient

was instantaneous. His swollen face gleamed, and an icy light like winter sunshine enlivened for a second his bleak eyes.

'Now as regards treatment: our gifted friend here has composed a mnemonic:

'Rub in blue butter
And drink the mercury in bumpers
Until you stutter.'

Now blue butter, which is mercurial ointment, might easily be found too strong for some skins. I would suggest the oleate of mercury.

Again he consulted his bit of paper –

'The glands adjoining your masseter
Are salivating by the litre;
And when you sail your love to meet her,
    In boat or barge,
Your sheets will do for the Blue Peter:
    Unguent. Hydrarg.!'

Sir Thomas put his arm on Birrell's shoulder, and with, 'Keep merrie, laddie, as long as you can,' left the ward.

Now I knew that nothing would convince Birrell that I hadn't given him and his mnemonics away. I couldn't have done so, as I told him, even had I wished, for the parts of 'Sindbad the Sailor' which he showed me did not contain any prescriptions, but were directed to certain phenomena of the sea, and to certain hallucinations of the whaler's crew,

'Where weighed Atlantics lift and pour
In thunder down on Labrador,
They heard, beyond a din and roar
    Like Thor's great mallet,
The calling of the Coal Quay Whore
    Which has no palate.'

There was reference to certain symptoms that were experienced by the whale who thoughtlessly swallowed the sailor. As far as I remember, they referred to the colouring effect of calomel on infants' stools, which turn green, and a suggested origin for Greenland from the effect of the mercury in Sindbad's system on the innocent cetacean.

'Where that cetacean defæcated
A continent was concentrated

From all the food evacuated,
    Which made no mean land;
And from its colour, when located,
    They called it Greenland.'

After all, you cannot memorise a whole poem when you have only been allowed to see part of it. I remember his comment on the side of the page, about the sailors hearing the calling of the lady who had no palate. It was written as a parody on the marginal glosses on the 'Ancient Mariner,' 'The sailors hear the siren voices.' And I remember his description of the storm, which seems to have been pretty bad.

'The sea rose up, the South Wind snorted,
The ship by Davy Jones was courted;
Rolled she to starboard, then she ported
    With many a shudder,
And, when the waters broke, aborted
    And dropped her rudder.'

He was a bit of a wax after the ironical cheers he got from class, and particularly from the hardly suppressed titters of the nurses.

## II
### [THE NLI VERSION]

O what a wondrous paradox
A sailor who escaped the rocks
Was wrecked by going down the docks
    When safe ashore
And brought to light a hidden pox
    And Hunter's sore.

It's all damned for good old Homer
To make Ulysses such a roamer
He had a wife to show at home her
    A long-lost face
But not lost longer than this rower
    And full of grace.

And nothing greater Virgil's planned –
Aeneas tossed on sea and land
Arrives at Carthage city and
    The queen depraves

And to make a city stand
    He rides the waves!

Sing me the Sybil, the Sailor
Who took them both aboard his whaler
Until they could no longer bail her
    And most amusing
The song may prove, — a right regaler,
    O Muse, if you sing.

For many a minor bard I wean
Has sung 'The Soldiers of the Queen'
Or raised the Lim'rick rhyme obscene
    But none did rise
To sing 'The Wearing o' the Green'
    Between the eyes

Till I, in spite of disregard
Vaunted the rower verdant scarred
And sang the sailor evil-starred
    Who, by degrees
Passed from the journal Hunter hard
    To tertiaries


III

[A CHORAL SONG OF SEALS IN THE SURF SURROUNDING CRETE]

And in the syphilitic surge
The noseless porpoises did urge
A choral song that from the verge
For to soothe their troubles
They [the inhabitants] heard at intervals emerge
    Have drowned in bubbles.


IV

[ANOTHER FRAGMENT]

The sailor feels       Oh whales that swim & snort & blow!
the climatic rigor      Oh Walruses whose front-teeth show!
                       Oh Seals that still select a floe
                            To cool desire!
                       I don't know how the Hell you go
                            Without a fire.

V
THE VOYAGE OF THE MORBID MARINER

i

Many a minor Bard I ween
Has sung the Soldiers of the Queen
Or raised the Limerick ryhme obscene
But none did rise
To sing the wearing of the Green
Between the eyes.

ii

Until a syphilitic Bard
Vaunted the [? voices mad scar'd]
And sang the Sailor [? evil star'd]
Who by degrees
Passed from the [? primal] Hunter's sore
To Ter[tiaries].

iii

Oh what a wonderous Paradox
A Sailor who escaped the rocks
Was wrecked when going down the docks
When safe ashore
He brought to light a hidden pox
And Hunter's sore.

iv

Ah did he when he weighed his anchor
Weigh all the consequences of chancre
I do not think that he would hanker
To hide his bowsprit
Or if he met her would he thank her
For what is now [? split].

v

Ah Sindbad 'twas an evil wind blew
When first you met that low caste Hindoo
You put your trust and penis into
On that occasion

Your glands must have been roughly handled
Causing abrasion.

### vi

Through which you [? were enucleated]
While cheaply you copulated
Then whilst the poison
You lay off [? incubated]
And noticed startling [? indurated]
Upon your glands

### vii

You thought a bit of sand got in
And worked its way beneath the skin
No! I was the symptom of the [? sin]
You should have [? hated]
And then the sore would not have been
Circumvallated.

### viii

If you had kept those dozen annas
To buy tobacco or bananas
You'd have what every healthy man has
And girls respect
As broad and brown as fine bananas
When it's erect.

### ix

But no! Just as the vessel luffed
Against the breeze your penis sloughed
And left you but a [? tiny tuft]
Of pubic hair
I do not wonder you were huffed
And tried to swear.

### x

The Captain then kicked up a rumpus
Because you tried to Pox the compass

The Doctor said give him [?]
Rub in blue butter
And drink the mercury in bumpers
Until you stutter.


xi

But worst of all they stopped your grog
And wrote down in the Captain's log
[?Worse] in a gray Mercurial fog.
And to the pole
The compass will not point but jog
Round Sindbad's hole.


xii

And day by day the vessel drifted
And lay like Wheat & Palen Syphiled
And never once the fog was lifted
Until too late [ ? ]
The sore of [ ? ] something shifted
Within [ ? ].


xiii

Despite the mucus in his [? molar]
The Seaman heaved the Syphilitic Sailor
Right over board and then a whaler
Or perhaps a shark
Engulphed him & grew somewhat paler
Than is a gourmet.


xiv

The mercury in Sindbad's system
Disturbed the whale who would have pissed him
But that his kidneys could not hold him
By normal rules
So Sindbad poxed what he did [? list] him
The whale's green stools.

VI

THE NENIE OF SINBAD, THE MORBID MARINER

Invocation of the Muse

Sing me the Sea, the Syph, the Sailor,
Who took them both on board his Whaler,
Until they could no longer bail her:
And most amusing
The Song will prove, a right regaler,
O Muse, if you sing!

It's all damn fine for good old Homer
To make Ulysses such a roamer.
He had a wife to show at home her
A long lost face:
But not lost longer than his vomer,
And full of grace.

In Virgil is there anything grand?
Aeneas, tossed on sea and land,
Arrives at Carthage City, and
The Queen depraves;
And then, to make another stand,
He rides the waves!

And many a rumour bard I ween
Has sung 'The Soldiers of the Queen'
And raised the Limerick rhyme obscene;
And none did rise
To sing 'The Wearin' of the Green'
Between the eyes.

Till I, in spite of disregard.
Vaunted the vomer verdant scarred
And sang the Sailor Evil-starred
Who, by degrees,
Past from the primal Hunter hard
To Tertiaries.

Ah, did he when he weighed his Anchor,
Weigh all the consequences of chancre?

For if he did, he would not hanker
To hide his bowsprit
Nor, if he met her, would he thank her
For what is now spilt.

Ah, Sinbad 'twas an evil wind blew
When first you met that low-caste Hindu
You put your trust and penis into!
On that occasion
Your glans must have been roughly skinned too
Causing abrasion

Through which you were inoculated
While cheerfully you copulated,
And, when the poison incubated
You lay off Cannes
And indeed something indurated
Upon your glans.

You thought a bit of sand got in
And worked its way beneath the skin!
No! It was the sympton of a sin
You should have hated.
And then the sore would not have been
Circumvallated!

If you had kept those dozen annas
To buy tobacco or bananas,
You'd have, what every healthy man has
And girls respect:
As broad and brown as five havannas
When its erect.


## [Delightful Thing]

Delightful Thing that Book of yours
Which, while I slept, the Post did bring:
Of old forgotten far off cures,
Delightful Thing.

Crude Mercury, it seems to sing,
Mixed in the salts on many [indecipherable ? a sting]

Brought inwardly a hallowing
Delightful Thing.

O undulating loves and lures!
Your joys are gone – and for your sting
After some – (– Mercury endures –)
Delightful Thing.


## [The Prostate]

The prostate is expensive
Here both Love and Lust are mated;
But O it never costs so much
As when enucleated.


## [On ENT Specialists, Colleagues in Dublin]

Down we lay him Mr. Graham,
It's always uncertain with Mr. Curtin,
You never know with Mr. Keogh,
It's only Woods who delivers the goods,
If that's not derogatory to Oliver Gogarty.


## [Therapeutic Thought]

Hydrarg. perchlor. and Pot. Iod.
For those who don't believe in God.


## [On looking at a Portrait in the Royal College of Physicians]

John Magee Finny
My fee is a guinea
The branchial cleft closes late
In the finny tribe –
That's why that fellow
Always talked through his neck.

## Patients

The Spud has got a gadget bright
For each man's motor car:
'It points to left, it points to right,
It shuts – and, There you are!'

The Spud has got a new moustache –
No product of his brain –
To left and right it points to mash
The girls; but, ah! In vain!

## To John Kidney who died of Glomerular Nephritis

Oh, what's in a name if the calling
The essence of fact has not seized?
The fact in this case was appalling:
The name was diseased.

From the walls of the flesh which immure in
The body as tubes do their lumen,
Came urine, and, mixed with the urine,
Were clouds of albumen.

And though by the doctors unbidden, he
Passed out through these tubes to his goal:
Albumen and coma and kidney
Secreted his soul!

For there came on the Dies Suprema
Which comes unto all who draw breath,
Death ushered in by oedema,
Oedema and death.

## To his Friends when his Prostate shall have become enlarged

(To Dr. Young, of John Hopkins, Baltimore, an expert pre-eminent in relieving the disorder)

*To such an extent has Medical Jurisprudence missed the deteriorating effect of prostatic enlargement on the mind and character of the afflicted that many a decent citizen has been arraigned, imprisoned and disgraced by a misunderstanding of what should be a matter not for Law, but for hospitalization and surgery. In fear lest he be afflicted and that the Law may not be more lenient before his death, the following lines, anticipating criticism, have been composed with grave jocundity and dedicated by the Author.*

Bear with me, Friends, when, ill-defined,
The mortal part shall touch the mind
And men shall think askance at me
And my post-cocious potency;

– When the gland sets my loins on fire,
Urging inordinate desire,
And from the sea 'neath which it lies
A thousand Venuses arise;

And I am contemplating rape
And growing careless of escape,
And Lust, not Art, engrosses me:
For who writes old men's Poetry?

When I persist in aping youth
In spite of the derisive truth:
'The only night life he can lead
Are frequent risings from his bed.'

When I am trailed from street to street,
Then let your kind committee meet
'We loved him young for his large heart:
Stand by this hypertrophic part.'

Thus may the town be set at ease
And learn to pity my disease,
Till I, with undishonoured head,
Join the uncopulating Dead.

## [Poets' Ward: From the Meath Hospital]

I sickened with the clear intent
To aid my printer, Seumas
And gain the rare advertisement
Of writing works posthumous.

So pale as that most watery bard
Who wrote above Rathangan
I took up lodgings in the ward
That saw the last of Mangan.

But you write of dying wicked
Before you print or stick it
When if you live to print the text
You'll certainly die wretched.

## The Psyching of Mum

Last week our Mum saw Dr. Brown,
The best psychiatrist in town;
He stretched her out for she paid cash down
    For psychoanalysis.
He stretched her out on a kind of couch
That doctors use when they note each grouch
From old maids, tired out wives and such
    As seek psychiatry.
He asked, 'Is there anything on your mind?'
Mum said, 'Not much but I feel inclined
At times to murder my eldest child.'
    And that was meaning me.
The door of the doctor's waiting room
Had a large key hole and his voice did boom
Till I couldn't but hear, so don't assume
    I eavesdropped at the door.
Mom said, 'On the whole, he's a good little boy;
But I will admit he can manage to annoy
Me till my life is devoid of joy

And I want to live no more.
'Since that is the case,' the doctor said,
Just give him a sock on his curley head
And you won't feel half so inhibited.
    [indecipherable]'
'I couldn't do that, though sometimes I would,
For something says that it's not so good
To murder one of the human brood
    Especially one's own.
'There's no such thing as good or bad,
Or right or wrong for it's all a fad
Derived from Church, your Mother or your Dad,
    Forget it and relax.
When you realise that you can laugh, Ha, Ha!
The blame goes back to your old Granda
As his goes back to his Grandmamma
    All scientific facts.
    A kind of innate tax
Since Mom is back she is acting very odd
She says there's no such thing as God,
That he doesn't belong to our period
    But superstitious folks.
She says that Sex is the only thing;
But it will not stand inhibiting
When she kilts her skirts for the Highland fling.
She says that I am in love with her
To Oedipus she will refer:
She says I am jealous of my own Father
    And don't know what to do.
She says that our cook loves a nasty cuss,
A fellow by the name of Narcissus
She won't cook no more food for us.
Father has loaded his birding gun;
He's keeping a date with Dr Brown
The best psychiatrist in town
He said lots more but his voice was low
Then poor Mum moaned, 'It was long ago'
He sounded as if he had said, 'Wot Ho!'
    And could not see [?our] joke.

## To Poets

Although you sing of Life and Love
It's strange that where you fail is
In giving us a rendering of
The vita sexualis.

## Too Late

Had she told me before she disordered me,
Had she but told me of it in time
I might have got salt and pills of white mercury
But now I'm cut off in my prime.

## [Conversation with Tom Casement in the Palace Bar, 1945]

Gone are those days I well remember
  Gone are those days so full of fun
Now all my limbs are growing stiffer,
  Did I say all? Well . . . all but one.

MONTO POEMS

## *The Hay Hotel*

There is a window stuffed with hay
Like herbage in an oven cast;
And there we came at break of day
To soothe ourselves with light repast:
And men who worked before the mast
And drunken girls delectable:
A future symbol of our past
You'll, maybe, find the Hay Hotel.

Where are the great Kip Bullies gone,
The Bookies and outrageous Whores
Whom we so gaily rode upon
When youth was mine and youth was yours:
Tyrone Street of the crowded doors
And Faithful Place so infidel?
It matters little who explores
He'll only find the Hay Hotel.

Dick Lynam was a likely lad,
His back was straight; has he gone down?
And for a pal Jem Plant he had
Whose navel was like half a crown.
They were the talk of all Meck town;
And Norah Seymour loved them well;
Of all their haunts of lost renown
There's only left the Hay Hotel.

Fresh Nellie's gone and Mrs Mack,
May Oblong's gone and Number Five,
Where you could get so good a back
And drinks were so superlative;
Of all their nights, O Man Alive!
There is not left an oyster shell
Where greens are gone the greys will thrive;
There's only left the Hay Hotel.

There's nothing left but ruin now
Where once the crazy cabfuls roared;

Where new-come sailors turned the prow
And Love-logged cattle-dealers snored;
The room where old Luke Irwin whored,
The stairs on which John Elwood fell:
Some things are better unencored:
There's only left the Hay Hotel.

Where is Piano Mary, say,
Who dwelt where Hell's Gates leave the street,
And all the tunes she used to play
Along your spine beneath the sheet?
She was a morsel passing sweet
And warmer than the gates of hell.
Who tunes her now between the feet?
Go ask them at the Hay Hotel.

L'ENVOI

Nay; never ask this week, fair Lord,
If, where they are now, all goes well,
So much depends on bed and board
They give them in the Hay Hotel.


## [A Stanza to be added to 'The Hay Hotel']

Shall Becky Cooper be forgot
Have I forgotten Liverpool Kate
And all the foam she used to frot
Were she for one night celebrate?
I often tried to dam that spate
When 'Fuck me like a horse!' she'd yell
And who was I to remonstrate
Before I sought the Hay Hotel.


## [Poem attributed to 'Barney']

Though it is 'hotel' all right,
No one ever stayed the night,

For we always came so late
That the night was out of date,
When the sun indecent lit
Summerhill and Britain Street.


## [On seeing Athletes in Monto]

Refraining not for any prize
I saw our young men play with punks,
The speedy lads with twinkling thighs
Who beat the world between their drunks:
Long Irvine trained by Tommy Monks,
And Pindy Clegg and Windy Way:
The best who wrinkled running trunks
Of all the patrons of The Hay.


## [On the Keeper of a Bawdy House]

O there goes Mrs Mack;
She keeps a house of imprudence,
She keeps an old back parlour
For us poxy medical students,
To show, to show
That we are medical students,
To show, to show,
That we are medical students,
To show, to show
That we medical students don't give a damn.


## The Old Pianist

(*He affirms the legend that the Prince of Wales,
afterwards Edward VII, when stationed at the
Curragh Camp visited the Kips, the red light
district of Dublin.*)

There was a time I was not found
Outside the pubs in slants of light,

Forgotten when the drink goes round,
Unwelcomed as a drizzling night,
Insulted by each half-bred shite
Who drinks, as if 'twas drink he feared –
I who played up to wild delight
In days before the Kips were cleared.

It was not with a whistle then
I kept the insteps off the floor.
Oh, no! Be God I played for men,
Masters alike of horse and whore;
When life was like a long encore
Of 'Here's the Best' and 'What is yours?'
You could not drown my playful score
No matter how you laughed with whores.

I played the night the Prince of Wales
Up from the Curragh came disguised,
We got the tip to reef our sails,
And yet let on we were surprised;
Poor Mrs Mack was paralysed,
She grew so lady-like and stately,
And got herself so bowdlerised
She lost her grip of things completely.

The Prince was not for bed that night
Had it not been for our Fresh Nelly
Who got herself so yelping tight
That in she came and slapped her belly;
'Ye're all so damn stuck up. I tell ye,
That no thinks of sticking up
His ballocks where there's quaking jelly:
'Twould be the making of that pup!'

'Excuse me gloves!' sez Mrs Mack,
Then whispered, 'Christ, when I get after
That mouldy whore, I'll break her back!'
The Prince, he simply roared with laughter,
And said, 'I hope you have not chaffed her
On my account. It would be grand
To take, although I bump the rafter,
A bird with such a Bush in hand.'

Mack muttered, 'O the bloody bitch
To burst into a lady's parlour
With no respect for Kings and sich!
You'd think Yerself was Nosey Barlow:
Enough to bring my lucky star low,
And make you think me common stuff!'
The Prince said, 'Who in Monte Carlo
Has such a belly, bubs or buff?'

The slavey we sent up to hear
Said Nelly said 'Your Royal Highness
I only took a sup of beer
To cure my modesty and shyness;
When Mother Mack put on such finesse
She almost made me want to puke,
You'd think she only let to line us
An odd Archbishop or a Duke.'

'Don't mind me, Kiddie, if I'm shy,
Beat me to death, and then I'm mastered;
There's not a hair on either thigh;
This belly never bore a bastard;
My bubs are round and alabastered,
And firm enough to crack a flea,
And when I come the sheets are plastered
Like Holland with the Zuyder Zee.'

I played to drown the chandelier
That chattered on the parlour ceiling.
'By Gob he's making Nelly rear
And all the better for good feeling.'
'But soon the plaster will be peeling',
Sez Mack, 'before he rings her bell.'
I said, as one romance revealing:
'What Nelly peels she plasters well.'

While this short time was going on,
Then up and spoke a bold equerry,
'Be kind enough to send me one
Well quartered lass to make me merry.
I'd like to offer you a sherry,
But since His Nibs is on a beano
All drinks would be derogatory
Below a Pommery and Greno.

'Send up Piano Mary here,'
Sez Mack, 'and then send up a bottle;
She is a dreamy little dear,
But she can bend the strongest wattle,
Your spine will know what tunes that mott'll
Strum on it like a piano player's
She is the best thing in the brothel,
Since Nelly's cooling down upstairs.'

'Be Christ', sez Mack, 'the Kip's in luck
When even them on guard gets randy:
Go out and say I'll stand a fuck
To that plain clothes man choked with brandy,
How are you standing, Napper Tandy?
I used to think, it sounds a farce,
The Sun of Heaven shone from your bandy . . .
Shone from – by Heaven – your bandy arse!'

This grandeur moidered Mrs Mack.
Sez she, 'The Prince has brought me luck.
I feel me auld form comin' back;
I'd like to stand yez all a fuck.
Come on in here, me plain clothes buck,
I have a way with warty boys.'
Sez he, 'I'm here on duty stuck,
And duty interferes with joys.'

It was enough, as home he druv,
To make a man of feeling wince
To hear each lewd 'Good night, me love.
Good night, me love. Good night, sweet Prince.
Has Nelly put yer back in splints;
And will ye tell the Jersey lily
That Dublin can, at all events,
Take London on and fuck it silly.'


## [Piano Mary's Fashion of Faithfulness]

He lay upon me head to tail
And wriggled in his joy
But it was all to no avail –
I'm true to Billy Boy!

He put me standing on my head
More muscle to supply
But little cared I what he did
I'm true to Billy Boy!

## [Forgiveness of Sins]

Tell each pleasant little harlot
Tho' her sins be black as scarlet,
Noted by an infant scrivener
All her sins shall be forgiven her!

## [The Days when we were Young]

If Ousley were alive to-day
He'd sing of days when we were young;
How Elwood tumbled in the Hay
And how Fresh Nelly champed her tongue:
His fiddle string is long unstrung
And I am in a parlous way
But here's 'The Days when we were young!'
And here's that hostel called the Hay.

# LOVE AND BEAUTY

---

## To —— To Powder Her Neck

Powder your neck lest there be seen
The marks where kissing lips have been,
But have a care the powder be
Matched to your round neck's ivorie
Lest by the difference of hue
Suspicion fall on me & you.

## To Stella

Stars by the light they shed
   Only are known,
Songs by the verse they wed
   Time have outgrown;
And that my verse may be
Shining with love of thee,
   Light me alone.

Life to the lute of Love
   Only will sing,
Few are the songs that move
   After the Spring;
And if the Spring be frore —
Spring that so soon is o'er —
What shall the Winter store
   From harvesting?

461

## To Lilian to Cozen Time

O who can stay the car of Day
   Careering to the West?
Or bid the moon not sink so soon
   Before she bares her breast?
Could Sun and Moon like us commune
   As we together lie:
The golden day would always stay
   The moon would never die.

But ah, each birth of heaven and earth
   By Time is onward driven.
And ere the sun's embrace the moon
   Grows faint within her heaven.
Why think you, Dear, that Time will spare,
   That spares not moon or Sun
And friendly prove to parted love
   If now we be not one?

## Song

Make me a mirror with those eyes
   That bashfully disown
The love enkindled images
   That lighten in mine own
That I may see that Love denies
'Tis not an image in your eyes.

## [Fragment]

If I were throned on Venus' star
Earth might shine a star to see
But since that tender [? state is] far
Be thou the Queen of Love for me . . .
All the world sings

## Love and Death

Like those vestals of the sky
Fallen before the day goes by:
Limbs to wear the velvet green,
Hearts that have sufficed a queen,
Or unsated Sappho even –
Matchless too – O God of heaven!
What has happened to all those? . . .

Why must Time be past to prove
To a lover what is Love? . . .
And our secret hearts declare
Dead are all the fairest fair.


## [A Lover's Lament]

Not the lightness of the air
Which the smallest pinion stirs,
Nothing know I light and fair
With a motion like to hers
Not the leaf that fans the bud
Kindling on the swinging linde
Mete her matchless maidenhood
And can satisfy my mind.

Slender as the Spring-time moon,
Pure and slender bright and fleet
Furthest from the plenilune
With one star beneath her feet
Goes she always in the sun
Pure and slender bright and free
Thoughtless as she hastens on
That she leaves the night to me.

She must ever hasten on
We may never meet and rest
As the azure-sandalled moon
Flies the night adown the West

Since we are the thralls of Time
Let me love her for her flight
Though the love that turns to rhyme
Leaves me wrapped around with Night.

## If Love were all sufficing who would sing?

I sit in darkness now that thou art gone
And though the heaven above fills up with day
My sky of life is barren of a sun
For thou, my sun of love, remains't away
True, thou hast promised swiftly to return
But I grow darkest as that sunrise nears;
The sun of light needs little thought to burn
But for the sun of love — what hopes and fears!
Since thou cans't make my hours of love too short
That cans't not ever make those hours too long
Desist from changing those short hours for sport
With a night that is than thee more strong
Help not the night! That never yields a boon
Grieve as thou mays't it cometh all too soon.

## Enchantment

*[indecipherable]*
*Trying magic the Poet is himself spell-bound*

Song is my only hope
To bring again to sight
Her dark hair's wavy crop
That floats the fingers up,
The grey eyes veiled in light,

Bright mists, such as in clear
And early frosty skies
Prevent the rising star
Of Venus; and they are
Before no other eyes.

I cannot make a spell
With salt and honey-cake;
But words may do as well,
Sweet words and multiple,
If duly used to make

Enchantment that shall bear
Distinctly into view
The tall and debonair,
Lovely young shape and rare,
I owe my singing to.

So, Heart, sing on until
You see again, beneath
The long dark lashes' thrill,
Her eyes with laughter fill;
And then – the lovely teeth,

That tell, what portraiture
Has never yet imparted:
O half my Lady's lure!
That she is most demure,
Demure when merry-hearted.

[2 lines indecipherable]
Of Beauty she'd be graced
With Beauty by her taste
And her long throated melodious voice –

And swallow's wings unstirred
The eyebrows long and sweet,
The nose wistfully blurred;
But how make with a word
The little hands and feet?

The hands, the feet, the ears
Ineffable! The notes
A shepherd thinks he hears –
And he is filled with fears –
Of most intricate flutes,

May make, when singled out
And heard in thymy lands,

The little convolute
Pink shells; and then denote
Her little feet and hands.

Her hand that pushes back
The hair beneath the brow,
Or her dark dresses' slack —
O Magic, white and black!
Who's the Magician now?

## Winifred

Spring, and the thin blue Springtide air
  Shone round me as I rowed
Between the meadow borders where
  A freshening water flowed;
The young leaves on the willow sprays
  Scarce hid the linnets green,
And pink and white in orchard ways
  The blossoming clouds were seen,
And pink and white her sweet face was,
  Her brown hair blown half free,
Who, when I landed on the grass,
  Brought out the ale to me.
She said her name was Winifred,
  And soft the accents came,
As if, with all its white and red,
  A blossom told her name.
She was so fair a maid to love
  That — why I cannot guess —
I saddened growing conscious of
  My very happiness,
Though then to me no God could give
  A greater blessing than to live.

Autumn now has come and ends
  The bright months, and the year,
More coloured than the spring, descends
  To its gold sepulchre.
The living leaves shall spread no more,
  To drink the thin blue air;

Summer has garnered in her store
    And all the world is bare.
And with the leaves deciduous
    The days have fallen between
That time when heaven was beauteous
    And all the world was green.
But now that too my heart receives
    The soft maturing breath
Although I have not like the leaves
    Some golden thought of Death,
I find that it is more fulfilled
    That days fallen between
The careless time it first was thrilled,
    Under the shadows green:
It makes me think of spring new spread
    To hear the name of Winifred.

## Dolly

Dolly has a double chin,
Dolly's hair is brown,
Dolly's at a little inn
Far away from Town.

When she tends the diary,
And she makes the bread,
And she calls you early
When the cream is laid.

Tall she is and slender,
Wanton, wayward, light
But her heart is tender
As the glow of night.

When the cocks are crowing
And the day begins
You can hear her going
With the milking tins.

When the pigeons thunder
In the noontide heat
She will go down under
And a tankard get.

When the folk are talking
Sitting at their doors,
She will come out walking
Past the sycamores

Hard it is to catch her
She is so aware
But you cannot match her
Here nor anywhere.

I will go for summer
To that little inn
Fearing a new-comer
Might be lodged therein.

Goodbye, Melancholy
And my lady friends
I will talk with Dolly
When the eve descends.


## [My Love]

When you'll see Rose and Lily link
In Beauty and bright the Pink;
When you'll see eyes that have the light
Of stars and interstellar night,
When you'll see all the fretted beams
Abstracted from the beds of streams
And confluent wave into one,
You'll see my Love's reflection.

When you'll see in the April wind
A linnet on the leafless linde
When you'll behold the fountain's crest
That dances whiles it seems to rest
You'll see the windless poplar move
That is the motion of my love.

## Molly

Molly through the garden
  Laughed and played with me,
And the gate unbarred in
  To the rosery.

Just she said to show me
  How the roses grew,
And when she would show me,
  Ask me if I knew

Which of all was fairest,
  Crescent bud or rose,
Till I guessed the rarest
  She would not disclose.

Laughing little lady,
  All her features shone
Like a star whose body
  And whose soul are one.

So I went intending
  To please her if I could,
Pondered then, and bending
  Pointed to the bud.

But the moment after
  Saw her face illumine
With a peal of laughter
  Reaching for the bloom.


## [A Compensatory Poem]

God made the rat
And then above
The rat he placed
The playful cat
For GOD IS LOVE.

## [Like Thoughts of Youth framed in an ageing Mind]

There is such life in you, a word you'll find
Will set me budding like an April tree
Forgetful of the fall of leaf to be,
Unmindful of the leaves that fall before
My apple sweetens from a bitter core.

## Secret Lovers in Vienna

What they did, who may tell?
But I do think 'twas nothing more
Than you and I have done before
With Bridget and with Nell.

## Jack and Jill

'Oh, come where running water
    Is tumbling down a hill!'
But the parson's daughter,
    Replied with, 'Jack and Jill!'
'Oh, Jack and Jill went up and down;
    And long ago are dead;
But I can never break my crown
    Because I've lost my head.'
'Jack and Jill are never gone:
    They stand for you and me.
And I don't want to tumble down,
    Or any hill to see.'
She laughed at me so sweetly
    That then I took my cue
And bore with her quite meekly
    Because full well I knew
When Love's reduced to laughter
    In valley or on hill,
There'll be tumbling after
    Jack meets Jill.

## The Peace of Life

How could his blindness save the Bard
From Love's gold head and length of limb,
When, past the flames of men who warred
His Helen reappeared to him.

Memory was mother of his Muse:
And thoughts of what blithe ways were hers,
Did angry heaven with earth confuse
Throughout his thronged hexameters.

The heart that fashioned men of pith,
Had strength for truth, but lesser joy
To sing of Beauty couching with
The meanest warrior of Troy.

Yet were it not for pain of Love
Song had not been a salve therefore
No hand had been stretched from above,
And not a sound along that shore.


## To Helen Beauclerk

Women are our subconscious selves,
Materialisations of our souls
Regions where faery queens and elves
Disport beyond Reason's controls;
And, as I am not one who delves
Deep into self, I love to see
Beauty, exceeding my poor self's,
Increased by objectivity.

You of the lovely learned name,
You of the most mellifluent fingers,
Force me, soul's bankrupt that I am,
To call on souls of earlier singers:
Dan Chaucer's, and on his who tells
How Helen ruled the Dardanelles:
For it takes more than I am worth
To sing you and to body forth.

## For Emily

God made a lady out of lightning
Playing on the edge of a night in the South:
You can see it still in her dark eyes' brightening
And the flicker when she smiles at the corner of her mouth.
Quick are her thoughts as her lithe arms' gestures;
Lighted is her face by the flame that in her glows;
Nothing is concealed by the drawing of her vesture's
Folds at wrist or shoulder, or the ripple of her clothes.
Quick is her speech and low, yet, to me listening,
I can but hear its sweetness, for the meaning in my brain
Takes time to bloom as the colour in the meadows
Waits to show what rainbows hid in April rain.

## [Venus is dead]

Barbers distraught by the thought of ladies' love-locks!
Passion-pale attendants in a dry goods store!
Venus is dead. But, be this the way that love talks,
A way not quite so subtile is the way I should prefer.

## Goodbye

If you saw your face as I
Saw it when you said Goodbye:
With the hair about it lit
Where the sun had Titianed it;
And the eyes that glowed and shone
With that other inner sun,
Chalices that held a wine
From the wild immortal vine
Glowing in the double cup
That a mortal hand holds up;
You would know, for you have wit,
Why I lingered saying it.

## [A Question]

Where have all great lovers gone?
Beauty as elect and rare
As when towns were trampled on
And a Macedonian hack
Monarch of Rome's bravest men
Walks today, and takes the air –
Can it be Love's joy is done
Since the mighty triumvir.


## The Blackout

She threw herself back in her chair;
I saw the lamplight on her hair,
Her hair that shone so black and bright,
There never was a blacker sight.
I looked and wondered and adored it,
Searching for similes to record it,
When suddenly the sirens shout
And all the room is blackened out.
Yes, all was darkness, yet I swear
The room was brightened by her hair,
As some sweet influence makes bright
A moonless and ambrosial night.

When I am blotted out from here
To wait in death the great 'All clear',
If I am left with any wit
Or thought at all, I'll think of it,
Think of her hair and win delight
To know that darkness can be bright.


## He accounts for the Skyscrapers

If Helen burned the 'topless towers'
    When things in Troy looked hopeless,
I said, where lovelier Helens dwell

The towers will be more topless:
I never saw such girls as yours
    But do not be afraid
Of Beauty, for you have as well
    A better Fire Brigade!

## The Getting of Gargantua

Grandgousier with Gargamelle
To do The Two-backed Beast did
Prepare religiously and well,
And this is how they feasted:
His arms around her waist he put
And gripped her by the buttock
While she, reciprocating rut,
Him, down by the arse-gut took.

Back and forwards goes the sea;
The planets go and come back:
He fleshed his Weapon featously
And gently drew his bum back;
Then in and out and in and in
With most ferocious yearning
They waged a battle chin to chin
That badly brooks adjourning.

They mutely moved; and when his Sword
With double hair was hilted,
She surged right up against her Lord
And winced; but never wilted.
Until Life's spring implacable
Was filled to overflowing,
His Balls her Bum belaboured well
As if to set it going.

He let it like a geyser go
Or like the Blue Rhine rising
Through wells tumultous with snow,
And pumped between her thighs in
The glue that grew Gargantua

With buttocks that impelled him
Well worthy of his doughty Da
And of her womb that held him.

His Horn was cornicopious,
Her Belly firm and rounded,
And thus Gargantua for us
Was hammered, forged, and founded.
So pray God send before you're spent
A Belly nicely cambered
And leave you to the Argument,
And me, not unremembered.


## To his Boar Cat Rodilardus

I might have known who know your way
From your demureness in the day,
O too demure to be devout!
The way you'ld go when you got out.

Why in the planatery gloom
When men for their own joy make room,
Do you the ambrosial night disturb
With cries no magic spell can curb?

Is it because you look before
And would Love's bitter end deplore?
But why bemoan what you enjoy
And with the Now the Then alloy?

Is there no present time at all
But Past and Future tinct with gall?
Or must your Present only be
Remorse mixed with anxiety?

For God's sake love, and don't reflect
Or you will be Love's derelict
Bankrupt and battered out of Love
If from delight your thought can move!

Ah! but it may be that you yearn
For Love beyond the Future's bourne
Behind the Past's – for 'Love Supreme',
A sabre-toothed despairing dream.

Of fronds like claws through which the sun
Striped you with yellow and with dun;
Of curbed allurements in the dust,
Rhythms and hieroglyphs of lust.

Of nights when you through torrid groves
Stalked your excruciating loves,
And raised with dyspareuniac roar
The eye-brows of the Ichthyosaur.

Howe'er it be, I won't complain
If Darwin touched you on the brain;
Only I wish you had kept your song
Till Evolution proved him wrong.

Nothing for me can love enhance
Like Love's ancestral, high romance;
But I thank God my ancestors
When they made Love omitted roars.

I know how Love and Death can deal
The double pang that lovers feel:
Paola's love was past a joke
When both were skewered at a stroke!

I know well how Augustus John
In lighter moments carries on,
But never heard I such a roar
From painter or from paramour.

As yours, Cassandra to our cost
As if all lunar towns were lost;
As if Isaiah's brood surprised
Were all together circumcized!

Perhaps in your non-Conformist way
To Love's delight you scream to say –
As my school-master used to do –
It hurts me more than it hurts you!

Surely your cry did Antony mark
Curdling the awed Egyptian dark;
And when the great Queen had him calmed
Pray that you might be well embalmed.

But I must take it half resigned
Bulgarian milk-like to my mind
Lest anger into love intrude
And raise too high the pressure of blood.

Truly it seems to me absurd
O Round-eyed as Athena's Bird!
O Undelighted in the dark,
Love's Martyr and Hieresiarch!

To sound the converse of all joys
By turning feeling into noise,
To mock the screech-owl thus, and prove
The long calamity of Love!


## [For a Collection of Cat Poetry]

Lady, when you rub your face
In private room or public place,
And reprimand each curl that strays
   With tactful pat,
See that you do it with the grace
   Of Tib, my cat.


## News

'Now, what's the news?' I asked her. She tried to make replies,
And while she gently chattered, her lashes veiled her eyes;
She may have had but little or much from which to choose;
I was a fool to ask her. Herself was all the news!
The only thing that mattered. Herself was all the news!
She was the news of all that sings when God is on His way;
She was the news of starry things that wake when eve is gray;
The news of poplars leaning when morning breezes move.
She was the latest bulletin from out the world of Love.

She brought me awful messages from Love's imperious lords
Who use our mortal bodies as the poets harpsichords;
And, when we love each other in our kindly human way,
Our loves are but an echo of the lordly notes they play.
She was the news of sunlight that strikes the mountain lawns
And shows you, as they pass across, the light-foot, dappled fawns;
The news of apples blossoming – her elbow meant to me
The branch that grows akimbo on a homely apple tree.
She was the news of golden heads that know the time to wait
When father is expected, and to gather at the gate;
Of all that Love has painted or sung or sanctified –
The long resounding organ and the windows, vermeil dyed.
She could not tell what news she brought. (I hoped she did not know
I cared not what he said or what Matilda said to Joe.)
No wonder she was hesitant before my questionings.
Can any woman be aware of all the news she brings?
The things the mailman carries are far beyond his ken.
How can a woman be aware of all she means to men?

## Love to Anne on Her Wedding Day

*(To Anne O'Neill Kinkead on Her Wedding Day –
April 29, 1944)*

God Bless the bride! and may she see
Long life and wide prosperity;
And build up in her husband's name
A home like that from which she came;
And, if her parents miss her curls,
Pay them back well with boys and girls.

## On the Pier

Dear, when we part no hearts shall be broken
Though I still have some pain at heart
At leaving you. By the same token
No pain shall you feel when we part
Though from my love I shall be parted,
With yours you will go hand in glove,
You who in love are still whole-hearted,
Yourself the object of your love.

## My Dreams

I saw my dreams move in the street;
A few of them were tall and stately;
A few vivacious, swift, petite;
But one outdid the others greatly:
Like to a goddess was her walk,
Her airy brows were clothed in beauty;
It were a sacrilege to talk
Of love; you could but bend in duty.
As for the others, O ye gods!
Ninety to one's an understatement;
Hundreds to one were better odds,
Amazed I stood and watched the scene,
Their ugliness had no abatement
I dreamed, my dreams were only bright smears
Compared to these, I must have had nightmares.

## The Dream

I saw my dreams walk in the street
And one was proud and calm and stately;
And two were raven-haired, petite;
They looked as they'd been laughing lately.
The air was mild, and all around
Me I could hear their gentle babble;
It seemed there was but little sound,
The place was quite devoid of rabble.
I crossed the street to ask the proud,
The calm, the tall, the lovely woman
If we had met; but I was cowed:
Her gaze had something superhuman.
The brunettes laughed; and she was gone!
This thought deserves but little kudos!
If the Ideal leads us on,
To lead at all it must elude us.

## Tardy Spring

I had a date with Spring.
She put me to the test
By wayward loitering
Then turning up half dressed:
A little smock she wore
Of pink and white peach blossom,
A smock that did far more
To show than hide her bosom.
The way she wore it on
Her barely curving belly
You'd think she had been drawn
By Sandro Botticelli.
And, oh, her rippling hair!
Her hair was long and yellow;
It lightened all the air
As doth the early willow.
I thought, with much surprise,
She looks so young and wildish,
With April in her eyes
And gangling limbs still childish,
She never meant to meet
In time for us to marry;
And that delayed her feet,
And that's what made her tarry.
She smiled and said, 'I'm here.
I kept the time we dated.
Now is there anywhere
To go to and be mated?'
I said, 'In brain and tongue
Of yours not yet has sap lain.
Who'd marry one so young
Unless he were a chaplain?'
She shook her upraised arm,
And up her smock of pink went,
I saw, for all her charm,
A juvenile delinquent.
She said, 'You are too brash
To meet and scorn a lady:
You old, white-headed trash!
You old cane-sugar daddy!
Supposing I am slow

In coming into action,
You cannot say that snow
To Spring is an attraction.
I have another date.'
She swished her scanty habit.
But she will pullulate
When I am old and crabbed.
I did not try to match
Her words, but muttered, '*Pardie!*'
When snow is on the thatch
No wonder Spring is tardy.


## [Amazons: a Fragment]

Those who regard as most inhuman
The seeming nonchalance of women
And who would have them [ ? ]

Thanks be to God those days are over
That saw the Amazonian lover.
The Amazons of warlike mien
Had once a year to yield to men.


## In a Bus

Spare it no more! That's just as far
As you should go in saving cloth
Though cloth must now be saved for war,
Hardly a mouthful for a moth
Is on your knees. The Highlanders
Don't show their knees as you do yours;
And they show theirs, for to their knees
They bring both friends and enemies.

The stores have not begun to stint
A trellis or a jungle print;
A pin check or a play-suit dress
A printed crêpe or Inverness;

Or pastel dreams with colors set
In aqua, rose, blue, violet,
Glen plaid or tailored navy moire
Or anything you may require –
Forgive my French pronunciation
Exactness would be affectation –
So I can't see why you should lay on
Restrictions when they're none on rayon.

Civilisation's said to rest
Largely on keeping women dressed.
By not exposing its foundations
During these structural alterations
You can promote its maintenance;
Why any girl with commonsense
Would, with priorities at play,
Keep something for a rainy day.

Why don't you go and ask your Granny
For petticoat or Paisley shawl
And if she says she hasn't any,
Gently persuade her to recall
Some old oak chest where lavenders
Preserve some petticoat of hers.
Try if the painted chest of drawers
Cannot relieve this want of yours,
I'm sure your dear old Grandmamma
Would help to hide your femora.
If you won't wear it, turn it in.
Maybe 'twill make a parachute;
And you can keep, down to your shin,
The same dress level of your skirt.
I'm not too brave; but gladly I
Would as a paratrooper float
Embroidered down to earth from sky
In a tempestuous petticoat.
Methinks the petticoated Japs
Would just be due for a collapse
If I came gently from the clouds –
A petticoat above the shrouds
And yelled to make them quite offended:
'This way the Son of Heaven descended!'

## Song

I played with Love at hide-and-seek;
   Where do you think I found him?
In the dells of Mary's cheek
   Where pink and white enwound him.
She ceased to smile as I came close,
So let the dimple-dweller loose
To hide in haffet curls of hair
And coil himself deep in her ear.

I softly sang to lure him out;
   What do you think I told him?
I told that wanton gadabout
   I would not even scold him;
But love him well and let him be
If he put in a word for me.


## In the Garden

Perfect beautiful momentary blossoms,
I who am momentary cannot long endure
The tension of your beauty, the knowledge that embraces
Beauty yet to come, beauty gone before;
The uninterruptible implacable procession
Of Beauty moving onward from the fountain to the bourne.
Therefore I take comfort and walk for a few paces;
So I go where Beauty goes, I care not to return.

# LIFE AND DEATH

---

## [A Query]

Could he who passed with aimless luck
Exams until he came to mix
The end and means, at last he stuck
To pass the Styx?

## [The Land of the Young]

If I recalled, would tears asperge
The night Theleme saw you Panurge?
But magic was far more in vogue
The night you passed to Tir na oge!

'Twas but a dim religious dream
The night you vanished in Theleme:
But you outsoared the power of Logue
The night you passed to Tir na oge.

Jack Morrow thought that things were strange,
Jim Geoghegan felt a coming change:
But Hyland eyed you like a rogue
The night you passed to Tir na oge.

We sat as two whose thoughts half lingered
Twixt stage and barmaid softly-fingered,
But Bailey's thoughts were 'Thirim pogue'
The night you passed to Tir na oge.

Why should a soul like yours delay
For pigmies to play out the play?
Wrapped in Howard's heroic tog'
You praeter-passed to Tir na oge.

You left aside the mantle green
By which you walk this straightened scene,
But left it to your old friend Gog
The night you passed to Tir na oge.

Your cloak fell first? – But why presume
On a green thought in a green-room?
Empedocles thus left his brogue –
The night you passed to Tir na oge.

Whether, my friend, we all must go
The sprightliest souls can hardly know,
But you with poets shall collogue
When you have passed to Tir na oge.


## Upon a Friend who died Distraught

'In the beginning was,' he said –
Since the merry man is dead,
Take it for his epitaph –
'Not the Logos, but the Laugh!'


## [A Noble Trace]

Where are all the great elks gone
Whose antlers seen against the sun
Seen on the sky line?
Deep in the moor's embrace
Is left a noble trace
Of the heraldic grace
To mark their high line.

## [What else is Joy?]

I saw the merry freshet of the Spring
Against the azure of the sky afar.
Primrose and daffodil and evening star,
In the clear light when light was lengthening,
Pouring on earth its procreant cataract,
Lovely, and filled with waves of life unseen,
As fresh a Spring as there has ever been
In spite of the Springs that have been wrecked.

But I who could remember many waves,
And many a girl grown into lengthy dress
All withered now, or widowed, held my breath,
Sickened at Nature laughing on her graves;
But what have I to do remembering?
What else is Joy but mockery of Death.

## Serenity

Since you are human, do not hope
    For life exempt from fear and pain:
Ask, rather, for the strength to cope
    With fear, and courage to sustain.

Brave men there were who played their part
    And cast off fear before the grave –
Witness King Richard Lionheart;
    And fameless men can be as brave.

It rests with you alone. It rests
    With you from gods to win the palm
Because your way of life suggests,
    If not their ease, at least their calm.

## Twilight Street

I took a house in Twilight Street
That leads to Twilight Lake.
My friends were all surprised at me

And asked why I should take
Such a house in such a street.
'It's quiet and discreet,'
I said, 'As such a house should be
That looks on Twilight Lake.'


## Reading at Night

Sleep drooping in its flight drew drowsily
Its wing across a word, or two, or three,
Pressing them softly down on the page
Faint as the fossil from another age,
The fluted shape alone, the shell, the trace
Of what was wonder to an earlier race:
Meaning which even morning scarce can find,
So long the lapsus since it slipped the mind,
Something left printed there since time began,
A thought prewritten for the waking man.


## Where

Where are all the roses gone
That made the air so very sweet;
And, lest the tale be incomplete,
Where are the briars they grew upon?
And girls without comparison,
Where are they now that were so feat:
The young and old, strong and effete,
And all the Springs that brought them on?
The mind of man asks, Where and Whence,
Caught within Time's sharp calendars;
But it may range and range it will:
There is no Time between the stars;
But we, by Time's omnipotence,
Are trapped and stayed till all is still.

## [Philosophising]

'Oh! Boys, avoid Philosophy,
Or with it light your pipe;
It indicates senility;
But when you're rotten ripe
And in the sere and detoxed state,
Then smoke it, and expatiate.'

## Autumnal

The pine leaves hang against the sky;
Against the blue, the sombre trees.
I must regard them well for I –
When dead I wonder what one sees.

## The Graveyard on the Hill

The cheerfulest acre a corpse can enter
Is the bright little graveyard by Dummerston Center
That stands where the mountains around are up-thrown
In the Land of Green Hills on a knoll of its own
With a low gray wall of local stone.

Dummerston churchyard and church are apart,
Here is a cemetery after my heart,
Open and blithe as the day's eyelid,
Open and honest where nothing is hid,
Where it is innocent still to be dead.

The space is clear, it is plain to view
Unshadowed except for a cypress or two;
The only cemetery I can recall
Where roses flow over a long stone wall
And the gravestones stand in the sight of all.

Life and death here, if simply viewed,
Are largely a matter of attitude:
A simple matter, my Friends, at that:

The Quick stand up and the Dead lie flat;
And a stone stands over their habitat.

The Dead lie down; but their stones stand up
To stake a claim in Life at the top –
In the hearts of the living, when all is said,
Is the only place we can find the Dead;
Their stones are their prayers to be well bestead.

I look and wonder to see these stones
Like brave ghosts facing a life in the sun's
Glory unmuffled, who first made the grave
A source of horror as if to enslave
Life by its terror, and daunt the brave.

If they were wakened and set on the plain,
What could life be but 'The Same Again?'
'The Same Again?' And they worked enow
Why make their backs again bend to the plow?
Why put the apple dropt back on the bough?

The Same Again with its plowing and sowing,
Mowing, and things that keep country folk going:
Up with the sun, and a break at noon,
Backs again bent till the day is done;
Their sons are now at it, so leave them alone.

Tight-lipped workers and scant of speech,
Helpful, and well-known each to each,
Spare of body and brown of chest,
Why should I trouble their well-worn rest,
I to whom work of all kinds is a pest?

All through my life on this earthly shelf
I never met anyone else but myself.
Here I may break from my selfish plight,
Here I may meet with my opposite,
Here I may lie and my life requite.

Bury me, therefore, where light earth falls
*Extra muros*: beyond the walls,
At the eastern angle as near as may be
To my favourite symbol, the apple tree,
Thus may they rest with the idler, me.

Whence, when the Angel's trumpet toots,
I will be only coaxed up from the roots
Provided I don't have to lift a hand,
And the idle angels will understand
And leave me alone in the rolling land.

## The Singing Well

There is beyond the dim blue hills
   A well that sings a faery song;
But all who hear it, legend tells,
   Cannot survive it very long:
Their hold on life cannot sustain
Its exquisitely faint refrain.

It sings of fairer life than ours;
   And holds this life of little worth
Where men are bound down all their hours,
   And, all their hours, are bound to earth,
Where Good is Evil's opposite
And Wrong is but opposed to Right.

Beyond the dim blue hills upthrust
   It tells of lands than this more fair
Where, whitely clad, in troops, the Just
   Move through the most pellucid air;
And all the trees are clear as ice;
And being there doth all suffice.

I too would go to seek that well;
   But I recall the Sirens singing;
And of the Kingdoms Lost can tell
   Whose music heard is Death's beginning;
I too would seek a life of bliss
Were I not reconciled to this.

*Gogarty's note: According to Chinese superstition
it was fatal to hear the music of a lost Kingdom.*

## *[Youth and Age]*

It dawned on me – I gave three cheers –
That youth is not confined to years.
I've seen the old act very youngly
And here's an old tree growing strongly.


## *The Kaleidoscope*

From fragments of gay childhood's days
And adult days of toil and hope,
And Love that moves through anxious ways
Time builds his brave kaleidoscope;
And we may see, when all's displayed
How are his lovely patterns made.

Is it not comfort then to know,
No matter what we do or are,
Whether we feel a blithesome glow
Or influence of malignant star;
Whether our days are saved or wrecked,
They all will shine in retrospect.


## *[Time]*

No wonder I can't seize the day,
For time presents a paradox.
It disappears while we're at work or play,
And when it reappears it mocks
All our attempts to get away.


## *His Epitaph*

Don't let death confuse you all:
Death is not unusual.

# ELEGIES

## On the Death of a Favourite Race Horse

The limbs that strove, the heart that pressed
With such intense desire,
Have reached a place of lasting rest,
Where they no more shall tire.

What aspiration fired the heart,
To what far goal it flew
I know not, nor may glean a part,
But only: – it was true.

And thou hast left – and what more falls,
To man to leave, or be – ?
In living mind's memorials
A noble memory.

## [Ode for Terence MacSwiney]

Put back your shoulders when you hear his name
And lift your heads, your name is honoured more
Than anyone has honoured it before
Since they who brought the battle-axes came;

And not the Roman who endured the flame,
Stood to the fire and burnt his bitter limb
(And the King kingly liberated him),
Not Scaevola outshines MacSwiney's fame.
For burning in his breast, the nation's will
Led by a courage that alone can cope
With torture, death and broadcast ravages,
Consumes, and beacons to the world until
Justice be guided to redeem our hope
Him fallen among unchivalrous savages.


## The Rebels

Not that they knew well, when they drew the blade
That breaks for victory if gain were planned,
You never gave without a trembling hand;
But when they heard of sacred truth waylaid,
And meanness with grandiloquence gainsaid,
And Freedom, in the name of Freedom, banned;
And Friendship in this foulness, this, England –
This was the cause of that good fight they made.

They heard your mobsters mouthing at the hordes,
Who care not so the fight increase their store,
Hawking your honour on the sandwich boards;
But theirs is safe, and to these things unlinked
They stood apart; and Death withholds them more,
Separate for ever and aloof – distinct.


## Arthur Griffith

He fought as many fights as Conn the Fighter;
    And all alone he fought
Without a friend to make his sword arm lighter,
    Unblindable, unbought.

He held his shield until the waves resounded,
    The men of Ireland woke.
He made the loud tyrannical foe dumbfounded
    And to relax his yoke.

Inglorious in the gap: by many a hater
    The scoffing word was said.
He heard from those who had betrayed him 'Traitor!'
    The cross-grained and cross-bred.

He shook from off him with a grand impatience
    The flesh uncomforted;
And passed among the captains in whom nations
    Live when these men are dead.

He's down, he's down! The silent heart is broken,
    Death's pang his forehead warps.
O let the foe snatch neither spirit nor token;
    But rally round his corpse.

## Micheál Coileáin

*'Multitudinous is their gathering, a great host with
whom it is not fortunate to contend the battle-trooped
host of the O Coileáin.'*

In the dark night I waited for the boat
That bore his body as its dearest freight;
And, with long time to wait,
I cast in mind our country's horoscope,
Striving to find the future from the past,
From courage to the people known by rote:
The laughing face, the unimpeded mind,
The heart that slew itself through being kind;
Until she loomed at last
With light on either mast,
And turned our Liffey to a Styx of hope.

How often had I lain awake and heard
The pent-up city trembling to the shot,
I shall forget it not,
And he alone the quarry for the lead
Of each licentious savage on him set?
How often have I prayed that still they erred
When through the streets they dashed
And house and house was smashed.
Now Death holds in a net
What England could not get
For forty thousand pounds upon his head.

What master spy, what bloodhound nosed him out?
Surely he is our country's supreme foe:
And surely he shall go
Down the memorial ages. He shall have
The fame of Judas who McMurrough clad.
What alien schemer or deluded lout,
What Cain has caught his country by the throat,
What devil to destruction could devote
The brightest heart we had
While he was yet a lad,
And his unblemished body to the grave?

When in the Mouth of Blossom* your lips paled
Then pale with resolution re-imbued
The gathering multitude
With whom it is not lucky to contend,
The Race becomes a Collins in this fray,
The bravest of your land are now enmailed;
So keep with Death your long-acquainted tryst
No death can make your famous soul desist
That was in danger gay
From pointing out the way
To walk with you ennobled to the end.

*Béal na Blatha.

## Threnody

Dead Lady Gregory
In the category
Of those whose old clothes and old mots
Relieved beggary.
Lord, let your Ray light
All of her ways:
She was a playwright:
Works were her plays.
Angel guards be at her
Side in this lurch;
She made the theatre
Tame as the Church.
Passion Play's Hero,
Spare Grandmamma . . .
Lillibulero,
Bullen an ah!

## In Memoriam of my friend
## Arthur Russell, Soldier and Airman

He had the kind and langorous air
Of gentle knights detached from fear:
And he was quiet in his ways,
He who could set the heavens ablaze
And overtake the setting sun
With speed and soar into his throne.
If modesty clothes bravery,
If gentleness activity;
If earth has ever been the pen
Of heaven-aspiring denizen,
Then Arthur comes into his own
From lowly things released and flown,
And stands for that haut chivalry
Which scorns the world and scales the sky;
So Death, which no brave spirit harms,
Let him pass out retaining arms.

## George Bonass

Lover of life, in days like these
You were a man we ill could lose,
You with your gay extemporaries
Fearless, a galliard of the Muse.
What times we had, what days and nights
With all their alcoholic rites!
Often you turned the night to day
For cricket teams that came to play.
The gait of going lacked no spurs
When you took on those cricketers.
If in the darkness you discern
The hasty ghost of Davy Byrne
All night until your man's brought in
Your breakfast – Scots and aspirin.
What though you wandered in your gait
You always kept your willow straight
Oh, sir, well blocked, well blocked! Well played

You were a right good bat and blade.
It's I am out; and stumped at that,
And you have carried off your bat.
Now that the stumps are drawn for you,
Whom shall I tell my secrets to?
You've gone to join the Bucks and Beaux
You've gone where all the good men go:
The florid boys with full-eyed faces
With girls who knew not what straight lace is.
Well for the Bard you made amends
Who wreaked his failure on his friends.
Fanning will miss you, so will Hogan,
And, by the station, starry Rogan.

## Panegyric on Lieutenant Commander Eugene Esmonde of the Fleet Air Arm

*Lieutenant Commander Eugene Esmonde, who crippled the* Bismarck *by torpedoing its rudder from the air and got a D.S.O., has been awarded (posthumously) the Victoria Cross for his attack on the German battleships in the English Channel. The official citation reads:*
   *'After being attacked by a strong German force Commander Esmonde, as the Squadron Leader, lost touch with his fighter escort and his plane was damaged, but he flew on serenely challenging hopeless odds, to encounter the deadly fire of the battleship cruisers and their escort, which shattered the port wing of his aircraft,' said the citation continuing:*
   *'Undismayed he led the squadron on through an inferno of fire and almost at once was shot down, but his squadron went on to launch a gallant attack in which at least one torpedo is believed to have struck a German battle cruiser and from which not one of the six aircraft returned.'*

I

Eugene well got! Well born, I mean,
Of Norman knights on the Irish scene
Who threw in their lot with the Irish lot
And with them for liberty turned and fought.

If all were told of the Clan Esmonde,
The best would be known of Ireland:
How the large demesnes that they held and ranged
Expanded and shrank as their fortunes changed:
From Wexford up to the Hurdle Ford;
Back again, beaten to Waterford.
Castles and towns as the centuries went
Changed; but one thing was permanent –
Estreated lands or retaken holds,
Followers slaughtered and forfeited folds;
Ennobled now with restored estate,
Or hanged for a rebel in Ninety Eight;
No matter what hazard had Time to give –
Freedom was Esmonde's perogative
And liberty loved with a courtly air
And everything gentle and debonair.

II

Of all the feasts that are jovial
A wedding feast is the best of all.
And now I am fondly recalling one
When your only sister married my son.
And the tents were set and the tables spread
On lawns with branches overhead
And the bright air lingered, with music plied
On fields by the Shannon's broad-margined side,
The wide still river too smooth for foam
As wide as the meadows around your home,
The lake-like river that shone full brimmed
And half the day with its shining rimmed
To lend some rays of immortal mirth
To your ancient home on the dreaming earth.
Why do I speak as if you were living,
You who gave all that you had for the giving:
Youth and courage and love to come
And a courtly life in an ancient home?
I speak of you living, for I cannot find
A place for Death in the deathless mind,
The immortal mind that can still make room
For the Past and ward from a final doom
All that is noble and worthy to last
In the Present; and water the roots of the Past.

I see you now as I wish to see
You in that season of jollity
When glasses were lifted and healths were approved
And dancing feet in a chorus moved.
With colour high and a mild surprise:
And wide, with black lashes, your dark gray eyes,
You helped each guest lest the fun should stop,
Keeping the old world customs up.
Who would have thought that the boy you were then
Would rank with the world's outstanding men;
And that there was hid by your gentle mien
A strong, unshakeable soul serene?
Or dreamt of a change from the sunlit swards
To skies all but solid with blazing shards?

### III

Volunteers, take up a torpedo plane!
– Aye, Aye, Sir! Esmonde is taking off.
I hope he can find a clear sea-lane:
It is hard to see through this screening stuff;
They have blackened the sea like a school of squids;
They have stippled the sky with their Amoit guns:
Their fire converges in pyramids.
Can you hear me? And now the land batteries roar.
They are laying their smoke screens down no more!
They have seen him! They must have seen him at once!
– If they saw him, he also has seen them, Sir.

### IV

'He flew on serenely': official report
Of official, precise, unexcitable men
Who tell a tale tersely as men who are
Convinced that words have no place in war.
'He flew on serenely'. And now I read where
It says you outdistanced your fighter escort,
And rode on serenely, Telefer!
And now a shell shatters your wing on the port.
Like a stalwart knight in a high romance
Who charges on with a broken lance,
Through yellow flames of a screaming hell
You led the squadron unafraid.
And, oh, but they rode it and rode it well!

Through waves sky high with the blasts of death.
With ear drums bursting and choking for breath
They pressed till their missiles were gallantly launched.
Were these the boys who were up with you
When you shattered the Bismarck's steering gear,
And gave her a wound that could not be staunched,
The boys who haven't got time for fear,
The boys with a difficult job to do?
'He is down, shot down!' I can hear them say.
'Eugene is gone. The Commander's dead!'
Aye; but they followed the way you led
Though the red sky cracked and the welkin burned
They struggled right on where the cruisers fled,
'And not a craft of the six returned.'
In the Fleet they call it 'the Air Arm's way'
I picked out the words of the part they played:
'Serene' and 'gallant' and 'undismayed'.

V

Dead when life was clear and fresh
With rosy cheeks and steadfast eyes
Deprived of form, unsheathed from flesh:
This is the mystery of mysteries.
Gone like a sunset in Spring:
That which was shapely has now no shape.
This is coming to everything;
This from which there is no escape.
What is it into which everything goes?
Where has the surly wind banished the rose?
Into the mind of God whence it arose.

VI

Better be blasted at Life's full height
When life is transcended and free from pain;
Better a death in the thick of the fight
Than a death rattle under a counterpane.
And he was youthful when entering in
To The Hall of Fame in the minds of men.
'True.' The fighting Gael will say.
'Who wants a straw death, anyway?'
But what of his Mother? What shall I tell her,
Looking at waves that remind her of loss,

Thinking of many a childish phrase,
Of helpless hands and benignant ways
Before the grimness of the sword?
Is there hearts' heal in any word?'
'His Majesty sends the Victoria Cross,
The highest award that the King can give,
With its simple legend inscribed, FOR VALOUR.
The rose reigns on through the Winter's pallor.
The child that you cherished forever shall live.'
And let her take comfort from this sure thing:
He is saved from the pain that her death would bring.

### VII

Should we for a lover of Liberty moan?
He died but for that which was bred in the bone.
Strong men have given him meed of regret,
Regret that brings into higher relief
All the grand things that are worthy of grief.
Things that humanity dare not forget
To him were becoming, so he has become
Ancestral, a youthful and procreant shade
Serene and gallant and undismayed.
Fame for a myriad men is dumb;
Yet fluent are the lips of Fame
For spirits elect and mettlesome:
'He had too much to give to doom:
Think of him as a branch in bloom,
A gentleman sans fear, sans blame.'

# Part 4

# THE PLAYS

# THE PLAYS

## INTRODUCTION

Not for nothing did *Blight*, Gogarty's first play to be written for and produced in the Abbey Theatre, have as its subtitle *The Tragedy of Dublin*, for it conveys a strong social message, indeed a political and economic one too. Gogarty had known and was appalled by the conditions of life experienced by the poor in Dublin from his medical student days on, particularly by the squalor of life endured by those who were compressed into the congested tenements. In sending the play to Lady Gregory, he wrote that it was intended to expose misapplied philanthropy, his other motive being to put a true picture of Dublin conditions on the stage. No disinterring of past Celtic heroes then, nor echoes of Synge's folk drama, but a Dublin doctor's desire to show how the poor were exploited, how the need was for preventive rather than remedial measures, and how hospitals, charity and charitable institutions provided an escape from responsibility. 'The only people who benefit from charity', says Tumulty in the third act, 'are the charitable people themselves'. And Gogarty linked their effects with those of political corruption.

Early in his career as a doctor Gogarty had made direct attacks on the situation of the poor and the system which caused it. Giving an address on 'The Need for Medical Inspection of School Children' at the Meath Hospital in 1911, he stressed the need to provide for the health of children. Schools should not be a menace to them: 'Torturing with teaching a little starving child affects both the mind and the body'. He

505

wanted school meals to be provided for children as well as medical examinations. A further address on the needs of children followed in 1913. He stressed the need for clean milk and for fresh air; the streets were full of mud and manure, 'dust and dessicated dung that pervaded houses and utensils'. Sanitation was disgraceful with the typical 'one common privy bemerded beyond use' which stood beside 'the one common water supply pipe which a corporation notice guards from waste'. Gogarty was to continue his personal crusade for amelioration of housing: as a senator he made twenty-seven speeches on the subject in one year.

The first two acts of *Blight* are set in a dilapidated tenement room. Stanislaus Tully, his sister, her crippled son and daughter are anticipatory of O'Casey's slum dwellers,especially those in *Juno and the Peacock*. Tully displays cunning in his use of compensation money (for the accident in which a bag fell on him) to buy the house and the neighbouring one for £100; fluent and eloquent,he becomes a politician, and in the third act is about to sell the houses for £2000, a considerable profit. 'Tenement property in Dublin', Tumulty remarks in the third Act, 'is like cheese that grows in value as it rots'.

The Dublin vernacular in the play is full of vitality. Tully, for instance, possesses a lively narrative skill:

Out comes my solicitor – a bald, big-headed, innocent-looking baby of a fellow, but as cute as six ould min. 'Have you any sensation in the legs?' sez he, in a whisper. 'Awful!' sez I. 'Nonsense' sez he, 'Ye don't feel them at all!' In the name of heaven! . . . Is it after me three weeks' suffering . . . ? 'That'll do ye' 'sez he, 'Remember now, not even if they stick you with a pin!' 'Is all me agony to go for nothing?' sez I. 'Which of us is conducting the case', sez he. 'On which of us did the bag fall,' sez I. 'That'll do ye now', sez he.

Tully uses oratical questions skilfully, as his defence of the wider social benefits of alcohol makes clear; he cites some of the city's buildings built by those who made their money by drink:

Did it ever strike you that nothing good was ever done by preaching in this town? What built Findlater's Church? Was it preaching or drink? Drink. And the new hostel in Hatch Street? Drink. What renovated St Patrick's and cleared Bull Alley? Drink. What gave us Stephen's Green – Drink – and the ducks swimming in it.

Tully's niece Lily's conversation with Miss Maxwell-Knox, the District Visitor, is smart and succinct. To Miss Maxwell-Knox's comment that 'The wages of sin *is* death' she replies 'The wages of sin is a month in the Locke'. The Locke Hospital specialised in venereal disease (Lily is later to contract syphilis) and Gogarty's play is the first to discuss this, 'the spread of the hidden plague in the city'. A reply to a Local Government Board letter on the subject is 'postponed' by the Board of the Townsend

Thanatorion, with Tully, now a member of the Board, pronouncing 'Let them that put themselves in the way of that disorder put up with it'. He wants the letter sent back to 'those evil minded blackguards in the Local Government Board that wrote it and tell them we won't have our city insulted'. Gogarty's final message is put in the mouth of Tumulty, a forthright and independent-minded Board member:

The less you spend on prevention the more you will pay for cure. Until the citizens realise that their children should be brought up in the most beautiful and favourable surroundings the city can afford, and not in the most squalid, until this floundering Moloch of a Government realise that they must spend more money on education than on police, this city will continue to be the breeding ground of disease, vice, hypocrisy and discontent.

*Blight* went down well with the Abbey audience and despite its topicality remains dramatically effective. Even more topical was *A Serious Thing,* a one act play mocking English inability to understand Ireland. The Centurion and two Roman soldiers, in khaki uniforms, to make the point clear, are guarding the tomb of Lazarus, whose resurrection symbolises Ireland's rebirth. This satiric play is a slight affair, but contains some digs at the interest of W.B. Yeats and his wife in the supernatural (it may have prompted his play *The Resurrection*) as well as some echoes of the speech of Talbot Clifton, Gogarty's rich and eccentric neighbour in Connemara.

*The Enchanted Trousers*, produced shortly after *A Serious Thing*, is much more effective in its farcical portrayal of the 'Department' (as Sir Horace Plunkett's organisation for Irish agricultural reform was known). A visiting committee is conned into approving Humphrey Heavey, an Irish actor who pretends to be an Englishman, as Minister for Potato Spraying; he then abandons his mother and schoolteacher brother who have thought up his role. The satire is directed not only at the 'Department's' habit of appointing Englishmen to high positions in its organisation, but also at accepted aspects of Irish and English national characteristics.

*Incurables* (1958) was written after a return trip back to Ireland after the Second World War. In it, Gogarty returns to his earlier attack on charitable institutions. His stay in America had, if anything, sharpened his satirical view, this time of Irish hospitals catering for the old. A hospital governor suppresses an elixir of restorative power because he thinks the country needs such homes for the old and feeble. The play was rejected by the Abbey Theatre (in 1951), regarded as 'too cruel' by Ernest Blythe, a Government nominee who was Managing Director of the theatre from 1941 to 1967, a very dull period in its history.

Gogarty has been regarded by some as the author of the very slight anonymous play *The Worked Out Ward*, (1918) which parodies Lady

Gregory's *The Workhouse Ward*. It has been published in Lady Gregory's *Comedies* (1970). I. It is included here in Appendices. He certainly wrote or worked on other plays in the late nineteen-thirties, among them *Wave Lengths*, the complete text of which was 'unaccountably' lost. The surviving portion is included here in Appendices. It suggests that this exploration of an idea that living voices could be captured from the ether was original and could have been very effective. The scope for blackmail is explored, and Gogarty's personal attitude to Joyce's treatment of him and his use of Gogarty's words in *Ulysses* appears to have shaped some of the play's thought about the potential tyranny of technology in the hands of the unscrupulous. Another play probably written about the same time was *Caerleon* or *The Camp of the Legions* of which two scenes of an act survive in typescript, possibly linked to Gogarty's book *I Follow St Patrick* (1938).

Lady Gregory had written to Gogarty in October 1919 with various suggestions for *The Enchanted Trousers* and her wish that the play should be as good as his talk — 'There ought not to be a bald sentence in it, there isn't in your conversation'. In both *Blight* and *The Enchanted Trousers* the speeches of his characters, lively and arresting, show his capacity for dialogue. In *Incurables*, included in *A Week End in the Middle of the Week and Other Essays on the Bias* (1958), Gogarty captured the accent of Dublin speech, quick, lively, imaginative. There is a good deal of coddin' in it as could be expected with the characters' backgrounds in the Coombe and Moore Street, famous for the repartee that flourished there. This is a lively sketch, tenser than his earlier plays. It reminds us that, as Lady Gregory had recognised earlier, witty conversational interchanges were what he could best bring to drama. But the charisma of creative conversation, the lure of the lyric and the power of prose that so successfully approximated to spontaneous speech occupied him more.

# BLIGHT

---

THE TRAGEDY OF DUBLIN
*An Exposition in Three Acts*

This play was first produced at the Abbey Theatre in Dublin, on 11 December 1917, with the following cast:

| | |
|---|---|
| STANISLAUS TULLY, a labouring man | Fred O'Donovan |
| MRS MARY FOLEY, his sister | May Craig |
| JIMMY, her crippled son | Michael MacLiammoir |
| LILY, her daughter | Irene Kelly |
| MISS MAXWELL-KNOX, a district visitor | Margaret Nicholls |
| MRS LARISSEY, a neighbour | Maureen Delany |
| MR BANNERMANN, landlord of tenement | Maurice Esmonde |
| JIMMY LARISSEY, a cabman | P. J. McDonnell |
| A LABOURER | Barry Fitzgerald |
| MEDICAL DICK | Arthur Shields |
| MEDICAL DAVY | Clement Garrick |
| CHARWOMAN | Dorothy Lynd |

Members of the Board of the Townsend Thanatorion:

| | |
|---|---|
| MR NORRIS GALBRAITH | Eric Gorman |
| MR TISDALL-TOWNSLEY | Fred Harford |
| MR MORPHY | Peter Nolan |
| MR WILLIAM MCWHIRTER | Hubert McGuire |
| MR TUMULTY | Louis O'Connor |
| GEORGE FOLEY, a discharged soldier | Bryan Herbert |

*Produced by Fred O'Donovan*

# BLIGHT

## ACT ONE

*Scene 1. – A dilapidated, beautiful room in a tenement house. Beds right, left and in front left. A clothes-line crosses diagonally, so that a hanging quilt drawn may screen a bed. Beside one bed is a jam-pot on a chair. Washstand and screen at foot between beds at window. A chair for cripple beside fire-place.*

TULLY (*lying in bed, right*). Eh, Mary, are ye awake yet? . . . Are ye awake, Mary . . . ? Mary, surely yer not asleep at this hour.

MARY (*lying in bed, left*). Well, then, indeed I'm not. Can't ye be awake for a minute without thinking that everyone else is asleep? Sorra much sleep I get between the children and yerself. I suppose it's a drink ye want?

TULLY. Go on; that's right! Why don't you say I'm drunk once for all and aise yer mind, instead of keepin' it in yer brain simmerin'?

MARY. Well if yer not drunk – yer fidgetin' for it. What is it you want?

TULLY. I want to know what's keeping little Jim.

MARY. How do I know what's keeping him except the weight of the jug. Don't ye know it's a shame to ask a child like that to go a public-house – to say nothing of the burden on his poor little limbs?

TULLY. Don't ye know damn well I can't show me nose out or I'd go meself? I, that am lying here trying to bear up this three weeks to take yez all out of poverty.

MARY. And sorra much ye ever bore; ye haven't as much patience as would get you caught in a shower of rain. How bad ye are can be judged from the food ye ate and the drink ye can lower.

TULLY. It's not for us to judge, Mary. That's a matter for the medical profession. Ye mustn't fly in the face of science. If ye could only realise the pain I'm bearing and the agony I'm in – and ye would realise it if ye heard what the doctor said to the solicitor. 'Shock,' sez he; 'collapse,' sez he; 'incapacitated' and 'complete prostration,' sez he; then ye would understand how mental suffering is far worse than mere physical suffering, and this will be me evidence: 'After hitching

511

wan bag on to the crane an' the ganger gave the signal to hoist, I was in th' act iv bendin' to tie the rope round the next bag to have it ready when the ring bruck and the bag that was hoisted fell on me spine and left me flat. I remember no more till I woke up in th' hospital a cripple for life, wid a pain in me back an' a drag in me walk that leaves me as wake as a cat when I cross the flure of the room.' Them's me symptoms, sorra bit alleviated, and it comes badly from me own sisther to doubt or contradict them, for if ye do yer contradicting yer own future.

MARY. I'm not doubting them. I hope ye'll be well compensated – though it's the only day's work ye ever did that the company's paying for – but it's no reason why ye should have sent that poor child out. How can his poor little back carry a full jug up three flights of stairs?

TULLY (*mimicking her*). How can his poor little back carry the buckets of slops ye send him down three flights of stairs with?

MARY (*with a gesture of despair*). Sure, what can I do? I can't get up and I can't leave the place in filth?

TULLY. Well then, why do ye run away wid the idea that because I wasn't stirring out of bed I wasn't working? There's many a wan works hard without putting a hand to a tool – brain working. Is it because I'm not running round clucking like a hen that ye think I wasn't working out a great idea? That's what I was at and ye'll see the result of it this very day if they give me compensation in the courts. Sure, my God, woman dear, don't ye know it's a rule of life the less the work the more the wages. Ye have only to look at the judges themselves and the Town Councillors.

MARY. A nice judge you'd make.

TULLY (*significantly*). No, but I'd make a likely town councillor.

MARY. That'll do yeh!

TULLY. If I get compensated according to me injuries I'll buy up Bannermann and go up for the election to the Ward the week afther.

MARY. Buy up Bannermann? Sure we can't even pay his week's rent. It's not likely he'll sell either.

TULLY. I said *if* I get compensation, then it's all plain sailing.

MARY. But Bannermann –

TULLY. Ah, leave that fellow to me! There are sanitary laws in existence that would wipe out Bannermann if they were only put in force. And I'll put them in force to force him to part with this house and the wan next door to it too, or I'm not Stanislaus Tully!

(*Enter* JIMMY.)

TULLY. Ah, Jimmy, I thought ye had forgotten yer uncle! (JIMMY *limps in with a washing-jug full of porter and carries it to the wash-stand, leaving it in the basin.*)

TULLY (*turning half out of bed*). Just walk up to the fireplace and back again until I show your mother the reasons I had for sending you out.
(JIMMY *goes back and loiters by door.* TULLY *rises and limps in imitation to close the door.*)
MARY. Mocking is catching.
TULLY. I know what's catching (*Ladles out a glassful of porter.*) – and who's going to catch it. The trial's coming off at twelve o'clock. I must get back now (*Returns to bed*) and wait for Jimmy Larissey and his cab.
JIMMY. Here's Miss Maxwell-Knox!
(TULLY *inverts a jam-pot over his glass of stout, gets under the bed-clothes hurriedly, and turns a card on the wall over bed, which reads: 'The Kingdom of God is within you.' Enter* MISS MAXWELL-KNOX, *consulting note-book.*)
MISS M-K. This is Mrs Foley's room?
MARY. Yes, Miss! Come in, Miss. God bless ye, Miss! Yer very welcome! Were ye able to get Jimmy into hospital?
TULLY (*in a weak voice, with his eyes fixed on card*). Come in, Miss! Yer very welcome, Miss – and so is anywan that's always doin' good. (*Louder.*) Get a chair for Miss Maxwell-Knox, ye little blackguard, Jimmy!
MISS M-K. I hope you are better to-day, Tully.
TULLY. Ah, I wouldn't say that; I wouldn't say that –
MISS M-K. Have you not got to go to court to-day?
TULLY. I have to be brought there, Miss. I hope to have the strength for the journey.
MISS M-K (*with a grim smile*). You know the source of all strength?
TULLY. Aye, indeed. But, incapacitated and completely prostrated as I am since the crane fell . . .
MISS M-K. No one is incapacitated from prayer nor from forgiveness and mercy. A sparrow cannot fall from the housetop without your Father knowing it, by which is meant that the poor are as important in His eyes as the rich. The poor, who are always with us.
TULLY. True for ye! It's on wan of them the bag fell. Now yer talking! The poor we have always wid us – an' it's high time something was done to stop it. As things are going, you'd think it was planned so that the poor would be always here. (MISS M-K *makes a gesture of horror.*)
MISS M-K. You shouldn't say that, you mustn't say that!
TULLY. But it's yerself that said it, and I'm axing is there to be no escape for the poor?
MISS M-K. 'They that are lacking shall have abundance.'
TULLY. That's all very fine and large. Look at us here – eight in a room when the childer's in. That's the only abundance we have.
MISS M-K. But God helps these that help themselves!
TULLY. How are we to help ourselves? How's Mary there to help herself

with her six children? Only for the Separation Allowance she and them might as well be in the workhouse, even if they could get themselves admitted. Only for that there'd be little for her, and me out of work.

MISS M-K. Yes . . . It's hard, but it gives occasion for fortitude. Without vicissitude that virtue would be lost. There is much that lies in your power to do and you neglect it. For instance, you should practise cleanliness, which is next to Godliness. Look at that little boy's face. (JIMMY *is waiting behind chair for lady to sit on.*) Just look at that little boy's face – the dirt of it, the neglect! Come here, my poor dear dirty little boy and I will help to clean your face. (*Takes him by the shoulder and makes to wash-stand, greatly to* TULLY'S *horror. Dips in her hand with washing-glove, and draws it out darkened with stout.*) Why, what is this? (*Smells it.*) Why, it's DRINK! Drink, you debauched, deceitful wretch! After all your promises and your pledge and the money I gave you for food! Drinking again . . .

(*Stamps her foot on the floor.*)

MARY. Be careful, Miss. That's wan of the rotten boards; ye might go through there for it's a bit dozed around the washstand. (TULLY *sits up in bed with resolute face of dignity offended, puts his hand for silence until he delivers his explanation.*)

TULLY. First of all, I'm not 'drinking' (*Imitates her accent.*) Secondly, it's not DRINK, for by that you mean drunkenness and self-indulgence.

MISS M-K. What is it then if it isn't drink?

TULLY (*composedly*). In spite of all your charitable work – and indeed I may say, your charity – it's sad to see how little you know how the poor live – or – how they don't live. I told you that when the childer comes in from school and Lily comes in from the laundry we'll be eight in this room. With the childer crying from the cold or hunger – as the case may be – how is the wage earner to get a night's rest in a bed where there isn't room to turn? Jimmy there and his big brother lies in my bed. With noise, misery and vermin rest is impossible, not to talk of sleep. Man, woman and child must live, sleep, dress, cook and eat and wash body and clothes in this wan place. Why don't you ask us why we are huddled here together without distinction of sexes? No, ye don't! That would raise one of these questions about capital and labour that touch upon vested interest and are so embarrassing. Ye prefer the cheap and easy cant about drink. Why do we drink? Because we want to sleep, because it's cheaper than chloroform! Who could stand this living hell without drink? Suppose ye had three childer in the bed with ye like Mary there and was expecting a baby, how are ye to get up and cook food? Isn't the milk of the city liquid filth, and if it wasn't wouldn't it get filthy standing in a room with all the slops – while a pint of porter is eating and drinking. Was it drink gave Jimmy his diseased hip? The worst thing drink does is that it brings us visits from the likes of you. For it's not to do good ye came here; ye kem here to get yer self-complacency stroked down wud the smoothing-iron of our vices. It's all drink, drink, and nothing else. Yer putting the cart before the horse, me lady. Poverty *first,* then dirt and disease and discontent and vice follow, and your preaching. Was it drink sent Georgie to the war for the sake of the Separation Allowance? Did it ever strike you that nothing good was ever done by preaching in this town? What built Findlater's Church? Was it preaching or drink? Drink. And the new hostel in Hatch Street? Drink. What put a roof on Christ Church Cathedral? Drink. What renovated St. Patrick's and cleared Bull Alley? Drink. What gave us Stephen's Green – Drink – and the ducks swimming in it! Drink doesn't keep us poor; but poverty makes us drink.

MISS M-K. But it's quite unfair to insinuate that if wine merchants and brewers elect to leave money to build churches, therefore religion depends on drink.

TULLY. No; but it's addicted to religion in an extraordinary way!

MARY. In the name of God, Stannie, what are ye saying to the lady? Don't mind him, Miss. He's excited about going to Court to-day, and his spine's injured – I wouldn't be surprised if it's getting up into his brain. He doesn't mean to be insulting. Besides, when he talks for the sake of speeching he can't help being offensive any more than one of them orators once he gets going. Stannie, ye ought to have manners enough to keep yer mouth shut before the lady.

TULLY. What do ye mean, Mary, be saying that I'm insulting? I never meant to give offence, but when she puts her hand into me night's rest and me morning's breakfast there it's enough to make any invalid – and invalids are always irritable – complain. I'm very sorry indeed, Miss Maxwell-Knox, if I said anything to hurt ye. If I had meant to be insulting I'd have handed ye back yer card (*Points to text.*) I only meant to say that without porter there would be no repose for the poor.

MISS M-K. But look at the harm it does, and the money it wastes that could be spent on other things! If I had known that you did not adhere strictly to your resolutions to be abstemious I would not have troubled you with my presence.

MARY. Ah, don't mind him, Miss! It's good ye are doing. If ye can only get poor little Jimmy into hospital.

TULLY. Surely ye wouldn't neglect your duty to extend a helping hand to the poor and weak and the weak-minded?

(*Enter* LILY *in fur coat. Looks boldly at* MISS M-K *and draws quilt hanging on clothes-line to screen her bed. Powders her face and whistles while arranging her hair.* MISS M-K, *seeing her, looks her up and down critically with lorgnette.*)

MISS M-K. The wages of sin is death.

LILY (*singing 'Hi tiddy li-i-ti. Carry me back to Blighty,' makes a gesture at* MISS M-K, *with her fingers and thumb.*)

MISS M-K. The wages of sin *is* death.

LILY. The wages of sin is a month in the Locke. (*Attempts to go out but is opposed by* MISS M-K.)

MISS M-K. Why are you not at the laundry doing *honest* work?

LILY. Because I didn't get *honest* wages – if ye want to know.

MARY. Lily is in a restaurant, Miss. Don't mind her, she'll be going out shortly.

LILY. I am. I'm in a restaurant and I get seven and six a week and two rounds of bread and margarine and a cup of tay, and free temptation, which is more than comes in other people's way. (*Making a face aside.*)

MISS M-K. May I inquire where you are going?

LILY. Will ye go look and ax?

MISS M-K. If I were you, my poor girl, I would not go on the streets.

LILY (*surveying her*). Sure, I'd know by the old beak of ye, ye wouldn't.
        (*Enter* MRS LARISSEY.)

MRS L. Will ye whist! Mary, here's Mr Bannermann for the rent.

MISS M-K. (*excitedly*). You are a matron, I presume and I appeal to you to add your influence to any influence for good that I may possess and join with me in preventing this young girl from living a life of viciousness and sin!

MRS L. If ye can't mind yer own business, ye can interview her father if he comes back from the fighting; meanwhile ye ought to turn yer activities on the landlord of these mansions who is coming up the stairs with a Notice to Quit for herself and the baby unborn in the bed there.
        (*Enter a boy.*)

BOY. Here's Bannermann, mother, to put us out!

MISS M-K. Good gracious, no! . . . I will sympathise, but –

MRS L. I suppose ye will go on talking about vice and calling me a matron and see this poor woman and her six children flung out into the street? That's what sends girls like Lily on the town, if ye want to know.

MISS M-K. What does it matter compared to the enormity of sin? Poverty is innocent. To be poor is no one's fault; but to be sinful, to brazen it out . . .

MARY. Well, all I can say is that when the Little Sisters of the Poor were here and seen Lily they made no remarks like that.

TULLY. No, nor the Vincent de Pauls!

MRS L. Arrah, will ye go 'long to hell and keep that kind of talk for them that sent her there. Do ye want that poor woman's child to be born in the streets? Mebbe ye'd prefer the workhouse. But I'll see that so long as there's breath in me body, nobody will put her out of this. (*Folds her arms.*)

TULLY. What's that ye are saying, Mrs Larissey, about Lily being sent on the streets? You'd think ye had as bad a mind as Miss Maxwell-Knox, who sees the devil or drink in everything, and sorra bit of good anywhere. Lily is as dacent a girl as there is in Gloucester Street!

MRS L. Wasn't it she that said it, the ould faggot. (*Going up to* MISS M-K.) If I'd a heard ye I'd a flung ye out body and bones meself . . . (*Enter* BANNERMANN, *collector.*) If it's good ye're after maybe ye'll explain to this fellow how Mrs Foley is to pay him 4/6 a week and keep her six children and the baby that's coming on the pay of her husband who got a job at the Front?

MISS M-K. Don't call it a 'job,' Mrs Larissey. He is fighting for humanity and civilisation, as every able-bodied man should be!

MARY. He's trying to keep a roof over our head.

TULLY. He's sorting letters somewhere in France.

MRS L. If, instead of criticising the poor, ye want to help them, will ye tell us how is Mrs Foley to pay 4/6 for her room and keep six childer – and one of them a cripple – on it?

BANNERMANN (*pinning Notice to Quit on the door*). I'm just pinning this to keep things in order. If ye pay before the week's out, well and good. I wish ye luck to-day, Stan.

TULLY. I'll see ye paid all right, Mr Bannermann. For peace sake, Miss Knox, or the love of God, go home out of that before Mrs Larissey gets – indignant.

LILY. So long. I'm off. (*To* MISS M-K.) Good-bye, Vigilance! (*Exit.*)

JIMMY (*calling after her*). Will ye have any chocolates for me, Lily, when ye come home in the morning?

MISS M-K. You can settle your own disputes. I shall no longer extend my help where there is nothing but ingratitude and ill desert. (*Exit.*)

MRS L. Good riddance. Sorra loss!

TULLY. Yes, that's the way, ye're always going on decrying the rich and forgetting to do anything to help yourselves from being poor. Ye can abuse Miss Knox to yer heart's content, but abuse is cheap and useless. If ye want to make the likes of her sit up ye must stand by yerselves, stand by me. Don't forget there's a vacancy in this ward, and I'm the man to fill it.

MRS L. Ye look better able to fill what yer in.

TULLY. Don't be facetious, Mrs Larissey. It's facetiousness that distracts ladies of wit like you from the serious things of life. Who can represent you better than one of yourselves, a man of the people and for the people – and I've already been promised strong support if the lawsuit comes off all right; but we'll want all yer wit to get me in.

BANNERMANN. Is it this ward ye intend to represent?

TULLY. Yes, it is! And sorra wan round here will have a chance against a democrat in a democratic constituency.

BANNERMANN. Dublin's looking for men with a stake in the city, and not lodgers to represent the Ward. How can property owners like myself afford to pay 12/- in the £ rates and keep a house like this in repair, if we have to support the likes of you on the Corporation?

TULLY. A stake in the city. Ye'd like to narrow the franchise, would ye? A tenement in a slum, that's what ye represent, and the day I'm elected Town Councillor the effect of my councilling will be pretty soon felt by you, me lad! I suppose you want to bully me poor sister out of 4/6 for a bed in a corner of this rotten room.

MRS L. Leave her alone till she gets little Jimmy into hospital, and God bless you, Mr Bannermann!

BANNERMANN. And even if I have a tenement house or two I am not the only corporator with an interest in tenements; and it comes well indeed from you, sponging here on your sister and devouring my rent in idleness and drink. (*Exit.*)

(*Enter a* JARVEY *and his friend.*)

JARVEY. Are ye ready, Stan?

TULLY. Ah, more power, me sound min. Come 'ere, me butties an' give us a hand. I'm that prostrated that I'm not able to move. D'ye think I'll be fit for the stairs? (*They help him out of bed.*) Put the left leg on the floor first – it's lucky.

JARVEY. Begorra, this is a five shilling job. Make it ten shillings if ye win and nothing if ye lose.

TULLY. Done me friend. I'm wid ye!

LABOURER. What about puttin' on yer Sunday blue?

TULLY. D'ye want me to be dressed up like a stockbroker? No begob? I'll go as the Company sent me home – tattered and torn and smashed up be the crane. (*They put on his boots.*) Where's me muffler, Mary?

MARY. Where would it be but where ye left it?

TULLY. I suppose it's on the piano with me clogs . . . Oh! be careful of me poor back!

LABOURER. Begob it would never do to waste a creak of it till we get you down to Green Street. (*He takes his crutch, they help him out.*)

MARY. Good luck to ye, Stannie!

TULLY (*on the stairs*). Heave easy, boys, ye carry Caesar!

# CURTAIN

## ACT TWO

*Scene — Same as in Act One.*

MARY. Is that you, Jimmy? (*Enter* JIMMY *with paper hat.*) See who's coming up the stairs. It's hardly time for yer uncle to be back yet. (JIMMY *goes out; re-enters.*)

JIMMY. Mother, here's Medical Dick from Phibsboro'.

MARY. Ye mustn't call the gentleman names, but learn to have respect for yer superiors. He's a very kind doctor and much better than the usual midwifery cases they send out.

(*Enter* MEDICAL DICK, *smoking a cigarette and carrying a bag.*)

MEDICAL D. May I come in, Mrs Foley? How are ye to-day?

MARY. Run out of this, Jimmy, and play on the lobby, that's a good child. (*Exit* JIMMY.) Won't you sit down?

MEDICAL D. (*drawing chair*). Ye aren't feeling any pains, Mrs Foley?

MARY. No sir — I think it will be a day or two yet. I'd like that it ud be you that would attend me if ye could, sir. Will ye be on duty all the week?

MEDICAL D. Well, I'm in a difficulty. I have to take out one more conduction case or they won't let me up for th' exam on Monday; and I have to go to Baldoyle, for my uncle has a sure thing running to win me back my fees. If I miss either you or it I'm done for.

MARY. So it's a race between the horse and the baby.

MEDICAL D. (*embarrassed*). Well, what I mean is . . . of course . . . there are other men on night duty that could relieve me; but I'm staying on duty specially watching you night and day, as it were, and exam or no exam, I'd be as careful of you as if you were — er — as if you were me first.

MARY. I'm sure ye will, sir! I'd like to have yerself, sir, ye were so lucky with the last — though ye came a bit late.

MEDICAL D. I'll send down a nurse that's a great pal of mine and she will let me know how ye are. If I'm out atself the porteress in the hall will

519

know where to find me.

(*Enter* JIMMY *excitedly*.)

JIMMY. Oh, mother, uncle's coming home! Half the street is after him and he has no crutch. (*Runs to window and looks out through the broken pane*.) Here's the cab coming round the bend!

MARY (*excitedly*). Is yer uncle in it?

JIMMY. No.

MARY. Ah!

JIMMY. No, he's sitting with his arm round the driver on the box; Jack Dempsey's marching in front like a band-conductor twirling the crutch. Mother, they're coming! Uncle's coming home! (*Runs excitedly through the door*.)

MEDICAL D. Are ye feeling weak, Mrs Foley?

MARY (*breathless*). No, it's only the palpitation I have when the wind gets congealed round me heart . . . Oh, I hope he's won! . . . It would mean such a lot to us all . . . Oh, if you please – if it isn't too much – would you mind puttin' yer head out to see what's happened?

MEDICAL D. What happened to who? (*Cheering heard from the street. Great noise in the hall*.)

MARY. Oh, I hear them on the stairs . . . he's won, he's won! (*Falls back in a faint*.)

(MEDICAL DICK *takes her pulse. Enter* TULLY, *thrust in with his two friends, cabman and labourer banging him on the back*.)

TULLY. Three hundred pounds!

MEDICAL D. Hush man! Mrs Foley has just fainted.

TULLY (*concerned*). It's nothing serious, I hope. Would a drop of this be any good? (*Produces naggin. Exeunt friends on tiptoe*.)

MEDICAL D. Open the window.

TULLY. Begob it ud be too bad if poor Mary went off before hearing of the wages for me one day's work.

MARY. Oh, I'm all right now.

TULLY. Break the news to her, break the news. (*Comes and whispers loudly*.) Three hundred pounds!

MARY (*smiling*). Please God it will do you good. Don't forget you promised to get little Jimmy looked after.

TULLY. Never fear, Mary. How are ye feeling now?

MARY. Grand again!

TULLY. Aye, I thought there was something reviving in three hundred pounds.

MEDICAL D. Claim under Workmen's Compensation?

TULLY. Begor it was – Employer's Liability.

MARY. How did ye do it, Stannie?

TULLY. Sit aisy there and I'll tell ye all. Mebbe, sir, you'll understand the medical words. I don't mind telling ye it's far from plain to me.

MEDICAL D. You can't expect medical terms to be plain and scientific at the same time?

TULLY. There was a shocking wrangling going on when we got down to Court. They smuggled me in quietly at the side-door, and I was kept ready to be produced. Out comes my solicitor – a bald, big-headed, innocent-looking baby of a fellow, but as cute as six ould min. 'Have you any sensation in the legs?' sez he, in a whisper. 'Awful!' sez I. 'Nonsense,' sez he, 'ye don't feel them at all!' 'In the name of heaven! . . . is it after me three weeks' suffering . . . ?' 'That'll do ye' sez he. 'Remember now, not even if they stick you with a pin!' 'Is all me agony to go for nothing?' sez I. 'Which of us is conducting the case?' sez he. 'On which of us did the bag fall,' sez I. 'That'll do ye now,' sez he. Then he pulls out me little bearded doctor while the big ones were swearing. 'Mind you, now; total absence of sensation, Tully,' he said, 'and I'm sorry to hear it.' 'Let yer legs swing loose,' sez he; 'keep thinking of yer knees all the time if they strike ye on the knee-caps.' 'Where does me spine come in?' I asked. 'I can demonstrate what I mean if you like, me lord,' I heard the big surgeon saying. 'Vivisection!' shouts me little doctor, who is as cute as a rat, 'ye'll subject my patient to no such indignity!' 'I did not mean on the plaintiff, my lord. Protect me from this abominable innuendo.'

MEDICAL D. What was the abominable innuendo?

TULLY. Wasn't he goin' to wriggle me spine before the whole court. 'I have too much surgical instinct for that, I hope,' sez the big surgeon, in a hell of a wax. 'It could all be accounted for by an attack of acute anterior poliomyelitis' sez he then. I looked round, but my solicitor had disappeared. 'Infantile paralysis in a man of fifty!' sez the ratty little doctor with the beard. 'Or spina bifida?' sez someone else. 'What's that?' the Judge snaps out: 'I've had enough of this (a poor man's Judge!) The injuries you mention are grave injuries anyway. Even if it were a case of infantile paralysis – which is a misnomer if a man has to wait to get it until he is forty-five – even if it could be got since the fall of the crane belonging to the company, while in the employment of the company and doing the company's work, the maximum sum I'm entitled . . .' 'Whist, me lord, my clients have settled by consent.' Then back comes my big solicitor, looking very aggrieved. 'I'm afraid three hundred pounds will hardly pay you for the loss of a spine,' sez he.

MARY. Well glory be to God for that anyway.

MEDICAL D. And did you say nothing?

TULLY. Iv course I did. I said 'How could I have put the chain round the bag if the sack was empty?'

MEDICAL D. Now what do you intend to do?

TULLY (*grandiosely*). I'm thinking of taking up social reform.

MEDICAL D. Why, it's only people with independent means can indulge themselves with social reform.

TULLY (*sarcastically*). Doctors differ, me lad. Doctors differ.

MEDICAL D. And why shouldn't they? So do diseases. When the public pay varying fees for opinions they are entitled to their money's worth. Surely you don't want doctors to be all as uniform as a box of Beecham's Pills?'

(*Enter* BANNERMANN.)

TULLY. Ah, never fear! Back again for yer four and sixpence?

BANNERMANN. I'm glad to hear ye were so successful.

TULLY. I don't doubt ye; but before me sister pays you the rent it's my duty to see that she's getting her money's worth, and not putting herself into the clutches of the law by paying you . . .

BANNERMANN. What are you talking about?

TULLY. If she pays 4/6 a week for this room before you make the floor safe, before you put a water-tap on the lobby, before you put the stairs and hall in a safe and sanitary condition, before you provide a water-closet for less than forty-seven people – male and female – before you disinfect the kitchen where old McLoughlin died of typhus – which they called enteric in the death certificate – before you whitewash the passages and repair those windows, she will be guilty of complicity in a plot against the health of the city, from which even your nephew the Sanitary Inspector, will be unable to extricate her.

BANNERMANN. Plots against public health! You are talking through your hat! There's no such thing.

TULLY. What, no public health?

BANNERMANN. Whether there is or not, no one would believe in a plot against it. I must trouble you, Mrs Foley, for this week's rent and three weeks' arrears.

TULLY. You can take your choice now. Serve your process for the rent and wait till ye get it. There's not a lodger in the place will pay ye now until I give the word, and that word won't pass me lips until ye put this verminous warren into the semblance of a habitation fit for even the lowest grade of human beings. It's not that ye haven't been told about it often enough.

BANNERMANN. So that's yer game! A no-rent campaign against house-property holders!

TULLY. It's very far from being a game, it is a solemn protest from your tenants against the delay in carrying out repairs. I have said nothing against over-crowding. Do you know how many souls sometimes take – what I can't call shelter – under this roof? Do you? You don't, and you the landlord. And ye don't know either what the Inspector of Dangerous Buildings has in his mind with regard to this ramshackle edifice. Let me tell you he was down here photographing the crack over the hall door lately with a minister and one or two of the boys.

BANNERMANN. That'll do ye now. None of yer bluff! Let *me* tell *you* that it wasn't the Inspector that was doing the photography, but the Georgian Society. I heard Professor Mahaffy himself saying that he never seen such a house.

TULLY. It ud be hard for him. Is there any harm in asking you what it cost you?

BANNERMANN. Well, there is not. This and – you know I acquired the adjoining edifice recently – well, this and that stood me in, what with structural alterations to make it suitable for single-room dwellings, the best part of £320.

TULLY. God help you (*deprecatingly*.) God help you! When ye come to put this house in a sanitary condition it will cost ye another £320.

BANNERMANN. Put yerself in my position as a landlord. I want to get a reasonable interest on the money invested.

TULLY. I wouldn't be in your position for the whole street.

BANNERMANN. And I don't want to throw good money after bad, even if I had it to throw away. I wouldn't be at all sorry if I disposed of the whole estate to-morrow.

TULLY. Wouldn't ye now? Ye'll be hard set to find a buyer, I'm thinking. Nobody dare touch it but a member of the Corporation, and they have so many irons in the fire that they're nearly putting it out.

BANNERMANN. Weren't you saying that ye intended to go up for the Ward yerself?

TULLY. Yes, but you know. No decent man likes getting mixed up in these elections. If it weren't that I am more or less forced to go forward in the Ward's interests, I wouldn't think of public life.

BANNERMANN. But you would have a better chance if ye had a holding in the Ward.

TULLY (*slowly and slyly*). Ah . . . that's what yer driving at! I'm not sure that the responsibility of being the owner of your property wouldn't be worse than the responsibility of representing the Ward.

BANNERMANN. What responsibility are you talking about? Don't you know you'd be on the pig's back if you once got on the Corporation?

TULLY. Is that all ye know? Well, I'll tell ye the responsibility. The representatives of a poor Ward like this have a great charge. If Merrion Square and the respectable parts of the town got to know of the conditions under which the poor live they'd be down on me like a hundred of bricks – it ud be worse than the bag on me back.

BANNERMANN. Rest easy if the public spirit of Dublin is all ye have to fear!

TULLY. Ye talk as if there was neither care nor knowledge in the city. Who framed the sanitary regulations? D'ye think the doctors don't know what should be and what shouldn't? Who sends all the money out of the town yearly for missions and acts of Christian charity? D'ye think that the God-fearing people would rise up with holy indignation and denounce me if they found me only as much as representing conditions such as you own? D'ye want me to believe that there's neither science nor charity nor the love of God in Dublin? D'ye want me to believe that all the clergymen and doctors that live by humanity are no more humanitarians than your nephew or yourself? D'ye want me to believe it's to China they'd be sending to save babies if they knew that here, under their very noses, 4 or 5 babies are perishing every day of the week. Why, my God, man, ye never know the day that saving babies might become fashionable and the society ladies be rushing down half stripping themselves for charity in the Theatre Royal. It's a fine ye ought to give me to relieve ye of yer responsibility and take the property out of yer hands.

BANNERMANN. And a nice reception they'd get if they did come trying to do good. Look at the way you treated Miss Maxwell-Knox.

MARY. Stanislaus, wouldn't it be better for us to take a cottage in the country? There'd be fresh air for Jimmy and room for the children to play.

MEDICAL D. But country bred children cannot stand conditions in the towns.

MARY. God forgive me; mebbe it would be better if there was no towns.

TULLY (in a whisper). If it warn't that herself is aginst it I might make ye an offer. How long have ye held them?

BANNERMANN. Six years.

TULLY. Oh, you've sucked the juice out of them. I thought of offering you a hundred pounds.

BANNERMANN. What! for the two?

TULLY. No, fifty for the wan.

(BANNERMANN walks up and down uncertain.)

TULLY. Mind yerself there, the floor isn't safe. Maybe you'll kill a few children if ye shake the ceiling off the room below.

BANNERMANN. For ready money – that is, cash down – I might see my way to parting with the house you're in for £100.

TULLY (producing a roll of notes with pain from his back pocket, and holding up one). D'ye see that fellah? Take it now and escape before the whole place collapses.

BANNERMANN. Put another £25 to it.

TULLY. What! and not leave meself enough to get the place cleaned! (BANNERMANN *shakes his head.*)

TULLY. I'll toss ye for ten or twenty.

BANNERMANN. Done. I'll give you the title if you let me go next door. (*Exit.*)

MARY. In the name of God, what do ye mane?

TULLY (*pointing mysteriously to earth*). Whisht, Mary, there's a gold mine underneath. Yer sleeping on a gold-mine. Wait until they try to improve the street. Slum's soil's as valuable as the sacred earth of Glasnevin Cemetery. Even if it wasn't, ye'd never know when the Government might take it into their heads to blow the place up and pay for it afterwards. (*Shouts from street, 'Speech, *TULLY*!' Cheering. '*TULLY*, a speech!!'*)

TULLY (*jerking his trousers*). Oh, begob, it's up to me now! (*Runs to basin for refreshment.*)

(*Increased shouts. Leans sideways from basin and shows himself at window. Roars of applause. Wipes his mouth and throws up the sash. His crutch is thrown in.*)

MARY. God save us, are they mad? What's that?

TULLY (*lifting crutch and putting it aside*). A memoir of me dead life. Whist now, Mary, and hear me address me constituents. Boys, I'm glad to see you. Glad to be able to address you all together as I would address everyone of you singly if I had the chance in the course of a day's work; that is, as labouring man to labouring man, as friend to friend (*Cheers.*) We have been living a long time together and enduring things a long time together that we don't intend to endure any longer (*Cheers.*). We've stood interference (*Cheers.*), and bullying (*Cheers.*), and oppression (*Loud cheers.*), and we've borne them all in patience (*Cheers.*), and, what is worse, in conditions that were not fit for pigs much less human beings (*Cheers.*). But now there is an end to all that (*Cheers.*). Those days are gone for ever, as if by a miracle, and why? The answer is very simple: why is there an end of misery and oppression? Because we know our own power *now* (*Cheers.*). We know what it is to work together. Who is it that the capitalists and rulers of the world are organised and plotting to keep under? Men like you and me; hard-working labouring men. How can they do it? Because the people are divided and they are united. But against a united people where are they? But if we are to be rulers we must organise ourselves. Union is strength (*Cheers.*). You are out to beat Capital. We are out to beat Capital even as I bet it (*Cheers.*). How is it to be done? We can't all represent ourselves. We chose a man we know; above all, a man we can trust – a man that knows what he's up against, a man that cannot be codded by any amount of cajoling. A man that will not play you false; better still, a man whose interests and your interests are identical: a man, therefore, that cannot play you false. (*A Voice:* 'How is yer back?') Nobody can say yer not fit to govern yourselves if ye send me to Cork Hill. If I yield to pressure and accept the heavy responsibility of representing you and your homes and tender children, our darling little ones, in this Ward, it's because I know what I'm doing (*Cheers.*). Because I have a stake in this Ward. Not much of a stake, but enough of a stake to be able to announce to you that the arrears of rent, for instance, in this house need not be paid. (*Cheers.*) Small though it be, the men who hold bigger stakes forsake the citizens – it's not in the Corporation you'll find Iveagh and Jamieson, but in the Kildare Street Club. If I go forward and do my duty how will ye know it? The coal fund will be there to inform you. And you can trust a man who owns a house among the people to look after the interests of the people. It doesn't do to cry: 'Down with the rich!' and forget to say: 'Up the People!' We need but stick together and we'll shake Capitalism off our back as a terrier shakes canal water out of its hide. (*A Voice:* 'As you shook off the sack.') Talking about cranes (*Laughter.*), reminds me we have a weight to lift off all our backs (*Cheers.*) Off the back of each worker, wife and child in the city of Dublin. And that takes me further. Dublin is the capital of Ireland and we are the citizens of the capital city of Ireland, and we won't tolerate any foreign ascendancy (*Loud cheers.*) – no, nor what's worse, local ascendancy (*Increased cheers.*). Ye'll hear people sneering at the tenements of dirty Dublin. Well, let me tell them that many a good man was brought up in a tenement (*Cheers.*). When they want their battles to be fought isn't it to the tenements of Dublin they have to come? Wasn't it out of this very house that me own brother-in law went out to the front (*Cheers and cries of 'Up Tully!'*) If we're poor itself, we're proud, and we won't be insulted. We ask only for our rights and nobody's bloody criticism. You'll hear a lot about 'dirty' Dublin and the Corporation, but was it the Corporation broke the men who built these houses and left them derelict? (*'No!'*). Was it the Corporation made people so poor that whole families were glad enough to shelter in a garret or back kitchen? Give everyone his due. It wasn't the Corporation but England done it with the Act of Union. Here, within eight hours of the self-styled Capital of Civilisation, a state of living exists worse than could be found amongst the most benighted tribes of savages and enough to justify their annihilation if it was. Where were the slums when Ireland was a nation? (*Cheers.*); and it's the Corporation will put an end to them (*Cheers.*) Don't forget there was a Corporation in Dublin before ever there was a tenement house. The only thing that stands between us and tyranny is the Corporation, and it's for the sake of the city in which I was born, and for the sake of the locality in which I was reared, and for the sake of my friends and associates that are making a determined stand for freedom and Ireland a Nation that I ask ye for all our sakes and Ireland's sake to rally round me at the poll. Oh, Dublin, how I love you! How my heart heaves for you, Gloucester Place! (*Breaking down.*) Further I can't trust myself to speak. Don't desert me, boys (*Cheers.*). (*Shuts the window and moves to washstand for a drink.*)

MARY (*moved*). Well, ye said one true word anyway when ye blamed England.

TULLY. And why wouldn't I? Isn't it better to blame England than have the boys blaming me? It's only when you're dealing with the people that you find how complicated life can be. They must have something to blame and something to praise, like the gods in the Queen's Theatre. The great secret of politics is to provide them with heroes and villains, and to take care that the villains are far enough away and the heroes within reach. (*Slaps himself on the chest.*)

MARY (*disillusioned*). But weren't you in earnest?

TULLY (*seeing her disappointment*). Oh, iv course I was! I was only explaining the statesman's point of view.

(*Enter* CABMAN, LABOURER *and* MRS LARISSEY, *slightly drunk.*)

MRS L. Aw, me sweet Stannie! Who'd have thought it iv ye! (*Goes up to him admiringly to put her hand under his chin.*) Aw, me sweet child's face! Didn't he larrap it into them, boys!

CABMAN. Begob, I never heard the like of it, and it's not wanst or twice that an orator stood on the top of me cab. Begob, he pumped it up at them in fine style. There was a head on that speech like a pint of stale stout.

MRS L. He belched it out of him like a foghorn.

TULLY. That'll do ye, boys. Now that that's all done and over we mustn't forget our lawful debts. (*Pays* CABMAN.) And that'll celebrate the occasion (*To* LABOURER.)

LABOURER. It was one of them fine reassuring speeches that kept its meaning to itself.

CABMAN (*withdrawing with* LABOURER). I hope I'll soon be laving ye as far as Cork Hill.

MRS L. Did ye hear him, Mary? Wouldn't it put a bull's heart in ye to hear him? The spits of him itself was like a shower iv rain.

MARY (*disconsolate*). Aye, indeed, I heard him.

MRS L. And why wouldn't ye. They say there's no one going up agin him after that.

MEDICAL D. Look here, Tully, you're no fool, an' now that things have changed with you I want you to get two jugs and two basins for this poor woman.

TULLY. Two jugs and two basins? For what?

MEDICAL D. For antiseptic lotion.

TULLY. Antiseptic? What do ye mean, Doctor?

MEDICAL D. I mean that in this case we must run no risk of infection.

TULLY. Sure the typhus is gone out of the house long ago.

MEDICAL D. It's not typhus I want to guard against, but you must provide basins for lotions so that the usual antiseptic precautions may be taken.

TULLY. Ah, now Doctor, if I was you, I wouldn't mind them. Sorra much good they did to little Jimmy an' him born in the Rotunda in an antiseptic chamber wud seven antiseptic doctors standin' around him an' the matron; an' look at meself, where was the basins when I was comin' into the world, I that have a constitution like a horse – fresh as a two-year-old – after gettin' three hundred pounds worth of a belt on me back.

MRS L. Be said be the doctor, now, Stannie, an' don't fly in the face of nature.

TULLY. Well, have it yer own way, Doctor. Sure they'll do for election afterwards anyway. (MEDICAL D. *is ready to go out*.) I'll go out with ye now an' you can show me the kind you want. (*Exit with* MEDICAL DICK.)

(*Enter* JIMMY.)

JIMMY. Ah, mother, sure ye won't send me in to hospital again? When I went in last year they only fed me on milk and they wouldn't let me out for the christening.

MRS L. Whist now, this time 'twill be different wud yer uncle in the Corporation; they'll give ye ducks' blue eggs, an' yellow butter an' barefooted potatoes.

JIMMY. I don't want to go.

MRS LARISSEY. Whist now, go in like a good boy. Wouldn't th' angel be surprised if he found you here when he kem wud the little baby?

JIMMY (*sniffing and going towards door followed by* MRS L., *who is putting on his cap*.) Th' angel ought to be used to it in this street.

CURTAIN

## ACT THREE

*Scene — The Boardroom of the Townsend Thanatorion. A well-furnished room — large table, fitted for writing in centre; walls hung with portraits of elderly gentlemen; several chairs. Two young men in white coats sitting at fire — legs sprawling over chairs and smoking.*

MEDICAL DAVY. But do you tell me you could get it in the lip?

MEDICAL DICK. Of course you can! You can get it anywhere — it mixes with the blood.

MEDICAL DAVY. Well, that's extraordinary! . . . There was a good-looking lassie in the dispensary yesterday when Johnny was taking it and he pointed it out in a sore on her lip. Unless he told us we would not have believed it, and even then a few of us were doubtful, for, of course, nobody believed the lady. She said she got it from a teacup.

MEDICAL DICK. What was she like?

MEDICAL DAVY. She was round and rosy. Oh! a fine scrumptious piece . . . she lived in Gloucester Street.

MEDICAL DICK. What was her name?

MEDICAL DAVY. Ah! that'll do ye now!

MEDICAL DICK. But, damn it all, if she's got it in the lip . . .

MEDICAL DAVY. Oh! . . . Her name was Lily Foley, and they sent her to the Locke.

MEDICAL DICK. Lily Foley!, There'll be hell about that when her uncle hears it; he is one of the Corporation star turns and represents the Public Health Department on this Board. I remember attending her mother on a midwifery job. She was a nice little girl . . . it's a damn shame!

MEDICAL DAVY. So it is; but what the devil is one to do?

MEDICAL DICK. What the devil did they do about small-pox! Isn't every child in the country taken before it's able to talk and injected with cow-pox? Wouldn't it be just as simple and neither dirty nor dangerous to test a drop of everybody's blood, and then we'd know

529

how to get rid of it, once we knew where it was? How can it be avoided until its whereabouts is known?

MEDICAL DAVY. But can that be done?

MEDICAL DICK. Of course it can! D'ye mean to say ye've never heard of Wassermann's test?

MEDICAL DAVY. Of course I have. That's what they did to me when I only had sciatica. But why isn't it done?

MEDICAL DICK. Because of our imported hypocrisy and because we haven't the courage to face facts; because we won't realise that prevention is better than cure, because charity must prey on suffering; because we mix morals even in our medicine.

(*Enter* CHARWOMAN *with duster and bucket; sniffs the smoke and opens the window; kneels to scrub the floor.*)

CHARWOMAN. Ye're a nice pair wud yer Wild Woodbines destroyin' the sterilization and the Board comin' up!

MEDICAL DICK. What! Is there another Board to-day?

CHARWOMAN. Wouldn't ye know that be the fire being lit? Wouldn't ye know it by my presence here, I that have been appointed charwoman to the Hospital Board?

MEDICAL DICK. That was a nice job anyhow, Mrs Larrisey!

MRS L. What d'ye mean?

MEDICAL DICK. Appointing you Charwoman to the Board of this hospital with work for only one day in the week.

MRS L. Be the terms of my appointment I should work only one day in the week, and I wouldn't only for the matron.

MEDICAL DICK. Ah, ah! is she down on you too?

MRS L. She has me in early in the mornings the Board's sitting, acting as lady's maid if ye please, fittin' her into her stays.

MEDICAL DICK. Only one day's work and a friend of the Matron — that's what I call striking it lucky, Mrs Larissey. I hope when I'm qualified they'll give me a sinecure position.

MRS L (*offended*). Sinecure position! None of yer jeering: All I will say is that when you're qualified, and the matron gets into her new corset, a great future will be overhanging the Dublin poor.

MEDICAL DAVY. Don't mind him, Mrs Larissey; he's never in earnest. Tell us what's the Board meeting for now.

CHARWOMAN. What's the Board for now, and they after gettin' thirty thousand pounds be ould MacNab's death, an' they sackin' wan another and rulin' wan another out of order to see which of them will have the spending of it? An' without that at all they'll be sittin' on the soldier for sleepin' in the flower-bed all last night. Thirty thousand pounds! Ho, that will build a new operating theatre. Ay, and a wing for skin trouble, or an observation ward where they put you in to wait for a disease.

MEDICAL DAVY. Which of them will get it? Ten to one McWhirter will grab the lot and do all the plumbing of the place over again.

MEDICAL DICK. Tisdall Townsley will buy a few old Masters to hang in the corridors. I heard him say the hospital would be complete if they acquired Rembrandt's lesson in anatomy to hang in the Board room. What would you say, Mrs Larissey, to the lesson in anatomy.

MRS L. Ye'd better ax the matron – I'm thinking if they spent a few hundred on letting out the childer for fresh air from the childer's ward they'd be less need to be building wings. The poor sees little of it anyway.

MEDICAL DICK. O, I'm surprised, Mrs Larissey; the Board charwoman of all people to doubt the efficacy of the hospital for treating sick children.

MRS L. It's fresh air I'd give them and no treatment. What's the good of feeding the little creatures for a few days and then throwing them back where they caught the diseases. It's like spittin' on a herrin' when the sea's dried up.

MEDICAL DICK. Evidently you are a believer in prophylaxis, Mrs Larissey.

MRS L. Is it any business of yours what religion I am? (*Whisking the duster at them.*) Be off out o' this if ye don't want the Board to be sitting on the pair of ye too!

    (*Exit Medical Davy, singing*):
> 'As I was going down Sackville Street
> Who did I meet but Sandy O,
> His kilt had fallen down to his feet
> Leaving him bare and bandy O!'

    (*Exeunt Students on left. Enter frock-coated gentlemen, pompous, fussy and middle-aged.*)

CHARWOMAN (*taking up the refrain she polishes the floor*):
> 'In came the nurse with a poultice hot,
> Who was it for but Sandy O!'

NORRIS (*1st Gent.*). Good gracious, what an atmosphere! Who is responsible for this?

CHARWOMAN. I dunno, sir, it must have been the man that was mending the telephone this morning. (*Exit, leaving bucket under table.*)

    (*Enter second Old Gentleman.*)

TISDALL (*2nd Gent.*). Ah, good morning Norris.

NORRIS. Good morning, good morning. Just give me a moment while I turn on this electric fan. Ah, it's you Tisdall. Glad to see you. Glad you were able to come. I wonder who'll be third.

TISDALL. Oh, yes, I forgot. Third man in, of course, takes the chair. Ten to one it will be that impossible fellow, Tumulty. I have actually seen him lurking round corridors, watching to be third man in. I think, as I have always thought, and I say it once again, that it is a perfectly absurd rule. I, as senior member, ought to be chairman, *ex officio,* and then we would not always have Tumulty in except when he thinks he can discover a scandal in the hospital to embarrass his colleagues on the Board. Just for curiosity's sake, let us watch the door.

NORRIS. You'll find he'll not be late this morning, since there is so much money at our disposal.

TISDALL. Well, he surely cannot expect any of this money for some madcap scheme of turning Merrion Square and the best places in the city into schools for Ragged Children.

NORRIS. Here's someone coming now!

(*Enter* CHARWOMAN *who takes bucket from under the table.*)

CHARWOMAN. Excuse me, gentlemen; I'll take this with me in case it might be interfering with the action of your feet.

(*Exit, wiping her nose on the end of her apron.*)

NORRIS. What a dreadful country.

TISDALL. Quite hopeless.

NORRIS. Quite.

(*Enter corpulent gentleman, with air of gargantuan mirth, he wears florid buttonhole, and carries magnificent walking-stick.*)

MORPHY (*3rd Gent.*). Ha, my gallant colleagues. And how are you all to-day? Getting into harness for a little clear thinking, and administrative thought?

TISDALL. Oh, Morphy, deuced glad to see you. Glad it was you who arrived third. We don't want our meeting presided over by that crank, Tumulty. If McWhirter and Tully arrive we'll have a quorum without him.

NORRIS. Somebody is coming now.

(*Enter* TULLY, *wearing frock-coat, bowler hat, brilliant blue tie and yellow boots.*)

TULLY. Good morning, gentlemen. It's a soft day.

MORPHY. Well, but salubrious nevertheless. I walked this morning about half a mile. The air was delicious, the scenery delightful and divine. One never realises how undulating Raheny is until one walks. O, the panorama of the Wicklow hills!

TULLY. Yes, I heard it's a good thing to be perambulating about before breakfast, for them that can afford to live a bit out of the town, but for men like McWhirter and meself we've got to keep our nose to the grindstone and our shoulder to the wheel, so to speak.

TISDALL (*seeing* NORRIS *closely scrutinising picture*). Who would you say that was by, Norris. (NORRIS *looks closer, without answering.*] Would you attribute it to some 18th century master.

(NORRIS *looks still closer, but does not reply.*)

TISDALL (*with diffidence*). Perhaps I am wrong?

NORRIS (*rubs his fingers on canvas, then smells his fingers*). Ha! Hum! Mastic varnish – I thought so.

TISDALL. Who do you think painted it?

NORRIS (*sternly*). Restored first, varnished afterwards.

TISDALL. Extraordinary how you perceived that!

NORRIS (*talking to himself*). I think I can detect a certain wilfulness, a certain playfulness in the painter.

TULLY. It must be a great picture. You took such a good look at it!

NORRIS. Yes, yes, I was trying to catch the master's meaning. When you look at a picture you should always ask yourself: 'What did the artist mean by it?'

TULLY. Indade now, it id be hard to tell that. I suppose he meant that the ould fellow drank too much port. What d'you think?

NORRIS. Now, now, I join issue with you at once. You are making – pardon me if I speak rather with emphasis, not to say assurance – you are making a mistake common to amateurs seeking an interest in the picture whereas you should look for it in the spectator. Forgive me won't you, if I thought it worth while to get you right? I feel very strongly on this matter.

TULLY (*scratching his head*). I suppose you must be worked up like that or you'd see nothing. Is the spectator not to look at it at all?

(*Enter* MCWHIRTER, *carrying despatch box.*)

TULLY (*relieved to change the subject*). How are ye to-day, McWhirter?

MCWHIRTER. A'll not tell ye.

MORPHY. Ho, ho! Why not, McWhirter . . . why not? Surely you hadn't a late night?

MCWHIRTER. A prefer to keep ma counsel to masel.'

MORPHY. That is a new departure from your old habits, McWhirter.

MCWHIRTER (*cheerfully*). A'm upset by McNab's death.

NORRIS. Yes, yes, it was extraordinarily sudden.

MCWHIRTER. And besides, when there's business to do a' make it a rule to keep ma personal feelings aloof from it.

MORPHY. Yes, yes, let us proceed. I take the chair. Be seated gentlemen. Read the minutes of the last meeting, McWhirter.

MCWHIRTER. If ye will permit me to make a remark, Mr Chairman – I think yer haste is indecent. What about a resolution of condolence with the relatives of our late colleague – Mr McNab – which is called for all the more as he left them no money, a man from my own town too, with whom it was a pleasure to work.

MORPHY. Of course, but all in its due time. It would be most unbecoming to let the minutes of the Board succeed to a solemn resolution which it would be better to leave separate, outstanding and apart.

NORRIS AND TISDALL. Hear, hear!

TULLY. I'm with you, Mr Morphy.

MCWHIRTER. That's an very well. I know ye want to make a speech.

NORRIS AND TISDALL. You must yield to the ruling of the Chairman.

TULLY. Obey the chair.

MCWHIRTER. I'll obey nobody, but a'll read the minutes of last week's meeting. (*Reads.*) 'The 156th meeting of the public Board of the Townsend Thanatorion was held on the 5th instant, Mr Tumulty in the chair.

'It was proposed by Mr Norris-Coote.

'Seconded by Mr Tisdall-Townley.

'That the thanks of the Board are due to Mrs Dickenson-Digby for the present of a male canary to the Children's Ward. The motion was supported by Mr Morphy, who made a few trite remarks on the subject of singing birds and childhood.'

TISDALL. 'A few trite remarks!' Morphy spoke most excellently as he always does – excellent and eloquent, with well-chosen words.

MORPHY. As Chairman I cannot naturally comment, but . . .

NORRIS. McWhirter's comments should not be entered on the minutes.

MCWHIRTER. Well, ye'd better get a paid shorthand writer if ye expect me to put down every member's speech. If ye'll turn your thoughts from elocution I'll get on with the minutes . . . Proposed by Mr McNab – the late lamented –

NORRIS. Is 'late lamented' in the minutes?

MCWHIRTER. How could it be mon – sure he wasn't dead – 'and seconded by Mr Tisdall – That in view of the increasing demand on the resources of the Hospital by the sick poor, and the valuable relief extended to so many of them, the thanks of the institution are given to all those who came forward with gifts and donations on Pound Day, *videlicet:*

Mrs Odlum – Eggs.

Mrs Tottenham Young – Cut chrysanthemums.

Mrs Harriet-Batt – One pound of bees-wax for the dancing-floor of the Nurse's ballroom.

Mrs Chiltern Pim – A pair of mittens.

O'Callaghan-Davis, Esq. – Newspapers.

Mr Forrester – A vegetable marrow.

Miss Eric Littleby – Playing cards and newspapers.

Mrs Globe-Terry – A Japanese lanthorn.

These voluntary and totally unsolicited contributions are themselves the best evidence of the strong spirit of Christian practice and principle which has always inspired and actuated the patrons of this Hospital.

CHAIRMAN. Quite so.

MCWHIRTER. A motion of thanks to the Matron for her efficient management of the Christmas entertainments was passed unanimously, with the exception of Mr Tumulty. The probationers were interviewed and addressed by the Board on the high dignity of their calling.

NORRIS. These are the young ladies that Tumulty wishes to turn into dairymaids to secure a clean supply of milk.

MCWHIRTER. The enquiry held to ascertain why the electric light failed at the Nurses' Ball revealed the fact that some of the resident students had been tampering with the electric switches. Apologies were formulated by Mr Morphy and directed to be posted to the visitors who had suffered inconvenience – Mr Tumulty objecting. The students were interviewed and admonished. The Board rose at a quarter to 12.

CHAIRMAN. All those who are in favour that these minutes should be signed say 'aye.'

ALL. Aye.

TULLY. Pass them round from right to left.

CHAIRMAN. Why, you would think you were directing a decanter of port.

TULLY. How bad it 'ud be!

(*The minutes are circulated and signed,* MCWHIRTER *lends his pen, which reaches* NORRIS.)

NORRIS. A quill pen, please! I refuse to encourage the use of these detestable American fountain pens.

MCWHIRTER. That's signed more important documents than you'll ever be likely to sign.

NORRIS. That may be, that may be; but it is beside the point.

MCWHIRTER. What's the point?

NORRIS. The point is that it is new fangled and vulgar.

MCWHIRTER. G'lang!

CHAIRMAN (*rapping the table*). Order, gentlemen! Order! There's a letter here from the Local Government Board calling attention to the urgent necessity of adopting some scheme for preventing the spread of the hidden plague in this city.

NORRIS. I think considerations of good taste counsel us to ignore it.

TULLY. Mark it 'read.'

MCWHIRTER. How can I mark it 'read' if I don't read it and how can I read it if it is to be ignored?

TULLY. Let them that put themselves in the way of that disorder put up with it.

TISDALL. But in cases where the innocent suffer for the guilty.

TULLY (*impatiently*). Why should decent people be asked to put their hands in their pockets to pay for the blackguarding of blackguards?

CHAIRMAN. Perhaps if we postpone its perusal until we ascertain the attitude of other great establishments in this matter.

TULLY. One would think we were the Locke Hospital.

NORRIS. Talking of the Locke or Westmoreland Hospital reminds me — what a beautiful facade it has! One of the most typical examples of its century in the city!

TISDALL. Ah, yes, the Georgian period and thereabouts. What is the next item on the agenda?

TULLY. I'd send that letter back to those evil-minded blackguards in the Local Government Board that wrote it and tell them we won't have our city insulted.

MCWHIRTER. Would ye prefer it stricken with the plague?

THE OTHERS. Hush, the chairman is about to address us.

CHAIRMAN (*with sudden solemnity*). It is my melancholy duty now, without any distraction or delay to propose a vote of condolence to the relatives of our late colleague, Mr William McNab, to whose public spirit this hospital and *therefore* the suffering poor of this city, are indebted for the sum of thirty thousand pounds.

> (*Enter* TUMULTY, *the others motion to him not to interrupt. He sits apart near the door by which he had entered.*)

CHAIRMAN. His relatives are to be condoled with, for the loss . . .

MCWHIRTER. I should think they are!

OTHERS. Hush!

CHAIRMAN. For the loss of a man of whom it may be well said from our point of view, in the words of the Swan of Avon (*Hear, hear.*), 'Nothing in his life became him like the leaving it.' (*Applause — chairman flattered.*)

TULLY. More power.

CHAIRMAN. He died —

MCWHIRTER. He did so —

CHAIRMAN. He died full of years and honours. He sat only last week in our midst. Yesterday we were summoned to hear the reading of his will. Apparently in vigorous health, he was called away from the institution which owes him so much, and in which he took such a deep, lifelong, and I might say, absorbing and undivided interest (*Hear, hear.*) One day in our midst, another —

NORRIS (*whispering*).

CHAIRMAN. A mere slip of the tongue, a *lapsus linguae*.

NORRIS. Be that as it may, there is all the more need of precision in speaking. In our midst, might mean inside us.

CHAIRMAN. Indeed! Very well then. One day *amongst* us, another day he is gone. Who can account for that? Who can presume to plumb or fathom the inscrutable designs of Providence? I ask you, who?

TULLY. There I leave ye!

CHAIRMAN. He will be lowered to rest, but will arise, as a lasting memorial in, I hope, some edifice, some additional ward, wing, or building, as his enduring monument, so that others who come after him and us, others who take their honoured place like those who are gone before (*Points to portraits.*) may point to it and say, reminded by it of him, his charity, his goodness, his solicitude for suffering, his fatherly tenderness for those less endowed with the world's goods – *Si monumentum requiris, circumspice.* (*Applause. Chairman bows.*)

NORRIS (*rising*). In seconding, with all willingness, the remarks –

MCWHIRTER. How do you spell *circumspice?*

NORRIS. In seconding the remarks of our respected and eloquent chairman, I am at the disadvantage natural to whoever would follow a Demosthenes, but yet, keenly sensitive to my own shortcomings (*No, no!*) and only urged on by what is indispensable and necessary, the fact that a motion must be seconded – let this be my excuse.

MCWHIRTER. I hope you won't say that these are not trite remarks.

NORRIS. Ignoring the interruptions of one whose *res angusta domi* in youth preclude him now even in affluence from an appreciation, or indeed a comprehension of the humanities and amenities, not to say even the civilities of gentle life, I persevere in my support of my learned, able, and more eloquent colleague.

MCWHIRTER. If yer meaning me – ye'r not meaning me!

NORRIS. For a long time I have cherished a scheme, and I think our chairman too has seen the necessity for it – a scheme by which a long-felt want may be supplied and a great need may be filled in this very hospital. Everyone knows, everyone regrets, everyone agrees that a mortuary chapel, decent and befitting this great institution must be erected if an urgent need of the hospital is not to be ignored, if the dead are to be treated with the respect which is their due, a respect which I have always entertained for them during the course of a long life, from which now nearing the end of it (*No, no!*) I refuse to be divorced. In what better or more becoming way could our late lamented colleague be commemorated than by the erection of a mortuary chapel? If Dublin is rich in anything it is rich in ecclesiastical architects and artists.

TULLY. Hear, hear.

MCWHIRTER. It's all ecclesiastical.

NORRIS. Gentlemen, let a pious fane arise over the poor dead, let the splendours of stained glass break with glorious variegations the hodden grey of their common lot; let Roman Catholic and Protestant share a communal sleep.

TULLY. Hear, hear to that!

TISDALL. This is a matter that had better be discussed in Committee.

CHAIRMAN. Excuse me, Tisdall, by your leave we will go into committee to decide to what use the thirty thousand pounds may be put.

TISDALL. There is as yet no pergola in the grounds of the Nurses' Home.

NORRIS. Oh, that's a trivial matter.

TISDALL. Excuse me, it is not! The grounds have not yet been purchased – though long promised.

MCWHIRTER. That's being taken up by Mr Tully who is negotiating for the purchase of the derelict houses beside the Home.

TULLY. That's right. I hope to have the matter closed this week, though I am afraid the party is holding out for £2,000.

NORRIS. Are we in committee?

CHAIRMAN. Oh, we are . . . I think we are.

TISDALL. I have no objection to support the project of building a mortuary chapel consistent with the dignity of this hospital if – firstly – I have some assurance that ample funds will be left for the very necessary improvements of the Nurses' Home and – secondly – that a second and *separate* mortuary chapel be provided for the Protestant dead . . .

MCWHIRTER (*heatedly*). And what d'ye think is going to happen to the Nonconformist dead?

NORRIS. That is a vexed question!

MCWHIRTER. D'ye think I'm going to let them lie in a compromising position between yer stained-glass windows?

CHAIRMAN. Oh, gentlemen, gentlemen, something can be arrived at surely – some agreement –

MCWHIRTER. There'll be no agreement, I'm telling ye! I'll have no stained glass nor any kind of embellishmentations.

CHAIRMAN. But surely –

MCWHIRTER. Surely what? Ye'll surely find a falling off in the attendance of patients in this hospital if ye try any religious intolerance here . . .

CHAIRMAN. Perhaps Mr Tumulty will give us his views?

MCWHIRTER. Yer not going to evade the issue like that! A'm telling ye unless ye provide a third and *separate* mortuary chapel with muffled glass for Nonconformists this Hospital will be boycotted, and a'll see to it. Ye'll be wanting music next.

NORRIS. Surely the decorations of the dead-house cannot influence the attendance in the out-patient department.

MCWHIRTER. Well, why are ye building one?

NORRIS. Because it is a longfelt want.

MCWHIRTER. If Roman Catholics can feel it, d'ye think that Non-conformists can't?

TISDALL. Wouldn't muffled glass suggest plumbing?

MCWHIRTER. It may suggest plumbing, but it doesn't suggest Popery. I'll have no Popery, living *or* dead!

CHAIRMAN (*in resonant voice*). Well now, gentlemen, the time has come for clear-thinking. Why hurt anyone's feelings, when there is ample means at our disposal to satisfy the requirements of all you three gentlemen? What is there to prevent us providing a tripartite mortuary building shaped like a shamrock, the symbol of Trinity and of our common Apostle . . .

MCWHIRTER. Well, why didn't ye say that before?

CHAIRMAN. I wished to hear all your views.

TULLY. Ah! me sound man!

NORRIS AND TISDALL. A shamrock-shaped chapel! An excellent idea!

CHAIRMAN (*pleased*). And now if Mr Tumulty would give us the benefit of his views, unanimity, that rare condition, might be reached.

TUMULTY. I have listened long enough to this and your other fatuous schemes. In no town is charity vainer or more misplaced. When I think of the vast, useless sums that are spent yearly in the name of charity and nothing comes of them, but misery continues unabated –

CHAIRMAN. You must remember now that money left specifically to this Hospital cannot be allotted to your pet purposes, for instance, to build schools in the best parts of the city.

TUMULTY. I have spent the morning trying to calm a discharged soldier who called last night while his little boy was dying in the children's Ward and he was refused admission.

MCWHIRTER. How d'ye propose to run an hospital without regulations?

TUMULTY. He will speak to you himself.

(*Preparing to call him in. Consternation of Board.*)

CHAIRMAN. I do not know that the deliberations of this Board are open to the public.

OTHERS. Certainly not!

TUMULTY. What! You haven't the moral courage to face the parent of one of your patients! Well, whether you like it or not, I'll bring him in. A little reality will do you good.

NORRIS. But surely you will rule him out of order, Mr Chairman.

TISDALL. If we were not in committee . . .

MCWHIRTER. Let him come in – what harm can he do?

TULLY. I'd like to know who he is first.

TUMULTY. He is a man who left his young family to go out to fight. He returned late last night to find the house his room was in derelict and his son dying in this hospital. His eldest daughter cannot be traced.

He went out to fight for you and the continuance of a system that betrayed him, did his son to death and sent his daughter to hell.

CHAIRMAN. Now, now . . . let there be no confusion of thought. It is quite evident that unless his son was already ailing in the first place he would not have been admitted to this institution, while his treatment, once he is admitted, is entirely a matter for the medical staff –

NORRIS. Which was never found wanting (*Hear, hear!*)

TISDALL. I am quite sure of that . . . It's no fault of the medical staff.

NORRIS. Day and night, night and day, with unrelaxing attention and vigilant eye, they watch over the health of the poor of this city.

TUMULTY. He was refused admittance to his dying boy.

CHAIRMAN. This is a charitable institution, and as such is governed by certain rules and regulations which have been found by long practice to be satisfactory.

TUMULTY. Why should this man be insulted by charity? Are the lives of the poor to depend on the sufferance of your good-will? Is charity to be ever an escape from responsibility?

BOARD. Our responsibility!

TUMULTY. Yes. The responsibility goes with the Revenue. Those who hold a County's money are responsible for a County's welfare. The Government holds most of it – you hold some of it, and in such proportions you are responsible, for it is obtained under the pretence of its being useful to the community.

CHAIRMAN. First of all that is inaccurate. The money has been left to us for the poor of Dublin.

TUMULTY. Why conclude at once that there is no other way of investing it for their benefit than in this hospital? Are the channels of charity to be so fixed and the means of relief to be so stereotyped by custom that the poor can get nothing from charitable bequests but an hospital or a Carnegie library? To establish one bed in this hospital costs £300, a tenement can be bought up and demolished for half that. If you spend £20,000 in getting rid of the surrounding plague spots, you will be able to close a wing of this foundation and so economise.

CHAIRMAN. If you refer to McNab's bequest it can only be put to the well-known aims and purposes of this hospital, which are –

NORRIS. Close the hospital. What a preposterous proposal.

MCWHIRTER. Ah, he's not serious.

TUMULTY. I am serious. I have sat and listened to you as patiently as I could this morning seriously proposing to spend thousands of pounds on three dead-houses when a few hundred pounds could buy up and destroy the very tenement house which caused the disease from which this poor man's son died. As long as you leave the corpse-converting slums, all the money spent in charity might as well be spent in decorating dead-houses, which are a symbol of the inefficiency and fatuousness of the whole system.

NORRIS. Hold on! Might I be allowed, Mr Chairman . . .

TISDALL. I think I can answer . . .

CHAIRMAN. Allow me, gentlemen. Now Tumulty, you are not really just. We have given up our time – remember there is no compulsion – most of us at great personal sacrifice and entirely on account of our public spirit, to manage a public charity.

TULLY. That's an Oliver for his Roland!

CHAIRMAN. Remembering now that it is not incumbent on any of us to do so . . . a little clear thought will show you . . .

TUMULTY. A little clear thought will show you that if you go on building wings and hospitals the time will come when you'll have to get someone to leave you money to build slums to keep up the supply of patients. All your charity only yokes another horse in the hearse.

(*Enter* GEORGE FOLEY, *a discharged soldier dressed in plain clothes.*)

MCWHIRTER. As a matter of fact, we are just negotiating about buying up two houses adjoining the Nurses' Home for fifteen hundred pounds.

TULLY. I'm afraid we'll have to pay £2,000.

SOLDIER. Two thousand!

TUMULTY. I have known for some time that Mr Tully, the representative of Public Health on this Board, had interests in tenement property; and now his own brother-in-law – this unfortunate soldier – has informed us that he owns the two houses. Will you take no action?

TULLY. Welcome back, George. Did the censor let you pass? How are all the boys at the front?

NORRIS AND TISDALL. One of our heroes! Get him something – give him something – give him – a chair.

NORRIS. Gallipoli, I suppose.

TULLY. Sortin' letters in France?

SOLDIER. Two thousand pounds! I'll stop that game anyway. That fellow got them two tenements for wan hundred pounds.

NORRIS AND TISDALL. Now, a little patience – a little patience, my good man, just a little patience and you'll be heard.

SOLDIER. I've had enough of patience.

NORRIS. Hush, hush, you are overwrought; we must make allowances for you.

TISDALL. Assuredly we will make allowances for one that fought for liberty, faced the barbarian and all – that sort of thing.

SOLDIER. Liberty be damned, what do I get from liberty? I haven't a house over my head! Where's my wife? Where's my poor girl? Where's my son and the baby that was born when I was away?

NORRIS. Dear, dear, did you lose a second child. This is unusually sad.

TISDALL. Added to the list of infantile mortality I suppose.

SOLDIER. The baby's dead, and that fellow there that I kept before ever he had a job, wouldn't put out a hand to save them.

TULLY. It was summer diarrhoea killed the baby, if ye want to know. D'ye expect me to go out on the streets wid a sweepin' brush to prevent the dust getting into the milk? It's the Cleansing Department you ought to blame if ye blame anybody, and not me that only represents the Committee of Public Health.

SOLDIER. All I know is that a curse is on you for your treatment of human beings. Ye'll be all wiped out and not one of ye left. The strong races that look after their own and that have homes to fight for will overwhelm ye. Yes! the men that's not starved into fightin' will beat hell out of ye for ye don't deserve to live the way ye treat mankind. How can ye win when you're killing your own. The curse of God is on ye all and ye'll feel it – for ye have neither sense nor pity – the curse of God is on ye all – for ye don't care. (*Exit.*)

CHAIRMAN. Dear, dear, not a word of gratitude, not a sign of recognition either for the kindness of the nurses or the surgical staff!

TUMULTY. The tragedy is that you are all so well meaning. Can there be no reform without revolution?

TISDALL. Reform? Surely you do not mean that we are to be reformed. How are we to blame?

TUMULTY. As usual where the system is rotten no one is to blame; but you are all to blame, for you are all part of charity's ineffectual farce. The only people who benefit from charity are the charitable people themselves. Take this case of Tully's tenement houses –

CHAIRMAN. Now, now, you must remember the empty houses are to be acquired at a valuation, regardless of the individuality of the owner, which is never allowed to enter into the consideration of the Auditors of this hospital. To the second part of your question the answer is in the negative.

TUMULTY. The full houses cost Tully one hundred pounds.

TULLY. Is that as true as everything else ye said? How d'ye know what I paid for them? To hear ye talk wan would think 'twas a crime to own a tenement house. Mebbe they'd be in full blast as microbe factories still if any wan else owned them but meself. Wasn't it I meself that got them condemned the moment the first suspicion crossed me mind . . .

TUMULTY. The first suspicion of the Hospital extension scheme?

TULLY. Is that an observation for one gentleman to make to another? Mr Chairman, I must ask ye to protect me from this abominable innuendo. The only way to escape comment at the hands of this gentleman is to strip yerself of all yer possessions. Somewan must own property. There must be somewan to pay the rates on it, and provide the Hospitals with their grant.

CHAIRMAN. Quite so, quite so, Mr Tully. Mr Tumulty is hitting at the very roots of property quite unwittingly I am sure.

TULLY. Like one of them bloomin' socialists.

CHAIRMAN. Property discharges very numerous obligations indeed, not the least of which is charity; as the poet has phrased it – 'and so the whole round earth is every way. Bound with gold chains about the feet of God.'

TULLY. As I was going to say if I was let, the moment the first suspicion that they were unsanitary crossed me mind I reported them meself and got them condemned.

TUMULTY. Tenement property in Dublin is like cheese that grows in value as it rots.

NORRIS. Mr Chairman, I rise to a point of order. A discussion upon tenement houses has been started with the object of making a most unseemly attack on Mr Tully, whose public spirit leaves nothing to be desired. I have yet to learn that it is the function of a Hospital Board to buy up tenement property which is not absolutely essential for its scheme of expansion and in this we are supported by the example of the great religious houses in this country.

MCWHIRTER. The island of saints and doctors!

NORRIS (continuing). We buy only the houses necessary to enable us to grow. Our Institution has been established for the relief of suffering. How can it discharge its functions if suffering does not exist?

TISDALL. Quite so, quite so! I should say that any other discharge of its functions would be absolutely *ultra vires, ultra vires*.

TULLY. Aye, that would a bit of *ultra violet* right enough.

MCWHIRTER. Aye, and perhaps lead to our being mandamused in the King's Bench with costs.

TUMULTY. Oh, there you go, piling institution upon institution until you lose sight of the idea which was originally responsible for your existence, until the spirit that created you lies dead in the letter, until the whole country is one mass of charitable edifices. Where is charity going to end, relief to begin?

TULLY. Ah, there's something in what he says. Of course, we could appoint one of our number who has a knowledge of slum conditions to acquire twenty thousand pounds worth of houses.

CHAIRMAN. Really, Tumulty, this is going too far.

TULLY. Now yer talking! I propose that he be no longer heard.

TUMULTY. Oh, don't bother, I'm going to leave. I just want to point out that all your benevolent formulism only makes the position more and more hopeless. The less you spend on prevention the more you will pay for cure. Until the citizens realise that their children should be brought up in the most beautiful and favourable surroundings the city can afford, and not in the most squalid, until this floundering Moloch of a Government realise that they must spend more money on education than on police, this city will continue to be the breeding-ground of disease, vice, hypocrisy and discontent. I leave you to erect your tripartite edifice over the children of the city of blight.

(*Exit* TUMULTY.)

NORRIS. Dear, dear!

TISDALL. What appalling ideas!

NORRIS. Where did he get them and who is paying for them?

TISDALL. Ha, I am afraid there is a great deal of money being spent to no good purpose in this city.

NORRIS. German gold.

CHAIRMAN. A mere idle dreamer – quite unable to appreciate organisation.

NORRIS. Exactly. He has not the responsibility of administration.

TULLY. Did ye hear what he said to me?

NORRIS. Indeed we did, and I think we owe it to you to express our appreciation of the dignified way in which you bore with it.

TISDALL. Extraordinary restraint.

CHAIRMAN. Quite remarkable.

TULLY. If it wasn't that I was a gentleman among gentlemen, for two pins I'd have given him a clather on the beak.

MCWHIRTER. Let's pass a resolution about it.

CHAIRMAN. An excellent suggestion.

NORRIS. Very well then; give me the privilege! I beg to propose: – That we, the Members of the Board of the Townsend Thanatorion, desire to place on record our sympathy, surprise and disapproval at the unprovoked attack made upon our respected colleague, Mr Tully, by Mr Tumulty and that notwithstanding the confidence of this Board remains unimpaired in Mr Tully, our esteemed friend and honourable colleague.

(*All arise and shake hands with* TULLY.)

## CURTAIN

# A SERIOUS THING

*A Play in One Act*

This play was first produced at the Abbey Theatre in Dublin, on 19 August 1919, with the following cast:

| | |
|---|---|
| A CENTURION | Philip Guiry |
| FIRST ROMAN SOLDIER | F. J. McCormick |
| SECOND ROMAN SOLDIER | Arthur Shields |
| LAZARUS | J. Hugh Nagle |
| A VOICE | |

*Produced by Lennox Robinson*

AUTHOR'S NOTE: Following the practice of writers and painters who coloured themes with their own day, as he did who called Hector 'That sweet Knight,' and as they who depicted men with hounds and matchlocks on the road to Calvary, the Players may be represented in uniforms most suited to the character of the piece. It seemed good to the Manager of the Abbey Theatre to present the first three characters in Khaki, which is well known and widely distributed.

# A SERIOUS THING

*Scene — The tomb of Lazarus to the left in a wall which crosses the back of the stage obliquely. On the Lintel is written 'Lazarus,' and on the wall topical catch-calls such as 'Up the Rebels' and 'Give them Gadara' are scrawled; to these graffiti a wag has added 'up' before the name on the tomb. The foreground is rocky.*

*Time — Seven hundred and eighty-five years from the Founding of the City.*

*First Roman soldier enters from the left and takes up a position as sentry by the wall. After looking about he sighs and sits down on a rock.*

FIRST ROMAN. Well, well; twenty years' decent service and here I am! But it's a great time in the world's history anyway — even if it isn't in mine. And here's the paper they send round to tell us how great are the times we're living in — I keep it to console me (*Takes it from his pocket.*) It's well to be supplied with the world's news here in this God-forgotten part of the Empire. 'The wife of Pilate had a dream.' Well, I wouldn't put it past her! It doesn't say who she dreamt about.
    (*Enter Centurion.*)
    (*He jumps up to attention as the Centurion enters and salutes him by bringing his thumb to his umbilicus with a circular motion and wagging the extended fingers.*)

CENTURION (*he is quite a boy, and he speaks in a most affected manner*). Hah! Lookey here now! You see now! These are your instructions. You are stationed here to prevent illegal assemblies, seditious speeches and all that kind of thing. You see? The movement must be prevented from spreading. Report to me at the change of guard. But, *but, but,* if anything serious occurs meanwhile you are to report direct to Pontius Pilate (*He points out left with his cane.*), on your own responsibility. Because, because, you see, the Governor takes quite a personal interest in the Government.

FIRST ROMAN. Yes, Sir.
    (*Exit* CENTURION.)

FIRST ROMAN (*Looking after him; after a pause, significantly shaking his head*). The wife of Pilate had a dream. Well! there's no accounting for taste.
    (CENTURION *re-enters hurriedly.*)

547

CENTURION. Oh by Jove, I had nearly forgotten. There should be two of you on guard. Shouldn't there? I think it is . . . who else is there?

FIRST ROMAN. Obadiah, Sir.

CENTURION. Bai Jove, you are perfectly right; yes, of course, Obadiah, quite recently recruited (*with reassured authority.*) – Now, then, where is Obadiah?

FIRST ROMAN. He's coming up the hill, Sir.

CENTURION. There's no disciplining these damn local recruits. For two straws when the fellow comes I will call him 'Civilian.'

FIRST ROMAN. Oh, don't do that, Sir.

CENTURION. Well, I don't want to be too severe. But this unpunctuality deserves it.

FIRST ROMAN. Quite right that, Sir; but he might take it that you were demobilizing him, and desert.

CENTURION. You don't mean it! The unprincipled beast. There's no making these Jews soldiers.

(*Enter Obadiah, the* SECOND ROMAN.)

SECOND ROMAN (*addressing First and speaking with marked Jewish accent*). It vos so hot!

CENTURION (*turning suddenly: sharply*). Why are you late?

SECOND ROMAN (*fumbling to salute with hand raised to forehead*). It must be the distance, Sir; I counted a thousand paces from the barracks, and lo and behold! it vos longer when I got here.

CENTURION. Don't let this occur again or you will be sent on police duty to Gadava. Now lookey here! These are your instructions. D'ye see? You are stationed here to prevent illegal assemblies, people passing without permits, seditious speeches and all that kind of thing, and to report to me at the end of guard. *But* if anything of a serious nature occurs, the Governor wishes to be informed at once. Is that clear?

SECOND ROMAN (*scratching his head with the hand still raised to salute*). Will we permit the beginning of the speeches before they become seditious?

CENTURION (*puzzled: After a pause, emphatically*). There must be no sedition. You two are the cordon sanitaire. There must be no sedition, either in thought, word or deed.

SECOND ROMAN. But how will we know?

CENTURION. What! You don't know what sedition is? Then the sooner you learn the better! Do your duty and report.

SECOND ROMAN. Aw! But eef . . .

CENTURION. Now shut up. . . . Report to me or to the Governor.

(*Exit.*) (SECOND ROMAN *brings his hand to his side with a slap.*)

FIRST ROMAN (*turning to Second with profound contempt*). Well, you're a nice omadhaun anyway!

SECOND ROMAN. Vell. How vos I to know? The speeches may not begin with sedition, and he did not say there was to be no speaking. Are we to forbid every kind of speech? Is no one to utter a word? Vhere then is freedom of speech?

FIRST ROMAN (*looking in direction in which* CENTURION *went, and then seating himself cautiously on a rock with a sigh of content*). If there is to be no assembly, how can there be seditious speeching? Did ye ever hear a speech without an audience? And if there was itself, what kind of an idiot are ye that ye can't make a mental note of it? Didn't ye hear him telling ye that we are the cordon sanitaire?

SECOND ROMAN (*about to seat himself opposite, but changes his mind and merely rests his spear (rifle) against the tomb*). – What is a cordon sanitaire?

FIRST ROMAN (*pointing significantly to spear or to rifle*). I'd not leave that there if I were you.

SECOND ROMAN. It's just like you to be afraid of a corpse! He's as dead as a door-nail.

FIRST ROMAN. I'm not afraid, but it would be better for you to be caught sitting on duty, than to be found without your spear (or rifle) in this district.

SECOND ROMAN. Ah, that is true. I will sit down. (*Takes spear (or rifle) and sits down opposite* FIRST ROMAN.) But you did not answer: vot is the Cordon Sanitaire?

FIRST ROMAN (*in very measured tones, with contempt*). You don't know? Ye could never tell? And what would you be after doing if ye did?

SECOND ROMAN. *Aw! But* . . .

FIRST ROMAN. 'Aw! But.' It's yer 'Aw buts' that got you snubbed. It's no wonder he couldn't stand you.

(*Jerks his thumb in the direction of* CENTURION'S *exit.*)

SECOND ROMAN. Ah, I do not mind a mere boy! You know the song? (*Sings*):

'Julius who conquered Gaul
By a boy was conquered!'

FIRST ROMAN (*with profound contempt*). Tell me, is the tune your own?

SECOND ROMAN. Ah, you vos humbugging me.

FIRST ROMAN. Aren't you a nice specimen to be comparing yourself to Julius Caesar?

SECOND ROMAN. I was meaning that I did not mind snubs from a young brat like that. (*Points in direction of Officer's exit.*)

FIRST ROMAN. No, ye can't be insulted, for you have neither dignity nor self-respect, nor even a superficial knowledge of the regulations.

SECOND ROMAN. Have I not?

FIRST ROMAN. No; or you would not be keeping up the old form of salute after the Proclamation has forbidden it.

SECOND ROMAN. Is that so?

FIRST ROMAN (*producing paper*). 'Army Regulations. Section K. 10 over X. to the 57th Cap. Tib. 1003. Officers and men will take note that after this date in giving and returning salutes the right hand is not to be raised to the forehead as heretofore, but is to be brought smartly to a level at and no higher than the umbilicus.' D'ye hear that?

SECOND ROMAN. Ah, yes! I see the reason – oh, yes, very subtile!

FIRST ROMAN (*solemnly*). Well, if you see the reason in an Army regulation you ought to be in the Pioneers – you are the first.

SECOND ROMAN. Is it meant to remind us that an army marches on its belly and to eat well?

FIRST ROMAN. No.

SECOND ROMAN. Perhaps it is to prevent the men losing confidence.

FIRST ROMAN. In what way?

SECOND ROMAN. By drawing attention to the officers' foreheads.

FIRST ROMAN. It shows how little you know.

SECOND ROMAN. Do you know?

FIRST ROMAN. I do. Tiberius has sprained his elbow taking the salutes of so many marches past of our perpetual victories, and now he can only raise his hand to his navel. And what's good for him ought to be good enough for you if you could be got to have discipline.

SECOND ROMAN. It doesn't take much discipline, does it, to guard a tomb?

FIRST ROMAN. It's not only guarding a tomb we are, but guarding the interests of the Roman Empire. D'ye think Imperial Rome is afraid of a corpse? Our great Empire fears nothing, living or dead.

SECOND ROMAN. Vell, why are we here?

FIRST ROMAN. To preserve peace and stamp out sedition.

SECOND ROMAN. But it is because we are here that the people are seditious.

FIRST ROMAN (*firmly and rather oratorically*). And because they are seditious we are here.

SECOND ROMAN (*with an irritating smile*). So the effect is an excuse for the cause?

FIRST ROMAN. There's no excuse for anyone objecting to law and order. Surely you don't sympathise with illegal assemblies, seditious speeches, with blackguardism like that recent cattle-driving in Gadara and all that orgy of crime? (*Pointing over his shoulder.*)

SECOND ROMAN. Ah, but eef a man walks straight he is arrested for illegal drilling, and if he walks crooked, for being drunk, and if he remains still he is asked to move on. Be just before you sit in judgment.

FIRST ROMAN. Don't talk nonsense. Do you think justice could have any effect on a lot of rebels? Answer me that. What are you thinking of? Answer me that.

SECOND ROMAN. I'm thinking it's an extraordinary thing that every country we occupy seems to be inhabited exclusively by rebels.

FIRST ROMAN. The sooner you begin to think in terms of Universal Altruism the better. D'ye think that I who spent my life spreading civilisation am going to risk my pension, (and the chance of selling my Government farm) for an excitable crowd of Jewmen who never saw a Gaul! Look at that! (*Points to ribbon.*) That was for suppressing the riot in Dalmatia. Look at that! (*Points to another ribbon.*) I got that on the Bosset river from Marcus Lepidus himself.

SECOND ROMAN (*taking off his helmet and showing his head*). I got that from the skelp of a bottle coming off duty one night. It doesn't show as much as a ribbon, but it is an honourable scar.

FIRST ROMAN. Gah, ye'll never be a soldier.

SECOND ROMAN. Vell, why was I made one?

FIRST ROMAN. Ye have neither discipline, courage or self-control.

SECOND ROMAN. Well, what did you want to conscript me for?

FIRST ROMAN (*producing paper, contemptuously*). It's a pity that you were not with Varus. Perhaps you'd like to hear Caesar's speech in the official report. (*Declaims.*) 'Sedition has been banished from the Forum, corruption from the Campus Martius and discord from the Senate House. Justice, equity and industry have been revived in the state; authority has been given to the magistrates, majesty to the Senate and solemnity to the Courts of Justice. Virtuous acts are honoured, wicked deeds are punished, the humble respects the powerful without deriding him; the powerful takes precedence of the humble without condemning him. When were provisions more moderate in price? When were the blessings of peace more abundant? Augustan peace diffused all over the regions of the East and the West, and all that lies between South and North preserves every corner of the world free from all dread of predatory molestation. The cities of Asia have been repaired; the provinces have been blessed by the humanity and consideration of their Governors. And this Province in particular by having Pontius Pilate and the Lady Claudia to assist him in promoting the peace and welfare of the district of his administration.'

SECOND ROMAN. Can't ye stop doping yourself with that stuff and give your intelligence a chance?

FIRST ROMAN. 'Honours promptly reward the deserving and the punishment of the guilty if slow is certain.'

SECOND ROMAN (*slyly*). Tell me, is the tune your own?

FIRST ROMAN. No, but I'll take good care that no damned nonsense undermines the government of Rome. Isn't every place benefited?

SECOND ROMAN. Yes, we have had more crucifixions and domiciliary
   visits, and they say the problems of government are likely to increase?
FIRST ROMAN. It's the garrisons that are likely to be increased.
SECOND ROMAN. Quite so. They are the problems.
FIRST ROMAN. None of your damned nonsense.
   (*Noise of a mob is heard from behind.*)
   (*Both spring to arms.*)
   (FIRST ROMAN *goes to back at right and looks over wall.*)
   (SECOND ROMAN *does likewise.*)
FIRST ROMAN. They're at it again, one of their processions, but it doesn't
   seem to be in military formation and it doesn't look as if it were
   coming up in our direction. (*Sits down, carelessly.*) The Seventh are in
   charge below and can look after it anyway.
   (*The* SECOND ROMAN *is looking excitedly over the wall.*)
   Perhaps you'd like me to read you another little extract from the
   public orator for the day (*Reads.*) 'Our responsibility is enormous. In
   the absence of agreement on any matter of political or social reform,
   the Roman Government is directly responsible for the shaping and
   conduct of Galilean affairs, and its policy must be guided by two
   supreme considerations – the welfare of Galilee and the safety of the
   rest of Imperial Rome and of the whole Empire. Under no pressure,
   external or internal, can it consent to father or promote any policy
   that might impair the one or imperil the other. The welfare of Galilee
   depends on good government – which means equal justice and
   opportunity for all, firm administration of the law, protection for life
   and property, and the free development of the country's intellectual,
   material and spiritual resources, moral education, in fact.' Are ye
   listening? 'At the present time Galilee's condition is such that any
   political experiment must involve the greatest danger. If it should
   satisfy disaffection the Empire would be betrayed; if it should fail to
   satisfy disaffection, no good and much harm would be done. There
   remains, then, the course which duty and interest alike dictate – firm
   and honest government under the existing Constitution. With that
   responsibility of the Roman Government neither Persia nor Africa
   has any right or, as we believe, any desire to interfere.' (*Looks and
   finds* SECOND ROMAN *inattentive.*) Will ye come down out of that and
   don't be getting the wind up.
SECOND ROMAN. There is a small dark man coming out of the crowd,
   and he seems to be coming in this direction.
   (FIRST ROMAN *rises.*)
   He is the cause of all the excitement. I have reported him several
   times already.
FIRST ROMAN. What can an unarmed man do against Rome?

(*Sits down again on rock.*)

SECOND ROMAN (*greatly relieved*). As I was about to say. This place is very quiet (*Sighing nervously.*) We'll be off duty very soon now, won't we? (*Sits down near tomb.*)

FIRST ROMAN. I'd like to know what you'd have done if I weren't here. You're the kind of fellow that could manage to be afraid even of a corpse.

SECOND ROMAN (*assumed carelessness*). Vell, there is not much kick in a corpse.

FIRST ROMAN (*dourly*). It's one of them out of the way at any rate. If they were all there there'd be a chance for a decent state of affairs.

A VOICE (*calls loudly*). Lazarus!

(*The* FIRST ROMAN *springs up at the alarm, and with rifle (or spear) at the ready moves warily in the direction of The Voice. As he does so, the stone of the tomb bursts open behind him and part of the wall falls on* SECOND ROMAN. *As he looks back at it the Voice calls out*): 'Come forth.' (*A corpse rises and comes blindly like a sleepwalker from the tomb in the direction of the call.*)

FIRST ROMAN. Halt!

SECOND ROMAN (*who runs to* FIRST *for protection, flinging himself on ground impeding him by grasping his feet*). Help!

FIRST ROMAN. Halt! And present your permit. Halt! Or I fire (run you through).

SECOND ROMAN (*looking up with his face beside* FIRST ROMAN's *feet*). Oh, don't strike fire, that might make it worse! Don't fire on the dead.

(*Exit* LAZARUS.)

FIRST ROMAN (*calling out*). All right, Lazarus! I can identify you. Ye'll be courtmartialed for being within a military area without a permit. (*To* SECOND ROMAN.) Let go my leg, and get up to blazes out of that and make a mental note of the speech.

SECOND ROMAN (*sitting up dazed*). Yes, but he was dead and buried three days.

FIRST ROMAN. Then put on your gas-mask. Isn't he infinitely better that way than alive?

SECOND ROMAN. He has risen from the dead.

FIRST ROMAN (*reminiscently*). I wouldn't be at all surprised if Pilate's wife hadn't a hand in this! as sure as dreaming goes with spirit-rapping.

SECOND ROMAN (*amazed*). And he was dead and buried three days . . . I think I'll go away (*Rising.*) I'll go away out of this.

FIRST ROMAN. And join the movement, will you? Ah, man, have sense, take up yer musket and try and have some self-respect. It's only a dead Jew.

SECOND ROMAN (*takes up musket and looks at it*). I'll ask the officer what's the use of a thing like this when death itself cannot stop the movement. (*Throws it against wall again.*)

FIRST ROMAN (*looking at it*). What! You refuse to shoulder the burden of civilisation.

SECOND ROMAN. What has your civilisation ever produced to equal this movement out from death?

FIRST ROMAN (*after a pause, suddenly*). What! Is that the movement he was referring to? The movement in the limbs of the corpse! Rising from the dead?

SECOND ROMAN. The dead has risen!

FIRST ROMAN. Well, if this thing spreads I'll send in my resignation.

SECOND ROMAN (*slowly*). And join the movement with me?

FIRST ROMAN (*scornfully*). Certainly not! But I'll send in my resignation, because where any Jew can rise from the dead is no place for a decent Roman. What's the use of all my service? If there is to be no more death, there can be no more valour. What's the use of discipline? What's the good of bravery? What becomes of fortitude and manhood and even common decency?

SECOND ROMAN. But it is splendid, splendid, no more death, hurrah . . . I will not be afraid now. I will have valour, hurrah, hurrah!

FIRST ROMAN. I'll see Pilate about it, it's a damned serious thing.

(*A murmur of amazement and applause is heard from the distance.*)

SECOND ROMAN. Oh, please, please, do not see Pilate, he might spoil it. . . . He would stamp out the movement. (*Dancing.*) No more death! (*Enter* CENTURION.)

CENTURION. What's all this about? What has happened here?

SECOND ROMAN. No more death!

CENTURION (*ignoring him and turning to* FIRST). Well?

FIRST ROMAN (*pointing to tomb*). He came and went down to join the meeting, Sir.

CENTURION. Who came out?

FIRST ROMAN. Lazarus, Sir.

CENTURION. Why was he not challenged?

FIRST ROMAN. He was, but he refused to stop.

CENTURION. Why was he not killed?

FIRST ROMAN. Because he was already dead.

SECOND ROMAN (*exultingly*). There is no more death!

CENTURION (*puzzled and incredulous*). Do you mean to say (*Pointing to open tomb.*) that the corpse rose, broke open that tomb and defied you sentries?

FIRST ROMAN. That's it, Sir. A very serious affair, Sir, under the regulations. Sir; I must report the matter directly to the Governor.

SECOND ROMAN. He wants to restore death. Don't let him, Sir.

CENTURION (*evidently puzzled, walks up and down stopping to think at intervals. Aside: 'What an extraordinary country!' Suddenly to First Roman*). Tell me, you weren't expecting this?

FIRST ROMAN. No, Sir!

CENTURION. You weren't thinking of . . . this kind of thing? That is to say . . . there was no suggestion in your mind of anything of the sort? Think carefully now. Are you quite sure?

FIRST ROMAN. Nothing that I am conscious of.

CENTURION. Ah, but there may be something you were *subconscious* of. *Sub-conscious*, you know. Nearly everything is sub-conscious.

FIRST ROMAN. No, Sir.

CENTURION. Tell me. Were you ever wounded in the head?

FIRST ROMAN (*glancing at Second and drawing himself up*). Certainly not, Sir.

CENTURION. No sunstroke or that kind of thing?

FIRST ROMAN (*curtly*). I was never unconscious in my life, Sir.

CENTURION. And you are not a member of any psychological society?

FIRST ROMAN. No, Sir.

SECOND ROMAN. I was wounded in the head, Sir.

FIRST ROMAN (*silences him with a scowl*). Yah!

CENTURION. Now, I want to ask you a question which you are to forget as soon as answered. (*With secrecy.*) Were there any ladies about here?

FIRST ROMAN. No, Sir.

CENTURION. Nor a lady?

FIRST ROMAN. No, Sir.

CENTURION. How very extraordinary! (*To himself.*) Still it will hardly do to tell her husband. (*To First Roman*): You will see, there may be people involved in things who have no interest in the administration, who are, in fact, more interested in spiritualism than in Government, and they might be greatly embarrassed if a complaint were to be made to the Governor about what is probably only a case of direct appearance after all, and a most successful experiment, you must admit.

FIRST ROMAN. With all due respects to you, Sir. If this movement amongst the dead is not stamped out, what is to become of Rome? No death, Sir, no Glory. No bravery, Sir. Cowards would be as good as ourselves, Sir. Look at that! (*Points to* SECOND ROMAN.) Then there's the matter of my medals. They'll lose all their value if resurrection becomes general – and I have gained a few in my time.

CENTURION (*hesitatingly*). Of course, but you would be compensated. Still I think on the whole. . . . It's hardly a matter for Pilate. I will call myself and make tactful enquiries at the Government House. You may have been present at a seance without realising it, and you must not take it too seriously.

SECOND ROMAN (*thinking that he hesitated*). Yes, Sir! It's an excellent movement, Sir, to get rid of death, don't tell Pilate.

FIRST ROMAN. It may not be serious, Sir; but ye see, if this kind of thing is allowed to go on it will put an end to warfare.

CENTURION. Now, now, I really can't see how the abolition of death would put an end to warfare.

FIRST ROMAN. Well, Sir, speaking as a plain soldier, Sir, I would object to working overtime or fighting after death.

CENTURION. Aw, of course, by Jove, yaas, so it would!

FIRST ROMAN. And then, Sir, if the Jews had a standing army or an army that would stand, there'd be no end to a campaign, Sir, if any Jew could rise from the dead. And apart from the fact you couldn't inherit any property you'd have no way of distinguishing yourself, Sir.

CENTURION. By Jove, no, you are quite right. It would be impossible to live in a world without end of non-commissioned Jews!

FIRST ROMAN. And impossible to get out of it, Sir.

(*Loud cheers are heard and a shout: 'Ah! me sound Lazarus!'*)

You see, Sir. We may be late with our report.

CENTURION (*after reflecting*). You are quite right. It is a serious thing. Come with me to the Governor. It's a matter for the greatest tact.

SECOND ROMAN. No, no. I vill not go to Pilate, I vill not die.

(*He runs off right.*)

CENTURION (*looking after him*). It seems to have undermined discipline already.

FIRST ROMAN. It would undermine a lot of things if there were no death.

CENTURION. Yes, after all, it is the restraint of death that gives life a style. It's Death that gives Life dignity.

FIRST ROMAN. Yes, Sir. Death's a great disciplinarian. It keeps the troops in order. But, of course, we are not exempt ourselves.

CENTURION. Oh, well, no. But the switch has no terror for the schoolmaster. . . . Ha, just listen to the disorder the resurrection has given rise to! I must speak to Claudia about this. (*Renewed cheers, and shouts of 'Up, Lazarus!'*) She should have been more careful. An experiment like this is likely to increase disaffection.

FIRST ROMAN. They are an upsetting, unruly lot in these parts.

CENTURION. What the country wants is firm administration of the law and protection of (*Looking at open tomb.*) death and private property, and 'free development of the country's intellectual resources, moral education, in fact.'

FIRST ROMAN. Yes, Sir.

CENTURION. It's no place for spiritualism. On to Pilate.

(*Exeunt.*)

## CURTAIN

# THE ENCHANTED TROUSERS

*A Play in One Act*

This play was first produced at the Abbey Theatre in Dublin, on 25 November 1919, with the following cast:

| | |
|---|---|
| HUMPHREY HEAVEY, an unemployed actor | Peter Nolan |
| ANDREW HEAVEY, his brother, a National School Teacher | Arthur Shields |
| MRS HEAVEY, their mother | Christine Hayden |
| OFFICIAL 1 | Michael J. Dolan |
| OFFICIAL 2 | Brian Herbert |
| OFFICIAL 3 | J. J. Lynch |
| OFFICIAL 4, their Secretary | J. Hugh Nagle |
| PILE, an English invalid suffering from pre-war shock | Philip Guiry |
| and | |
| ARTHUR | Eric Gorman |

*Produced by Lennox Robinson*

# THE ENCHANTED TROUSERS

*Scene — Clare-Galway, Ireland.*

*A room in a country National School which is used as a sittingroom by the teacher's family on occasions such as this.*

*Half the blackboard is overhung by a map of the Tonic Solfa, Regulation literature hangs in cards on the walls, e.g.:*

> A CONTINENT is a COUNTRY
> inhabited by FOREIGNERS

> An ISLAND is LAND
> surrounded by a NAVY

*Time — Anyday in Ireland*

HUMPHREY. Let me see, let me see now (*Looks in glass in lid of his make-up box and fixes in a monocle.*) That ought to do for a Duke's face. Making one's self up is a great help, even though one is only rehearsing. This will be no easy novel to adapt. That's the worst of the novelists who write about the passionate life of the spirit — they never see how difficult it is to represent the high interior conflict in an outward form consistent with its dignity. Let me see now. I have to spit and say 'Damn' (*Looks about and spits into fireplace. Says in a rehearsal voice*): 'Damn.' That won't do either. It seems both must be done together because it reads: (*Refers to a yellow and black book and declaims somewhat pompously*): 'Damn it,' said the Duke as he spat in the grate, 'What would life be without culture?'

(*His Mother — MRS HEAVEY — enters and looks on amazed.*
HUMPHREY *continues with exasperation*): —
Should the Damn be before the spit or the spit before the damn? It's perfectly impossible to damn and spit at the same time — I wish to Heaven I was acting in a Cinema or in a noble play of Japan. It must

559

be a nonchalant spit.

MRS HEAVEY. Well, if that's the kind of playacting that goes on in England, it's no wonder that she is where she is. And I wondering how me grate got all rusty. Spittin' indeed. A nice thing to bring over here to this clean country where we're not allowed to spit even on or off the tram.

HUMPHREY (*pocketing monocle*). Oh, Mother, I was just rehearsing a new adaptation for the Fall.

MRS HEAVEY. Well, I'll trouble you not to do it again as long as you're here. (*She wipes the side of the grate with the fender brush.*) Ye might be opening the window to let out the tuberculosis.

HUMPHREY (*he goes towards window and turns*). It's only a play, Mother. A society novel I'm trying to adapt.

MRS HEAVEY. Don't talk to me about Society when what you want is common decency. If that's the kind of society ye keep it's no wonder that it can't keep you or you wouldn't be back here out at elbows and out at heels depending on your poor old mother that's worn her fingers to the bone stitching to keep body and soul together.

HUMPHREY. You are pleading for the theatre of commerce now.

MRS HEAVEY. What? Is it me pleading for a theatre?

HUMPHREY. You are making money the measure of Art.

MRS HEAVEY. Am I? I'm thinking the lads beyond have taken the measure of your art and bundled you out.

HUMPHREY. I am still confident that it is good.

MRS HEAVEY. Handsome is that handsome does.

HUMPHREY. Although it may be hard to act, the conception is fine. The old Duke spitting into the sinking fire and inveighing against life in the name of culture. Life that is tolerable only as a revelation of the personality, an expression of culture. Life that only reveals a meaning when considered aesthetically. It is as fine a thing as the death of Onogi and his wife who committed hari-kari together as if to recall Japan back by a grim gesture to its old cult of the warrior when the tradesman was threatening the Nation's will. It is legitimate Art, a comedy of manners.

MRS HEAVEY (*emphatically*). Manners maketh man and want of them the fellow.

HUMPHREY. Mother, you are as bad as Carlyle for the sincerity of your platitudes.

MRS HEAVEY. Is cursin' and spittin' legitimate art?

HUMPHREY. Mother, you do not understand. I was reading over the character I may have to play, that of the Duke Du Vain Desir. One of the grand old Norman stock who is ruined by the loss of his richest mistress.

MRS HEAVEY. A nice Duke you'll make. Imagine a duke spittin'.

HUMPHREY. Yes, if you had read the book you would understand that it is symbolic, the result of the unconscious mental process of a dream – an evidence of repression that escapes the psychic censor and expresses dissatisfaction and disgust.

MRS HEAVEY. Well, it's no wonder. But if you would only try to act your brother who works honestly night, noon and morning, teaching the children, and saving the crops, you could hold your head up with the best of them and there'd be something to show for your play acting; and I wouldn't have to express my dissatisfaction and disgust at your makin' a laughin' stock of yourself before the neighbours.

HUMPHREY. That in itself is an achievement.

MRS HEAVEY, Which? Is it being laughed at?

HUMPHREY. Quite so. Anyone can be a tragedy.

MRS HEAVEY. What are you saying?

HUMPHREY (*grandiloquently*). It is given to few to achieve comedy.

MRS HEAVEY. It's your mocking and sneerin' that has left you where you are, leanin' your weight on me an' spongin' on your brother whom ye ought to be imitating. You that can't get a job even in England where there's nothing but jobs.

HUMPHREY. But you have a bad word to say even of him. He reads too much in books that are not good for him.

MRS HEAVEY. Well, it would be better for you to be giving him a hand than painting your face and spittin' into the grate.

HUMPHREY (*to himself*). 'Art is its own exceeding great reward.'

MRS HEAVEY (*dusting grate*). Unfortunately. It's a reward that's always in arrears.

(*Enter* ANDY HEAVEY.)

ANDY. Whist, whist now, Mother, you'll have to go out of the Schoolroom. There's a Visiting Committee coming here to sit in it in no time.

MRS HEAVEY. A Visiting Committee? To sit on whom?

ANDY. An Appointments Committee.

MRS HEAVEY. But what appointment are they after? The only people that are coming here are coming here to settle about the potato spraying, and that's not till next week. Mebbe somebody wants to be a porter at the Workhouse?

ANDY. Here, Humphrey, lend a hand to put the benches back in their place. (*He carries benches to R. while* HUMPHREY *walks up and down reading the book and gesticulating.*)

MRS HEAVEY. Lend a hand, is it? Sorra much help he'll be. What d'ye think he was at but spittin' and damning, rehearsin' a play for England in the Fall.

HUMPHREY. What's the Appointments Committee for, Andy?

ANDY. To appoint a Minister of . . .

MRS HEAVEY. Another minister and nobody goes to church but the Coastguard!

ANDY. A Minister of Potato Spraying.

MRS HEAVEY (*indignantly*). Potato Spraying – as if any yardboy could not do that. What do they want a Minister to do it for?

ANDY. Oh, it's a big appointment for someone to control all the potato blight in Clare-Galway.

MRS HEAVEY. An appointment, is it? Oh, I see. That means another job for another Englishman.

ANDY. I wouldn't say that, Mother. They might do with a Scotsman. There's many a one might be lured over for £1,200 a year.

MRS HEAVEY (*after a pause*). But Glory be to God, you might have a chance yourself. (ANDY *makes a gesture of deprecation.*) If ye hadn't why would they be coming here? It's a good sign if they are taking over the schoolhouse for a Spraying Depot.

ANDY. Put that out of your head. It's because it has the only large room in this part of the country. They're only going to meet here to make the appointment. Look where you left your knitting.

MRS HEAVEY. But aren't you the only educated man in this part of the country? Who else is there? Sure, they couldn't give it to an omadhaun . . . and the police Sergeant's not allowed to take it.

ANDY. If they can't find an Englishman here they'll bring one with them. Unless, unless (*Pointing at* HUMPHREY.)

MRS HEAVEY. Unless what? Don't be mystifying me. (ANDY *continues pointing at* HUMPHREY.) What! Is it Humphrey? Why, he doesn't know a potato from a sod of turf.

ANDY. No, but he should know an Englishman. And if he can't *act* one after all the time he's been play-acting in England . . .

MRS HEAVEY (*seizing the idea*). Shure, of course, he should. Shouldn't ye, Humphrey? Could ye bring yerself to stretch yer Art as ye call it on acting an Englishman for the laddoes from Dublin?

HUMPHREY. But what would the Appointment Committee say?

ANDY. I know the kind of people who are on this Committee: Englishmen from Killiney. They'll be delighted at meeting any kind of Englishman. The more Cockney the better. It would be a relief to them to think they had found the genuine article at last. They are tired acting an imitation themselves. They might remodel themselves on you and give you the job.

MRS HEAVEY. And it wouldn't be the first job that was given by mistake.

ANDY. And if he doesn't know how to act an Englishman after all his play acting and his high life in London, well, he's not good even at work of his own choosing.

MRS HEAVEY. Troth, and he ought to know, God knows. D'ye hear that, Humphrey? If you don't know how to act? Surely, ye will act.

HUMPHREY (*undecided*). . . . but they'd never believe in me.

MRS HEAVEY. Yes, they would, Sonny. Try and do it for your poor old Mother's sake.

HUMPHREY. Do you think any sane body of men would confer an appointment worth – how much is it worth?

ANDY. £1,000 a year at the very least.

HUMPHREY. On an unknown man.

ANDY. Wait till ye see them before ye call them sane. Besides, doesn't everyone start by being unknown? Surely you don't think anyone would get a job for being found out?

HUMPHREY. No, but it will mean jail if I am found out.

MRS HEAVEY. Jail for playing the Englishman! Are you out of your senses? Chairman of the Prisons' Board at the very least.

HUMPHREY. But what do I know about spraying?

MRS HEAVEY (*aside*). Spraying. Look at the grate.

ANDY. When did a job in Ireland depend on proficiency?

HUMPHREY. That's all very fine: but suppose they asked me what copper sulphate was? What do I know of Chemistry?

MRS HEAVEY. Begorra, judging by the lads that comes down here I think the more ignorant ye are the better.

HUMPHREY. That's all very well; they have only to talk about the climate, but suppose they ask me what a microbe is. What do I know of bacteriology? Suppose they ask me what causes blight and I don't appear to know?

ANDY. Causes, causes. Nobody enquires into the cause of anything in this country. They juggle with effects. Besides they'll think your ignorance is merely a pose. They'll never believe you. They'll think it's the usual modest pose. Every Englishman is in a worse predicament than you'll be. Not once or twice in his rough island story but he has been so for centuries. He never knows what moment his armies may peacefully penetrate and annex some highly civilised country. He never knows the moment he may be called on to be superior to the most cultured race in existence. How does he protect himself, what does he do? What do you know about chemistry? What did he know about Hindustani? What do you know about copper sulphate? What did he know about Arabic? And yet he owns India and Egypt. Do you think he learnt their language before taking over those countries to save them from themselves? Not at all.

HUMPHREY. Then what did he do?

ANDY. He became the opposite.

HUMPHREY. To what?

ANDY. To everything. Language, culture, knowledge, civilisation itself. He has had to become the negative to so many peoples and things that he has had no time for self-progress.

HUMPHREY. But will I have to blight the potatoes first and spray them afterwards?

ANDY. You must get yourself into the state of mind that no matter what you do it is good for the country. You must carry out your instructions and administer the law. In other words, you'll be forced along in accordance with your own interests.

MRS HEAVEY. But there's no blight in Clare-Galway.

ANDY (*in solemn parody of an official utterance*). And is that any reason why Clare-Galway should be deprived of the benefits of the preventive and precautionary methods of modern science? Who can tell the day it might break out? Get rid of it before it comes.

MRS HEAVEY. Begorra, if he talks like that he'll do nicely. That's like the way they go on in the Castle taking precautions against things that never was.

HUMPHREY. But how am I to get rid of the Committee and keep the £1,000 a year?

ANDY. By complete lack of knowledge – total ignorance. Owing to the exigencies of representative Government a member of the Cabinet never knows what he may have to take on, so he keeps his mind an unprejudiced blank. You do the same and add a little rudeness and pretend to think that the Commissioners are as illiterate as a Board of Education or some such Body. Act the Englishman, then they will not expect much of you. For they know that in England it's bad form to be intelligent.

HUMPHREY. What. Eh?

ANDY. Hasn't England been worshipping stupidity for a hundred years? Call anything that is unpleasant irrevelant. Mix sentimentality with valetudinarianism. Substitute for language inarticulate sounds. Act, *act*, that's all you have to do. You'll have the most sympathetic audience in the world. But, above all, don't you forget to be sympathetic – it saves the Treasury and secures your salary.

MRS HEAVEY. Well, now, indeed if he can't do that.

ANDY. You'll have the most appreciative audience for an Englishman in the world. An Irish audience, who, instead of criticising you will be finding points to admire and be looking to you for a lead.

HUMPHREY. But I don't want to turn myself into a negation personified. What about my self-respect?

ANDY. Self-negation is at any rate a preservative for self-respect. It keeps the personality away from wear. And the best way to preserve it is as an actor playing the fool.

HUMPHREY. Is a fool and an Englishman synonymous?

ANDY. Now, now, now – no politics. The first thing to do is to select a good name for yourself, something that will be full of the genius of the language and racy of the soil. Something restrained and unpretentious. A monosyllabic name.

MRS HEAVEY. I never heard of a gentleman with a name of one syllable.

ANDY. Remember, we're talking of England. Now the commonest sound in the language is S. So it must be a name commencing with S. Sharp, Stubbs, Smith or Slow. Smith's too common and is never found with a Christian name; Sharp is not in the character. The choice lies between Stubbs and Slow. Slow is a rotund, solid, self-respecting name. What about Mr Slow? It's a good name for a Government official.

HUMPHREY. I think I will use my own stage-name to avoid unpleasantness.

ANDY. What is it?

HUMPHREY. Siegfried Stott.

MRS HEAVEY. Oh, well, you might take a decent name when you're about it.

HUMPHREY. But Siegfried Stott is a Saxo-Anglican name, that's why I choose it to compliment the Anglo-Saxons. It has a hint of Opera in it.

ANDY. Mother, it will do very well. Think of the American papers. Political news by our Irish Correspondent. 'Stott sprays. Blight delays,' and the headlines in the Tuam Herald. 'Mr Stott who sprayed all the tubers in the West had the honour of being invited to dine with His Excellency at the Viceregal Lodge.'

MRS HEAVEY. Oh, if he gets a meal out of it you can call him anything you like.

HUMPHREY. Just a moment. Suppose I am Siegfried Stott. How can I account for my presence in this God-forsaken part of the country? Imagine anything with a name like Stott being found in a bog in Clare-Galway.

ANDY. Why not? Couldn't you be over for the Shootin'? Haven't you taken the whole moor and are damned disappointed with the sport? You expected partridge with all the tillage.

HUMPHREY (*ruefully*). Do I look much like a man who was disappointed with sport?

ANDY. No, not yet, but wait until you are dressed for the part. Wait until you put on the toga Brittanica. The dress suit for the country: a Norfolk jacket, knickerbockers and a pair of spats.

HUMPHREY. And where am I to get all that rig out, we haven't time – and we couldn't get them if we had?

ANDY. Well . . . I could . . . Let me see?

MRS HEAVEY. I'll tell ye. Ever since the King's visit there are six suits of plain clothes down at the barracks and all of them knickers.

HUMPHREY. But you surely don't think that it would deceive anybody to dress me as a plain clothes policeman?

ANDY. Of course it would. Your feet are quite small.

MRS HEAVEY. Well, all I can say is that the clothes made the six peelers look like loyal civilians, though they forgot their disguise and stood to attention as the King passed.

HUMPHREY (*turning*). But damn it all, man, that's not the point. Do you think I'll submit to be rigged up like a common constable?

ANDY. Why not? (*Singing.*)

'Love turned Jove into a swan
All for the love of Leda,
And he a bull o'er meadows ran
To carry off Europa.'

HUMPHREY. But this is very far from being a love affair.

MRS HEAVEY. Hush, now, Humphrey. I'll get you the *sergeant's* suit. His Norfolk jacket and his knickerbockers. He was promoted Sergeant the day after I sewed the double seat into them.

ANDY. Yes, do, Mother, before he becomes unreasonable and begins to argue about a mere matter of raiment. Don't be a minute, Mother. (*Signs to her to hurry.*)

(*Exit* MRS HEAVEY.)

HUMPHREY (*profoundly dejected*). I do not intend to go through with this. It is perfectly absurd.

ANDY. My dear fellow, you have only to play a part. Are you not an actor?

HUMPHREY. Yes, but where's my part? If you only had time to write down what to say when they ask me my qualifications.

ANDY. D'ye mean to say that you're going to let them talk? You must assume the initiative. Warn them that they will drive you out of the place if they talk shop or mention a problem or a crisis.

HUMPHREY. What crisis?

ANDY. I don't know, but Officials are always provided with a crisis; that is, an extenuating circumstance to excuse mental confusion. You must seize the conversation.

HUMPHREY. What conversation?

ANDY. Well, that comes well from one who has lived so long in England. Sport or your health are the only topic of conversation. Be a bowel and give even your thoughts time to digest themselves before you speak. The Commissioners will supply the words and the cues. Besides, if necessary, I shall stand behind them by the blackboard and point out with the pointer the sounds you are to make in reply. (*He points on the blackboard*.) Think of me. I shall have to play the idiotic Irishman with his dudheen upside down to draw off from them the awful weight of their own gravity. Don't think you are the only actor in the piece?

HUMPHREY (*scrutinising the blackboard*). The tonic solfa! Well, absurd as the trousers are as a means to advancement, the tonic solfa is more ridiculous.

ANDY. There you go again. Absurd and ridiculous. Those words reveal an attitude of mind only found in subject races. Ridiculous – evoking laughter; laughter is a refuge. Don't you know you must never laugh or give rise to laughter? Imitate Punch. Of course you may smile, but only when taking the offensive. You know the old Irish Triad – the three things to be dreaded: The horns of a bull, the heels of a stallion, the smile of an Englishman. Why, man, it's sinister.

HUMPHREY. But to keep to the point . . . the tonic solfa. How is that to help me?

ANDY (*soliloquising*). 'to keep to the point'. (*More alertly*.) How is it to help you? Quite simply. I point to the vowels; never mind the consonants, they are only used to modify the grunts. You repeat. (*He points with a pointer*.) Oh-eh-ah. According as I point them out. Nobody can deny those are the chief ingredients of the English language and comprise nearly all conversation, with a few barbarisms, such as 'beastly' and 'awfully', frequent 'quites', a few 'damns', and the ten platitudes added.

HUMPHREY (*expostulating in argument*). But surely you have not reduced the English language to that.

ANDY. No, I haven't, but the English themselves have.

HUMPHREY. But where is the language that managed to produce Shakespeare?

ANDY. But where is the manager that dare produce him now?

HUMPHREY. Ah, yes. Only too true – quite true.

ANDY. Then, by the way, that was a splendid and quite natural contribution of your own. 'To keep to the point'. I'll just put a point on the board and do that. (*points with the pointer*.) Where you are to say 'keep to the point'. What about a little rehearsal? Suppose they come into the room saying (*He walks to the door and ENTERS as if one of the Commissioners*.) 'Fact is we have to make a very careful and exhaustive selection.'

HUMPHREY. Exhaustive. When there's nobody for the job?

ANDY (*tapping the blackboard and prompting him*). O. O. O. Remember that's the only possible reply to official language.

HUMPHREY. O?

ANDY. Yes. Now I'll anticipate some of the conversation and indicate the answers. You repeat. Don't mind the D or the R. 'Well, Mr Stott, what kind of sport have you been having (*Points to the Re.*) in this rather God-forsaken wilderness?'

HUMPHREY. Eh?

ANDY. I was just wondering if you had knocked out any sport in this beastly place. (*Points to Do.*)

HUMPHREY. Oh!

ANDY. Yes, there used to be some salmon fishing (*Points with exaggerated emphasis to Fah.*); but it is ruined.

HUMPHREY. Ah?

ANDY. Yes, yes. Have you not heard? A most regrettable affair. The salmon came up out of the sea and devoured the eggs in the new hatchery and nearly committed race suicide in spite of the efforts of the Fishery Department to preserve them. (*Points to Fah.*)

HUMPHREY. Ah.

ANDY. You'll do splendidly; why there's not an easier language to learn than modern English when you are properly dressed for it. 'O, eh? Ah.'

(*Enter* MRS HEAVEY *with a parcel.*)

MRS HEAVEY. I asked the Sergeant's wife to lend them to me to make a pattern of. They say they're in an awful state.

HUMPHREY. Then that settles it. I will not put them on.

MRS HEAVEY. Not the trousers, dear, but the Commissioners. The Sergeant was talking to their chauffeur and he says there's a surplus that has to be got rid of before the end of the financial year, and it's next week.

HUMPHREY. A surplus?

MRS HEAVEY. Yes, and if they don't elect somebody at once there'll be no way of spending the money, and if they send it back they'll not get it from the Treasury next year, and besides there might be an inquiry about former years' extravagance and their wages might be docked, so they'll have to elect you. They've had to hold the election a week before the advertised time. That's why they're here today and not next week.

ANDY. You're in luck. They're in a bad corner. Demand double salary, bonuses and that kind of thing.

MRS HEAVEY (*who has been unwrapping parcel*). There's a double seat in them, for I put it in myself.

ANDY. Hold them up, Mother. (*She does so.*) There you are, Humphrey, when you enter that, you enter England.

'This seat of Mars,
This fortress built by Nature for herself

Against infection and the hand of war.'
Come on. (*Takes him by the arm.*) Put them on. Adopt your country. Become naturalised. Assume your pride of place. Dictate culture by remaining silent: become superior and inaccessible, monopolise civilisation – set a goal for the world to strain to. Wrap yourself in the Imperial gloom of this two-legged limbo – get into the trousers.

(ANDY *takes them from her and gives them to* HUMPHREY, *at the same time pushing him behind the screen formed by the blackboard, partly.*)

ANDY. Stay behind there now and change your nationality.

MRS HEAVEY. If we only had a pair of shoes with the tongue hanging out he'd do.

HUMPHREY (*from behind screen*). I'm thinking I'll have my tongue hanging out before I'm done. (*Pause.*).

MRS HEAVEY. The Sergeant is rather a full man. Do you think they'll fit him?

ANDY. Oh, the baggier they are the better.

HUMPHREY. It's hard enough to get my own off – over my boots.

ANDY. Get on with the trousers. (*Pause.*)

HUMPHREY. If Mother asks Nellie for her shoes I think I'll be able to fit into them.

(MRS HEAVEY *makes a sign of collusion to* ANDY *and exit.*)

ANDY. Get on with the trousers. (*Pause.*)

HUMPHREY. Do you wear them with a belt or braces?

ANDY. Get on with the trousers.

HUMPHREY. I say. Must I take off my – must I wear these things next to my skin?

ANDY. Get on with the trousers. (*Long pause.*)

HUMPHREY (*brightly to gain time*). I say. What about having them disinfected? Couldn't you put them in the oven for a while? Pasteurise them or do something to sterilize them? There's no knowing what may happen . . .

ANDY. Get on with the trousers.

HUMPHREY (*suddenly*). Can't I play the part of a Scotsman and wear a kilt?

ANDY (*losing patience*). Damn it, man, think imperially and get on with the trousers.

HUMPHREY. I am thinking imperially and I think that things like these will put an end to the Empire.

ANDY. What do you mean?

HUMPHREY (*sharply*). Keep to the point.

ANDY (*delighted*). Oh, you'll do.

(*Enter* MRS HEAVEY. *She gives shoes to* ANDY *who throws them over screen.*)

ANDY. Here are the shoes, catch.

MRS HEAVEY (*who is looking through window*). There's three of them now and a little fellow. The first is a round comfortable stock of a man. He might be a widower, he wears white spats.

ANDY. Spats! Humphrey! By Jove, I never thought of that. Be sure to put your spats over your shoes. They will hide the tongues and give you tone.

MRS HEAVEY. Hurry up, the're looking for the house.

ANDY. Time enough, Mother. They have seen it long ago, for it's the only one in the place.

MRS HEAVEY. Mebbe you're right, they're walking round one another. I suppose they can't come in till they find it officially.

ANDY. You can't expect officials to be unanimous about anything, except the reason for their own existence. Are ye nearly ready, Humphrey?

MRS HEAVEY. There's a tall thin looking one and a fellow in a motor coat.

HUMPHREY (*pulling*). By George, and (*Pause.*) by Gad.

ANDY. Have you both legs in?

MRS HEAVEY. They have a poor little devil of a fellow with a hard face like a lady that breeds dogs, and they're all asking him questions.

HUMPHREY (*sings some Cockney catch*).

> 'Away with the fife and the drum,
> And the posters that all of us know
> Where a horrible sergeant says "Come,"
> And a horrid old woman says "Go".'

ANDY. You might be getting the golf clubs out of the hall, Mother. (*Exit* MRS HEAVEY.) (*After a pause anxiously.*): If it's a matter of a buttonhook or if I could assist you in any way. . . .

HUMPHREY (*muttering to himself and grunts with satisfaction*).

(*Enter* MRS HEAVEY *with golf clubs.*)

MRS HEAVEY (*to Andy*). Here's the lump of sugar for you to be trying. Couldn't he be practising indoors like Mr Soape the R.M. used to do on wet days?

(HUMPHREY *with monocle in eye emerges in elaborate sporting costume, stands trimming himself in middle of stage.*)

Well, good heavens. If he isn't for all the world like the auld fellow that blew the tail off the red setter at the Shoot at Moore Hall.

ANDY (*admiringly*). Splendid. I always knew you had acting in you. Don't forget to sit on these fellows thoroughly with your double seat. What will you be doing when they come in? Would you like me to go out and meet them and say that there's an English gentleman in the house, or will you be reading a book?

HUMPHREY (*rudely ignoring him: extending his arm without looking at his Mother and speaking imperiously, in a voice completely changed*). The brassey please. Aw. Thank you. (*He takes it without looking round, puts it under his arm and begins to search his pockets.*)

ANDY (*showing his amazement at the change in his manner*). I asked you would you require anything to read.

HUMPHREY (*shortly*). Naw. I have my own literature here, thank you. (*Produces paper and begins to unfold it.*)

    (HUMPHREY *sits at end of bench, crosses his legs.*)

MRS HEAVEY. How do you like that salmon fly in your cap Humphrey? The sergeant is a bit of a sport, and he wore it for the King.

HUMPHREY. Aw!

    (*Voices are heard without.*)

MRS HEAVEY. Here they are. Well, God help them anyway when they see that. (*Points to* HUMPHREY.)

HUMPHREY (*indicating a place on the floor*). Put the ball on the tee. Will you?

ANDY (*comes forward and lays a lump of sugar at his feet*). Here you are.

MRS HEAVEY (*whispering to* ANDY). There's only one thing that might ruin him. They nearly always have a genuine Englishman trapezing around with them for his health. What'll happen Humphrey if he is confronted with one of them lads?

ANDY (*taken aback: slowly*). His rudeness will save him; it is most convincing already and it's his only chance. (*Smiles with admiration.*) D'ye hear, Humphrey? If they have the usual invalid from England act as rudely as you can or tell him a smutty story and he'll be convinced.

HUMPHREY. Mind your own business. (*Assumes a stance and addresses the ball, taking an elaborate grip on club held over his head.*)

MRS HEAVEY (*astonished*). Surely you're not going to give them a larrup of that?

ANDY. Hush.

HUMPHREY (*shouting as Officials enter*). 'Fore.'

    (*They fall back. Presently one comes cautiously forward.*)

    (*Exit* MRS HEAVEY *throwing up her hands.*)

1ST OFFICIAL (*looking about him*). What is this? There must be some mistake.

    (*Enter* 2ND OFFICIAL.)

2ND OFFICIAL. I do not know. (*To* 3RD OFFICIAL *who is entering.*) What is this? Is there a mistake?

3RD OFFICIAL (*after a pause to* 4TH OFFICIAL *who is entering*). Do you know what this is? Is there a mistake?

4TH OFFICIAL (*who speaks slowly and monotonously*). This is the

Schoolhouse; but I will look it up. (*Producing map; they gather round and look at the map. Enter* PILE *leisurely and sits R front.*) Yes, it must be the Schoolhouse; there are only two other buildings and they are under different departments.

1ST OFFICIAL. What Departments?

4TH OFFICIAL. The Prisons Board and the Poor Law.

ANDY. Begob and begorrah, your Honours. There's only the Workhouse and the Jail, and the Workhouse is full of poor ould people beyond their work, and the Jail's empty, for there's no criminals.

2ND OFFICIAL (*who has been examining* HUMPHREY). I fear we are disturbing this gentleman.

    (HUMPHREY *stands with legs apart, 'addressing' the ball.*)

1ST OFFICIAL. What do you mean 'no criminals?'

ANDY. No, indade. When the law couldn't make them the people advertised for the sake of the jail, but there was no answers. It was a great loss to let the jail go, for the town grew up around it, but we're looking forward to the next Coercion Act when we'll be forced to be prosperous again.

1ST OFFICIAL. What nonsense! No crime.

ANDY. No, aren't the judges boxing wan another with white gloves at every sessions on the Bench?

HUMPHREY (*loudly*). Aw, by George. An Irish bull, oh by Gad. (*Laughs loudly, the Officials grin.*)

4TH OFFICIAL. No, it says quite definitely here on the map. The National School. You can see it there (*To* 3RD OFFICIAL) in Clare-Galway.

1ST OFFICIAL (*with asperity*). How the deuce can we be in two places at the same time, Clare? Galway?

HUMPHREY. Unless he's got an Irish map. Aw.

3RD OFFICIAL (*sotto voice to* ANDY). Who is this gentleman?

    (*Indicating* HUMPHREY.)

ANDY (*loudly in exaggerated brogue*). I dunno, yer Honour. I think he's on a holiday from the Kildare Street Club or the Ballast Office.

3RD OFFICIAL. Ah, yes, the Irish Lights' Board.

1ST OFFICIAL (*fussily*). Are we all here?

3RD OFFICIAL. No, Arthur hasn't arrived yet.

2ND OFFICIAL (*who has been wandering around*). Of course it's *the* schoolhouse or at any rate *a* schoolhouse. It doesn't need a great knowledge of mathematics to recognise chemistry when one sees it. (*Points to tonic solfa on blackboard.*) It's surprising what a lot of children have to learn nowadays.

ANDY. Aye, indeed, yer honour. It's getting harder every day since the Government commandeered the Alphabet and had the Rule of Three raided by the Police.

2ND OFFICIAL. Whatever are you talking about?

ANDY. They said that the Rule of Three was seditious literature: that one province should rule and not Three.

4TH OFFICIAL. The question of locality is settled. I have located ourselves on the map here.

3RD OFFICIAL. What are those squares?

4TH OFFICIAL. Those are the plots. (*He closes map made like a series of panoramic views.*)

3RD OFFICIAL. Oh? Where's Arthur?

ANDY. Sure, sure, ye haven't lost yer way?

HUMPHREY (*wielding club*). When you're quite done inspecting the school, I will go on with my practice.

>(1ST, 2ND *and* 3RD OFFICIALS *surround the* 4TH *and whisper, then they shove him forward.*)

4TH OFFICIAL (*slowly, in an even tone, affecting a deliberate manner*). I fear, sir, there has been some mistake. The Irish Government has taken over a schoolhouse which happens to be *this* schoolhouse in the barony of Ballynarragh in order to select and appoint a suitable person as Minister of Potato spraying.

HUMPHREY. I happen to have taken over the bally shoot and this is the only bally place where one can stay.

1ST OFFICIAL (*aside to* 4TH). Who is this person?

>(*The* 4TH OFFICIAL *does not answer as he is being questioned by the others.*)

2ND OFFICIAL (*from the group of three gathered at back of stage*). What I can't understand is that there are no applicants . . . And where's Arthur?

4TH OFFICIAL (*turning round*). I have letters from all the Irish Members here. (*Indicates despatch box.*)

2ND OFFICIAL. Can we have omitted to advertise the appointment by any chance? Was it duly advertised? We are bound to give due notice beforehand.

4TH OFFICIAL. It was not advertised.

2ND OFFICIAL. What?

3RD OFFICIAL. What?

3RD OFFICIAL. Eh, what?

1ST OFFICIAL. Eh, what?

2ND OFFICIAL. Good gracious. And if not why not?

4TH OFFICIAL. For the simple reason that it was so anticipated for their friends by so many members of Parliament so long beforehand that I felt we were quite within our rights to anticipate them by electing first and advertising afterwards.

2ND OFFICIAL. Quite so. Nothing could be fairer.

4TH OFFICIAL. Besides there are urgent State reasons why we should elect to-day.

HUMPHREY. Do you call it fair in Ireland to walk into peoples' houses? In my poor damned country – nine-tenths of which are rotten but one-tenth quite sound – an Englishman's home is his castle.

3RD OFFICIAL. Where's Arthur?

1ST OFFICIAL (*from the group of three in background*). Ask the gentleman if he is staying here.

HUMPHREY (*defiantly*). Make no bally mistake about that. I am.

2ND OFFICIAL (*aside*). He exhibits great firmness. That's the man for this country. Firm and resolute.

(*All the Officials are together at background taking counsel.*)

1ST OFFICIAL. But who is this person?

2ND OFFICIAL. I have a shrewd suspicion.

1ST OFFICIAL. Well, then, for goodness sake, speak out. Who is it?

2ND OFFICIAL. It may be the new Chief Secretary.

4TH OFFICIAL. What?

3RD OFFICIAL. What?

1ST OFFICIAL. Eh, what?

2ND OFFICIAL. I wouldn't be at all surprised.

1ST OFFICIAL. But how are we to know? It would never do not to know.

2ND OFFICIAL. If only Arthur were here. He knows them all. In fact, he's a regular roué for Chief Secretaries.

ALL (*after a pause to* 1ST OFFICIAL). Go forward and explain.

(*They push* 1ST OFFICIAL *forward.*)

1ST OFFICIAL. Sir, I take it that you are a stranger here and not yet in office? (HUMPHREY *who is leaning back on golf stick rises on his toes.*) Then when I explain the position you will see that there has been no intentional invasion of rights. We in Ireland have to work under considerable difficulties. One of which, I regret to say, is causing you some inconvenience. There is so little housing accommodation for the various Departments that in places such as this we are forced to avail ourselves of whatever accommodation lies at our disposal. We often have to use the National School buildings for temporary Government offices in Congested Districts. May I take it that you are a stranger here and not yet in office?

HUMPHREY (*he is standing with his back to door C. He points over his shoulder with golf club*). Imagine a grouse moor in a congested district. Oh, I say. You are a funny lot over here. (*Breaks into a loud guffaw.*)

1ST OFFICIAL (*turning to the* 3RD). This is preposterous. Either he goes or I go.

HUMPHREY. Oh, inspect away. I'll try and bear it for the sake of the empire. Don't mind me.

(*The* OFFICIALS *circle round him,* 2ND OFFICIAL *following* 1ST *and so on.*)

2ND OFFICIAL. As there are no applicants, it might be no harm to explain the position to him a little more tactfully, a little more clearly. (*Looks at* 1ST OFFICIAL.) If we only had Arthur. But I'm afraid Arthur is overworked.

1ST OFFICIAL. It is a matter for common intelligence, not tact.

3RD OFFICIAL (*starting after* 2ND *very deliberately*). No, Arthur is not overworked, but he has been doing too much lately.

HUMPHREY (*following them with his eyes in amazement*). I'm afraid my native stupidity is upsetting you.

3RD OFFICIAL. He didn't mean to say that.

1ST OFFICIAL (*still exasperated and walking a little faster*). I am quite capable of explaining myself, thank you.

(*Enter* ARTHUR *in a frock-coat walking straight into right corner.*)

ARTHUR (*cheerily*). By George, and so this is where you all are?

4TH OFFICIAL (*as if from a reverie wearily*). Cheerio.

1ST OFFICIAL. Well, at last, Arthur.

2ND OFFICIAL. We are saved. Here's Arthur.

3RD OFFICIAL. Arthur.

ARTHUR. Am I in time for the election? Is this the successful candidate? Congratulations, congratulations. (*Approaching* HUMPHREY.) I have still the pleasure of learning your name.

HUMPHREY. Stott, sir. Stott. Stott, Stott. (*He keeps practising with the golf club and lump of sugar left.*)

2ND OFFICIAL (*taking him by the arm and walking him across front of stage and round* HUMPHREY). Hush, Arthur. We were just about to explain the situation to this gentleman, but a slight misunderstanding has arisen. He has taken the school, and it seems he is staying here.

HUMPHREY (*as they are going behind him*). Yaas. I've got the shootin' and fishin' – such as it is.

2ND OFFICIAL. We have had to make use of this building. (*Ominously.*) How it came to be rented as a shooting box is a matter for the Board of Education.

ARTHUR (*stopping centre*). Learning something every day, eh? But the fishing has gone to the dogs here, eh? (*Affably.*) Is this your first visit to this poverty-stricken country, Mr Stott?

HUMPHREY. Yaas, and it is likely to be the last.

ANDY (*drawling*). God help us. How does it support the likes of us at all, at all, at all?

ARTHUR. Oh, come, come, Mr Stott. You must not judge us in a hurry. What kind of sport have you been having?

(*A consultation is going on all this time in a corner of the stage right back.*)

HUMPHREY. Bad, by George.

ARTHUR. Quite so. Quite so, bad, quite so. We must try and make that right. The grouse are gone to the dogs.

ANDY. Yes, yer honour, they do be saying them collie dogs is the divil for grouse.

ARTHUR. What I was going to suggest to you, Mr Stott, is to have a try for rabbits. Particularly since the Department have improved the breed. (4TH OFFICIAL *plucks his sleeve.*) Just a moment. Pardon me just a moment, Mr Stott. (*Consults with* 4TH OFFICIAL *whispering.*) As a stop-gap.

ANDY. He might have got a skelp at a buck hare if we went out before the Daylight Saving Bill. They never leave their forrums now since they changed the time.

HUMPHREY (*visibly in a better humour*). Irish wit, by George.

ANDY (*encouraged by their attention*). Yes, indeed. There was a young gentleman sent down here from the Department of Agriculture and Technical Instruction, a bit of an artist. He was offering a reward for glow worrums. (*He makes gestures, as if catching flies.*) 'For,' sez he to me on the quiet, sez he, 'Pat,' sez he, 'I have the interest of Ireland at heart, so I have,' sez he, 'even though I come from Killicrankie; and what's more, the interest of Irish sport at heart, and if we can wanst manage to cross the buck rabbits wid the glow-worms, we'll get a breed,' sez he, 'that can be shot at nights by the light of their own scuts.'

HUMPHREY (*loudly*). Ow, I say. Paddy is pulling our leg. Ow. I say.

(*All the* OFFICIALS *are in a better humour.*)

ARTHUR. Mr Stott. If I might request the honour of your attention without taking up too much of your valuable time, I might be able to make a suggestion which having merited your consideration, might lead to your taking a more favourable view of our country and be not without a little interest to yourself.

2ND OFFICIAL. Isn't Arthur amazing?

ARTHUR. We find ourselves − not for the first time indeed − in a very responsible position, one fraught with the greatest possible benefit to the country, but, at the same time, calling for the exercise of the greatest delicacy and tact.

2ND OFFICIAL. Arthur is perfectly marvellous.

ARTHUR. In short, Mr Stott, we had to add to the personnelle of the Irish Administration; I find it had not been added to when I congratulated you.

HUMPHREY. Oh, an Election, by George. Why not elect one of yourselves?

ARTHUR. Simply because we are already overburdened with work, and in any case it is a position just recently created, well remunerated; and we always endeavour to give the country the benefit of the election if we can possibly manage to find anyone possessing the necessary education and breadth of view to fit him for the post, but the people are extremely backward, and it would not be quite becoming if we were to elect one of ourselves.

HUMPHREY. Too much like Home Rule, by George, eh, what?

ARTHUR. It is not that, not that. But if you lived at all in this country you would come to realise that all questions of Government are questions of the greatest perplexity. We have a most ungrateful people to deal with, and since the unavoidable cessation of emigration the administration of the Government finds itself accordingly hampered, therefore in order to secure perfect impartiality in administration and to leave no cause for charges of favouritism or precipitancy in making appointments, and we have often to recourse to co-opting whenever possible someone who will not be embarrassed by local associations or family ties. There's Mr Pile here who has been persuaded to help us. Let me introduce you to Mr Pile, late fellow of New College, Oxford. Doubtless, you have seen the motto over the Holywell Gate, 'Manners maketh man,' Mr Stott, this is Mr Pile – fellow of New – author of 'The Judicious Use of Manures' and 'The Prolegomena to Peace.' (PILE *who is sitting forward right on a chair with his legs crossed bows distantly and crosses his legs in opposite position.*)

HUMPHREY (*puts out his hand while* PILE *refuses, bowing stiffly.* HUMPHREY *is visibly affronted*). Oh, yaas, manners maketh man and want of them the fellow – of Oxford, eh? (*Laughs loudly.*) Eh, what? Now that is really good. (*Looks about for approval.*) (*To* ANDY.): Damme, Paddy, don't you see that, where are your Irish wits? You see Oxford manners are . . . (*Laughs with satisfaction.*) Oh, it's really subtle.

ARTHUR (*pained but persistent*). My other colleagues here, I am sure, would be delighted if you could find it in you to accept a position which we all should be unanimous in offering to you – Minister of Potato Spraying.

HUMPHREY. My dear sir, I'm over here for rest and change, not to work. (*Swings club jauntily.*)

ARTHUR. Quite so, but this would involve no work, that is to say, no effort or physical strain as it is purely administrative.

HUMPHREY. What would I have to do? (*This is followed by a stir of satisfaction amongst the other* OFFICIALS.)

ARTHUR. I've no instructions. But the Secretary can give you details. If you could signify your approval of our suggestion it would clear the path either for the discussion of details and salary or for our plans to be put into execution at a later date.

HUMPHREY. Salary, eh? Well, I might consider it if it is to aid the Empire?

(*The* SECRETARY *comes forward. He speaks methodically.*)

SECRETARY. The salary on which we had determined was to have been £1,000 a year.

HUMPHREY. Totally inadequate. Come, come now. You must think Imperially.

(*The* OFFICIALS *whisper to* SECRETARY.)

1ST, 2ND, 3RD OFFICIAL (*one after the other*). Quite so.

4TH OFFICIAL. We must think Imperially.

SECRETARY. Well . . . But in view of the distance of the district and the difficulty of administering it, it has been decided to offer double the salary to the Minister on the understanding that he is to appoint two resident assistants who may be male and female — at half the salary originally allotted for the one assistant whom in the first instance it was decided to appoint.

HUMPHREY. Ho. District; is it large? (*To* 4TH OFFICIAL.): I say, let's have a look at that collapsible plot of yours (*Pulls out and consults a map.*) If there was any decent fishing here I might consider it.

ARTHUR. I am sure you could arrange with the Fishery Board to let you have a little sport. The Department are all very harmonious and pull well together, I am glad to say.

HUMPHREY. Would the potatoes be likely to interfere with me in the execution of my duty in spraying them? (*Good-humouredly.*) Eh, what? Eh, what? Ha, ha. (*They all join in the laugh.*)

ARTHUR. We may take it then, Mr Stott, that you will accept the office of minister of this District.

HUMPHREY. You may take it that I'll take the £2,000 a year all right. There's nothing like being candid, is there?

3RD OFFICIAL. And you'll probably after a little experience make a most excellent minister.

HUMPHREY. Will the Government supply the spraying stuff?

3RD OFFICIAL. Certainly, certainly. That's under the Minister of Munitions. We hold a monopoly of all the Copper Sulphate in the world.

HUMPHREY. Haw! But what about the water? Don't you use water and that kind of thing?

3RD OFFICIAL. Unfortunately, we have only too much rain water here.

HUMPHREY. Aw. You may have a quantity, but not quality.

3RD OFFICIAL. Quite so. It can be imported from England.

2ND OFFICIAL. If he's as good as Arthur he'll do. Will you give the Secretary your address, Mr Stott?

HUMPHREY. Oh, by Gad, I haven't a card, but Stephen's Green, the United Arts' Club, Stephen's Green, will find me.

4TH OFFICIAL (*taking it down*). The United Service Club?

HUMPHREY. Oh, no. The United Arts' Club. I am only a temporary member, but it contains a lot of distinguished people who tell me they prefer it to the D.B.C.

(*Enter* MRS HEAVEY.)

MRS HEAVEY. Might I be after offering yez all a cup of tay?

(*The* OFFICIALS *refuse gracefully*.)

(*To* PILE.): Wouldn't ye like a little weenshey cup to lay at the back of yer heart? (OFFICIALS *prepare to go*.)

ARTHUR. Well, Mr Stott, good luck to you. You'll find you'll not be overburdened this year, at least, and by this time next year your assistants should have a good working knowledge to go on with. Would you care to join us in a motor run? We have to do a little inspection of the district, and about ten miles further on there's a rather good hotel. (HUMPHREY *shakes his head*.) No. Then I can speak unofficially. I'd be very glad, Mr Stott, if you would come along with me and dine.

2ND OFFICIAL. If you go along with Arthur he'll get you a bang at some jolly fine cock to-morrow afternoon.

PILE. You must promise to have a meal with me at my hotel.

HUMPHREY. Oh, eh. Ah. Charmed. Later on perhaps. Later on. Charmed. Oh, aw.

ARTHUR. Very well, then. We must hold you to that. (*Exit* 2ND OFFICIAL.) My congratulations were not so out of place, it seems, after all. (OFFICIALS *exeunt*.)

4TH OFFICIAL (*last to leave and gravely with exaggerated emphasis*). Au bientot. (HUMPHREY *turns round slowly to look after them as they go*.)

MRS HEAVEY. Well, I couldn't believe my ears and I listening all the time. It's too good to be true. Andy, me dear, think of us with £2,000 a year.

ANDY. He carried it off magnificently.

MRS HEAVEY. When Andy is one of your assistants and I'm the other you might appoint your sister Nellie as yer under secretary and bring her to London. Mightn't he do that for her, Andy?

ANDY. Now that he's got it he doesn't seem inclined, I'm thinking, to be too flahoulyah with it. What about giving us a lift, Humphrey?

HUMPHREY. Corruption!

ANDY. What?

MRS HEAVEY. What are you saying – corruption?

ANDY. Who's corrupt?

HUMPHREY. You are both corrupt.

MRS HEAVEY. Well, now, listen to that!

HUMPHREY. Yaas, it's your national failing, I'm afraid.

MRS HEAVEY. Well, now, you've a chance to cure it by giving us all a job under your new regime.

HUMPHREY. I refuse to have my administration sullied by favouritism.

MRS HEAVEY. Well, it's a nice state of affairs when it's corruption to do a turn for one's own flesh and blood. Can't you have a little reason?

HUMPHREY. Reason? Why should I have anything that might disagree with me?

ANDY. Ah, for God's sake, man, stop fooling and have some intelligence.

HUMPHREY. Intelligence? The damned thing the Jews have. Certainly not. I prefer integrity.

ANDY. None of your English Hypocrisy!

HUMPHREY. Don't decry the evidence of a great nation's religious sense.

MRS HEAVEY. What are we to do at all, at all?

HUMPHREY. Think imperially and act! (*Exit* HUMPHREY.)

ANDY (*going to door to look after* HUMPHREY). Well, he's off out of this anyhow. He's gone off with the Sergeant's trousers.

MRS HEAVEY. I'm thinking it's the trousers is gone off with him. The Sergeant was promoted for cheering the day he put them on. And now look at what they've done for Humphrey.

ANDY. Trousers indeed! It was I did it. And to think of his damned impertinence turning on me and telling *me* to *act!* But I'll say this . . . If he ever dares to come round about this place again and I don't care what position he holds – I'll break his face.

MRS HEAVEY. Hush, Andy. Don't talk like that! I have as much right, maybe, as you to be angry with him,

ANDY. Well, and what'll ye do?

MRS HEAVEY. Never mind him, Andy. Leave him to God and (*shaking her fist.*) He'll play hell with him.

## CURTAIN

# INCURABLES

*A Play in One Act*

This play was included in Gogarty's *A Weekend in the Middle of the Week and Other Essays on the Bias* (1958).

CHARACTERS
(in order of appearance)

PAT, a patient paralysed from the waist down
A HOSPITAL PORTER (non-speaking part)
MIKE, a patient, suffering from locomotor ataxia
GEORGE DALY, the Hospital's Groundsman
MRS DURKIN, a patient in a bath chair
EAMONN LOPEZ, a.k.a. EDDIE BRIGHT, a patient
(who was suffering from Bright's Disease)
MR VERSCHOYLE, THE GOVENOR of the Hospital
THE MATRON of the Hospital

# INCURABLES

*Scene. The grounds of a large hospital. A tree, umbrella-shaped like a weeping elm, in the centre of the stage. It is about a third of the stage's width. A dense myrtle bush to the left adjoining wing. The floor is a lawn. The background suggests a distant building. There are seats around the tree.*

PAT (*seated under the tree with a rug round his knees, smiles reminiscently*). Ah, begorra, yes. (*A uniformed porter passes. Pat looks at the sky, then at the porter.*) Them was the days! (*The porter looks back wondering.*) Aw, Janey Mack! (*The porter looks again.*) Along the back beach when the wind was blowing and the horses running and every jockey with a different colour coming along like hell! (*Exit the porter.*) Them was the days, and the thunder on the turf! God be with the times; and God be with Baldoyle! And Red Maurya selling cockles and never troubling to lace her shoes. I never seen her since. Mebbe it's in the workhouse she is. She'd be like a shrunk apple if I seen her now, and her eyes glazed with the palsy like a window in a snug. For God's sake look who's comin'.
 (MIKE *enters advancing unsteadily pushing a lawn mower to maintain his balance.*)
PAT. The auld blackguard that can't balance but has to go chasing himself.
MIKE (*retreats and advances balancing. He runs the lawn mower against the seat*). Up and hooray! Was there ever such weather? Who were ye saying was in the workhouse? Who's shrunk?
PAT. It's a mighty fine humour you're in this morning. You must have been reading *Christian Dying* by Sylvester Stott.
MIKE. And why wouldn't I be merry on a day like this?
PAT. Oh, then you're easily pleased if all you want is fine weather to make ye lep like a flounder. Go aisy now or ye'll cut the toes off me feet.
MIKE. And would ye know it if I did? Hasn't the feeling gone out of yer feet this five years? Usen't you be sayin' that ye had two feet in the grave but that you were all right so long as it wasn't yer head?

583

PAT. Before ye sit down just roll that up in front of me till I get a whiff of the cut grass. (*Sings.*) 'And the ramble through the new-mown hay.'
  (MIKE *sets the lawn mower adrift and, balancing, half-falls into the seat.*)
PAT. Ye'll break your neck if ye keep tripping about like a spavined goat. What the hell has brought you out at all? Don't ye know that if the lawn mower is found here ye'll be kept in like the last time they found you stretched out when ye let the roller fall into the greenhouse? If ye can't walk without support, sit still like meself.
MIKE. Whist now. George will be wheeling Mrs Durkin this way soon and I'll get him to leave it back where I got it.
PAT. He will in me neck.
MIKE. Of course he'll take it back. Many's the chaw I gave him.
PAT. Yer a hard chaw yerself.
MIKE. Cheer up now, me hearty, and give us again. (*Sings.*) 'The ramble through the new-mown hay, Titty fol loll!'
PAT (*surly*). It's a bloody fine ramble you'd take through the new-mown hay if ye couldn't scut behind the mowing machine and then ye'd be likely to overtake it with yer 'festination' and trying to catch up with yer centre of gravity, or whatever the doctors say is wrong with you, you that can no more walk than a twelve-months' child.
MIKE. Well, I like that from one who can't walk at all. Paralyzed from the hips down. Well, God's will be done. But tell us who was it you were sayin' was in the Union like a withered apple and I coming in.
PAT. I wasn't saying anyone was in the Union. I was only recollecting a walk I had one fine morning thirty good-looking years ago, before you died from the hips up.
MIKE (*humoring him*). You must have been a warty boy thirty years ago.
PAT. I was walking one morning from Weldon's to the Murroch of Baldoyle. D'ye know the Murroch? And I see a fine strap of a red-haired woman comin' towards me.
MIKE (*interested*). Red, did ye say?
PAT. Red, beggora, with the sun behind her like the light on a dun cow's rump. 'Good morrow,' sez I. 'Good morrow,' sez she, smiling a bit and letting on to be passing but not getting out of my way all the same. 'And what might ye be doing in a fine still morning like this?' sez I. 'Mebbe it's pickin' cockles I am,' sez she. (*Nudging* MIKE.) Picking cockles, mind ye, with her back to the beach.
MIKE (*avidly*). Go on! Go on!
PAT. 'Yer done now anyway,' sez I. 'Look behind ye. The tide's in.' 'Oh, my!' sez she, laughing with a little laugh as if it didn't matter a damn. 'I suppose I'll have to wait now,' sez she, 'till it goes out.'
MIKE. Yes! Yes?

PAT. 'That's about the only thing *we* can do now is to wait,' sez I. Never letting on (*Nudging* MIKE) but that I thought picking cockles was the most important thing on God's earth . . .

MIKE (*finishing the sentence*). *We* can do. Were you picking cockles?

PAT. No, you idiot. But I was adapting myself. 'If ye don't want to go back empty-handed and lose the whole day, ye must wait now till the tide gives us a chance,' sez I.

MIKE (*avidly*). Yes, yes, yes.

PAT. 'But where can we wait?' sez she. 'In here,' sez I, 'if the grass isn't damp. There'll be no one to disturb you if ye waited a week, and ye'll hear nothing but the lark singing or mebbe the whistle of a train.'

MIKE. Go on!

PAT. 'But it wouldn't do if it was damp,' said I. 'I can put me shawl on the grass if it is itself,' sez she.

MIKE (*excitedly*). Yes.

PAT (*leisurely*). 'Well, whether it's damp or not, the dew never did any harm,' sez I. 'When the sun's a bit stronger it'll be as dry as a rick of hay.'

MIKE. So it would! Go on!

PAT. So in we went through a hedge, I holding the branches out of her way – I noticed that she had no stockings on – and she spread her shawl under a bush.

MIKE. Oh boy!

PAT (*putting his thumbs in his armpits, sings*.) 'Chantez, ma belle!'

MIKE (*impatient*). But what happened then?

PAT (*very leisurely*). 'There's one consolation,' sez I. 'There's no hurry about the tide. It is not likely to go out with a click.' 'Time and tide wait for no man,' she sez, with a little laugh. 'That's true,' sez I, to keep up the conversation and so on while we were sitting on her shawl.

MIKE (*disappointed*). Aw! What good were ye?

PAT (*bringing his hand down on* MIKE'S *hat, revealing a bald head*). Aren't ye the lascivious, evil-minded auld devil to be lookin' for harm under every bush? It's you and the likes of you has the place that it's not worth living in.

MIKE (*sniffing for smut*). I only meant to ask . . . I only wanted to know what ye were talking about while the tide was running out.

PAT. Aye. And when I began telling ye, ye asked me what good was I.

MIKE. Well, what was it about?

PAT. A'll not tell ye! as the Scotsman said when they asked him the morning after his marriage how he was.

MIKE. I only wanted to know.

PAT. Ye only wanted to know. And do ye think I'd tell ye even if your wishes came off?

MIKE. I only wanted to know.

PAT. What? And what do ye want to know?

MIKE. I only wanted to know, is it that that has ye pondering on the past?

PAT. When I had my day I didn't treat it as the future when I had it.

MIKE. Isn't it a pity that ye have not a bit of it left? It couldn't have been picking cockles that turned ye into a mermaid with no feelin' in yer feet. (*Laughs, shaking himself.*)

PAT (*sotto voce*). That'll do ye now.

(*Enter* GEORGE *the groundsman, wheeling* MRS DURKIN *in a bath chair. She is almost completely covered by the chair's apron and her shawls.*)

MIKE. Aw! Me sound man George!

GEORGE. Good morrow, me. This is a fine sound healthy morning.

MIKE (*raising his hat*). How are ye this morning, Mrs Durkin?

GEORGE. She can't hear you. She's full of dope. (*Moves on.*)

MIKE (*in an excited whisper*). Eh, George. Whist! Come here a minute. Shove her into the myrtles for a minute and put the lawn mower back for me like a decent man and I'll give ye a chaw.

GEORGE (*obeys; then, mockingly sententious*). The matron sez that ye are all to conduct yourselves with due decorum, for the Angel of Death has visited us bringing sorrow in his train. Which means that there's another stiff in the mortuary.

PAT. Who is it?

GEORGE. Auld Bright's.

PAT. Aw. Poor auld Bright's! Who'd have thought that he would be the next, and he as red and as hearty as a forge fire.

GEORGE. Them are the lads that go. They are so full of life that they can't stand the pressure of it. They want to spend it, and they spend themselves. The fellows that go about currying favour with death by looking like corpses, they don't go sudden like poor old Bright's.

MIKE (*sententiously*). A great loss to Ireland.

PAT. Arrah, who?

MIKE. Eddie Bright's.

PAT. For God's sake?

MIKE (*mockingly sententious*). Aye; and a great loss to Gaeldom, the same Eamonn Bright's. There's many we could have spared sooner than Eamonn. The country won't be the same again now he's gone. (*Turns up his eyes.*)

PAT. Well, you may console yourself. Is the country ever the same for two minutes? To listen to you one would think that he had invented

Death and went off himself on purpose. For God's sake be honest and sensible and don't be trying to read onto a tombstone more than there's under it.

MIKE. I'd give a lot to have him back for the sake of The Cause.

GEORGE. Well, and you'd lose a lot if he did come back. Wasn't it you who drew him in the sweep on the morning's deaths? How much of yer three quid that ye won would ye give for the sake of The Cause?

PAT (*sits up alertly*). So that is what has you in such unholy good humour this day of our Lord?

MIKE. I didn't know he was dead.

GEORGE. Oh, no. I suppose you thought that the three quid was yer auld-age pension?

PAT. Three quid! Did he win three quid?

GEORGE. He did. He drew old Bright's who went off with the Angel of Death bringing sorrow in his train.

MIKE. Well. Hadn't ye all a fair chance yerselves?

GEORGE. Well, we wouldn't hide it if we won.

MIKE. And who did you draw, Pat?

PAT. That'll do ye. Ye won't draw on me, I'm telling you. (*Shivers in disgust.*)

GEORGE. There's not a shake out of ye yet, Pat, in spite of yer two feet in the grave. (*Laughs.*)

PAT. Mind ye, old Bright's got a long run. He was the favourite this six weeks.

GEORGE. Well he's stretched at last and Mike has the winnings. It'll cost half a crown to get that lawn mower left back. It's confined to the ward he'll be if it's found, as sure as my name is George Daly.

MIKE (*anxiously*). Is the Governor coming his morning?

GEORGE. He's showing the Matron round. He might be here any minute now. (*Looks as if to see if they were approaching.*)

PAT. For the love of Mike give him the half dollar if you don't want to be locked up.

(MRS DURKIN *sneezes.*)

MIKE. For the love of Mike, George Daly, shove her further into the myrtles, and back with the lawn mower quick!

GEORGE. When you part and not before. (*He shoves the bath chair in out of sight.* MIKE *fumbles for half a crown.* GEORGE *takes it and exits with lawn mower.*)

(*Enter* GOVERNOR *with the* MATRON.)

GOV. (*to* PAT). Well, how are we this morning, Pat? You all right?

PAT. Speaking for myself, sir, it's only half of me that's right. I can't speak for yourself, sir, at all.

GOV. What? What?

MIKE. He's paralyzed, sir, from the waist down. And he's walkin' on wool. So there's only the upper part that can be right.

MATRON. Now how did you get here, Mike?

MIKE (*embarrassed*). I – ah – well, I had to follow me centre of gravity. And it landed me here, mam.

GOV. (*to* MATRON). What is this case?

MATRON. It is a case of locomotor ataxia, which makes the victim keep on racing after his centre of gravity. Always trying to catch up with himself.

GOV. Ah, quite. Do you come from the Curragh, my good man?

PAT. No, sir, he comes from Baldoyle, and he may have caught cold in his spine lying under a hedge on the road from St. Doulough's down to the Back Strand.

MIKE (*embarrassed*). Don't mind him, sir. He comes from Moore Street, but I was born in the Coombe.

GOV. (*to* MATRON). No hope, I suppose.

MATRON. Not the least; locomotor ataxia. (*To the men.*) When there is no hope the best thing is to be resigned.

PAT. Right, mam. Since we're incurables, it would be the height of ingratitude to get better and upset the charitable institution.

MATRON. That will do, Pat.

GOV. Well, don't despair. We have been so well endowed by the government that something may come of it, something may come of it.

MIKE (*sotto voice*). Now yer talkin'.

GOV. We are already getting results with our experiments. That last experiment, the six hundredth and seventh one, is surprising. Already the Russian experts in the Donnybrook laboratory have revived dogs that have been dead twenty-five minutes.

MATRON. They asked my permission to work in the mortuary this morning.

GOV. You gave it to them, I hope? (MATRON *nods*.) We will take a look into the laboratory where they are working on that elixir of life, or six-oh-seven as they call it.

    (*Exeunt.*)

    (MRS DURKIN *sneezes.* PAT *and* MIKE *start.*)

MIKE. What's an elixir of life?

PAT. A bottle to buck you up.

MIKE. Didn't you hear him saying they were reviving the dead?

PAT. Aye, a few auld dogs. They're always torturing dogs for our sakes.

MIKE. But this is reviving them and bringing them back to life.

PAT. That's what I'm telling you. Isn't that the worst torture of all?

MIKE. What?

PAT. To be dead twice?

> (*At right side wing as one faces the stage, the lid of a coffin appears and is withdrawn. After sufficient time to engage the attention of the audience, enter* EAMONN BRIGHT. *He is apparently naked but screened by the coffin lid. He comes in making growling sounds.*)

MIKE. Jumping Jehoshaphat!

PAT (*who is sitting to* MIKE'S *right and has not a fair view*). What's wrong with you?

MIKE. Bright's!

PAT (*sitting about*). Conistanthu? It's the laddo himself. He that has Bright's disease. Begor, them specialists from Moscow has revived more than dead dogs. Where are ye going, a cara?

BRIGHT. I am going to see my attorney.

PAT. He's as good as dead!

MIKE. They said . . . I thought . . . How are ye feeling? Ye'll catch cold with no clothes on but a plank.

BRIGHT. I'm as good as dead, am I? I'll see about that. I ought to be from the way I was treated for pneumonia. I woke up stark naked on a stone slab, with a hose pipe in my arm and tuppence on me eyelids, and three bearded Sheenies waiting for me to wink them off. And me name spelt wrong on me coffin lid. I'll have the law on the whole bloody place. Nice treatment indeed for an invalid, to be put out of doors with the dead.

MIKE. Sheenies? Is that the way to talk about our most modern scientists? I'd say nothing about it, Eamonn, if I was you. Slip back to the ward and make them give you a cup of G.Y.E. It's vitamins you want.

PAT. It cures pimples.

BRIGHT. Does it, begob? I won't stop until I have the law on them all.

MIKE. You may have been revived, and you ought to be thankful.

BRIGHT. And who the bloody hell said I was dead?

MIKE (*embarrassed*). I don't know. I heard that they were doing a lot with dogs.

BRIGHT. I'm a dog, am I? For two pins I'd give you a clatter with this lid. (*Stands behind it showing inscription:* EAMONN LOPEZ, AGED 56. R.I.P.) My name is Lopez, an old ancient Irish name. And what have I to do with R.I.P.?

PAT. Aisy now. Don't you expect to rest in peace?

MIKE. No. Nor let anyone else rest either.

BRIGHT. I'll not rest until I get substantial damages.

MIKE. Arrah, for what?

BRIGHT. Indecent exposure.

PAT. If you don't catch your attorney before he goes to lunch, you won't see him for a week.

BRIGHT (*holding the lid horizontally as he goes off, hurriedly*). Begorra, you're right. I never thought of that.
> (*Exit.*)

PAT (*cogitating*). Ireland's made up now. And Gaeldom's reimbursed! But listen to me, Loco, or whatever you are, there must be great goings on in the Research Foundation.
> (MRS DURKIN *sneezes.*)

MIKE. Is there?

PAT. Isn't there? There's your great Gael that you have given so much to see back again. And what about your winnings? What about your winnings? I ask you.

MIKE. Whist.
> (*Enter* GOV. *and* MATRON. *The* GOV., *who was grey and past middle age, and the* MATRON, *who was skinny, are much improved. The one is twenty years younger and the* MATRON *aggressively buxom.*)

MATRON. But if this goes on we shall have no cases for our beds.

GOV. I would not say that. I would not say that. There will always be the poor and decrepit in this country who will be objects of charity. It would hardly be fair to them to make them able-bodied all of a sudden if they were not prepared to work. Have you seen the gardener, my men? If he passes, you might say that the dahlias want watering, or to be bedded out.

PAT & MIKE. We'll tell him, sir.

MATRON. What do you mean?

GOV. I mean that this country is not prepared for this discovery, for the present it must not be released.

MATRON. And that we must keep it in the dark?

GOV. We must not let the elixir get out.

MATRON. May I not have some for my herbaceous border?

GOV. Better not. Better not. Tropical results!
> (*Exeunt.*)
> (*Enter* GEORGE *with watering can.*)

GEORGE. Did ye see that auld blackguard?

PAT. He's just gone out with the Matron.

GEORGE. Dammit. I don't mean Verschoyle, but auld Lopez whom we called, because he had it, Bright's.

MIKE. He's gone out too.

GEORGE. Where?

MIKE. To see his attorney.

GEORGE. Coddin' apart, where's he gone? Has he gone at all? The Moscow specialists revived him, and off he goes without as much as by your leave. And they're blaming me for leaving the gates open and letting him out.

PAT. Mr Verschoyle is blaming you.

GEORGE. Me?

PAT. It seems that there's something wrong with the dahlias.

GEORGE. Let me tell you and him that the Dalys were always decent people and they are all right. What's wrong with them?

PAT. Oh, nothin'. Nothin'. It seems that they want watering and to be bedded out.

GEORGE. Beddin' out?

MIKE. He's only coddin'. It's the flowers he meant. Get the watering can.

PAT. Don't go, for the love of God. Here, George, here. Come here. Listen. You may not know it but it all fits in. This idiot doesn't see it or he'd give you the rest of his three quid and be glad to part.

GEORGE. It's his no longer, now that auld Bright's is not dead.

PAT. It'll be yours, George, if Mike has a spark of sense. For neither he nor me will want it if he does what I'm going to say. Those lads that the government brought over have discovered something good. I'm able to take notice.

GEORGE. And what did you notice?

MIKE. A red-haired woman thirty years ago.

PAT. For the love of God, shut up. This is serious. George, Mike's two pounds seventeen and sixpence are yours if you go into the laboratory and bring us out a bottle marked six-oh-seven. If it isn't in the laboratory it may be in the dead house where they were working all the morning on auld Bright's.

GEORGE. You haven't told us what you noticed.

PAT. Jaysus! Is it necessary? I noticed that the Governor got suddenly twenty years younger and that the Matron put on in half an hour (*Pointing to his breast*) – what d'ye call it? – embonpoint. I noticed that Eamonn Lopez or auld Bright's as we used to call him is up and out and he was dead this morning, and I noticed that the only anxiety of the Gov. and Matron was to keep the discovery dark and in the hands of the hospital. It makes everything grow. He wouldn't give it to her for the herbaceous border. It's too tropical it would be, he said.

MIKE. Begor, if you had it you'd show us something tropical.

PAT. Out with the sweep money or I'll take it off you myself.

(MIKE *reluctantly takes coins from many pockets.*)

GEORGE. But how the hell am I to know the right bottle? The whole place is full of shelves. Between test tubes and retorts and pipettes I wouldn't know where I was. There are hundreds of bottles and they're all the same.

PAT. Count until you come to six-oh-seven. Or better still, pinch the last bottle on the highest shelf.

MIKE. If he gets the wrong one, do I get me money back?

GEORGE. It's your funeral, not mine.
>     (*Exit.*)

MIKE. I wonder did it really revive Bright's.

PAT. Ye're always thinking about your money. He was dead all right, if that's any consolation to you. And so you won the sweep. Now listen to me. It will be plain sailing if we get the bottle. I'm only half-dead, and you're only creeping.

MIKE. I'm not creeping but sprinting. I wish I could creep. Do you think it will cure Parkinson's disease? And where will we rub it in?

PAT. I'll get George to rub it into the small of me back where the feeling meets the numb. You can have it rubbed into your head for a trial.
>     (MRS DURKIN *sneezes.*)

MIKE Or we might try it on her.

PAT. It might be too dangerous.

MIKE. It might be that.

PAT. Well then – (*jerks his thumb in the direction of* MRS DURKIN) – ladies first, say I. And I've always said it.
>     (*Enter* GEORGE, *excited.*)

PAT & MIKE. What's up.

GEORGE. Oh, be jabers! Dead rabbits and guinea pigs leppin' all over the place and the auld baboon with the glazed eye gone daft from only just a little rub of it into the butt of his tail. This must be the stuff. (*Shows strange phial.*)

PAT (*reading label*). Poison, be jabers. (*Hands it to* MIKE, *in a changed voice.*) You paid your money like a man. The first shot is yours.

MIKE. But after you. I don't want to take advantage of a few quid. I'll try it when it has done you good.

PAT. For heaven's sake, don't be flying in the face of science and blocking the progress of modern research. If it were left to the likes of you, we'd get nowhere.

MIKE. But it's labelled 'poison'.

PAT. Was there ever anything good that came out of a bottle that we were not told was poison? Take it, George, and give him a rub of it like a decent man.
>     (GEORGE *takes the phial and after some play rubs it into* MIKE's *scalp. Immediately a great crop of hair takes the place of the bald skull. (A rubber cap is removed, showing the hair it hid.)*

MIKE (*putting his hand up and feeling the hair*). Holy Smoke. Is it crepe that's on me or hair? That's the stuff. What do I look like?

GEORGE. Hairy enough.

PAT (*amazed*). You look like one of them Eyetalians from Abyssinia or a barber's apprentice. Here, give it to me.

MIKE. George, give us a good rub of it into the small of my back.

(GEORGE *rubs*.)

MIKE. Now let me stretch my limbs and test me equilibration. I'll go backwards first. (*He takes two paces backward and then marches in mock military goose-step fashion forward.*)

PAT. Eh? Here! Where are ye going? If you keep going on like that you'll find yourself in Arbour Hill.

MIKE. And I wouldn't care.

PAT. I suppose not if it were for The Cause, but you're forgetting something. What about me? Give us a lick of it, George. (*He pulls his shirt up over his head.* GEORGE *rubs his spine.*)

PAT (*breathing a sigh of relief*). Test me knee jerks, George. (GEORGE *taps him under the knee cap. A boot flies off with the resulting kick.*) Oh boy! (*He stands up in riding breeches with the laces untied and unlaced boot and does a few dance steps.*) 'And the ramble through the new–mown hay.' What do I look like?

MIKE. You look like the Gaelic League. But fasten yer breeches and adjust yer dress before leaving. (*Remembering.*) What about the old lady under the myrtles?

PAT. Give it to me and I'll give her a dart of it.

GEORGE. But we don't know what's wrong with her or where to rub her.

PAT. Ah, leave that to me.

(*He goes over and pulls the bath chair into view and pours some of the fluid down the back of* MRS DURKIN'S *neck.*)

PAT. That seems to have given her a thrill. (*He pours again.*)

MRS DURKIN (*wakens slowly. Looks round and at the bath chair*). A perambulator – for the love of God!

PAT (*recoiling in fright*). So it worked.

MIKE (*watching* MRS DURKIN, *renovated and comely, throwing off the apron of the bath chair and appearing in apron and shawl as a cockle gatherer*). Well, I should say it did.

PAT. Are ye all right, Mrs Durkin?

MRS DURKIN. Who d'ye mean? (*She advances slowly and as if menacingly from the chair.*) Which of yez called me Mrs Durkin? (*Looking about.*) And how did I get into the Phaynix Park?

PAT. We're not in the Park.

MIKE. Hould yer whist.

MRS DURKIN. Which of ye swiped my basket of cockles?

PAT (*tentatively*). Ye haven't a grey hair on you, Norah.

MRS DURKIN. And can it be? You're the young fellow that kept sloothering me at the back of St. Doulough's till the tide went out and came in again.

PAT. And you took me up to Weldon's and stood me a few pints.

MIKE. The pair of ye made the most of yer time.

(*Enter the* GOVERNOR, *running.*)

GOV. (*shouts*). Close all the gates! A great theft has occurred! Close the
   gates. Let no one out. Call the police. Everybody must be searched.
   (*Exit.*)

GEORGE. Now ye see what ye've let me in for. This means the loss of
   my job. What am I to do with this? (*The phial.*)

PAT. Shove it into the watering can. (GEORGE *puts the phial into the can.*)
   And pretend that you are watering the dahlias or the grass even.
   Here, hand us up that rug. Sit down, Mike. Mrs Durkin, get behind
   the tree. Now what do you think of that for scientific research?
   There's nothing to beat the mind of Man, barrin' the bees.
   (*Noise and loud voices off.*)

GEORGE. Be jabers, the police! (*To* PAT.) Now you see what you've let
   me in for.

PAT. Don't lose yer head, man. Behave as if it was no concern of yours.
   Water the grass! Pretend to be doing yer usual work. Go on,
   nonchalant-like.

A SERGEANT'S VOICE OFF. Each patient must be questioned separately and
   seriatim.

(MRS DURKIN *and* PAT *and* MIKE *are seated under the tree.* GEORGE *waters
   the grass, beginning at the root of the tree.*)

PAT (*sotto voice*). Attaboy, George!

(*The tree grows down gradually; the grass rises up until the trio under the tree are
   enclosed in the growing greenery. They are gradually obscured. One of them
   sings, and the song diminishes like the Volga boatmen's song. The light
   diminishes with the song.*)

SONG

It's only a matter of Time
Till grass will cover us all.
Like waves that flow with an undertow,
The grass will cover us all.

The green will win in the end,
And cover us all with green;
On friend and foe the green will grow
And cover us all with green.

We are cured of all disease,
Of Faith and Hope and Strife,
Of Love and legal pleas:
We are cured even of Life.

(*Fading.*)

The grass will win in the end
And cover us all with green
(*Fading, almost indistinguishable*)
   and all with green
      win in the cover us all with green.

(*When the light comes on, for a moment, there is nothing but greenery*).

CURTAIN

# APPENDICES

# Appendix 1

## *The Ballad of Oliver Gogarty*

Come all ye bould Free Staters now and listen to my lay,
And pay a close attention, please, to what I've got to say,
For 'tis the tale of a Winter's Night last January year,
When Oliver St John Gogarty swam down the Salmon Weir.

As Oliver St John Gogarty one night sat in his home,
A-writin' of prescriptions or composin' of a poem,
Up rolled a gorgeous Rolls-Royce car and out a lady jumped,
And at Oliver St John Gogarty's hall-door she loudly thumped.

'Oh, Oliver St John Gogarty,' said she, 'now please come quick,
For in a house some miles away a man lies mighty sick.'
But Oliver St John Gogarty to her made no reply,
As with a dexterous facial twist he gently closed one eye.

'Oh, Oliver St John Gogarty, come let yourself be led,'
Cried a couple of masked ruff-i-ans, puttin' guns up to his head.
'I'm with you, boys,' cried he, 'but first, give me my big fur coat,
And also let me have a scarf – my special care's the throat.'

They shoved him in the Rolls-Royce car and swiftly sped away,
What route they followed Oliver St John Gogarty can't say.
But they reached a house at Island Bridge and locked him in a room,
And said, 'Oliver St John Gogarty, prepare to meet yer doom.'

Said he, 'Give me some minutes first to settle my affairs,
And let me have some moments' grace to say my last night prayers.'
To this appeal his brutal guard was unable to say nay,
He was so amazed that Oliver St John Gogarty could pray.

Said Oliver St John Gogarty, 'My coat I beg you hold.'
The half-bemoidered ruff-i-an then did as he was told.
Before he twigged what game was up the coat was round his head,
And Oliver St John Gogarty into the night had fled.

The rain came down like bullets, and the bullets came down like rain,
As Oliver St John Gogarty the river bank did gain;
He plunged into the ragin' tide and swam with courage bold,
Like brave Horatius long ago in the fabled days of old.

Then Oliver St John Gogarty a mighty oath he swore
That if the gods decreed that he should safely reach the shore,
By the blessed martyr Oliver and by the two St Johns,
He'd present the River Liffey with a pair of bloomin' swans.

He landed and proceeded through the famous Phaynix Park;
The night was bitter cold, and what was worse, extremely dark;
But Oliver St John Gogarty to this paid no regard,
Till he found himself a target for our gallant Civic Guard.

Cried Oliver St John Gogarty, 'A Senator am I!
The rebels I've tricked, the river I've swum, and sorra the word's a lie.'
As they clad and fed the hero bold, said the sergeant with a wink:
'Faith, thin, Oliver St John Gogarty, ye've too much bounce to sink.'

## Lines on the Sinclairs [by George Redding]

*from* As I was Going Down Sackville Street *(1937)*

It is a thing to wonder at, but hardly to admire,
How they who do desire the most, guard most against desire:
They chose their friend or mistress so that none may yearn to touch her,
Thus did the twin grandchildren of the ancient Chicken Butcher . . .

> 'Two Jews grew in Sackville Street
> And not in Piccadilly,
> One was gaitered on the feet,
> The other one was Willie.
>
> 'And if you took your pick of them,
> Whichever one you chose,
> You'd like the other one more than him,
> So wistful were these Jews.

'They kept a shop for objects wrought
By Masters famed of old,
Where you, no matter what you bought
Were genuinely sold.

'But Willie spent the sesterces
And brought on strange disasters
Because he sought new mistresses
More keenly than old Masters.

'Two Jews grew in Sackville Street
And not in Piccadilly,
One was gaitered on the feet,
The other one was Willie.

'And if you took the pick of them,
Whichever one you choose,
You'd like the other one more than him,
So wistful were these Jews.'


## As I was Going Down Sackville Street

As I was going down Sackville Street
   Hey, Ho! Me Randy O.
Three bloody fine whores did I chance to meet
   With me gallopin' rearin' Randy O.

I chose the wan wid the curly locks
   Hey, Ho! Me Randy O.
I went with her, but she gave me the pox
   In me gallopin', rearin Randy O.

Then off to Mercer's I did go
   Hey, Ho! Me Randy O.
Wid me prick in me hand and me balls to show
   And me gallopin' rearin' Randy O.

'Three inches of this you'll have to loose
   Hey, Ho! Your Randy O.'
Oh, leave me the stump to play wid the whores
   And me gallopin' rearin' Randy O.

In came the nurse wid a poultice hot
    Hey, Ho! Me Randy O.
Sez she, 'Young man, lay this on your bot
    And your gallopin', rearin' Randy O!'

Oh, Nurse, Oh Nurse! It is too hot!
    Hey, Ho! Me Randy O.
'Ye didn't say *that* when gettin' the pox
    In yer gallopin', rearin' Randy O!'

But now that I'm well, I feel quite game
    Hey, Ho! Me Randy O.
If I meet wid me whore I'll have her again
    Wid me gallopin' rearin' Randy O.


## *The Maunder's praise of his strolling Mort*

Doxy, oh: thy glaziers shine
As glimmar, by the Salomon!
No gentry mort has prats like thine
No cove e'er wap'd with such a one.

White thy gambles, red thy gan
And they quaroons dainty is;
Couch a hogshead with me then,
In the darkman's clip and kiss.

# Appendix 2

# THE WORKED-OUT WARD

---

PERSONS
JOHN DILLONELL
STEPHEN GWYNERNEY } *Political paupers.*
MRS HOULIHAN. *A countrywoman*

*Scene — A Political Ward in an Irish city. The two old politicians should be in bed.*

JOHN DILLONELL. Isn't it a hard case, Stephen Gwynerney, myself and yourself to be left out in the cold, and it be the Peace Day of St. Woodrow, and the elected Sinn Feiners attending on the Peace Conference?

STEPHEN GWYNERNEY. Is it sitting at the Conference you are wishful to be? Let you raise up the Party, if you're able to do it, not like myself that has Unionism, the same as tin-tacks within in my inside.

JOHN DILLONELL. If you have Unionism within in your inside, there is no one can see it or know of it to be any different from my own Provincialism that is propped up with rameis, and the Party that is twisted in its ideas the same as an old cabbage stalk. It's easy to be talking of nationality and independence, and they maybe not to be in the Party at all.

STEPHEN GWYNERNEY. To open me and analyse me you would know what sort of a Unionist and West Briton I am in my heart and in my mind. But I'm not one like yourself to be orating and boasting and bluffing the time Conscription was at hand, thinking to get a bigger share than myself of the popularity and the votes.

JOHN DILLONELL. That's the way you do be picking at me and faulting me. I was an Irishman, and a good Irishman in my early time, and it's well you know that, and both of us reared in Constitutionalism.

STEPHEN GWYNERNEY. You may say that, indeed. We are both of us reared in Constitutionalism. Little wonder you to have good nourishment the time we were both rising, and you to have been brought up away from Trinity, the time I was floundering there.

JOHN DILLONELL. And you didn't get away from Trinity, I suppose, and get my principles from the Party, letting on they to be your own? For you were always a cheater and a schemer, grabbing every political stunt for your own profit.

STEPHEN GWYNERNEY. And you were no grabber yourself, I suppose, till your Party and all your votes wore away from you!

JOHN DILLONELL. If I lost it itself, it was through the crosses I met with and I going through the war. I was never a Trinitarian West Briton like yourself, Stephen Gwynerney, that ran from all nationalism and turned Imperialist unknown to your Chief.

STEPHEN GWYNERNEY. Imperialist, is it? And if I was, was it you yourself led me on to it, or some other one? Is it in my own college I would be to-day and in the face of the Gwynerney family, but for the misfortune I had to be joined to a bad Party that was yourself. What way did my credit go from me? Spending on fencing, spending on votes, making up lies, putting up sham fights, that would keep your followers from coming through desperation on to the Sinn Fein side, and every intelligent man in Ireland from seeing through your game.

JOHN DILLONELL. O, listen to you! And I striving to please you and be kind to you, and to close my ears to the abuse you would be calling down upon the Party. To ruin your credit, is it? It's little credit there was for my poor beasts to ask of the country. My God Almighty! What were you but a Trinity shoneen?

STEPHEN GWYNERNEY. And what do you say to my recruiting campaign, that your henchman destroyed on me, the time that Lynch was stumped and the Sinn Feiners making gaps in his speeches.

JOHN DILLONELL. Ah, there does be a great deal of gaps knocked in a distracted party. Why wouldn't they be knocked by the Diehards, the same as were knocked in the Liberals by Lloyd George?

STEPHEN GWYNERNEY. It was the Diehards, I suppose so, that gave up the Home Rule Bill? And compromised on recruiting, and petitioned President Wilson himself from the Mansion House, after denying Ireland to be an international question?

JOHN DILLONELL. And what happened myself the day I tried to run a pro-Irish policy? Two brazened dogs that rushed round making recruiting speeches against me. I never was the better of it, or of the start I got, but wasting from then till now!

STEPHEN GWYNERNEY. Think you were a pro-German Sinn Feiner they did, that had made his escape out of Frongoch. Sure any Britisher with life in him at all would be roused and stirred seeing the like of you going Sinn Feining.

JOHN DILLONELL. I did well taking a line against you that time. It is a great wonder you not to have gone over to Flanders, but the laws of England is queer. Isn't it a bad story for me to be wearing out my days beside you the same as a spancelled goat. Chained I am and tethered I am to a man that is ransacking his mind for pro-Ally lies!

STEPHEN GWYNERNEY. If it is a bad story for you, John Dillonell, it is a worse story again for myself. A semi-neutral to be next and near to me through the whole four years of the war. I never heard there to be any great name on the Dillonells as there was on my own race and name.

JOHN DILLONELL. You didn't, is it? Well, you would hear it, if you had but ears to hear it. Go across to Ballaghadereen, and down to Tipperary, and you'll hear of Dillonell.

STEPHEN GWYNERNEY. What signifies Ballaghadereen and Tipperary? Look at all my own generation buried in Trinity College. And what do you say to St. Columba's College and Brasenose, Oxford? Aren't they apt to have knowledge of a superior race? Was a Dillonell ever Regius Professor of Divinity, or chaplain of T.C.D.?

JOHN DILLONELL. It is a pity that you are not in any of those places this minute, that you might be quitting your brag and your chat, your unionism and your imperial ways; for there is no one under the rising sun in Ireland could stand you. I tell you you are not behaving as in presence of an Irish nation!

STEPHEN GWYNERNEY. Is it wishful for my resignation you are? Let it come and meet me now and welcome, so long as it will part me from yourself! And I say, and I would kiss the book on it, I have one request only to be granted, and I leaving it in my will, it is what I would request, nine furrows of the House of Commons, nine ridges of political molehills, nine waves of the *Irish Times* to be put between your Party and mine, the time we are elected again.

(MRS HOULIHAN *comes in with a parcel. She is a country-woman with orange, white and green shawl. She stands still a minute. The two old politicians compose themselves.*)

MRS HOULIHAN. I never was in this place at all. I don't know am I right. Which, now, of the two of ye is a Nationalist?

JOHN DILLONELL. Who is it calling my Party name?

MRS HOULIHAN. Sure amn't I your mistress, Molly Hibernian Maguire that was, that is now Kathleen in Houlihan.

JOHN DILLONELL. I didn't know you till you pushed anear me. It is time
indeed for you to come and see me, and I in politics these thirty years
or more. Thinking me to be no credit to you, I suppose, among the
tribe of Parliamentarians. I wonder at Sinn Fein to give you leave to
come ask am I living yet or dead?

MRS HOULIHAN. Ah, sure, I buried generations of great Parliamentarians.
Parnell himself was the last to go. Sure we must go through our
crosses. And he got a wonderful lever on the English; it would
delight you to hear his like in Westminster again. My poor Charles
Parnell! A nice clean man, you couldn't but admire him. Very severe
on the English, and he wouldn't touch a compromise.

JOHN DILLONELL. And is it in Ireland you are living yet?

MRS HOULIHAN. It is so. A wide lovely house I have, four beautiful
provinces, and harbours and industries, and minerals. It is what I'm
thinking yourself might come and look after me. It is no credit to me
now, you to be going to Westminster at all.

JOHN DILLONELL. What luck could there be in a place and a statesman
not to be in it? Is that a new national programme you have brought
with you?

MRS HOULIHAN. It is so, the way you'll be tasty coming back to the
people of your own country. Sure you could be keeping the fire of
nationality in, and stirring the nation to a sense of its own dignity,
and dealing yourself with the problems of the day, developing our
industries, fostering our culture, and maybe leading the country to
prosperous independence. For when Parnell died, Westminsterism
died.

JOHN DILLONELL. Let me out of this! (*He spreads out the national programme
and tries to grasp it.*) That now is a good idea . . . if I could only adopt
it.

STEPHEN GWYNERNEY (*alarmed*). And is it going to abstain from
Westminster you are, John Dillonell?

JOHN DILLONELL. Don't you hear I am. Going to work, I am, in the only
place where I can get every good thing for Ireland.

STEPHEN GWYNERNEY. Ah, John, is it truth you are saying, you to go
from Westminster, and to leave the people, the English people, and
people from the best universities, and they having a great liking for
us. You'll be craving the talk. Not to be lying at Westminster would
be the abomination of misery!

JOHN DILLONELL. Look now, Kathleen . . . It is what I often heard said,
two Irish Parties at Westminster to be better than one. If you had an
old programme full of holes, wouldn't you put another under it that
might be as tattered as itself, and the two parties together would make
some sort of a decent show.

MRS HOULIHAN. Ah, what are you saying? There is no holes in the policy I brought you now, but sound it as the day I spun it.

JOHN DILLONELL. It is what I'm thinking, Kathleen . . . I do be weak an odd time. Any point I would carry, it preys upon my mind. Maybe it is a hard thing for a man that has spluttered on the floor of the House for thirty years to go changing from place to place.

MRS HOULIHAN. Well, take your luck or leave it. All I asked was to save you from the harm of the year. Give me back my fine programme so (*gathers up the parcel*) till I'll go look for men of my own! Yourself and your Party, that never left fighting and scolding and attacking one another! Sparring at the English like young pups, and then coming docile to the heel of your masters. It's mad I was to be thinking any good could be got of you, and you the slave of habits, and the admirer of Imperial England. It's queer in the head you've grown from asking questions in Parliament; your heart's not with your own people.

STEPHEN GWYNERNEY. Let her go so, as she is so pro-German and disloyal, and look for men of her own – God help them! We could not go with her at all.

MRS HOULIHAN. It is too much time I lost with you, and dark days waiting to overtake me on the road to freedom. Let you stop together, and the back of my hand to you. It is I will leave you the same as God left the Jews!

(*She goes out. The old politicians are silent for a moment.*)

STEPHEN GWYNERNEY. Why wouldn't it be wide? What would you know about Ireland? Whatever sort of a house you had in it. was too narrow for the growth of your brains.

STEPHEN GWYNERNEY. Stop your impudence and your chat, or it will be worse for you. I'd bear with the mere Irish as long as any man would, but if they'd vex me, I would conscript and coerce them as soon as an Englishman!

JOHN DILLONELL. That Sinn Fein may chew you from skin to marrow bone! (*Seizes the* Freeman's Journal.)

STEPHEN GWYNERNEY (*seizing the* Irish Times). By cripes, I'll put out your pin-feathers.

JOHN DILLONELL. You factionist! You sorehead! You West Briton, you!

STEPHEN GWYNERNEY (*hurling phrases from the* Irish Times). Take this so, you defeatist, you Bolshevik, you flaunter of Ireland's shame.

(*They throw the* Irish Times, Freeman's Journal, *and all the abusive words in their respective political vocabularies at one another.*)

## CURTAIN

# Appendix 3

*FROM*

# WAVE LENGTHS

*(an incomplete version)*

---

## ACT II SCENE 3

*Magnificent Offices like a great Bank: Wave Lengths Limited, New York. Large posters on back wall.*

SAM KLAWSENHAMMER *(overdressed, lolling in a chair. Beside him is a smaller one. A low desk in front. He picks up the telephone).* Have you recorded? Show her in. SOUSE *peeps through door at back of stage, seeing lady shuts it quickly.*

    *A tall lady with blue in her whitening hair is ushered by a female clerk carrying notes.* SAM *rises and motions lady to chair. His air is that of a consulting physician, so is his get-up. He takes the notes and dismisses the female clerk. He sits back in his chair turning the pages back over the book.* This record of your vibrations shows that it took place on the 18 kilocycle band I should think. Let me see. Exactly. *(Turns pages.)* Now we require date and place for the recovery of the confidence or whatever you wish to have put beyond recall. Beyond recall. *(He rises and takes up telephone.)* Prepare a silica safety disc of . . . *(Turning to customer.)* You know you can wear it as a bangle, or a locket. We advise our clients to put them in a safety vault deposit box. They are not exposed to wear and tear.

LADY. Do they need to be renewed?

SAM. Madam, our remedy is absolute. Absolute. Once the etherial voices are gathered and canned, I mean preserved, I mean absorbed. They never can be collected again just as the scent of the rose can never turn back into the flower. And as nothing grows or increases that is to say increments in the ether no method known to man can bring the words you uttered out of the air again. Once you have purchased your Wave Length. I may say though, and you are at liberty to exercise your privilege of extending no confidences to any members of the staff — I may say also, that it makes it easier, that is to say facilitates the seizing and preservation of the sounds, it makes the research less difficult for our scientists, if you repeat as far as you can remember the words you wish recalled. In the next room there is a confidence cabinet into which you may speak.

LADY. I see. But it is not so much what I said as what I did . . .

SAM. Did, did? We have no remedy for that. Words not deeds! Words not deeds. They can be recalled but deeds. Why we wouldn't be here if it were not for deeds whereas words. They might be flirting yet.

LADY. I think I will confide the whole matter to you if it will hasten the delivery of the Wave Length. A young man asked me to marry him and to divorce my husband. Of course I refused and told him so.

SAM. There's nothing dishonourable in that. Why do you want that recovered?

LADY (coyly). It was the way I told him. I wouldn't like it to come to [the] ears of my husband.

SAM (firmly). Never. Now we have the modulations of your voice and their vibrations all worked out in these notes. When you enter the next room an attendant will conduct you to the recording cabinet. Speak into it with if possible the same energy or fervour or whatever you used. The words will be transmitted and when you come into the outer office the disc with the price attached will be waiting for you. Make a note of our address for future use.

LADY. There will be no future use. He deceived me. I saw him taking some young cloak-room attendant — she looked just about as cultured as that — out in the car I gave him. I'll never speak to him again. Once I get my Wave Length, I'm through.

SAM (rising). Madam, the Company feels it a privilege to serve you. In the next room which is dark to avoid light waves you may unburden your mind. (Pushes a bell. ATTENDANT conducts LADY to door at back. Exeunt.)

SAM. Poor old girl. Some gigolo; and she's afraid that if he gets a hold of her loving cooings he'll blackmail her. Well it is for people of her temperament that the company does its best work. It comforts, reassures and replaces them firmly on their pedestal of self respect. Next please. (Presses bell.) Enter ATTENDANT leading a very smartly *dressed woman, slim, about fifty.* SAM *goes through the usual dignified deferential acting. When they are seated:*

SAM. And now Madam?

LADY (*speaks out quite boldly*). I am married to a man who once held a position in Society somewhat above my own. I find myself envied by many women, some of them women of great wealth. As my husband is about the same age as myself and as I have been married a few times before I met my present husband, it has occurred to me that some evil-minded woman wishing to cause trouble may avail herself of this new invention and send my husband a broadcast of the confidences interchanged between me and my other husbands. I have come to put that out of any woman's power.

SAM. (*nodding approval*). And your decision is perfectly right – laudable. That is what our firm is for, to co-operate in saving people of fine character from repetition. When I say 'repetition' I am not alluding to your previous marriages, but to the fact that we are now in the presence of an invention which can repeat conversations of long ago. I quite agree that there is danger particularly since you move in wealthy circles.

LADY. Pardon. I must correct you: *Above* wealthy circles.

SAM. Above wealthy circles. All the more incumbent on you to protect your present husband from a broadcast of the confidences and conversations which passed between you and your former husbands, I mean consorts.

LADY. I have nothing to hide but if it would help to explain, nothing kills love more surely than a formula. Now it is not my fault that there is only one word for love in the English language and that is love. There are no degrees in the word itself. So if I have used it as a term of endearment to one or two of my former husbands and my present one gets to hear of them (he has been so protected all his life that he has very little understanding of these affairs) he might come to think that I had a formula, a patter, a set of set phrases about love and that they meant nothing. Every husband likes to think that a woman only married before in order to love him better. I don't want my husband to think he is just one more spectator at a play.

SAM (*understandingly*). He might imagine himself on a line so to speak.

LADY. Oh, nonsense. But he might detect a leit motif, if you see what I mean.

SAM (*sighing deeply*). Ah, yes. Ah, yes indeed. It has broken up many a happy home.

LADY. What do you mean? What has broken many a happy home?

SAM (*smiling knowingly*). We need not go into that; but I see what you mean.

LADY. What do you mean? What do you mean? What has broken up many a happy home?

SAM. Need I say it?

LADY. Certainly.

SAM. The leit motif.

LADY. The leit motif! What has that got to do with it. Perhaps you don't even know what leit motif means.

SAM (*smiles knowingly*). Don't let us discuss it.

LADY. I asked you what you mean by a leit motif breaking up happy homes. What is a leit motif?

SAM. It's a form of birth control.

LADY. Nonsense. It's a musical term referring to the hidden theme in the music.

SAM. Oh yes. The same old tune on the same old fiddle.

LADY. You don't inspire confidence. There are shortcomings in your education.

SAM. You don't have to have confidence in me. It is in our engineers you should have confidence who are at the present moment draining the ether of every expression of the word love you ever uttered. Nobody will be able to remind you or cast it up to your husband.

LADY. But there were some occasions when I said 'I don't love you'. They might be left to my credit.

SAM. 'I don't' is good enough. We can't discriminate. It might help us if we knew how long you were engaged before your last marriage.

LADY. 'Engaged!' I was betrothed.

SAM. How long were you betrothed before the conjunction.

LADY. What do you mean? Conjunction.

SAM. It's a term for marriage among the nobility.

LADY. You are either insolent or a fool.

SAM. I didn't mean to be. Will you follow the attendant etc.
  (*Exeunt* LADY *and* ATTENDANT. SAM *rings, rings again. Enter another* ATTENDANT.)

SAM. Have you any idea who that lady is?

ATTENDANT. No, Sir, she said nothing.

SAM. Nonsense, she must have spoken.

ATTENDANT. No, Sir.

SAM. But how did she learn the procedure? How did she know that she was to come in here?

ATTENDANT. I told her maid, Sir.

SAM. Her maid. So she had a maid. Go out and have a word with the maid. Tell her what it is all about and she may tell you something. See?

ATTENDANT. Yes, Sir. She might want a permanent Wave. (*Exit.*)
  (*Enter* SOUSE *bursting through door at back.*)

SOUSE. Now listen, Sam. What's the good of my firm working on you to teach you English, manners and behaviour good enough to make you a receptionist, if you insult the first great lady that comes in?

SAM. I don't get you.

SOUSE. You mean you don't comprehend. But what did you mean by asking how long it was before the conjunction took place.

SAM. That was all right. I remembered hearing of how an editor corrected a reporter for writing that certain royal persons were 'engaged' when he should have said 'betrothed'. 'We speak of the copulation of mice but the conjunction of elephants', he said. She corrected me about 'engaged' so I came back with 'conjunction'. That's all right.

SOUSE. Well it's just not all right. And there's another thing, Sam. How often have I asked you not to send me only the old women. It's bad enough to sit shut up in a cabinet in the dark room. But if I have to listen to nothing but old women past love but loving to talk about it, I'll quit.'

SAM. Now Sammy, take it easy. Your own Publicity firm drew up the scheme for putting this across. There must be a secret cabinet, it said, into which they can talk and get it off their chest. They are not to be bound to do this but they must be given the option. You have only your own firm to blame. You suggested yourself for the cabinet.

SOUSE. There's nothing wrong with the firm; but yesterday I sat all day and there was only one good-looker who put her head in. Quit sending me old ones.

SAM. Orl right. Orl right (*Bell rings*). We can't select our customers. Suppose the Unknown Soldier's widow called, would you refuse to see her?

SOUSE. No. But, Sam, what are you getting at? How would we know that she was the Unknown Soldier's widow?

SAM. We wouldn't. That is why I say that we can't select our clients.

SOUSE. I know we can't. But send me something out of the ordinary Sam, and don't press the old ones to talk into the cabinet. Let them pass right through. (*Bell rings again.* SAM *takes it up.*)

SAM. 'Sez they are inseparable?' Well ask him to let the lady come first. (*To* SOUSE.) You had better get back in there.

SOUSE. Now, remember: no old ones.

SAM. Old ones? Now what do you think the company is? A White Slave Traffic Outfit? Hell. Get back to the dog-house. You proposed it yourself. You're getting nuts.

SOUSE. See here, Sam. That's no language to use to me. Look at the Firm's instructions. 'The Receptionists must use dignified and courteous language and show a fatherly consideration for all concerned'. You have the book of words.

SAM. Who's breaking the rules? You come butting in. I might have been in the middle of an interview for all you cared. Don't spill the beans when we're making good (*Telephone rings.*) Do your stuff Sammy and I'll do mine. (*Listens to phone.*) 'Says they're inseparable . . .' Who's inseparable? (*Waves* SOUSE *away.*)

SOUSE. Well I'll go back for the session, but remember no old ones (*Exit back stage.*)

SAM (*into telephone*). Well, if he says that he can wait, ask the lady to come in first. (*Enter a gaudy blonde.*)

SAM *rises with a suppressed exclamation. Bows. The* LADY *extends her hand.* SAM *bows over it with exaggerated courtesy. Leads her to chair. To the* ATTENDANT.)

SAM. May I have the lady's vibrations?

(ATTENDANT *hands notes.* SAM *seats himself.*)

SAM. Will you permit me to read this as I report on your vibrations?

LADY. Why, certainly.

SAM. Strong and recurring. Now will you be kind enough to tell me how the Company can serve you?

LADY. It's like this. I want my Wave Length for some words I said to an old acquaintance of mine about a week ago, or nine days ago, that is, it was in the early hours. It would be eight or nine days ago.

SAM. The exact date is of little importance. Our instruments pick up sounds no matter how old they are. You spoke of an old acquaintance.

LADY. Well, he was not so much of an old acquaintance of mine as an old fossil who was an acquaintance. And I called him a lot of names and used language.

SAM (*sententiously*). Ah, we should never speak in anger but count up to 100 first.

LADY. You've got me all wrong. It's not of the bad language that I'm ashamed but of the terms of endearment.

SAM. They shall be recalled and cancelled from the ether. You will never have them cast up as unpleasant reminders that you lavished love on an unworthy object.

LADY. That's O.K. by me. You see I'm going to be married and if the old stiff gets to hear that I pretended he was my Uncle he may put me on the air and my boy friend could not bear it. The old stiff often said that he could never find anyone like me and that if anyone took me away from him, what wouldn't he do.

SAM. And you want to get away from him?

LADY (*with a shrug of disgust*). Yes. He's getting balmy. Last week he started dressing up in my clothes . . .

SAM. The attendant will take you to the next room. (*Rings.* LADY *exits with* ATTENDANT. *Bell rings.* SAM *picks up telephone.*)

SAM. Oh, yes. Inseparable nothing, show him in.

SAM (*after business with telephone*). Show him in. (*Enter a* GIGOLO. *He is loudly dressed exactly as* SAM. *Bridegroom's large tie. Blue-grey double breasted waistcoat, spats, etc.*) Well and what can I do for you?

GIGOLO. I want to get my words back. If her husband got to hear them he might divorce her and where would I be then.

SAM. You must make yourself a little clearer. Am I to take it that you have been flirting with a married woman?

GIGOLO. That's all right. It's the husband who might take it seriously. I did ask her to divorce him. I didn't mean a word of it. I'm engaged to a blonde. I want my Wave Length. Will it cost much?

SAM (*rising in righteous indignation*). Wave Lengths such as yours can be obtained in Woolworths. The Company has no use for characters as common as yours. You would want a Wave Length every week. Good day.

GIGOLO. I only meant to . . . (SAM *turns his back. The* GIGOLO *slinks out, the door opens as he nears it. Exit.*)

SAM (*jumps up, goes to mirror, undoes his tie taking out pin and ties it again in simpler fashion. Remembers his spats*). It seems to me that this company must guard itself against recruiting Wave Lengthers. It would lose finality and authority if it had to traffic with people who kept on repeating themselves. That is a danger. We want select people out of the ordinary. (*His desk bell rings. He picks up telephone.*)

(*The door at back bursts open, enter* SAMMY).

SAMMY SOUSE. That was Fifi. What the Hell is the game anyway? Why the Hell did you send her in to me. She's quitting. Going to marry a guy who got an automobile from his Aunt. What did you send her in for? That's what I'd like to know.

SAM. Be reasonable Sammy Souse. You kept on grousing because old women were your only confidents. And the first blonde I get I thought would please you. How was I to know that it was Fifi? How was I to know? She'll marry no gigolo for if I'm not mistaken he was here a minute ago looking for his Wave Length to save him from being shown up. Sammy.

SAMMY SOUSE. So what?

SAM. 'Where are your brains! So what?' We'll turn the Sound Restorer on to him now that we have his voice vibrations and we'll do it in the presence of Fifi. That will end that. This invention is by no means phoney.

SAMMY SOUSE. The brain is all right. I get you. But we ought to start right now.

SAM. Don't you see that it can't be done until we have the cooperation of Leopold and the Professor? That we should have any time now. Take it easy, Sammy, and go back to your mystic closet. (*Bell keeps ringing*). We must get on with the work.

SAMMY SOUSE. Let me know when we have hooked up with Mr Professor. You will, won't you, Sam?

SAM. Sure, partner.

  (*Exit* SAMMY SOUSE.)

SAM (*picks up telephone*). Inseparable nothing. Show him in.

  (*Enter* GHANDI *and his goat. He leads the goat behind him with a leash. This he gradually shortens as he drags goat through door. When he has hauled goat beside him, he subsides in sitting posture cross-legged on floor. Enter* ATTENDANT.)

ATTENDANT (*hands notes*). He said that they were inseparable and he would not leave it in the cloak-room. These are Mr Ghandi's notes.

SAM. Oh, all right.

  (*Exit* ATTENDANT.)

GHANDI. Please.

SAM. Now how can Wave Lengths Limited serve you, Mr Ghandi? You know we are a world wide corporation and we know of no restrictions on our philanthropic activities, age, race, boundaries, hemispheres, empires, nothing. Now all you have to do is to invoke our aid. Here we are to give it to you.

  (*Enter* ATTENDANT. *She holds door open.*)

ATTENDANT. Mr George Bernard Shaw.

  (*Exit* ATTENDANT. *Enter* G.B.S. *with writing pad.*)

G.B.S. I saw Mr Ghandi coming in here and I thought that I would follow him and give him some information and advice on vegetarianism and the interior. And Indian economy. What contribution is she making to armament production. Is the standard of living rising with her war aims? There are many questions which Mr Ghandi and I could discuss to the great advantage of the audience.

SAM. Mr Shaw may I remind you that you are in the offices of a semi-philanthropical company which has been formed to release the public from the dread of having their past speeches cast up at them. We can do nothing for you because everything you have ever said you have also written. We cannot erase the written, only the spoken word.

G.B.S. There is only one thing worse than a semi-philantropical company and that is a totally philantriopican one. I regard the whole thing as a prodigious hoax. Who cares what he has said. The memory of the public is only as long as the time between the edition of its newspapers.

SAM. That remark is uncalled for. You are unique and may be regarded as a sad exception from the kindly race of men. Why, even your love letters can be published. Therefore if you will permit me to discuss his problem with Mr Ghandi . . .

G.B.S. Ghandi has no problem because he has no property. Of course if he has ventured into politics that is a different thing. Politics is the father of all problems. Even so I cannot see why he should wish to have any of his past speeches taken off the record. All he wants is a crisis. In a crisis everything is justified. Now if you were to supply Mr Ghandi with a crisis it would not be necessary for him to correct himself.

SAM. I must remind you once again that you are in the offices of Wave Lengths Limited.

GHANDI. Yes, Mr Shaw. I am honoured to make your acquaintance. You are well-known in India.

G.B.S. I am well-known everywhere. I cross all the frontiers. As a dramatist I am known in every civilised country. I am second only to Charlie Chaplin who goes beyond me – and civilisation.

GHANDI. India knows you as a vegetarian.

G.B.S. If England had your climate, I would have solved the problem of the standard of living. It is an effort to maintain the standards of living that sends countries to war. You have solved it with your goat.

GHANDI. And yet we in India with the lowest standards of living in the world are subjected to the highest proportional taxation. The Government would tax my loin-cloth but that they are too prudish. They know that I and my millions of followers would discard our loin cloths if they were taxed.

G.B.S. If they tax your turban you can use it as a loin-cloth.

SAM. I don't know where all this is leading. But I guess if there is nothing else to tax they'll tax his goat. Whether you approve of it or not Mr Shaw, you are taking up a considerable portion of my time which is the Company's time. I am sure you would not willingly interfere with a man's right to work.

G.B.S. Certainly. I deny anyone's right to work wrong.

SAM. Perhaps you will permit Mr Ghandi to go into the next room.

G.B.S. Well, if Mr Ghandi prefers mumbo-jumbo to me, I would very much like to accompany him and see what hocus pocus you have staged in there. (SAM *rings and signals attendant to lead off* GHANDI. *Exit* GHANDI *and goat.*)

SAM. Unless you contribute to the Company whether you will accept your Wave Length or not, I cannot permit you to occupy the Company's premises or to take up any more of my time.

G.B.S. I would be condoning a felony were I to contribute to it.

SAM. I suppose that was the reason you said 'Press' when they passed the plate to you in Church.

G.B.S. I represent the Press everywhere even when in Church. The only difference is that I have an audience among the members of all religions. The parson has only the audience of his congregation. The parson uses a strongly stylised form of language. I use journalism only. Journalism is the language of the living and kinetic. The parson's language is static and archaic.

SAM. Would you like to be seated Mr Shaw – I can send for a higher chair.

G.B.S. I am well able to rise from any chair. Let me tell you that I consider this Wave Length idea of yours to be one of the greatest frauds ever perpetrated on a gullible public. If it were only symbolical it might be excusable. For symbolism is an excuse for anything. But to propose in real earnest to take words out of the ether so as to prevent anyone from getting them and selling the sponge to the speaker is nothing short of criminal blackmail. I am well aware that Marconi thought that he was listening-in to voices of the dead, but that was when he was on his death bed. It is not scientifically impossible to recover such words. Let me warn you that if you recover any of mine which I have not already published, I shall expect to be paid royalties. It may interest you to know that I have anticipated Marconi and whoever is behind this fraud because I alone can bring up the speeches of past heroes and heroines and adjust them to the stage as it is at the present day, in its decline of course. Take my *Androcles and the Lion* for example. In that play you have the voice of Caesar not perhaps as he actually spoke but as he should according to the laws of the drama have spoken. And that is truly according to artistic truth. It would never do for a Roman Emperor to be presented to the present day public without preparing him to meet the present day public with its prejudices and preconceived notions due to the ignorance of historians. Therefore in the only way Caesar could speak comprehensively, I have produced him. It is to me and not to you that the public should come to have their speech adjusted to the ever-changing present. There is no need for Wave Lengths. It is not waves we want but stability. If the public memory could last even ten years there would be no wars. Every so-called statesman would be discredited out of his own mouth and displaced before he could do much harm. It is a company for public reminders you should form and not this company with its unjustifiable suggestion that a man is safe if he cannot be reminded of what he said. It will be interesting to see what reactions will be caused by this well advertised fraud of yours. When it gets into the Reich, Rome and Tokio, for instance, and the public hear what the Son of Heaven said when he was educated at Oxford, then there will be fun. I am prepared to stand back and laugh at poor mortals with their ignorances, bigotries and beliefs. They should be fooled into peace and not into war.

*(Shouting and scuffling heard off. The door at back bursts open again. Enter* SAMMY SOUSE *followed by* GHANDI *and goat.)*

SAMMY SOUSE. Well a bloody old goat. Now look here Sam. I've stood this . . .

(SAM *directs his attention to* SHAW.)

SAM *(to* G.B.S.*).* My partner was not alluding to you, Mr Shaw.

SAMMY SOUSE *(to* G.B.S.*).* Do you own the goat?

G.B.S. I am afraid that I have not got further than a goatee. I am glad to see that you did not remain long in there Mr Ghandi.

GHANDI. It is the wrong place for the restored speeches. I do not want my speeches obliterated. Though I have changed my attitude I have not changed my heart. I want to find out how many promises have been made by the numerous Vice-roys of India and what they have said among themselves. This is a place for forgetting speeches. I want them called back.

SAM. You'll have to get in touch with the parent company. But it must be done through us.

G.B.S. What you have [is] a company facing both ways. One can obliterate and repeat.

SAMMY SOUSE. Now get this right. This Wave Lengths Limited does an infinite lot of good. Whether it can actually insure people from their Past and there are very few people like you Mr Shaw with no Past but a perpetual Present, it can give them new heart and a sense of security particularly as we deal with people whose past words nobody would think of picking up. We give them a sense of importance and so increase the sum of human dignity and we teach them to have a becoming reverence for words. The less likely they are to be put to the test, the greater is their security.

G.B.S. In other words the more bogus the better. I didn't catch your name.

SAMMY SOUSE. Souse of Souse, Sticklinger and Spread, Publicity Inc.

G.B.S. Now that is most interesting. The fact that such companies as yours exist is proof of what danger this country is in. Publicity has become synonymous with Perfection in the mind of the Public. Never since the Sophists of Ancient Rome was there a civilisation carried on flimsier foundations. Publicity may well be your undoing. Everything is Publicity even this war. And wars cannot be won by advertisement. And the public mind has become [so] susceptible that it mistakes notoriety for the solid article. Let us go Mr Ghandi. You are the only thing in the country that represents basic fact.

SAM AND SOUSE. Ah, come now. Be fair-minded, Mr Shaw.

G.B.S. This is no time for fairmindedness. We are at war.

## CURTAIN

# ACT III SCENE 1

*N.B. These scenes with the heads of Governments need not be produced. They can be recorded just as a radio-play is recorded. It may be better thus because to produce living celebrities on the stage is unconvincing. Besides, it is not drama.*

*The stage is divided vertically into two with almost identical arrangement of tables, furniture, etc. During the conversations of one side those of the other are heard and the scenes appear alternately by a system of blacking the one out for the moment. The dialogue is given separately. It is left to the producer to decide whether this is better than separate scenes in serial. The scene in the British House of Commons committee room 13 is given here separately pending the choice of the producer. If he approves of two separate scenes or a series of sandwiched scenes, this will not preclude that choice.*

*Council Chamber in the Reich.* GOEBBELS *and* VON RIBBENTROP *seated at a large council table capable of seating ten or twelve.* RIBBENTROP *examining a paper similar to the one used by* MONTGOMERY *in preceding scene.*

RIBBENTROP. I have asked Fritz Hirsch to report on this.

GOEBBELS (*looking at the advert for Wave Lengths Limited, reads*). LET NO ONE REMIND YOU. GET THE ETHER DRAINED. It looks to me like one of those American humbugs that take advantage of the superficial knowledge of science in the nation and exploit it by unscrupulous advertisement. You remember the stampede in New Jersey caused by Orson Welles and his talk of invasion by men from Mars? And then there was Dr Abrams Mystic Box.

RIBBENTROP. Some Jewish racket.

GOEBBELS. That is not quite to the point. The point is that the Mystic Box could never have robbed a public that was not sufficiently intelligent to know: 1, that the base of all matter was electrical and 2, that the Goeben and Breslau were able to jam the radio of the British Navy.

RIBBENTROP. Explain.

GOEBBELS. With those concepts fixed in the public mind, it was quite easy for the unscrupulous exploiter Abrams to fool the public by his Mystic Box. He suggested that, as all matter was electric, he could block the radiations of disease by blocking them in the same way that the two German battleships blocked the British wireless. This proposal to remove all traces of former speech from the ether is on the same lines of exploitation: by dishonest suggestion.

RIBBENTROP (*takes up telephone*). Hirsch is in attendance. We must call Hirsch. He is our best authority on wireless and all the possibilities of wireless. Show him up.

(*Enter* FRITZ HIRSCH. *He salutes.*)

HIRSCH. Excellenz.

RIBBENTROP. Be seated Herr Dozent. We have here a copy of the American periodical with the notice which you saw. I am anxious to have your report.

HIRSCH. Excellenz, my report may be divided into two or, rather into a report on a scientific possibility and a piece of audacious nonsense. It is within the bounds of possibility to recover the voices of the past. It is utter nonsense to suggest as Wave Lengths Limited suggests that voices once recovered, cannot be recovered again. There is no material that can absorb ether just as there is nothing that can absorb light.

RIBBENTROP. Thank you Herr Dozent. But this makes the thing all the more serious for us. While we are not for the moment interested in oblitering old voices, we are very greatly interested in preventing the words we use at present from being overheard. Is it possible without a microphone in this room that they could hear us in Washington or London?

HIRSCH. Merely a matter of improved technique.

GOEBBELS (*in a whisper*). Then this is serious.

HIRSCH. Pardon, Excellenz. It will not save you to speak in a whisper.

RIBBENTROP (*beginning to whisper then correcting himself*). Is there no way of preventing it, Herr Dozent. I do not mean by buying our Wave Lengths but by some means that I hope you can suggest.

HIRSCH. There is.

RIBBENTROP AND GOEBBELS (*together*). What?

HIRSCH. By kidnapping the inventor or by the destruction of the machine. There is no other way. No way in which to prevent every word from being heard. The inventor whoever he is has simply dispensed with a microphone. We can be overheard.

GOEBBELS (*looking at his watch*). That's a nice prospect Hirsch. In a minute the Supreme Command meets to take its orders from the Führer. Are our discussions and decisions to be open to the world?

HIRSCH. If I might suggest the use of note-paper . . . (*Enter* FLUNKEY.)

FLUNKEY. The Supreme German Commander. His Excellenz Field Marshal General Walther von Brauchitsch!

(*They rise, bow and salute.* GOEBBELS *indicates a seat. Exit* FLUNKEY.)

GOEBBELS. You are as punctual as a doctor at a consultation.

VON BRAUCHITSCH (*smiling grimly*). There is a good deal to be said for timing Herr Excellenz.

(HIRSCH *makes timid little reminders.*)

RIBBENTROP (*pushing over advert to* VON B). By the way . . .

(*Enter* FLUNKEY.)

FLUNKEY. His Excellenz Field Marshal Wilhelm Ritter von Leeb.

(*They rise, bow and salute.* VON LEEB *takes off great coat many wrappers, gloves etc. and hands them to* FLUNKEY *who exits with a pile of clothes.*)

VON LEEB. I perceive with pleasure that I am not the last. It would never do to arrive after the Führer. Would it, gentlemen?

RIBBENTROP. It is somewhat doubtful if we can deliberate at all.

VON LEEB. As a matter of fact things have got a little way beyond deliberation . . . Take Leningrad, for instance.

(HIRSCH *wildly excited but not venturing to address so august an assembly tries to push the paper in front of* VON LEEB. VON LEEB *smiles condescendingly and nods in a friendly way.*)

RIBBENTROP. We are in danger of being overheard.

VON LEEB. Overheard by whom? (*Enter* FLUNKEY.)

FLUNKEY. Field Marshal Fedor von Bock! (*Welcome procedure as before.*)

GOEBBELS. Herr Ribbentrop has a message for you.

VON BOCK (*suspiciously*). I would prefer to receive the message in the presence of all my comrades-in-arms. There have been too many interferences of a semi-private nature for which no one can be saddled with –

(HIRSCH *writhes.*)

VON BRAUCHITSCH. The expert here has abdominal pain. Attention.

(*Enter* FLUNKEY.)

FLUNKEY. Field Marshal Karl von Rundstedt.

(*Exit* FLUNKEY *with great coat as before. Welcome as before.*)

VON BRAUCHITSCH. As I was saying Herr Dozent Hirsch has abdominal pain. I have a fellow feeling, I know the symptoms. Are you in pain my friend?

HIRSCH (*faintly*). May I speak? Have I your permission to address you?

VON BRAUCHITSCH. Gentlemen, are you willing to hear the Herr Dozent? (*Chorus of guttural assents.*)

HIRSCH. Excellenz, for God's sake do not speak. Hold no council this evening. Every word said in this room can be overheard in the

Chancellories of America and London. A new method of recording has been perfected by which words out of the past can be heard and with much less technical equipment, words as they are being spoken can be recorded and rebroadcast. I would not have ventured to interrupt your deliberations but that I feel and feel it deeply that no War Council could take place unless you want to inform London and Washington and Chiang Kai Shek of your plans. Silence I implore.

GOEBBELS (*in answer to looks of incredulity*). He is the Dozent of Electric radiations in the University of Berlin.

(*Enter* FLUNKEY.)

FLUNKEY. Mein Führer. Commander in Chief of the Armies of the Reich. Generalissimo.

(*They sit unmoved. Fingers on lips.*)

HITLER. Is this your way of expressing your loyalty? Is this insubordination. Why do you put your fingers to your lips. Are we overheard?

(*They all nod frantically.*)

HITLER. By whom? (*Enter* FLUNKEY.)

FLUNKEY. Col. General Johannes Blaskowitz.

HITLER. What is the idea, Blaskowitz?

BLASKOWITZ. Heil Hitler!

HITLER. I have asked a question.

BLASKOWITZ. I was delayed by the ice. I meant no disrespect. I trust the Führer and the assembled Supreme Command will excuse me.

THE SUPREME COMMAND. *Hush!*

HITLER. Why were you listening in?

BLASKOWITZ. I was not listening in.

HIRSCH. Führer, I obtained permission to speak. I would never have ventured were it not for the sake of the Fatherland and that I have great abdominal pain.

GOEBBELS. Führer, a new means of recording conversations has just been perfected in an island off Nantucket by a Dr Frengly. It is not His Excellenz Col.-Gen. Johannes Blaskowitz who is listening to us now but the whole world of democracy. We dare not broadcast our deliberations. I move that you adjourn the meeting or conduct it in silence with written notes.

HITLER. Send a gun-boat! Send a destroyer, send two destroyers to capture that machine. Gestapo! Before it falls into the hands of that commercial syndicate which is known as the British Empire.

RIBBENTROP. Führer, according to Dozent Hirsch you are forewarning America. You are being overheard.

HITLER. Is that true, Herr Dozent?

HIRSCH. Führer, it is true. May I ask your permission to leave the Council Chamber, before I become involuntarily irreverent?

(HITLER *nods. Exit* HIRSCH.)

HITLER (*speaking to all nations*). We will purchase the machine by peaceful means and save it from being turned into some vicious little engine for the corruption of the world.

GOEBBELS. The Herr Dozent was greatly agitated. It may be that he has taken the invention greatly to heart and can realise its potentialities more than we or it may be that nervousness has brought on an attack of abdominal pain. Or both.

HITLER. There is nothing like a little purgative to cure abdominal pain. My Italian friend the ersatz Caesar has tried castor oil on his Italians.

VON RUNSTEDT. That accounts for it!

HITLER. For what, Field Marshal?

VON RUNSTEDT. For the fact that they have been relaxed ever since.

HITLER. We must give no offence until we take the offensive. (*Tremendous cheering from off.*)

VON BRAUCHITSCH. What is that? (*Going to window and looking out.*)

HITLER. The Unter den Linden is packed. (*Shouts as of a multitude off.* 'Heil Hitler!' 'On to Rome! On to Italy. It's warm there.')

(*The assembled persons look at each other.*)

GOEBBELS. Hirsch was perfectly right. We have been overheard and our remarks have been relayed in almost instantaneous broadcast. The public must have been informed hours ago that our deliberations would be made public.

HITLER. The meeting is adjourned *sine die*. (*Prepares to leave. All stand and salute. Exit* HITLER.)

(RIBBENTROP *stretches for the paper.* GOEBBELS *snatches it.*)

VON BRAUCHITSCH. The invention is no fake. I am wondering if the Wave Length part of it may not be true.

(*The generals and* GOEBBELS *and* RIBBENTROP *all seem anxious. They rise and study the advert for Wave Lengths Limited as if it were a map.*)

## CURTAIN

## ACT III SCENE 2

*(Scene 1 if run alternately with Scene 1 set in Reich)*


CHURCHILL *and* BRENDAN BRACKEN *discovered seated.*

CHURCHILL. The older I grow the more incredible things become. Now Bracken, as Minister for Information inform yourself how much truth there is in what you have told me and report at once to me. How am I to know that it is not a figment of your Irish imagination?

BRACKEN *(producing paper with W.L.'s advert).* I have informed myself. Here is their advertisement.

CHURCHILL. You go to an advertisement for your facts! You should have sent for a radio expert and asked him what this means. It is true that Marconi said something, as it says here, about recapturing voices from the past. Inconvenient as that might be for some people, it is not half as inconvenient as the possibility of being able to listen–in and to eaves'–drop on all our present sessions.

BRACKEN. It cuts both ways. We could listen–in to Hitler.

CHURCHILL. I'm sick of listening to Hitler. Get me a trustworthy report. An expert's report. And not something out of your own head or your own office. Nothing fanciful, my dear Bracken.

BRACKEN. What about Beaverbrook?

CHURCHILL. Surely you do not suggest that he is the antithesis of imagination?

BRACKEN. No but he is in the way of getting facts. His newspapers . . .

CHURCHILL. There was an American humourist who described an Admiral who had lost his way at sea being compelled to send ashore for a newspaper to get his bearings. It seems to me that you are in a somewhat similar predicament when you have to send for a newspaper man to tell you what you should know yourself.

BRACKEN. But Beaverbrook is an expert. He was one of the first to

625

investigate the possibilities of Television. I was at Cherkley when he demonstrated the first well-known television set . . .

CHURCHILL. Let us send for Beaverbrook. (*Telephone rings wildly.* CHURCHILL *signs to* BRACKEN *to pass the receiver.*)

CHURCHILL. What? Who? Is that you Beaverbrook? The very man! I was thinking of you a moment ago. About to ask you to drop in. What? A matter of the most profound importance. You cannot speak of it over the phone? Or over anything. What the devil do you mean? If you cannot speak of it why ring me. You know that I am a busy man nearly as busy as yourself. As a matter of fact I was about to send for you. Now it is you who send for me. You have Goering and Von Brauschitsch at Cherkley. Did they arrive by parachute? Their voices. Very well, Max. In that case I will come along. (*Hangs up.*) Come with me, Bracken. I have heard of the King sending for his Prime Minister, never of a Prime Minister sending for the King. Yet here we have Beaverbrook sending for the Prime Minister. Says he hears voices. Is he getting like Hitler or Joan of Arc. Riddle me that Bracken. Come along. (*Telephone rings.*)

CHURCHILL. So they can be transcribed. I have no radio but I can have one brought in. No. How could I? But you can talk and give the meter to the mechanic yourself. Bracken, ring for the radio. (*Hangs up.*)

BRACKEN (*rings*). So the Prime Minister will not go to his Cabinet Ministers after all?

CHURCHILL. It was the very thing you were describing to me as a possibility. Sorry if I suggested that it was your Irish imagination. It is not any longer just a possibility but a fact. Beaverbrook heard the German Supreme Command at a meeting with Hitler and they are just as perturbed about it as we. When the radio comes the man can get the private Cherkley wave length and we shall hear all that went on in the Reich without leaving the room.

BRACKEN. That's resource for you. There never was a more resourceful or practical man than Max. He can speed things up. His name should be used as a verb for getting things done. 'Beaverbrook it.'

CHURCHILL. What about 'beaving it up' on the lines of 'heaving it up?' 'Beaver up that output;' or more simply 'beave it up.'

BRACKEN (*as door opens and mechanic pushes his tackle in before him*). It will be interesting to see how he beaves up his transmission from Cherkley to this.

(*Enter* MECHANIC *with radio.* MECHANIC *keeps on his cap with peak back.*)

MECHANIC. Where do you want this 'ere set up?

BRACKEN. Don't you think that you might take your cap off in the presence of the Prime Minister?

MECHANIC. Wot are we fighting for? 'Ats off? Where would we be without his 'ats?

BRACKEN. Plug it in there and get Cherkley 00 and tune into the kilocycle band that will be announced. Then clear out.

(*After a lot of fiddling and trying to get Cherkley, the* MECHANIC *tunes in and the voice of* BLASKOWITZ *is heard.*)

THE VOICE. Heil Hitler!

MECHANIC. Wot's all this?

BRACKEN. It's got nothing to do with you. You may clear out.

MECHANIC (*as he exits*). Heil Hitler, not arf!

(*The conversations are repeated as from the 'Heil Hitler' of Act III Scene 1 [page 620] to the end. The voices of course are repeated without being labelled except where the speakers address one another.*)

CHURCHILL. As clear as day. Not a syllable slurred! They might have been shouting in Hyde Park. They arrived at no decision. They were forewarned that they could be overheard. Good Heavens, there are infinite possibilities in this!. We must act at once. Go immediately Bracken and find out where the inventor lives. If he has parted with his invention to the United States Government, and if he has not, on what terms will he part with it.

BRACKEN. It says here 'in an island off Nantucket'.

CHURCHILL (*consulting map*). That might be any island off Long Island: Fisher's Island, Block Island, Plum Island, Gardiner's, Ram Island. This brings us nowhere.

BRACKEN. That was Hitler's voice ordering a destroyer, two destroyers to be sent to seize the machine. They must know where they are going.

CHURCHILL. If they don't they have Fifth Columnists who will soon give them the required information. We cannot seize the property of any American citizen. We can pay for it. We will pay for it.

BRACKEN. What about leasing it?

CHURCHILL. There is no doubt about it. Beaverbrook was right.

BRACKEN. Sorry to interrupt, so was I right, too.

CHURCHILL. It is an invention of the gravest importance. And we must get it or it will get us.

BRACKEN. What have we got to hide. Our principles are known over the whole earth.

CHURCHILL. Now don't fly off in a gust of oratory. It is true that we have principles and that we stand by them very often to our own detriment. It is against the unprincipled peoples we are fighting. We have not gone back on our word to Ireland. We have not seized her territory or commandeered her ports.

BRACKEN. No; but you are ruling her out of the market cutting her prices. The English never defeat their enemies, they disqualify them 'As Dooley says'.

CHURCHILL. Another Irish buffoon.

BRACKEN. No, a half fellow countryman of yours this time, Peter Findlay Dunne.

CHURCHILL. To continue, we cannot send battleships to raid America and steal this invention as Germany stole the bomb sights. But we can send an Admiral to call and interview the inventor and suggest that at least he may share his invention with us and with the United States. We have to keep our plans secret from the enemy. Military decisions are what we have got to hide. And now back with you to your Ministry of Information. You have done pretty well.

## CURTAIN

## ACT III SCENE 3

*Cottage gable as in Act I, Scene 1.* RAYMOND *and* BIANCA.

RAYMOND. He was only on a pleasure trip, Bianca. I saw him get off the boat. He may have come out of curiosity or he may have heard rumours of your Father's invention and thought it worth his while to stay around and find out.

BIANCA. You are joining in with Daddy who hates him now. After all he floated the Company.

RAYMOND. I don't want to go into it all over again. But what he did was to take the honest invention of your Father and to associate his good name with a dishonest company and at the same time bind your Father to recover the voices and to make scandalous examples of anyone who refused to be blackmailed by Wave Lengths Limited. I am afraid that he has committed a felony and that your Father is tied up in it.

BIANCA. You are only saying this because you think that I love him.

RAYMOND. I am afraid you do.

BIANCA. What difference would that make to you?

RAYMOND. It would make every difference.

BIANCA. How?

RAYMOND (*missing it*). He is not worthy of you. He is a cheat and an exploiter. He did not hesitate to put your Father within the reach of the law while all the time he was making love to his daughter.

BIANCA. I suppose that if he is not worthy of me, it means that you are?

RAYMOND. I can work for you, Bianca.

    (DR FRENGLY'S *head appears.*)

THE PROFESSOR. So there you are billing and cooeing as it should be. As it should be. When I was Raymond's age I would have considered myself fortunate if I could win the friendship of a charming companion in the sweet of the year.

RAYMOND. I am afraid I have not got that good luck.

THE PROFESSOR. She's but a lassie yet. Bide your time, Raymond. Bide your time.

BIANCA. Daddy, may I go down to the harbour? I will be back in time to give you your lunch. There is a crowd about the harbour.

THE PROFESSOR. Well if you are not satisfied with listening to them from here run along, but leave me Raymond. I can give him some transcriptions. (*Exit* BIANCA.) Raymond, since you last helped me, I have obtained rather amusing and valuable results. Recently as you know I announced on the radios of Berlin that there would be a meeting of the Führer with the Supreme Command and that its transactions would be broadcasted. Apparently it was taken for a hoax until the crowd assembled and overheard all that went on, even to the radio expert's groans when he got an attack of appendicitis. I have by this time identified von Brauschitsch's voice. Come in and I will dial him up as he talked to Hitler. Come in. (RAYMOND *enters cottage*.)

VOICE. I take a very serious view of this. Not, mein Führer, that I would exceed you in anything, much less in taking things seriously. But do not think it a mark of disrespect if I take a very serious view indeed. This invention would dissolve army discipline and soften any army. Consider what would happen if troops were to listen-in on our calculations of the cost of any military operation in terms of their lives.

HITLER. Thanks to Hirsch we are surrounded by a lower dome of reflection, a deflecting umbrella in a magnetic field. We are safe from international eaves'-dropping. You are right in taking a very serious view. No nation could continue the struggle for *Lebensraum*. Every move in a general's mind would be anticipated and countered. There could be no war. Peace would break out on earth. What then?

VON BRAUSCHITSCH. Then the Jews who thrive in peace would rule the earth.

HITLER. Nonsense. They thrive on war. Don't you see it?

VON BRAUSCHITSCH. Well. But I am only a soldier with a military training.

HITLER. You would think that it required a metaphysical training to agree with me.

VON BRAUSCHITSCH. Hirsch has assured you that we are sound proof? And yet Hirsch laughed at Wave Lengths Limited.

HITLER. Two different things. One purported to absorb past voices. This Hirschian roofing is composed of a network of jamming waves. Why are you so concerned?

VON BRAUSCHITSCH. Because when we were not protected but exposed, as it proved, to the hearing of the town – and who knows how much further? You threatened to send a destroyer to confiscate the property of an American inventor. Has he not been forewarned by your threat?

HITLER. Von Brauschitsch, you are very clever. I thought of that and denied my intentions immediately.

VON BRAUSCHITSCH. So whom are you sending?

(Enter DR FRENGLY [the PROFESSOR] and RAYMOND arm in arm.)

HITLER. Captain Otto Niedelmyer of the destroyer Tirpis and Capt. Kurt Freuhling of the destroyer Adofind.)

DR FRENGLY [THE PROFESSOR]. So you see, Raymond, they think that they are sound proof. And I certainly am forewarned by Hitler's threat. This is rather a lonely Island. I do not weigh very much. It would be comparatively easy to kidnap me and to carry me off to a waiting submarine, any night, instruments and all.

RAYMOND. But, dear doctor, do take precautions or let me get precautions taken for you. You must think of Bianca if you won't think of yourself.

DR FRENGLY (smiling and shaking his head). No, Raymond you are a good boy to take such care of me. But if there be anything in my invention it will take care of me and of itself. I must work late this night.

(Enter BIANCA hastening.)

BIANCA. Who do you think they have arrested? A man called Clitterhouse who said that he was a member of Wave Lengths Limited and that he had come to call on you. He had a short-wave set and he was listening in to Lord Haw-Haw when they caught him.

THE PROFESSOR (cogitating). Let me see. Let me see. I think that I heard the voice of Clitterhouse when they were founding the fraudulent company. Bianca, would you care to listen and to try if you can to recognise it. You have heard Clitterhouse of course?

BIANCA. Yes a few moments ago when they were leading him away. He was very frightened and expostulating very loudly.

THE PROFESSOR. Well, take seats and I will repeat the company's meeting or rather a part of it where were can identify Clitterhouse. (Exits into cottage.)

THE VOICES. Mr Chairman, may I indulge the hope that Mr Souse will give my colleague and me at least the opportunity of justifying ourselves and me the chance of establishing my bona fides with you Gentlemen, and my goodwill . . .

BIANCA. Why it's Leopold!

THE VOICES. A word with my Colleague will convince him. I have failed to do so. (CHAIRMAN.) Will you talk to his partner and ask him what it's all about. Satisfy yourself, or don't satisfy yourself; but don't come in and tell me, Sam and expert Clitterhouse that we're a lot of bloody fools. Thank you, Mr Chairman.

BIANCA. Yes he speaks like that under his breath and mincingly.

SOUSE. What does he want me to do?

(*Telephone rings.*)

BIANCA. Oh, how distinctly you can hear the telephone.

THE VOICES. Excuse me, Gentlemen. Is that you Bianca? Yes, Dear. Oh, I had no time to say goodbye. But have patience, Dear. This is very important. Ask your father to the phone for a minute. (SAM'S *voice.*) Is Bianca blonde?

LEOPOLD'S VOICE (*continued*). Cut it out. There is nothing like that. She is just a means to an end. It is. Yes. It is important.

BIANCA (*weeping*). Daddy. Daddy. I don't want to hear any more. 'A means to an end'.

## CURTAIN

# ACT III SCENE 4

*The Cottage. Dawn.*

> DR FRENGLY [THE PROFESSOR] *and* RAYMOND *are discovered fastening a large packing case upon the lawn.*

DR FRENGLY. You were a good boy, Raymond, to work with an old man all night. You know all I can impart to you. You are my scientific heir, the inheritor of all my methods. Take this to Washington. Offer it to the Government. If it is too modern for them, offer it to the Navy. Or to the Army. Give a demonstration. It will put them in the advantageous position of being always forewarned. It is all we can do. They will see to it that they are forearmed. This is no time to offer the historical research of which it is capable to any of the Universities. It does not require the rehearsal of the death of Caesar to teach people, now that civilisation can be assassinated and the work of generations undone by a series of treacherous stabbings. This duplicate is smaller than my original but somewhat clumsy apparatus; but it has the advantage of being portable. I have taken care that the patents do not fall into lay hands. The police will take it beyond the reach of Fifth Columnists and spies. Take it to the station. Here I must await the day and what it may bring. I have one, nay, I have many things for which to be grateful, but one is that by means of my machine Leopold's duplicity was discovered and you are reconciled to my little girl.

> (*Exit* RAYMOND *with case on a barrow.*)

RAYMOND. Goodbye, Sir.

DR FRENGLY (*quoting to himself*)
> 'He gave man speech and speech created Thought
> Which is the measure of the Universe.'

> (*The sounds of the chugging of a naval launch come from the machine within.*)

633

DR FRENGLY. I wonder which navy will get here first. That sounds like German words of command. (*Sounds*)

*Stemmen Sie das fuss uber das galender. Stemmen Sie! Herr Leutnant Also.

> (DR FRENGLY *looks at his watch. He sits somewhat languidly. The wash of waves is heard. Day brightens. Two German sea Captains enter with drawn revolvers.*)

CAPTAIN OTTO NEIDELMEYER. Do I address Dr Frengly?

DR FRENGLY (*without rising*). You do. But whom do I address?

CAPTAIN OTTO NEIDELMEYER. You address Capt. Kurt Freuhling here and Capt. Otto Neidelmeyer, in my own person.

DR FRENGLY. You are trespassing on private property.

CAPT KURT FREUHLING. There is no private property when universal values are at stake. Just as there must be no private instruments to intrude on and to upset secret deliberations and to make private councils common property. We are here to take you and your apparatus on board a destroyer. If you comply you will not be hurt. If you resist we have orders to wreck the apparatus and ensure that you can never build another one.

DR FRENGLY. Kurt and Otto. Now where did I hear those names? One moment, Captains Courageous. One last revolution of the dials. Oh, no. I have no intention of turning away on my own native soil from any invaders, be they uniformed or clad as spies. One moment. You can look at me through the glass door.

CAPTAIN OTTO (*to* CAPTAIN KURT). Keep him covered.

FEMALE VOICE. Otto, Otto, Darling. you will bruise my lips. Why must you be so frantic.

OTTO'S VOICE. Karin, loveliest. I have orders to sail at once on a secret mission. I did not mean to be so rough.

FEMALE VOICE. And leave me to the gloomy love of Kurt.

OTTO'S VOICE. That old plum is under secret orders too.

KURT (*to* OTTO *in amazement.*) My wife, you scoundrel!

OTHER FEMALE VOICE. Kurt you are not old. Your face may be purple but it is the lovely purple that the sea takes on at evening when I sit on the quay of Cherburg praying for your safe return. You have such serene and gentle ways, not like my wildebeast, Otto.

OTTO (*to* KURT.) My wife you scoundrel.

> (*Alarm sirens sound from the sea. In the distance at the side of the cottage two closely moving destroyers can be seen far off: scarcely seen owing to fog.*)

---

*Editor's Note:* "Werfen Sie das Fass über das Geländer. Werfen Sie! Herr Leutnant!"
(This is what the author probably dictated to the stenographer in America who seems to have typed phoenetically.)

KURT TO OTTO. Two enemy ships hard by. Two British battleships. No salvos!

(*Exeunt. Enter* THE PROFESSOR.)

DR FRENGLY. (*smiling*). I have always held that idle words are the cause of half the woe in the world.

(*Enter two British Admirals.*).

ADMIRAL HALYARDS-TOPPENHAM. Dr Frengly, I presume?

DR. FRENGLY. To whom and to what do I owe this intrusion?

ADMIRAL HALYARDS-TOPPENHAM. Dr Frengly, we do not intend to intrude on you or to trespass on your property. But at the present time we have to act in such a way as to afford you protection from piratical raiders. We had to act with caution and forego the usual preliminaries of politeness before making a call. This is Captain Gasket-Spurling.

(*The* CAPTAIN bows. FRENGLY *rises and shakes his hand.*)

CAPTAIN GASKET-SPURLING. How do you do, Professor.

ADMIRAL HALYARDS-TOPPENHAM. To continue, Professor, we bear a proposal from His Majesty's Government to you. We would like to make an offer of remuneration to you for the inclusive use, that is limited to the use by your Government, or for the exclusive use of this invention of yours for the duration of the War. If you have already offered it to your own Government, well and good. If not, we are open to negotiate with you, always bearing in mind that we do not intend to withhold any information which it may bring from the USA Government. Eh, Spurling?

CAPTAIN GASKET-SPURLING. Quite, quite, Sir. And of course Dr Frengly will believe us when we assure him that we intended no trespass. We had to anticipate trespass from elsewhere.

DR FRENGLY. Gentlemen, you are too late.

BOTH SEAMEN. Too late! Have you been raided?

DR FRENGLY. Very nearly so.

BOTH SEAMEN. Germany?

DR FRENGLY (*nods.*)

(BOTH SEAMEN *look at each other.*)

ADMIRAL HALYARDS-TOPPENHAM. Are we too late?

DR FRENGLY. No. No. No. There was a raid this morning shortly after dawn. I had anticipated it from orders I heard given. I and my apparatus were to be kidnapped and taken aboard a destroyer, in fact aboard two destroyers and conveyed to Germany.

CAPTAIN GASKET-SPURLING. How did you escape, Sir?

DR FRENGLY. There was no need to escape. The captains overheard each other's wives talking and thought fit to fight it out on board their battleships. That's all.

ADMIRAL HALYARDS-TOPPENHAM. Compromising conversation. What they call in England *crim. con.* Eh?
    (*Laughs.*)
CAPTAIN GASKET-SPURLING. Jolly good instrument, what? Reminds me of a story told of an Admiral who in order to protect his wife while at sea sent a letter to a lieutenant informing him that his intentions to her were no longer welcome. The lieutenant wrote back. 'I got your circular this morning, Sir.'
    (*Cannonade heard from the sea. The seamen start.*)
ADMIRAL HALYARDS-TOPPENHAM. Enemy action? Damn, I wish I had brought my spy-glass.
    (*Puffs of smoke descried dimly out at sea.*)
CAPTAIN GASKET-SPURLING (*as* FRENGLY *rises.*) Got a pair of binoculars, Sir?
    (*Exit* FRENGLY.)
ADMIRAL HALYARDS-TOPPENHAM. Doesn't sound like our guns though it is hard to tell the timing at this distance.
    (*Enter* DR FRENGLY *with a pair of binoculars which he hands to the* ADMIRAL.)
DR FRENGLY. Would you care to have a look through these (*cannonade continues growing.*)
ADMIRAL HALYARDS-TOPPENHAM. Our ships are not in action. Nor are the men at stations. I can't make it out. Can you, Spurling?
CAPTAIN GASKET-SPURLING. By Gad!
ADMIRAL HALYARDS-TOPPENHAM. What do you see, Spurling.
CAPTAIN GASKET-SPURLING. Seems incredible to me. Sir have a look.
    (*Hands over binoculars.*)
ADMIRAL HALYARDS-TOPPENHAM. It is incredible. Two German destroyers sinking one another!
DR FRENGLY. Which goes to show that if Hitler has no use for women his Navy has.
ADMIRAL HALYARDS-TOPPENHAM. What's that? What's that?
DR FRENGLY. They are fighting a duel with battleships instead of pistols. To prove that the Navy as a whole stands for sex. Would you care to have me record the remarks on board your ship?
ADMIRAL HALYARDS-TOPPENHAM. Thank you. No. I rather fancy that I can guess them. There will be few assertions of regret. I will dial on to the village and see if I can pick anything up. There's the church. A young fellow is talking to the parson. Why, it's my assistant's voice. But she has consented and I feel that her father won't object.
PARSON. All the better then, and all the more easily you can get her parent's permission which you understand I must ask for in cases where the bride is very young.

ADMIRAL HALYARDS-TOPPENHAM (*to* DR FRENGLY). So there is to be a marriage in your family, Professor.

CAPTAIN GASKET-SPURLING. My felicitations, Sir.

[*At this point some of the TS is missing. Presumably* ADMIRAL HALYARDS-TOPPENHAM *has seen two Italian battleships and hands the binoculars to* CAPTAIN GASKET-SPURLING, *asking him to confirm what he has seen*].

CAPTAIN GASKET-SPURLING. Their washing is hanging out to dry.

ADMIRAL HALYARDS-TOPPENHAM. In all my life, I never heard of such a thing in any Navy.

DR FRENGLY. Washing their dirty linen in public. It may be symbolical. (*Dials.*)

ITALIAN VOICE. We can talk about Marconi who was the first to point out the possibility of the thing. Then invite him on board and off we go.

ADMIRAL HALYARDS-TOPPENHAM. What was all that?

DR. FRENGLY. Just another little plot to kidnap me and take me on board.

ADMIRAL HALYARDS-TOPPENHAM. What, on a battleship dressed like that! What do you intend to do? Shall I sink 'em?

DR FRENGLY. Well, for the sake of peace! (*dials*) (*cannonading heard*).

CAPTAIN GASKET-SPURLING. They are doing the very thing that the Germans did. Committing suicide with ships!

ADMIRAL HALYARDS-TOPPENHAM. By Gad Dr Frengly. You are right. War cannot continue in the face of a machine like yours. But where are the French Navy?

DR FRENGLY. They would not mind. You see it's more or less normal among the French.

CAPTAIN GASKET-SPURLING. How about the Japs, Dr Frengly?

DR FRENGLY. No nation may hope to defeat a great nation by surprise. This instrument made in America, is designed to catch treachery by the throat.

CAPTAIN GASKET-SPURLING. To give the Son of Heaven hell, in fact? Doctor, I think that between us we have got something as you would say.

(*Both* SAILORS *shake the Professor's hand.*)

DR FRENGLY. Gentlemen, I have a request to make. Will you breakfast with me in the morning? There is a wedding in my family and it would make the picture perfect if you were to attend it. It is not without significance or symbolism that the first authentic voice I identified out of the Past was this . . . one moment (*exits into cottage. His head appears at the little window. Disappears*). Just a moment. (*Noise of radio, then*)

FROM FAIREST CREATURES WE DESIRE INCREASE
THAT THEREBY BEAUTY'S ROSE MIGHT NEVER DIE

(THE SEAMEN *look at one another.*)
ADMIRAL HALYARDS-TOPPENHAM. Sounds like a seed catalogue, eh?
CAPTAIN GASKET-SPURLING. Sounds like amateur theatricals in Ireland.
ADMIRAL HALYARDS-TOPPENHAM. On the other hand it may be as he says, symbolical.
CAPTAIN GASKET-SPURLING. Quite. Sir, quite.
(*Enter* DR FRENGLY *with drinks.* THE SEAMEN *rise.*)
THE TWO SEAMEN. Till to-morrow, then (*shake hands.*)
DR. FRENGLY. Till to-morrow, Gentlemen. (*They raise their glasses.*)
THE TWO SEAMEN. Here's to the stars and stripes.
DR FRENGLY. The dawn is diurnal.
              But the stars are eternal.

# Appendix 4

# THE CONTENTS OF SINGLE VOLUMES OF GOGARTY'S POETRY

*HYPERTHULEANEA* (1916)
To the Muse
The Feast
To George Russell
To a Mushroom
To his Friend the Apothecary Poet
The Isles of Greece
To an Aviator
To an Art Critic
To M.—
Westward
To his Friend to Try another
  Tavern
Urbs Intacta
To Kasimir Dunin Markievicz
Spirat adhuc Amor
On first looking into Kraft-Ebing's
  Psychopathia Sexualis
Sonnet: When the Clearance was
  intended to the City
'Memento Homo quia pulvis es' (at La
  Trappe)
To the Rev. George O'Neill
The Two Despairs
To a Clever Little Lecher
Conscription
To an Amphisbaenic Friend
To a Bearded Dealer in Old Objects of Art
The Dandelion
Helen's lamp
A Line from Rabelais
Epitaph
Epilogue

Poems from *SECRET SPRINGS OF DUBLIN SONG* (1918)
Spring in Dublin
A Double Ballad of Dublin
To Citizen Elwood in South America
Rondeau
The Poet to the Physician [by Seumas
  O'Sullivan]
The Physician Replies
To Carson, Swimmer of Sandycove
From 'The Queen's Threshold'
The Old Man Refreshing Himself in the
  Morning
On the Death of his Aunt
Praise and Friendship
The Question. I.
The Reply. II. [by Seumas
  O'Sullivan]
Threnody on the Death of Diogenes, the
  Doctor's Dog
The Pilgrimage to Plunkett House
A Lament for George Moore
To George Moore on the Occasion of
  his Wedding

Poems from *THE SHIP AND OTHER POEMS* (1918)
[illustrated by Jack B. Yeats]
The Centaurs
The Ship
The Old Goose
The Image Maker
Castle Corrib

Aphorism
To Reformers
Marcus Curtius
The Crowing of a Cock

*WILD APPLES* (1929)
New York: Jonathan Cape and Harrison
    Smith
Introduction by A.E.
The Crab Tree
Galway
With a Coin from Syracuse
Portrait With Background
Upon Horan
Portrait
Portrait
Portrait
After Galen
Portrait
When It Is Too Late
Portrait
The Yacht
To the Moon
The Waveless Bay
On Troy
To Berkeley
To a Friend
To Æ. Going to America
To W. B. Yeats
Marcus Curtius
Song
Fresh Fields
Kingdoms
To the Fixed Stars
To Some Spiteful Persons
The Plum Tree by the House
Melsungen
This Kip
To the Maids Not to Walk in the Wind
Ringsend
The Weathercock
Petersen Lane
O Boys, O Boys!
To Reformers
To a Cock
Praise
The Nettle
The Ship
The Phœnix
The Emperor's Dream
A Pithy Prayer Against Love

The Crowing of a Cock
Hertes Hele
Verse
Lullaby
Liffey Bridge

*WILD APPLES* (1930)
Dublin: Cuala Press
Preface by W.B. Yeats
The Crab Tree
Galway
With a Coin from Syracuse
Portrait with background
Portrait ['Lights on her gaudy hair']
Another Portrait [Jane W— 'She does
    not seem to care']
When it is too Late
After Galen
To some Spiteful Persons
To Æ going to America
Aphorism [Ringsend]
A Pithy Prayer against Love
Farewell to the Princess
Petersen Lane
Sandymount
Dedication
Kingdoms
To Moorehead, Blind
Per Iter Tenebricosum
The Oak-Wood
The Conquest
The Exorcism
Excommunication
Off Sicily
Lambay
Castle Corrib
The Image-Maker
To Death
To the Fixed Stars
Nymphis Et Fontibus
Tot Milia Formosarum
The Plum Tree by the House
Release

*SELECTED POEMS* (1933)
New York: The Macmillan Company
*Shapes of Earth and Sky*
The Crab Tree
With a Coin from Syracuse
Portrait with Background
Non Dolet

APPENDICES – THE CONTENTS OF SINGLE VOLUMES

Connemara
Praise
Good Luck
The Casting
The Oak Wood
Dunsany Castle
Dedication
Colophon

*OTHERS TO ADORN* (1938)
London: Rich and Cowan
*Shapes of Earth and Sky*
The Crab Tree
With a Coin from Syracuse
Portrait with Background
Non Dolet
Virgil
Golden Stockings
Portrait [Diana clothed]
The Waveless Bay (Kiltymon)
Nymphis et Fontibus
The Phœnix
To the Lady — (Who acted Queen
    Elizabeth for the screen)
Kingdoms
O Boys! O Boys!
I Tremble to Think
To the Moon
To Petronius Arbiter
Non Blandula Illa
Fresh Fields
The Plum Tree by the House
Melsungen
Liffey Bridge
The Ship
To the Lady —
Earth and Sea
Sunt apud infernos tot milia formosarum
Ringsend [after reading Tolstoi]
Marcus Curtius
To a Cock
Concerning Hermione
    I.    The Conquest
    II.   The Exorcism
    III.  Excommunication
    IV.   Silence
    V.    A Sound
Centaurs
Anglers
To the Liffey with the Swans
High Tide at Malahide

Per Iter Tenebricosum
The Mill at Naul
The Image-Maker
To Ethne
Off Sicily
The Old Goose
Verse
Reflection
Lullaby
The Emperor's Dream
Palinode
To Death

*Wit and Satire*
After Galen
On Troy
To Some Spiteful Persons
To a Boon Compan ion
To the Maids not to Walk in the Wind
To a Mushroom
The Nettle
A Pithy Prayer Against Love

*Cavalier Accents*
Tell Me Now
Begone, Sweet Ghost
Perfection
Gaze on Me

*Personal*
To a Friend
To A.E. Going to America
To W.B. Yeats who says that his Castle
    of Ballylee is his Monument
To My Friend the Rt. Hon. Lorcan
    Galeran (A great householder)
To My Portrait, by Augustus John
To Augustus John
To the Poet W. B. Yeats, Winner of the
    Nobel Prize 1924
Back from the Country
Panurge
Choric Song of the Ladies of Lemnos
'Aeternae Lucis Redditor'
Limestone and Water
New Bridge
I Wonder
Europa and the Bull
Thrush in Ash
Applied Poetry
Sub Ilice

New Forms
Women
To Ninde
To 'Aphrodite'
Leda and the Swan
Release
Faithful even unto Freud
Domi
To Edward Moreton Drax, 18th Baron
    Dunsany
Farewell to the Princess
Alas!
To James Stephens
And So On
Death may be very Gentle
To Shadu 'L-Mulk
Connemara
Praise
Good Luck
The Casting
The Oak Wood
Dunsany Castle
Dedication
Colophon

*ELBOW ROOM* (1939)
Dublin: Cuala Press
The Forge
The Blackbird in the Town
Elbow Room
Applied Poetry
All the Pictures
To Lydia
Thinking Long
Fog Horns
Time, Gentlemen, Time!
Sung in Spring
Angels
Anachronism

*ELBOW ROOM AND OTHER
    POEMS* (1941)
New York: Duell, Sloan and Pearce
It has not proved possible to obtain a
copy of this volume nor to see a list of
its contents. The edition was limited to
75 copies of which 60 were printed (L,
p.298). The Editor and publisher would
very much like to hear from anyone
who possesses a copy. It is likely that the
contents are the same as those of *Elbow*

*Room* (1942) published by the same
New York firm. The Library of
Congress does not have a copy nor
do the New York Public Library and
the Berg Collection. The Houghton
Library, Harvard University, does not
include the book in its large Gogarty
collection nor does the Ellen Clark
Bertrand Library at Bucknell University.
The title is not listed in the *National
Union Catalog* pre 1956, nor in the
*Cumulative Book Index* 1938–1942, nor
in the *American Book Publishing Record*
vol. 7, Cumulative 1876–1949.

*ELBOW ROOM* (1942)
New York: Duell, Sloan and Pearce
The Forge
The Blackbird in the Town
Elbow Room
All the Pictures
To Lydia
Thinking Long
Fog Horns
Time, Gentlemen, Time!
An Appeal from the Judgement of
    Paris
A Prayer for His Lady
For a Birthday
The Eternal Recurrence
To an Old Lady
To a Friend in the Country
Sung in Spring
Angels
Anachronism
The Isles of Greece
High above Ohio
'Aeternae Lucis Redditor'
Elegy on the Archpoet William Butler
    Yeats Lately Dead

*PERENNIAL* (1944)
Baltimore, Maryland: Contemporary
Poetry
Dedication: To James Augustine Healy
Perennial
Croker of Ballinagarde
Song made by Sir Dinadan for Sir
    Tristram That an Harper Might Play It
    Before King Mark
Remembering Albert Spickers

High Tide at Malahide
Suburban Spring
Leave-Taking
Between Brielle and Manasquan
To Major Eugene F. Kinkead
Elegy to the Archpoet William Butler
    Yeats, Lately Dead (with notes)
High above Ohio
The Mill at Naul
Leda and the Swan

*PERENNIAL* (1946)
London: Constable & Company
Dedication: To James Augustine Healy
Perennial
To Major Eugene F. Kinkead
The Water Lily
The Dragon Fly
Improvements
If Sight Were Sound
Croker of Ballinagarde
Oughterard
The Apple Tree
Bill Baveler
Dawn in Vermont
The Airman's Breastplate
Between Brielle and Manasquan
High Above Ohio
Remembering Albert Spickers
Elegy on the Archpoet William Butler
    Yeats Lately Dead
Glenasmole
Farrell O'Reilly
Song made by Sir Dinadan for Sir
    Tristram That an Harper Might Play It
    Before King Mark
Leda and the Swan

*UNSELECTED POEMS* (1954)
Baltimore, Maryland: Contemporary
    Poetry (Volume 10 in Distinguished
    Poets Series, ed. Mary Owings Miller)
Adam and Eve
Farrell O'Reilly
Noah's Ark
Ars Longa

One World
Dispute between the Head and Heart of
    the Poet
The Phoenix and the Unicorn
Job's Healer
Without Venus
A Report on the Sexless Behaviour of
    Certain Microscopic Individuals

*PENULTIMATE POEMS*
To a Moth
Free Will
The Village of Plandome
Sodom and Gomorrah
Before Psychiatry
Perfection [This has the same title as
    another poem in *Collected Poems*]
Whodunit who didn't
Supersonic
Make us aware
Full Circle
Misgivings
When
A Wish
The Eternal Feminine
Psychoanalysis I
Psychoanalysis II [This has been added to
    the text from a TS in Bucknell]
The Changeling I
The Changeling II
The Weathercock [appeared in *Wild
    Apples* (1929)]

Poems in Gogarty's list for this volume
    which appeared in *Unselected Poems*
    (1954)
The Phoenix and the Unicorn
Adam and Eve
Without Venus
A Report on the Sexless Behaviour of
    Certain Microscopic Immortals
One World
The Dispute Between the Head and the
    Heart of the Poet
Without Venus

# ACKNOWLEDGEMENTS
# AND ANNOTATIONS

# ACKNOWLEDGEMENTS

I would like to express my appreciation to those libraries which have allowed me access to unpublished material and provided texts of various editions and individual printings of Gogarty's poems. My thanks are also owed for permission to publish various poems in this edition, and for this I record my gratitude to the following libraries and individuals whose collections have contributed copy texts (the Notes on the text for Part Three gives details of the sources used):

The Ellen Clark Bertrand Library, Bucknell University; the Beinecke Rare Book and Manuscript Library, Yale University; the British Library, London; the Library of Congress, Washington; the Carl A. Kroch Library, Cornell University; the Miller Library, Special Collections, Colby College; Special Collections, the University of Delaware Library; the Gilbert Library, City of Dublin Library, Dublin Corporation Public Libraries; Dublin City Archives; the Collection of the late Oliver Duane Gogarty S.C.; the Collection of Professor Warwick Gould; the Houghton Library, Harvard University; the Lilly Library, Indiana University, Bloomington, Indiana; the Collection of Professor Brendan Kennelly; the Collection of Professor J. B. Lyons; the Mercer Library, the Royal College of Surgeons in Ireland, Dublin; the National Library of Ireland, Dublin; the Library of the University of North Carolina, Chapel Hill; the Harry Ransome Humanities Research Center, the University of Texas at Austin; the Royal Hibernian Academy of Arts; the University of Reading Library; the Collection of Professor Colin Smythe; the James A. Healy Collection, the Stanford University Libraries; the Library of Trinity College, Dublin; and the Collection of Guy St John Williams.

I have had generous and very welcome assistance from individual librarians and should like to acknowledge my indebtedness to them, in particular to:

Mr Charles Benson (Trinity College, Dublin); Dr Claire Blinn (Centre d'Etudes Supériences de la Renaissance, Tours), Mr Michael

649

Bott (University of Reading); Ms Mary Clark (Dublin City Archives), Ms Nancy Dagle (Bucknell University); Mlle Géraldine D'Amico (Ambassade de France, Londres), Mr C. J. Lance Dubosq (Cornell University); Ms Sarah Dodgson (The Athenaeum); Ms Beatrice M. Doran (Mercer Library, Royal College of Surgeons in Ireland); Ms Doris Dysinger (Bucknell University); Mrs Deirdre Ellis-King (Dublin Corporation Public Libraries); Ms Madeleine Gaughan (Mercer Library, Royal College of Surgeons in Ireland); Ms Susan Halper (Harvard University); Ms Maureen D. Heher (Yale University); Ms L. Rebecca Johnson (University of Delaware); Ms Maire Kennedy (Dublin Corporation Public Libraries); Ms Lorna Knight (Cornell University); Ms Brid Leahy (Dublin City Archives); Ms Jane Maxwell (Trinity College, Dublin); Mr Alan McMillan (The Presbyterian Historical Society of Ireland); Ms Leslie Morris (Harvard University); Mr Timothy Murray (University of Delaware); Ms Veronica Morrow (Trinity College, Dublin); Dr Eilis Ni Dhuibhne (The National Library of Ireland); Mr Tim Noakes (Stanford University); Mr Padraig O'Cearbhaill (The Placenames Branch, Ordnance Survey, Ireland); Ms Mary O'Doherty (Mercer Library, the Royal College of Surgeons in Ireland); Ms Teresa O'Donnell (Archivist, Guinness Ireland Group); Dr Donall Ó Luanaigh (The National Library of Ireland); Ms Felicitas O'Mahoney (Trinity College, Dublin); Mr Seán Ó Seanóir (Trinity College, Dublin); Mr David Power (Trinity College, Dublin); Ms Rose Reddy (Trinity College, Dublin); Dr Raymond Refaussé (Representative Church Body Library, Dublin); Ms Nancy Rinehart (Colby College, Maine); Ms Alexandra Rogers (Harry Ransome Humanities Research Center, University of Texas at Austin); Mr William George Simpson (Trinity College, Dublin); Ms Gillian Smith (Mercer Library, Royal College of Surgeons in Ireland); Mr Malcolm Taylor (The Vaughan Williams Memorial Library, the English Folk Dance and Song Society); Mr John E. White (University of North Carolina at Chapel Hill) and Dr Frances Wood (Oriental and India Office Collection, the British Library).

The Preface by W. B. Yeats to the *Collected Poems* is reprinted from the introduction to the *Oxford Book of Modern Verse 1892–1935*, and the Prefaces by W. B. Yeats to *An Offering of Swans* (1923) and *Wild Apples* (1930) are all reprinted by permission of A. P. Watt Limited on behalf of Michael B. Yeats, and Scribner, New York, a Division of Simon & Schuster Inc. A. E.'s Preface to *Selected Poems of Oliver St. John Gogarty* and his Introduction to *Wild Apples* (1929) are reprinted by permission of A. M. Heath Limited on behalf of the Estate of Diarmuid Russell. The publishers have been unable to obtain permission to print the Preface by Horace Reynolds as attempts to find his heirs have failed. They would be grateful for any information concerning them. I am much indebted to the British Academy for a generous Research Grant and to the Royal Society of Edinburgh for a Travel Grant. These awards have greatly facilitated the research and travel involved in the completion of this edition.

I have been given unstinting assistance in annotating the poems and plays, in solving some of the many problems of identification of people, of places and of quotations. To those who gave me so much generous help and encouragement I extend heartfelt thanks. They include: Professor Thomas Acton; Professor Michael Alexander; Dr Sarah Alyn-Stacey; Professor Peter Bander-van Duren; Dr Moff Betts; Dr Angela Bourke; Professor Brian Boydell; Professor Terence Brown; Dr Maurice James Craig; Professor Anne Crookshank; Professor Adèle Crowder; Professor Christopher Crowder; Sir Kenneth Dover; Mr Mark St. John Ellis; Professor Roy Foster; Professor Gerard Gillen; Mr Andrew Goodspeed; Professor Warwick Gould; Dr Tony Green; Miss Charlotte Hartwell; Mr Leslie Hayward; Mr Michael Holroyd; Dr John Izod; Dr Bo Jeffares; Mr Antony Kamm; Professor Brendan Kennelly; Professor Donal Kenrick; Mr Declan Kiely; Professor Adele King; Professor Antony Levi; Professor John Luce; Professor J. B. Lyons; Professor W. J. McCormack; Professor Brian Charles McGing; Mr Alasdair Macrae; Mrs Daphne Maxwell; Mr R. E. Newell; Mr and Mrs Oliver O'Brien; Professor Robert Mahoney; Mr Omar Pound; Professor Hans Reiss; Mr Stewart F. Sanderson; Professor Masaru Sekine; Mr William George Simpson; Professor Colin Smythe; Dr Bruce Stewart; Dr David Sutton; Dr Loreto Todd; Ms Deirdre Toomey; Major General Christopher Tyler; Professor J. R. Watson; Professor Robert Welch; Mrs Anna MacBride White; Professor Harry White; Mr Guy St John Williams; Professor Colette Winn; Dr Robert Woof and Professor Barbara Wright.

I should like to offer special gratitude to some of those listed above who have been so unfailingly resourceful and unstintingly patient in aiding my research: to Andrew Goodspeed, who is preparing an edition of Gogarty's letters; Declan Kiely, whose bibliographical skills are outstanding; Jack Lyons, medical historian par excellence, whose biographical insights into Gogarty's life are unique; Daphne Maxwell, whose historical and topographical knowledge has proved invaluable; Colin Smythe, scholarly publisher, wise, tolerant and incisively informative; Bruce Stewart, excellent bibliographer and critic; Deirdre Toomey, whose ability to track down the obscure is inimitable; and Bob Welch, who is so knowledgeable about Irish poetry.

Where individual poems in *Penultimate Poems* are marked G in the *Notes on the Text* the texts of these poems were part of the collection of Gogarty's son, the late Oliver Duane Gogarty S.C., and were very kindly supplied for the present edition by Francis Warner.

My wife, Jeanne, has helped in the reading of difficult manuscripts and provided her usual stimulus and support during what has been a very pleasurable period, of getting to know more about the minutiae of Gogarty's most rewarding writing, something ever increasingly appreciated over many years.

A.N.J.
Fife Ness, 2001

# CHRONOLOGY OF
# GOGARTY'S LIFE

1878    Oliver St. John Gogarty, eldest son of Dr Henry Joseph Kelly Gogarty and his wife Margaret (neé Oliver) born at 5 Rutland Square, Dublin on 17 August.

1890    Oliver goes to the O'Connell School, North Richmond Street, Dublin (convenient to the family's country residence, Fairfield House, standing in 7 acres in Glasnevin).

1891    Death of Dr Henry Gogarty.

1892    Oliver goes to Mungret, a Jesuit School near Limerick.

1893    Oliver goes to Stonyhurst College in Lancashire.

1896    Matriculates, Royal University of Ireland.

1896–7    Boarder at Clongowes Wood College, Co. Kildare while studying for First Arts Examination, Royal University of Ireland (an examining body). Successful in sport: plays for Bohemians in their (soccer) Cup Final, winning gold medal, wins 3 mile cycle race, bowls impressively in Clongowes first eleven, notably in match against Dublin garrison.

1897    Passes First Arts Examination, R.U.I.

1897    Enters Trinity College, Dublin.

1898    Fails second Arts Examination in all subjects, R.U.I. 15 July awarded Royal Humane Society's Bronze medal for rescuing Dennis Brody from the Liffey. Passes examinations in Botany and Zoology, T.C.D.

1899    Begins clinical work at Richmond Hospital. Wins several cycling events at College Races, June, and later 20 mile Championship of Ireland. Fails to rescue John Meeke from drowning at Balbriggan, Co. Dublin (owing to clumsy handling of rescue boat sent to help his efforts), 4 August. Awarded Royal Humane Society's vellum certificate for having saved

653

|      | man from drowning at Blackrock, Co. Dublin, 19 October. |
|------|--------|
| 1900 | Wins various cycling events. |
| 1901 | Meets James Joyce. Awarded Royal Humane Society's vellum certificate for rescuing Max Harris, a would-be suicide, from drowning in the Liffey, June. Suspended by the Amateur Athletic Society for bad language when three other racing cyclists tried to ram him. |
| 1902 | Fails anatomy and physiology. Wins Vice Chancellor's Prize for English Verse (T.C.D.): 'In Memoriam Robert Louis Stevenson'; wins Royal University's gold medal for English Verse: 'Byron'. |
| 1903 | Studies midwifery and gynaecology at the National Maternity Hospital, Holles Street. Wins Vice Chancellor's Prize for English Verse (T.C.D.): 'The Death of Shelley'. |
| 1904 | Spends two terms at Worcester College, Oxford. Takes possession of Martello Tower, Sandycove, 17 August. S.C. Trench, and possibly J. S. Starkey (Seumas O'Sullivan), stayed there and James Joyce from c. 7 to 15 September). |
| 1905 | Fails anatomy. Mother insists he make a week's retreat in a Cistercian Monastery. Wins Vice Chancellor's Prize for English Verse (T.C.D.): 'Cervantes: Tercentenary of Don Quixote'. |
| 1906 | Briefly in New York, June. Marries Martha Duane ('Neenie'), daughter of an American Civil War pensioner, of Ross Dhu, Moyard, Connemara. Co. Galway, August. |
| 1907 | Completes Finals, June: in addition to M.B. gains M.D. by thesis. First son Oliver Duane ('Noll') Gogarty born at Fairfield, 23 July (d. 1999). In London, October 11, for some days before visiting Nuremberg en route to Vienna for further study in Otology and diseases of the nose and throat. |
| 1908 | In Dresden for holiday over New Year, back in Vienna by end of January. Returns to Dublin, takes 15 Ely Place, setting up as an ENT Specialist, and 'sports a motor' (an Argyll, to be followed by a 40/50 hp Rolls-Royce in 1912 and, later, a Mercedes Benz). Has appendix removed. Honorary Consultant at Richmond Hospital. |
| 1910 | Takes Fellowship of Royal College of Surgeons, Ireland. |
| 1911 | Appointed ENT Surgeon to Meath Hospital, Spring. |
| 1915 | Seriously ill (? typhoid fever) in Meath Hospital, convalesces at Seaview, Sorrento Road, Dalkey, a cottage in which the Gogartys live between 1915 and 1917 while 15 Ely Place is let and consulting rooms moved temporarily to 32 St Stephen's Green. |
| 1916 | *Hyperthuleana*. |

1917    Buys Renvyle House, Connemara (family holidays previously
        spent with Mrs Gogarty's sister at Garranbaun House, Moyard,
        Co. Galway).
1918    *The Ship and Other Poems*. First night of *Blight* at the Abbey
        Theatre, 11 December.
1919    *A Serious Thing* and *The Enchanted Trousers* staged at Abbey
        Theatre.
1922    Writes poems on deaths of Arthur Griffith and Michael Collins.
        Member of Senate, Irish Free State.
1923    Escapes from attempted assassination at Chapelizod and swims
        down the Liffey to safety, 19 January. Renvyle House burned
        down, 19 February. Transfers practice to London, but attends
        Senate meetings in Dublin. *An Offering of Swans*.
1924    Returns to Dublin. *An Offering of Swans and Other Poems*. At
        Tailteann Games awarded poetry prize for *An Offering of Swans*;
        3rd in archery competition; his *Tailteann Ode* set to music by
        Louis O'Brien.
1925    Two of his poems included in the *Oxford Book of English Verse*.
        In January at St Moritz, took part in a race down the Cresta
        run. In October on a pilgrimage to Rome in a party headed by
        President Cosgrave and the Bishop of Killaloe, which was
        received by the Pope.
1926    Buys Dunguaire/Dungory Castle (King Guaire's dun or fort), a
        16th century tower (unroofed) and bawn at Kinvara, Co.
        Galway.
1928    *Wild Apples*. Proposes the formation of the Irish Aero Club.
        Renvyle being rebuilt.
1929    *Wild Apples*.
1930    *Wild Apples*. Opens Renvyle House as hotel.
1932    Foundation member of Irish Academy of Letters.
1933    Unhurt after crashing plane when landing at Baldonnel
        Aerodrome, Co. Dublin, 23 July.
1936    Seventeen of his poems included in the *Oxford Book of Modern
        Verse*.
1937    *As I was Going Down Sackville Street*. Loses libel action brought
        by Henry ('Harry') Sinclair who was awarded £900 damages
        for two passages in *As I was Going Down Sackville Street*.
1938    Sells 15 Ely Place to the Royal Hibernian Academy. *Others to
        Adorn*; *I Follow St Patrick*.
1939    *Tumbling in the Hay*; *Elbow Room*. Wins libel action against
        Michael Joseph Ltd and their printer for defamation of character
        in Patrick Kavanagh's *The Green Fool* (1938). Applies to join
        RAF but considered too old. Goes to America, September.

Strenuous lecture tour ends in December.

1940 *Going Native*. Tries to join up in Canada but again considered too old. Begins to write for various American journals and publishers. Takes apartment in E 61st Street, New York.

1941 *Elbow Room and Other Poems; Mad Grandeur*.

1942 *Elbow Room*. In Barnert Hospital, Paterson, New Jersey for treatment for rectal polypi, February.

1943 Visits Robert Flaherty at Black Mountain Farm, Green Mountains, Vermont, July.

1944 *Perennial*. At Rocky Ridge, Maryland, spring and early summer.

1945 *Mr Petunia*. Transport difficulties mean he misses his daughter Brenda's marriage to Desmond Williams of Tullamore in June. Spends summer and autumn at Renvyle.

1947 In Dublin, May; in Renvyle, summer; returns to New York, September.

1948 *Mourning Became Mrs Spendlove*.

1949 *James Augustine Joyce*. Spends most of summer at Renvyle; returns to New York, September.

1950 *Rolling Down the Lea; Intimations*. Spends some of the winter in Florida; later in Ireland, bankers pressing for sale of Renvyle House Hotel.

1951 *Collected Poems* (U.S. Edition, 1954).

1952 Renvyle House Hotel no longer viable as family-owned concern.

1953 Visits Ireland.

1954 Elected Fellow of the Academy of American Poets. *It isn't This Time of Year at All*. Considers bidding for the Martello Tower.

1955 In Ireland, broadcasts for Radio Eireann. *Start from Somewhere Else*.

1956 In Dublin for Golden Wedding Anniversary, August.

1957 In hospital New York (cardiac symptoms), April. Plans to return to Ireland for good the following year. Considers buying a house with three acres of land at Ticknock, County Dublin. Mrs Gogarty in a nursing home. Collapses (heart attack) en route to dinner with Ben Lucien Burman at a Chinese Restaurant, 19 September. Dies in Beth Israel Hospital, New York, 22 September. Subsequently buried in Ballinakill Cemetery, between Letterfrack and Cleggan, County Galway.

1958 Mrs Gogarty ('Neenie') buried by his side. *A Weekend in the Middle of the Week*.

1963 *W. B. Yeats: a Memoir*.

# ABBREVIATIONS IN NOTES
# AND NOTES ON THE TEXT

(i) The following abbreviations are used in the Notes; they also indicate the sources of copy texts when they are placed after the titles of poems in Notes on the Text (where some other sources are given in full). Grateful acknowledgments for permission to use these sources are made on page 649. Other volumes referred to are included in this list.

B:          Ellen Clarke Bertrand Library. Bucknell University.
BK:         Collection of Professor Brendan Kennelly.
BL:         The British Library.
BLYU:       The Beinecke Rare Book and Manuscript Library, Yale University.
C:          Carl A. Kroch Library, Cornell University Library.
CC:         James A. Healy Collection, Colby College Library.
CS:         Collection of Professor Colin Smythe.
D:          University of Delaware Library.
DM:         Dublin Corporation Public Libraries (the Gilbert Library).
G:          Collection of Oliver Duane Gogarty.
GW:         Collection of Guy St. John Williams.
HD:         The Houghton Library, Harvard University.
HRHRC:      The Harry Ransome Humanities Research Center, University of Texas at Austin.
JC:         James Carens, *Surpassing Wit. Oliver St. John Gogarty, his Poetry and his Prose* (1979).
L:          J. B. Lyons, *Oliver St. John Gogarty. The Man of Many Talents* (1980).
L (1976):   J. B. Lyons, *Oliver St. John Gogarty* (1976).
LJAM:       J. B. Lyons, *James Joyce and Medicine* (1973).
LJJ:        *Letters of James Joyce*, ed. R. Ellmann, II (1966).
MLTT:       *Many Lines to Thee: Letters of Oliver St. John Gogarty to G. K.*

|          | *A. Bell . . . 1904–7*, ed. James F. Carens (1971). |
|----------|------|
| NLI:     | The National Library of Ireland. |
| NY:      | *The New Yorker.* |
| NYT:     | *New York Times.* |
| O'C:     | Ulick O'Connor, *Oliver St. John Gogarty. A Poet and his Times* (1964). |
| S:       | Stanford University Libraries. |
| T.C.D.:  | The Library of Trinity College, Dublin. |
| US:      | American Editions. |
| YP:      | *Yeats's Poems*, ed. A. Norman Jeffares (3rd edn, 1996). |

(ii) Abbreviations for titles of Gogarty's volumes of poetry in Notes and Notes on the Text.

| H      | *Hyperthuleana* (1916). |
|--------|------|
| TS     | *The Ship and Other Poems* (1918). |
| SSDS   | [Poems in] *Secret Springs of Dublin Song* (1918). |
| OS 23  | *An Offering of Swans* (1923). |
| OS 24  | *An Offering of Swans and Other Poems* (1924). |
| WA 28  | *Wild Apples* (1928). |
| WA 29  | *Wild Apples* (1929). |
| WA 30  | *Wild Apples* (1930). |
| SP     | *Selected Poems* (1933). |
| OA     | *Others to Adorn* (1938). |
| ER     | *Elbow Room* (1939). |
| ER 41  | *Elbow Room and Other Poems* (1941). |
| ER 42  | *Elbow Room* (1942). |
| P      | *Perennial* (1944). |
| CP     | *The Collected Poems* (1951; 1954). |
| UP     | *Unselected Poems* (1954). |
| PP     | *Penultimate Poems* (unpublished; included here in Part Two). |

(iii) Abbreviations for titles of some of Gogarty's prose works referred to in Notes and Notes on the Text.

| SS   | *As I was Going Down Sackville Street* (1937; 1994). |
|------|------|
| TH   | *Tumbling in the Hay* (1939; 1996). |
| GN:  | *Going Native* (1940; 1941). |
| MG   | *Mad Grandeur* (1941; 1943). |
| RL   | *Rolling Down the Lea* (1950). |
| I    | *Intimations* (1950). |
| TTY  | *It Isn't This Time of Year at All* (1954). |
| SSE  | *Start from Somewhere Else* (1955). |
| WMW  | *A Weekend in the Middle of the Week* (1958). |
| YM   | *W. B. Yeats: A Memoir* (1963). |

# NOTES TO PART ONE

---

## *Collected Poems*

ODES AND ADDRESSES

**'Ode'**
sub-title: The Tailteann Games were held in Dublin in August 1924; the ancient Aonach Tailteann was a fair or festival held at Tailte, near where the River Blackwater joins the Boyne. Gogarty's Ode was awarded a prize. The musical setting was by Louis O'Brien: (1978–1958) who was born in Dublin into a well-known musical family. His father, Richard Vincent O'Brien, a noted musician, trained among others William Ludwig, the great Wagnerian baritone, who was for many years a principal singer with the Carl Rosa Opera Company. Louis' siblings were all involved in music. His brother Vincent was a distinguished Irish musician who trained John McCormack, Margaret Burke Sheridan and James Joyce.

Educated at the O'Connell Schools, North Richmond St., Dublin, Louis studied music under his father and at the early age of sixteen was appointed organist of St. Macartan's Cathedral, Monaghan. Afterwards he was organist at St. Joseph's Church, Berkeley Road, Dublin, and from there transferred to St. Andrew's, Westland Row, where he remained as organist and choirmaster until his death. He also taught music in Belvedere College, directing the orchestra for its annual performances of Gilbert and Sullivan operas.

In 1924 he won the Tailteann gold medal for this setting of Oliver St. John Gogarty's 'Ode' for solo, chorus and orchestra. Dr Charles Woods of Cambridge University, the judge appointed by the Tailteann Music Committee, thought highly of O'Brien's setting, describing it as racy of the soil. When the work was first performed in the Theatre Royal, Dublin, an orchestra of 60 musicians and choir of 400 voices was employed. The musical setting could not, for reasons of space, be included in this edition, but copies of it are obtainable from Colin Smythe Ltd.
*Tara:* the seat of the High King of Ireland, a complex of earthworks and mounds north east of Navan, County Meath.
*King Leary:* the High King of Ireland (Irish, *Laoghaire MacNeill*) in the fourth century

659

(438–453AD), the son of Niall of the Nine Hostages (so called from his taking hostages from vassal peoples after three of his sons, Eogan, Conall and Enda, had razed Emain and subjected Ulster to their rule; Niall, himself born of a British mother, raided Roman Britain and probably died on one of these predatory raids. He and his father Eochu are the earliest historical kings of Tara. See T.F. O'Rahilly *Early Irish History and Mythology* (1946) p. 234. He was converted to Christianity by St. Patrick; a lively account of this was given in Muirchú's life of the Saint, written about two hundred years after his death. See Alannah Hopkin, *The Living Legend of St. Patrick* (1989) pp. 40–44.

*Meath:* county north of Dublin.

*Conn:* Conn Cetchathach, the Hundred Fighter, or Conn of the Hundred Battles, a legendary pre-Christian Gaelic king who established a kingdom near Mullingar, then transferred his seat to Tara, becoming High King of Ireland.

*McRoy:* Fergus MacRoy (or MacRoigh), King of Ulster, gave up his throne for a year to his step-son Conchubar (or Conor) MacNessa, but Conchubar held on to the throne; the story of his wife Ness tricking Fergus out of power is told in *The Book of Leinster.* Fergus afterwards became the lover of Maeve, Queen of Connacht, married to Ailill (or Ailell).

*the wooden sword:* a reference to an episode in the *Tain Bo Cualgne.* Ailill, husband of Queen Medb (Maeve) of Connaught, suspected her of having an affair with Fergus MacRoy and told his own charioteer Cuillius to watch them. When they were sleeping together Cuillius took Fergus's sword out of its sheath and brought it to Ailill who gave it to him to keep in his chariot. When Fergus found his sword was gone he cut a wooden sword from a tree. See Thomas Kinsella's translation of *The Tain* (1970, paperback edn) pp. 103–110 and 118. Gogarty also refers to the episode in his TTY, Ch. 32, the image of Fergus and his useless weapon coming into his mind when he could not reach his revolver when being kidnapped by gunmen in the Civil War who intended to execute him.

*MacNessa's:* Conchubar (or Conor) MacNessa, King of Ulster, the central figure in *The Fate of the Children of Usna.*

Gogarty's refreshing critical comment on the 'Ode' to Mrs Mary Owings Miller, made twenty years later on 18 February 1944, was that it was 'rather tripe.'

**'Virgil'**

*Mantua's meadows:* an echo of the Latin epitaph on Virgil's (70–19 BC) tombstone which begins '*Mantua me genuit . . .*' (Mantua was my birthplace).

*Imperial Rome:* Virgil went to Rome at sixteen to study rhetoric and philosophy. His farm was confiscated when the victorious triumvirs were settling their disbanded soldiers on the land; when Arrius, a soldier who had been given the land, refused to give it up and assaulted him, he went to Rome where he received compensation. At Rome Virgil became a friend of Maecenas, who proved a munificent patron; he gave him a villa at Naples and a country house near Nola.

*to found a city:* In his epic the *Aeneid* Virgil provided an illustrious beginning for Rome, linking it with Aeneas, the Trojan hero; the work was undertaken at the request of Octavian (the Emperor Augustus).

*the woodland deities:* a reference to Virgil's *Eclogues* (or *Bucolics*), ten pastorals modelled upon those of the Greek poet Theocritus (c.310–250 BC); it may also extend to the *Georgics*, his four books dealing with country life, a guide to agriculture embellished with mythology and philosophy.

*Pan:* an ancient Arcadian shepherd-god, a son of Hermes (but his mother varies in different legends). He had goat legs and horns and was amorous. Virgil describes one of his conquests in *Georgics* III, 391–393.

*Sylvan:* Sylvanus or Silvanus, the Roman god of uncultivated land, who was also a god of agriculture and woods.

**'To "Aphrodite"'**

*Aphrodite:* the Greek goddess of love and beauty, a daughter of Zeus who was also a goddess of the sea (in Roman mythology she was Venus).

*Pandemian:* available to everyone (Greek, *pandemios*, of all the people).

'To Ninde'

*Title:* the poem was addressed to Emily Miner in the *Irish Statesman*, 21 September 1929.

*Helen:* Helen of Troy, wife of Menelaus, King of Sparta. In Greek legend she deserted her husband, accompanying Paris, son of Priam, King of Troy, to Troy, thus causing the Trojan war which was ended by the Greeks sacking the city after a ten year siege.

*Dian . . . fawn she slew:* Diana, an Italian deity, later associated with Artemis, the Greek moon-goddess, patroness of virginity and hunting.

*limb in Melian land:* Melos, an island in the SW Aegean Sea, was the centre of early Aegean civilisation. The statue known as the Venus de Milo was found there.

*Coan seas:* Cos or Kos, an island in the SE Aegean Sea, famous for literature and medicine and art (Apelles the Coan painter was known for his painting of Venus).

*Praxiteles:* a fourth century BC Greek sculptor whose work included statues of Aphrodite at Cos and at Cnidus.

**'For a Birthday'**

*Helen:* see note above, this page.

**'To a Cock'**

*Troy:* see note on Helen above, p. this page.

*his who fought to save the fatal Queen:* Jupiter and Semele.

*gifts of fire:* Semele, loved by Jupiter, was persuaded by Juno, his consort, disguised as Semele's nurse, to ask Jupiter to come to her in the same majesty with which he approached Juno. Horrified, he acceded to Semele's request. She could not withstand his majesty (clouds, lightning, thunderbolts) and was consumed by fire. Her unborn child Dionysus, saved from the flames, was brought to term in Jupiter's thigh.

*The Argive Valleys . . . her limbs:* in Homer and Virgil the Greeks besieging Troy were called Argives, especially those from Argos, (a city in SE Greece in the Peloponese dominated by Argos in the 7th Century BC), hence Helen of Troy, the Greek wife of Menelaus, King of Sparta whose running off to Troy with Paris, son of King Priam of Troy, caused the Trojan War.

*Grace O'Malley's:* Grace O'Malley, also known as Granuaile, (c.1530–1603) married Donal O'Flaherty of Bunowen Castle in 1546, her father being chief of the O'Malley clan. She took control of her husband's business; after his death she defended Hen's Castle ('the oldest mortared castle in Ireland. It was built by Roderick O'Conor's sons and the son of William Fitz-Adelm, the original de Burgs'. TTY, p. 23). Her husband was called the Cock and the Castle 'was called after her who had raised its siege,' when her husband was locked up in the castle earlier. (RL, p. 158) in Lough Corrib and began her career as a pirate and trader. She later married Richard Burke of Rockfleet Castle in Clew Bay, County Mayo, where she defeated an English expedition in 1574. Imprisoned in 1577, she returned to Connaught in 1579. In 1593 she sailed up the Thames and negotiated with Elizabeth I, gaining all her requests. See Gogarty, I, pp. 122–132, for discussion of her, and see also Anne Chambers, *Granuaile. The Life and Times of Grace O'Malley* (1979) cited also in note on 'The Old Goose', p. 685. She is sometimes regarded as a personification of Ireland.

*Leda:* a queen in Sparta, the mother of Helen (of Troy) and Pollux, by Zeus who visited her in the shape of a swan (cf Gogarty's poem 'Leda and the Swan' p. 144).

*Semele:* see note above, p. 661.

*Each Sabine dame:* The Sabines, dwelling NE of Rome, were invited to a spectacle; the subsequent rape of the Sabine women was part of oral folklore; it led later to the Sabines settling in Rome.

*Hercules aflame:* Deianira his wife, jealous of his attachment to Iole, sent him the tunic of Nessus which poisoned him; he appealed to Jupiter and lay on a burning pyre: this was surrounded by dark smoke and Jupiter conveyed the immortal parts of Hercules to heaven.

**'To my friend, the Rt. Hon. Lorcan Galeran (A Great Householder)'**
The poem first appeared in *Hyperthuleana* (1916) addressed to William McElroy, see p. 199.
Title: *Lorcan Galeran:* He is based upon the well known Dublin character Larkey Waldron who lived in some state in Killiney, County Dublin:

> 'Who is Larkey?' you will rightly ask. He is a brother of General Waldron but he lives in his own right. Don't mind George Moore when he writes of "the obscene bulk of Larkey Waldron." I admit that Larkey is a substantial man; he weighs four hundred pounds and over, but then he is a stockbroker to the Catholic Church; and St. Thomas Aquinas was no lightweight and yet he wrote the *Summa* and fixed the school. Larkey has to do sums for the bishops and archbishops and invest money for the Little Sisters of the Poor. He lives sumptuously in a beautiful house on Killiney Hill.
>
> Yes: Larkey is a great fellow in every sense. He sits in his office in Anglesea Street with two telephones and four mantelpieces by Bossi in the room. He wears a skullcap of black silk topped by a large pink rhododendron. He hasn't seen his feet for years. (TTY, p. 125.)

In *Mr Petunia* (1946) p. 21 Gogarty describes him as self-important and pontificating, 'a rolling tun of a man'

*What Shakespeare and Sam Johnson wrote . . . clear thinking:* 'You won't be surprised now to hear that Larkey's hobby is clear thinking; and Dr Johnson' (TTY, p. 125.)

*Agamemnon:* a King of Mycenae, (brother of Menelaus, King of Sparta) who led the Greeks at the siege of Troy.

*Big-bellied as the Trojan Horse:* it contained within it the Greeks who emerged from it at night (when the Trojans were feasting, thinking the Greek fleet had left and the siege had been abandoned), opened the gates of the city to the returning Greeks and began the massacre of the Trojans.

*Orpheus . . . all but clasp Eurydice:* in Greek myth Orpheus, a poet and lyre-player, married to Eurydice, sought her in Hades after her death and was allowed by Pluto to bring her back to earth on condition he did not turn and look at her before they reached the upper world. He almost succeeded but turned to look at her at the last moment and so lost her.

*Marathon:* referring to a messenger, Pheidippides, who ran 150 miles in two days to Sparta to seek help for Athens, bringing the news of the Persian landing at Marathon in 490 BC, hence any large or arduous task. The Athenian army marched to the Plain of Marathon and their ensuing victory on land prompted the still formidable Persian fleet to retreat to Asia.

*'What did you say that Shakespeare said?*
*The book is somewhere on my shelves':*

> A dinner with Larkey Waldron . . . when the ice-pudding, served half-way through it, transformed your stomach into hemispheres, and the dinner began again for a conquest of a New World: the butler sent in mid repast to the library to verify a quotation which was forgotten with the next mouthful . . . (SS, p. 253.)

*God helps those:* Galeran may be attributing to Shakespeare the proverbial 'God helps them who help themselves'.

*Tiberian peace:* that of the Roman Empire, from Rome being on the Tiber, but for an alternative explanation see note on the phrase, p. 691.

*Magee:* William Kirpatrick Magee (1868–1961). Assistant librarian at the National Library of Ireland (1895–1921), he wrote several books, using the pseudonym John Eglinton. See further note on him below (p. 726).

*Clarke:* Gogarty's friend Tom Clarke (1857–1916) revolutionary, first signatory of the *Proclamation of the Irish Republic,* executed in 1916, might be meant here but this reference is probably Austin Clarke (1891–1974), poet, playwright and novelist.

*silent Hone:* probably Joseph Maunsell Hone (1882–1959) a director of the publishing house of Maunsel and Company, and biographer of Swift, Thomas Davis, George Moore and W.B. Yeats. He was not greatly given to easy conversation. Gogarty elsewhere refers to his 'quiet ways and his delicate health, which assured old age' (It did) TTY, p. 153. It is, however, remotely possible Nathaniel Hone (1831–1917), the Irish painter, is intended here.

*Parnassus' second peak . . . Your cousin:* Parnassus is a mountain in central Greece, sacred to Dionysus, Apollo and the Muses. The Castalian spring and Delphi are on its slopes. Here the 'second peak' refers to McDonald, a Dublin architect, Waldron's cousin, another heavy-weight, who

> weighed at least four hundred pounds, as became a cousin of Larkey Waldron. His collar was twenty inches around: his mouth was open, and his whole face turned upwards, for, even though your neck has taken over, you must breathe. He was gasping when I met him. To give him time to catch his breath, I stood and waited. Was he leaving his office or entering it? What did it matter? He was breathing easier now.
>
> "How is Larkey?" I asked.
>
> After a moment he gargled in his deep bass, "Splendid. You should see him since his cure. A child can speak to him. I don't believe in this slimming. Tell me, do you?"
>
> "Which side is he slimming?" I asked.
>
> "I must hurry," he said, as if to explain his breathlessness, and stepped into his office. (TTY, p. 124.)

### 'To James Stephens'

Title: James Stephens (?1880–1950) poet, novelist, short-story writer and brilliant talker, was born in Dublin, where on the death of his father and remarriage of his mother he was sent to an orphanage; he worked as a typist and clerk in the office of a Dublin solicitor, Mecredy, from 1896 (see note on 'Macready'; p. 734). He lived in Paris from 1912 to 1915, then returned to Dublin as Registrar of the National Gallery of Ireland until 1924, moving to England in 1925. He was the author of *The Charwoman's Daughter* (1912), *The Crock of Gold* (1912) and *The Demi-Gods* (1914). Joyce thought Stephens should complete *Finnegans Wake* if he could not finish it himself.

### 'To a Friend'

*A.E.:* the pen name of George Russell (1880–1935), derived from the Greek Aeon: a mystic poet, novelist and painter, he was a leading figure in the Irish co-operative movement, editor of the *Irish Homestead* (1905–1923) and then of the *Irish Statesman* (1923–1930).

### 'To the Lady –'

*your gables . . . Oxford:* Garsington Manor, home of Sir Philip and Lady Ottoline Morrell, outside Oxford.

*a poet:* W.B. Yeats and his wife were friends of the Morrells.

### 'To A.E. going to America'

Title: see note on A.E. above, this page.

*Du Bellay . . . Lyrè home:* Joachim du Bellay (1522-1660), born at Lire in Anjou, French poet and prose writer, was a member of the Pleiade, for which he wrote a manifesto in 1549, rejecting medieval linguistic traditions and advocating a return to classical and Italian models.

*Plutarch . . . Chaeronea:* Plutarch, (c.AD 46–c.AD 120) Greek biographer and philosopher, was born and resided mainly in Chaeronea; he studied at Athens; under Hadrian he was procurator of Achaea and an Athenian citizen. He is best know for his *Lives* (AD 105–115), anecdotal and ethical, of soldiers and statesmen.

**'To W.B. Yeats who says that his Castle at Ballylee is his Monument'**
Title: Yeats bought a Norman tower and cottages at Ballylee in County Galway for £35 in 1917; he and his wife supervised alterations to make the buildings habitable. 'In Memory of Major Robert Gregory' (YP, p. 144), completed in 1918, records them as 'Almost settled' in. Yeats called the tower Thoor (Irish *tur*, a tower) Ballylee; he and his family spent their summers there until 1929.

*Dun Angus:* Dun Aengus, a Celtic fort, high on Inishmore, the largest of the Aran Islands, on the cliff edge.

*O'Flaherty . . . Auchnanure:* Auchnanure (Irish, *Achadh na niubhar*, the Field of the Yews) Castle is three or four miles beyond Moycullen, north west of Galway City. The castle was built in the late fifteenth century or early sixteenth century: it was destroyed by Sir Edward Fitton in 1572. Then, rebuilt, James I granted it to Hugh O'Flaherty in 1618. It was held by the O'Flaherty family until the end of the century. See Sir William Wilde, *Lough Corrib and Lough Mask* (1867). Augustus John wanted to buy it: the complications are tellingly recorded by Gogarty (SSE, p. 124). One brother owned it and would sell but another controlled the right of way and might block access. Gogarty described it as being in ruin, 'supported by only a shank of rock for the limestone was eroded by the bog water in the small stream that flowed by it.' It has recently been restored very successfully.

*he who told how Troy was sacked . . . Burd:* Homer. Seven cities claimed to be his birthplace. Burd, obsolete except in ballads, is a poetic word for woman; here, Helen of Troy.

**'To my Portrait, by Augustus John'**
Title: Augustus John (1878–1961), English Bohemian artist who met Gogarty in 1912 and painted him twice in 1917; they were friends though highly critical of each other.
Epigraph: remembered inaccurately from Shakespeare, *Antony and Cleopatra*, IV, viii:

> Cleopatra:     O infinite virtue, com'st thou smiling from
>                      The world's great snare uncaught?

*Elysian skies:* in Greek myth Elysium was the dwelling place of the blessed after death, hence, as adjective relating to Elysium, delightful, glorious, blissful.

*woman great with child:* a reference to John's painting of his wife and his mistress Dorelia. See note on Francis Macnamara, p. 694 and Gogarty, TTY, pp. 150 *et seq.*

*Troubadours:* lyric poets who flourished from the 11th to the 13th centuries, mainly in Provence and North Italy; they wrote mainly of courtly love in complex metres.

**'To Augustus John'**
*Silenus's:* he was chief of the satyrs, often portrayed riding drunkenly on a donkey. The reference here may be to King Midas who mixed wine with the waters of a fountain from which Silenus was accustomed to drink, got him completely inebriated and, after keeping him ten days, restored him to Bacchus, who then gave Midas the power of turning everything he touched to gold.

*Lettergesh:* situated in the parish of Ballnakill, County Galway, a mountainous region along the coast between Tully and Lough Muc.

*your driving:* Augustus John was taught to drive by Gogarty simply putting him in a car and telling him to drive off (see Gogarty TTY, p. 212). He did drive off, at high speed, and only came to a stop when he ran out of petrol by Lough Fee. The coast road from

Leenaun to Tully Cross runs beside Lough Fee and Lough Muc.

*Helen's throat . . . our Lady of the War . . . ten years?:* a reference to the Trojan wars, fought over Helen, which lasted ten years.

*Achill:* Achill Island, an island off the west coast of County Mayo.

*Leda:* see note above, p. 661.

*Sordello: (b.?1200)* an Italian troubadour.

*Robin Hood:* a legendary English outlaw; according to tradition he lived in Sherwood Forest and robbed the rich to give to the poor.

*'Evening in the Highlands':* A painting lost when the Royal Hibernian Academy was shelled by a British gunboat in the 1916 Rising. A clue to the identity of the painter is provided in SS (1994 edn) pp. 124–5:

> He [Sir John Simon (1873-1954), Home Secretary 1915–16] knew Dublin. He had been over for the Compensation Claims Committee. The Royal Hibernian Academy had been burned and the artists who had lost pictures at its exhibition were claiming for them. He did not know how the Artist Gray, a painter of Highland cattle, arrived at the estimate of his loss. Or, rather, he did discover it. Gray . . . claimed for the loss of a characteristic work. He could not make up his mind. It was a great picture. If it had not been in the Royal Hibernian Academy it might have been in the Tate Gallery . . .

And, being asked how much it was worth, he found it hard to assess its value. It was time to adjourn for lunch. Gray met a friend in the nearest pub; they decided on getting a reward in proportion to the needs of the occasion, and, on the Commission's sitting being resumed, Gray explained that in his picture there were twenty cattle on the hillside . . . 'And at fifteen pounds per head that would work out at three hundred pounds, besides those hidden in the mist'. The painting was probably by a son of Charles Gray (?1808–1892), born in Greenock, who exhibited from 1837 on in the Royal Hibernian Academy, and was known for his views of Scottish scenery. He had several sons, Edwin Landseer, Alfred, Gregor, James and Charles Malcolm. Of these Alfred (1864-1924) seems the most likely, his many listed paintings including several landscapes with cattle, 'A Highland Herd in the Grampians', 'Highland Cattle, Dee Side', 'Highland Mist' and 'Evening West Highlands' as well as many evening scenes in Scotland.

*'The Stag at Bay':* A painting (perhaps nearly as well known as his 'The Monarch of the Glen') by Sir Edwin Henry Landseer (1802–73), English animal painter whose favourite subjects were well known through the excellent engravings of his paintings of dogs and deer by his elder brother Thomas Landseer (1796–1880).

*Your London agent:* Michael Holroyd suggests that this was a private joke probably referring to Jack ('Curly') Knewstub who managed the Chevril Gallery where until the late 1920s Augustus John, William Orpen, Charles Conder, William Rothenstein and others showed their work. The 'forehead numb' suggests their being at loggerheads.

**'To the poet W.B. Yeats, winner of the Nobel Prize 1924'**

*a town of the North:* Stockholm. See W.B. Yeats, *The Bounty of Sweden* (1924), for an account of his receiving the prize there.

*a Dolphin:* See Yeats's poems 'Sailing to Byzantium', 'Byzantium' and 'News for the Delphic Oracle', YP, pp. 301, 363 and 461.

*Town of your birth:* Yeats was born in Dublin in 1865.

*granite hills:* the Dublin mountains.

*the Roman of old . . . Pyrrhic slaughter . . . Sabine waters:* Pyrrhus, king of Epirus, defeated the Romans at Heraclea in 280 BC, at Asculum in 279 BC but suffered very heavy losses in doing so (giving rise to the description a Pyrrhic victory; 'one more such victory and we are lost' he is reported to have said after Asculum. A battle at Benevento was then drawn in 275 BC. The year Pyrrhus died, 272 BC, the Romans created the

Anio Vetus, a 40 mile aqueduct supplied by the river Anio bringing water from the Sabine hills to Rome. Gogarty had probably been reading Plutarch's *Life of Pyrrhus*.

*his back to a poet he gave:* Arion (c.628–625 BC) of Lesbos spent most of his life at the court of Periander, tyrant of Corinth. After a profitable trip to Italy and Sicily he either leapt or was thrown overboard by the crew on his return journey and carried to land by a dolphin, one of many who, attracted by his singing, were playing about the ship.

*Venus' heel:* see notes on pp. 661, 669 and 675 above. Aphrodite was widely worshipped as a goddess of the sea, and was sometimes represented as accompanied by or drawn by dolphins. See, for instance, the 'Triumph of Galatea' (1511–12) in the Farnesina by Raphael (1483–1520) based upon a poem by Poliziano, but which was taken by many to represent Venus, where two dolphins are drawing her in a shell-shaped vessel. 'The Triumph of Marine Venus' by Nicholas Poussin (1594–1669) in the Philadelphia Museum of Art shows her drawn in a chariot by dolphins.

*Julian race:* relating to Caius Julius Caesar (100–44 BC) Roman general, statesman and historian.


EARTH AND SEA

**'The Forge'**
*blacksmith . . . Queen of Love:* Venus (Aphrodite) was married to Vulcan (Hephaestus) the lame blacksmith god.

*Master of those who know:* Professor Henry Stewart Macran, Fellow (1892) and professor of Moral Philosophy (1901) at Trinity College, Dublin. He wrote *Lectures on the History of Ancient Philosophy* (2 vols, 1856) and *Letters on the Development of Christian Doctrine: Doctrinal and Practical* (2 vols, 1859). He influenced Gogarty as an undergraduate and is described affectionately in TH and SSE where this conversation is recorded:

> 'I always blame the woman', the professor was saying. 'Yes, at my time of life, the woman is to blame.' This was something new, quite new to me, to whom love then was all a 'wonder and a wild desire.' The thought of blaming women for anything but being the unwilling transmitters of social diseases was very far from my thought. ['Too Late', p. 453, is then quoted]. This shocking idea must have appeared on my face because the Master of Those who know (about wines, too) said, 'Have a little more sauterne.' We sat and sipped while the Master expounded about women and why he blamed them. I was so innocent, or, if you like, ignorant, that I imagined that it was his wife the Master had in mind.

This passage suggests that the poem 'McGurk,' p. 369, may be about Macran.

*a Titan god:* Titan was one of the older Greek gods, probably pre-Hellenic; they battled against Zeus, son of Kronos and Rhea, and were gigantic in size.

*Pegasus:* the immortal winged horse of Greek legend, sprung from the blood of Medusa, one of the three gorgons. The poet Ovid (43 BC–AD 17) related a legend in which Pegasus lived on Mount Helicon, a mountain in Boeotia sacred to the Muses; by striking it with his hoof he created the fountain of Hippocrene, after which the Muses made him their favourite.

*take off . . . the heavenly horse:* Pegasus: hence Gogarty (who was Ireland's first amateur aviator) is about to compose a poem by riding Pegasus.

**'Sung in Spring'**
*our ship is a rotor:* perhaps a glancing reference to an innovative German-built rotor ship, propelled by two tall vertically rotating metal cylinders, of the nineteen-twenties or thirties.

**'The Dublin-Galway Train'**

*Nil obstat: nil* or *nihil obstat* (Latin, nothing hinders) a phrase used by Roman Catholic censors to declare publication inoffensive to faith or morals.

*Athlone:* Athlone (Irish *ath,* a ford) on the River Shannon is virtually in the centre of Ireland, seventy-eight miles west of Dublin.

*walled Maynooth:* Maynooth, in County Kildare, is fourteen miles west of Dublin; its castle dates from c.1176. The 'Truth' is taught in St. Patrick's College, a seminary founded in 1796, subsequently a constituent college of the National University, now styled the National University of Ireland, Maynooth.

*the meadow . . . Druidical Nooth:* (Irish *machaire,* a plain) the plain of Nooth in Maynooth (Irish *Magh Nuadhat* or *Maigh Nua* is from *Nuadhat,* a King of Leinster).

*Mullingar:* Gogarty's note glossed it as the Square Mill; in County Westmeath, it is approximately fifty miles from Dublin.

*Moate . . . a manmade hill:* Moate is about sixty-eight miles from Dublin, ten miles east of Athlone in County Westmeath, so called from the Great Mound, the moat of Graine-og, Young Grace, by tradition a Munster princess. In RL Gogarty explained the word: 'In Ireland they call all the tumuli 'moats' . . . They get their name probably from the Norman word 'motte' meaning a mound. There are many words of Norman French that have passed into the language.'

*The Shannon:* see Spenser, *Fairie Queene,* IV, Canto XI, 41: 'The spacious Shenan spreading like a sea'.

*Cromwell . . . 'to hell':* Oliver Cromwell (1599–1658) offered the choice of 'To Hell or Connaught' to the defeated Catholic Irish landowners. Those whose lands were expropriated were meant to be given land in Connaught and Clare but in many cases did not receive any.

*And now, Goodbye:* Gogarty is recognising the difference between western and eastern Ireland.

*Ballinasloe:* Gogarty's note: 'The Place of the Hostings'. It is ninety-four miles from Dublin.

*Connemara . . . sons of Conn:* see note on Connemara below, p. 673.

*Athenry:* The Ford of the Kings (Irish *ath,* ford; *nry,* of the Kings) about one hundred and nineteen miles from Dublin.

*Oranmore:* Gogarty's note: 'The Great Shore': south of Galway about a hundred and thirty miles from Dublin.

*Lady Philippa of Merlin Park:* she was the second daughter (b. *c.*1857) of Charles Wyndham, 7th Earl of Harrington (b. *c.*1809) who married Elizabeth de Pearsall, by whom he had six sons and six daughters. Philippa Lester Stanhope married William Sharp Waithman of Merlin Park, Galway; they had a son and a daughter, the son, Captain Waithman, living with his wife in Merlin Park until it was acquired for a hospital and they moved to a small house at Murrough. Merlin Park was built near Galway City for Sir Charles Blake *c.*1807–8; it was subsequently sold in the Encumbered Estates Court in 1852.

*Daly's of Dunsandle:* Castle Daly (Irish *Dún San Dail,* Sandal's fort or dun) is in Loughrea, County Galway. John Acton Daly assumed the surname and arms of Daly in lieu of his patronymic Blake by royal licence in 1837. The Dunsandle here, however, is more likely Dunsandle of Anthenry, County Galway, built for Denis Daly MP in the late eighteenth century: it was sold in 1954 and dismantled in 1958. See the Knight of Glin, D.S. Griffin and N.K. Robinson, *Vanishing Country Houses of Ireland* (1988): the destruction was 'a major loss to Ireland's architectural heritage'.

*The Galway Blazers:* a famous Irish hunt.

*Morty Mor . . . the principal works of Galway town:* Morty Mor McDonough/McDonagh,

'Big Martin', who died before 1950 (see Gogarty, ch. 2, *RL* (1950). Thomas McDonagh and Sons Ltd owned general and grocery stores at Merchants' Road and Flood Street, Galway, with a Fertiliser and Manual works at Quay Street, Galway as well as a branch in Tuam. Gogarty described him as dressed in black, 'for, since clergymen wear it, black commands respect; and as the greatest employer in the town, respect was his due.'
*Waeshael!:* or Wassail, Anglo Saxon; be in good health.
*reasty:* rancid.
**'The Blackbird in the Town'**
*Finn:* Finn MacCumhail (MacCool) leader of the Fenians, killed on the Boyne AD283.
*Letter Lee:* Gogarty read Standish O'Grady, *Finn and his Companions* (1892), admiring Finn as a hero and poet. Ch V gives Finn's poem composed to show his poetic skill – he had been learning the mysteries and skills of poetry by the river Boyne – and this praises the singing of the blackbirds. Cf Gogarty's remark to Yeats 'You remember the quotation from the Early Gaelic, "The music Finn loved was the Song of the Blackbird of Letterlee?"' I, p. 16, Gogarty may have got this from 'Cride's Lament for Cael' (see Myles Dillon, *Early Irish Literature* (1948), p. 39, which links the blackbirds with Letter Lee: 'Sad is the note of the thrush in Dromkeen and sad the music of the blackbird in Letterlee'. The original Irish form of the name is found in two poems in the *Fianaíocht* cycle of the early modern Irish period. Each refers to the music of the blackbird. The location of the place is unknown; it probably means 'The Hillside of the Calf'.
*The Bird of Valour . . . the bird untamed:* 'The blackbird was called the bird of valour by the ancient Irish who used them to fight instead of gamecocks'. See I, p. 16.
**'If Sight were Sound'**
*Aurora:* Roman goddess of the dawn.
**'The Crab Tree'**
*Lough Neagh:* a lake in SW County Antrim, the largest lake in the British Isles.
**'To the Liffey with the Swans'**
Gogarty released two swans on the Liffey in gratitude for the river's having borne him to safety in January 1923 when he escaped from IRA gunmen. See pp. 599, 729 and 773. Gogarty's account of the kidnapping can be found in Ch. XXXII, 'You Carry Caesar', of TTY, pp. 174–184. This is how Brendan Considine described the events of 12 January 1923 from the point of view of the Republicans who had captured him as a hostage and would have probably have shot him as a reprisal for the Free State Government's execution of Republicans:

> 'During the course of the Civil war a situation had arisen whereby prisoners held by the then Free State Government were being executed by way of reprisals for certain military activity pursued by the Republicans. With a view to counteracting this policy of reprisals it was decided by Headquarters Staff of the republican Forces to apprehend certain personages of influence and power who were known to be strong supporters of Government policy and who publicly condoned these acts of reprisal. Among those listed appeared the name of Dr St John Gogarty, who was duly taken into custody. To the credit of his captors the operation was carried out under very great risk since his home was situated in the shadow of Goverment Buildings. Those in charge, in accordance with instructions, treated their prisoners with every respect. As to the prisoner, he behaved with great courage and with the utmost confidence and discussed with his captors many subjects of mutual interest, interspersed with wit and humour which were part of his make-up. The manner of his escape was in keeping with his general conduct during his detention, confident and courageous.' (*Irish Literary Portraits*, ed. W.R. Rodgers (1972) p. 161).

*a king's . . . daughter:* Leda, beloved of Zeus, who appeared to her in the guise of a swan (cf 'Leda and the Swan', p. 144).

*doubled bird:* the swan and Zeus combined.
*the Twin Sportsmen:* Castor and Pollux. Pollux was fathered by Zeus, Castor by Tyndareus, the husband of Leda, a Spartan king.
**'The Water Lily'**
*Cyprian birth:* Aphrodite, the Greek goddess of love and beauty (or Venus, her Roman counterpart) was born out of the foam of the sea.
*Cyprian:* Aphrodite was born and worshipped near Cyprus.
*patines:* patin or patine, a variant of paten, a plate.
**'The Dragon Fly'**
*Ephemeral . . . ephemeris:* lasting only for a short time (from Greek ephemeros, lasting only a day). Ephemerid is the usual form for an insect (including mayflies).
**'Liffey Bridge'**
*Ben Edair:* the hill of Howth, forming the northern arm of Dublin Bay.
*Hurdle Ford:* early name for Dublin, Baile Atha Cliath (Irish *Baile*, town/city; *atha cliath*, ford of the hurdles, or hurdle work, see note p. 762) and see also RL, p. 60:

> 'I remember how laboriously I tried to dig out from the Irish of *The Youthful Exploits of Finn*, the story of how that son of Cumhall drowned the youths of Dublin while they were bathing in the Plain of Life. That was the way "Liffey" was spelt then. It was wider and shallower then than the fifty yards width of it that flows unheeded now.'

**'The Plum Tree by the House'**
*The Forbidden City:* normally Lhasa, Tibet, famed for its inaccessibility and hostility to strangers, though there is a remote possibility Gogarty may be referring to a walled area in Beijing, China, enclosing the Imperial Palace, also called the Forbidden City.
**'Suburban Spring'**
The title of the poem was 'Springtime in Munsey Avenue' when it first appeared in the *New Yorker*, 8 May 1943.
**'Perennial'**
*that gowned man . . . Tyrrellus noster:* Robert Yelverton Tyrrell (1844–1914), Fellow of Trinity College, Dublin, who befriended Gogarty when he was an undergraduate and through whom he met several other dons. Tyrrell held professorships of Latin, Greek, then Ancient History; he is best known for his edition of the *Correspondence of Cicero*. cf 'Aeternae Lucis Redditor' p. 187.
**'Thrush in Ash'**
*Hebe:* in Greek myth, a goddess of youth, love and spring; the daughter of Zeus and his consort Hera, she was made cupbearer of all the gods by Hera. Zeus, however, gave her office to Ganymede when she fell in an indecent posture when pouring nectar for the gods at a festival.
*Ida:* Mount Ida, the highest mountain in Crete, associated with the worship of Zeus.
*the Tuscan:* 'The Magi' is not specific enough for a clear identification but Gogarty probably knew of Benozzo Gozzoli's elaborate 'Journey of the Magi' (fresco cycle 1459 Palazzo Ricardi, Florence) from one of the countless Medici reproductions and may have assumed it was a panel painting.
*Lancinate:* pierce or tear.
**'The Apple Tree'**
*The Logos:* in philosophy, reason, argument (Greek *logos*, a word) especially personified as the source of order in the universe. The reference to God in 1.11 suggests that there may be a possible sense here of the Divine Word (the second person of the Trinity). See the Bible, John I.1, 'In the beginning was the Word, and the Word was with God, and the Word was God".

**'Lullaby'**
*Cloth of Gold:* specifically cloth woven from silk threads interspersed with gold, or else from gold threads alone.
**'Angels'**
*Pompeii:* an ancient city in Italy, SE of Naples, buried by an eruption of Vesuvius in 79 AD. Excavations have revealed some of its mural paintings, mainly in small panels, of naturalistic figures and landscapes.
*Hermes:* in Greek mythology the messenger of the gods.
*Olympus:* a mountain in Macedonia in Thessaly, the residence of the gods.
*four fountained island;* Hermes flew from Olympus (where Zeus was holding counsel) to bring Calypso Zeus's command to her, to release Odysseus (see Homer, *Odyssey* 5, 27ff). Calypso's island, Ogygia, had four springs (*Odyssey* 5, 70-71). His mission was thankless as Calypso was reluctant to obey.
*Dante:* Dante Alighiere (1265–1321) a Florentine poet, author of the *Vita Nuova* and *la Divina Commedia* and other works, one of Gogarty's favourite poets.
*reasty:* rancid.
*Georgian Dublin:* known for its finely proportioned squares, terraces and public buildings. Its wide streets arose from the activity of the Wide Streets Commission set up in 1758.
*Raheny:* an area midway between Dublin and Howth.
*Portmarnock:* an area north of the isthmus linking Howth to the mainland at Sutton.
*Dundrum:* south of Dublin, now a suburb, at the foot of the Dublin mountains.
*O'Donnell:* Red Hugh O'Donnell (c.1571–1602) born in Donegal. Captured and imprisoned in Dublin Castle, he escaped in winter over the Dublin and Wicklow mountains in 1591, was inaugurated as The O'Donnell in 1592, shared in Irish victory at the Yellow Ford in 1598, agreed to the impetuous plans of Don Juan d'Aquila (leader of the Spanish forces which had come to Ireland) which led to the Irish defeat at Kinsale in 1601. He was poisoned with the knowledge of if not at the instigation of Sir George Carew.
*Sandals of Hermes:* they were winged to enable him to go wherever he pleased speedily.
**'Song made by Sir Dinadan for Sir Tristram that an Harper might play it before King Mark'**
The poem is prompted by the medieval romance in which a knight, Tristram, the nephew of King Mark of Cornwall, fell in love with his uncle's bride Iseult, an Irish princess (in another account she was the daughter of the King of Brittany), after they mistakenly drank a love potion. Chapelizod on the Liffey is named after Iseult. Gogarty wrote the poem for Christopher Stone, describing it as one which 'Chaucer, Malory and Swinburne begot', probably referring in Swinburne's case to his romantic poem *Tristram of Lyonesse* (1882). Stone (whom Gogarty met at Oxford) shared a cottage at Burford in the Cotswolds with Compton Mackenzie who edited and owned *The Gramophone* and later became Stone's brother-in-law. Stone, known for his BBC broadcasting, owned Field Place (Shelley's birthplace in Horsham, Sussex). See TTY, p. 185 and 'At Burford', p. 367.
*incipit citharista:* the cithara (a four-stringed instrument, a lyre or guitar) player begins.
*Hic calcibus citharistam ejiciunt:* they eject the cithara player with kicks at this point.
**'Dunsany Castle'**
*Tara . . . royalist ground:* because Tara in County Meath, north of Dunsany Castle, was the residence of the High Kings of Ireland. For Gogarty's friend Lord Dunsany see note on him below, p. 704.
**'Croker of Ballinagarde'**
Title: 'Boss Croker': Richard Welstead Croker, of Tammany Hall fame, was a wealthy

American of Irish origin, a fanatically keen owner of race horses. His horse Orby won both the Irish and the English Derby in 1907. Glencairn, his house in Sandyford, County Dublin is now the residence of the British Ambassador to Ireland. Gogarty records him ordering his library to be filled with a thousand volumes of Algebra to decorate its walls (TTY, p. 11).

*Ballinagarde:* Ballynaguarde House, Ballyneety, County Limerick, the seat of the Crokers, was built in 1774. The family came originally from Linehan, Devon. The *County Book Series* describes the ruined house 'with statues all standing naked in the open air'. There was a proposal to bring Hercules to Limerick, 'but a committee of inspection having studied him carefully fore and aft decided he would never do for the confraternities.'

*the Tipps:* the Tipperary Hounds, a hunt dating from 1820. See *Bailey's Hunting Directory* (1998–99). Gogarty, whose father had Richard Burke, Master for forty years, as a patient, commented on the Tipperary Hounds in TTY as being unlike any other Irish pack:

> in that they hunt in the season five times a week instead of the weekly runs of the Royal Meath, the Kildares and other hunts. And the Tipperary Hunt was exclusive; it had few members but all were devotees. Its headquarters were at a small hotel in Fethard which kept an excellent chef. Dr Stokes lived in the hotel and he was a fixture, an authority of some kind, probably a veterinary surgeon. Next to the Master, the chief member was Dan Maloney of the well-formed body and the ruddy face. When he blew his nose it took about sixty seconds to regain its deep purple hue. The Master lived at the Grove and there were hunters by the dozen in the stables as well as the pack in the kennels. All the members had to be endowed with independent means, for it costs money to hunt and to do nothing else. The Master had lots of money; so had his neighbour Lord Waterford, another leathery man and somewhat of a rival with his own pack.

*Horse Show award:* the Royal Dublin Society's Horse Show held in Dublin in August, centres upon equine affairs and is a great social occasion.

*Beastings:* US spelling of beestings, the first milk secreted by a mammal after parturition.

**'New Bridge'**

*New Bridge . . . the oldest bridge:* Newbridge (Irish, *Droichead Nua*), County Kildare, had its New Bridge built over the river Liffey in 1308. The town developed after the building of a cavalry barracks there in 1816. The New Bridge was succeeded by a three-arched concrete bridge in 1936.

*Eternal City . . . Settimo Severe:* the arch in Rome built in commemoration of Lucius Septimus Severus (AD 193–211) and his deeds. He defeated the Parthians and occupied Mesopotamia, but failed to achieve much in Scotland before dying in York.

*The Sabine ridge:* probably a reference to the Anio Vetus (see note on 'Roman . . . gold . . . Sabine water' above, p. 665).

**'Glenasmole'**

Title: *Glen na smol* (Irish, the Valley, or Glen, of the thrushes) in SW County Dublin, through which the river Dodder flows (see Christopher Moriarty, *Down the Dodder* (1991)). The Dodder, an eighty-six mile long river, rises on Kippure, County Wicklow and flows into the River Liffey at Ringsend, Dublin.

*Bohernabreena:* (Irish, *bothar*, road; *breena/Bruighean*, a royal house of public hospitality), the site of two artificial lakes, reservoirs supplying water to Dublin, in Glenasmole, County Dublin. There was a house on the Dodder, two miles from Tallaght, *Bruighean Da Derga*, destroyed by pirates in the early Christian era; no trace of it remains but it has left its name on the town land, Bohernabreena, the road of the *Bruighean* or Mansion.

*Lochlann galleys:* (Irish *Lochlann* Norse/Scandinavian) an allusion to the Viking raids on

Ireland which began in 795. (They fortified an area above the Liffey in Dublin which became their chief centre; they also developed townships in Wexford, Waterford, Cork and Limerick. Their dominance ended with their defeat at the Battle of Clontarf, outside Dublin, in 1014.) Gogarty's 'Foreword' to the poem in *Contemporary Poetry* IV. 4, Winter 1946, comments:

> Glenasmole is the Gaelic for 'The Valley of the Thrushes.' The poem refers to a saga that tells how some Scandinavian marauders ambushed and burned a hostel, Bohernabreena, on the River Dodder near Dublin in which sat a remnant of the super-human, half magical race of Gaelic warriors which the old poets love to describe. The spear of the leader had to be kept cool in a cauldron, for it grew to a white heat at the approach of a battle.
> Bohernabreena means the Hostel by the wayside 'boher' or road.

**'Limestone and Water'**
*Parian stuff:* marble from Paros, a Greek island in the Cyclades, in the S. Aegean Sea.
*The castle:* probably a generalised image but it could apply to Yeats's tower at Ballylee, County Galway (cf 'In Memory of Major Robert Gregory', YP p. 235: 'The tower set on the stream's edge'), to Auchnanure, O'Flaherty's castle, see note above, p. 664, or to Gogarty's own unroofed tower, Dungorey or Dunguaire Castle (King Guaire's dun) in Kinvara, County Galway, which he bought in 1926.
**'Anachronism'**
*A dark man:* Homer.
*Achilles' deadly path:* Achilles, son of Peleus and the sea deity Thetis, was the foremost warrior at Troy. Homer's *Iliad* is based on his wrath at Agamemnon's taking his captive Briseis; he withdrew his forces from the Greek army but returned when his friend Patroclus was killed by Priam's son Hector.
*the bow one man alone:* in Book XXI of Homer's *Odyssey* the suitors for Penelope, Odysseus' wife, fail to string Odysseus' bow, a test she set them. He, however, disguised, easily manages this before beginning his slaughter of the suitors.
*in the sea immersed:* in Book VI of the *Odyssey,* Odysseus, lost for two days and nights in the sea after he left Calypso, arrived at the land of the Phaeacians in Scheria, washed up by a great wave.
**'Sub Ilice'**
Title: from Latin *ilex,* a holm-oak.
*Alba Longa:* in the Alban Hills, 12 miles SE of Rome, an ancient city destroyed by the Romans in 600 BC.
*Soracte:* a mountain in Etruria sacred to Apollo, visible from Rome.
*'vides ut':* Horace *Odes* I.ix. *Vides ut alta stet nive candidum Soracte* . . . Do you see how Soracte is standing glistening white with snow?
*Flaminian Way:* a road in Italy running north from Rome to Rimini, constructed in 220 BC by Gaius Flaminius, a Roman general (d. 217 BC) defeated by Hannibal at Trasimene in 217 BC.
*confiscated farmstead:* see note on Virgil above, p. 660.
*his friend in Rome:* probably Gaius Cornelius Gallus (*c.*69–26 BC), a poet and politician introduced into Virgil's tenth *Eclogue* as an Arcadian shepherd. A friend of Augustus, he was influential at Rome, and is thought to have brought about the restoration of his friend Virgil's farm or to have had him compensated for its loss. It had been confiscated in 44 BC when land round Cremona was distributed to veterans of the civil wars.
*Mastersinging races:* meistersingers were members of various German guilds organised to compose and perform poetry and music. Gogarty may have had Richard Wagner's (1813–83) opera *Die Meistersinger* of 1868 in mind.
*colour . . . Titian preferred:* Titian (Tiziano Vercelli, ?1490–1576), Italian painter of the Venetian school, used a reddish-gold colour for the hair of many characters in his

religious and mythological paintings.

*veniemus urbem:* (Latin) we will come to the city.

*Virgil's birthplace:* see note on him above, p. 660.

*Idyll's ilex:* Virgil's *Eclogues* (or *Bucolics*) were modelled upon the *Idylls* of Theocritus and Gogarty is here using the word Idyll for them.

*Menalcas:* He appears in *Eclogues* III and IV.

*Phyllis:* name used in some pastoral poetry.

*the Idyll: Eclogue* III.

*Vis ergo inter nos:* a quotation from Virgil, *Eclogue* III: are you willing, then, that we should have a trial between us, by turns, what each can do?

*vicissim:* Latin, in turn. Gogarty is glossing it in advance with 'turn about's'; the inverted comma after 'about's' makes it seem a possessive whereas the sense is: 'turn about' is '*vicissim*'.

*Dodder:* see note above on 'Glenasmole', p. 671.

*Virgil led a soul estranged:* In Book VI of the *Aeneid* Virgil has Aeneas, in accordance with the order of and accompanied by the Sibyl of Cumae, visit the underworld where he meets his father Anchises who prophesies the future greatness of Rome. He also meets Dido, who committed suicide when he left her at Carthage and is not reconciled to him. He returns to his ship through the Ivory Gate.

**'Oughterard'**

*Oughterard:* a village about 15 miles NE of Galway, about a hundred and fifty miles from Dublin.

*Jim Sweeney, the Sergeant and Father McNulty . . . running dog Finn:* It has proved impossible to identify these characters, the Presbytery records in Oughterard not having been kept; the running dog Finn (a greyhound or whippet) does not seem to have been recorded locally or elsewhere; he is not in the earlier issues of the *Greyhound Calendar* in the British Library (1928). There is a possibility that the Rev. Stephen McNulty who served mainly in Ulster (from 1920 at Castlebillingham, Armagh, from 1925 at Leggan, Dromore) might have been a curate for a year or so at Oughterard. From 1916–1925 the Parish Priest at Oughterard was the Rev. James Craddock.

*black Morty Mor:* see note above, p. 667.

**'Connemara'**

*Connemara:* a coastal region in County Galway, called after the descendants of Conn the Hundred Fighter, See note on him above, p. 660.

*West of the Shannon . . . the Suck:* the country west of Athlone, on the Shannon, has often seemed wild, mysterious, different to Irish writers, such as the novelists Maria Edgeworth, Lady Morgan, Charles Robert Maturin and James Joyce (in his story 'The Dead'). Gogarty is intensifying the difference between Connaught and the east of Ireland by going further west, to Ballinasloe on the Suck. The note on Cromwell (with his 'to Hell or Connaught' p. 667), may suggest the difference is due to the forced movement west of those largely Catholic Irish whom Cromwell expelled from their lands.

*the Suck:* the Shannon's largest tributary, a river rising near Castlereagh in County Roscommon and flowing through Lough O'Flynn, Ballymoe and Ballinasloe to join the Shannon above Banagher.

*Ballinasloe:* a town in County Galway about twelve miles SW of Athlone.

*The Seaside sons of Conn:* see note on Connemara above.

**'Dawn in Vermont'**

Title: Gogarty thought Vermont the county of America that most resembles Ireland (RL, p. 172). See his praise of a brook in leafy Vermont (I p. 79) which indirectly refers to Yeats's poem 'Vacillation,' IV, YP, p. 367.

**'Nymphis et Fontibus'**
Title: (Latin) to Nymphs and Springs.
**'The Phoenix'**
Title: The Phoenix is a legendary Arabian bird, said to set itself on fire and rise from the ashes every five hundred years. Gogarty once nearly succeeded in having it put on the Irish Senate's list of protected birds in the Wild Birds Protection Act.
*Atlantides:* fabulous islands (Greek, plural of Atlantis, the fabulous island).
*epinikian:* victorious, triumphal (Greek *epi*, above, near to; *nike*, victory).
**'High Tide at Malahide'**
*Malahide:* a village, now virtually a suburb, on the sea coast north of Dublin.
*Lynn Doyle:* pseudonym of Leslie Alexander Montgomery (1873–1961) a comic writer; born in Downpatrick, he was a bank manager in Dundalk, County Louth; he is known for his Ballygullion stories, Ballygullion being a fictional townland.
*Conn:* see note above, p. 660.
*Swords' River:* Swords, a village, now a suburb, in north County Dublin on the Dublin Belfast road with a long history of being burnt by the Danes (in 1012, 1016, 1130, 1138, 1150 and 1166. In 1185 it was sacked by O'Melaghlin, the King of Meath).
**'The Isles of Greece'**
*her lovely city:* Mitylene, a port in Lesbos, Sappho's birthplace, an island in the E. Aegean Sea off the NW coast of Turkey. The Greek poetess (*b.c.*650 BC) fled from Mitylene (the chief town of Lesbos) to Sicily (*c.*596 BC) but returned to Mitylene later. Lesbos was known as a centre of lyric poetry, led by Alcaeus (7th century BC) and Sappho.
*nota bene:* Latin, make a note; note well; take notice, a phrase calling attention to something important.
*hetairai:* educated courtesans.
*Girton girls:* Girton, a Cambridge College, originally for women students, opened at Hitchin in 1869 and transferred to Cambridge in 1873.
**'The Waveless 'Bay''**
*Kiltymon:* on the Wicklow coast near Brittas Bay.
**'Fog Horns'**
*Dark Pool to White Ford:* Dark Pool is a name for Dublin, (Irish, *Dubh* dark/black; *linn*, pool.) *Linn* is an ancient word meaning not merely a pool but a 'riverpool', in this case formed by a confluence of the Liffey and the Poddle, or the Bradoge; in Gogarty's view, the former flowing under 'The Dolphin', the other coming down from under Grange-gorman, and entering 'Anna Liffey at the end of east Arran Street' (RL, p. 59). The water gets its dark colour from the bogland through which it flows for much of its course. Mary Clark has suggested that 'White Ford' may have been the White Bank near the mouth of the Liffey, the 'Dark Pool' being higher up the river. It was called white because of the number of shells on it and because of the sands being generally contrasted with the darker, often wetted colour of the rest. In Corneille's map of 1804 it appeared as a narrow ridge about 700 metres long, stretching SW from the South Wall, which it joined 800 metres E of the Pigeonhouse Fort with a 90 metre junction. See J. W. de Courcy, *The Liffey in Dublin* (1996).
*Howth:* see note above, p. 669.
*Ben Edar:* Howth, see note above, p. 669.
*the Lea:* a meadow, meadow land. Cf Spenser, *Faerie Queene*, IV, Canto XI, 41: 'There was the Liffey rolling downe the lea.' Nearer the sea were the marsh and sandbanks at the mouth of the Liffey before it was confined by quays.
*Moore Street:* a street running parallel to the west side of O'Connell Street, Dublin, which joins Henry Street and Parnell Street, formerly the resort of 'shawlies', women

who sold fish and flowers.

*Dark Linn:* Irish, *linn,* a pool (see note on *Dark Pool* above); but Black Linn is also the highest point of Howth Head, 560 feet in altitude.

*the Rinn:* Irish, point or headland.

**'Between Brielle and Manasquan'**

Title: *Brielle and Manasquan . . . Barnagat's still Bay:* These are in Monmouth County on the Atlantic coast of New Jersey, resorts with some commercial fishing; Brielle is near the mouth of the Manasquan River. (R.L. Stevenson wrote part of *The Master of Ballantrae* in Manasquan in 1888.) Barnegat Bay extends about thirty miles along the coast; entered from the sea through Barnegat inlet it is protected by Island Beach peninsula and Long Beach Island. Barnegat is a village about two miles inland from Barnegat Bay. Gogarty stayed with the Spickers family (see p. 709) who had a house there.

*Bristol's:* blue and green glass were specialities of the Bristol glass makers.

**'The Ship'**

*Valparaiso:* Chile's main port, in central Chile.

*the Andes' blue . . . city set:* Valparaiso is set on a wide bay of the Pacific with the high Andes mountain chain behind it.

**'Off Sicily'**

*Venus' heel . . . Foam-Born Queen:* Venus, goddess of love, the Roman equivalent of Aphrodite (Greek, *aphros,* foam) was born from the sea.


SATIRES AND FACETIAE

**'O Boys! O Boys'**

*a young fellow of old . . . wonderful town:* Marco Polo, see note on him, p. 686.

**'Ringsend'**

*Ringsend:* area south of and bounded by the Liffey, a mile from the centre of the city, where the Dodder joins the Liffey; it was largely a working class area in the late nineteenth and early twentieth centuries.

*Tolstoi:* Count Leo Nikolayevich Tolstoi (1828–1910), the Russian novelist, aesthetic philosopher, moralist and mystic, author of the novels *War and Peace* (1863–69) and *Anna Karenina* (1874–76). Gogarty may have been reading his *What is Art* in which he argued that only simple works constitute great art. He made over his fortune to his wife and lived poorly as a peasant under her roof.

**'After Galen'**

*Galen:* a Greek physician, anatomist and physiologist (Latin, Claudius Galenus, ?130–?200 AD), who codified the medical knowledge of his time; his authority continued until the Renaissance.

**'To a Boon Companion'**

This poem was addressed to Seumas O'Sullivan (see note, p. 692) when included in *T.C.D.*

*Alcmena's chesty son:* the Greek hero Hercules, son of Zeus and Alcmena. Smitten by her charms Zeus took on the guise of her husband Amphitryon, a Theban prince, when he had gone to war to avenge the death of his father-in-law's son, this having been the condition of his obtaining the hand of Alcmena, daughter of the King of Mycenae.

**'To an Old Tenor'**

*Melfort Dalton:* James Joyce portrayed D'Alton as Bartell D'Arcy. D'Alton resided at 4 Seaview Terrace, Clontarf, Dublin. The *Post Office Directory* (1901) also lists him at 68 Gardiner Street, Dublin.

*Chanticleer:* the cock who figures in 'Reynard the Fox' (?*c.*1200) and in Chaucer's 'Nun's Priest's Tale' in the *Canterbury Tales.* The word can also be used as a name for a domestic cook.

*GPI:* General Paralysis of the Insane.

*St Joseph's Old Maid's Home:* St Joseph's Asylum for Aged and Virtuous Females, Spinsters, on Portland Row (Numbers 4–8), which runs from Duke Row to Buckingham Place, Summerhill, Dublin, founded in 1836 'for the benefit of aged single females of unblemished character under the care of Nuns, the Poor Servants of the Mother of God'. See note on *Blight,* p. 767 (where it is 'the hostel on Hatch Street')

*Waes-hael:* see note above, p. 668.

*Non nobis:* (Latin) not for us.

**'To a Mushroom'**

*Silenus' bad example:* Silenus was noted for his drunkenness. See note, p. 664.

*Augustan:* relating to the period and the poets of the reign of the Emperor Augustus Caesar, hence to any period or author noted for refinement and classicism.

**'To the Maids not to Walk in the Wind'**

*from foam . . . as Venus:* see notes, pp. 661, 669 and 675.

**'A Pithy Prayer Against Love'**

*Priapus:* a fertility god, said to be the son of Aphrodite and Dionysus. He appeared as a grotesque deformed creature in his statues, usually placed at the doors of houses or in gardens. See further note on Priapus in notes on 'George Moore's Garden Shrine' p. 742.

*Jack Falstaff:* Sir John Falstaff in Shakespeare's *Henry IV,* a fat, witty, self-indulgent braggard; good natured but in the *Merry Wives of Windsor* his vices expose him to indignity and mortification. He decides to make love to the wives of two gentlemen living at Windsor, Ford and Page, because they have the command of their husbands' purses. He sends identical love letters to both wives, who contrive his misadventures – at Ford's house, when Ford arrives, Falstaff is hidden in a basket with dirty linen and tipped into a ditch; at a second assignation he is disguised as the fat woman of Brainford and beaten by Ford. A final assignation is arranged in Windsor Forest where Falstaff is attacked and pinched by mock fairies and beaten by Ford and Page. See Gogarty's poem 'Applied Poetry' p. 140 dealing with Doll Tearsheet and Mistress Quickly who grieve for him.

*Hippocleides:* Herodotus, the Greek historian (*c.*480–425 BC), tells the story (VI.128) of how Hippocleides, chosen suitor for the daughter of the tyrant Cleisthenes, ordered the flute players at his wedding to play a dance, and ended up standing on his head and gesticulating with his legs; his intended father-in-law remarked 'Son of Tisander, you have danced your marriage away'. 'It doesn't bother Hippocleides' was the reply.

*cordax:* Greek, cordax, an indecent dance, particularly in comedy.

*ου φροντίς!:* no bother (Greek, *ου,* no/not; *φροντίς,* bother). Gogarty is quoting Herodotus directly here.

**'The Three':**

**'Faith'**

*Brian O'Lynn:* See Gogarty's limerick on him below, p. 357.

**'Hope'**

*Surgeon MacCardle:* John Stephen McArdle (1859–1928) FRCSI (1884) of 72 Merrion Square, Dublin, Surgeon of St Vincent's Hospital, Professor of Surgery, Catholic University School of Medicine, President of the Irish Medical Association and author of *Operative Surgery for Students* (1894). He was a pioneer in abdominal surgery. A Dublin character, known as 'The Surgeon' or 'Johnie Mac', he was often host at lavish lunches in the Dolphin Restaurant and fond of galloping in the Fifteen Acres in the Phoenix Park.

**'Choric Song of the Ladies of Lemnos'**

*Tirynthian groom:* Hercules (Greek Heracles) the hero known for his twelve labours, was, according to tradition, a Tirynthian. Tiryns is on a rocky hill in the Argive plain, two and a half miles north of Nauplia and a mile from the sea.

*Lion's fell:* a lion's skin. Hercules was sometimes portrayed bearing a club and wearing the skin of a lion he killed at Mount Cithaeron as a cloak, but the garment is more often attributed to the lion he killed at Nemea, the first of the labours imposed upon him by Eurystheus, to whom Hera (angered by Zeus boasting about the son Alcmene would bear him) tricked Zeus into giving the rule of Tiryns and Mycenae which should have come to Hercules.

*The Town of Death:* Hades, from which Heracles stole Cerberus, the infernal watchdog, showed him to Eurystheus and then returned him to the Underworld.

*the Triple Dog:* Cerberus, a monstrous dog guarding the entrance to the lower world; known as the dog of Hades, he had three heads and a mane or tail of snakes.

*Alcestis:* a daughter of Pelias, she married Admetus, who forgot to sacrifice to Artemis at the Bridal Feast, and saw an omen of imminent death. He was saved from this by Alcestis promising to die on his behalf (no one else offered to do so). Admetus received Hercules hospitably despite his grief at her death and Hercules fought with Hades (or with the death spirit Thanatos) and got Alcestis back from the underworld.

**'Europa and the Bull'**

*Archer Goddess:* Artemis, or the Roman equivalent, Diana.

*Alabaster Palaces of Minos:* Minos, a legendary King of Crete, son of Zeus and Europa, who became supreme judge in the infernal regions. His vast palace in Crete was at Knossos.

*Dells of Ida's island:* Mount Ida, a mountain in central Crete, hence here Crete.

*Would turn into a Ford*: satiric comment on Ford cars as symptomatic of a mechanical mass production age.

*Sidonian Shore:* Sidon on the coast of Phoenicia, a city known from the first century BC for its purple dyeing and glass blowing.

**'The Old Woman of Beare'**

Title: This is an early Irish poem, frequently translated. See, for example, *The Penguin Book of Irish Verse*, ed. Brendan Kennelly (1970) pp. 31 and 62.

*Fresh Nellie:* a Dublin whore.

*Mrs Mack:* a well-known brothel keeper. See 'The Old Pianist', p. 456.

*Mrs Lepple:* another whore. See Gogarty's 'The Hay Hotel', p. 454 and 'The Old Pianist', p. 456.

*warty boys:* See W.B. Yeats's comment in a letter of 22 May 1936 to Dorothy Wellesley that 'warts are considered by the Irish peasantry a sign of sexual power', *Letters on Poetry from W.B. Yeats to Dorothy Wellesley* (1964 edn., p. 63).

*Femen's stone:* (Irish, *Sid al Femen*) the home of Bodb in *The Wooing of Etain*. See Myles Dillon, *Early Irish Literature* (1948). In *The Children of Lir* Aoife visits a neighbouring Danaan King Bor the Red (also Bodb) who lived at a lonely place by Lake Derryvaragh in County Westmeath. *Bodb Derg* was a son of the Dagda.

*Bregan:* perhaps Bregon. Ith, Miled and he were people of the mythical Milesians. Their relationships are confusing. T.W. Rolleston, *Myths and Legends of the Celtic Race* (1911), describes Ith as the grandfather of Miled, dwelling in a great tower which his father Bregon had built in Spain. In another version Bregon is described as the son of Miled, father of Ith. Bregia is the great plain lying to the east of Tara, between the Boyne and the Liffey (Irish *Mag Breg*, said to have been named after Breaga, son of Bregon and uncle of Mil. Bregia is a Latinised form of *Breg*).

*Bregan's Chair:* obscure; perhaps Bregon, father of all the Milesians, is implied, or a Bishop, Saint Brogan; yet again it may be a local place name. See Kuno Meyer's translation of this poem:

> The stone of the Kings on Femen
> The chair of Ronan in Bregan
> Tis long since storms have reached them:
> The slabs of their tombs are old and decayed

See also Frank O'Connor's translation:

> Femon Brega, sacring stone,
> Sacring stone and Ronan's throne,
> Storms have sacked so long that now
> Tombs and sacring stone are one

Rónán was a king of Leinster *c*.600 AD, the son of Aedh. His death is recorded in the *Annals of Ulster* and by the Four Masters under three dates, 610, 619 and 629 AD. See Myles Dillon *The Cycle of Kings* (1946).

*McHugh:* he was Hugh McNeill, who at one time taught Classics and Romance Languages at St Patrick's College, Maynooth. See James Joyce, *Ulysses* (1992 edn) pp. 156–189 (The *Evening Telegraph* office). Lenehan whispers a limerick about him into Stephen's ear:

> There's a ponderous pundit MacHugh
> Who wears goggles of ebony hue.
> As he mostly sees double
> To wear them why trouble?
> I can't see the Joe Miller. Can you?

[A Joe Miller is slang for a joke. Stephen Dedalus then remembers Gogarty's phrase]: In mourning for Selhurst, Mulligan says 'Whose mother is beastly dead' (*op. cit.*, p. 170).

*Alma's reedy ford:* Other translations of the poem give 'the sea' or 'the wave of the Great Sea' See Kuno Meyer's translation:

> They row and row across
> The reeds of the Ford of Alma

### 'Job's Healer'

*the Comforters of Job:* In the Bible Job was smitten by boils 'from the sole of his foot to his crown'. Various friends, 'comforters' attempted to explain his affliction. See Job 4 and 5; 8; 11; 15; 18; 20; 22; 32; 34; 35, 36 and 37.

*the whopping Whale:* See the Bible, Jonah 1:7 and 2:10. Jonah was fleeing from a command of the Lord when the ship he was in was threatened by a storm. He was thrown overboard: 'Now the Lord had prepared a great fish to swallow up Jonah, and Jonah was in the belly of the whale three days and three nights'.

*Confluent furunculosis:* a skin condition characterised by multiple boils.

*Leviathan:* a monstrous beast, a sea monster. See Job 41: 1–34, Psalms 14:14; 104: 26 and Isaiah 27:1; and see also Milton, *Paradise Lost*, VII, 412:

> There Leviathan
> Hugest of living Creatures, on the Deep
> Stretcht like a promontorie sleeps or swimmes . . .

*Behemoth:* a monstrous beast, probably a hippopotamus. See Job 40:15–24.

*Borrow an axe . . . kill your mother:* an echo of the anonymous 'Lizzie Borden':

> Lizzie Borden took an axe
> And gave her mother forty whacks;
> When she saw what she had done
> She gave her father forty-one.

LOVE AND BEAUTY

**'Dedication'**
*He . . . Caesar's ear':* Virgil, see note on him above, p. 660.
**'Tell me Now'**
*Amorous Triumvir:* Mark Antony (?83–30 BC) a Roman general who served under Julius Caesar in the Gallic wars and became a member of the second Triumvirate. He defeated Brutus and Cassius at Philippi in 42 BC, repudiated his wife for Cleopatra, queen of Egypt and was defeated by his brother-in-law Octavian (Augustus) at Actium in 31 BC.
*Abydos' bay:* Abydos, an ancient Greek colony on the Asiatic side of the Dardanelles (ancient name, the Hellespont). Leander, a youth of Abydos, used to swim across to visit his beloved, Hero, a priestess of Aphrodite at Sestos; he was drowned in a storm and then she killed herself by throwing herself into the sea. The story has been told by Marlowe in *Hero and Leander*. Byron emulated Leander in swimming the Hellespont.
**'Thinking Long'**
Entitled 'To Parmenis' in NYT, 11 October 1939, Parmenis being a character in *Going Native* (1941) who likes being rude. She gives the narrator/hero 'one in the eye' on their first meeting. She is the daughter of a clergyman who christened her Parmenis 'because her surname was Innes'. She is the niece of the vicar with whom the narrator/hero is staying; there is a funny episode (based on Irish/English differences) when she bids him to her bedroom. See Ch 12, GN, pp. 187–219.
**'Concerning Hermione'**
**I. The Conquest**
*The Conquest:* presumably the Norman invasion of Ireland.
*eight hundred years:* The Normans arrived in Wexford in 1169, Strongbow, (Richard de Clare, 2nd Earl of Pembroke, c.1130–1176), crossing in 1170.
*hucksters:* cf Yeats's '[Introductory Rhymes]', YP, p. 263:

> . . . blood
> That has not passed through any huckster's loin.

**II. Exorcism**
*The Queen it is death if one sees . . . merciless dart:* Artemis, who set Actaeon's dogs on him, to kill him, after he had seen her bathing naked. (There is, however, a remote possibility that Persephone (more properly described as a Queen, as wife to Hades) could be intended. In Homer's *Odyssey* II, 632–5 Odysseus says he wants to stay in Hades and see more ghosts but is afraid Persephone might send up to him the 'gorgon head of some terrible monster' which, presumably, would turn him into stone. If one saw Persephone one was already a ghost in Hades except for the few heroes who made the descent and returned to upper air, viz Hercules, Oydsseus and later Aeneas). If Artemis is intended, Gogarty might also have been thinking of *Odyssey* V.121 seq. where Calypso reproaches Hermes (who has brought her a message from Zeus that she must send Odysseus on his way immediately) about the cruelty of the jealous gods, citing the case of Artemis killing Orion with her darts when Dawn had fallen in love with him. See *Odyssey*, 5, 121–4.
*The Queens whom the young man judged:* Paris, son of Priam, King of Troy, was exposed on Mount Ida (his mother Hecuba having dreamed she would bear a torch which would burn down the palace at Troy), grew up as a shepherd, and married Oenone. But at the marriage of Peleus and Thetis the goddess of discord threw a golden apple among the gods and goddesses, and the final contenders for it came down to the claims of Hera, Aphrodite and Athena. Paris was appointed to be judge and when the

goddesses appeared naked before him, he gave the apple to Aphrodite as she promised him the most beautiful woman in the world. He therefore visited Sparta and persuaded Helen, the wife of King Menelaus, to elope with him to Troy.

*changed to a reed or a laurel*: in classical Greek mythology Syrinx, a nymph, ran away from Pan. She begged the Earth or the river nymphs to help her; she became a reed-bed from which Pan made his pipes. Daphne, daughter of a river god, rejected the advances of Apollo who was pursuing her; she prayed for help and was turned into the laurel which bears her name.

*Arundel walls*: an 11th century castle in West Sussex. The second Earl (Thomas Howard, ?1585–1646) was a patron of learning and the arts.

**V. 'A Sound'.**

*Joyous Gard*: Launcelot's Castle in the Arthurian legend (Malory placed it at Anneck (Alnwick?) or Bamborough, on the NE English coast).

**'Release'**

*To Calypso*: Calypso, one of the daughters of Atlas, a nymph who reigned in the island of Ogygia, received Odysseus hospitably when he was shipwrecked, offering him immortality if he would stay with her.

*the messenger . . . Pieria . . . the order from above*: this follows Homer's *Odyssey*, Book V. Zeus ordered Hermes to convey to Calypso the need for Odysseus to return home. Hermes dropped down to the Pierian range and skimmed the sea till he reached Ogygia. Pieria is a region of ancient Macedonia west of the Gulf of Salonika.

*Odysseus, free*: After staying seven years with Calypso he was allowed to depart and resumed his journey back to Ithaca.

**'Melsungen'**

*Melsungen*: a town on the Fulda, twelve miles south of Kassel, in the former Prussian province of Hesse-Nassau.

**'Send from the South . . . '**

*the great Gulf . . . Summers for the North*: a relatively warm ocean current, the Gulf Stream (or North Atlantic Drift), flows from the Gulf of Mexico northeastwards off the Atlantic coast of the US, bringing warmer water towards the west of Ireland and NW Scotland.

**'Begone, Sweet Ghost'**

*young Actaeon*: see note above on 'The Queen it is death if one sees' p. 679. When the hunter Actaeon saw Artemis and her attendants bathing naked she turned him into a stag and he was devoured by his own hounds.

**'Good Luck'**

*Apples of gold the Hero dropt*: Milanion (or in some versions of the legend, Hippomenes) to whom Aphrodite had given three golden apples from the garden of the Hesperides.

*Atalanta*: she was so delighted by the golden apples she stopped briefly to pick them up so Milanion won the race and married her. The race was with Atalanta; whichever of her suitors outdistanced her would marry her; those whom she distanced were to be killed by her dart.

*cordial . . . Iseult*: see note above, p. 670. When Tristram is bringing Iseult (Isoud in Malory's *Le Morte Darthur*) and Bragwaine her attendant to King Mark's court, Isoud's mother has given Bragwaine a love potion to be given to King Mark. On the ship Tristram and Isoud find the flask containing the love potion and drink its contents in ignorance and as a result love each other for the rest of their lives.

*he who kept the unwitting tryst*: Tristram, sent by his uncle King Mark to Ireland to request Iseult in marriage.

*Western gold . . . posset*: apples or a love philtre.

**'Applied Poetry'**

*Doll Tearsheet*: a character in Shakespeare's *Henry IV*.

*Youth's a stuff will not endure:* Quotation from Shakespeare, *Twelfth Night* II, iii.
*Gross Sir John:* Sir John Falstaff, see note, p. 676.
*Doll and Quickly:* Doll Tearsheet and Mistress Quickly, the servant of Dr Caius, a French physician, characters in Shakespeare's *Henry IV* and *The Merry Wives of Windsor*.
*The Bard . . . our pleasant Willie:* Shakespeare.
*Love can't be made by proxy . . . Heigh with orthodoxy . . . o'er the dale:* an echo of Shakespeare, *The Winter's Tale* IV.II.I:

> When daffodils begin to peer
> With heigh! the doxy, over the dale . . .

*Full honoured and respected*
*We meet our troops of friends:* Another Shakespearean echo, from *Macbeth* V.iii.22:

> And that which should accompany old age
> As honour, love, obedience, troops of friends . . .

### 'To Shadu 'L-Mulk'
*Khalil Shah:* this author has not been traced in any English or French bibliographies of Persian literature or reference books, nor have any scholars of Persian literature who have been consulted recognised the name of the author or the poem. Gogarty may, it has been suggested, have found some pastiche or spoof presented as a Persian poem and possibly thought it genuine – or else invented author and poem himself.

### 'Leda and the Swan'
Leda, a queen of Sparta, mother of Helen and Pollux by Zeus, who visited her in the shape of a swan. Her other twin son Castor was by her husband Tyndareus.
*Leda's Mother:* Eurythemis, whose husband was Thespius.
*Lacedaemon:* another name for Sparta or Laconia.
*All that Trojan brightness;/Agamemnon murdered;/And the mighty twins:* Helen, Leda's daughter, was the cause of the Trojan war. Agamemnon was murdered by his wife Clytaemnestra and her lover Aegisthus on his return from Troy. The mighty twins are Castor and Pollux, the Dioscuri. After the death of Castor Pollux spent half his days with his brother in Hades, half with the gods on Olympus. They were made the constellations Gemini by Zeus, which never appear together, one rising when the other sets and so on alternately. Pollux became god and patron of boxing, Castor excelled in the management of horses. They were regarded as the patrons of sailors. In Roman times they were thought to have led Roman armies in various battles. Cf. Yeats's 'Leda and the Swan' (YP, p. 332):

> A shudder in the loins engenders there
> The broken wall, the burning roof and tower
> And Agamemnon dead.

Cf also W.B. Yeats, *A Vision:* 'I imagine the annunciation that founded Greece as made to Leda, remembering that they showed in a Spartan temple, strung up to the roof as a holy relic, an unhatched egg of hers; and that from one of her eggs came Love and from the other War' (*A Vision* (1990 edn). p. 260, and see also notes, ibid., pp. 391 and 400).

### 'Faithful even unto Freud'
*Freud:* Sigmund Freud (1856–1939) Austrian psychiatrist, the originator of psychoanalysis, based on the free association of ideas and analysis of dreams.
*seven maids:* the seven daughters of Atlas, placed as stars in the sky to save them from Orion's pursuit (another legend says this was after they killed themselves in grief over the death of the Hyades, their half-sisters).

682                                   NOTES TO PAGES 148–152

*Saladin:* Saleh-ed-Din Yusuf ibn Ayyuh (?1137–93) Sultan of Egypt and Syria who opposed the crusaders, capturing Acré, Jerusalem and Askelon.
*The Moor:* Muslim people of North Africa of mixed Arab and Berber descent who established their power in N. Africa and Spain: in the eighth century they were converted to Islam. They had a considerable effect on Spanish architecture.
*Maiden in a castle wall:* this stanza has some echoes of Tennyson's *The Lady of Shalott*.
*Corinthians:* dissolute people. Corinth was known for its profligacy.
*Aphrodite's house:* Aphrodite was the goddess of love.
**'Farewell to the Princess'**
*The Mandarin of T'Sow:* probably Ts'ao Shuang (d. 249 AD) who, raised to high office by the Emperor Ming Ti, sought military renown, heading an expedition against the rival house of Shu, but failing ignominiously. He took to riotous living after the Emperor's death, appropriating some of the Emperor's concubines; he was put to death for being involved in a treasonable conspiracy. Gogarty may possibly have had in mind Ts'ao Ts'ao (AD 155–220) who distinguished himself in a campaign in 184 AD. He overcame many chieftains, defeating Hu Pu who had assassinated Tung Cho, his master, against whom Ts'ao Ts'ao had created a movement of various officials. He campaigned successfully against Yuan Shao and his sons, was ennobled as a prince. The Emperor Hsien Ti was largely controlled by him and after the death of the Empress (whom Ts'ao Ts'ao had put in prison for plotting against him) he proclaimed his own daughter Empress. He created large armies and enforced strict discipline on them. See Herbert A. Giles, *A Chinese Biographical Dictionary* (1898).
*The Duke of Ting . . . twenty ladies . . . The Lord of Lu:* Duke Ting ruled in Lu (a small state founded in the twelfth century BC) from 509 to 495 BC. He appointed Confucius (Latin name of Kung Fu-tse (551–479 BC) to govern the town of Chung-Tu in 501 BC. The Chinese philosopher, who had been a teacher since 531 BC, reformed social behaviour and brought about the prosperity of the state, celebrated for its culture, but incurred the jealousy of its neighbours. They engineered a breach between Confucius and the Duke. Confucius left Lu in 497 and did not return until 485 or 484 BC; recalled by a new Duke he did not re-enter political life. The Duke of Ting's support of Confucius and his good government had been diverted by a gift of eighty beautiful girls and a hundred and twenty-five horses. See Friedrich Hirth, *The Ancient History of China* (1908).
**'Women'**
*Dryades:* Dryads, hamadryads and meliae were tree-spirits in Greek mythology, the first two originally belonging to oak trees (though dryad came to mean any tree nymph), the last to ash trees.
**'I Wonder'**
*Lethe:* forgetfulness, from Lethe, the river in Hades that caused forgetfulness in those who drank its waters.
*Time's Magnificat:* the Magnificat is the hymn of the Virgin Mary (see Luke I:46–55) used as a canticle; here Time's celebration is not linked to a similar outburst of praise.
**'With a Coin from Syracuse'**
*Syracuse . . . the fountain Arethuse:* Arethusa, a nymph, the daughter of Oceanus, bathed in the river Alpheus; the god of the river fell for her and pursued her. She appealed to Diana who changed her into a fountain in Syracuse.
*Pherenikos:* the name (it means victorious, Greek, φέρειν to carry off; νίκη victory) of a racehorse of King Hiero of Syracuse mentioned in Pindar, *Olympian Odes:* I.29.
*blood . . . can suddenly go wild:* cf Yeats's 'To a Young Girl' (YP, p. 242) and 'A Bronze Head' (YP, p. 464). Was there a common source for the Sicilian coin? Cf a letter of 6 December 1926 from Yeats to Olivia Shakespear (at the time that he was chairing the

Irish Senate's Committee which chose Ireland's coinage), commenting on an early photograph of her: 'Who ever had a like profile? – a profile from a Sicilian coin'.
**'Portrait'**
*(Diana Clothed):* Diana was the Roman counterpart of Artemis; see last line of poem and note on her below, this page.
*Toxophilite:* an archer.
*amice:* or almuse, a fur lined hood or cape worn by certain religious orders.
*chlamys . . . Artemis:* a short flowing cape (Greek, χλαμύς a mantle) Artemis, twin sister of Apollo, was the virgin goddess of hunting and the moon.
**'Perfection'**
*the ball left-handed:* the poem was reputedly written to Helen Wills Moody, the American who was world tennis champion. See note on her, p. 705.
**'Portrait with Background'**
*Dervorgilla's . . . daughter:* Dervorgilla, daughter of the King of Meath, left her husband Tergernan (Tiernan) O'Rourke in 1152 to live with Diarmuid (Dermot) MacMorrough, King of Leinster. Their daughter Eva married Strongbow, Richard de Clare, 2nd Earl of Pembroke (*c.*1130–1176).
*of all the Leinstermen Ri:* Dermot (Irish *Ri*, king) who appealed for help from Henry II of England after he had been banished from his kingdom. Henry gave him an army under Strongbow.
*Strongbow and Henry:* After Strongbow (see previous notes) came to Ireland, he offered his Irish conquests to Henry to appease the latter's jealousy of his success. Henry was crowned King of Ireland during his stay there (1171–72).
*that maddened Tristram:* he fell in love with Iseult, bride-to-be of his uncle King Mark. See notes on 'Good Luck' p. 680.
**'An Appeal from the Judgement of Paris'**
*Young Idalian lout . . . the apple . . . the pippin:* Paris who was brought up as a shepherd. See notes on him above, p. 679.
*Venus . . . the pippin . . . young Leda's swan-white daughter:* see note above on p. 680. The pippin refers to Paris giving Aphrodite (Roman, Venus) the golden apple in the contest between the three goddesses, see note below, this page. Helen was Leda's daughter.
*Nor had Troy gone down in slaughter:* Aesacus the seer prophesied that the son of Priam and Hecuba, about to be born, would be the ruin of Troy. Agelaus, Priam's chief herdsman, was given the task of killing the child but exposed him on Mount Ida instead where he survived, having been suckled by a she-bear. Agelaus finding him five days later brought him home in a wallet (hence his name Paris). His identity was revealed when he performed well at the games in Troy. Despite the priests of Apollo demanding he should be put to death Priam declared it better for Troy to perish than his wonderful son should die.
*that nude Idalian crew:* Paris had asked Hermes (who had brought the three goddesses to Mount Gargarus, the highest peak of Ida, where Paris was herding cattle) whether he should judge them clothed or naked. Hermes told him it was for him to decide the rules of the contest, and Paris decided they should disrobe which accordingly Hera, Athene and Aphrodite did.
**'Golden Stockings'**
A poem about Gogarty's daughter Brenda. See Introduction, p. 14.
**'Praise'**
*It cost a man his Muse.*
*When Rome went down:* This may refer to Lucan (AD 39–69), known for his *Pharsalia*, a heroic poem describing the struggle between Caesar and Pompey. Nero was jealous of

his success and forbade him to recite in public; he was compelled to commit suicide for his part in the conspiracy of Piso. This identification depends upon Gogarty indicating Rome's decline under Nero.

**'I Tremble to Think'**
This poem was reputedly written to Gogarty's wife Neenie (nee Martha Duane, of Ross Dhu, Moyard, County Galway) whom he married in 1906.


LIFE AND DEATH

**'The Airman's Breastplate'**
Epigraph: ( . . . *the Lorica or breastplate of St Patrick* . . . ) Despite tradition, the Breastplate, sometimes known as St Patrick's Lorica, has nothing to do with the Saint: it is an eighth century composition intended to be used as a charm before a journey: 'Today I gird myself with a great strength.' See *A Golden Treasury of Irish Poetry, AD 600–1200*, ed. and translated by David Greene and Frank O'Connor (1967).

**'Panurge'**
Panurge was one of the main personages in Rabelais' *Pantagruel*. He was cunning, witty and in the later books a coward and buffoon, a 'very dissolute and debauched fellow, if there were any in Paris: otherwise and in all matters else, the best and most virtuous man in the world'.
*the Master dreamed:* in *Pantagruel*.
*Ilissus' verge:* Ilissus, a river in Attica, flowing east and south of Athens to join the Cephissus; it has its source on Mount Hymettus. Ovid has a fine description of it in *Ars Amatoria* III. 687–694.
*the boar-cat Rodilardus:* a name created by Rabelais (literally rouge red; lard) for Panurge's cat.
*the fornicating Friar:* Francois Rabelais (?1496–1553?). A novice of the Franciscan Order, he read widely; he fled to the Benedictine House near Orleans, befriended by the Bishop of Maillezais; he entered the University of Montpellier to study medicine and became a physician in Lyons, where he began to write; his *Pantagruel* appeared in 1532. That year a popular book was *The Great and Inestimable Chronicles of the Great and Enormous Giant Gargantua*. Rabelais wrote a new *Gargantua* in 1534. He later went to Rome, taught at Montpellier, was in Paris and Turin, fled to Metz when the Sorbonne condemned his final book; he was then in Rome and later in Paris.

**'Time, Gentlemen, Time!'**
The poem may have been prompted by an incident recalled by Yeats and Gogarty (the following version is quoted from the Reynolds papers, HD) when Macran (see notes on him pp. 666 and 731), highly intoxicated, was put into a cab at night by a firm waiter (at Jammet's restuarant and bar in Nassau Street) and stuck his head out of the window to shout 'Closing Time – Time – Time! What's Time? You don't know, you dirty brutes! Time is the moving Shadow of Eternity.'

**'Centaurs'**
*Lyaeus:* the releaser or the looser from care; epithet of Bacchus (Greek, λυαῖος).
*Chiron:* the wise and kindly centaur who taught many Greek heroes in their youth.

**'Anglers'**
*Ching Chih Ho:* an eighth century AD Chinese author who wrote a work on the conservation of vitality. He took office under the Emperor Su Tsung of the Tang

dynasty but was banished, later to be pardoned in a general amnesty. However, he became a wandering recluse, taking to the woods and calling himself 'The Old Fisherman of the Mists and Waters'. He spent his time angling without bait, not wishing to catch fish. When offered a house by a friend, he replied 'I prefer to follow the gulls into cloudland rather than bury my eternal self beneath the dust of the world'. See Herbert A. Giles, *A History of Chinese Literature* (1901), p. 191. The image of the baitless hook is used in 'To a Trout', p. 167.

**'The Old Goose'**
*Patrick's frozen Reek:* Croagh or Cro-Patrick, Patrick's Heap, a mountain near Westport, County Mayo, on the summit of which Patrick is reputed to have fasted and to have banished snakes from Ireland.
*islands:* this may refer to the many islands in Clew Bay overlooked by Croagh Patrick.
*a Queen, Armed, amorous and holy:* possibly Granuaile. See note on her above p. 661 and see Anne Chambers, *Granuaile. The Life and Times of Grace O'Malley c.1536–1603* (1988 edn) pp. 11–12, 15–19.

**'Non Blandula Illa'**
Title: Not those charming things. An echo of the Roman Emperor Hadrian's (AD 76–138) poem *'Ad Animam Suam'* (To His Spirit). In the poem *'animula'* is used as a term of endearment, only in the vocative; *vagula* means hastening away or wandering:

> Animula vagula blandula
> Hospes comesque corporis
> Quae nune abibis in loca
> Pallidula rigida medula
> Nec ut soles dabis jocos!

Alexander Pope's (1688–1744) translation shows some of the parallels between Hadrian's poem and Gogarty's:

> Ah fleeting spirit! wand'ring Fire,
> That long hast warm'd my tender breast
> Must thou no more this frame inspire?
> No more a pleasing, cheerful guest?
> Whither, ah whither art thou flying!
> To what dark, undiscover'd Shore?
> Thou seems't all trembling, shiv'ring, dying,
> And Wit and Humour are no more!

The 'Anima Vagula' chapter in Walter Pater's *Marius the Epicurean* (1885) is referred to several times by W.B. Yeats. See *Memoirs* (ed. Denis Donoghue, 1972) pp. 36, 42 and 95.
*A sea-grey house:* possibly Renvyle, Gogarty's house in County Galway, on the sea's edge beside a small lough. He bought it in 1917.
*Berserks:* ancient Norse or Viking warriors who worked themselves into a frenzy before battle and fought with insane fury and courage.

**'The Ho Ho Bird'**
Possibly derived from Hoh hot, or Hu ho-hao-t'en, a city in N. China, former capital of Guiyan province, now capital of Inner Mongolian Autonomous Region.

**'The Emperor's Dream'**
*A Phoenix:* see note, p. 674.

**'The Mill at Naul'**
Naul: an area in north County Dublin, four miles inland from Balbriggan, about

eighteen from Dublin, known locally as The Naul (Irish *'n-aill*, the cliff). The mill and mill buildings are still standing. The original castle was built by Stephen de Crues in the early thirteenth century.

**'Palinode'**
Title: a poem in which the poet recants something he has said in a previous poem.
*the merry Attic blade's Remark:* Aristophanes (?448–380 BC) the Greek comic dramatist who satirised leading contemporary figures, Socrates and Euripides among them, in his plays.
*'A gentle man . . . Shades':* Sophocles, the Athenian tragedian (*c.*496–406 BC) characterised in Aristophanes, *Frogs*, 82: ὁ δ'ἔὐκολος μὲν ἐνθάδ', ἐὐκολος δ'εκει. Gilbert Murray translated this as 'Content with us, will be content in Hell', G. Hookham Frere as 'An easy-minded soul and always was'.

**'Domi'**
Title: at home (Latin).

**'All the Pictures'**
Title: 'pictures' meaning films. See Gogarty's article 'On seeing "All the Pictures"' (Guest Editorial) in *Rotarian*, November 1942, p. 7. This describes his relief at his patient's abruptness in accepting the sentence of death: There is no graver moment in the life of a doctor than when he has to give this news:

> With a judge it is different. In law the criminal is guilty. In medicine it is an innocent victim who has to be condemned.

The incident took place in about 1922:

> long before we called the movies 'the pictures'. The very fact that he was the first in my memory to use the words as a metaphor of external nature, that he had the courage to be so detached increased my admiration. . . . He had transcended himself when he called life 'the pictures'. He had made the discovery that life is a play. He had removed himself from the stage to become spectator.

**'Sunt apud infernos tot milia formosarum'**
Title: From Propertius 3.2.63, a prayer to Persephone for his mistress as the crisis of her illness passes: 'Make your clemency last, Persephone: be content with the countless beauties who dwell within your kingdom'. Sextus Propertius (*c.*48 BC–15 BC), the impassioned Roman elegaic poet, had (like Virgil) some of his property confiscated by the Triumvirs, but won the support of Maecenas at Rome. His mistress Cynthia was his main inspiration.
*China's halls/To Polo:* Marco Polo (1254–1324) Venetian traveller whose father and uncle brought him on their second trip to China in 1271; they again visited Kublai Khan, the Mongol Prince, who took to Marco and sent him as an emissary to various countries in Asia. He was governor of Yang Chow for three years. He returned to Venice in 1295. His *Travels* describe different Asian states, particularly that ruled by Kublai Khan.
*Great Magellan:* Ferdinand Magalhães, Portuguese navigator (*c.*1480–1521) who reached the Pacific by the strait named after him; his ship completed the first navigation of the world, though he died in the Philippines.

**'Per Iter Tenebricosum'**
Title: from Catullus III, 11–12:

> *Qui nunc it per iter tenebricosum*
> *Illud, unde negant redire quemquem*

This relates to Lesbia's sparrow: 'Now it's over forever, down that dark tunnel [or alleyway] he's going from where, they say, once vanished you never return'.

*Lesbia's sparrow:* Catullus, the Roman poet (see note on him, p. 740) wrote poems to Lesbia, who was Clodia, the wife of Q. Calcilius Metellus; she encouraged him at one time but on returning to Rome from Verona he found her involved with another man and wrote a final letter of farewell to her.

**'Marcus Curtius'**
*Marcus Curtius:* Mettius Curtius (4th Century BC), a noble Roman youth who is said to have ridden his horse into a chasm which had opened in the Forum in 362 BC, because the soothsayers had said it could only be filled by throwing into it the most precious treasure of Rome.

**'Non Dolet'**
Title: No cause for grief (Latin: *doleo*, I grieve); or, it does not hurt; see Swinburne's use of the Latin for a poem with a similar title in his *Collected Political Works,* (1924) I, p. 869).


ELEGIES

**'To Petronius Arbiter'**
*Proconsul of Bithynia:* Petronius Arbiter (1st century AD) thought to be the Caius Petronius described by the Roman historian Tacitus (*c.*55–120 AD) as *'arbiter elegantiae'* (the judge of taste) at Nero's court. He aroused the jealousy of another of Nero's circle, Tigellinus, who brought about his banishment. He was ordered to commit suicide.

**'Bill Baveler'**
*The Brown Stone Tavern Keeper:* not, so far, identified.

**'Farrell O'Reilly'**
*Farrell O'Reilly:* a friend of Gogarty's father ('both came from Royal Meath').
*Kilbeg:* O'Reilly's place in County Meath. Gogarty describes it at the end of Ch 2, TTY:

> It was a garden with many beehives. There was a well in the middle of the yard but the door of it was always locked. The Liss or fairy palace . . . stood in a field in front of the house, a raised square with a few twisted thorn trees on it which no man dare cut down. It seemed harmless: 'Ah but just you wait till night.' But I was sent to bed long before that.

*Moynalty:* a plain in County Meath (Irish, *magh-nealta*, the plain of the flocks). It is also the ancient name of the flat county lying between Dublin and Howth, *sean-mhagh ealta Edar.*

**'Aeternae Lucis Redditor'**
Title: Restorer of Eternal Light (. . . Robert Yelverton Tyrrell . . . ) see note on him above, p. 669. The Latin title echoes that, Professor J.R. Watson has suggested, of a hymn attributed to St. Ambrose, 'Aeternae lucis conditor', Gogarty having made use of the variant in sound and sense to pay tribute to Tyrrell, who is the restorer (Latin *redditor* from *reddo*) of light as opposed to the creator *(conditor* from *condo*). For the text of the hymn see H.A. Daniel, *Thesaurus Hymnologicus* (1855), I, p. 39, and Don Matthew Britt, *The Hymns of the Breviary and Missal* (1948), pp. 20–22. Ambrose also wrote a more popular morning hymn 'Aeterne rerum Conditor' (O Eternal founder of all things). The 'lucis' version, however, is the only one in the metre used by Gogarty. Both hymns are mentioned in Samuel W. Duffield, *Latin Hymn Writers and Their Hymns* (1889), p. 507, as well as 'Lucis Creator Optime' (p. 509), attributed to Gregory the Great (p. 57). All three hymns were popular 'classics.' See Ruth E. Messenger, *The Medieval Latin Hymn* (1953).
*Janus:* the god of the doorway, an ancient Italian god who was guardian of the city

gates and private doors. The gates of his temple were left open in war, closed in peace.
He is represented as having two heads facing in opposite directions.
*Virgilian calm:* Virgil lived into the period of peace established by Caius Julius Caesar
(63 BC–14 AD), the first Roman Emperor from 27 BC until his death. He was
venerated by the senate and the people and had the title of Augustus conferred on him.
Gogarty is here equating the Edwardian peace with the peace established by Augustus.
This is parallel to Yeats's 'Nineteen Hundred and Nineteen' (YP, p. 314):

> . . . A law indifferent to blame or praise,
> To bribe or threat; habits that made old wrong
> Melt down, as it were wax in the sun's rays;
> Public opinions ripening for so long
> We thought it would outlive all future days.

*the Great Wall:* probably any defence against those seeking to destroy a civilisation, such
as the Great Wall of China, constructed as a defence against the Mongols in the 3rd
century BC and rebuilt in the 15th century AD, or the various Roman walls built in
Rome, England and Scotland: the Wall of Aurelian (AD 271–5), a 12 mile wall round
the city of Rome; the 37 mile wall of Antoninus running from the Forth to the Clyde,
built in AD 142. It was evacuated in an orderly way, unlike Hadrian's wall, 80 miles in
length, erected in AD 122–8, running from Wallsend-on-Tyne to Burness-on-Solway.
This wall was overthrown in AD 196. Restored in AD 200–25 by Severus, it was
abandoned after attacks by the Picts, Scots and Saxons in AD 367–9, and finally
evacuated in AD 383–8. Gogarty probably had the last of these walls in his mind.
*Stygian shore:* the Styx, a river of Hades, the lower world, hateful, gloomy (from Greek
6τύγειν, to hate) over which Charon ferried the shades of the dead. According to
Virgil, *Aeneid* VI, 439, the Styx encircled Hades nine times ('. . . *et noviens Styx interfusa
coercet*').

**'Elegy on the Archpoet William Butler Yeats lately dead'**
Title: Yeats died on 28 January 1939
*the laurel crowned me:* Gogarty's note read 'The Irish Academy of Letters, founded by
W.B. Yeats and G.B. Shaw, crowned the author's work, *Wild Apples*, some years ago'.
See 'On being elected to the Irish Academy of Letters' (p. 353). Yeats gave Edmund
Dulac a lively account of Gogarty's high spirits at an Academy Dinner in May 1937:
Gogarty was in the chair and made a speech . . . 'We are at a great historic moment, a
moment as important as that which saw the birth of Elizabethan lyric and its music,'
and then at intervals he jumped up and made another speech, sometimes about the
Elizabethan lyric, sometimes that he might say 'Did you once see Shelley plain?' and
then at his fourteenth speech, Starkey ('Raggle Taggle'), who was quite as drunk as
Gogarty ran and stood between the tables waving a fiddle about his head and cursing
us, 'Damn you all, damn, I say damn, I have gone all over the world looking for people
who "just enjoy themselves."' Then glaring at Gogarty, who was trying to silence him,
'I am a fiddler, I am not a movement, I am a fiddler, I am a bloody fiddler – Hell!'
Then he began to play getting as much noise as possible out of his fiddle with Gogarty
beaten down. After that our proceedings lacked method, somebody sang 'Who fears to
speak of Ninety-eight' at the piano and Gogarty continued to make speeches when
ever anything could be heard; he denounced De Valera, various personal enemies and
repeated old ballads. Fortunately I had turned out the waiters and stood with my back
against the door so there was no danger of their returning. Everybody had enough
bottles beside him.
*troubled Euripides:* Euripides (480–406 BC), the Athenian tragedian whose plays were
realistic and rationalistic; he focussed attention on human minds and emotions, open to

scepticism about the conventions, religious beliefs and traditions of his time.

*Unvexed Sophocles:* Sophocles (496–406 BC), the Athenian tragedian who represented men as they ought to be; in Mathew Arnold's phrase 'he saw life steadily and saw it whole'.

*Ossian [Oisin] in Faery lands:* Oisin, a legendary Gaelic warrior and poet, visited three islands spending a hundred years on each with the fairy goddess Niamh. Cf. W.B. Yeats, *The Wanderings of Oisin*, YP, p. 1 and notes, *ibid.*, pp. 483–489.

*dark Ferdia's strain:* This is ambiguous. Ferdia was a friend of Cuchulain but had to fight against him, being part of the army of Queen Maeve of Connaught. The strain may also refer to the music played to the two warriors, to soothe them at sunset each day after their single combat, when they put down their weapons, treated each other's wounds and remained friends till the morning when they resumed fighting. Yet again Ferdia could be regarded as a member of the supernatural race 'that hosts in the hills.'

*of the tower:* Gogarty's note read '"Of the tower" is a term derived from falconry. It means a hawk at the top of his flight and ready to swoop'.

*Dulac:* Edmund Dulac (1882–1953), French-born naturalised British artist and book designer, a friend of Yeats. See note on Helen Beauclerk, p. 757.

*lost egg:* the egg in Sparta was alleged to have survived to the time of Pausanias (fl. c.150 AD), the Greek traveller and historian. See Pausanias 3.16.1 and Cf W.B. Yeats, *A Vision and Related Writings* (1990), p. 105: 'During the reign of the Antonines tourists saw it hanging by a golden chain from the roof of a Spartan temple. Those of you who are learned in the classics will have recognised the lost egg of Leda, its miraculous life still unquenched.' See note on this passage, *ibid.*, p. 39.

*Herodotus:* the Greek historian of the fifth century BC whose only surviving work is *The Persian Wars*.

*stranger mysteries . . . the decease/Of Caesar, Christ and Socrates:* a reference to Yeats's ideas in *A Vision*. See 'The Great Year of the Ancients,' *A Vision* (1990 edn), pp. 243, 264.

*Adonais: Adonais, an Elegy on the Death of John Keats:* (1821) a poem by Shelley written in Spenserian stanzas. See lines below characterising it as 'Shelley's cosmic sermon'. Shelley pictured the many mourners of Keats, the Muse Urania, Dreams and Desires, Sorrow and Pleasure, Morning and Spring and the fellow poets, all bringing their tributes to the bier of Adonais. The lament then turns into a triumphant declaration of the poet's immortality.

*Burns on Captain Grose . . . on Henderson not Grose:* Burns wrote two poems on Captain Francis Grose, '[Ken ye aught o'Captain Grose?]' and 'Epigram on Capt. Francis Grose, the celebrated antiquary' but the poem preferred here is 'Elegy on Capt. M———— H————, A gentleman who held the Patent for his Honours immediately from Almighty God!'. The epitaph to this last poem has eight four-line stanzas, the final line of each ending with a description of Matthew Henderson as a man, prefixed with different adjectives: 'great', 'poor', 'brave', 'bright', 'kind', 'true'and in the penultimate stanza, 'queer', the final line's adjective being 'rare'. Gogarty remembers a conversation with Yeats about *Adonais* in *Going Native* (1941), p. 17:

> Wait a moment,' he said, checking my rapture. 'Burns wrote an elegy on somebody or other in which he says "Matthew was a *queer* man." You remember?' So there was Yeats giving up the whole of the *Adonais* for the sake of one single word that conveyed without mantlings, directly and immediately, the character of the man. Yes, I did remember the lines whence it came –
>
>> If thou hast wit, and fun, and fire
>> And ne'er guid wine did fear, man;
>> This was thy billie, dam and sire,
>> For Matthew was a queer man

*'blind and ignorant town':* a quotation from W.B. Yeats's 'To a Wealthy Man who promised a Second Subscription to the Dublin Municipal Gallery if it were proved the People wanted Pictures' (YP, p. 202).

*City Fathers . . . a horse:* Dublin Corporation conferred the Freedom of the City on Boss Croker, his horse *Orby* having won both the Irish and the English Derby. See note on him, p. 670. Gogarty's note comments that Croker had a Tammany Hall career, that the City Fathers gave him the Freedom of the City but refused Gogarty's suggestion that they gave a similar honour to Yeats.

*Pegasus:* In Greek mythology the winged horse sprang from the blood of the Gorgon Medusa; he struck Mount Helicon (see note on it, p. 666) with his hoof. He aided the hero Bellerephon, who caught him with the aid of Athena, and tried to fly off to heaven on him. See note on him, p. 666.

*Dean Swift . . . equine state:* In the Fourth Book of *Gulliver's Travels* Swift portrayed the horses, the Houyhnhnms, as endowed with reason and contrasted them with the disgusting Yahoos, brutal beasts in the shape of men and women. Jonathan Swift (1667–1745), educated at Kilkenny College and Trinity College, Dublin, the first great Irish prose writer, author of *A Tale of a Tub* (1704) and *Gulliver's Travels* (1726) whose satiric political pamphlets included the *Conduct of the Allies* (1713), the *Drapier's Letters* (1724) and *A Modest Proposal* (1729). His poems and his *Journal to Stella* convey his humour and wit engagingly.

*Clear bright rill:* 'that turbulent little mountain stream' in Weston St John Joyce, *The Neighbourhood of Dublin* (1913), p. 151, where he calls it the Owen Dugher (The Ordnance Survey anglicises it as Owendoher) which flows down the side of Cruagh Mountain, its rocky bed suggesting the name for the village of Rockbrook, near Yeats's house, Riversdale, a former farm house outside Rathfarnham, County Dublin.

*Tyrrell, Mahaffy and Macran:* See notes on them, pp. 669, 701 and 666.

*golden Russell:* see note on him, p. 663.

*England's great hearted Laureate:* John Masefield OM (1878–1967), appointed Poet Laureate in 1930, was a friend of W.B. and Jack B. Yeats.

*murmured metre till the end:* Gogarty's note read: 'Lady Dorothy Wellesley in her book *Letters on Poetry from W.B. Yeats to Dorothy Wellesley,* tells how when unconscious, dying, his lips still murmured rhyme. See p. 194 for his footnotes.

# NOTES TO PART TWO

## Notes to *Hyperthuleana* (1916)

Title: Hyperthuleana: Beyond the Beyond. Thule was the most northerly island in Europe.

**'To the Muse'**

*Grace in Botticelli:* a reference to Sandro Boticelli's (1444–1510) painting *Primavera* (Spring) in the Florence Academy.

*Queen, the Italian's:* Botticelli was born and lived in Florence.

*Church Street:* Church Street Old runs from Arran Quay to Constitution Hill (King's Inns), Dublin, Church Street New from Bow Street to Smithfield.

**'The Feast. To my Right Honourable Friend William McElroy (a great householder)'.**

This is an early version of the poem which appears in *Collected Poems* as 'To my Friend, the Rt Hon Lorcan Galeran (a Great Householder)'; the text is sufficiently different from that in *Collected Poems* to justify the whole poem being included here. See notes on p. 662. Gogarty dedicated *An Offering of Swans* (1923) to McElroy, whom he described among the Scotsmen who seemed to him the most humorous and most amusing men he had met:

> One of them was named McElroy, who came to Belfast to be married there. That was on a Wednesday. I called him on Sunday from Dublin by long distance telephone, little hoping that he and his bride would still be in their hotel. Italy I though was more likely. A room in the Excelsior in Naples giving on a bed of Neapolitan violets! The desk put me through. Astonished, I asked 'How are you Mac?' 'Ah'll not tell ye!' he said (SSE, p. 86). Elsewhere Gogarty described him as one of the most generous and enthusiastic men he had ever met (TTY, p. 99).

*the Kairos:* καιρός (Greek): the right point of time.

*Tiberian peace:* Tiberius Claudius Nero (42 BC–AD 37) had a brilliant military career before succeeding Augustus as the second Emperor of Rome. The first eight years of his rule, according to Tactius, were marked by just government, frugality and care for the interests of the provincials. He followed the foreign policy of Augustus, abandoning the project of conquering Germany and settling several disputes by diplomacy.

Alternatively, the peace of the Roman Empire could be meant, see note, p. 663, with reference to Rome being situated on the Tiber cf. 'Domi' l.26, p. 178.

**'To George Russell'**
Title: see note on Russell, p. 663

**'To a Mushroom'**
*Silenus' bad example:* In Greek mythology he was satyr-like, fat, jolly and much given to drunkenness. See further note, p. 715.
*caves of Cheddar:* Cheddar Gorge, a pass through the Mendip Hills near Cheddar, a village in North Somerset: it is known for its stalactic caverns and rare limestone flora.
*Dead Sea fruit:* the apple of Sodom, of attractive appearance, but turning when grasped into dust and ashes, possibly the fruit of *Solanum Sodomeum*. Cf. Thomas Moore, *Lalla Rookh* (1817), 'The Fire Worshippers' II:

> Live Dead Sea fruits that tempt the eye,
> But turn to ashes on the lips!

and Byron, *Childe Harold's Pilgrimage* (1812–18) Canto III, 34:

> Like to the apples on the Dead Sea's shore
> All ashes to the taste.

Dedication: for note on Francis Ledwidge, see p. 744.
This earlier version of the poem, also included in *Collected Poems*, contains eight stanzas more than the later version and reverses the order of its last two. It has therefore been included here.

**'To his Friend the Apothecary Poet (To make something up for him')**
*when you compound:* the poem is addressed to J.S. Starkey ('Seumas O'Sullivan', 1879–1958), educated Wesley College and Catholic Medical School before becoming apprenticed in his father's pharmacy. Essayist, poet, whose *Collected Poems* appeared in 1940, and editor of the *Dublin Magazine* (1923–58).
*'Brave dead singer of the Vine':* probably Virgil, whose *Georgics*, Book II, deals with viticulture. Professor J.V. Luce has pointed out the Tennysonian echo in his 'To Virgil' III:

> Thou that singest wheat and woodland,
>     tilth and vineyard, hive and horse and herd;
> All the charm of all the Muses
>     often flowering in a lonely word.

*Herbert's:* George Herbert (1593–1633) English clergyman and poet, seemed at first likely to have a worldly career but took orders in 1630 and became the parish priest at Bemerton in Wiltshire. His verse is almost all contained in *The Temple* (1633); it expresses humility and an ideal of service, its serenity sometimes shot through with dramatic touches, sometimes written in an expostulary tone arising out of convinced and convincing faith.
*No thought of Newman's:* Cardinal John Henry Newman (1801–90) who broke with evangelism – he was vicar of St Mary's, Oxford – to join the Roman Catholic Church in 1845; he became a Cardinal in 1879. He was Rector of the Catholic University in Dublin (1854–58).
*Browningish:* Robert Browning (1812–89) an English poet who brought a sense of the bizarre into his poetry. Gogarty probably objected to his puns and occasional clever rhyming (rather than his spiritual insight), the realism of which often produced staccato effects.
*the brew . . . Shakespeare* and *Ben and all the Mermaid Crew:* Shakespeare and Ben Jonson

were not ignorant of tavern life; the Mermaid tavern, in Bread Street, London, was the meeting place of the Friday Club, (started by Sir Walter Raleigh) and was frequented by its members and other writers. It is well celebrated in 'Master Frances Beaumont to Ben Jonson'.

### 'The Isles of Greece'

*To W.K. Magee:* William Kirkpatrick Magee (1868–1961), an assistant librarian at the National Library of Ireland (1899–1921), who wrote under the pseudonym of John Eglinton (see poem p. 389 and notes pp. 726 and 735), edited *Dana* and wrote several books including *Anglo-Irish Essays* (1917) and *Irish Literary Portraits* (1935).

*Ringsend:* at the lower reaches of the Liffey, originally a port in its own right.

*Davy Jones:* the spirit or devil of the sea (Davy Jones's locker is the bottom of the ocean, regarded as the grave of the lost or buried at sea).

*Montenegro:* a republic bordering on the Adriatic, declared a kingdom in 1910, and united with Serbia, Croatia and other territories in 1918 to form Yugoslavia.

*Lepanto . . . cross . . . swamp the crescent:* A port in west Greece, scene of a naval battle in 1571 in which the Turkish fleet was defeated by the fleets of the Holy League.

*Nota bene:* Latin, note well, see note above, p. 674.

*Mytilene:* a port on the Greek island of Lesbos, known as a centre of poetry in classical times, mainly for the 7th century BC lyric poet Alcaeus and the 6th century BC poetess Sappho.

*Rhododendrons:* the name is derived not from Rhodes but from Greek *rhodon*, rose and *dendron*, tree.

*Calypso . . . got the slip:* Calypso, a daughter of Atlas, who lived alone on the island of Ogygia, fell in love with Odipseus when he was washed up on the island. He yearned to return to Ithaca and his wife Penelope and refused her offer to make him immortal if he stayed with her. Zeus sent Hermes to command her to let Odysseus go.

*Homer:* the Greek poet, author of the great Greek epics, the *Iliad* and the *Odyssey*. Reputedly blind, he was probably born in a Greek colony in Asia Minor, the epics being composed, probably, between 850–800 BC.

*Ajax . . . Salamis:* a Greek hero of the Trojan War; he killed himself when the armour of Achilles was given to Odysseus. His father was Telamon, King of Salamis.

*Paul:* (first century AD) the apostle of the Gentiles, a Pharisee who persecuted Christians, but on his way to Damascus had a vision which converted him to Christianity. He is the author of the Epistles to the Galatians, to the Romans, and to the Corinthians, and possibly other epistles as well.

*Pilate:* Pontius Pilate was Roman Procurator of Judea and Samaria (AD 26–36) during which time Jesus Christ was crucified, at his assent in response to Jewish demand. See the Bible: Matthew 27:1–24; Mark 15:1–15; Luke 23:1–25; John 18: 29–40, 19:1–16.

*Cook's:* Thomas Cook (1808–1892), pioneer of organised tours; the internationally famous company bearing his name still exists.

*looked on Life . . . Steadily, and drank it whole:* an echo of Matthew Arnold's 'Sonnet to a Friend' 1.14 in which he is praising Sophocles 'Who saw life steadily, and saw it whole.' It anticipates the implied criticism of Arnold's classicising in the penultimate stanza.

*Plato:* Plato (*c.*427–347 BC), the Greek philosopher, developed his idea of Utopia in *The Republic*.

*Arnoldizing:* a suggestion that Matthew Arnold, the English poet and critic (1822–88), weakened classical legends in his treatment of them.

*Ionian thalattaliths:* marine rocks (Greek *thalassa*, sea, *lithos*, rock).

### 'To an Aviator'

*thyrsus:* in Greek myth, a staff or wand wound round with ivy and vine leaves, usually tipped with a pine cone, borne by Dionysus (Bacchus) and his followers (Bacchanals).

**'Westward'**
Dedication: Francis Macnamara, a County Clare landlord 'whose thought was occupied for a number of years by a great work on philosophy he intended to write' see Patricia Boylan, *All Cultivated People, A History of the United Arts Club, Dublin* (1988), p. 65. One of his daughters, Caitlin, married the Welsh poet Dylan Thomas. His other daughter Nicolette Devas wrote of him in *Two Flamboyant Fathers* (1966).

**'To his Friend to try another Tavern'**
*Euphumistic calls*: possibly misprint for euphemistic.
*Delahunt's*: the name of a public house, called after its owner. Several existed in Dublin, among them those in Baggot Street Lower and Lower Camden Street.
*bona fide*: (Latin, in good faith) genuine travellers, bona fides, (who had to be five miles from home) were allowed by the licensing laws to drink after hours; a public house serving them was sometimes known by this name. The legislation was abolished in 1960, as it tended to encourage drinking and dining. See note p. 750. This suggests the public house was outside Dublin, as it was probably written to J.S. Starkey who lived in Rathmines at the time.

**'To Kasimir Dunin Markievicz'**
Title: Count Kasimir Dunin Markievicz (*b.*1874), the second son of a Polish landowning family in the Ukraine. He studied art in Paris where he met Constance Gore-Booth from Lissadell, a 'Big House' in County Sligo. They were married in 1900 and lived a bohemian life in Dublin until 1908 – normal family life for the Markievicz family ended then with her involvement in Irish politics and his increasingly frequent visits to Poland where he endured much in the 1914–18 war and Russian Revolution. He later worked in Warsaw and returned to Ireland to be at his wife's deathbed in 1927.
*him who taught proud Hector's overlord*: presumably the centaur Chiron who taught Heracles. Heracles installed Hector's father Priam as King of Troy in place of his father Laomedon. Laomedon had cheated Heracles of his pay for rescuing Hesione from a sea monster. (He had earlier cheated Poseidon and Apollo of their pay, for, respectively, building the walls of Troy and guarding his cattle).
*Roland for its Oliver*: an effective retort or retaliation. Roland was the greatest of the twelve paladins (or peers) who attended Charlemagne (Oliver was another); he died at Roncevalles in 778 AD.

**'Spirat adhue Amor'**
Title: Love is still alive, from Horace (see note on him p. 714) *Odes* IV, IX, 10–12:

> . . . *spirat adhuc amor*
> *Vivuntque commissi calores*
> *Aeoliae fidibus puellae*

(The love of the Aeolian maid still breathes and her passion, confided to the lyre, lives on).
*Merlin*: an ancient British prophet and magician, a hero of the Arthurian legend.
*the queen*: Helen of Troy.
*Abydos' flood*: Abydos, a Greek colony on the Asiatic side of the Dardanelles (or Hellespont) the scene of the legend of Hero and Leander. Leander, a youth from Abydos, drowned in the Hellespont in a storm on one of his nightly visits to Hero, his beloved, a priestess of Aphrodite, who killed herself after Leander died in the storm.
*him who clasps his love . . . nether scene*: probably Orpheus who sought his wife Eurydice in Hades but failed to bring her safely back to earth because he broke the condition that he should not look back at her.
*Stephen's Green*: St Stephen's Green, Dublin, south of the Liffey, in Gogarty's time

surrounded by many houses of the well-to-do. Gogarty had his consulting rooms there for a time.

*Ajax:* a fierce Greek hero who fought at the siege of Troy, the son of Telemon, King of Salamis, see note above, p. 693.

*twenty-one:* then the legal coming of age.

**'On first looking into Kraft-Ebing's *Psychopathia Sexualis*'**
A witty parody of Keats's sonnet 'On first looking into Chapman's Homer'

*Shebeen:* a place where alcohol is sold illegally.

*Quay was coaled:* workers unloading coal from ships at the Coal Quay on the Liffey were well known for using obscene language.

*Kraft-Ebing:* Freiherr Richard von Krafft-Ebing (1840–1902), born at Mannheim, a German specialist in nervous diseases, and a professor in Vienna.

*Macran:* Henry Stewart Macran. Professor of Philosophy at Trinity College, Dublin. See note on him pp. 666 and 731.

**'Sonnet. (When the Clearance was intended to the City)'**
Title: the Dublin Metropolitan Police caused the closing and demolition of some of the kips in 1908. Another version of the title read 'On the demolition of Tyrone Street by the Police in 1908.' Tyrone Street was the name given to Upper Mecklenburgh Street in June 1886. The residents of the Street sought this change because they were 'members of the respectable working classes' and wished to dissociate themselves from those who lived in 'the houses of Lower Mecklenburgh Street [which] are used for improper purposes and inhabited by persons of the worst character' (*Dublin Corporation Reports* (1886) II, p. 45. In time the new name of Tyrone Street became infamous and had to be changed to Waterford Street in 1911 which it is still called (*Dublin Corporation Reports* (1911) III, p. 123.

*Hercules:* in classical myth Hercules was known for his strength and for performing twelve immense labours.

*Jove . . . Danae:* Jove (Zeus) came to Danae as a shower of gold and begat Perseus on her. She was imprisoned in a brazen tower by her father Acrisius, King of Argos, because an oracle had foretold the king would be killed by his daughter's son. Danae and Perseus were cast adrift in a boat on the sea and borne to the island of Seriphos, where they were well treated by King Polydectes.

**'Memento Homo quia Pulvis es (At La Trappe)'**
Title: from the Bible (Genesis 3:19). For dust thou art, and unto dust shall thou return; *cf.* The Book of Common Prayer, Order for the Burial of the Dead, 'dust to dust'; and Longfellow 'Excelsior', 'Dust thou art: to dust returnest'.

*her daughter:* possibly a glancing reference to James Stephen's *The Charwoman's Daughter* (1912).

Dedication: for note on James Stephens, see p. 663.

**'To the Rev. George O'Neill**
(Who resigned from the Feis because of a Kissing Song)'
Title: Rev. George O'Neill. Born in Dungannon in 1863, O'Neill became a Jesuit in 1880. Professor of English Literature in the Royal University of Ireland (1901–9), then Professor of English Language at University College, Dublin, he moved to Australia in 1923 and died in Sydney in 1947. A Wordsworthian and Baconian, he published many articles and reviews, his several books including *Could Bacon have written the Plays? A Study of Characters* (1909), a translation of Jacobus de Voraigne, *The Golden Legend* (1914) and *Essays on Poetry* (1919). An address he gave at the Mayo Feis was published as a booklet entitled *Ireland as a Teacher of England and Scotland.*

*Feis:* Irish, a meeting or annual assembly. Here probably the *Feis Ceoil*, an annual musical competition.

*Horsel and Wagnerian melody:* The Horselberg is in Thuringia. Tannhauser, a German minne singer of the 13th century, rode by the Horselberg in Thuringia, was attracted by a woman in whom he recognised Venus; he spent seven years in revelry in a cave into which she had beckoned him. He sought absolution from the Pope in Rome, who told him it was as impossible for him to be forgiven as for his dry staff to blossom. But after three days, it did so. Tannhauser, then sought by the Pope, could not be found; he had returned to Venus.

*reiterated 'Pudding and Pie':* a nursery rhyme, hence 'reiterated': 'Georgy Porgy Pudding and Pie / Kissed the girls and made them cry.'

**'The Two Despairs'**

*Hell's river . . . Hope's wreckage:* a reference to the Styx (Greek στυγεῖν, to hate; hence στυγνός hateful) a river in Hades over which the shades of the dead were ferried by Charon. See notes on Charon, obol and Styx below, p. 700.

*the parsley crown:* Victors in the Isthmian and Nemean games were crowned with garlands of parsley (see, for example, Juvenal 8, 226).

**'To a Clever Little Lecher'**

This is one of several poems included about William Sinclair; the others are included in Part III see pp. 399–401 and see also 'To an Amphisbaenic Friend' below p. 215 and notes on the Sinclair brothers pp. 740–41.

**'Conscription'**

*The pen . . . sword:* See Edward George Bulmer-Lytton, first Baron Lytton (1803–1873), *Richelieu* (1839):

> Beneath the rule of men entirely great
> The pen is mightier than the sword

Dedication: *W.O.* is Sir William Orpen (1878–1931). Born at Stillorgan, County Dublin, he studied at the Dublin Metropolitan School of Art and the Slade School, London. Known for his Irish genre subjects as well as his fine portraits, he was a war Artist in the First World War and was an official artist at the Peace Conference. The poem is commenting on his being a war artist.

**'To an Amphisbaenic Friend'**

Title: *amphisbaenic:* from Greek *amphis*, both ways, and *bainein*, to go, hence able to move backwards or forwards – in classical myth the amphisbaena was a poisonous serpent with a head at each end.

*That Greek . . . Juvenal despised:* See Juvenal, *Satire* 3, 78, a famous passage attacking foreign immigrants in Rome: 'Queritis, I cannot abide a Rome of Greeks and yet what fraction of our dregs come from Greece.' The particular Greek, *graeculus esuriens*, of Juvenal led to Samuel Johnson's lines in *London*:

> All sciences a fasting monsieur knows
> And bid him go to Hell, to Hell he goes.

which were derived from Juvenal's

> *Omnia novit Graeculus esuriens*
> *In caelum iusseris ibit*

*King Billy's nose:* William III, William of Orange (1650–1702), who defeated James II at the Battle of the Boyne and became joint ruler with his wife Mary II (the daughter of James). Mary died in 1694; he was succeeded in 1702 by Anne, James II's second daughter (1665–1714).

**'To a Bearded Dealer in Old Objects of Art'**

This is another teasing poem to William Sinclair. See note on him, p. 741.

**'Helen's Lamp'**
*Paris:* the son of Priam, King of Troy, who brought Helen, wife of Menelaus, King of Sparta, back to Troy with him, thus provoking the Trojan War.
**'A Line from Rabelais'**
This poem was written at Christmas 1909, dated thus on part of MS, NLI.
*Faire and softly passeth Lent:* Curiously enough Urquhart, *The Works of Mr Francis Rabelais* (1653), whose translation Gogarty admired, did not translate this line directly from the Prologue of the Fourth Book (addressed *'aux lecteurs beneroles'*): *Bien et beau s'en va Quaresme!* [*Carême* in modern French] rendering the line thus 'twill be fair anon'. Either Gogarty translated the original or he may have read W.F. Smith's translation of Rabelais, *The Five Books and Minor Writings* (2 vols, 1893), which gives 'Fine and fair goes Lenten Air'.
*sprent:* scattered or sprinkled, from an arcaic verb sprenge, to scatter or sprinkle.
Dedication: for note on George Moore, see note below, this page.
**'Epilogue**
To the People of Ireland in the Coming Times'
The subtitle echoes W.B. Yeats's 'To Ireland in the Coming Times', YP, p. 85.

# Notes to *Secret Springs of Dublin Song* (1916)

**'Spring in Dublin'**
The poem is reminiscent of Swift's poems 'A Description of the Morning' and 'A Description of a City Shower'.
*sidecars . . . Glasnevin:* hired horse drawn vehicles . . . Glasnevin, an area north of Dublin, in Gogarty's youth still regarded as countryside.
*a play by Synge . . . gloom and squalor:* Gogarty was not in sympathy with the drama of John Millington Synge (1871–1909) which presented a stark if poetic tragi-comic view of Irish country life in such plays as *In the Shadow of the Glen* (1903), *The Well of the Saints* (1905), *The Playboy of the Western World* (1907) and *The Tinkers' Wedding* (1909). *Riders to the Sea* (1904) was a tragedy.
*Cork Hill:* the seat of Dublin's municipal government, the City Hall. Completed in 1879, it adjoins Dublin Castle on the high ground west of Dame Street. The civic offices are now situated on the much disputed Quay site below Christ Church Cathedral.
*the Stock Exchange:* the Dublin Stock Exchange was founded in 1789 and is now situated in Anglesea Street, Dublin.
*ducks now splash:* St. Stephen's Green's lake is populated by ducks and water-hens with gulls as well seeking food from passers-by. Cf. Yeats's 'Demon and Beast' YP, p. 293.
*Rathfarnham's lanes:* Rathfarnham, a small village, now a suburb in South Dublin, at the foot of the Dublin Mountains.
*George Moore:* Moore (1852–1933), the Irish novelist who had lived in Paris, originally intending to be an artist, then in London, earning a living by writing (as the income from his father's estate in County Mayo proved very small) before returning to Ireland, living in Ely Place, Dublin (where Gogarty was a neighbour from 1900 to 1910.) His famous trilogy *Hail and Farewell* (1911; 1912; 1914) gives an amusing, often malicious account of his friends and associates. He spoke freely of his love affairs, accounts which were received with scepticism, wittily voiced by Susan Mitchell:

> 'Some men kiss and tell. Some men kiss and do not tell.
> But Moore tells and does not kiss' (RL, p.111)

## 'A Double Ballad of Dublin'

*Inchicore . . . hurdles:* beside the Liffey, Dublin being known as the Ford of the Hurdles (*Baile atha Cliath*) see note, p. 762.

*the ridge of the hazels:* the name (Irish, *Drum Cuil Coille*) for the hill upon which the ancient city of Dublin was built. See George A. Little, *Dublin before the Vikings* (1957) p. 37. It was a spur of the Eiscir Reada, the Gravelridge of Riding, probably the earlier Irish highway leading from Dublin to Galway. It can be seen from the riverside from the stretch of old city walls, along the southern side of Cork Street near St Audoen's Gate.

*Bishops divide the Episcopal chair:* presumably a reference to the fact that Dublin has both a Catholic and a Protestant Bishop.

*Asthore:* Irish term of endearment, my treasure, my darling.

## 'To Citizen Elwood in South America'

Title: John Elwood, known as Citizen Elwood, see note on him, p. 725.

## 'Rondeau'

A poem playing on the echoes of Moor, More and Moore.

*Your ancestors:* George Moore's family was originally protestant, the first marriage into a Catholic family occuring in the eighteenth century. A son of this marriage, George Moore the merchant, passed as a Catholic in Spain; he was the novelist's great-grandfather, who returned to Ireland from Alicante with a large fortune which enabled him to build Moore Hall, overlooking Lough Carra in County Mayo. Gogarty is suggesting a Moorish relationship through the Spanish connection, something emphasised by the supposed ancestors sacking Baltimore.

*Baltimore:* a small seaport with a troubled history, situated in the Barony of Carberry, County Cork, east of Mizzen Head and due south from Bantry. The town was burnt down in 1537 in revenge for one of the O'Driscolls (chiefs of Baltimore for several centuries) having seized a vessel full of Spanish wine that had sought refuge in the harbour. It was plundered again in 1631 by two Algerian galleys led up the intricate channel to its port by a Dungarvan fisherman, subsequently executed for his treachery. Over two hundred of the inhabitants, mostly English settlers, were carried off into slavery, the town sacked and plundered. Thomas Davis (1815–1845) commemorated the second attack in the last poem he wrote, 'The Sack of Baltimore':

> The yell of 'Allah' breaks above the prayer and shriek and roar –
> Oh, blessed God! the Algerine is Lord of Baltimore . . .

*O'More:* the O'More. 'The' prefixed to the surname indicates the head of an Irish clan. (The O'More clan has a contemporary leader).

*bois and boulevard:* a reference to George Moore's youth in Paris. See note on him p. 697.

## 'To Carson, Swimmer of Sandycove'

*Murray's haven:* a pub called the Arch kept by 'watery-eyed Murray' in Sandycove: at the end of the Dalkey tram line, it was convenient to the Martello tower. It has been called 'The Arches', 'Journey's End', 'O'Brien's', and is now 'The Mariner'. Gogarty remarked in TTY that he and his friends used to visit it in the evenings.

*Carson:* Alfred E. Carson, who lived at 2 Sandycove Avenue West, known for his all the year round swimming; he swam every day from the Forty Foot to Bullock Harbour and back, and sometimes swam to Dalkey Island and rested there for an hour before swimming back. 'Strangers seeing his clothes on the rocks' writes Mervyn Wall, 'would frequently raise the alarm that a man had been drowned'. Carson appeared about 1906 in the Kingstown Police Court to answer summonses, he had in breach of the township's by-laws entered the sea at the Forty Foot Hole after 9.00 am without a bathing costume. The case was seen as an attempt to restrict the immemorial right of the regular Forty Foot swimmers to bathe without costume whenever they felt like it. Carson's counsel argued that the Forty Foot was 'open' and the Forty Foot being the property of Lord Carysfort was not governed by laws applying to public bathing places. The case was decided in Carson's favour. The right to swim there without costume is now restricted to times before 9 am; women were strictly debarred from entry. See Mervyn Wall, *Forty Foot Gentlemen Only* (1962).

*For what dost thou, O Carson, care for cold . . .*
*The Bobbie weakened by the rathe lanthorn?* This refers to Carson's winter swimming, when he could be seen picking his way to the water's edge of the Forty Foot (the 'banks of granite' surrounded the deep pool at Sandycove) with a lantern. The Bobbie was a young zealous policeman on duty, a newcomer to the neighbourhood, who, when the place was covered in snow, was, according to Mervyn Wall:

> shocked to see a naked man clearing away the snow to put his clothes down, so he ordered Carson to dress himself and accompany him to the Dalkey Police Station. Carson without a word did as he was told, and his arrival there in the custody of the most junior member of the local police force caused intense amusement as he was very well known as a local figure of standing and good repute. He was immediately released. (*Forty Foot Gentlemen Only* (1962), pp. 15–16.)

*O Golden Carson:* probably, Professor Lyons has suggested, a reference to his bronzed complexion.
*McCurdy:* this is probably Gogarty's contemporary at Trinity College, Dublin, F. McCurdy Atkinson, who won several Vice Chancellor's Prizes in English Prose (in 1903, for 'The Scandinavian and the Celtic Geniuses as seen in Mythology and Legend'; in 1904 for 'Mythology – theories as to its origin and development'. He became a journalist in London and is mentioned in Joyce's *Ulysses*. See note on McCurdy, p. 734.
*Griffith's towel:* Arthur Griffith (1872–1922), Gogarty's great friend, used to swim with him in the Forty Foot Hole at Sandycove, sometimes extending their swimming to Bullock Harbour further south along the coast. See Seán T.Ó Ceallaigh, 'Arthur Griffith', *The Capuchin Annual* (1966) p. 136: 'Gogarty challenged Griffith to swim across Dublin Bay from the Martello Tower at Sandymount. Griffith accepted. The two men swam out half way across the bay. Gogarty got the idea that the double journey might be too much for his friend, so he himself pretended to be tired and told Griffith he was giving up. Griffith protested but Gogarty insisted, turned back and Griffith followed him'. (Sean T.O'Kelly (1882–1966) held several ministerial posts (1932–45) before becoming president of the Irish Republic (1945–59). He was one of Gogarty's first patients, operated on by him in the Richmond Hospital in 1902.) Griffith founded *Sinn Fein* (1905) and was the first President of Dail Eireann. Gogarty had known him 'since the days when his first movement for freedom began in *An Stad*, Cahill McGarvey's little tobacco shop opposite Findlater's Church at the corner of North Frederick Street', about 1899; later Griffith used to have a few 'large ones' with his friends 'in the Bailey of an Evening.'
*Starkey:* James Sullivan Starkey (1879–1958) who wrote under the pseudonym Seumas O'Sullivan. See note on him, p. 692.
*that stroke* the trudgeon. See note below on 'trudging'.
*the Adelaide:* one of Dublin's main hospitals, now moved out from the central area of the city to the Tallaght region in S.W. County Dublin.
*Gordon:* possibly Thomas Eagleston Gordon, who graduated there in 1890, was appointed Professor of Surgery, Trinity College, Dublin in 1916, President of the Royal College of Surgeons, Ireland, 1928. He wrote on abdominal surgery, orthopaedics and the hypertrophied prostate gland; he lived at 8 Fitzwilliam Square.

See J.B. Lyons, *An Assembly of Irish Surgeons* (1984) pp. 80–81.

*that Gordian knot:* may indicate that he corrected an umbilical hernia in the Adelaide Hospital.

*Starkey mingled:* in his role as an apothecary.

*Nereus:* a sea god, father of the Nereides, lived in the depths of the sea.

*Proteus:* an old man of the sea who looked after the flocks of Poseidon; he had the gift of prophecy but, when questioned, assumed different shapes to avoid those who wished to consult him.

*the quaint Calypso:* a sea nymph who detained Odysseus for seven years on her island of Ogygia.

*trudging:* using the trudgeon stroke, with over-arm action as in the crawl with a scissors kick, named after John Trudgen, an English swimmer who invented it.

*Kirke-like:* Kirke and Lyons were two local fishermen who sold lobsters to Gogarty and his friends in the tower; see TTY, Ch. III.

*Poseidon:* in Greek mythology god of the sea, a brother of Zeus and Hades.

*Charon:* in Greek mythology the ferryman who ferried the souls of the dead over the rivers Styx and Acheron to the infernal regions.

*obol:* Charon's fee, usually placed under the tongue of the dead to pay him.

*Styx:* a river of Hades (or the lower world), hateful and gloomy. See note above, p. 696.

**'From "The Queen's Threshold"'**

Act I (Interrupted)

*Queen Mary:* this (in view of 1.12) may refer to the wife of George V, who became King in 1910. His consort, whom he married in 1893, was formerly Princess Victoria Mary Augusta Louise Olga Pauline Claudine Agnes of Teck (1867–1953). Gogarty met her during the period he practised in London after his kidnapping in 1923 (while living in England he returned to Dublin, armed, accompanied by armed detectives, to attend Senate meetings).

*the Allies:* in the 1914–18 war the powers of the triple entente, France, Russia and Britain along with other countries allied to them against Germany.

**'The Old Man Refreshing Himself in the Morning'**

Partially parodying W.B. Yeats's 'The Old Men Admiring Themselves in the Water', YP, p. 134, which begins 'I heard the old, old men say' and ends:

> 'I heard the old, old men say
> All that's beautiful drifts away
> Like the waters'

*lithia:* the oxide of lithium, L10, short for lithia water, often prescribed for gouty conditions in the nineteenth century.

**'On the Death of his Aunt
(To the Gravediggers to enter her gently)'**

*the widow of a worthy brewer:* she 'had not only the *Almanac de Gotha* by heart but *Burke's Landed Gentry* as well'.

*a sable bottle with two Saint Andrew's crosses:* the product of her husband's brewery, possibly stout.

Cf a passage in Joyce's Ulysses (1992 edn), p. 52:

> The aunt thinks you killed your mother.
> That's why she won't.
> *Then here's a health to Mulligan's aunt*
> *And I'll tell you the reason why*
> *She always kept things decent in*
> *The Hannigan famileye*

**'Praise and Friendship'**
'The Reply' is by Seumas O'Sullivan, see note on J.S. Starkey, p. 692.
*Redding's, terse:* George Redding (1882–1944), an Ulsterman who worked in Guinness's brewery, Dublin, from 1901, a sought-after position. He was in the Forwarding Department (1910–1923). He was subsequently transferred to London, and was Head of the Cooperage Section at Park Royal from 1936 until his death in 1944. He was known for his witty unpublished verse. One of Gogarty's drinking companions in Fanning's Public House in Lincoln Place, he used to attend Gogarty's Friday evenings in Ely Place. He wrote 'Two Jews in Sackville Street,' the cause of the libel action brought against Gogarty in 1937 who had included the lines in his SS. Redding was not troubled in advance about the case (see Lyons, L, p. 184). One poem he did publish was to Gogarty (*Irish Statesman*, 23 July 1927) with whom he kept up a lively correspondence when Gogarty was in America, In SSE Gogarty described him as

> born in the North. He was appointed by examination of course to the great brewery of Guinness which has a cathedral-like solemnity about it. It narrowed his style because his poems were never published. There must be others but I remember 'So few but roses all!' He was a 'strong silent man'. He hated humbug and therefore hated the twins Harry and Willie [the Sinclair brothers, see pp. 740–41]. Harry, bald and dignified, Willie a bearded gadabout.

**'Threnody on the Death of Diogenes, the Doctor's Dog'**
Title: *the Doctor's:* the poem mourns the death of a dog belonging to Sir John Pentland Mahaffy (1939–1910), a Fellow of Trinity College, Dublin, who became Professor of Ancient History (1869) and Provost (1914–1919). Mainly known for his scholarly works on Greek life, literature and history, he was a dominating and witty conversationalist. Gogarty wrote well of him in SS and TTY.
*Greece:* a reference to Mahaffy's *Rambles and Studies in Greece* (1878).
*the seed of a King:* Mahaffy, who was rather a snob, was proud of his contacts in the regal world of Europe. See R.B. McDowell and W.B. Stanford, *Mahaffy* (1972).
ὦ χαῖρε,ὦ κύον! Farewell, dog (Greek, χαῖρε to greet or bid farewell; κύον dog).
*Persephone:* a daughter of Zeus and Demeter, she was carried off by Pluto (Hades) when gathering flowers in a vale of Enna in Sicily and made his Queen in the lower world. Demeter wandered the earth in search of her, and Zeus agreed to her return on condition she had eaten nothing in Hades. She had, however, eaten some pomegranate seeds there. She was finally allowed to spend six months of the year on earth, six in Hades.
*Mock turtle:* soup made in imitation of turtle soup, or a calf's head dressed with condiments and sauces to resemble a turtle.
*'Conversation':* a reference to Mahaffy's *The Principles of the Art of Conversation* (1889).
*Bion:* a pastoral poet (*c*.100 BC–?) of Smyrna who ended his life in Sicily where he was poisoned; he is best known for his lament on Adonis on which Shelley modelled his 'Adonais'.

**'The Pilgrimage to Plunkett House'**
*Piers Plowman-like:* In *The Vision concerning Piers Plowman*, a middle English alliterative poem, the poet, wandering on the Malvern Hills, sees a vision of a high tower and a dungeon and a 'fair field full of folk'. Piers Plowman offers to guide them on their pilgrimage to St Truth.
*Plunkett House:* 84 Merrion Square, Dublin, presented to Sir Horace Plunkett (1854–1932) in 1908, to be the headquarters of the Irish Agricultural Organisation Society. See Trevor West, *Horace Plunkett: Co-operation and Politics, an Irish Biography* (1986).
*a man of beard and brawn:* George Russell (see note on him, p. 663) who sported a fine bushy beard.

*Mananaun:* Mannanan MacLir, son of the Irish sea god Lir; a shape changer, he rode his horses, the sea-waves, as though over a plain.

*the wall with gods is quick:* Russell painted the walls of his upstairs office in Merrion Square with his images of visionary beings, as he had the walls of the house of the Theosophical Society in Ely Place, Dublin.

*gombeen men:* shopkeepers who practise usury.

*High-Priest Registrar:* Russell. As a visionary poet he could read the omens; the 'High-Priest' is probably ironic, but the 'Registrar' reminds us of how very practical he was.

*Dana:* a legendary goddess of the Tuatha de Danaan, mother of all the gods who inhabited Ireland before the coming of the Milesians.

*Banba:* one of a triad of goddesses, the sisters Erin/Eire, Fodhla and Banba, who married the Milesian invaders MacGreine, MacLecht, and MacCuill. Their names are also names for Ireland.

*the cream . . . separated milk:* the Irish Co-operative movement established creameries; by 1891, 15 had been established. See Trevor West *Horace Plunkett, Co-operation and Politics* (1986), pp. 29–35.

*Rathgar:* Russell lived in Coulson Avenue, Rathgar, a south Dublin suburb.

**'A Lament for George Moore'**

*Ely Place:* where Moore (and Gogarty) lived in Dublin, a cul de sac, a street away from St Stephen's Green. Gogarty's former house, Number 15, is now the Royal Hibernian Academy. See note on Moore, p. 697.

*A.E.* George Russell, see note on him above, p. 663.

*Virgo Magee:* see note on him above, p. 663, and p. 726.

*Edward Martyn:* Martyn (1859–1923) an Irish landlord and playwright, who lived at Tulira Castle, County Galway. A cousin of George Moore, he was co-founder with Lady Gregory and Yeats of the Irish Literary Theatre. He admired Ibsen's theatre of ideas but left the movement that led to the creation of the Abbey Theatre, supporting first the Theatre of Ireland then the Irish Theatre, for the production of works concerned with contemporary Irish life and plays in Gaelic, and also of continental plays in translation.

*Your firstlings:* as Moore was writing *Hail and Farewell* he used to read selected passages to friends, something which caused considerable unease among his friends and acquaintances.

*Catholic . . . seceded:* In 1903 Moore wrote to the *Irish Times*, declaring himself a Protestant, a gesture prompted by his dislike of authoritarianism in Irish Catholicism.

*still the light . . . light from:* an echo of Robert Burns, 'The Vision' (1785), Duan Second:

> But yet the light that led astray
> Was light from Heaven

*Les Dames aux Temps jadis:* 'Ballade des dames du Temps Jadis' in *Le Grand Testament* (1461) of Francois Villon (1431–?). Born in Paris, he graduated in 1452, fled from Paris after fatally wounding a priest in a brawl. He joined a criminal organisation. Pardoned in 1456, he took part in a robbery, fled to Blois, was sentenced to death for another crime but released as an act of grace. He continued to be in trouble for theft and brawling and finally left Paris after another sentence of death was commuted to banishment. Nothing more is known of him after that. His poetry was realistic, full of irony and vitality; it gave new energy to medieval verse forms – ballades and rondeaus – through his sharp observation of contemporary life.

*Hazardous and harmless lover:* see note on Moore above, p. 697.

*Come back to Ireland:* after completing *Hail and Farewell* Moore had left Dublin in 1911, to live for the rest of his life in Ebury Place, London. Gogarty may be echoing 'Come back to Erin' here, a popular nineteenth century song of the parlour variety composed by 'Claribel' (Charlotte Arlington Barnard).

*Playboy unguessed at:* the hero of Synge's *The Playboy of the Western World* (first staged in 1907), Christy Mahon, deludes villagers in County Mayo with his boast that he has killed his father. He is turned upon when his father turns up. The play blends an exposure of the locals' gullibility with the unreality of Christy's boasting about his prowess and the reference to the *Playboy* emphasises the 'harmless' aspect of Moore as a lover.

## Notes to *The Ship and Other Poems* (1918)

Title: *Castle Corrib:* Gogarty may have been thinking of the savage fighting around Lough Corrib in the time of Grace O'Malley (Granuaile, 1530– c.1603). See notes on her, pp. 661 and 685.

## Notes *to An Offering of Swans* (1923)

**'When the Sun Shines'**
Gogarty added a note to the poem (originally 'To Mary on Howth Summit'): 'we see this in the mystics Blake [and] Novalis'
**'Please drive slowly through Little Waltham'**
Title: Little Waltham in Essex is on the A130, about four miles north of Chelmsford and about six and a half miles south west of Braintree.
*Waterloo:* a small town in central Belgium where British and Prussian forces under the Duke of Wellington and Blucher routed the French under Napoleon in 1815.
*Robin Hood:* a legendary English outlaw; according to tradition he lived in Sherwood Forest, Nottinghamshire, and robbed the rich to give to the poor.
*'Amor':* Rome spelt backwards (Latin *Roma*, Rome) is *Amor*, love.
**'The History Examination'**
*The Eagle . . . the Idaean boy:* Ganymede, a beautiful youth, was tending his father's flocks on Mount Ida in Phrygia when, at the command of Zeus, an eagle carried him up into heaven to become cup-bearer to the gods in place of Hebe (see note on her, p. 668).
*Fergus . . . the wooden sword:* In Irish legend Fergus was King of Ulster until his mistress Nessa tricked him into letting her son Conor (Conchubar) rule in his stead for a year; Conor proved so popular Fergus went into exile hunting in the woods. See note on the wooden sword, p. 660.
*Lancelot his scar:* Lancelot, one of the Knights of the Round Table, the lover of King Arthur's wife, Queen Guinevere. Having gone secretly to a joust in Winchester he agreed, though remaining faithful to Guinevere, to wear the sleeve of Elaine, the Fair Maid of Astolat, who had fallen in love with him. He was wounded in the tournament by his kinsman Sir Ector de Maris.
*Liffey's last, sweet reach:* at Chapelizod, Dublin.
*Poppaea's . . . hair:* Poppaea Sabina, then wife of Sabinius Otho (her second husband) was the mistress of the Roman Emperor Nero (37–68 AD); he married her in 62 after banishing his wife Octavia on a trumped up charge and then having her put to death. Otho subsequently became Emperor in 69 AD after his troops lynched the Emperor Galba, Nero's immediate successor. Gogarty's most likely sources could have been Pliny 11–41 or Juvenal.
**'Folia Caduca'**
The Latin title means fallen (*caduca*), leaves; (*folia*).

# Notes to *An Offering of Swans* (1924)

**'To Edward Moreton Drax, 18th Baron of Dunsany'**
*one who loves the muses:* Lord Dunsany (1878–1957), dramatist and writer of fiction; a landowner in County Meath, he served in the Coldstream Guards in the Boer War, in the Royal Inniskilling Fusiliers in the First World War and later in the War Office, London.

**'Slanting Light'**
*Danae . . . stream of gold:* In Greek myth, the daughter of King Acrisius of Argos, Danae, was confined by him in a brazen tower because an oracle had foretold the king would be killed by his daughter's son. Zeus, who was enamoured of her, came to her there in a shower of gold. Her son Perseus acidentally killed Acrisius, giving him a fatal wound with the discus he had thrown at funeral games at Larisa. Despite the cruel treatment he had received from Acrisius Perseus had borne his grand-father no ill will.
*the shaw:* shaw is an arcaic word for a thicket, a copse or grove.

**'Seven concerning Hermione'**
**'VI A Privilege'**
*Poictiers:* Poitiers, a town in southern central France, capital of the province of Poitou until 1790.

**'VII A Miracle'**
*Pygmalion:* in Greek legend a king of Cyprus and a sculptor who fell in love with a statue of a beautiful woman that he had made; in answer to his prayer Aphrodite gave the statue life.
*chryselephantine:* ancient Greek statues made of or overlaid with gold and ivory (Greek, *krusos*, gold; *elephas*, elephant, hence ivory).

**'Early Morning – Germany'**
*a golden head . . . Brenda:* Gogarty's daughter Brenda (b. 1912). A sculptress, she married Desmond Williams of Tullamore in 1945.

**'To a Trout'**
*Thyades:* a name for the Bacchanals (or Maenads), from Thyas, the first woman to be the priest of the god Bacchus.
*hookless bait:* cf 'Anglers' p. 167.

**'To the Lady——'**
The poem is addressed to Sarah Bernhardt (1844–1923), the famous French tragedienne, who played the eponymous Queen Elizabeth in a silent film in 1912.
*Gloriana:* one of the names under which Edmund Spenser (?1552–99) indicated Queen Elizabeth in his *Faerie Queene*.
*Diana:* the virginal Roman goddess associated with the moon and with hunting, the equivalent of Greek Artemis.
*Artemis:* the daughter of Zeus and Leto, twin sister of Apollo, she was a Greek goddess with whom Diana is linked. A huntress, she lived in perpetual celibacy in Moesia, in the area of Dacia, south of the Danube.
*Graces . . . triune:* in Greek mythology the three graces were three sisters, Aglaia, Euphrosyne and Thalia, givers of charm and beauty. Triune means three in one (Latin *tria* three, *unus* one).

**'Pankration'**
Title: a dangerous sport of the ancient Greeks combining boxing, wrestling, kicking, strangling and twisting.

**'And Now'**
*the Dacian Constantine:* Flavius Valerius Constantinus, Constantine the Great (?280–337), the first Christian Roman Emperor; he moved his capital to Byzantium which he

renamed Constantinople. Born in Naissus, Upper Moesia, he was the son of Constantius Chlorus and Helena, who was probably his concubine, whom he had to put away in order to marry Theodora, daughter of Maximilian. Constantine was an outstanding general, an administrator and legislator of energy and integrity.

**'Lambay'**
Lambay, an island off the north coast of County Dublin, north of Ireland's Eye and Howth.

**'Relativity'**
*Einstein:* Albert Einstein (1879–1955) American physicist and mathe-matician, born in Germany. He formulated the special theory of relativity (1905) and the general theory of relativity (1916) and made major contributions to the quantum theory.

**'Medicus Poetae'**
Title: the doctor (Latin *medicus*) to the poet (Latin *poetae*)
Addressed to his friend J.S. Starkey ('Seumas O'Sullivan') see note on him, p. 692.

**'To Tancred'**
*Tancred:* Francis Willoughby Tancred, whom Gogarty met with Grattan Freyer in London at the Cafe Royal during his stay at Oxford. He worked in the Stock Exchange and wrote various volumes of poetry; he ended up in a mental hospital. Gogarty writes on him in TTY, giving a lively anecdote in Ch. 33 of how, at Gogarty's request, Tancred was allowed out to a dinner party in London, an order issued by 'she who must be obeyed', the doctor in charge of him, Travers, imposing the sole condition that Tancred should return by midnight – 'A Cinderella part'. He is mentioned in the verse letter to Dermot Freyer, p. 394.

# Notes to *Wild Apples* (1928)

**'Portrait' ['You in your apple tree']**
The poem is written about a neighbour's daughter.

**'Portrait'**
*Jane W:* Jane Waring.
*Helen, your foster town:* Troy, destroyed by the Greeks at the end of the Trojan War. It is her 'foster town' because she left her husband Menelaus, King of Sparta, and ran away with Paris, son of King Priam, to Troy.
*Grand Rapids:* a city in S.W. Michigan.
*Scamander's place:* Scamander is a river in Asia Minor flowing into the sea near Troy. It is called Xanthos (yellow) by Homer in the *Iliad*, where Achilles fights it; the river was driven back by fire sent by Hephaestus.
*Araby the Blest . . . the Phoenix nest:* see note on 'The Phoenix', p. 674.

**'To George Redding'**
*George Redding:* see note above, p. 701.
*Helen Wills:* Mrs Helen Wills Moody (b.1905), an American tennis player who was Wimbledon singles champion eight times between 1927–1938, also winning the US title seven times and the French title four times; both a novelist and a painter, she was a friend and admirer of Gogarty who went to see her playing at Wimbledon and brought her to visit Yeats in Dublin, having persuaded her to play in the Fitzwilliam Open tennis tournament there in which she beat Thelma Jarvis, the English player. Gogarty then took her off to stay at Renvyle, County Galway: 'Yes, Dr Gogarty was the reason I went to Ireland'. See Ulick O'Connor, *The Fitzwilliam Story 1877–1977* (1977). Gogarty's poem 'Perfection', see p. 153, may have been written to her.

*Senorita d'Alvarez:* Madame (Marguerite Alvarez de Rocafuarte) d'Alvarez (d. 1933), an opera singer educated in Paris, the daughter of the Marquis de Rocafuarte and Marie Poupard de Neuflize, who lived in London. She sang in La Scala, Milan, the Chicago Opera House, Westminster Abbey and the London Opera House, Covent Garden.

*Countess Bezzi Scali:* Contessa Maria Christina Bezzi-Scali (1900–1996) was the second wife of Marchese Guglielmo Marconi (1874–1937) whom she married in 1927. He was the inventor of the persistent wave system of wireless telegraphy (1906) whose transatlantic wireless telegraph service began in 1907. He was awarded the Nobel Prize for Physics (1909). Born in Bologna, he had an Irish mother and had married Beatrice O'Brien, daughter of the fourth Baron Inchiquin in 1905, the marriage being dissolved in 1924.

*Catullus:* See note on him, p. 740.

**'The Yacht'**

*Pindus:* a chain of mountains in northern Greece which separate Thessaly from Epirus, Pindus being celebrated as sacred to the Muses and Apollo.

*rock bred Homer's isle:* Chios, an island in the Aegean Sea which asserted (among other claimants) that it was Homer's birthplace.

**'To Reformers'**

*Kubla Khan:* Kublai Khan (?1216–94), Mongol emperor of China, the grandson of Genghis Khan. He completed his grandfather's conquest of China, overthrowing the Sung dynasty in 1279 and founding the Yuan dynasty which lasted until 1368. See note on p. 712.

**'The Crowing of a Cock'**

*Spengler:* Oswald Spengler (1880–1936) German philosopher of history, author of *The Decline of the West* (1918–22) which argues that civilisations go through cycles of growth and decay.

*withers at the top:* an echo of Swift's remark 'I shall be like that tree, I shall die at [the] top', cited by Edward Young, *Works* (1789) III, p. 196. Gogarty may have got the image from Yeats's 'Blood and the Moon', YP, p. 367, a poem written in 1927, first published in Spring 1928 in *The Exile* and later in *The Winding Stair* (1929).

# Notes to *Wild Apples* (1929)

**'Galway'**

*her I owe my being to:* probably a disguised reference to his wife, Neenie, who came from Moyard, County Galway. See 'I tremble to think', p. 159 and note on p. 684.

*Salthill:* A seaside suburb of Galway city.

*Eyre Square:* at the centre of Galway city.

*The Spanish dames:* a reference to Galway's trade with Mediterranean ports. There is a 'Spanish Arch' there still.

**'Upon Horan'**

Title: Horan: this may have been either John William Horan, MB,B.Ch,BAO (National University of Ireland, 1915) or James Mulvihill Horan, L., LM (Royal College of Physicians, Ireland, 1912). But a version entitled 'Upon Moran' exists in C, which suggests Gogarty may also have been expressing dislike of D[avid] P[atrick] Moran (1869–1931), the 'Irish Irelander', proprietor and editor of *The Leader* which he founded in 1900. His increasingly illiberal views appeared in *The Philosophy of Irish Ireland* (1905).

**'To Berkeley'**
George Berkeley (1685–1753), Irish philosopher, educated at Kilkenny College and Trinity College, Dublin, Bishop of Cloyne, whose works include *Essays towards a New Theory of Vision* (1709), *A Treatise Concerning the Principles of Human Knowledge* (1710) and *Dialogues between Hylas and Philonovs* (1713). He thought that only particular things exist and since they are only a complex of sensations if we take from them that of which we have perception nothing remains. He thought spirit the only real cause or power.

**'This Kip (le bourdel où tenons nostre estat – Villon)'**
The quotation from Villon is from the 'Ballade de la Grosse Margot', the line ending three stanzas and the envoi. For Villon see note, p. 702.
*kip:* possibly a word of Danish origin, a brothel. In a TS (C) Gogarty annotated kip as a corruption of kip where women were kept and added: cf Goldsmith 'rattling a whore in a kip'.

**'Petersen Lane'**
Title: At right angles to City Quay on the Liffey, Dublin, the Lane runs to Townsend Street.
*great pines of Norway which make up the masts:* an echo of Milton's *Paradise Lost*, I, 292–4:

> . . . the tallest pine
> Hewn on Norwegian hills, to be the mast
> Of some great admiral . . .

**'Hertes Hele'**
Title: 'Hertes Hele' (archaic), Heart's wellbeing, Heart's ease.
*the alley called after the Dane:* Gogarty's MS (T.C.D.) reads 'Dane in Dublin is a general term for Scandinavian'.

## Notes to *Wild Apples* (1930)

**'Sandymount'**
Title: a largely coastal suburb three miles south of the centre of Dublin.
*Lambay:* see note p. 705.
*The mail boat . . . come in:* into Dun Laoghaire harbour from Holyhead; the afternoon one then arriving between 5 and 5.15 pm.

**'To Moorhead, Blind'**
*Moorhead:* Dr Thomas Gillman Moorhead, (1878–1960), Regius Professor of Physics in Trinity College Dublin, who fell when emerging from a train at Euston Station in 1926 and immediately became blind, his (bilateral) retina having become detached; he continued to teach, chair committees and entertain generously. Gogarty organised a group of friends who took it in turns to walk with Moorhead on Saturday afternoons, usually in the Dublin mountains. Moorhead wrote *Surface Anatomy* (1905) and *A Short History of Sir Patrick Dun's Hospital* (1942).

**'The Exorcism'**
*The Queen it is death if one sees:* see note, p. 679.

## Notes to *Selected Poems* (1933)

**Colophon'**
Title: *Colophon:* generally a publisher's emblem on a book, also an inscription at the end of a book (generally showing the title, printer, date etc.) Greek κολοφών, a finishing stroke).

*the high boot:* the buskin (Greek κόθορνos) was a thick-soled boot worn by actors in classical Greek tragedies.

*before the Fool comes on:* tragedies were generally followed by a satyric play in the fifth century up to the middle of the fourth century BC. These were usually of a grotesquely comic character.

## Notes to *Others to Adorn* (1938)

**'Reflection'**

*gombeen man:* a shopkeeper practising usury (from Irish *gambín*, interest on a loan).

*Mullingar:* a town in N Central Ireland, the county town of County Westmeath.

*Ringsend:* see note above, p. 675. The river Dodder meets the Liffey at Ringsend where the Grand Canal system has its three locks, Camden Lock, Buckingham Lock and Westmoreland Lock.

*the IXth Lock:* Gogarty's liking for the two canal systems, and the Ninth Lock in particular, appears in a passage in SS:

> . . . the banks of the canal . . . are lovely even now, in spite of their neglected elms and the garish hoardings which are allowed to deface the only boulevards we possess. Old elms, open and half hollow, which were planted to be conduits for water in days before cast-iron or earthenware could be made, gauntly stand in their decay, more sinned against than sinning, and shelter by night the fugitive loves of a city, as the Bard said when he compared a lady whose reputation was disputed to the trees on the canal. The path is lovely because it runs beside the long water over-arched by bridges of cut stone which complete their ellipse by reflection in the calm water. From Dublin to the Shannon, one hundred miles away, these two great examples of Eighteenth-century engineering extend. They cross valleys and enter marshes, such as those which alone could hold up the onsweep of the Roman roads. Lonely through the rich brown bogs they run, to little towns whose white cottages brighten the pale green water, and on through short borders of sheltering trees. Reliable, unleaking, linking Dublin to the largest river of the three kingdoms, to the 'lordly Shannon spreading like a sea. . . .'
>
> When my mind longs for that peace which is Death's overture, I think of myself as a lock master at one of the country locks beyond the edge of Dublin, where the sound of living water never ceaseth. I would appoint myself to the Ninth Lock, which is not far from Clondalkin. There is a great stretch of water on one side and a well-appointed public-house where one might rest and spend some of the three pounds a week between boats. With a well-chosen form of peculiarity or moroseness one might preserve the privacy of the inner man . . . (SS p. 48).

## Notes to *Elbow Room* (1939)

**'Applied Poetry'**

The first sixteen lines of this poem (printed here in *Elbow Room*) were not included in 'The Isles of Greece. Applied Poetry (Lesbos)' in *Collected Poems*, which begins 'Marble was her lovely city', a section included as ll.17–44 of 'Applied Poetry' in *Elbow Room* (1939) but not printed in this present version of the poem in *Elbow Room*.

*Aspasia:* (fl 5th century BC) born in Miletus, was the gifted intellectual and vivacious mistress of Pericles (*c.*490–429 BC) the Athenian statesman, responsible for encouraging Athenian architecture, sculpture, music and drama.

# Notes to *Perennial* (1944)

**'Dedication: to James Augustine Healy'**
*James Augustine Healy:* a New York friend of Gogarty, praised – along with Dr Maloney, Judge Campbell, John Quinn, Cornelius Sullivan, Major Kinkead, James A. Farrell and Dr McCartan – as one of the citizens of the United States who have encouraged the arts of Ireland, enlightened patrons. See I, pp. 180–181.
*Yeats . . . the cares of old age and loss:* Yeats wrote of his old age in many poems from *The Tower* (1928) on; he also wrote of the loss of friends after they were dead and also of the loss of love and of civilisation. See also 'What was Lost', YP, p. 430. In 'The Tower', YP, p. 305, the question is put:

> Does the imagination dwell the most
> Upon a woman won or woman lost?

The agony is faced in 'Nineteen Hundred and Nineteen' *op. cit.*, p. 315.

> Man is in love and loves what vanishes,
> What more is there to say?

Yeats also lamented the loss of personal vigour in several poems.
**'Remembering Albert Spickers'**
Lieutenant Albert Spickers, a pilot in the United States Army Air Corps, was killed in the crash of a bomber at Akron, Ohio on 3 October 1942. Gogarty wrote the poem for his parents Dr and Mrs William Spickers. William Spickers was a leading surgeon in New York with whom Gogarty used to lunch at Sardi's or the Russian Tea Room at West 57th Street.
*Pindaric tongue:* Pindar, Greek lyric poet (?518–?442 BC) was born near Thebes.
*Delphic or Olympian throng:* Pindar was particularly known for his poems celebrating victories at various games, some of which were sung at the place of victory, some when the visitor had returned home. The Pan-Hellenic Games were held at Delphi every eighth year until 582 BC, after that every third year of each Olympiad. The Olympic Games were held in honour of Zeus at Olympia in Elis every four years; they were founded in 776 BC and abolished in 393 AD (or 426) by the Emperor Theodosius.
*Coeur des Lions:* like Richard I (1157–99) of England, a brave man to whom the epithet *coeur de lion*, lionhearted, was applied.
**'To Major Eugene F. Kinkead Sometime Sheriff of Hudson County, New Jersey'.**
*skaith:* probably scath or, occasionally, scaith. It means shadow or darkness. Good triumphs in spite of the support evil can get from the dark. The word can also mean 'veil' so that evil may hide itself, but good will overcome it.

# Notes to *Unselected Poems* (1954)

**'Adam and Eve'**
*Hermann Goering:* Hermann Wilhelm Goering (1893–1946), German Nazi leader and Field Marshal who commanded Hitler's storm troops and mobilised Germany for war from 1933 as Prussian Prime Minister and Commissioner for aviation. Sentenced to death at the Nuremberg trials, he committed suicide.
*Bernard Shaw:* George Bernard Shaw (1856–1950) Dublin born Irish wit, playwright and man of letters, Nobel Prize winner. See note on him below, p. 772.

*Spironema pallidum:* the spirochaete bacterium that causes syphilis.

*caudal anaesthetic:* equivalent to the epidural anaesthetic used in childbirth.

*flammen werfer:* (German), flame thrower.

*thoracoplasty:* plastic surgery of the thorax or surgical removal of ribs or part of them to permit the collapse of a diseased lung. Gogarty is applying medical terminology to Eve's being made out of Adam's rib. See Genesis I:20–23.

*Lilith:* in Talmudic literature, Adam's first wife (in the Old Testament and Irish folklore she was a female demon who attacked children).

*Old Freud:* see note on him, p. 681.

*Oedipus complex:* a group of emotions, usually unconscious, involving a child (usually a male child) desiring to possess the parent of the opposite sex sexually, to the exclusion of the parent of the same sex.

*Dresden after Delph:* the china made at Meissen near Dresden since 1710 is delicate procelain ware, mainly used for decorative objects whereas Delph (or delf or delft) is earthenware, tinglazed, made in England and Holland, getting its name from Delft, a town in the SW Netherlands, where it was made since the 17th century (generally with blue decoration on a white ground).

### 'Noah's Ark'

*'Becoming Childers everywhere':* an echo of 'Haveth Childers Everywhere', from James Joyce's *Finnegans Wake.* The Finnegan of the book is Humphrey Chimpden Earwicker (H.C.E.) who keeps a pub in Chapelizod, Dublin. H.C.E. stands for the universality of the character, the initials applied as Here Comes Everybody. Howth Castle and Environs and Haveth Childers Everywhere.

*his own son-in-law:* See the Bible, Genesis 9:20–27 which only mentions Noah's getting drunk. Is Gogarty confusing him with Lot here? See note below, p. 711.

### 'Ars Longa
### (To W.B. Yeats)'

*Coan . . . Hippocrates:* the most celebrated physician of the ancient world (c.460–357 BC) was born in Cos, one of the Cylades.

*'Life is short and art is long':* a translation of the Latin, *'vita brevis, ars longa'*, the opening phrases of Hippocrates, *Aphorisms 1*, where he remarks of medicine: 'The life so short, the art so long to learn, opportunity fleeting, experience treacherous, judgement difficult'. Gogarty corrected this standard translation in I, p. 11: 'It is due to Hippocrates to correct a mistranslation of one of his great aphorisms. His Greek suffered through its Latin translation. "Ars longa" is not what he said. It was for the poet Chaucer correctly to translate it: "The life so short, *the craft* so long to learn."'

### 'One World'

*the cow jumped over the moon:* from the nursery rhyme:

> Hey diddle diddle,
> The cat and the fiddle,
> The cow jumped over the moon;
> The little dog laughed
> To see such sport,
> And the dish ran away with the spoon

*. . . from mental strife*

*I will not cease:* An echo of William Blake's preface to *Milton:*

> I will not cease from Mental Fight,
> Nor shall my Sword sleep in my hand,
> Till we have built Jerusalem
> In England's green and pleasant land

**'Dispute between the Head and Heart of the Poet'**
*Heart but I am too old*
*Now for this questing:* the poem is reminiscent of Yeats's 'A Dialogue of Self and Soul' (YP, p. 346):

> Why should the imagination of a man
> Long past his prime . . .

though it takes an opposite attitude to the second part of that poem's 'I am content to live it all again.'
**'The Phoenix and the Unicorn'**
*The Mountains of the Moon:* in Ruanda, hence meaning impossibly far away.
'Without Venus'
*The Queen of Sheba:* a queen of the Sabeans who visited Solomon (see the Bible, Kings 10:1–13). In some accounts she came from Ethiopia (In the *Kebra Negast* she slept with him); the Sabeans, however, occupied the SW corner of Arabia (modern Yemen). Gogarty may have been influenced by Yeats's poems 'Solomon to Sheba' and 'On Woman'. See YP, pp. 240, 250. In *Autobiographies* (1955) p. 464, Yeats wrote that the love of Solomon and Sheba must have lasted 'each divining the secret self of the other' . . . or . . . creates a mirror where the lover or the beloved sees an image to copy in daily life'.
*hara kari:* a non Japanese variant of *hara-kiri.*
**'A Report on the senseless behaviour of certain microscopic Immortals'**
*Paramecium:* any freshwater protozoan of the genus Paramecium, with an oval body covered with cilia, feeding through a ventral ciliated groove (Greek, *paramekes* elongated).
*Grave where . . . thy sting:* cf the Bible, Acts 15:55 'O death, where is thy sting? O grave, where is thy victory?'

# Notes to *Penultimate Poems*

**'To a Moth'**
*imps:* enlarges. Imp, a term originally from falconry, to graft feathers on to a broken wing, hence to extend, add to.
*fields of Dis:* Dis is another name for Orcus or Pluto, the Roman name for the god of the underworld, hence the fields of Dis are the abode of the dead (Greek, Hades).
**'The Village of Plandome'**
*Plandome:* a village in Nassau County, south east of New York on the north shore of West Long Island on Manhasset Bay, just north of Manhasset.
**'Sodom and Gomorrah'**
*Title:* Sodom and Gomorrah were destroyed by God with fire and brimstone for their wickedness. See the Bible, Genesis 19:24.
*no employment for a Modom:* as the city was known for its homosexuality there was no need for a brothel keeper.
*Lot:* one of those who left Ur of the Chaldees for Haran; he accompanied his uncle Abraham when they left for the land of Canaan. Lot, however, chose to move east to the plain of Jordan while Abraham moved to Hebron (see the Bible, Genesis 13:8-18). After the destruction of Sodom and Gomorrah when Lot and his two daughters had left Zoan and were living in a cave in the mountains the daughters made him drunk and slept with him in turn. The elder had a son, Moab, by him, the younger a son, Ben

Am. (See Genesis, 19:31–38). Hence Lot saw himself as his own son-in-law.

*pillar of salt:* Lot's wife, contrary to God's instructions, looked back at the destruction of the cities and was turned into a pillar of salt.

**'Supersonic?'**

*juke boxes:* Gogarty was telling a story in New York in a bar on Third Avenue to five or six friends sitting in a booth with him but when he was about to come to the point:

> a young man, sitting by the bar, went over and placed a coin in a jukebox. All hell broke loose. The expression on Gogarty's face changed; he became very sad, a combination of sadness and anger, and he said, 'Oh dear God in Heaven, that I should find myself thousands of miles from home, an old man at the mercy of every retarded son of a bitch who has a nickel to drop in that bloody illuminated coal-scuttle.'
> (*Irish Literary Portraits*, ed. W.R. Rodgers (1972), p. 164)

**'Full Circle'**

*Ghenghis . . . Karakoram:* Genghis Khan (?1162–1227), a Mongol ruler whose empire extended from the Black Sea to the Pacific, founded Karakoram in Mongolia in 1220. It was later destroyed by Kublai Khan.

**'Psychoanalysis II'**

*an ax:* an echo of the anonymous "Lizzie Borden": see note, p. 678.

**'The Changeling (I)'**

*Arcturus:* the brightest star in the constellation *Boötes*, a red giant.

*claws of the bear:* see note above (Arcturus from Greek ἄρκτος, bear; οὐρός, guard or keeper).

**'The Changeling (II)'**

This version is probably earlier than 'The Changeling (I)'. Unlike that poem, it is told in the first person and is more personal. Gogarty's parents lived in 5 Rutland [now Parnell] Square, Dublin, and 'the' father of 'The Changeling (I)' and 'the' mother are here 'my' Father and 'My' Mother.

*Arcturus:* see note above on 'The Changling (I)'.

# NOTES TO PART THREE

*Notes to Poems Published in Journals*
*and Unpublished Poems*

ODES AND ADDRESSES

**'Ode of Welcome'**
This ode welcoming the Irish Yeomanry regiment arriving home in Dublin from the
Boer War in June 1900 was published in *Irish Society*. The initial letters should be read
downwards. Although Gogarty disclaimed authorship in later life (he named Jack Lester
as the author in a letter of 27 August 1954 to Horace Reynolds) it has long continued
to be attributed to him by many of his friends and is included here because of that and
his earlier implication that he was responsible for it.
**'In Memoriam: Robert Louis Stevenson'**
Title: Robert Louis Stevenson (1850–94): Scottish novelist, poet, essayist and travel
writer.
*jocund Chaucer:* Geoffrey Chaucer (?1345–?1400), poet, secret service agent and
controller of customs in the Port of London, travelled to Italy in the King's service and
was attached to various embassies in France and Italy. His longer works include *Troylus
and Cryseyde* and *The Legende of Good Women* as well as *The Canterbury Tales.*
*Samoan grave:* In 1888 Stevenson, his wife and Lloyd Osborne, her son by a previous
marriage, set out for the South Seas and settled in Samoa where he bought the Vailima
property and temporarily recovered his health. He died and was buried in Samoa in
1894.
*Goldsmith and . . . Scotland's darling son:* Oliver Goldsmith (1728–1774) Irish poet,
playwright, novelist and essayist; Robert Burns (1757–96) the Scottish poet.
*Treasure Island:* the romance which made Stevenson famous in 1883; it had previously
appeared as a serial in *Young Folks* from 1881 under the title 'The Sea Cook or Treasure
Island'.
*Tusitala:* The Teller of Tales, Stevenson's Samoan name.

713

**'To his Extraordinary Friend George Kennedy Allen Bell'**

*Title:* . . . Bell. Gogarty met Bell (1883–1958) at Oxford where he was an undergraduate at Christ Church; he became Dean of Canterbury and then Bishop of Chichester in 1929.

*Rose and Crown:* a public house in Wimbledon.

*the Bard:* Algernon Charles Swinburne (1887–1909), English poet and critic, the eldest son of Admiral and Lady Jane Swinburne. He was educated at Eton College and Balliol College, Oxford, which he left without taking a degree. In 1879 after a breakdown caused by an intemperate life he lived in the care of his friend Theodore Watts-Dunton in semi-seclusion at No 2, The Pines, Putney. Gogarty and Bell shared an enthusiasm for Swinburne's work when they were at Oxford. Bell had told Gogarty (who had earlier tried in vain to pay his respects to Swinburne but been foiled in his attempts by Watts-Dunton) of how he had himself attempted to intercept Swinburne on his short journey from the house in Putney to the Rose and Crown in order to present him with a copy of his own poem which had won the Newdigate Prize at Oxford.

*Aeschylus . . . Gela . . . Aitna:* Aeschylus (525–456BC) born at Eleusis near Athens, the father of Greek tragedy, died at Gela in Sicily. He wrote a play *Aetnae* in honour of the city founded by Hieron in 476 BC.

*Rotten Row:* a road in Hyde Park, London, a fashionable resort for riders. The derivation is probably from a row or road of rotten earth (or bark) suitable for a riding-track.

*poet-Yeats-like:* Yeats affected a poetic loosely tied bow tie as a young man.

*Balliol . . . Genesis . . . Guinnesses:* Swinburne was at Balliol College from 1856 to 1859: he obtained a second class in classical moderations in 1858. 'My Oxford career' he commented, 'culminated in total and scandalous failure'. See Harold Nicolson, *Swinburne* (1926). He became a nihilist in religion and a republican in politics soon after arriving at Oxford. *Guinnesses* suggests his over-enthusiastic drinking habits before Watts-Dunton eventually imposed a regime upon him

*Homer . . . Horace . . . Arguitur laudibus vinosus:* a reference to Horace (Quintus Horatius Flaccus (65–8 BC), the Roman poet), *Epistles* I.19.6, *Laudibus arguitur vini vinosus:* Homer is convicted as a wine lover.

*winedark:* an epithet applied to the sea by Homer (οἶνοψ).

*Pindar's barmaid:* Pindar (*c*.522–*c*.440BC) the chief lyric poet of Greece, born near Thebes, capital of Boeotia; his triumphal Odes are divided into four books celebrating victories won in the Olympian, Pythian, Nemean and Isthmian games.

*'αριϭτον ὕδωρ:* the best water.

*the beverage for him:* whisky.

*Keats . . . claret . . . winking at the brim:* from Keats, 'Ode to a Nightingale':

> Full of the true, the blushful Hippocrene,
> With beaded bubbles winking at the brim.

He wrote to Benjamin Bailey on 14 August 1819 that his friends 'should drink a dozen of claret on my tomb'.

*pints of 'plain':* Guinness.

*sling-y:* presumably Helicon, the sanctuary of the Muses.

*glabrous . . . Phoebus' bays:* glabrous or smooth laurel leaves. Phoebus Apollo was the god of poetry.

*Trench:* see note on him, p. 739.

*Hyperion:* Keats's poem, written in 1818–19. There were two incomplete versions of it. In the first, Hyperion's aid is sought by Saturn who is debating with the Titans about how to recover his fallen realm; in the second the poet has Hyperion's fate (the last of the Titans, he was dethroned by Apollo) revealed to him in a dream. In Greek mythology Hyperion was a son of Uranus and Ge, one of the Titans. He married Thea by whom he was father of Aurora, the Sun and the Moon.

*The Tower:* The Martello Tower Gogarty occupied at Sandycove, see note p. 734.

*northwards to Howth:* Howth was on the opposite, northern side of Dublin Bay from Sandycove.

*Hamancos:* This was probably a misprint for Namancos, as Gogarty may have been thinking of Milton's *Lycidas* here:

> Or whether thou, to our moist vows deny'd,
> Sleep'st by the fable of Bellerus old,
> Where the great vision of the guarded Mount
> Looks towards Namancos and Bayona's hold.

In a letter to G.K.A. Bell (*MLTT*) Gogarty alludes to the Martello tower that 'looks towards Ben Edair [Howth] if not Namancos hold'.

*Professor Dowden:* Professor Edward Dowden (1843–1913) born in Cork, was educated at and became the first Professor of English Literature (1867–1913) in Trinity College Dublin. He wrote books on Shakespeare, Shelley and Southey and was an effective minor poet.

*hydromel:* mead.

*inturreted:* in the Martello tower.

*Sandycove:* the area surrounding the tower, about seven miles south of Dublin.

*Silenus' den:* the Martello tower. Silenus was a satyr-like elderly companion – a fosterfather – of Dionysus: Sileni (they often were referred to in the plural) were like satyrs – except that they were older, wiser and drunker – expert in music and when captured given to prophecy. Silenus was the chief comic character in the satyr plays that followed tragedies on the Athenian stage.

**'Beginning of a poem to G.K.A. Bell'**

*a cloven rock:* The rock surrounding the Forty Foot Hole, a men's swimming place at the sea's edge at Sandycove, is granite.

**'Foreword (to Ireland)'**

*Moynalty's leas:* Monalty is in County Meath; lea is a meadow or field. See note, p. 674.

*Moher:* the Cliffs of Moher, in County Clare.

*Horace tells . . . How they who lacked a sacred poet:* See Horace, *Odes* 4, 9, 25ff:

> Vixere fortes ante Agamemnona
> Multi; sed omnes illacrimabiles
> Urgentur ignotique longa
> Nocte, carent quia vate sacro

'Many brave men lived before Agamemnon all unwept and unknown, lost in the distant night since they lack a divine poet . . .'.

**'Ireland's Welcome to the Fleet'**

Title: A photograph of Lord Charles Bereford was accompanied by a note in *Ireland:* 'The Channel fleet consisting of eight first-class battleships and four cruisers under the command of Admiral Lord Charles Beresford, KCVO, KCB will visit Dublin during the Horse Show week' (see 'The Horse Show' below, p. 319).

*the hand that steers you:* Lord Charles Beresford.

*lords of Waterford:* Lord Charles William de la Poer, 1st Baron Beresford (1848–1919), British Admiral born at Phillipstown, County Offaly, was the son of the fourth Marquis of Waterford.

*the Bay:* Dublin Bay, where the Channel fleet assembled in 1904.

### 'Cervantes: Tercentenary of Don Quixote'
This was the poem with which, for the third time, Gogarty won the Vice Chancellor's Prize for English Verse in Trinity College, Dublin.

*Your rare Knight:* Don Quixote de la Mancha has had his wits disordered by reading old romances and imagines he is called upon to roam the world on his old horse Rosinante in search of adventures.

*Sancho:* Sancho Panza, a rustic, both shrewd and credulous, whom Don Quixote lures into being his squire by promising him the governorship of an island.

*his Lady's name:* Dulcinea de Toboso, a good looking girl in a neighbouring village.

*Cervantes:* Miguel de Cervantes Saavedra (1547–1616), Spanish novelist and dramatist, who lost the use of his left hand at the Battle of Lepanto, was taken by pirates and imprisoned at Algiers for five years.

*his that shook the broad Athenian stages:* Aristophanes (*c.*448–380BC) the great Athenian poet who caricatured contemporary figures and their comments on current affairs in his lively, outspoken comedies.

*Parnassus:* a mountain in central Greece, in N.W. Boeotia, sacred in ancient times to Dionysus, Apollo and the Muses. On its slopes were Delphi, the site of the famous oracle, and the Castalian Spring, believed to be a source of inspiration.

### 'The Horse Show'
Title: the Royal Dublin Society's Horse Show, held annually in Dublin in August, a major social event.

*Daughter of the ocean:* Poseidon with his brothers Zeus and Hades drew lots to divide the rule of the universe, Zeus receiving heaven, Hades the underworld and Poseidon the sea

*his gift . . . to Hellas:* When Poseidon and Athena were in competition for the patronage of Attica Poseidon created a spring of seawater on the Acropolis at Athens, Athena caused an olive tree to grow nearby. The judges thought her gift more useful and she became patroness of Athens. Poseidon, enraged at this decision, flooded the plain of Attica. The Athenians, however, continued to honour him as well as Athena. In this poem Gogarty is drawing on later Roman poets' views that Poseidon's gift to Athens was the horse.

*World outspeeding horses:* Poseidon was agreed to have been the founder of horse racing.

*Star of Eve:* Venus, the second star in order of distance from the sun, the morning or evening star.

*Hellas . . . Olympian loam:* the Olympic games, founded in 776BC in honour of Olympian Zeus, were reorganised to include chariot racing and races for single horses in the early years of the seventh century BC.

### 'Ode on the Bicentenary'
Title: written on the bicentenary of the Medical School in Trinity College, Dublin.

*Old Fortress:* Trinity College, Dublin, founded by Queen Elizabeth in 1591.

*John Stearne:* the founder of the Irish College of Physicians in 1660, Stearne (1624–1669), after becoming a Fellow of Trinity College, Dublin in 1643, studied medicine at Cambridge (1643–49) and at Oxford. He lectured in Hebrew and was Professor of law in 1660, becoming Professor of medicine in 1662.

*Anne:* Queen Anne (1665–1714), the last Stuart sovereign, was a daughter of James II.

*Nicholson:* Henry Nicholson entered Trinity College, Dublin at the age of seventeen in 1667, graduating with a Bachelor's degree in medicine in 1674; he was the first lecturer in Botany in Trinity College, Dublin, 1711, and is said to have written a book on the Botanical Garden in Dublin in 1712.

*Helsham:* Richard Helsham (?1682–1738) was Fellow Medicus at Trinity College, Dublin 1706/7; one of the first four lecturers in medicine in 1711 (with Hoyle, Griffith and Thomas Molyneux) and a Fellow and President of the King's and Queen's College of Physicians, he was the first Professor of Natural and Experimental Philosophy in 1724 and succeeded Thomas Molyneux as Professor of Physics (1733–38). Swift's physician, he was praised by Swift (see Pope's *Works* IX, 94) as ingenious, good-humoured, a fine gentleman and an excellent scholar who entertained his numerous friends 'often and liberally'. He blamed earlier philosophers who disregarded experiments and published his *Lectures on Natural Philosophy*.

*Molyneux . . . Two fames:* William Molyneux (1656–1698), educated at Trinity College, Dublin, a distinguished scientist who wrote on optics and mathematics. Associated with the Royal Society and the Dublin Philosophical Society, he helped to found the Royal Dublin Society.

*the hangman burned:* it has been generally held, but not correctly, that Molyneux's *The Case of Ireland Started* (1698) met this fate: the legend was first popularised by Charles Lucas (1713–1771), the founder of *The Freeman's Journal* (1763–1923).

*Hoyle:* Richard Hoyle (?1681–1730) entered Trinity College, Dublin in 1696 at the age of 15, becoming President of the King's and Queen's College of Physicians and Professor of Anatomy.

*Cunningham:* Daniel James Cunningham (1850–1909), an Edinburgh graduate, was Professor of Anatomy at Trinity College, Dublin (1883–1903) and at Edinburgh University (1903–1909). He wrote a *Manual of Practical Anatomy* (2 vols, 1893–94).

*Griffith:* Robert Griffith (?1663–1719), a fellow of the King's and Queen's College of Physicians, was appointed the first King's Professor of Medicine in 1717, a post established by the bequest of Sir Patrick Dun; see note below. His examiners included Richard Helsham and Thomas Molyneux (brother of William, see note above, this page).

*Sir Patrick Dun:* Irish physician, born and brought up in Scotland (1642–1713) was five times President of the Dublin College of Physicians, an MP in the Irish House of Commons (1692–1703) and Physician General to the Army (1705). He left money to fund a Professorship of Physic in the College of Physicians. His portrait was painted by Kneller. Sir Patrick Dun's Hospital in Grand Canal Street, Dublin, was named after him and established out of funds from his estate.

*Goldsmith:* see note on him above, p. 713. He qualified as a doctor (after leaving Trinity College, Dublin he attended medical lectures at Edinburgh and Leyden) acted briefly as a physician at Southwark in 1756 before becoming a writer.

*stooped ere conquering:* a reference to Goldsmith's famous comedy *She Stoops to Conquer* (1773).

*the lucid Dean:* Jonathan Swift (1667–1745), Dean of St Patrick's Cathedral, Dublin (1713–1745). See note on him, p. 690.

*Cheyne-Stokes's respiration:* alternating shallow and deep breathing named after John Cheyne (1777–1836), a Scottish physician who had been an army surgeon before acquiring a lucrative practice in Dublin in 1809; he was subsequently appointed Physician-General to the Forces in Ireland; and after William Stokes (1804–1878), who studied medicine at Edinburgh and Dublin. Physician to the Meath Hospital in Dublin, he edited the *Dublin Journal of Medical Science* and was Regius Professor of Medicine in Trinity College, Dublin, from 1845.

*atheroma:* a fatty deposit on or within the lining of an artery, often causing an obstruction to the blood flow.

*Metchnikoff and Osler:* Elie Metchnikoff (1845–1916) a Russian bacteriologist in France; winner of the Nobel Prize, he formulated a theory of phagocytosis. Sir William Osler (1849–1919), Regius Professor of Medicine at Oxford (1904–1919); a Canadian, he was educated at Toronto and Magill; his *The Principles and Practice of Medicine* (1891) went through many editions.

*Peasant grew to Overman:* possibly a reference to Nietsche's theory of the *ubermensch*, superman (1896).

*Since that old doctor, when*
*He ruled as mayor beside his town,*
*Your strong foundation fastened down,*
*That sinks not in the fen:* Alderman Thomas Smith, an apothecary (the description of him as 'doctor' is typical of the period, meaning he practised the crafts of leeching and healing), a wealthy Dublin citizen who was Mayor when Trinity College was established in 1591. He laid the foundation stone on 13 March 1592 on the site of the supressed Augustinian Monastery. Students were first received in the original buildings in 1594, these being of red brick surrounding a courtyard (none of them have survived). The 'fen' refers to the marshy ground spreading inland from the Liffey at the time (on which snipe reputedly continued to be shot well into the eighteenth century). See Colm Lennon, *The Lords of Dublin in the Age of the Reformation* (1989), pp. 68, 76, 271, 270-271. See also Douglas Bennett, *Encyclopaedia of Dublin* (1991), p. 220, who states that the marshy ground extended from the present Burgh Quay to Townsend Street. The river Steyne flowed into the sea at the present junction of Hawkins and Townsend Streets; a stone in College Street marks the spot; the land was reclaimed in 1663 when Mr Hawkins built a sea wall there.

*Stokes who stood so firm:* Whitley Stokes (1763-1845) Regius Professor of Medicine, Trinity College, Dublin (1830-43), who was suspended for his nationalist opinions (1798-1800).

*that Stokes:* Sir William Stokes (1839-1906), son of William Stokes (1804-1878), Professor of Surgery at the Royal College of Surgeons of Ireland 1872, President 1886-7, and surgeon to the British Forces in Natal 1900.

*Graves:* Robert James Graves (1796-1853), physician to the Meath Hospital, founder of the Park Street School of Medicine and Professor of Medicine to the Irish College of Physicians; he gained a great reputation by his *Clinical Lectures on the Practice of Medicine* (1848). He travelled with Turner in the Alps and Italy. He is known for Graves Disease, a hyperactive thyroid gland.

*Hamilton . . . Wordsworth's friend:* Sir William Rowan Hamilton (1805-1865), best known for his mathematical theory of quarternions. A polymath, he was appointed Superintendent of Dunsink Observatory and Professor of Astronomy at Trinity College, Dublin, while still an undergraduate, shortly afterwards becoming Astronomer Royal for Ireland. He wrote on optics and dynamics and was well-versed in Arabic, Persian and Sanskrit. Gogarty was aware that Hamilton, like himself, had won the Vice Chancellor's prize in English Verse more than once. He continued to write philosophical poetry and was President of the Royal Irish Academy (1837). He accompanied Wordsworth on his tour of Ireland in 1829.

*Fitzgerald's:* George Francis Fitzgerald (1851-1901), a Fellow of Trinity College, Dublin and distinguished mathematical physicist (author with Lorenz of the contraction in relativity theory). He attempted to fly a Lilienthal type glider in 1895 from a ramp in the College Park, and developed an electro-magnetic theory of radiation.

*Wright:* Wilbur (1867-1912) and his brother Orville Wright (1871-1948), Americans who designed and flew the first powered aircraft in 1903 at Kitty Hawk, North Carolina.

*Icarus:* in Greek myth the son of Daedalus (the Athenian architect and inventor who built the labyrinth for Minos on Crete; it housed the Minotaur), with whom he escaped from Crete, flying with wings made of feathers and wax. Despite his father's warning, he flew too near the sun, the wax melted and he fell into the Aegean and drowned

*Iveagh the Munificent:* Edward Cecil Guinness, 1st Earl of Iveagh (1847–1927), third son of Sir Benjamin Lee Guinness, spent most of his large fortune upon philanthropic projects. Most notable was the provision of decent accommodation for the poor, especially those who lived in the wretched slums between Christ Church and St Patrick's Cathedral, in the Iveagh Buildings. The Iveagh Trust founded a play centre for the children of the poor who had previously spent their days on the streets. The building in Bull Alley was known as the Bayno (from beano, a feast) from the cocoa and buns fed to the children between three and fourteen who made 7,820,520 visits to the Play Centre which taught sewing, dancing, art, cookery, singing and swimming. The population in the area has declined; the building is now the home of the Liberties Vocational School.

**'The Injection: To Lord Dunsany'**
Title: Lord Dunsany. See note on him, p. 704.

**'To Her Most Gracious Majesty'**
Title: see note on Queen Mary, p. 700.
*House in Miniature:* a reference to Queen Mary's famous dolls' house, now at Windsor Castle.

**'To Maurice Baring'**
Title: Baring (1874–1946), fourth son of Baron Revelstoke, was educated at Eton College and Trinity College, Cambridge. He held various diplomatic posts, became a war correspondent and wrote poems, short stories, novels and books on Russia.

**To Stuart Benson'**
Title: Stuart Benson (1877–1949), an American sculptor born in Detroit, Michigan, had two portraits in the Salon d'Automne in 1932, and one, Portrait du peintre Touchagues, in the Salon des Tuileries in 1935. In his thirties and forties he lived in Clos de Pére. His bronze head of Gogarty is reproduced as a frontispiece in *Perennial* (1944). See O'C, p. 229 for an account of Gogarty flying to Paris in 1928 from Dublin when a pupil of Rodin offered to do a sculpture of him; he left at four one afternoon, sat for the artist till midnight, flew back at four-thirty in the morning to receive his patients in Dublin at ten-thirty. (He used to hire Irish Army Air Corps planes upon occasion).

**'To Madame Chiang Kai-Shek'**
Title: born Soong Mei-ling in 1897, she was the second wife (1927) of the Nationalist Chinese President Chiang Kai-Shek. In the US from 1908–1917 she publicized his cause in the West; she was the first Chinese and the second woman to address a joint session of the US Congress in 1943. On 14 June 1943 Madame Chiang Kai-Shek arrived by train in Ottawa; she was received by the Earl of Athlone, the Governor-General, and Princess Alice and the Canadian Prime Minister, Mackenzie King. She was given cheques for Chinese relief by the Red Cross and Junior Red Cross. She addressed both Canadian Houses of Parliament during her three day stay. The poem appeared on the front page of the paper with a subheading in brackets which read: (Dr Gogarty, distinguished Irish poet, novelist and literateur, now living in New York, has written this tribute to Madame Chiang exclusively for *The Gazette*, and especially to welcome Madame Chiang to Canada today).

**'To the Grand Daughter of Lord Dunsany, aged two, in the Garden of Dunsany Castle'**
Title: the Dunsany residence in County Meath
*Mother's eyes:* see following note.
*Randall Plunkett:* Randall Arthur Henry Plunkett, 19th Baron Dunsany (1906–1999), Lt. Col. Retd. Indian Cavalry. By his first marriage to Mrs Vera Bryce (divorced in 1947) he had a son; the daughter referred to in this poem was the only child of his second marriage to Mrs Sheila Katrin Victoria Foley.

EARTH AND SEA

**'Poem from Oxford'**

*the trout at Godstow Bridge:* a well known inn near Oxford, on the Thames.

*the fines unless that I landed soon:*

See the somewhat similar situation in Gogarty's GN:

When you swam into Wuggins [Worcester College, Oxford] by way of the Provost's lake and disturbed the nesting swans and got us all gated . . . I could not help recalling the scene near midnight one long-vanished summer, between the bridges of the canal behind the college, the silhouetted bowler hats of the proctors converging from each side; and the amazement of a local Ariadne deserted on the bank as I took unobtrusively to the waters which drowned love. It was better, I reflected as I swam away that she should be astonished than that we should be surprised. (p. 29).

**'Ringsend'**

*the Quay:* Ringsend until the seventeenth century was a port in its own right; between 1707 and 1728 the great South Wall was built along the Liffey as far as the Dodder (where Sir John Rogerson's Quay ends).

**'The Little Dark Wood'**

The poem was originally entitled 'Roisindhu', an allegorical name for Ireland, the Little Black Rose, but also, as Gogarty tells us in Chapter 26 of TTY, describing Renvyle, 'the house', it means the Little Dark Wood:

> Geologically it was a wonder: a storm beach enclosed a little lake which was fed by a little brook that fell from a rocky rise on the south side. The lake was forty yards from the house, the house was less than a hundred yards from the sea. In the lake was a little peninsula wooded still with the last specimens of old Irish fir trees. It was called Roisindhu, the Little Dark Wood and it gave its name to the lake. Above it rose Letter Hill, a mountain that, as the mists of morning lifted, could be seen plum-blue, reflected in the lake.

The chapter heading is 'A Sea-Grey House' and it describes Renvyle House, Connemara, County Galway, purchased by Gogarty in 1917, burnt down by the Republicans in the Civil War, rebuilt with an Irish Free State government grant and opened by the Gogarty family as a hotel in 1930.

*sallies:* willows.

**'Out of Dublin'**

*Mulhuddart:* situated on the right bank of the Tolka, one and a half miles from Blanchardstown.

*Clonee:* in the parish and barony of Dunboyne, on the Dublin–Navan road, seven miles NW of Dublin.

*Rogers:* Pat Rogers of Balfstown, Ratoath, County Meath, a renowned horse dealer and trainer, whose sons George and Charlie carried on his traditions as dealers and trainers.

**'With the Coming-in of Spring'**

*Feast of Brigid:* February 1st; Brigid (or Bridget or Bride), patron Saint of Ireland after Patrick, and protectress of those engaged in dairy work died c.525AD. Born at Faughart, near Dundalk, she established the first nunnery in Ireland in County Kildare. The Patron Saint of poets, blacksmiths and healers, she is also venerated on the continent, notably in Alsace, Flanders and Portugal. Legends about her include her multiplication of food – butter for the poor, bathwater turned to beer for thirsty clerical workers and cows giving three milkings a day for bishops to drink.

*Claremorris:* (or Clare; Irish *clar chlainne Muiris*, the plain of the family of Murris) is situated in the parish of Kilcoman, the barony of Claremorris, County Mayo. It is on the road from Ballinrobe to Castlerea, fourteen miles SE by S from Castlebar, one hundred and seventeen miles (W by N) from Dublin.

*Balla:* (or Ballagh) about six miles east of Castlebar, County Mayo in the Barony of Claremorris, on the Castlebar–Claremorris road.

*Kiltimagh:* about six miles north of Balla.

*Ballinamore:* (Irish, *Bel-an-atha-moir*, the Mouth of the Great Ford) is about thirty miles north west of Carrick on Shannon in County Leitrim, in the Barony of Carrigallan.

*Carra:* (Carra Lough, overlooked by the ruins of Moore Hall, George Moore's family residence; the 'weir lake' beside the Ballinrobe–Castlebar road, County Mayo) . . .

*Gallen:* (or Gillen) is a parish in the Barony of Garrycastle, County Offaly, six miles NE of Banager on the road to Ferbane) . . . *the Gap of the Two Bushes:* these places, as Gogarty tells us in his highly comical account of George Moore's funeral, his 'ultimate joke', I, p. 23, come from James Stephens's 'magnificent reincarnation of blind Raffery's [Anthony Raftery or Antoine Rafterai (1779–1835) the blind wandering Irish poet] 'County of Mayo' with its wonderful rendering of internal assonances:

> I say and swear my heart leaps
> up like the rising of the tide
> Rising like the rising wind till fog
> and mists must go
> When I remember Carra and Gallen
> close beside,
> And the Gap of the Two Bushes
> And the wide plain of Mayo

See also I, p. 115 for a slightly different version of the poem.

*Killaden:* from the last stanza of Stephens's translation of Raffery's poem: 'To Killaden, then, to the place where everything grows that is best'. See also Frank O'Connor *Leinster Munster Connaught*, p. 298 'Killaden's the place where everything pleases'.

**'Tradition'**

*Inis Fail:* Ireland (Irish *inis*, an island; *fal*, genetive *fail*), the stone monument at Tara which 'was supposed to shriek on the rightful inauguration of the rightful monarch of all Ireland'. See Patrick S. Dineen, *An Irish-English Dictionary* (1927).

**'By a Stream in Bergen County'**

Title: Bergen County is in New Jersey, U.S.A. Its county seat is Hackensack

**'The Green Glint'**

Cf a passage in TTY concerning magic in the West of Ireland where this incident is described (TTY, p. 223).

**'Flyer in Manhattan'**

*Mt Rainier:* the highest mountain (14,410 feet) in the Cascade range in W. Washington State.

**'To Girls to go Harvesting'**

*foison:* a plentiful supply or yield (from Latin *fusio*, a pouring out).

**'And no Farther' [an unpublished version]**

*Hoover:* Herbert Clark Hoover (1874–1964), thirty-first President of the United States (1928–1932). A Republican, he opposed direct governmental assistance to the unemployed after the slump of 1929; this led to his defeat by Franklin D. Roosevelt.


SATIRES AND FACETIAE

**Dislikes and Disapprobations**

**'Epigram on Connolly'**

Connolly: presumably James Connolly (1868–1916). He founded the Irish Socialist

Republican Party in 1898; in America from 1903, where he founded *The Harp* (1907–10), he returned to Dublin in 1910, becoming head of the Irish Transport and General Workers' Union; in 1913 he led the Dublin transport strike with James Larkin and founded the Citizen Army. He was appointed commander of Republican forces in Dublin in 1916 and was subsequently sentenced to death by a court martial and shot in 1916. It is less likely that 'the player Connolly' (YP, p. 454) is meant, an actor who was shot in fighting near the City Hall in 1916.

**'[A Lock-In]'**
A Dublin lawyer wrote a novel in which he referred to Arthur Griffith and his fleas. Dublin rumour had it that the lawyer and his brother, a doctor, stayed at home on Easter Monday, 1916, when the Rising began, their mother having locked away their rifles under the stairs. The image of the fleas was likely to have been prompted by Yeats's poem 'To a Poet, who would have me Praise certain Bad Poets, Imitators of His and Mine', written in April 1909, prompted by what Yeats thought his friend George Russell's overpraising poets still writing in the Celtic Twilight mode, YP (1996), p. 189.

**'On his Mother's dishonest Solicitor, run over by a car, reputedly a Rolls-Royce'**
*solicitor:* 'Had I inquired into the credentials of my mother's attorney I would have found that he had been struck off the Rolls which is a rare disgrace for an attorney . . . [He was] an insinuating bony-headed little scoundrel who had robbed his way to seeming prosperity . . . He had met my mother at the altar rail, for he haunted the Jesuits' Church in Gardiner Street. That was enough for her. She had the utmost confidence in the rogue . . . [He] made away with the whole property before my mother's death' (TTY, p. 219).

**'On the Charges of his American Agent for Lecture Tours'**
A TS in T.C.D. contains these remarks written after the poem by Gogarty:

> When I speak of the voraciousness of lecture agents, I am thinking of Clarke Getts. After he had sent me out to the Middle West I sent him the following postcard [this poem]. I never got a reply. He had troubles of his own at the time. See also I, pp. 179–180 for Gogarty's general views on 'the devastating rapacity of American lecture agents'; he goes on to describe some of their machinations.

**'To a Lady Reviewer'**
This poem was prompted by Mary Colum's (1887–1957) review of Gogarty's *Elbow Room*, NYT, 12 April 1942. Mary, wife of Padraic Colum, went to America with him shortly after their marriage. She contributed to many journals and wrote *Life and the Dream* (1928; 1947; 1966).

LIMERICKS

**'[The Virginal Kip-ranger]'**
Title: Gogarty had several names for Joyce, the Virginal Kip-ranger, Dante, or Kinch, which he used according to his mood.
*The Kips:* Nighttown, the red light district of Dublin. Ulick O'Connor remarks that the word was probably derived from the old Danish Dublin 'Keep' or 'Area cordon' and adds that the place was probably unique in that it was licensed by the police, quoting the *Encyclopaedia Britannica* to the effect that the police permitted 'open brothels confined to one area, but carried on more openly than in the South of Europe or even Algiers', O'C, p. 54.

**'On James Joyce'**
*Monasterboice:* the site of a Celtic style monastery with decorated high crosses in County Louth.

**'On James Joyce's brother, Stanislaus'**
*Kinch:* a name Gogarty called Joyce at times.
**'On Parker the Grinder'**
Title: grinders were unofficial coaches or tutors, paid by undergraduates – and, indeed,
by candidates for Fellowship on occasion – in Trinity College, Dublin, some of whom
had rooms in the College, 'Parker' having his ground-floor room in a house to the east
of the square called Botany Bay. 'You could take out grinds with him in almost any
part of the BA, Trigonometry, Astronomy, Algebra, almost anything' (TH,
p. 31) 'Parker' may have been based on Brown, a talented classical scholar and grinder
who had rooms in Botany Bay.
James Carens suggests in *Surpassing Wit* (1979) that the last line might have read 'Astride on
a prostitute's hips'. Parker appears again in TH, as the short cut not only to BA but MB:

> Now Parker's a jolly good soul
> And he keeps mercury in a bowl
> Since the transit of Venus . . .
> Affected . . .

The mercury alluded to was used to find the nadir in Botany Bay, though the place itself was
the opposite of the zenith as far as houses and appearances went (TH, p. 30).

**'On Ryan, a fellow student'**
Title: the limerick is attributed to 'Emerson E.' 'Ryan', Gogarty remarks in TH, was

a very hard-working student, off his chump and up in the Asylum [the Richmond Asylum,
Dublin], for that's where they put Ryan when he found out too late his mistake in confusing
the celestial with the terrestrial. It never occurred to him that anyone could be so base as to
represent for the sake of simplicity all the stars as level, ignoring the difference in the distances
from the earth and putting them all at the same level on the surface of a globe – a globe
which you were supposed to look at from the outside, though everyone knew we were inside
it and under the dome of stars.

*The Richmond Asylum:* a government grant was made for its establishment in 1810. It
was opened in 1815, the second lunatic asylum after St Patrick's Hospital was established
by Dean Swift in the eighteenth century. (See Marcus Renber, *State and Private Lunatic
Asylums in Ireland: Medics, Fools and Maniacs 1600–1900*, Institute of History of
Medicine, Cologne; J.D.H. Widdes, *The Richmond, Whitworth and Hardwicke Hospitals,
St Laurence's Dublin 1772–1972* (1972) and *The House of Industry Hospitals 1772–1987 –
A Closing Memoir*, compiled and edited by Eoin O'Brien, Lorna Browne and Kevin
O'Malley, 1988). It became Grangegorman and is now known as St Brendan's.
**'The Young Man from St John's'**
Gogarty disclaimed authorship of this limerick in a letter to Horace Reynolds in 1952,
but it has so frequently and persistently been attributed to his Oxford days that it is
included here. By 1927 he had told Reynolds that he did not write many limericks, his
reputation amongst his friends for doing so being founded upon their attributing them to
him; but in a letter to Reynolds of 8 March 1927 he wrote 'Do not think by this that I
would repudiate "unbaptised rhymes" or that I have grown uncivil, as narrow natures
would/ And call those pleasures evil/ Happier days thought good.'
Letter (HD papers) cited in *L*, p. 321.
**'On Miss Horniman'**
Title: Annie Elizabeth Fredericka Horniman (1860–1937) met W.B. Yeats through their
membership of the Hermetic Order of the Golden Dawn. They became good friends
and this led to her buying for the Irish National Theatre Society the disused theatre in
Abbey Street, Dublin (part of which had been a morgue) in 1904, paying the players'

salaries the following year. She was not sympathetic to nationalist and popular plays and sold out to the Irish directors on generous terms in 1910 after the theatre had stayed open during the period of mourning after the death of Edward VII. She then turned her attention to repertory theatre in England, Manchester greatly benefitting from her help. Niáll (Neil) Montgomery, son of Gogarty's friend James Montgomery atttributed this limerick to Joyce.

**'The Young Lady of Chichester'**
Title: Gogarty's friend of Oxford days G.K.A. Bell (1883–1958) was elevated to the see of Chichester in 1929. See Gogarty, TTY, p. 63.

**'On being elected to the Irish Academy of Letters'**
Title: The Academy, Yeats's brainchild, was founded in 1932; its main purpose was to protect Irish writers from the Censorship Board. Gogarty was elected a member. See note on p. 688.

**'On a fallen electrician'**
Title: prompted by the death of an electrician who fell to his death from a Nassau Street, Dublin, rooftop when repairing an illuminated advertisement for Oxo.

**'The Fussy Boys'**
*Ferrar.* Gogarty is probably alluding here to the New York publishing firm of Farrar Strauss [& Giroux], founded in 1946.

**'Of Daniel O'Connell, who, it is rumoured, begot many bastards'**
*Daniel O'Connell* (1775–1847) achieved Catholic Emancipation in 1829, and was known as the Liberator. cf Yeats's comment that 'We never had any trouble about O'Connell. It was said about O'Connell, in his own day, that you could not throw a stick over a workhouse wall without hitting one of his children, but he believed in the indissolubility of marriage and when he died his heart was very properly preserved in Rome' (cf also Yeats's poem 'The Three Monuments', YP, p. 335), *The Senate Speeches of W.B. Yeats,* ed. Donald R. Pearce (1960), pp. 97–98.

**'Brian O'Lynn'**
Title: Brian O'Lynn appealed to Gogarty's imagination. In his novel *Mad Grandeur* (1943) he quoted the first two lines of this limerick, contrasting the coaches, the fashion and other signs of wealth of those attending the Curragh races in County Kildare with the figures representing Dublin's 'poverty and squalor unmatched by any city in Europe'. In SSE Gogarty quotes two stanzas about O'Lynn whom he elsewhere described as life's great optimist:

> Brian O'Lynn with his wife and his ass
> Were crossing a bridge as the legends aver;
> The bridge it collapsed and the trio fell in:
> 'There's land at the bottom', said Brian O'Lynn.

and

> Brian O'Lynn had a house to be sure,
> With the stars for the roof and the bog for a flure:
> A way to go out, and a way to come in;
> 'It's mighty convenient,' said Brian O'Lynn.

**'The Young Fellow at Bray'**
Title: Bray, County Wicklow, on the coast 12 miles south of Dublin, once a fashionable resort, now virtually a suburb of Dublin.

**'A Professor of Trinity Hall'**
Horace Reynolds rejoiced in this as a parody of Riemann's and Einstein's non-Euclidean mathematics.

PARODIES

### 'Parody of Swinburne's "Itylus"'

The poem takes ll. 45–47 from Swinburne's 'Itylus' (*Collected Poetical Works* (1924), I, pp. 54–56) altering l. 48 ('The feast of Daulis, the Thracian sea') to 'Thou art classic, romantic is Gogarty'.

*Itylus:* the son of Aedon, married to Zethus, King of Thebus. She was jealous of her brother's wife Niobe who had six sons and six daughters, and tried to kill one of the sons. However, she killed Itylus by mistake. Zeus changed her into a nightingale, whose song is Aedon's lament for her son Hylas.

*Itylus:* Swinburne wrote a ballad, 'Itylus', on the subject in *Poems and Ballads,* first series (1866).

### 'William Dara thinks of the sin of his childhood and is sorrowful'

The poem parodies W.B. Yeats's 'The Pity of Love', YP, p. 75. It was 'Sent to the Wandering Aengus'. Aengus was the Celtic god of love and Gogarty's use of 'The Wandering Aengus' as a name for Joyce derives from the title of another Yeats poem, 'The Song of Wandering Aengus'. Yeats's poem 'The Pity of Love' ends thus:

> The cold wet winds, ever blowing,
> And the shadowy hazel grove
> Where mouse-grey waters are flowing,
> Threaten the heart that I love.

### 'To Elwood Poxed'

Title: John Elwood, known as Citizen Elwood, a friend of Gogarty and Joyce, and a member of the group of students described in *Tumbling in the Hay* (1939) as meeting in the portico of the National Library (where Joyce taxed Elwood with inscribing his name in pencil on the backside of the Venus of Cnidus in the pillared colonade of the National Museum opposite the Library) was a chronic medical student who eventually took the Licentiate of the Apothecaries Hall in 1915 and practised medicine at Carrowbehy in his native area of County Roscommon. Gogarty comments in TTY that he was called the Citizen to ridicule his advanced views, 'an ebullient fellow who always had a quizzical smile in his eyes and around his shapely mouth'.

### 'Parody of "To Althea from Prison"'

The poem follows the first two lines and the fifth of Richard Lovelace's poem closely:

> Stone walls do not a prison make,
> Nor iron bars a cage;
> Minds innocent and quiet take
> That for an hermitage;
> If I have freedom in my love,
> And in my soul am free;
> Angels alone that soar above
> Enjoy such liberty.

The comment on Jehovah in Gogarty's note is repeated by Joyce, attributed to Buck Mulligan in *Ulysses* (1992 edn), p. 257:

He rattled on
– Jehovah, collector of prepuces, is no more.

### 'The Policeman is bathing – to Girls to have no Fear but Caution'

*His anger . . . comforted:* These lines parody W.B. Yeats's 'The Folly of being comforted', YP, p. 130:

O heart! O heart! if she'd but turn her head,
You'd know the folly of being comforted.

## 'Lack of Knowledge'

The poem was probably provoked by 'John Eglinton' not including in *Dana* a poem by
Gogarty that he had promised to publish. *Dana* ran from May 1904 to April 1905; a
monthly, it was critical of Catholicism's role in Irish society and of the Gaelic League's
exclusivity. 'John Eglinton' was the pen name of William Kirkpatrick Magee
(1868–1961), a celibate Assistant Librarian in the National Library of Ireland. He had
said, when sexual indulgence was being discussed, 'I never did it' which became a
joking catch phrase among Gogarty, Joyce and their friends. The poem parodies
Burns's 'John Anderson my Jo':

John Anderson my jo, John,
   When we were first acquent;
Your locks were like the raven,
   Your bony brow was brent;
But now your brow is beld, John,
   Your locks are like the snaw;
But blessings on your frosty pow,
   John Anderson my Jo.

John Anderson my jo, John,
   We clamb the hill the gither;
And mony a canty day, John,
   We've had wi' ane anither:
Now we maun totter down, John,
   And hand in hand we'll go;
And sleep the gither at the foot,
   John Anderson my Jo.

Gogarty's MS note on the poem read: 'This is most ecclesiastical. The schoolmen equate knowledge for temptation etc'.

**'Languorous Lotus-Land'**

A parody echoing Tennyson's 'The Lotus Eaters'.

*O'Leary harboured:* possibly John O'Leary (1830–1907), the old Fenian leader who returned to Dublin having spent the last part of his gaol sentence in Paris in exile; he had a strong influence on Yeats. In this case the poem may be contemplating him bereft of his impressive beard (see the drawing of him by John Butler Yeats in William M. Murphy, *Prodigal Father* (1978) p. 141, or, probably, this is the O'Leary described in SSE:

> Now O'Leary, though a very mild albeit a shrewd businessman on land, owned a yacht on which he became a regular devil. He used to shanghai his friends and when he got them on board, abuse them outrageously. Why the change in his character let psychologists explain; there is no room for them here. It seemed that Kevin [Smith, who worked at 'Cantrell and Cochrane's the soda water people over the way from Fanning's public house'] went on board O'Leary's yacht with a large paper sticking out of his breast pocket. 'What have you got there?' asked O'Leary. 'My mother's marriage lines, so you will have to modify your language when you address me.'

*Huysmans:* Joris Karl Huysmans (1848–1907), French novelist of a decadent school, known for his novel *A rebours* (1884).

*O si quis piorum:* from the peroration of Tacitus (*c*.55–120), *Agricola*, a life of the Roman statesman and general who conquered Britain (77–86AD), the opening sentence of the last chapter (46):

> *Si quis piorum manibus locus, si, ut sapientibus placet, non cum corpore extinguntur magnae animae, placide quiescas, nosque, domum tuam ab infirmo desiderio et muliebribus lamentis ad contemplationem virtutum tuarum voces, quas neque lugeri neque plangi fas est.* (If there be any habitation for the spirits of the just; if, as philosophers will have it, the soul that is great perish not with the body, may you rest in peace and summon us, your household [Agricola was Tacitus's father-in-law] from weak repining and womanish tears to the contemplation of those values which it were impiety to lament or mourn.)

*tendebat manus:* Professor J.V. Luce suggests that this refers to the passage in Virgil's *Aeneid* VI, 314 describing the souls in Hades waiting for Charon to ferry them across the Styx: *Tendebantque manus ripae ulterioris amore.* They stretched out their arms in longing for the farther shore

*dear old days:* an echo of Horace, *Ars Poetica*, 173, *laudator temporis acti*, a praiser of past times.

*Walter Pater:* Pater (1839–94), English essayist and critic who advocated the love of art for its own sake. His works include *Marius the Epicurean* (1885), *Studies in the History of the Renaissance* (1873) and *Imaginary Portraits* (1887).

*asphodelian:* the asphodel appears in Greek legend

*that City Asphodelian,* probably so called because of the asphodel giving its name to the Plain of Asphodel, the dwelling of most of the shades in Hades. See Homer, *Odyssey* II, 539 and 24, 13. It is a ghostly grey weed suiting the grey existence of those in the Underworld.

*Syphilitic city . . . River Goh:* a reference to Gomorrah. See note p. 711.

*dolce far niente:* (Italian) a pleasant idleness.

*cherubim in . . . Yo Yohimbum:* possibly a reference to Yohimbine or Yohimbenine, an alkaloid used as an adrenergic blocking agent, obtained from an African tree, the Yohimbe. It is reputed to be an aphrodisiac.

*The bird of loudest lay . . . Leone tree:* cf Shakespeare, *The Phoenix and the Turtle*:

> Let the bird of loudest lay,
> On the sole Arabian tree
> Herald sad and trumpet,
> To whose sound chaste wings obey.

## 'Five Parodies'

### II

A parody of William Blake's (1757–1827) 'The Tyger', in *Songs of Experience*:

> Tyger! Tyger! burning bright
> In the forests of the night
> What immortal hand or eye
> Could frame thy fearful symmetry?
>
> In what distant deeps or skies
> Burnt the fire of thine eyes?
> On what wings care he aspire?
> What the hand dare seize the fire?
>
> And what shoulder, & what art,
> Could twist the sinews of thy heart?
> And when thy heart began to beat,
> What dread hand? & what dread feet?

*Helicon:* A mountain in Boeotia, Greece, the location of the springs of Hippocrene and Aganippe, believed by the ancient Greeks to be the source of poetic inspiration and the home of the Muses.

### III

*Gethsemane:* the garden where Christ was betrayed on the night before his crucifixion. See the Bible, Matthew 26: 36-56.
*Metempsychoser:* metempsychosis is the migration of one soul to another or the entrance of a soul after death into a new cycle of existence in either a new human or animal body.
*Marsyas:* a satyr or silenus, a musician and inventor of music for flute or oboe. He challenged Apollo to a contest in music, which Apollo won, and, taking advantage out of an agreement that the winner could do what he liked to the loser, flayed him alive.

### V

*Dr Wood:* presumably Woods, Sir Robert Woods (1865–1938) whom Gogarty admired greatly. See note on him below, p. 753 (In view of this the 'down' is surprising, 'Woods' being possibly a hasty choice of a rhyme for 'concludes').
## 'Pax Britannica'
Pervasive echoes of William Wordsworth (1770–1850), 'The World is too much with us' (1807), ring through this poem:

> The world is too much with us
> Getting and spending we lay waste our powers . . .

The rhymes of both are very similar. Wordsworth uses ours, boon, moon, hours, flowers, time . . . be, outworn, lea, forlorn, sea, horn, us.
*Gossoons:* (Irish) boys, serving boys.
*Earl Kitchener of the Cartoons:* probably a reference to the poster of Kitchener pointing, with the words 'Your country needs you'. Horatio Herbert Kitchener, 1st Earl Kitchener of Khartoum (1850–1916) was born near Ballylongford, County Kerry. He

served in the Sudan campaign, routing the Khalifa at Omdurman (1898); commander in South Africa (1900–1902), he became commander of India (1902–1909) and Secretary for War (1914) before he was lost with HMS Hampshire, mined off Orkney in 1916.

**'Parody of Arthur O'Shaughnessy's Ode'**
Here is the text of the Ode:

> We are the music-makers,
> And we are the dreamers of dreams,
> Wandering by lone sea-breakers,
> And sitting by desolate streams;
> World-losers and world-forsakers,
> On whom the pale moon gleams:
> Yet we are the movers and shakers
> Of the world for ever, it seems.
>
> With wonderful deathless ditties
> We build up the world's great cities,
> And out of a fabulous story
> We fashion an empire's glory:
> One man with a dream, at pleasure,
> Shall go forth and conquer a crown;
> And three with a new song's measure
> Can trample an empire down.
>
> We, in the ages lying
> In the buried past of the earth,
> Built Nineveh with our sighing,
> And Babel itself with our mirth;
> And o'erthrew them with prophesying
> To the old of the new world's worth;
> For each age is a dream that is dying,
> Or one that is coming to birth.

**'A Scotsman speaks to William Shakespeare'**
Padraic Colum recalled that Gogarty was very fond of lowland Scots, 'not only Burns but minor poets around Burns whom he could repeat with gusto'. *Irish Literary Portraits,* ed. W.R. Rodgers (1972), p. 144.


LIGHT-HEARTED VERSES

**'To William Dawson'**
Written to William James Dawson, a fellow undergraduate at Trinity College, Dublin, who had won the Vice Chancellor's Prize for Latin Verse in 1904 and 1905 and for Greek Prose in 1906. He had boasted that his father, a Limerick man who became Lord Mayor of Dublin (1882–1883), read 'chapters' of Sappho before going to bed. His father (1842–1917) moved his bakery from Limerick to Dublin; he was High Sheriff of Limerick (1876–7), M.P. for Carlow, (1880) and became Collector of Rates for Dublin Corporation in 1891, dying in office. See Gogarty TH, p. 114 for a polished account of the couplet's composition given to Mahaffy. William Dawson, who wrote as 'Avis' in *The Leader*, composed the ballad, denigratory, in fine Dublin style, about how Gogarty made his escape from the gunmen by swimming the Liffey on 12 January 1923, and sang it at the Arts Club in Dublin; it was sung to the air of 'The River Roe' or 'The Winding Banks of Erne'. It was originally circulated in typescript and later published in

O'C and in *More Irish Street Ballads* collected by Colm O'Lochlainn (1965). See Appendix, p. 599, and, for Gogarty's account of the kidnapping, TTY, pp. 177–182.

**'Idea for the Ending of a Poem'**

A letter to Joyce announced that Gogarty had 'a poem yet in the head of the Father Chaos-Elwood'. (See note on him, p. 725). The end of it, he remarked, would be the three lines in the text.

**'To the Wandering Aengus'**

In his letters 'from the Bard Gogarty', partially parodying Yeats, to James Joyce, who had asked Gogarty for money, Gogarty replied that he was short of money himself. He had earlier lent so much to Joyce that he lacked the fare back to Dublin (he was at Oxford from January to June 1904). The letter announces that he has 'only ten bob [50p in contemporary currency] here for the term' and that 'in town here I owe about £20'.

Title: Upon occasion Gogarty called Joyce 'the Wandering Aengus'. (Aengus was the Irish god of love). The poem was prompted by W.B. Yeats's poem 'The Song of Wandering Aengus', YP, p. 93. The 'beloved' may have been suggested by Yeats's 'He bids his Beloved be at Peace' or 'A Poet to his Beloved', YP, p. 96 and p. 98 and by his 'He hears the Cry of the Sedge', *ibid.*, p. 102.

**'At Burford'**

Title: Sir Compton Mackenzie, the Scottish novelist and journalist (1883–1972) and his future brother-in-law, Christopher Stone (see note, p. 670) had taken a cottage at Burford in the Cotswolds where Gogarty visited them.

**'The Spud' (to George Redding)**

'The Spud' may be 'Spud' Murphy, Dr Cyril James Murphy M.D., F.R.C.P.I., Physician to the Meath Hospital, Dublin.

*his Mayo mud:* The Spud appears as the Bud, a projector, in SS, pp. 32–33: You have a chance to come in on it now . . . we have an option on 'Mrs McNulty's holding'. In answer to the question what is it he replies '. . . You don't know that there are about three hundred million tons of it, of the finest quality in the world lying untouched in Mayo and the deep-sea slip at Port Na Cloy! One hundred pounds a ton f.o.b., and there you go'. Why, he is asked, is he going to Paris, can't he ring them up? To which he replies 'My dear Sir, my very dear Sir, who can do business with Paris satisfactorily by long-distance telephone?' 'It' is kaolin or china clay. There is a world shortage, he says, the Cornish mines are petering out. 'We must all be in first on the ground floor'. See also SS, p. 76, which indicates that the project of exporting kaolin has become a boring topic.

*Kaolin:* a fine white china clay, a feldspar or aluminium silicate, used to treat diarrhoea, also employed as a poultice. It is a disinfectant, a detoxifier generally. It is also used in the manufacture of bone china and hard paste porcelain.

*Boul Mich':* the Boulevard St. Michel, the chief thoroughfare in the Latin Quarter which begins at the Place St. Michel and leads south to the Carrefour de l'Observatoire, passing the Cluny Museum, the Sorbonne and the Luxembourg Gardens. It was largely known for its Bohemianism and the many students' cafes which line it.

*There I leave you:* This was a characteristic phrase frequently used ('playing for safety as is his wont', TTY, p. 98, and see also p. 105) by Laurence O'Neill (1874–1943). His father, John, a Dublin corn factor at 18 King's Inn Street, moved the successful and expanding business into Smithfield Market at the turn of the century. Laurence joined the family business as a young man and was involved in its management till his death. Elected to Dublin City Council in 1911, he was subsequently elected Lord Mayor of Dublin in 1917 and served consecutive terms of office until 1924 when the Minister for Local Government abolished the City Council until 1930. O'Neill was then elected as a Councillor and served until 1936. He had also been a T.D. (1922–25) and a Senator (1929–1936). A skilled negotiator, he averted a threatened General Strike in 1920 and one in the drapery trade in 1921. Gogarty, however, probably chiefly remembered him for his action in another sphere: 'Larry O'Neill, the little fellow in black knickerbockers and the lump of white wool in his left ear, who was President of the Amateur Athletic Association and, afterwards, chronic Lord Mayor, had suspended me for bad language at the Furzy Glen corner [of the Phoenix Park] where all the cyclists from Ulster crashed. It is remarkable how gloomy fools impress the Irish public.' (TTY p. 58). Elsewhere he is characterised as 'The chronic Lord Mayor' (TTY p. 105).

**'George Redding's reply: The Mayo Spud in Paris'**
George Redding's (see note on him, p. 705) reply to the previous poem; Gogarty quoted it in SS, p. 84 with the following comment on Suzanne:

> Where did George get 'Suzanne' I asked.
> 'That reminds me,' said Joe. 'They are all Suzannes'
> 'Are they?'
> At Boulogne, at Rouen and Amiens, I never met anyone who was not Suzanne.'
> 'Why?'
> '*Nom de guerre*, I presume.'

**'McGurk'**
Title: McGurk is presumably a similar sounding name, chosen to resemble that of Macran (see note, p. 666) who was Professor of Moral Philosophy at Trinity College, Dublin, and became a friend of Gogarty, who called him the Master of Those who Know. The McGurk Macran equation is made clear in SS, pp. 321–324. He is depicted affectionately and appreciatively elsewhere by Gogarty, notably in Chapter XVI of TH, which describes a philosophical discussion between them in the garden of Fairfield, the Gogarty family's house outside Dublin. *Inter alia* Macran expounds Hegel's views and is helping the young Gogarty to think clearly. He also appears in the account of a picnic near Lough Bray in County Wicklow in SS, pp. 318–324.
*a Janus:* the Roman god of doorways, passages and bridges, Janus is depicted with two heads, facing opposite ways (hence Janus-faced, two faced or hypocritical)
*unmoralised, unmarital:* See the comment on Macran in TTY, p. 62:

> In Dublin he [George Kennedy Allen Bell (see note, p. 715)] met Macran, and he learned that his ideas of philosophy – moral, of course – were sometimes a cause of anxiety to his wife. This he recorded:

> > You could be all things but a good
> >     and wifely man;
> > And that you would not if you could,
> >     We know, Macran.

**'That City'**
*Guadelquiver:* or Guadalquivir, the chief river of Spain, 348 miles in length, rising in the Sierra de Sequra flowing west and southwest to the Gulf of Cadiz.
*'Little breezes dusk and shiver':* From Tennyson, 'The Lady of Shalott':

> > Willows whiten, aspens quiver,
> > Little breezes dusk and shiver . . .

. . . *the cenotaph of Keelin*

*Where the widowed wife is kneelin'*: This may be a reference to a graffito in the lavatory behind Nelson's Pillar, Dublin (SS, p. 78).

> Here lies the grave of Keelin
> And on it his wife is kneeling;
> If he were alive, she would be lying
> And he would be kneeling.

There was a version in a pub in Dalkey, 'but it is corrupt' (SS, p. 79). This may have been in 'The Arch' see note, p. 698.

*Nolan Wheelan:* James Valentine Nolan Wheelan S.C. who was reputed to have gone through two fortunes. He was an Oxford soccer blue and a friend of Gogarty's wife Neenie (L, p. 190).

*Nolens volens:* (Latin) whether willing or unwilling.

*Maurice Joy:* see note on him, p. 738.

*Connolly:* see note on him, p. 721.

*Richard Lynam:* described as the 'King of the Kips' in SS p. 87 and as 'a lively lad' in 'The Hay Hotel', p. 454, he was a well-known Dublin bookmaker.

*Sinbad:* Sindbad of the Sea, or Sindbad the Sailor, one of the tales of the *Arabian Nights*. A rich young man of Baghdad, Sindbad wasted much of his fortune in riotous living, undertook several sea voyages as a merchant and had various marvellous adventures. See Gogarty's use of him pp. 436 *et seq.*

Lethe: one of the rivers of Hades. Drinking it obliviated memories of past lives

Matthew Arnold: see note on him, p. 693.

**'Fragmentary Question'**

*Panurge:* see note: p. 684.

*Macran:* see note: p. 666.

*Pan:* see note: p. 680.

**'Ad Priapum'**

See note on Priapus, p. 676.

**'A Trinity Boat Song'**

Written for the Dublin University Boat Club.

*the river:* the Liffey, on which the Boat Club had its clubhouse at Islandbridge.

**'T.W. Wilson on Homophony'.**

Title: *T.W. Wilson*: unidentified

*Sedley:* Sir Charles Sedley (?1639–1701), a wit, and fashionable profligate, wrote three comedies – the best of them *The Mulberry Gardens* (1668) – and two tragedies as well as some songs, among them 'To Celia', where he rhymes 'aim' and 'them', 'have' and 'crave', and 'To Chloris' where he rhymes 'sit' and 'beget', 'when' and 'pain', and 'insensibly' and 'fly'.

*Rossetti:* Dante Gabriel Rossetti (1828–82), poet, artist and translator, founded the Pre-Raphaelite Brotherhood with Millais, Holman-Hunt and four other artists. He wrote poetry from 1847, including 'The Blessed Damozel'. His *Poems* appeared in 1870, his *Ballads and Sonnets* in 1881.

**'A Rejoinder to George Redding's "The Quiver"'**

Gogarty quoted Redding's poem in TTY, p. 35.

*Marie Stopes:* Marie Carmichael Stopes (1880–1950), pioneer advocate of birth control, the author of 70 books of which *Married Love* (1918), in particular, caused much controversy.

*Boyd-Barrett:* Dr Joseph Boyd-Barrett, a Dublin doctor and close friend of Gogarty, who graduated in medicine at the Royal University of Ireland in 1907. Mrs Boyd-Barrett's address is given as 10 Tivoli Terrace, South Kensington in the P.O. Directory for 1907. Boyd-Barrett had his consulting rooms in 79 Merrion Square, Dublin. The 'holy brother' was 'one of three brothers whom an overpious mother ruined, remarked Gogarty, 'The holy brother spent his days in church kneeling and his nights begetting children, his wife was redheaded and his quiver full'.

**'Comment on Thomas Bodkin'**
Bodkin had written to Gogarty on 7 September 1916: 'These verses of yours would hurt his feelings if he [Waldron] saw them. If he saw them with my name linked thereto he might arrive at the conclusion that I in some way suggested or was responsible for them. However I presume you were only joking when you told me of your intention [of dedicating his poem on Waldron (p. 44) to Bodkin]'.
*Bodkin:* Thomas Patrick Bodkin (1887–1961), born in Dublin, was educated at Belvedere College, Clongowes Wood College and the Royal University of Ireland. Called to the Bar in 1911, he became Director of the National Gallery of Ireland (1927–1935) and Director of the Barber Institute and Professor of Fine Arts, Birmingham University (1935–?1952). His books include *The Approach to Painting* (1927) and *Dismembered Masterpieces* (1945). See Anne Kelly, 'Thomas Bodkin at the National Gallery of Ireland' *Irish Arts Review Yearbook* 1991–1992 pp. 171–177, and Aidan Dunne and Michael Smith, 'Modernist Man', the *Irish Times*, 26 June 1999.

**'Tom Greene of Gort an Tochain'**
*Tom Greene:* not identified.
*Gort an Tochain:* This should perhaps be amended to *Gort an Tochair*, 'the Field of the Causeway'. *Gartatocher,* the anglicised form of the place-name, is the name of two extant farmlands in Counties Mayo and Clare respectively.

**'In the Stud-farm'**
In sending the poem to Compton Mackenzie Gogarty wrote 'Enclosed calculated to keep men's minds on horse-breeding in this blood-stock country. Also, slyly aimed at a friend who has introduced a youth to her menage'.

**'Talk (at all levels)'**
*Nineveh:* the ancient capital of Assyria on the river Tigris opposite the present city of Mosul. It was destroyed in 612 by the Medes and Babylonians.
*Memphis:* a ruined city in N. Egypt, an artistic and administrative centre, sacred to the worship of Ptah.
*Babylon:* the chief city of ancient Mesopotamia, settled about 3000 BC.

**'Diary Entry'**
*Trip no further:* cf Shakespeare, *Twelfth Night*, II.iii:

> Trip no further, pretty sweeting;
> Journeys end in lovers meeting,
> Every wise man's son doth know . . .

**'The Buck'**
This poem was probably from the period when Gogarty was writing his novel *Mad Grandeur* (1941); he included 'Buck' Whaley (Thomas Whaley (1766–1800), an Irish politician and eccentric) in it and wrote a ten page TS on him (now in Bucknell University Library). Gogarty was himself sometimes described as a twentieth century buck and Joyce's caricature portrayal of the youthful Gogarty in *Ulysses* as Buck Mulligan is well known. Tiger Roche appears also in TH, knocked out in Mrs Mack's brothel, pp. 263–265, and in *Mr Petunia* (1946) pp. 10–11 Gogarty describes him as the last of the eighteenth century swordsmen and duellists, the swashbucklers or 'bucks' and his death is descibed on p. 22.

**'A Poem by Simon Swishback'**
See A. Norman Jeffares, 'Know Your Gogarty', *Yeats Annual*, 14, 2000, pp. 298–305.

## SOME MARTELLO TOWER POEMS

**'Murray'**
Title: Murray kept a public house near the Martello Tower in Sandycove first rented initially at Gogarty's suggestion by Joyce, then by Gogarty from the War Office (See note MLTT, p. 19). Gogarty, who provided the furniture, described it to G.K.A. Bell:

> In this tower there are four rooms one large one above, and three below. Two of these are only pantries one containing a well; the other is copper-sheeted and was a magazine when the place was used as a fort. The upper chamber . . . is reached by a ladder stairway and is about 20 feet off the ground. The walls are 9 feet thick and the door massive. But, the best place of all is the roof. It is circular . . . and has a parapet all round. The parapet is about 6 feet high but there is a ledge, a yard wide which when one stands on it enables one to see comfortably over the wall leaning arms on it . . . The view is splendid. (MLTT, p. 30).

See note on 'Carson, Swimmer of Sandycove', p. 698, and 'Carmen Carsonii', and 'Carson' below.

**'Carmen Carsonii'**
Title: The Song of Carson. Alfred E. Carson was known as an all-the-year-round swimmer, who lived at 2 Sandycove Avenue, Sandycove, see note p. 698.
*Murrays:* the Arch, Murray's public house. See note on previous poem, and p. 698.
*Starkey:* Gogarty's friend James Sullivan Starkey ('Seumas O'Sullivan'). See note on him, p. 692.

**'Carson'**
*the Muglins:* barren rocks seaward to the north of Dalkey Island, on which a foghorn was installed. Smaller rocks are named Lamb Island, Clare Island and Maiden Rock. It was an adventurous swim for Carson on account of the currents.

**'McCreedy'**
This is Gerald Mecredy (1884–1946) B.A., M.B., D.P.H., Gogarty's fellow student at Trinity College, Dublin. His sister, the late Mrs R.W. Archer, described him in a letter to one of her daughters as having frolicked in the Martello Tower, clad only in top hat and dress shirt. There is an extant photograph of him naked with other contemporaries (possibly his brothers) in the Tower; they are climbing on each other's shoulders, making a human pyramid against the stone wall. The name was frequently misspelt as McCreedy or Macready; the doctor's father, a solicitor, employed the youthful James Stephens in his offices in Merrion Square. See note, p. 663. For Gogarty's account of how Stephens sacked himself from the firm see TTY, p. 196.

**'McCurdy'**
Title: *McCurdy*: Frederick McCurdy Atkinson, Gogarty's contemporary at Trinity College, Dublin. Like Gogarty, he had the distinction of winning Vice Chancellor's Prizes, in his case for English Prose in 1903 ('The Scandinavian and the Celtic genius as seen in Mythology and Legend') and in 1904 ('Mythology – theories as to its origins and development'). See James Joyce *Ulysses* (1992 edn), p. 277:

> – Longworth and McCurdy Atkinson were there . . . Puck Mulligan footed featly, trilling:

> *I hardly hear the purlieu cry*
> *Or a Tommy talk as I pass one by*
> *Before my thoughts begin to run*
> *On F. McCurdy Atkinson,*
> *The same that had the wooden leg*
> *And that filibustering fillibeg*
> *That never dared to slake his drouth,*
> *Magee that had the chinless mouth.*

> *Being afraid to marry on earth*
> *They masturbated for all they were worth*

– . . . Longworth is awfully sick, he [Buck Mulligan] said, after what you wrote about that old hake Gregory.

**Ernest Victor Longworth**: (1874–1935), Barrister and Editor of the *Dublin Daily Express* to whom Joyce was introduced by Lady Gregory in 1902; he wrote some reviews in the paper. See *Ulysses* (1986 edn) p. 177:

> Longworth is awfully sick, he said, after what you wrote about that old hake Gregory. O you inquisitional drunken jew jesuit! She gets you a job on the paper and you then go an slate her drivel to Jaysus. Couldn't you do the Yeats touch?
> He went on and down, mopping, chanting with waving graceful arms – The most beautiful book that has come out of our country in my time. One thinks of Homer . . .

[Buck Mulligan is here thinking of Yeats's comment on Lady Gregory's *Cuchulain of Muirthemne* (1902). See vol. VIII of Yeats's *Collected Works* (1908) pp. 133 *seq*: 'I think this book is the best that has come out of Ireland in my time'].
*Magee* ('John Eglinton'), see notes on pp. 663 and 693 and see 'Lack of Knowledge', p. 359, was present earlier in the Library Episode in *Ulysses* where Gogarty's poem about him is partially quoted (*ibid.*, p. 276):

> Puck Mulligan, panamahelmeted, went step by step iambing, trolling:
>
> *John Eglinton, my jo, John.*
> *Why won't you wed a wife?*

The lines beginning 'I hardly hear the purlieu cry' were probably by Gogarty, who obviously enjoyed parodying Yeats (see poems in *Parodies* section above) and is here echoing the opening lines of Yeats's *Baile and Aillinn*, YP, p.121:

> *I hardly hear the curlew cry,*
> *Nor the grey rush when the wind is high,*
> *Before my thoughts begin to run*
> *On the heir of Ulad, Buan's son,*
> *Baile, who had the honey month.*

Vivian Mercier remarked in this connection that this represents the Irish tradition of parodying in full career, travestying the lines of a great poet as soon as they are published. The time [in *Ulysses*] is supposedly 1904, the place the National Library of Ireland; 'Baile and Aillinn', the poem parodied, formed part of *In the Seven Woods* which Yeats published in 1903 (*The Irish Comic Tradition*, 1991 edn, p. 210).

## SEUMAS O'SULLIVAN POEMS

**'Sandycove Lines'**
*Starkey's:* see note on Starkey p. 692.
**'Advice to Seumas O'Sullivan'**
Title: Seumas O'Sullivan, see note on Starkey, p.692.
*stuck me again:* Gogarty failed his medical examinations in both 1904 and 1905; he was repeatedly failed by Professor Andrew Francis Dixon (d. 1913) in his second MB examination as deficient in anatomy.
*hydrog Psichon:* Hydrogen peroxide; but was it a hint of Hydrargyrum, mercury, which was a heroic purgative for syphilis, often indicated in the second stage?
*a Chronic:* the name for a student who failed examinations repeatedly – sometimes

deliberately as in the well-known case of a famous rugby international player who had been left an income for as long as he was a medical student at Trinity College, Dublin. Modern universities tend to be less tolerant of students who fail to proceed with their courses in a reasonable time (though their presence among the student body was often beneficial).

*Medea . . . poisonous pastures:* in Greek mythology Medea, the daughter of Aetes, King of Colchis, fell in love with Jason, who came to Colchis in quest of the Golden Fleece. She helped him to obtain it and they left for Greece, Medea first tearing her brother Absyrtus apart and leaving his mangled remains for their father to see. At Colcos she restored Jason's father, Aeson, to health by boiling him in a cauldron with magic herbs. When driven from Colcos (Medea, having encouraged the king's daughters to kill their father Pelias and boil his flesh in a cauldron, then refused to restore him) Jason and Medea fled to Corinth, where he deserted her for the King's daughter Glauce. She revenged herself by killing the two children she had by Jason and destroying Glauce. Later she married Aegeus, father of Theseus, whom she planned to poison but instead finally escaped to Asia.

*Pharmacopea:* the pharmacopoeia, an authoritative book which contains lists of medical drugs with their uses, dosages and formulas.

*Mareotic mere:* The Mareotic Sea, or Lake Mareotis, south of Alexandria, Egypt. See Shelley's *Witch of Atlas*, LVIII where the witch glided down the Nile

> By Moeris and the Mareotid lakes
> Strewn with faint blooms like bridal chamber floors

and Yeats's 'Demon and Beast', YP, p. 293,

> O what a sweetness strayed
> Through barren Thebaid,
> Or by the Mareotic Sea . . .

In SS, p. 50 Gogarty quotes 'The silted Nile mouths and the Moeritic Lake'.

*experientia docet:* (Latin) experience teaches

**'To Stark to leave Rathmines'**

Title *Stark . . . Rathmines*: J. S. Starkey (see note p. 692) then lived in Rathmines, a suburb south of Dublin.

**'Invitation to my dear Stark'**

Title: the invitation was to suggest he should accompany Gogarty on his 'annual rest cure'

*Duke Street . . . shawls:* the lanes off Duke Street, Dublin, were at the time a poor quarter. The women who sold flowers, fruit, vegetables or fish were known as shawlies from their black shawls.

*Rathfarnham:* see note to previous poem.

*sheets of foam . . . corded balls:* the poem parodies Matthew Arnold's 'The Scholar-Gypsy':

> . . . and unbent sails
> There, where down cloudy cliffs, through sheets of foam,
> Shy traffickers, the dark Iberians come;
> And on the beach undid his corded bails

**'In Loco'**

*Kochler:* Colin Smythe has suggested this may be a disguised name for Thomas Goodwin Keohler (Keller, after 1914) (1874–1942), a poet and member of the Theatre of Ireland Company from May 1906.

*we were na fou:* an echo of Robert Burns's 'Willie brew'd a peck o'maut':

> We are na fou, we're nae that fou,
> But just a drappie in our e'e

*Anacreon:* a 6th century BC lyric poet (?572–?488BC) of Teos in Ionia, who lived mainly at Samos but went to Athens at the invitation of the tyrant Hipparchos. See note below on 'A Whiskey below Par,' p. 749.

**'To Starkey by "John Eglinton"'**
These lines are put in the mouth of 'John Eglinton', the librarian W.K. Magee, see p. 735.

*the Quays:* probably a suggestion here of a red light area.

*Byrne:* J. F. Byrne, a friend of Gogarty and Joyce, who quarrelled with them and with another friend, Cosgrave. He is the model for Cranly in James Joyce's *A Portrait of the Artist as a Young Man.* Joyce's brother Stanislaus had a particular dislike of Byrne whom he called 'Thomas Square-Toes' and described as having an impenetrable mask like a Cistercian bishop's face.

*sea-born Carson:* see note p. 698.

*McCurdy:* see note on him, p. 734.

*Lyster:* Thomas William Lyster (1855–1929), the Librarian of the National Library of Ireland, described by Gogarty in SS:
'a lovable man . . . His brown beard moved a little as he smiled, with cheeks fresh as a child's while his whispering, diffident, feminine voice invited us in'.

*Orpheus:* a legendary pre-Homeric poet and lyre-player, who failed to get Eurydice his wife back from the infernal regions because he looked back at her and broke the condition imposed by Pluto and Persephone for her release. After this he separated from the society of mankind, and the Thracian women, offended by his coldness, tore him in pieces and threw his head, still uttering the name Eurydice, into the river Hebrus.

**'A letter to Starkey from Dresden'.**
Title: See note on Starkey, p. 692.

*Sirmio . . . Sandycove:* Sirmio is a promontory on the southern shore of Lake Garda on which Catullus (see note on him, p. 740) had a villa. He gave a rapturous description of the place. See Catullus xxxii.I.

*St. Carson's Mount:* See note on Carson, p. 698. The Mount may be a jocular reference to Sandycove; see note on 'Hamancos', p. 715, where the guarded 'Mount' is the Martello tower.

*Murray's Custom House:* The Arch, a pub run by Murray, 'the big headed thin little publican', in Sandycove, 'the nearest licensed house to the [Martello] tower'. It wasn't, but was convenient enough, and close to the school where Joyce was teaching.

*Charon:* the ferryman who ferried the dead across the rivers Styx or Acheron to Hades.

*McCurdy:* see note on him, p. 699. He may by this time have become a journalist, and have been 'ordered up' by his Editor.

*Colum:* probably Padraic Colum (1881–1972), playwright, novelist, poet and folklorist; he and his wife Mary left Ireland for America in 1914; he remained there for most of the rest of his life but spent his last years in Dublin.

*Kettle:* Tom Kettle, a school friend at Clongowes Wood College, County Kildare, where Gogarty admired his prowess as a cyclist. In SSE he described him as outstanding, 'Young, buoyant, laughing, carefree and gifted with an astounding power of breaking through an enemy's front with a wit like lightning'. Kettle became MP for East Tyrone in 1906 and Professor of National Economics at University College,

Dublin in 1909. He bought arms in Belgium for the Irish Volunteers in 1914 but after the Easter Rising of 1916, of which he disapproved, he volunteered for service in France and was killed at Ginchy on 9 September 1916. Here Gogarty is referring to his curious, often contradictory, blend of liberal intellectualism and confessional catholicism. See Roy Foster, *Apprentice Mage* (1998), p. 298 and J.B. Lyons, *The Enigma of Tom Kettle* (1983), pp. 133–6.

*Pledge-bound Party:* the Irish Parliamentary Party upon which Parnell had imposed a pledge to sit, act and vote together. Here Gogarty is asking whether the Party is staying quiet on the issue of cattle driving, denounced in public by Kettle. John Redmond, who had led the Parnellite minority of the Irish Party after Parnell's death in 1891, and became leader of the re-united Party in 1900, had used Parnellism and its fervent supporters such as Hazleton (see following note). The party had become, however, conservative in outlook and was embarrassed by the issue of cattle driving. This was an agitation against graziers in the West supported by local agrarian radicals as well as rising members of Sinn Fein. The party while supporting the graziers had nonetheless to appear not to disagree with this 'Ranch War'. Professor Foster has drawn my attention to Paul Bew, *Conflict and Conciliation in Ireland 1890–1910: Parnellites and Radical Agrarians* (1987), who shows the Catholic Church was put under pressure by the issues which cattle driving raised (hence a possible split between Kettle who supported it and some of the Church leaders who condemned it – Kettle having asserted the morality of cattledriving in a defence plea in the Wicklow Assizes in 1907).

Gogarty is using the hazel as a term for cattle driving (with the punning line with Haztleon) as it was used by D.P. Moran (see note on him, p. 706) of *The Leader*, who was critical of the policy: 'At its best the "hazel" as a weapon of general use is two-edged. It strikes at more than the grazier's bullock' (*The Leader*, 18 January 1908). In other words Gogarty is asking if the Parliamentary Party is supporting Kettle ('the Kettledrum') or has it been dumb and stopped using the hazel switch though earlier having used ('exploited') Hazleton who stands as a symbol for Parnellite methods. Gogarty's own disapproval emerges in his account of how he made his way from the West to Dublin during the Easter Rising of 1916. He got as far as Mulligar by train: there the lines were cut and he hired a car which he was asked to share with the well-known Larry Ginnell, Member of Parliament for Westmeath and instigator of the 'hazel wand' treatment of the graziers:

> Cattle driving was then the vogue. Cattle instead of men were supposed to be the enemies of the country and those who owned cattle were to be punished by having their herds driven by the hazel ward. My own opinion was exactly the opposite. (TTY, p. 164).

*Hazleton:* Richard Hazleton, an Irish Parliamentary Party MP, a strong supporter of Parnell.

*Maurice Joy: Sir* Horace Plunkett's secretary and editor of *The Irish Rebellion of 1916 and its Martyrs* (1916).

*the end of Keats:* John Keats (1795–1821) died of consumption.

*Herrick:* Robert Herrick (1591–1674), lyric poet, was incumbent of Dean Prior, Devonshire (1629–47). Ejected in 1647, he had his living restored in 1662. His *Hesperides* contains 1200 poems – love poems, epistles, epigrams. Gogarty's lyric poetry has often been compared to his. His friend Tancred 'knew every word Herrick had written' and, when Gogarty himself first met Lord Dunsany at a Hunt Ball at Dunsany Castle, he quoted 'all Herrick's *Hesperides* and was about to start on his *Noble Numbers* when someone drew his audience away. Dunsany knew Herrick as well as I did.'

*Kelly's Quay:* This could be the premises or yard of S. Kelly, a coal merchant listed in Thom's *Dublin Directory* in 1927 and 1935 as being at 22 Hanover Quay (and 15 D'Olier Street), part of the Grand Canal Docks running from Forbes Street to Britain

Quay, or else a loading dock on the Royal Canal at 'Kelly's Bridge', Lock 9 (but now renumbered Lock 8). There may also be a glancing reference to *Kelly's Keys to the Classics*, a well known series of cribs.

*Mooney's:* a Dublin public house, still flourishing.

*Soracte:* a mountain in Etruria near the Tiber, about 26 miles from Rome, celebrated by Horace, Odes I,9.

*Childe Roland:* a reference to Robert Browning's (1812–1889) poem 'Childe Roland to the Dark Tower came'.

*buskin not the sock:* the buskin, a raised boot worn by actors in classical Greek tragedy; the sock, a light shoe worn by actors in comedy

*dismal state that Oxford man:* Richard Samuel Chenevix ('Dermot') Trench (d. 1909) son of a Colonel in the British army and a grandson of Richard Chenevix Trench (1807–1886), Archbishop of Dublin and author of over 40 works including *On the Study of Words* (1851). Gogarty first met Trench in Oxford where they were both members of the Saint Patrick's Club. He appears as Haines in Joyce's *Ulysses*; he was a fervent Irish nationalist and member of the Gaelic League, wrote a pamphlet, *What is the Use of Reviving Irish?* and taught Gaelic in his rooms at Balliol College, Oxford. Gogarty, who had him to stay in the Martello Tower at Sandycove, was warned about his depression and feared that, like his father, he might kill himself, as indeed he did, blowing his brains out in hopeless love of Lady Mary Spring-Rice.

*Wiener Wald:* a district in Austria, the Vienna Woods.

*Neptune's day:* Neptune, the Roman God of the sea (corresponding to the Greek Poseidon). The planet Neptune rotates in fourteen hours, so the 'day' may suggest that the time will go slowly till the friends meet again. 'Neptune' has probably been suggested by the earlier 'sent by sea' route of the letter to Ireland.

*Kepler:* this may refer to Johann Kepler (1571–1636) of Wurtemberg, the celebrated German astronomer.

**'At Woodenbridge'**

The caption of the postcard on which the lines were written was: 'Hounds at Woodenbridge, County Wicklow'.

**'Your Father's Hat'**

The poem was sent to Starkey in a letter of 9 November 1913. After two years in Wesley College, which he entered at twelve, Starkey spent two years in the Catholic University Medical School before becoming an apprentice in his father's pharmacy. See 'To his Friend the Apothecary Poet', p. 204.

**'Limited Edition'**

The poem is enclosed in a letter referring to Starkey's book including his poem 'The Wasp'. Gogarty writes 'Just as Smyllie was triumphing because his copy of your book is in the thirties, mine in the fifties (51) in came Whiston who had not received a copy. This throws out my theory that the last verses were printed for your enemies'.

POEMS CONCERNING DERMOT FREYER

**'Verse Letter to Dermot Freyer from Nürnberg'**

Title *Dermot Freyer.* Gogarty first made his acquaintance in London, and they corresponded frequently. The Gogartys stayed at Nuremberg on their way to Vienna in 1907. Freyer, then Major Freyer, opened a guest house or hotel on Achill in the early nineteen-twenties. See 'A Line from Corrymore' below, p. 395 for Gogarty's somewhat ironic description of it.

*Scythed Time:* Time was personified (for the first time in 1509) as an aged man, bald but with a forelock, carrying a scythe and an hour-glass.

*the Langham:* a hotel in London (now the Langham Hilton, still situated at 1 Portland Place, W.1) where Freyer and Tancred met Gogarty and his wife in October 1907 (he had married in 1906).

*he whose new-found verse:* Francis Willoughby Tancred was an undergraduate at Cambridge when Gogarty first met him.

*Catullus-like:* Caius Valerius Catullus (*c.*83–54BC), the Roman poet and epigrammatist who celebrated 'Lesbia' in his poems. She was Clodia, the notorious sister of Publius Claudius. Catullus had a country house at Sirmio on Lake Garda (Sirmione in Tennyson's 'Frater, ave atque vale').

*Les Belles Dames du temps jadis . . . their poet:* a rondeau (translated by Rossetti and Swinburne) by François Villon. See note on p. 702.

*Scaith:* (archaic) harm, damage.

*no married man:* Gogarty married Martha Duane of Galway in 1906; she accompanied him when he studied in Vienna 1907–08. The Duanes came to Connemara as followers of the O'Flahertys in the middle ages. See Tim Robinson, *Connemara* (1990).

*prostatic place:* Freyer must have been living at home at the time; the reference is to his father, Sir Peter Freyer (1851–1921), born in Connemara, who served in the Indian Medical Service before retiring in 1896 and then practising in Harley Street, London. He invented the prostate gland operation and wrote *Surgical Diseases of the Urinary Organs* (1908).

*Tancred:* see note above on 'new-found verse'.

*Hans Sachs:* Sachs (1494–1576), a shoemaker of Nuremberg, the author of 200 plays and much verse including meister songs. He appears in Wagner's opera *Die Meistersinger von Nurnberg*.

### 'A Villanelle of Thanks'

*a book of verse:* Freyer's *Rhymes and Vanities*.

*Misey Die:* possibly a contraction of the Latin miserere, the 51st Psalm which begins *'Miserere mei, Deus'* (Have mercy on me, O God).

*Iritis:* inflammation of the iris of the eye.

*Thamyris:* a Thracian musician, mentioned by Homer (*Iliad*, ii, 594), who challenged the Muses to a contest of will, and, when defeated, was deprived of his eyesight and melodious voice, while his lyre was broken.

*Maeonides:* a name applied to Homer sometimes, supposed to be a native of Maeonia (an early name for Lydia). Gogarty is remembering here a line from Milton (*Paradise Lost*, iii, 53) 'Blind Thamyris and blind Maeonides'.

*A poet's eye . . . fine frenzies':* cf Shakespeare, *A Midsummer Night's Dream*, v. i:

> The poet's eye, in a fine frenzy rolling
> Doth glance from heaven to earth, from earth to heaven . . .

### 'A Line from Corrymore'

Gogarty's picture of Major Freyer's guest house or hotel in Achill.

*delph:* See note on 'Adam and Eve', p. 709; here it is a chamber pot.

## JESTING ABOUT THE SINCLAIR BROTHERS

### 'To W.A.S.'

Title: W. A. S. is William A. ('Boss') Sinclair (d. 1937), who married Cissie Beckett (Samuel Beckett's aunt). His twin brother Henry was plaintiff in the libel action against Gogarty's *As I was going down Sackville Street* (1937) which Gogarty lost, the plaintiff being awarded £900 in damages. Beatrice Elvery, an accomplished artist; her sister; Cissie Beckett and Estella Solomons (who married J.S. Starkey) studied in Paris. Beatrice Elvery later married Lord Glenavy.

*old ivory:* the Sinclairs had an antique shop in Nassau Street, Dublin.
*your spouse:* Cissie Beckett.
*a second elephant house:* There was an effigy of an elephant over the doorway of J.W. Elvery's shop in Nassau Street, on the corner of Dawson Street. It dealt largely in sports goods.
**'Lines addressed to William A. Sinclair'.**
Title: see note above on 'To W.A.S.'
*Sink . . . Beard:* names applied jocularly to Sinclair by Gogarty and some of his (and the Sinclairs') friends.
**'Gretta'**
*ladies in Nassau Street:* presumably outside the Sinclairs' shop, hence the indecipherable first word in 1.1 may have been '*Sink*' (from Sinclair) or '*Boss*': names applied as in note above on 'Lines addressed to William A. Sinclair'.
*the Dalkey Tram:* The Dalkey tram (number 8) ran from Nelson's Pillar, passing along Nassau Street en route.
*a bargain sale . . . jade:* another reference to the Sinclairs' antique shop.
*the Bailey:* a chop house, now a restaurant, in Duke Street, Dublin.
*the Pine Forest:* in the hills south west of Dublin.
*Lamb Doyle's:* a pub at Ticknock in the hills overlooking Dublin.
*home to Howth:* Howth, the rocky promontory enclosing the northern side of Dublin Bay, where William and Cissie Sinclair lived.
**'Nocturne 7.15 pm'**
*Bailey to Bailey:* from the Bailey, the Dublin chop house or pub to the Bailey, the lighthouse at the end of Howth, indicating the Sinclair home there
*the Boss:* William Sinclair.
**'On William Sinclair'**
*the one-backed Beast:* from the euphemism for normal sexual coupling, 'the two-backed beast,' (used in 'The Getting of Gargantua,' p. 474).
*a blind:* a drunken spree, a binge.
*the Jew:* William Sinclair, see note p. 740.
*Argenti Nit:* argentum nitricum (nitrate of silver, or lunar caustic) used as a remedy.
*Finck:* sometimes used as a slang name for a Jew.


CLASSICAL THEMES

**'Beyond Hydaspes'**
Title *Hydaspes:* In conquering India Alexander the Great (356–323 BC) crossed the Indus and at the Hydaspes overthrew Porus, then created Greek colonies throughout the Punjab; he marched back through Baluchistan to Persia and later died at Babylon.
*topless tram:* Being open on top allowed the lower Sandymount trams to pass under a low railway bridge on the route.
*Sandymount:* formerly a village on the coast approximately three miles south of the centre of Dublin, now a suburb.
**'To a Sailor'**
*Monte Negro:* Montenegro, bordering on the Adriatic, was declared a kingdom in 1910, and united with Serbia, Croatia and other territories in 1918 to form Yugoslavia.
*Lepanto . . . Cross . . . Crescent:* Lepanto is a port in West Greece between the Gulf of Corinth and Patras, the scene of a naval battle in 1571 in which the fleets of the Holy League defeated the Turkish fleet.
*'nota bene' . . . Mitylene:* a port on the Greek island of Lesbos where Sappho, the Greek lyric poetess (?b. mid 7th century BC), was born; seemingly as a result of political

trouble there she went to Sicily where she died. See lines 9–11 of 'The Isles of Greece,
p. 205, for the *'nota bene'* – *'Mitylene'* rhyme. See note on 'The Isles of Greece', p. 693.
*Calypso:* one of the daughters of Atlas, a nymph who reigned in the island of Ogygia.
Odysseus, returning from Troy, was shipwrecked there and stayed seven years with her,
refusing her promise of immortality if he would remain with her.
*Ajax . . . Salamis:* Ajax, bravest, after Achilles, of the Greek army which besieged Troy,
was the son of Telemon, King of Salamis.
*excursions run by Cook's:* the reference is to the tours organised by Thomas Cook
(1808–1892); his company still survives.
*Life . . . Steadily:* See Matthew Arnold, *To a Friend* (1849): '[Sophocles] saw life
steadily, and saw it whole'.

**'Opening Lines of Oedipus Rex'**
Gogarty meditated a version of Sophocles' *Oedipus Rex* (of which these are the opening
lines) in which he would emphasise Thebes as the world city of Sophocles, as Troy is of
Homer. He was involved in Yeats's translations of Sophocles, reading him the Greek
and supplying a rough translation for him.
*Cadmus:* the founder of Cadmea, later called Thebes. He and his brothers were ordered
to find their sister Europa (kidnapped by Zeus) or not to return home. Cadmus took
advice from the oracle at Delphi which told him to give up the search and settle where
a cow would lie down. He built his town there, killing a dragon that was feasting on
the bodies of several of his men. Athena directed him to sow half of the dragon's teeth.
The armed men who then sprang from the ground fought each other until five brothers
were left who made peace with each other and with Cadmus. His marriage was
unfortunate, his children Actaeon, Semele and Ino coming to violent ends while Agave
tore her son Pentheus to pieces for spying on the Bacchants.

**'George Moore's Garden Shrine'**
Title: Gogarty sent this poem to G.K.A. Bell in a letter of 7 March 1905 from 5
Rutland Square, Dublin, remarking 'George Moore is having a Priapus made for his
garden. I sent him a little adieu "to Geo Moore" and then added the poem.'
*Corn . . . wine . . . quaint Priapus:* Priapus, according to Greek mythology, was the son
of Dionysus, his mother either Aphrodite or a local nymph. Disgusted with his
appearance his mother had ordered him to be exposed on the mountains, but he was
rescued by a shepherd and became the chief god at Lampsacus, his temple 'the asylum
of debauchery'. His symbol was the phallus and he was described as almost a phallus
provided with a grotesque body; his sacrifice was the ass, an embodiment of lust as
well as stupidity. His cult spread widely and he became a god of orchards and
gardens, his statues representing him as a (furry) misshapen man with enormous
genitals, holding a stick to scare birds, a club to drive away thieves, a scythe for
pruning and cutting corn; the statues were usually crowned with vine leaves. See 'Ad
Priapum', p. 372.
*Lampsacus:* once the site of a Phoenician factory reputedly colonised by Phocaea, this
city had a strategic position, guarding the eastern entrance to the Hellespont, which led
to its prosperity and historical significance (see J. B. Bury *A History of Greece* (1900;
1931) pp. 197, 378, 492, 503, 750–757). In the sixth and fifth centuries B.C. it was
successively under Lydian, Persian, Athenian and Spartan control, having some periods
of self-government in the fourth century.

**'In Haven'**
Title: See 'In Harbour' by Swinburne, *Collected Poetical Works* (1924) I, p. 529.
*Colchis promontory:* on the Black Sea, south of the Caucasus, whence Jason brought back
the Golden Fleece and Medea, the daughter of the King of Colchis, see note on her
above, p. 736.

**'Foreword for a proposed volume, *Ditties of No Tone*'**
*Aristophanes:* Aristophanes (*c*.448–*c*.380BC), the great Athenian dramatist whose comedies caricatured the leading personalities of his period and their views on current events. His plays were outspoken, exuberant and, at times, outrageous in their comedy.
*Martial:* Marcus Valerius Martialis (*c*.AD40–104), born at Bibilis in Spain, lived in Rome from 64 AD for 35 years before returning to Spain. He wrote 1500 short poems or epigrams, coarse but witty, which convey a sharp insight into Roman life.
*Rabelais:* see note on him, p. 684.
**'Talassio'**
*Romulus:* in Roman mythology the founder of Rome; he and his twin brother Remus, the children of Mars and Rhea Silvia, were suckled by a wolf after being abandoned in infancy. Romulus later killed Remus in an argument over the new city.
**'Four lines of [Sappho's] Greek'**
Gogarty's letter to E.H. Alton, Fellow, Professor of Latin and later Provost of Trinity College, Dublin, discussed his translation:

My dear Alton
Can you accept this—

Ἑσπέρε πάντα φέρων ὅσα φαίνολις ἐσκέδασ'
ἀνώς
φέρεις ὄιν, φέρεις αῖγα, φέρεις ἀπό ματερι
παῖδα

And is 'shepherds back' better than 'home'? And you bring the sheep better than 'you fold'? I want home for the cottage scene where the mother collects the child that wandered playing at the end of the lines. And yet, because 'back' came so naturally I find myself distrusting myself and putting too much mind into a correction. ['Bring with the 'i' in it is higher up the scale than 'fold'. (MS addition in ink)].

As Gogarty dashed off his Greek somewhat hastily the editor has substituted instead the text in *Greek Lyric* ed. David A. Campbell (1982), I, 104, p. 130. Campbell translates the passage more literally as: 'Hesperus, bringing everything that shining Dawn scattered, you bring the sheep, you bring the goat, you bring back the child to its mother'. (*Ibid.*, p. 105).
**'Good Luck'**
*Alexander:* see note p. 741.
*Caesar:* see note p. 666.
*Ghengis:* see notes pp. 706 and 712.
**'Happy and Glorious'**
*Pindarus:* Pindar, see note on him, p. 709.
*Happiness . . . own . . . Crown:* Gogarty is thinking of Pindar's *First Pythian Ode*, to Hieron (*Pyth.* I. 99 ff):

τὸ δέ παθεῖν εὐ πρῶτον ἄθλων
εὐ δ'ἀκούειν δευτέρα μοῖρ'
αμφοτέροισι δ 'ανὴρ
ὅς ἄν εγκύρσῃ καὶ ἔχη
στέφανον ὑψιστον δέδεκται

To fare well is the first prize
And the second portion to be well spoken of;
But whatever man can light on and seize both
Has received the highest crown

*meed:* an archaic word meaning reward or recompense.
**'The Supreme Crown'**
See notes above on 'Happy and Glorious', p. 743.
**'Dialogue'**
An imagined dialogue between Lord Dunsany (see note p. 704) and his protegé, the poet Frances Ledwidge (1887–1917) of Slane, County Meath, who was killed in the battle of Ypres. His cottage in Slane is now a museum devoted to him.
**'Hesperus, Thou Bringer of Good Things'**
*Hesperus:* the Evening Star.
*Who sang of love in Mitylene:* Sappho, see note p. 674.
**'To Catullus'**
*the Fortune that she meant to you:* In his poems Catullus poured out his passionate love for Lesbia. See note on him p. 740. The idea of writing a poem to Catullus may have been inspired by Swinburne's 'To Catullus' with its

> Love and the sense of kinship only bred
> From loves and hates at one with another

Swinburne, *Collected Poetical Works* (1924) II, p. 599. See also his 'Ad Catullum', *Ibid.,* I, p. 457.
*reasty:* another spelling for reesty, derived from dialect reast/reest to be uncooperative in a noisy way.
*Fishamble Street:* a street running from Castle Street to Essex Quay on the Liffey in Dublin, where Handel's *Messiah* was first performed.
*Fumbally Lane:* it runs from New Street (a continuation of Clanbrassil Street lower) to Blackpits, in Dublin. The name is a corruption (*c.*1789) of Bumbailiffs' Lane.
**'Locusts'**
*Parnassus Hill:* a mountain in Phocis, famous for the oracle of Delphi, was regarded as a favourite place of Apollo and the Muses.


RELIGIOUS THOUGHTS

**'Samain'**
*Amairgin:* Amergin was thought to be one of the sons of Milesius by Scota; he appears in the Red Branch cycle of tales as a druid. Gogarty described how 'Amairgin, the poet, gave to the Tuatha de Danaan the lower half of Ireland, that is the territory underneath earth and under the water outside the garish light of day. The sons of Mil received the upper part and once a year on the last day of October and the first day of November there is common territory between the two parts (TTY, p. 223).
*The Danaans:* the *Tuatha de Danaan*, the tribes of the goddess Danu 'the mother of all the ancient gods of Ireland'. They were regarded as masters of magic, 'and are said to have come from the isles of Northern Greece in time out of mind and to have bought their magic with them' (TTY, p. 223).
*that Beneath the Wave:* (Irish *Tir-fa-Thonn*) the enchanted underworld beneath the sea.
**The Song of the Cheerful (but slightly sarcastic) Jaysus'**
This poem, which Gogarty called 'a delightful satire on Commercial Christianity' was sent in copy form to James Joyce who used it in *Ulysses* (1922).
**'To Rabelais, the fornicating friar'**
*Panurge:* see note on him, p. 684.
**'Celibacy'**
*gay Thelemes:* the Abbey of Thelema, in Rabelais I, liii *et seq.*, was built by Gargantua to reward Friar John for his prowess in war. It was to be the opposite in every way of

ordinary monastries and convents, its only rule *Fay ce que vouldras* (Do what you like). cf GN where Gogarty's hero/narrator had had hopes the vicarage, where he is in bed with Parmenis, might have something in common with the Abbey of Theleme. He quotes the inscription over its door.

> Here enter not fond makers of demurs
> In love adventures

and tells her the Abbey was reserved for 'All noble sparks endowed with gallant parts' and goes on to quote 13 lines of Rabelais (in English translation).
**'Christ and the Money-Changers'**
See Matthew 21:12. 'And Jesus went into the temple of God, and cast out them that sold and bought in the temple, and overthrew the tables of the money-changers and the seats of them that sold doves'. See also Mark 11:15, Luke 19:45 and John 2:14–16.
**'Jonah and the Whale'**
*bona Fides:* I had no good faith in, no belief in.
*'What is truth?' asked jesting Pontius:* See Francis Bacon: 'What is Truth? said jesting Pilate; and would not stay for an answer' *Essays:29, 'Of Truth'*.
*Jereboam:* Jereboam II (8th century BC) thrust back the Syrians and reconquered Ammon and Moab.
**'Strong Men'**
*them who go down to the sea:* see Psalms 107: 23–24:

> They that go down to the sea in ships, that do business in great waters;
> These see the works of the Lord, and his wonders in the deep.

*After-wrath:* 'a part of the stock-in-trade of the churches so it had to go in' (part of a note to 'Dear Jim' [James A. Healy] in Gogarty's hand).
**'For as much as'**
*From the Persian:* It has not proved possible to identify a source for this quotation.
**'Then and Now'**
*'Pan is Dead!'* from Plutarch (*c*.AD 46–*c*.120), the Greek biographer and philosopher, *The Obsolescence of Oracles*, 419: 'The Great God Pan is dead'.
*sly sophists:* originally sophists were pre-Socratic philosophers, itinerant professional teachers of oratory and argument, ready to enter into debate on any matter; the word has come to mean someone using clever quibbling arguments which are unsound fundamentally.
*dryads:* in Greek mythology nymphs or deities of the woods.
*naiads:* nymphs dwelling in lakes, rivers, springs or fountains.

POLITICAL POEMS

**'Wie geht es Gagenhofer?'**
Title: as Gogarty altered the 'Gagenhofer' to Ganghofer, the poem relates to Ludwig Albert Ganghofer (1855–1920) whose later work could be classed as *'servilen Kriegspropagandisten'*, servile war propaganda, in his *Eiserneu Zither* (1914) and *Reise zur Deutschen Front* (1915). Professor H. S. Reiss has suggested his earlier work was of a Synge-like nature. The German means 'How goes it, Gagenhofer'.
*Macedonian man:* Alexander the Great, see note p. 741.
*Thetis's child the wrath:* the opening lines of Homer's *Iliad* with an address to the Muse: 'Sing me, O Muse, the wrath of Achilles . . .' Achilles was the son of Pelius by the nymph Thetis, one of the Nereides.

*the archer:* the Greek god Apollo, the patron of bowmen, to whom the sudden deaths of men were attributed; he fought on the Trojan side and was a bitter critic of Achilles.

*An Apollonian King . . . Muses:* Probably a reference to Apollo, in Homer's *Iliad* Book XXIV, addressing the other gods on the twelfth day of Achilles' dragging Hector's body round the barrow of his friend Patroclus, killed by Hector.

*Tiresian word:* Tiresias was a blind soothsayer of Thebes who revealed to Oedipus that he had murdered his father and married his mother.

*Ploughshare is the sword:* cf the Bible, Isaiah 2:4: 'And they shall beat their swords into ploughshares and their spears into pruning hooks: nation shall not lift up sword against nation neither shall they learn war any more' (cf Micah 4:3 and Joel 3:19 where the ploughshares are beaten into swords).

**'To Lord Dunsany'**

*against the Boer:* Dunsany served in the Coldstream Guards in the Transvaal in the Boer war.

*Plugstreet Wood:* First World War army colloquial (later historical) name for Ploegsteert, a Flemish village near Armentières. See Fraser and Gibbons, *Soldier and Sailor Words and Phrases* (1925).

**'To a German . . . after 1918'**

*Black and Tans:* a force first recruited in January 1920 to reinforce the police; also known as the Auxiliaries or Auxies, they were named Black and Tans after a famous hunt because of their motley uniforms; their brutal tactics in the guerilla warfare included intimidation and reprisals.

**'To Erskine Childers'**

*lean Spanish Knight:* Don Quixote. These lines were probably prompted by dislike of Eamon de Valera (1882–1975) who opposed the 1921 Treaty. In the ensuing Civil War Erskine Childers, D.S.O. (1870–1922), an Englishman who had espoused Irish nationalism and had been Director of Publicity for the Revolutionary Irish Government (1919–1921) and Chief Secretary to the Irish Peace delegation, was court-martialled and shot by the Free State Government forces for carrying a hand gun. He is known for *The Riddle of the Sands* (1903) as well as works of military history and strategy.

*Your leader . . . The rueful countenance:* references to Eamon de Valera (1882–1975) and his severe appearance. He led the opposition to the Irish Free State set up in 1922, which resulted in the Civil War. See R.F. Foster, *Modern Ireland 1600–1972* (1988) Chapters 20 and 21 for a succinct account of the period.

*Let me . . . fat:* a quotation from Shakespeare, *Julius Caesar*, I, ii, 192. Another poem, a sonnet printed in *The Freeman's Journal* in 1921, attributed to Gogarty (because of its opening lines directly parodying Wordsworth's 'Poems Dedicated to National Independence and Liberty', XIV:

> Milton! then shouldst be living at this hour;
> England hath need of thee

and continuing to echo the sonnet)
was direct enough:

> Childers, then shouldst be leaving at this hour,
> England hath need of thee beneath Big Ben.
> Thy sword is stagnant, so should be thy pen

(O'C p. 193)

**'Don't hang Hitler'**

*Hitler:* Adolf Hitler (1889–1945), Dictator of Germany, reputed to have been a housepainter and decorator during some of the years between 1904–1913. He committed suicide in 1945.

*Goering:* Hermann Wilhelm Goering (1893–1946), German military and political leader, ace pilot in the First World War, in charge of the Luftwaffe in the second. He was the first and only holder of the rank of Marshal of the Reich. He committed suicide after being found guilty at the Nuremberg Trials.

**'To Ireland Befooled'**

*Fildy Rue:* or Fiddledeeroo, a term of abuse meaning a wastrel, a turncoat or good-for-nothing. It almost certainly derives from the Gaelic song, *'Kill, fill a rúinó,* in which a mother addresses her son who has converted from the Catholic priesthood to become a Protestant cleric. This song, it is believed, was on the defection of Dominic O'Donnell who died as Rector of Carrigart, County Donegal, in 1793. She beseeches him to return to the faith of his upbringings, so, by extension, a Fildy rue or Fiddledeeroo is someone who has turned aside from truth and abandoned his integrity. See Thomas O Fiaich, 'Irish Poetry and the Clergy', *Léachtai Cholmcille,* IV, 1975, pp. 30–56.

*Mendicant O'Lynn:* See Gogarty's interest in Brian O'Lynn, pp. 117 and 355.

*Great Kings . . . beyond the Boyne . . . the Hundred Battle:* These were the rulers of Ulster; the hundred battles are the victories of *Conn Cétchathach,* Conn the Hundred Fighter. The northern half of Ireland was known in Irish literature as Conn's half, he and Mag Nuadat being supposed to have divided the country between them. See Thomas F. O'Rahilly, *Early Irish History and Mythology* (1946) p. 191.

*Niall brought the captives home:* Niall of the Nine Hostages, the founder of the Ui Neill dynasty at Tara, King of Meath at the time of Patrick's captivity.

*far lands flamed:* Niall made raids on Roman Britain and, in some versions of the legends about him, on continental Europe also.

*send the Great Earl back . . . who waits beneath Lough Gur:* Gogarty may have been confusing history and mythology here. The 'Great Earl' is *Gearoid Mór,* Gerald Fitzgerald, Earl of Kildare (1456–1513), for over thirty years effectively the uncrowned King of Ireland (with a hiccup in 1495 when Sir Edward Poynings subordinated the business of the Irish parliament to the English crown). But the Lough Gur legend refers to *Gearoid Iarla,* Gerald Fitzgerald, third Earl of Desmond (1338–1398). See David Fitzgerald, 'Popular Tales of Ireland', *Revue Celtique* IV, 1879–80, pp. 186–199. This Earl was thought to be a magician; he had a mysterious locked room in his castle at Lough Gur in County Limerick. After a magical experiment he disappeared beneath the surface of the lough (accompanied, in some legends, by his whole family); he is reputed to rise periodically and ride round the lough. See also Patrick Kennedy. 'The Enchantment of Geroidh Iarla', *Legendary Fictions of the Irish Celts* (1866), pp. 172–174, where the legends are attached to a later mid-sixteenth century Earl of Kildare, also a magician and a shape-changer. His wife asked him to change himself into a goldfinch; he did so but was then attacked by a hawk and disappeared from human sight. Once in every seven years this Earl 'rides round the Curragh of Kildare on a steed, whose silver shoes were half an inch thick the time he disappeared; and when these shoes are worn as thin as a cat's whisker he will be restored to the society of living men, fight a great battle with the English and reign King of Ireland for two score years'. He, however, is sleeping with his warriors under the Rath of Mullaghmast in County Kildare, not under Lough Gur. James Clarence Mangan in his translation of a 'Lament' for Sir Maurice Fitzgerald associated Lough Gur with the Fitzgerald family, whose banshee wailed over the lough:

> Oe'r Lough Gur that night, once-twice-yea thrice
> Passed a wail of anguish for the brave

**'Freedom'**
*A Dago's at the head of things:* a slighting reference to Eamon de Valera's parentage; he
was born in New York, the child of a Spanish father and Irish mother. Gogarty had a
profound dislike of him and his policies (see note above on Erskine Childers, p. 746)
which surfaced upon occasion in his prose works.
**'A Reply to Crazy Jane'**
*Our king's a modern king:* a reference to King George V (1865–1936). This poem replies
to Yeats's 'Crazy Jane on the King' quoted by Gogarty in SSE, pp. 126–7 with the
comment that it was 'not in Yeats's *Collected Poems* nor . . . anywhere but in my head
for he recited it to me.' Gogarty remarked that the Irish believed that their kings were
half magical: 'one glance if it fell on you would make you lucky for life. Yeats in his
unpublished poem 'Crazy Jane and the King', contrasting the Irish idea of kingship
with the English store-dummy king, has a line "saw the lucky eyeball shine."' (TTY,
p. 211). This is the text of the poem:

> *Crazy Jane on the King*
>
> i
>
> Yester-night I saw in a vision
> Long bodied Tuatha-de-Danaan
> Iron men in a golden barge,
> Those great eyes that never wink,
> Mirrored on the winking wave –
> That a righteous king should have –
> When I think of him I think
> May the devil take King George; –
>
> ii
>
> Saw the sages wait the king
> Seven fingers cautioning;
> Saw the common people surge
> Round a wave-wet landing-stair
> Banging drum & tambourine;
> Saw the lucky eye-ball shine
> On the lewd & learned there –
> May the devil take King George –
>
> iii
>
> Upon the moment he was gone,
> Nothing there could hold him down,
> Nor hammered iron of the forge
> Upon his body & his head,
> Nor that great troop I saw in a vision
> Long bodied Tuatha de Danaan
> But long or short when all is said
> May the devil take King George.

A later version read in 1.6 'Eyes' for 'That' and the third stanza was altered to

> iii
>
> Upon the blasts of music there,
> Up the gold & silken gear,

> Up the strong work of the forge,
> Up the light & laughing head
> Up bleak–midnight and a vision
> Long bodied Tuatha-de-Danaan –
> But long or short when all is said
> May the devil take King George.

For details of the history of the poem, first written in Rapallo early in 1929 and the first using the persona of Crazy Jane, see Richard J. Finneran, 'The Composition and Final Text of W.B. Yeats's 'Crazy Jane on the King', *I. Carbs* IV.2. Spring–Summer 1981, pp. 67–74. Yeats's poem 'Crazy Jane on the Mountain', *On the Boiler* (1939), blames George V for not insisting on Britain coming to the aid of the Czar of Russia and his family who were brutally killed at Ekaterinburg in July 1918. See Yeats's *Explorations* (1962) pp. 442–3 and *Letters on Poetry from W.B. Yeats to Dorothy Wellesley* (1940; 1964) p. 171. See Kenneth Rose, *King George V* (1983) for King George's attitude to the Russian royal family.

*Catullus:* see note on him, p. 740.

*Solomon:* King of Israel (*c.*1015–977BC), second son of David and Bathsheba, whose reign was outwardly splendid. He was known not only for his wisdom but for the number of his wives and concubines.

*Kubla:* Kublai Khan, Emperor of China. See note on him, pp. 706 and 712.

*Doorn:* near Arnheim, the Netherlands, where William II (1859–1941), the third German Emperor (1888–1918) settled with his family after he was forced to abdicate on 9 November 1918 after the collapse of the German armies.

*Kiplings:* Rudyard Kipling (1865–1936), sometimes regarded as a proponent of Imperialism.

## ON DRINKING

**'Sounds' (an earlier version)**
Gogarty used to meet various cronies in the public house kept by Fanning, the 'tall tavern keeper who had in his veins Cromwellian blood', in Lincoln Place, Dublin; they included George Bonass, George Redding, James Montgomery, Joe Boyd Barrett, Kevin Smyth and others.

**'Driving to the Ward'**
*the Ward:* an area bordering North County Dublin in County Meath, known for its stag hunt.

**'What might have been'**
*Arthur impotent:* possibly a reference to King Arthur.

**'A Large One deep in the Lamb Doyle'**
Title: *The Lamb Doyle* (or Lamb Doyle's): Doyle's public house at Ticknock, on a hill overlooking Dublin and Dublin Bay. Gogarty frequently drove up there to lunch after a morning's work in hospital.

**'In the Snug'**
*George:* either George Bonass or George Redding.

**'A Whiskey below Par'**
*Anacreon:* a late 6th century BC Greek poet born at Teos in Asia Minor who lived at Samos and at Athens. Known for his praise of wine, he died according to legend, at Teos at the age of eighty-five, choked by a grape stone.

*Inisowen:* Gogarty commented that 'Inisowen, of course is Irish whiskey' (I, p. 91).

**'Bona Fides'**
Title: Alcoholic drinks could be sold to genuine travellers outside the regulated hours
permitted by the licensing laws, travellers who had travelled five miles from the place
where they had spent the previous night. Bona fide (Latin, in good faith) travellers
were assumed not to have been able to refresh themselves during normal legalised
business hours. Many persons made journeys to public houses outside the city centre in
the suburbs for the purpose of drinking outside hours and were known as bona fides.
*the Lamb:* [Doyle] see note above, p. 749.
*Wiley Yeats:* W.B. Yeats.
**'Drink'**
Gogarty wrote to Starkey in the letter containing the poem 'I have found a substitute for
drink. It is a Dutch lager Z.H.B. and it produces the illusion of the Septembral Stuff
without the distress at Dawn'. The Grand Hotel might have been either that at
Greystones or the one at Malahide.
**'Hiking'**
I *with thine only eye:* This is an echo of an impromptu joke made by Gogarty on seeing
a friend enter a pub with a friend a patch where one eye had been removed. It echoes or
parodies the song 'Drink to me only with thine eyes . . .' The friend was Colonel
Charles Russell of the Irish Army Air Corps, a former R.F.C. pilot; the pub was the
Bailey.
II Pubis Regis is probably an invented name, anticipating the King's action in the next
line. But the idea of the spoof names continues in IV and V of this poem. See note
below on them.
'III' *The King and Tanner parted:* in the Ballad (see next note) the King asked the way to
Drayton Basset on encountering the tanner, and invited the tanner to accompany him
there, where he would pay the shot, an offer rejected by the tanner.
'III (Another version) The Ill Wind Inn' *The farting tanner and familiar king:* they then
exchanged horses, the tanner's having a cowhide saddle, and the tanner fell off. The
King finally presented the Tanner with Plumpton Park for three hundred years 'to
maintain his cow-hide'. Gogarty found this line in Herrick's (see note on him, p. 738)
poem 'To His Booke *Hesperides*'. (See F.W. Moorman's edition (1915) p. 155). Herrick
obviously knew the ballad source (it is in F.J. Child's *English and Scottish Popular Ballads*
(1898) V. pp. 75–77), 'The Ballad of King Edward the Fourth and the Tanner of
Tamworth', stanza 23 which contains these lines:

> The King took the tanner by the leg,
> He girded a fart so round;
> 'You'r very homely,' said the King,
> 'Were I aware, I'd laid you o' th' ground.'

'IV' *Melbury Bub:* It is in Dorset, called after an early owner William Bubbe who held
the manor in 1212 (A Bubbancumb near Melbury was mentioned in 1070; and there is
a Bubwith in the East Riding of Yorkshire, 6 miles E. of Selby).
'V' *Steeple Bumford:* Here Gogarty is possibly inventing the name, perhaps thinking of
Steeple Bumstead in Essex, first mentioned in 1261, though in his novel *Going Native*
(1941), p. 60, the somewhat auto-biographical hero is reading a newspaper in an
English rectory and records: 'A vacancy for an organist in Steeple Bumford! These
English names are so amusing. They always sound as if they were trying to say
something else – Broad Hintings?'
**'The Triumph of Time'**
I *rode in triumph through New Mexico:* cf Christopher Marlowe (1564–93), *Tamburlaine*

*the Great* (1590) Part I. II. V:

> 'Is it not passing brave to be a King
> And ride in triumph through Persepolis?'

MEDICAL MEDITATIONS

**'An invitation'**

An invitation to Dermot Freyer (see note p. 739) to visit Ireland, this 'isle of green access'.

*prostate . . . Peter:* a reference to Freyer's father, Sir Peter Johnston Freyer (1851–1921), who invented the prostate gland operation. After serving in the Indian Medical Service (1875–96) he became surgeon to St Peter's Hospital for Stone, London (1897–1914). He became C.B. and K.C.B. in 1917.

**'Song [of Medical Dick and Medical Davy]'**

Gogarty's Notes read:

[Stanza I] Notice the almost severe manner in which the legend opens. No details diminish the naked and sublime conception of the protagonists. There is a hint of ballad influence in the mannerism of the opening of Stanza II 'Outspoke'
Compare Homer: –

> τόν δὲ ἀμείβενος προσέφη
> πὸδας ὸικὸς Αχελλεος

Line iii Carefully observe the deprecatory past subjunctive tense in the 'I'd swap' for 'I would swap'. It is in order to avoid emphasis lest the bargain and sense of loss be too present to David. The name too is symbolical. Did not the stones of David overcome the ponderous Goliath?
line 4 The redundancy at commencement for continued disparagement of the coveted gift
Stanza III
Notice the catalepsis. The character of the thinker in the weight of verse
Stanza IV Idyllic
Virgilian and Theocritean-influence return to Nature
[indecipherable] the bovine Day.

In the Cornell MS the poem is dedicated:

> To
> James Augustine Joyce
> Scorner of Mediocrity and Scourger of the Babblement
> this work is
> Dedicated
> as I wish to have before my work
> the holder of the highest of contemporary names
> and the longest of contemporary tools

If at this late date handling a fragment of unsurpassed folk song I have failed to sustain that passion and lyric ardour which hurls into music at the opening lines of this masterpiece let me not be charged with presumptious interference but at least be credited with the good intention and accredited with a place among those mighty minds who have unsparingly endeavoured before the world to show what medicals are.

**'Sindbad'**

Title: Sindbad. See note on him, p. 732.

**(i) 'In Situ'**
Sir Thomas Myles (1857–1937), 'the best-looking man in Dublin with his cavalry moustache and his Herculean frame. He was a great Shakespearean. In his youth he was a great boxer'. Like Erskine Childers (see note on him, p. 746) using his yacht the *Asgard*, Myles used his own yacht *Chotah* for the same purpose, to land guns for the Irish Volunteers: 'I brought you these bloody guns to show that bloody Carson that two could play his game.' (a reference to the Ulster Volunteers running guns in April 1914).
*Hunter's sore:* called after John Hunter (1728–83), noted for his investigations of venereal disease.
*Coal Quay:* then a red light region of Dublin, by the Liffey. See Joyce's mention, in *Ulysses* (1992 edn) p. 274, of 'Rosalie the coalquay whore'.
*Davy Jones:* the spirit or devil of the sea.
**(ii) 'The NLI version'**
*Ulysses such a roamer . . . a wife:* In Homer's *Odyssey* Ulysses took ten adventurous years to return to Ithaca; he lost all his companions and was only acknowledged by his wife Penelope after he killed her suitors. She had remained faithful to him despite the importunities of her many suitors and the absence of any news of him during his protracted absence.
*Aeneas . . . the Queen depraves:* in Virgil's *Aeneid* Aeneas had a love affair with Dido, Queen of Cathage after he had been shipwrecked there.
*a city stand:* Aeneas left Carthage by order of the gods, and Dido committed suicide in despair. After seven years Aeneas reached the Tiber and established himself near the gate of Rome ('the city'). He married Lavinia, daughter of King Latinus, succeeded his father-in-law and was killed in a battle with the Etruscans. Descent of the Roman Emperors was traced back to him as founder of Rome by Virgil and other Roman authors.
*the soldiers of the Queen:* a popular Victorian song: 'We're soldiers of the Queen, my boys'.
*The wearing o' the Green:* a traditional street ballad *c.*1795 dealing with Napper Tandy (1740–1803), a popular nationalist hero. See note on him below, p. 755.

> I met Napper Tandy, and he took me by the hand,
> And he said, 'How's poor ould Ireland, and how does she stand?
> She's the most distressful country that iver yet was seen,
> For they're hangin' men an' women there for the wearin' o' the green

**(iv) 'Another Fragment'**
Sindbad had almost arrived at the North Pole in this stanza and is complaining of the weather. The captain of the ship is punished by Providence for throwing Sindbad overboard. The sailors are heading for death but, as a marginal note indicated the sailors 'hear the Syren voices'.
**'On ENT specialists, colleagues in Dublin'**
*Graham:* Thomas Ottiwell ('Togo') Graham M.C. (1883–1966). Born in Worcestershire, the second son of Professor Christopher Graham of Clare College, Cambridge, he moved to Ireland with his family and entered Trinity College, Dublin where he graduated BA 1905 and in medicine in 1906 (MD 1908). After further study at Vienna, Heidelberg and Freiburg he became Throat, Nose and Ear Surgeon at the Victoria Eye and Ear Hospital and the City of Dublin Hospital; he was consulting aural surgeon at Sir Patrick Dun's Hospital. He won his M.C. in supervising the evacuation of wounded soldiers under fire in a battle on the Piave in 1918. He was president of the Royal Irish

Academy of Medicine for 1951–1954. See J.B. Lyons, *An Assembly of Irish Surgeons* (1984), pp. 107–109.

*Curtin:* J. McAuliffe Curtin: Laurence John Curtin, graduated MD National University of Ireland, 1913, and studied at Vienna. He was Hon Throat Surgeon at the Dublin Skin and Cancer Hospital.

*Keogh:* Peter John Keogh, who graduated MD, BCh and BAO from the Royal University of Ireland (1908). He then studied in London, Berlin and Vienna and was an Ear, Nose and Throat surgeon in the Jervis Street Hospital, Dublin, as well as in the Children's Hospital in Temple Street and St Vincent's Hospital. See L, p. 78 for Gogarty's treating him as an object of derision: "'Oh – Keogh!" he would say, to the amusement of the students, shining a light on a damaged palate or tonsil bed. "Look at the snot doctor!" he remarked unfeelingly when the unfortunate Keogh emerged from his hall-door as Gogarty drove past.' L, p. 78.

*Woods:* Sir Robert Henry Woods (1865–1938) Professor of Laryngology and Otology, Trinity College, Dublin, whom Gogarty met in the Ear, Nose and Throat Clinic in the Richmond Hospital, Dublin, as a medical student. Woods, the first Dublin specialist in ENT surgery, became a friend and adviser; when he left a vacancy at the Richmond Hospital Gogarty was appointed to it. Gogarty greatly respected his master, and wrote a generous obituary of him in the *Irish Journal of Medical Science* in 1938, praising him as an unsurpassable surgeon, describing his greatness as moral greatness: 'the way he envisaged life made him great and remarkable'.

**'Therapeutic Thought'**

*Hydrarg perchlor:* mercury used, perhaps, as a heroric purgative in syphilis. See 'Delightful Thing' above.

**'On looking at a Portrait in the Royal College of Physicians'**

*Finny:* In 1900–01 Gogarty attended the lectures of the Professor of Medicine, John Magee Finny (1841–1922), King's Professor of the Practice of Medicine, Trinity College, Dublin; Physician to Sir Patrick Dun's Hospital; President of the Royal College of Physicians in Ireland and the Royal Academy of Medicine in Ireland.

**'Patients'**

*The Spud:* probably 'Spud' Murphy, see note p. 730.

'To his friends when his prostate shall have become enlarged'. A version in Gogarty's hand (see notes on the text for this poem, p. 809). added another stanza, with its last line 'My thoughts may dwell beyond Stead's Act.' William Thomas Stead (1849–1912), editor of the *Pall Mall Gazette*, inaugurated 'new journalism' and was responsible for the Criminal Law Amendment Act (1885).

**'Poets' Ward: From the Meath Hospital'**

Gogarty wrote this poem to Seumas O'Sullivan when into his third week as a patient in the Meath Hospital, Dublin, probably suffering from typhoid fever; he was then thirty-seven.

*Rathangan:* a reference to J.F. Byrne, 'Cranly' in Joyce's *A Portrait of the Artist as a Young Man* (1916).

*Mangan:* the Irish poet and translator James Clarence Mangan (1803–1849) died of cholera in the Meath Hospital, in the same ward in which Gogarty was later a patient.

**'Conversation with Tom Casement in the Palace Bar, 1945'**

Title: Tom Casement, a younger brother of Sir Roger Casement, served as an officer on sailing ships on the Australian route before acting as British Consul at Delagoa Bay in Portuguese East Africa. He became a friend of Smuts at the time of the Boar War, and on returning to Dublin, created the Coast Life Saving Service, establishing its store in Fleet Street, Dublin. He had no pension and no idea how old he was. He died after falling into the Grand Canal.

## MONTO POEMS

**'The Hay Hotel'**
Title: this establishment was patronised by late night dwellers in Monto or Night-town, the area of the Kips (a word probably derived from the Danish, Dublin's Keep or area cordon), the brothel district. Situated in Cavendish Row (originally Cavendish Street, called after William Cavendish, 3rd Duke of Devonshire, Lord Lieutenant 1737–45); it dates from 1753 and was renamed Cavendish Row in 1766; it formed one of the sides of Rutland Square, named after Charles Manners, Duke of Rutland (1754–87), Lord Lieutenant (1784–87); it was renamed Parnell Square in June 1911.); it got its name from the hay kept in one of its windows for the cab horses waiting for patrons to emerge. The hotel was run by the former butler and cook at Gogarty's parents' house, 5 Rutland Square.
*Tyrone Street:* see note on 'Sonnet: When the Clearance was intended to the City,' p. 695.
*Faithful Place:* it intersects Railway Street, which runs from Lower Gardiner Street to Lower Buckingham Street; originally Great Martin's Lane it was renamed Mecklenburgh Street then Lower Tyrone Street (see note on it above).
*Meck town:* the Monto or brothel area around Mecklenburgh Street.
*Fresh Nellie's gone and Mrs Mack:* a well-known whore and a well-known brothel keeper. See Joyce, *Ulysses* (1992 edn), p. 274 for mention of Fresh Nellie and Rosalie the coal quay whore as 'two gonorheal ladies'. See *Ibid.*, p. 599 for mention of Mrs Mack and see note on 'On the Keeper of a Bawdy House' p. 755 and the list of Madams in SS, p. 313, where Gogarty is fantasising about turning the Dublin banks into brothels and the brothels into banks.
*Hell's Gates . . . the street . . . gates of hell:* Although there was a Hell existing in eighteenth and nineteenth century Dublin it disappeared when Fishamble Street and the adjacent area was widened (See C.T. McCready, *Dublin Street Names Dated and Explained*). It was a partially arched passage leading from Christ Church Lane to Christ Church Yard, and had furnished apartments. It might be assumed that 'Hell's Gates' was probably a colloquial name for some alley or buildings off a 'street' in Monto, with Cavendish Row implied as the Street, as the name does appear in Directories. However, as 'Hell', the laneway off Christ Church Lane, was entered by a gate or gates (See Douglas Bennett, *Encyclopaedia of Dublin* (1991) p. 97) it may be argued that Piano Mary lived not in Monto but across the Liffey in this gated passage called hell.
**'A Stanza to be added to "The Hay Hotel"'.**
This stanza was added at the request of Dan Leahy, a bookmaker who complained that Becky Cooper had been left out of 'The Hay Hotel'.
**'Poem attributed to "Barney"'**
*Barney:* the name of a character in TH.
*Summerhill and Britain Street:* Britain Place (not Street) runs off Parnell Street which becomes, after Gardiner Street is crossed, Summerhill. Great Britain Street, however, was not far from Rutland Square 'on the boundary of Night-town' (L, p. 39) and became Parnell Street on 1 October 1911 following the unveiling of a statue of Charles Stewart Parnell (1864–91) in Sackville Street, now O'Connell Street.
**'On seeing athletes in Monto'**
See a passage in TH (p. 268):

> Across the street I saw two of our well-known Athletes. I began to think how unconvincing the words of the apostle, which he wanted to get the 'boys' of Greece, who were all athletic fans, would be to us or to some of our champions at all events. Though they strove for the mastery, they refrained from very little.

NOTES TO PAGES 456–459

*The Hay:* see notes on 'The Hay Hotel', p. 754.
**'On the Keeper of a Bawdy House'**
In TH Gogarty gives a prose picture of this well-known Dublin brothel-keeper:

> Her face was brick-red. Seen sideways, her straight forehead and nose were outraged by the line of her chin, which was undershot and outthrust, with an extra projection on it like the under-jaw of an old pike. There is a lot of rot talked about the effect of vice on the countenance. It gives some faces, if anything, a liberal look, but it largely depends on the kind of vice. Avarice was written by Nature's hieroglyphic on the face of Mrs Mack.

See also note on 'The Hay Hotel', p. 754.
**'The Old Pianist'**
*subtitle: the Curragh Camp:* In County Kildare about 30 miles from Dublin, a centre of army activity then and now.
*Mrs Mack:* see note on her above, p. 754. In TH, ch. xxii, Gogarty gives her comments on the old pianist:

> 'I don't know what things is coming to at all,' said Mrs Mack. 'Lookit that now.' I followed the direction of the bedizened arm, which pointed, as it seemed, to the centre of a bare floor covered with oilcloth which had been newly waxed. The room was empty save for two forms of benches on either side, and a pianist who sat with his face turned to the wall in front of a cottage piano on which stood a half-empty pint measure of stout. He sat on a revolving stool with his toes turned like the toes of an organist; and, judging from his inept legs and inturned toes, he was an advanced case of locomotor ataxia. But the poor are kind to one another; so are the whores. Doubtless in his day he had gone 'into the breach bravely with his pike bent bravely', and had come 'halting off'. But he had got a job as pianist at Mrs Mack's.

*Fresh Nelly:* a well known whore (who made unfavourable comments on James Joyce).
*Nosey Barlow:* unidentified.
*This belly never bore a bastard:* see Joyce, *Ulysses* (1992 edn) p. 528:

> Mr Mulligan, in a gale of laughter at his smalls, smote himself bravely below the diaphragm, exclaiming with an admirable droll mimic of Mother Grogan (the most excellent creature of her sex though 'tis pity she's a trollop): There's a belly that never bore a bastard.

And see also Gogarty, RL, pp. 18–19 and 23, where he introduces Mary Anne the hoyting girl of Cootehill [County Cavan] and her 'What's That.' Mary Anne 'was or is a "roaring girle" of Dublin who, as the song made in her honour – well, not exactly in her honour, but about her – says, "She doesn't care a damn." Later she is 'Good old Mary Anne, with all her liberality and large discourse and "There's a belly that never bore a bastard" . . .'
*Pommery and Greno:* Pommery is a brand of champagne, Greno is possibly Les Grenouilles, a dry white wine made in the Chablis region of France. In one version of the poem the drinks were called Click Ho and Shatoo Quim, Dublin pronunciations of Veuve Cliquot, a champagne, and Chateau d'Yquem, a sweet white wine (one of the greatest) from the Sauternes area of Bordeaux. Gogarty remarked of it that 'those who go to the races will pronounce it in their own way' (RL, p. 90).
*Piano Mary . . . that mott'l:* another well known whore. See 'Piano Mary's fashion of faithfulness' p. 459. Motte or mot is Dublin slang for a girl.
*Napper Tandy:* Jocose address. James Napper Tandy (1740–1803), a co-founder of the United Irish Society in 1792, fled to America in 1793, then went to Paris in 1798. Given command of a body of troops, he landed with them in Donegal, became insensibly drunk and was carried back to his ship. Captured in Hamburg, he escaped the death penalty as his arrest was held to contravene international law. Sentenced to death in 1801, he was freed at the intervention of Napoleon. He died at Bordeaux.
*moidered:* bothered.

*warty boys:* it was commonly supposed that warts were a sign of sexual potency. Cf
W.B. Yeats, *Letters on Poetry . . . to Dorothy Wellesley* (1940; 1964), p. 63, commenting
on a line in his 'The Wild Old Wicked Man', the 'Muses were women who liked the
embrace of gay warty lads. I wonder if she [Laura Riding] knows that warts are
considered by the Irish peasantry a sign of sexual power?'.
*Good night, sweet Prince:* from Shakespeare, *Hamlet,* V.ii.
*The Jersey Lily:* a sobriquet originating in Sir John Everett Millais' (1829–96) portrait of
her, attached to Lillie Langtry (1853–1929), an actress and one of the beauties of her
day, who was a close friend of the Prince of Wales.
**'The Days when we were Young'**
*Ouseley:* Gogarty sometimes wrote under the name Gideon Ouseley, liking the dactylic
echo of Gogarty and aware he was reversing his initials OG/GO. A connection of the
family, Gideon Ouseley was buried in Mount Jerome Cemetry, Dublin. He wrote
various Protestant religious pamphlets.
*Elwood:* see note on him, p. 725.
*Fresh Nelly:* a Dublin whore
*the Hay:* see note on 'The Hay Hotel' p. 754.


LOVE AND BEAUTY

**'To Stella'**
This was the first poem published under Gogarty's name.
**'Song [Make me a mirror with those eyes]'**
This is reminiscent of Ben Jonson's (1572–1637) song 'To Celia' in *The Forest* (1616)
which was frequently sung (sentimentally!) at Victorian and Edwardian musical
evenings:

>Drink to me only with thine eyes
>And I will pledge with mine . . .

**'Love and Death'**
Gogarty sent this poem to G.K.A. Bell in October 1904, remarking that it was 'of
course unfinished'. He entrusted it to Bell 'unfledged as it is' knowing he would 'not
sneer at its struggle to fly' MLTT, pp. 44–45.
**'Winifred'**
Winifred was Alice Steele, a barmaid in Islip, met during Gogarty's stay at Oxford. He
glossed the poem in a letter to G.K.A. Bell.

>The idea is this: the Present is almost as intangible as the Past when one tries to seize it for
>enjoyment. The very fact of Beauty being present overwhelms and numbs one from realising
>it is completely as one can realize (and regret it too) when it is in the Past. We must regret to
>realise. The Garden never appeared so beautiful until Adam was driven out. 'Our sweetest
>songs are those that tell of saddest thought.' [from Shelley, 'To a Skylark', 1.95].

**'A Compensatory Poem'**
Written as a compensatory poem for the 'old ladies' of the Society for the Prevention
of Cruelty to Animals, after Gogarty had shot a black cat which was stalking George
Moore's blackbird in Ely Place with an arrow. The cat survived.
**'Secret Lovers in Vienna'**
On two anonymous lovers who had clandestinely used a room in the house in Vienna
where Gogarty had given up a large part of their apartment ['the large chambers that
had been the apartment of Krafft Ebing, author of *Psychopathia Sexualis* and of course
the instigator of that enemy of the human race, Freud'] after his wife had left. On his

return from hospital he had noticed the black and yellow uniform of a coachman and a footman who sat on the box seat of an ambling brougham. He could hear 'the sounds of love-making intensely intimate coming from the other room. The lovers spoke English of all tongues – what a language to make love in!' This was so they should not be understood by the landlady, who had rented the room as a rendezvous, if she overheard them. Not wishing to eavesdrop he went out, slamming the door as he went, but inadvertently he had locked the lovers in. On returning later he found a hole large enough to permit a person to pass through this cut in the great door. 'What would all the secrecy and precautions have availed a lady from the palace of K. K. Franz Joseph if a lady in waiting or whatever she was had stayed out all night? Obviously the officer had used his sabre' (TTY, pp. 80–81).

**'Jack and Jill'**
The poem is based upon the nursery rhyme of Jack and Jill.

**'The Peace of Life'**
*The Bard:* Homer.
*Memory . . . mother of his Muse:* See W.B. Yeats, 'The Philosophy of Shelley's Poetry', *Essays and Introductions* (1961), p. 91: '. . . it was but the story of Prince Athanase and what may have been the story of Rousseau . . . thrown outward once again from that great Memory which is still the mother of the Muses, though men no longer believe in it'.

**'To Helen Beauclerk'**
Title: Helen Mary Dorothea Bellingham (*c.*1892–1969) was adopted as a baby by a family friend, Major Edmund de Vere Beauclerk. Educated at the Paris Conservatoire, she decided not to continue as a musician. When working on the *Evening Standard* she met Edmund Dulac (1882–1953) the French-born British naturalised artist, book illustrator and musician. Dulac was a friend of W.B. Yeats; he collaborated in *At the Hawk's Well* (1916) for which he designed masks and costumes and wrote the music. He wrote music for Yeats's broadcasts and for 'The Three Bushes' (YP, p. 414). Helen Beauclerk was introduced to Dulac by F. McCurdy Atkinson (see note, p. 699), a colleague on the *Evening Standard*, who remained a lifelong friend. After Dulac separated from his second wife in 1923, he and Helen lived happily together. He illustrated some of her novels, which included *The Green Lacquer Pavilion* (1926) and *The Love of the Foolish Angel* (1929). She translated Damille Hunabelle's *Philippine* (1955) and used Helen de Vere Beauclerk as her author's name. She died after a long incapacitating illness.
*Dan Chaucer's:* Geoffrey Chaucer (?1345–1400), now mainly known for his *Canterbury Tales*.
*his who tells:* Homer in *The Iliad*.
*the Dardanelles:* by implication, Troy.

**'Goodbye'**
*Titianed it:* turned it reddish-gold like the colour (sometimes called Titian red) of hair portrayed by Titian, Tiziano Vercelli (d. 1576), the Venetian painter.

**'A Question'**
*mighty triumvir:* Mark Antony, the lover of Cleopatra. See note on him, p. 758.

**'He accounts for the Skyscrapers'**
*the topless towers:* See Christopher Marlowe (1564–1593), *Doctor Faustus*, V. i:

> 'Was this the face that launch'd a thousand ships
> And burnt the topless towers of Ilium?'

**'The Getting of Gargantua'**
*Gargantua:* originally the name of a benificent giant in French folklore. Rabelais (see

note on him, p. 684) refers to the *Grandes Chroniques*, a chapbook incorporating legends about him, probably written by Rabelais himself. His *La Vie très horrificque du Grand Gargantua* (1534) was a preliminary volume to his *Pantagruel* (1532). Gargantua was the son of Grandgousier and Gargamelle, a prince given to hearty eating and drinking as befitted his gigantic size. He was studious, athletic, good-humoured and a lover of peace.

*the Two-backed Beast:* traditional euphemism for the act of copulation. Gogarty probably based the poem on a passage in Book One. See *The Works of Mr Francis Rabelais, Five Books of the Lives, Heroic Deeds and Sayings of Gargantua and his son Pantagruel,* translated into English by Sir Thomas Urquhart of Cromarty and Peter Antony Motteaux (1653):

> In the vigour of his age he married Gargamelle, daughter to the King of the Parapaillons, a jolly pug, and well-mouthed wench. These two did oftentimes do the two-backed beast together, joyfully rubbing and frotting their bacon against one another, in so far, that at last she became great with child, of a fair son, and went with him into the eleventh month . . .
> (Fraser Press Edn. 1970, p.34).

*And leave you to the Argument,*
*And me, not unremembered:* a handwritten comment on the last line (TS in HD) reads: 'the last line is evidently a reminiscence of the Homeric Hymns "the blind old bard of Chios' rocky isle/may not unremembered be".' The blind old bard is Homer.

**'To his Boar Cat Rodilardus'.**
Title: *Rodilardus:* the name given by Rabelais to a cat belonging to his character Panurge. It appears as the 'Alexander of Cats' in La Fontaine's *'Le Chat et le Vieux Rat'*
*dyspareuniac:* dyspareunia is difficult or painful coitus.
*Darwin . . . Evolution:* Charles Robert Darwin (1809–82), the discoverer of natural selection. His best known work *The Origin of the Species by means of Natural Selection* (1859) was followed by many other works, *The Descent of Man* (1871) the most influential of them.
*Paola's love:* Francesca, daughter of the Count of Ravenna, given by him in marriage to Giovanni Malatesta, fell in love with Paola, her husband's brother. The lovers were put to death in 1289. Gogarty met the story in Dante's *Inferno*, 5th canto, where Francesca tells how she was influenced by reading the tale of Lancelot and Guinevere. The story is also told in Leigh Hunt's (1784–1859) *The Story of Rimini* (1816).
*Augustus John:* see note on him, p. 664.
*Cassandra:* in Greek myth a daughter of Priam, King of Troy and his wife Hecuba; she was endowed with the gift of prophecy but was fated not to be believed.
*Isaiah's brood:* Isaiah was the first of the major Hebrew prophets; he lived in the eighth century BC.
*Antony:* Mark Antony (Marcus Antonius, 83–30BC), Roman General who served under Julius Caesar in the Gallic wars, became a member of the second triumvirate, defeated Brutus and Cassius at Philippi, and having repudiated his wife for Cleopatra, Queen of Egypt, was defeated by Octavian (Augustus), his brother-in-law, at Actium.
*great Queen:* Cleopatra (?68–30BC), queen of Egypt, mistress of Julius Caesar and later of Mark Antony. She killed herself with an asp to avoid being captured by Octavian.
*Bulgarian milk-like:* like yoghurt, regarded as calming.
*Athena's bird:* the owl.
*Hieresiarch:* one who is ranked highest.

**'Tardy Spring'**
*Sandro Botticelli:* The Florentine painter (1444–1510), who produced many works on classical subjects (The Birth of Venus, in the Uffizi; Primavera, in the Florence Academy; and Mars and Venus in the National Gallery, London) as well as numerous

devotional paintings (The Coronation of the Virgin, in the Florence Academy; the Madonna and Child in the Uffizi).

**'Amazons: a fragment'**

*the Amazons of warlike mien:* the Amazons were a mythical tribe of warrior women. According to Aeschylus they lived in the Caucasian mountains, and later on the river Thermodar which emptied into the Black Sea. Hercules defeated them and killed their queen. Theseus abducted Antiope, or Hippolyte, and took her to Athens; eventually he made a treaty with the Amazons who had followed them into Attica and entrenched themselves on the Areopagus.

*Once a year:* mythical accounts account for the perpetuation of their female culture by telling of their copulating at intervals with men of neighbouring tribes and rearing only the girl children.


LIFE AND DEATH

**'A Query'**

*the Styx:* in Greek mythology a river across which Charon ferried the dead.

**'The Land of the Young'**

*Theleme . . . Panurge:* the Abbey of Thelema in Rabelais, built and endowed by Gargantua (I.lii *et seq*) to reward Friar John for his prowess in the war with Picrochole. It was to be the opposite of conventional monasteries, its only rule *'Fay ce que vouldras'* (Do what you like) for the well endowed men and women admitted to it. See note on him p. 684. See also Swinburne, 'A Roundel of Rabelais', *Collected Poetical Works* (1924) II, p. 1234, for

> 'Theleme is afar on the waters . . .
> But the laughter that rings from her cloisters that knows
>     not a bar
> So kindles delight in desire that the souls in us deem
> He erred not, the son who discerned on the seas as a star Theleme'

*Tir na Oge:* (Irish) meaning the Land of Youth, the Hereafter, usually *Tir na nOge*.

*Logue:* Michael Logue (1840–1924), Archbishop of Armagh (1888), Cardinal (1893).

*Jack Morrow, Jim Geoghan, Hyland:* unidentified, also *Howard* in l.19.

*Bailey's thoughts:* possibly the Rt Hon. W.F. Bailey, a great party giver who loved 'to entertain anything that sang, painted, composed or acted'. Known as 'Greenroom Bailey', he had a large house, Number One, Earlsfort Terrace, Dublin with many bedrooms. In SSE, p. 57, Gogarty described him as a bachelor and a Land Commissioner: 'He had an income ample for his needs and more than ample so he took an interest in art, especially in the Abbey Theatre in which the two Miss Algoods could be seen acting and in the Greenroom between the acts. After the show he would ask the actors to Earlsfort Terrace and, of course, the parties had to be late, into the wee sma' hours in fact.' Because of his way of speaking he was known also as Hubble Bubble Bailey.

*Thirim pogue:* (Irish) I take a kiss.

*Gog:* presumably Gogarty himself.

*Empedocles:* a learned philosopher (d. *c*.430BC) of Agrigentum, Sicily, who plunged into the crater of Mount Etna, a weary man ready to die, 'the tarnished philosopher'.

*collogue:* (Irish) to confer confidentially.
**'Upon a Friend who died distraught'**
*In the beginning . . . Not the Logos:* See the Bible, Saint John 1.i: In the beginning was the word . . . Logos (Greek, a word) the divine Word, the second person of the Trinity.
**'A Noble Trace'**
cf Gogarty's comment: 'It was almost two thousand years ago that Finn and his companions ranged these hills . . . From the highest dells in the mountains rose the great antlered elks that drew down from the exposed heights to browse on the plains that made the Liffey a broad-margined stream. Those mighty heads shall be seen no more against the sky. They have passed in the eternal procession of the great things that are gone from the hills and forests of the ancient land.' (*Going Native* (1941) pp. 3–4). The impressively large skeletons of Irish elks in the National Museum in Kildare Street, Dublin, probably prompted both poem and prose.
**'What else is Joy'**
On the letter to Starkey enclosing these lines Gogarty wrote 'This is 1st shot. It may have been electric (see other side) [which was headed Siemens–Schuckert, the German firm which constructed the hydro-electric Shannon scheme which commenced operation in 1929] not an eclectic shock! Anyway you'll like 'wrecked'! But I suspect anything I didn't keep for years. This is 1st shot.'
**'Serenity'**
This poem had a sub-heading '(A thought from Meleager)' [(*c*.140–*c*.70BC), a poet and philosopher who lived mainly in Tyre and Cos, a master of the epigram, who collected the first large anthology of them] in the version sent to Michael Sadleir (1888–1957), since 1920 a director of Constable and Co, to be included in *Penultimate Poems*. A TS version attributed the thought to Menander (342–291/90BC), the Athenian writer of new comedies known for his characterisation, his renunciation of mythology in forming contemporary life, particularly love-plots.
*King Richard Lionheart:* Richard I (1157–1199 AD) King of England, *Coeur de Lion,* or the Lion Heart, known for his bravery, particularly as a leader of the third Crusade (1191) at Acre, at Joppa and on his advances to Jerusalem (a city he never saw) and later after being captured in Austria) in France warring against Philip. He was killed when beseiging the chateau of Chaluz.
**'Reading at Night'**
*lapsus . . . slipped the mind:* an echo of *lapsus linguae* (Latin, a slip of the tongue).
**'The Graveyard on the Hill'**
*Dummerston Center:* Dummerston is in Windham County, on the Connecticut River in South East Vermont. (See note on 'Dawn in Vermont' p. 673).

ELEGIES

**'Ode for Terence MacSwiney'**
Terence MacSwiney (1879–1920), an accountant, co-founder of the Cork Volunteers in 1913, who persuaded the Kerry Volunteers to give up their arms in 1916, became Mayor of Cork, was arrested and died in Brixton Prison after a hunger-strike lasting seventy-four days.
*the Roman who endured the flame:* Caius Mucius Scaevola, reputed to have failed to kill Lars Porsenna, and then, to show his indifference to pain, held his right hand in a fire (Scaevola, a diminutive of *Scaevus,* left handed).

**'The Rebels'**
The book in which this was included, *Aftermath of Easter Week* (1917), published by the Irish National Aid and Volunteers Dependent Fund to raise funds for those imprisoned in Easter Week 1916, was edited by Pieras Beaslai (1883–1965). He was imprisoned in Easter 1916 after taking part in the Rising and was later Director of Propaganda for the Irish Free State government in the Civil War. He wrote thirteen plays between 1906 and 1938, a biography of Michael Collins and a novel *Astionar* (1928).
**'Arthur Griffith'**
Title: See note on him p. 699, and Gogarty's account of his death, TTY, pp. 193–195.
*Conn the Fighter:* Conn the Hundred Fighter. See note on him, p. 660.
**'Micheál Coileáin'**
Title: Michael Collins (1890–1922), born in Cork, joined the IRB and the Gaelic Athletic Association in London; he fought in the G.P.O. in 1916, was interned and released. He organised the Irish intelligence system in the Anglo-Irish war; was Minister of Home Affairs (1918), and Minister for Finance in the first Dail Eireann (1919–22) and a reluctant member of the Irish Treaty delegations in 1921. In the Civil War, he was Commander-in-Chief of the Free State government forces, and was shot and killed in an ambush in County Cork on 22 August 1922.
*Judas . . . McMurrough:* seen as a Judas-like figure as he invited the Anglo-Normans into Ireland and gave his daughter in marriage to Strongbow (see note on him, p. 683).
**'Threnody'**
*Lady Gregory:* Lady Isabella Augusta Gregory (1852–1932), a widow since Sir William Gregory's death in 1892.
*old clothes:* Lady Gregory invariably dressed in black clothes.
*Lillibulero . . . Bullen an ah!:* Lilli-Burlero Bullen-a-la!, the refrain of a song written by Lord Wharton to satirize the Earl of Tyrconnel on his going to Ireland in January 1686–7 as James II's Lord Lieutenant. The song is included in Percy's *Reliques*. Percy called the words ones used by Catholics in the 1691 Rebellion. The words are mock Irish.
**'In Memoriam of my friend Arthur Russell, Soldier and Airman'**
Title: *Russell:* he was killed when the Fairey III F he was piloting crashed in the suburb of Rathgar, Dublin in October 1934.
**'George Bonass'**
Title: George R. Joseph Bonass (1886–1942), a barrister, was educated at Belvedere College, Dublin, and lived in 81 Wellington Road, Dublin. A keen cricketer, he was captain of Pembroke in 1920, having led the club's batting and bowling averages in 1919. He played for Ireland against the Military of Ireland in College Park in 1921, a two-day match abandoned when gunmen fired through the railings and killed a young girl spectator. When the Irish Cricket Union was reconstituted in 1924 he was its first secretary (1924–31).

He was warned off alcohol when a patient in the Meath Hospital, Dublin. Gogarty, however, brought him whiskey in a hot water bottle to escape the attention of the nurses. He wrote an affectionate portrait of him:

> George who smiled to himself, meant only the laughter that he himself originated which was not our idea of laughter at all. Laughter in Indignation House [Fanning's public house in Lincoln Place] had to be at someone else's expense and George was not given to hurting anyone. George, without bitterness, was a good soul . . . [He] had a deep voice, which gave him a way with the ladies. His eyes of burning brown perhaps helped. He wore a brown suit of Harris tweed with plusfours. He was, well, call it medium size (SSE, p. 63).

*the Ghost of Davy Byrne:* the owner of a public house, 21 Duke Street, Dublin, still popular.

*Fanning:* his public house, 'the Hostelry nearest the Back Gate [of Trinity College, Dublin] was known', Gogarty remarked in SSE, 'as Indignation House as Fanning was usually raging about everything', see note on him, p. 749.

**'Panegync on Lieutenant Commander Eugene Esmonde of the Fleet Air Arm'**
Title *Esmonde:* he was a connection of Gogarty, whose second son Dermot married Carmel Esmonde, Eugene's sister.

*the Hurdle Ford:* (Irish *Áth Cliath,* the Ford of the Hurdlework; the name implied a method rather than a material, *Áth Cliath* being a kind of causeway using a reef of rock that intruded into the Liffey. See George Little, *Dublin before the Vikings* (1957). Dublin is called *Baile Átha Cliath,* the city of the Hurdle Ford as well as *Dubh Linn,* the Dark (or Black) Pool.

*a torpedo plane:* a Fairey Swordfish, operating from the aircraft carrier Ark Royal.

*Telefer!:* Far-bearer, far-carrier or far-striker, an apparent coinage, on the analogy of the classical epithet 'Far-darter', or 'far-shooting', ἕκατος or ἑκατηβόλος, applied to Apollo; it implies as well as Esmonde outdistancing his escort, the range of the torpedo he carried on his aircraft, thus striking from afar. See Horace Reynolds's use of the word spelt as Taillefer, characterising Gogarty, charging 'with ardour, juggling his sword, a feather in his cap, a song on his lips' (p. xxviii).

*the Bismarck:* this German battleship, completed in 1940, was sunk when attempting to make her way to Brest from the Baltic.

# NOTES TO PART FOUR

---

## Blight

**Act One**

*Findlater's Church:* the Abbey Presbyterian Church in Parnell Square (formerly Rutland Square), Dublin. The roots of the congregation go back to about 1660, in Bull Alley (see note below) and to a Huguenot community which arrived in Dublin in 1690. The building of the present Abbey Church, opened in 1864, was made possible by the generosity of Alexander Findlater, a Dublin merchant.
*Christ Church Cathedral:* first built as a wooden structure by King Sitric Silkenbeard, it was replaced by the Normans with a stone structure in the 1170s; it was restored (1871–78) by the architect George Street, the restoration costs mainly met by Henry Roe, a wealthy Dublin distiller. It is now the Cathedral of the Diocese of Dublin and the Metropolitan Cathedral of the Southern Province of the Protestant Church of Ireland while St Patrick's is the Church's national Cathedral.
*hostel in Hatch Street:* St Joseph's Asylum for Aged and Virtuous Females, see note on St Joseph's Old Maids' Home, p. 676.
*St Patrick's and Bull Alley:* St Patrick's Cathedral, founded in 1190 by John Comyn, the first Englishman to become Archbishop of Dublin. It was extensively rebuilt after a fire at the close of the fourteenth century. Bull Alley runs from Patrick Street to Bride Street along St Patrick's Cathedral Gardens. The Cathedral was extensively rebuilt after a fire at the close of the fourteenth century. It was restored (1860–65) by Sir Benjamin Lee Guinness of Guinness's brewery, Dublin.
*Stephen's Green:* St Stephen's Green, a large public park largely surrounded by Georgian houses, in Dublin, the distance of Grafton Street and Westmoreland Street south of the Liffey.
*the Locke:* a Dublin hospital specialising in the treatment of venereal disease.
*Little Sisters of the Poor:* Roman Catholic order of nuns, the aim of which was to aid the poor.
*Vincent de Paul's:* members of a Roman Catholic Society for aiding the poor.
*Gloucester Street:* it runs between O'Connell Street (across Gardiner Street and

763

Buckingham Street) and Amiens Street, north of the Liffey, in Dublin, north of
Connolly Railway Station, formerly Amiens Street Station.
*Green Street:* where the court was situated. It is a continuation of Arran Street from
Upper Moore Street to Bolton Street.

## Act Two

*Medical Dick:* see text of 'Song' (Medical Dick and Medical Davy) p. 435 and note on
p. 751.
*Phibsboro:* a district in north Dublin in the parish of Grangegorman, the Barony of
Coolock, a mile north of Dublin on the Dublin–Navan road near the Royal Canal in
the North Circular Road area.
*Baldoyle:* known for its racecourse outside Dublin. Baldoyle Village is on the
Portmarnock Road, about half a mile from Sutton Cross, 'Formerly a bathing resort
and earlier a resort of smugglers, highwaymen and other undesirables'. See Weston St
John Joyce, *The Neighbourhood of Dublin* (1913). Gogarty gave Baldoyle the Irish name
*Baile dhu Gall*, the settlement of the Dark Strangers, in describing how his schoolfriend
Tom Kettle's family had settled around the village of St Margarets, having come as dark
strangers, a Danish family originally ('all Norsemen are called Danes') that had come
out of the sea along the Black Beach now Baldoyle, long before the Battle of Clontarf
(1014). That Battle broke the power of the Danish invasions. TTY, p. 20.
*Beecham's Pills:* a patent medicine.
*Professor Mahaffy:* see note p. 701.
*A memoir of me dead life:* a dig at George Moore's *Memoirs of my Dead Life* (1900).
*to the front:* the western front in the First World War.
*Act of Union:* the Act of 1800 uniting Ireland with England, passed by the Irish
Parliament in Dublin.
*Gloucester Place:* off Gloucester Street, see note above, p. 763.
*Cork Hill:* the site of the City Hall, the building housing Dublin Corporation, adjoining
Lord Edward Street, a continuation of Dame Street.

## Act Three

*the Rotunda:* Dublin's main maternity hospital, a complex of buildings in the south east
corner of Parnell Square.
*Medical Davy:* see note above, p. 751.
*Wasserman's test:* a diagnostic test for syphilis named after the German bacteriologist
August von Wasserman (1866–1925).
*Wild Woodbines:* cheap cigarettes made by W.H. and O.D. Wills, an English firm.
*Raheny:* an area bordering the sea between Dublin and Howth.
*the hidden plague:* venereal disease.
*Swan of Avon:* William Shakespeare.
*Si monumentum . . . :* if you would see his monument look around you. A Latin
inscription in St Paul's Cathedral, London, to the architect Sir Christopher Wren
(1632–1723) responsible for the new building replacing that burnt in the Great Fire of
London of 1666.
*res angusta domi:* in straightened circumstances. From Juvenal (*c.*55–140) III, 9.164.

> *Haud facile emergunt quorum virtutibus obstat*
> *Res angusta domi.*

See Dryden's translation:

Rarely they rise by virtue's aid who lie
Plung'd in the depths of helpless poverty.

*Carnegie Library:* Andrew Carnegie (1835–1919), the Scots-born American steel manufacturer, endowed public libraries, notably in Scotland and Ireland, and educational and research trusts.
*Oliver for his Roland:* a reversal of the phrase a 'Roland for his Oliver', an effective retort or retaliation. Roland (killed in battle at Roncevaux in 778AD) and his friend Oliver were paladins (12 legendary peers who were in attendance on Charlemagne). The friends had a prolonged and undecided single combat; at Roncevaux Oliver urged Roland to summon help by blowing his horn but he left it too late.
*ultra vires:* beyond the legal power or authority of a person, agent or corporation.
*ultra violet:* the part of the electromagnetic spectrum with wavelengths shorter than light but longer than X rays; as adjective, relating to or consisting of radiation in the ultra violet.
*Moloch:* in the Old Testament a semitic deity to whom parents sacrificed their children.

## A Serious Thing

*Gadara:* Palestine.
*Founding of the City:* in 753BC.
*Lookey here now! You see now! OK by Jove:* repeated as 'Bai Jove' in Centurion's next speech and meant to emphasise his Englishness. The 'Lookey here now' was a phrase often used by Gogarty's friend Talbot Clifton, who lived at Kylemore House, and was thus Gogarty's neighbour, Renvyle House being seven miles away. Gogarty described Clifton as 'having the wealth of Lytham St Anne's and the half of Blackpool behind him.' See accounts of him in SS, pp. 142–154 and 200–232.
*Omadhaun:* a fool, an idiot from the Irish *amadan*.
*cordon sanitaire:* a line serving to cut off an infected area, hence a buffer line or buffer zone.
*Pioneers:* the Pioneer Corps.
*Tiberius:* Tiberius Claudius Nero Caesar Augustus (42BC–37AD) who succeeded his father-in-law Augustus. He had a brilliant military career but became increasingly cruel and tyranical.
*recent cattle driving:* see note on *Pledge-bound Party*, p. 738.
*Marcus Lepidus:* Marcus Aemilius Lepidus (d.? 13BC) Roman statesman, member of the Second Triumvirate with Octavian and Mark Antony.
*Varius:* Publius Quintilius Varius (d. AD9), a Roman governor of Syria who suppressed the revolt in Judaea, and later committed suicide after being utterly routed in Germany by Arminius.
*Pilate's wife hadn't a hand in this! as sure as dreaming goes with spirit-rapping:* a dig at W.B. Yeats and his wife who were interested in spiritualism.
*aw, of course, by Jove, yaas, so it would:* more imitation of the affected speech of an Englishman.

## The Enchanted Trousers

*a noble play by Japan:* probably a reflection of W.B. Yeats's interest in the Japanese Noh theatre. Yeats wrote an Introduction to Ezra Pound's *Certain Noble Plays of Japan* (1916).
*Onogi and his wife:* this does not refer to any known Noh play; it may be invented or,

possibly, be derived from a Kabuki play.

*Killiney:* seaside area south of Dublin, north of Bray, County Wicklow.

*Tuam Herald:* a local paper, Tuam being a country town in County Galway.

*Jove . . . Leda . . . he . . . Europa:* see notes on Leda p. 681 and Europa p. 677.

*dudheen:* a short-stemmed clay pipe, from Irish *dúidín,* a little pipe.

*This seat of Mars . . . :* from a speech by John of Gaunt in Shakespeare's Richard II, Act II Scene I.

*the R.M.:* Resident Magistrate.

*Moore Hall:* the novelist George Moore's (1852–1933) ancestral home, at Ballyglass, County Mayo. It was burnt in 1923, and Moore lost his last link with Ireland; after living in Dublin from 1901 to 1911, he settled in London in Ebury Street. He had been a friend and neighbour of Gogarty in Ely Place, Dublin.

*an Irish bull:* a self-contradictory, inconsistent often arrestingly ludicrous statement. The classic account was given by Maria Edgeworth in her *Essay on Irish Bulls* (1802) and Mahaffy defined an Irish bull as a male animal that is always pregnant.

*Kildare Street Club:* Formerly on the corner of Nassau Street and Kildare Street (now amalgamated with the University Club on St Stephen's Green) it was a gentleman's club. Exclusive, its membership consisted mainly of landlords and members of the largely protestant ascendancy.

*Ballast Office:* a building on the corner of Westmoreland Street and Aston Quay on the Liffey. The Dublin Ports and Docks Board, which was responsible for control of Dublin's port, shipping and customs, occupied it.

*Holywell Gate:* in Oxford.

*Congested Districts:* The Congested Districts Board was established in 1891 to deal with the problems of West of Ireland.

*The United Arts' Club, Stephen's Green:* The club was founded in 1907 (A Dublin Arts Club was founded in 1892 and lasted five years. It met in 7 St Stephen's Green, the studio of John Butler Yeats) and first met in 22 Lincoln Place, moving to 44 St Stephen's Green in December 1910, thence to Merrion Square briefly before 3 Upper FitzWilliam Street was purchased. The Club is still situated there. See Patricia Boylan, *All Cultivated People* (1988) and P.L. Dickinson, *The Dublin of Yesterday* (1929).

*D.B.C.:* Dublin Bread Company, which owned several cafes.

*flahoulyah:* generous, casual. From *flaith* overgenerous, Irish *flaithúil.*

## Incurables

*Janey Mack:* a common Dublin expression.

*Baldoyle:* see note p. 764.

*Christian Dying by Sylvester Stott:* this title and author were probably invented by Gogarty. Stott appears in *The Enchanted Trousers* as Siegfried Stott, the acting name of Humphrey Heavey, an unemployed actor who pretends to be an Englishman and is appointed Minister of Potato Spraying by a visiting Appointments Committee. He calls it 'a Saxo-Anglican name with a hint of opera in it'.

*the ramble through the new mown hay, Titty fol loll:* originally a ballad, No 112 in R.J. Child's *English and Scottish Ballads* (1904), pp. 239–240, 'The Baffled Knight':

> 'You'd had me,' quoth she,
> 'Abroad in the field, among the corn, amidst the hay,
> Where you might had your will of mee,
> For, in first faith, sir, I never said nay?

There are many versions of the song, notably 'Blow away the morning dew' taken down in 1903. A third version of 1903 matches that of 1907 in which the lady is more forthcoming:

> If you'll wait till you come to my father's yard
> Where walls are built around O
> O here you can have your will of me
> And twenty thousand pounds O
> Ri fol the dol i day O Ri fol the dol i day

But then she locks him out of the yard. Another version collected in 1908 from the eighty-three year old Charles West at Rashill, Bromfield includes the maid 'All on some new mown hay' (the line is repeated three times with 'some' twice and 'the')

> As I walked out one May morning
> To view the fields so green o
> And there I spied a fair pretty maid
> All on the new mown Hay o
> Right fal the dal the day

Gogarty may have found the ballad in Child's edition which he seems to have read. Cecil Sharpe recorded a version by Alfred English, and two modern groups have made the song part of their repertoire. They are Martin Cathy and Dave Swarbuck of Skin and Bone, and, broadcast on 30 May 1999 in the BBC's *Something Understood* programme, The Watersons' 'Country Life', in their 'Rough Guide to English Roots Music', (RG Net 1018). In *Mr Petunia* (1946) p. 96 Gogarty has Plant make a song out of 'were ye never at the One-Eyed Man's?' which he hums to the tune of 'And the ramble through the new-mown hay'.

*the Union:* the South Dublin Union at Garden Hill, beyond Inchicore, Dublin, (of which the Editor's maternal grandfather, Alexander Fraser, was master in the late nineteenth and early twentieth century).

*a wartyboy:* see note on warts, p. 756.

*Weldon's:* a public house, no longer existing. Local opinion suggests it was situated on the present College Street in Baldoyle.

*the Murroch:* a Murragh or Murrough is a flat piece of land along the sea shore, a salt marsh (probably this is a marshy spit of land on the sea side of the Baldoyle to Portmarnock Road).

*Chantez ma belle:* from *Serenade*, by Charles François Gounod (1818–93). As well as composing operas, masses, anthems and hymns he was a popular songwriter.

*St Doulough's:* an ancient church built in the twelfth or thirteenth century, but founded by St Doulagh about 600AD. It has a massive stone roof, a well and a hermit's cell. It is on the Malahide Road near Balgriffin, about two miles inland from Portmarnock, County Dublin.

*Moore Street:* north of O'Connell Street, Dublin, known in the past for its 'shawlies', the women traders who had stalls and wicker baskets on wheels. See 'Fog Horns', p. 102.

*the Coombe:* a slum area of Dublin known for its liveliness, near St Patrick's Cathedral, once fashionable and with thriving industries; the weavers' guildhall has been restored and the run-down area is now being replanned. It was known for the Coombe Lying-in Hospital, opened in 1829, originally set in a stable at the back of Stephen Street; it was built with money provided by the brewers Sir Benjamin Guinness (1798–1868) and his son Sir Arthur E. Guinness (1840–1915). Apart from its former hospital (moved to Peter Street when the Adelaide Hospital came into being) the area is know for the song 'Biddy Mulligan the pride of the Coombe'.

*Conisthathu:* (Irish) How are you?

*a cara:* (Irish) friend. Used in correspondence as the equivalent of 'Dear Sir' or 'Dear Madam'.

*Sheenies:* a derogatory word for Jews.

*G.Y.E:* Guinness Yeast Extract (somewhat similar to Marmite or the Australian Vegemite in taste) produced by the firm of Arthur Guinness & Son, Dublin.

*Eamonn Lopez . . . Lopez, an old ancient Irish name:* a dig at Eamon de Valera's Spanish parentage (see note on him p. 748).

*Verschoyle:* the Governor, the name suggesting Anglo-Irish gentility.

*Eyetalians from Abyssinia:* a confused memory of the Italian conquest of Abyssinia in 1935–36; after the liberation in 1941 by British forces the Emperor Haile Selassie was restored to his throne. He was reputedly murdered some years later in a political revolution.

*Arbour Hill:* a military barracks in Dublin.

*the Gaelic League:* an organisation founded in 1893, with Douglas Hyde as president, to revive Irish as a living language.

*Phaynix Park:* the Phoenix Park in Dublin.

# NOTES TO APPENDICES

**'The Ballad of Oliver Gogarty'**
William Dawson (see note on him, p. 729) was the author of this skit which he sang at
the United Arts Club in Dublin (see Patricia Boylan, *All Cultivated People* (1988),
p. 141). The air to which it was sung is 'The River Roe' or 'The Wandering Banks of
Erne' by William Allingham (1824–1889). The kidnapping occurred in January, not
December as in the version of the air below which is taken from Colm O'Lochlainn's
*More Irish Sheet Ballads*, See *Notes on the Text*, p. 814, and, for the kidnapping, notes on
p. 668.

### THE LAY OF OLIVER GOGARTY

769

**'Lines on the Sinclairs [by George Redding] from *As I was Going Down Sackville Street*'.**

These verses were part of the two passages which Henry Morris Sinclair, in the action libel which he brought against Gogarty in 1937, declared were defamatory. In Gogarty's defence it was argued that the poems were part of Dublin folklore and it is now accepted that they were written by Gogarty's friend George Redding. See note on him, p. 701.

**'As I was Going Down Sackville Street'**

This is the version of an old Dublin Street ballad remembered by Gogarty. He told Horace Reynolds (who collected other examples of it) that Joyce heard and rescued it 'from oblivion and obloquy' in Faithful Place. Gogarty used it for the title of his autobiography, originally to have been called *The Flashing Phoenix*.

*Sackville Street:* now O'Connell Street, Dublin's main thoroughfare.

*Mercer's:* Mercer's Hospital.

**'The Maunder's Praise of his strolling Mort'**

This is a canting song. The vocabulary can be translated as: *Maunder:* beggar; *Strolling Mort:* a canter who pretends to be a widow; *Doxy:* a she-beggar, a whore, a trull, of 'the twenty-fifth Rank of *canters*, being neither maids, wives or widows; *glaziers:* eyes; *glimmar:* fire; *Saloman:* the Beggar's Sacrament or oath; *gentry mort:* gentlewoman; *pratts:* buttocks; *core:* man, also a rogue; *wap'd:* lay with; *fambles:* hands; *gan:* mouth; *quarrons:* the inside of the thigh above the knee; *couch a hogshead:* go to bed; *darkmans:* night; *clip:* embrace.

The source is Richard Head, *The Canting Academy; or Villanies Discovered* (1674) where the poem is entitled 'Canting Song' (See J. C. Holten, *The Dictionary of Cant* (1885) and B. E. Gent *The New Dictionary of the terms . . . of the Canting Crew* (1699) and consists of 7 stanzas; an English rhyming version is supplied. The first two stanzas, printed here, were among Gogarty's papers in Trinity College, Dublin. At first it seemed likely to have been an attempt of Gogarty's to write a parody of a canting poem, especially as Joyce, who inserted some of Gogarty's poems in *Ulysses*, had included the second stanza there (see *Ulysses* (1992 edn) p. 59). Gogarty altered the original title substituting 'Maunder' for 'Rogue' and dropping 'delight in' before 'praise'; he also (correctly) altered the Canting Song's 'parts' to 'pratts'. Joyce stuck to the 'rogue' in 'rogue's rum lingo' and quoted 'O my dimber wapping dell' from the seventh stanza of the original; he wraps the stanza round with prose:

> Shouldering their bags they trudged, the red Egyptians. His blued feet out of turnedup trousers slapped the clammy sand, a dull brick muffler strangling his unshaven neck. With woman steps she followed: the ruffian and his strolling mort . . . Buss her, wap in rogue's rum lingo, for, O, my dimber wapping dell. A shefiend's whiteness under her rancid rags. Fumbally's lane that night: the tanyard smells.

> *White thy fambles, red thy gan*
> *And thy quarrons dainty is.*
> *Couch a hogshead with me then.*
> *In the darkmans clip and kiss.*

> Morose delectation Aquinas tunbelly calls this, *frate porcospino*. Unfallen Adam rode and not rutted. Call away let him: *thy quarrons dainty is.* Language no whit worse than his. Monkwords, marybeads jabber on their girdles: roguewords, tough nuggets patter in their pockets.

## The Worked-Out Ward

This play has been attributed to Gogarty; it was published in 1918 by the Talbot Press, Dublin. It is included here somewhat tentatively; the title suggests a relationship with

Lady Gregory's *The Workhouse Ward*, published in her *Seven Short Plays* (1909), and the similarities are obvious, her play containing two old men and a small part for a woman, the staging only requiring two beds. The text is included in the Coole Edition of Lady Gregory's *Comedies* (1970).
*John Dillonell:* thin disguise for John Dillon (1851–1927), Irish politician, MP for Tipperary in 1880 and East Mayo 1885–1918. Imprisoned on many occasions, he was head of the anti-Parnellite party from 1896–99, and in 1918 of the remnant of the Nationalist Party.
*Stephen Gwyneney:* thin disguise for Stephen Lucius Gwynn (1864–1950), a man of letters (whose father was later Professor of Divinity at Trinity College, Dublin). He was Secretary of the Irish Literary Society in 1904, was Nationalist MP for Galway from 1906–18, and served with the Connaught Rangers in the First World War.
*the Peace Conference:* the conference at Versailles, 1918.
*Unionism:* the Act of Union between England and Ireland was passed in 1800 by the Irish Parliament in Dublin. Unionism opposed Home Rule (the Home Rule movement was founded in 1870) and nationalism. In 1918 the Unionist party was heavily defeated by Sinn Fein in the General Election.
*West Briton:* a term used abusively by Home Rulers and separatists by the early twentieth century; it had originally been used by those, Anglo-Irish largely, who approved of the Union with some pride. In Ulster the Unionist MPs set up a Unionist Council in 1905.
*Conscription was at hand:* On 18 April 1918 a Military Service Act passed at Westminster threatened conscription for Ireland. A conference at the Mansion House, Dublin concerted all-Irish opposition to this.
*Trinity:* Trinity College, Dublin, founded in 1591.
*shoneen:* someone who affects English ways, from Irish *seon*, John, hence John Bull, an Englishman.
*Lynch:* possibly Liam Lynch (1893–1923) who reorganised the Cork Volunteers in 1919, commanded a Brigade in the Anglo-Irish War, was a member of the IRA Supreme Council and opposed the 1921 Treaty. He became IRA Chief of Staff, resigned over seizure of the Four Courts but joined its garrison, commanded an Irregular division, and was shot by provisional government forces in 1923.
*President Wilson:* Thomas Woodrow Wilson (1856–1924), twenty-eighth President of the United States, responsible for America's entry into the First World War, known for his participation in the Peace Conference, his 'fourteen points' and championship of the League of Nations. The US Senate, however, rejected the Treaty of Versailles.
*St Columba's College:* a Protestant boarding school, situated outside Dublin beyond Whitechurch in the Dublin hills.
*Brasenose College:* an Oxford College.
*Mrs Houlihan:* she is *Kathleen ni Houlihan*, a traditional figure for Ireland. She is the main figure in Yeats's nationalistic play *Kathleen* (later *Cathleen*) *ni Houlihan*, first performed in Dublin in 1902.
*thirty years:* John Dillon sat as MP for East Mayo from 1885.
*the mere Irish:* term applied to the native (Hibernian) inhabitants (from the Norman-French *mère* (pure). Elizabeth I described herself as 'mere English'). It was used disparagingly later when confused with the English word 'mere'.
*Parnell:* Charles Stewart Parnell (1846–1891) leader of the Irish Parliamentary Party which rejected him because of his role in the divorce action taken by Captain O'Shea against his wife Katharine ('Kitty') who was Parnell's mistress.
*four beautiful provinces . . . :* an echo of W.B. Yeats's play *Cathleen ni Houlihan* (1902) where the old woman (Kathleen ni Houlihan) speaks of her four green fields ( the four provinces of Ireland; Ulster, Munster, Leinster and Connaught).
*the Freeman's Journal:* the *Freeman's Journal and National Press*: a daily newspaper,

representing middle class Catholic nationalist views.

*the Irish Times:* a daily newspaper, Conservative, Protestant and predominantly Unionist in its political views at that time.

## Wave Lengths
### (an incomplete version)

**Act II Scene 3**

*Unknown Soldier's Widow:* the Cenotaph in London is the tomb of an unknown soldier killed in the First World War.

*Ghandi:* Ghandi, Mohandas Karamchand (1869–1948) known as the Mahatma, 'of great soul', was an Indian nationalist leader born in Kathiawar, India. He studied law in London; in 1893 he went to South Africa where he opposed discriminatory legislation against Indians. In 1914 he returned to India and became leader of the Indian National Congress, advocating a policy of non-violent non-cooperation to achieve independence. Jailed several times, he attended the London Round Table conference on Indian constitutional reform. In 1946 he negotiated with the Cabinet mission which recommended a new constitution. After Independence (1947) he tried to stop Hindu-Muslim conflict in Bengal. He was assassinated by a Hindu fanatic in Delhi in 1948.

*Shaw:* George Bernard Shaw (1856–1950) Irish dramatist, essayist and pamphleteer, was born in Dublin; he left office work there in 1876 and joined the committee of the Fabian Society in London in 1882, becoming known as a journalist and music and drama critic. He began to write plays in 1885; among his early successes were *Arms and the Man* (1894), *Candida* (1897), *Man and Superman* (1903) and *Major Barbara* (1905). *Androcles and the Lion* (1912) and *Pygmalion* (1913) were followed by *Heartbreak House* (1919) and *Saint Joan* (1923). Shaw wrote over 40 plays, and was awarded the Nobel Prize for Literature in 1935.

*Chaplin:* Charlie: acting name of Sir Charles Spencer Chaplin (1889–1977) British film actor and director. Born in London, he developed his skills in comedy under Fred Karno with whom he went to Hollywood in 1914. He adopted a bowler hat, turned out with a moustache and a cane which became his hallmark in many successful silent films such as *The Kid* and *The Gold Rush*. His first full sound film was *The Great Dictator* (1940). He left the USA for Switzerland in 1952. He was awarded an Oscar in 1973 and was knighted in 1975.

*Marconi:* Gugliemo (1874–1937) see earlier note on Senorita d'Alvarez, p. 706. Born in Bologna he was awarded the Nobel Prize for Physics in 1909, was created a Marquis and became a Senator in 1929. He succeeded in sending signals by wireless telegraphy across the Atlantic in 1907. He died in Rome.

*Androcles and the Lion:* a play by George Bernard Shaw, described by him as as 'religious pantomime'.

*The Son of Heaven:* a title given to the Emperor of Japan. Hirohito (1901–1989) was Emperor from 1926 to 1989; his reign was marred by aggressive wars against China (1913–32 and 1937–1945) and against Britain and the USA (1941–1945). After very successful progress in the Pacific the atomic bombs dropped on Hiroshima and Nagasaki ended the war, which was already going against Japan. In 1946 when Japan was occupied by American troops under General MacArthur the Emperor renounced his mythical divinity and became a constitutional monarch.

*Oxford:* In 1921 Hirohito had been the first Japanese prince to visit the West.

**Act III Scene 1**

*Goebbels:* (Paul) Joseph Goebbels (1897–1945), a Nazi politician. A deformed foot absolved him from military service. A bitter anti-semite and powerful mob orator, he was an enthusiastic supporter of Hitler. He became head of the Ministry of Public Enlightenment and Propaganda in 1933 and expounded the radical aspects of Nazi ideas. During the war he had virtually become in charge of Germany (while Hitler busied himself directing the military side of the war). He and his wife committed suicide in Hitler's bunker in Berlin, having poisoned their six children.

*Ribbentrop:* Joachim von Ribbentrop (1893–1946), a German politician born at Wesel who became a member of the National Socialist Party in 1932 and Hitler's adviser on foreign policy. He negotiated the Anglo-German naval pact in 1935, became Ambassador to Britain in 1936 and Germany's Foreign Minister (1938–45). Captured in 1945, he was condemned to death at the Nuremberg trials and executed.

*Orson (George) Welles:* (1915–1985) an American film actor and director, born in Wisconsin, who made his acting debut in Dublin, before returning to the US to found the Mercury Theatre (1937). His radio production of H.G. Wells's *The War of the Worlds* was so realistic it caused panic in 1935. He wrote, produced, directed and acted in *Citizen Kane* (1941), a landmark in cinema technique. His most celebrated acting role was that of 'Harry Lime' in the film *The Third Man* (1949).

*Montgomery:* Bernard Law Montgomery, 1st Viscount Montgomery of Alamein (1887–1976), was educated at Sandhurst, served in the first World War and, after a succession of staff appointments, headed the 3rd division. After Dunkirk he led the 8th Army to victory at Alamein, the Axis forces being eventually driven back to Tunis. In the invasion of Normandy he attracted the German offensive to the British flank allowing the Americans to advance speedily. He was in command of the Occupation Forces, then was deputy Supreme Commander to the NATO forces.

*Dr Abrams Mystic Box:* Dr Albert Abrams (1863–1924) who obtained his medical degree in Heidelberg in 1882 and practised for many years in his native city, San Francisco, becoming Head of the Medical Clinic at Cooper Medical School there, published several books and achieved an international reputation. In 1910 he founded a mode of treatment known as Spondylotherapy, his book on it going through five editions. In 1910 his *New Concepts in Diagnosis and Treatment* developed his ERA (Electronic Reaction of Abrams) diagnosis, based upon the state of the body's electronic oscillations. The vibratory rates of different diseases were discovered by a drop of the patient's blood being tested in an apparatus (the 'box'), which basically comprised a condensor, a rheostat and an ohm meter, for diagnostic purposes, the treatment being by means of an oscilloclast (or magnetic interrupter). By 1923 over 3500 practitioners were using his methods; these caused much controversy, as Abrams had begun to make increasingly extravagant and dogmatic claims about his theories. ERA was investigated by the *Scientific American* in 1923. See Sir Thomas Horder, *A Preliminary Communication concerning the Electronic Reactions of Abrams* (1925) and *Abrams' Method of Diagnosis and Treatment* ed. Sir James Barr (1925). Barr considered Abrams a genius and an outstanding medical figure in the half century to 1925.

*Goeben and Breslau:* two Second World War German battleships.

*von Brauchitsch:* Walter von Brauchitsch, a German Field Marshal, responsible for Operation Barbarossa, the invasion of Soviet Russia.

*von Leeb:* Wilhelm, Ritter von Leeb (1876–1956), born at Landesberg, joined the Bavarian military service in 1895, studied at the Military Academy in Munich (1907–19112) and was an officer on the General Staff in 1914. A general by 1930, he was appointed General in charge of the artillery in 1934. He retired in 1938, was reactivated in 1939 and after serving in the west became a Field Marshal on the eastern Front. In conflict with Hitler in the winter crisis of 1941–1942, he was dismissed. Arrested by the Allies in 1945, he was sentenced to three years' imprisonment.

*von Bock:* Fedor von Bock (1880–1945), born at Küstrin, was a staff officer in the First World War. He commanded the German armies invading Austria (1938), Poland (1939) and the Lower Somme, France (1940). He was promoted to Field-Marshal, took part in the German invasion of Russia (1941) but was dismissed by Hitler in 1942 for failing to take Moscow.

*von Rundstedt:* (Karl Rudolf) Gerd (1875–1953) a German Field Marshal; born at Aschersleben he served in the First World War, became Military Commander of Berlin, and directed the German attacks on Poland and France in 1939. He was relieved of his command when the Germans were checked in the Ukraine and given a new one in France in 1942. He was recalled after the success of the Allied invasion in 1944 but then returned to direct the German offensive in the Ardennes. His ill health meant that war crimes proceedings against him were dropped.

*Chiang Kai-Shek:* editorially altered from the idiosyncratic TS version *Kang Chai Sheck.* See note on 'To Madame Chiang Kai-Shek' p. 719.

*Hitler:* see note on him, p. 746.

*Blaskowitz:* Johannes Blaskowitz (1883–1948), born at Peterswalde near Wehlau, was on the General Staff in the First World War. In 1938 he was in charge of Heeresgruppe III in Dresden which marched into Prague in 1939. General Commander (East), he came into conflict with Hitler because of a memorandum he wrote about the violent behaviour of the S.S. in Poland. Relieved of his command in May (1940) he was reinstated as Head of Command for the South of France. In 1944 General Commander of Army Group G, in 1945 of the Heeresgruppe H, and then of 'Fortress Holland', he escaped trial at the Nuremberg War Crimes Tribunal by committing suicide.

*My Italian friend, the ersatz Caesar:* Benito (Armilcare Andrea) Mussolini (1883–1945) who became known as Il Duce (the Leader). He was born at Romagna. In 1919 he helped to found the *Fasci di Combattimento,* a would-be revolutionary party, and became Prime Minister in 1922. By 1925 he had become a Dictator. His forces annexed Abyssinia (1935–1936) and Albania (1939) and the Axis between Italy and Germany was instituted. His declaration of war on Britain and France was followed by defeats in Africa and the Balkans; after the Allies invaded Sicily in 1943 he was overthrown and arrested in July. Rescued by German paratroopers, and in charge of a puppet republic, he was recaptured by Italian Resistance forces and shot.

*Castor oil:* administration of doses of castor oil was one of the methods used by the Fascists upon political enemies.

*Unter den Linden:* a broad avenue running through the middle of Berlin from Marx-Engels Platz to the Brandenburg Gate. The name means 'Under the lime trees'; in 1647 the Great Elector caused six rows of lime and nut trees to be planted along it; these were removed in 1675. It is lined by many university buildings and embassies as well as a library; museums are adjoined at the cathedral and the opera house.

### Act III Scene 2

*Churchill:* Sir Winston (Leonard Spencer) Churchill (1874–1965), British statesman and author, Prime Minister from 1940–1945 and 1951–1955. Born at Blenheim Palace, educated at Harrow and Sandhurst, he fought at Omdurman in 1898, and was a reporter in the Boer War. He held several ministerial posts; as First Lord of the Admiralty he was blamed for the Dardanelles disaster in 1915, but became Minister of Munitions in 1917. He was Chancellor of the Exchequer (1924–1929). He returned to the Admiralty in the Second World War; after Chamberlain's defeat he was Premier and Minister for Defence and led the nation to victory, his oratory inspiring his audiences at the blackest of moments. In 1951 Prime Minister again (after the

Conservatives were defeated in 1945), he then sat as a backbencher from 1955. He won the Nobel Prize for literature in 1953 and was knighted that year.

*Bracken:* Brendan Bracken (1901–1958), First Viscount Bracken (1952), was born at Killmallock and educated at Sydney and Sedburgh; he became Chairman of the *Financial News* and Managing Director of the *Economist* (1928–1945). Elected M.P. in 1929, he was Minister of Information from 1941 to 1945, and was First Lord of the Admiralty in the 'caretaker government' of 1945.

*Beaverbrook:* William Maxwell Aitken, 1st Baron (1879–1964) born in Canada, where he made a fortune before going to England in 1910. There he gained control of the *Daily Express* (1918) and the *Evening Standard* (1923). These papers put forward his imperialist views. He held several posts in Churchill's wartime cabinet.

*Joan of Arc:* Jeanne d'Arc, known as the Maid of Orleans (*c.*1412–1413), French patriot and martyr who was born into a peasant family at Domrémy. At thirteen she heard the voices of three saints telling her to rescue France from English domination. The Dauphin eventually allowed her to lead the army which relieved Orleans, with Joan at its head in a suit of white armour. She took the Dauphin to be crowned Charles VI at Rheims. She was captured and sold by John of Luxembourg to the English who tried her for heresy and sorcery and burned her at the stake.

*Fifth Columnists:* a phrase used to describe enemy sympathisers in the Second World War who might help an invader. The term was first used to describe rebel sympathisers in 1936 in the Spanish Civil War in Madrid when four rebel columns were advancing on the city.

*We have not seized her territory or commandeered her ports:* Britain respected Ireland's neutrality in the Second World War, having returned the 'Treaty Ports' to her before the war.

*'As Dooley says'* . . . *Peter Findlay Dunne:* 'Mr Dooley' was the creation of Peter Finley Dunne (1867–1936), an American humourist born in Chicago, a newspaper editor who created Mr Dooley as a satiric commentator on current events and personalities in an Irish–American vein.

### Act III Scene 3

*Der Führer:* a name by which Hitler (see note on him, p. 746) was known. It means the leader.

*lebensraum:* a slogan adopted by Germans, mainly Nazis, to justify their expansion beyond their borders into Eastern Europe on the grounds that their large increasing population needed more agricultural land to guarantee sufficient food production in future.

*Lord Haw Haw:* name given (because of his affected drawling accent) to William Joyce (1906–46). Born in New York City, he lived in Ireland as a child before his family emigrated to England in 1922. He founded the British National Socialist Party in 1937 and during the Second World War broadcast propaganda from Radio Hamburg. He was captured by British forces at Flensburg, tried and executed in London.

### Act III Scene 4

*He gave man speech and speech created thought which is the measure of the universe:* from Shelley's *Prometheus Unbound* (1820) Act 2, Scene 4, 1.172.

*Captains Courageous:* an ironic echo of Rudyard Kipling's (1865–1936) *Captains Courageous* (1897).

*Cherburg:* Cherbourg, a French naval base used by the Germans in the Second World War.

*From fairest creatures we desire increase,*
*That thereby Beauty's Rose might never die:*
From Shakespeare, Sonnet I.

# NOTES ON THE TEXT

Abbreviations, and in some cases full titles, immediately following the titles of poems indicate the sources of copy texts. Acknowledgements for permission to reproduce these copy texts are given on p. 649. Abbreviations are listed on p. 657. Significant variations in different editions, MSS or TSS are given below following the order of the poems in the List of Contents. Titles of poems supplied editorially to poems not given titles by Gogarty are enclosed in square brackets in the text throughout, though not elsewhere.

A TS list in B contains 44 titles of poems, possibly a potential list of contents for a projected collection; thirty-nine of these titles are of poems included in the present edition, twenty-six of them having been published in other volumes of Gogarty's poetry or separately. Some of the titles on the list, however, may refer to other poems (some taken from TSS, some from published sources) published here under different titles. (As the Notes on the Text dealing with individual poems indicate, Gogarty sometimes altered the titles of his poems.)

Thus 'Sitting Pretty' was probably an alternative title for 'In a Bus' p. 481; 'Contrast at the Movies' for 'Coming from the Movies' p. 349; 'Ireland Old' for 'To Ireland Befooled' p. 423; 'Dreams' for 'My Dreams' p. 479 (or possibly, 'The Dream' p. 479); 'Hill Brook' for 'The Stream" p. 339 (or, possibly, 'By a Stream in Bergen County' p. 338). So far no text has been found to match the title 'To the People of the Future who shall gaze on the Portrait of Ethel Mann [? Mannin] by Daniel Wilson'.

# PART ONE

ODES AND ADDRESSES
**Ode**
*Written at the request of the Irish Government
on the revival of the Taillteann (Irish Olympic)
Games.* The following variants occur in
the text of the separate publication,
published by Piggott and Company,
Dublin in 1924. The inconsistent use of
capitals and lower case at the beginnings
of lines has not been listed. Another text
was included in the official programme of
the games but its variants have not been
included here.
Title: Aonach Tailteann 1924. Prize Ode
Dedication: To my Mother
Before 1 OPENING CHORUS
2 . . . will
3 God! The . . . of his . . .
4 Holds and . . . till
5 . . . face, of . . . be drained
7 . . . numb
8 . . . heart . . . sustained
Between 8 and 9 no space
9 . . . conflict . . .
10 . . . best
11 . . . field
12 . . . that is . . . test
16 . . . totter to the ground
Between 16 and 17 SOLO OR SMALL
CHOIR
18 . . . wide eyed steep
20 . . . deep
21 where are noble men and horse
22 . . . Ah! . . . rein
26 . . . again
Between 26 and 27 no space
27 Aye their . . . now
26 omitted
28 . . . still
30 . . . knows
31 . . . they
HERALD
33 . . . King
KING LUIGUAID
34 . . . were
35 . . . strong

36 . . . air
38 . . . brave
39 . . . retold
41 . . . old
Between 41 and 42 no space
42 . . . peace . . .
43 . . . path
44 . . . charioteer
45 . . . Bards
46 . . . race
47 . . . dames
48 . . . face
49 . . . open'd Tailteann Games
THE KING OF THE SOUTH
51 King, . . .
53 there, isled in grass the . . . grow
54 . . . below
55 . . . low.
57 . . . of fairy land.
59 . . . black
60 . . . flocks
61 . . . rocks
62 With the stout
63 . . . deep breathed . . .
64 King we . . .
65 Who will . . . breathe,
66 As . . . to its . . .
67 . . . men, reversing . . . foes
68 . . . track
70 . . . bards . . . dead . . .
71 In the green dun . . . year.
72 The summer comes . . .
73 And, . . . interval,
74 . . . and to men
75 . . . glory and then
76 . . . them, . . . soon
78 . . . come O King where . . . sped
79 . . . still – foot dead.
80 . . . from king the . . .
81 . . . land
83 . . . hearts are . . .
85 . . . down
Between 87 and 88 no space
89 . . . gold
90 . . . barque
91 . . . seen by poets' eyes

94 . . . wings . . . fly
SONG OF THE BARDS
96 . . . sport, but song
97 . . . renown
98 . . . strong
99 . . . courage strives unknown.
100 . . . makes . . .
102 . . . defeat
103 . . . heed.
Between 103 and 104 no space
104 We have driven . . .
105 . . . years
106 . . . gives way . . .
107 . . . charioteers
109 . . . respite
110 . . . earth's
Between 111 and 112 no space
111 Into the . . .
113 . . . Conn
114 . . . hundred battled wrath
115 . . . on
116 . . . Queenly . . .
117 . . . thorn
118 . . . Mac-Roy
Between 119 and 120 no space
121 . . . race
122 . . . how supernal force
123 . . . courage, strength and grace.
125 Where Ocean . . . loam
126 . . . turf
127 . . . foam
Between 127 and 128 no space
128 . . . shield of song
129 . . . Kings
130 . . . 'gainst . . .
133 . . . date
134 . . . undo
135 . . . fate.
FINAL CHORUS
136 New . . . prairie hill
137 . . . drain
139 . . . chief's puts . . . main
140 Come . . . race
141 . . . still
143 . . . games of strength and skill
Between 143 and 145 no space
145 . . . light
146 . . . hand
148 . . . Ireland
149 welcome, Brothers, . . .
150 . . . land . . . hail:

151 . . . tho' . . . set
152 . . . gael.
The following variants occur in *Poetry: a Magazine of Verse*, LVIII, V, August 1941.
62 Where stout lowlanders, and wild without fear
66 . . . near its close
81 . . . colored . . .
101 . . . dead,
113 . . . Conn
122 . . . how supernal . . .
140 Come . . .
**To the Moon**
The first version of the poem is quoted in WA 28 as follows:
    O born before our birth began
    Throughout thy clear and frozen vales
    Beyond the listening ear of men
    Aloft may sing – what nightingales
2 . . . vales   WA 29
**To the Fixed Stars**
Title: 'To the Fixed Stars (Lux Perpetua)' WA 29; WA 30
2 . . . Moments rest . . .   WA 30
3 . . . watch, with   WA 30
6 . . . age-long hours:   WA 29
7 . . . Life   WA 29
10 . . . Well!' WA 29; Trusting to . . . well!'   WA 30
11 . . . respite.   WA 29; WA 30
13 . . . seems to rest,   WA 29; WA 30
15 . . . best   WA 29
19 . . . suns   WA 29
**Virgil**
4 . . . Burnished the . . .   OS 23
6 . . . rhyme   OS 23
7 . . . Roman air   OS 23
**To Lydia**
12 . . . As a wing! . . . in *NYT*, 8 August 1939;   ER 42
**To a Cock**
2 . . . go,   WA 29; SP; OA
3 . . . squalour, . . .   WA 29
5 . . . use   H
10 . . . destroy:   H; WA 29; SP; OA
12 . . . Desire,   H; Desire; WA 29
22 . . . peace;   WA 29
25–32 omitted   WA 29
37 . . . cry, Absurd   WA 29
38 . . . are;   WA 29
40 . . . Leda?   WA 29

42 . . . to say:   WA 29
44 . . . Nature.   WA 29
52 . . . bird, or   WA 29
53 . . . Beast; . . .   WA 29
56 . . . murder!   WA 29
58 . . . beast, . . . dove,   WA 29
59 . . . Love;   WA 29
60 . . . gladdest:   WA 29
61 . . . spent   WA 29
62 . . . arbitrament:   WA 29
63 . . . repent,   WA 29
65 . . . Came;   WA 29
66 . . . dame;   WA 29
67 . . . aflame;   WA 29
68 . . . Dawn to Heaven   WA 29
70 . . . do, burning bright:   WA 29
71 Not, for . . . plight,   WA 29
72 . . . Kathleen, Kevin   WA 29
74 . . . low,   WA 29
75 . . . Love . . .   WA 29
76 . . . all!   WA 29
77 . . . hacked,   WA 29
78 . . . city, sacked,   WA 29
80 . . . wall!   WA 29
82 . . . the Dawn . . .   H
84 . . . Strife . . .   WA 29
86 . . . Death, . . .   WA 29
87 . . . way,   WA 29
88 . . . Life . . .   WA 29
91 . . . neck; and   WA 29
92 . . . tempter!   WA 29
94 . . . get!   WA 29
95 . . . yet,   WA 29
98 . . . Love's . . . wing;   WA 29
100 . . . refulgence!   WA 29
101 . . . you're . . .   WA 29
102 To give your spirit birth H;
    Gogarty's handwritten correction in H
    (copy 2) reads 'To bring your spirit to
    life'
105 . . . gained,   WA 29
108 . . . ashes!   WA 29
110 . . . denied;   WA 29
112 . . . flashes!   WA 29
116 . . . heather's!   WA 29
Dedication: . . . 'To Augustus John'
    omitted in CP
**To My Friend the Rt. Hon. Lorcan
Galeran**
An early version of this poem entitled
'The Feast. To my Right Honourable

Friend William McElroy (a Great
Householder)' is printed on p. 199.
3 . . . a Feast's,   OS 24; OA; . . . Feasts
    SP
4 . . . is filled with Guests!   OS 24; OA;
    SP
10 What . . . said?   OA
11 . . . fill proceed . . .   OA
13 . . . commands   OS 24; SP
24 Big bellied . . .   OS 24
46 A chewing . . .   OA
47 . . . out,   OS 24; SP; Well . . . out
    OA
48 . . . gout.   SP; OA
55 . . . heard   OS 24
56 . . . word.   OS 24
64 . . . Earth!   OS24; OA; SP
69 Earth   SP; OA
73 And mounted . . . dome   OS 24;
    OA; SP
78 Resounding like . . .   SP; OA
**To a Friend in the Country**
Title: as above in CP contents list; title in
text omits 'in the country'
8 . . . brown   ER 42
**To the Lady –**
Title: . . . To the Lady . . .   OS 23; To
the Lady –   SP; OA
10 . . . like a shrine   OS 23
14 . . . was spring's   OS 23
**To A.E. going to America**
Subtitle: [from the Irish Statesman 9,
1928, p. 457] supplied in The Living Age,
March 1928
1 . . . West:   WA 30
4 . . . proportion power . . .   WA 30
4 . . . guessed The Living Age, March
    1928
5 Who . . . The Living Age, March 1928
11 . . . as back from Rome   WA 30
12 . . . Lyré . . .   WA 30; The Living
    Age, March 1928
**To W.B. Yeats who says that his
Castle of Ballylee is his Monument**
1 To Stones . . .   WA 28; WA 29
**To my Portrait by Augustus John**
18 . . . women . . .   OA
27 . . . lose confidence . . .   OS 24; OA;
    SP
**To Augustus John**
26 . . . reach   OA

37 . . . I am wrong,   OA
78 . . . picnic . . .   OA
**To the Poet W.B. Yeats, Winner of the Nobel Prize 1924 (To Build a Fountain to Commemorate his Victory)**
The following variants occur in the *Literary Digest*, 19 January 1924: Title: To W.B. Yeats to Build a Fountain to Commemorate his Victory
4 . . . hand,
5 . . . Earth,
8 . . . stone,
11 . . . you, . . . birth,
13 . . . spills:
16 . . . old
22 . . . treasure; and
23 . . . walls;
24 . . . spalsh
26 . . . wash;
28 . . . the wave
29 Till the Dolphin tumbles and reels;
30 . . . Poet . . .
31 . . . Venus' heels
32 . . . song.
33 . . . place,

EARTH AND SEA
**The Forge**
22 . . . clamour,   ER 42
23 No space after this line   ER
35 . . . for the wheels to roll   ER
35 . . . to cool   ER 42
40 . . . or two   ER
71 . . . he can't create;   ER
**Sung in Spring**
10 . . . spars   ER
27 On . . .   ER; ER 42
30 . . . ships   ER 42
35 . . . oceans   ER; ER 42
38 . . . an never ending . . .   ER
49 She makes . . .   ER
55 . . . were . . .   ER
**The Dublin-Galway Train**
The following variants occur in *Contemporary Poetry*, VII. no. 2, summer 1947:
1–3 set in italics
Space between 3–4
3 . . . ranges.
4 . . . Wellenough . . .

Space between 25–26; 26–39 indented
36 . . . meadow of – nobody knows who was Nooth.
48 . . . towsled . . .
Space between 51–52; 52–55 indented
63 . . . linked . . .
Space between 67–68
84 To Athenry . . .
105 . . . percieve
130 The harnassed . . .
Space between 131–132
133 and 134 omitted
143 . . . washael, . . .
**The Blackbird in the Town**
7 . . . Bird of Valour. See notes, p. 668
21 . . . transcendant   ER 42
**If Sight were Sound**
The following variants occur in *Contemporary Poetry*, IV. 1, Spring 1944:
6 . . . silk pavilion?
8 . . . three tops . . .   [presumably a misprint]
21–25 omitted
**The Crab Tree**
Title, in *Irish Statesman* 10 Dec 1927: 'Wild Apples'
1 . . . Crab-tree,   WA 28; WA 30
3 . . . thin soil   WA 30
13 . . . of Persia   WA 50
27 . . . of a glory   OA 38
**To the Liffey with the Swans**
4 Transformed beloved . . .   OS 23; OA; SP; *An Anthology of Irish Literature*, ed. David H. Greene (1954)
6 . . . royal feather   OS 23
9 . . . doubled Bird   OS 23
11 . . . wonder stirred:   OS 23
**Liffey Bridge**
3 . . . name,   OS 23
4 . . . vapours; and . . .   OS 23
6 . . . and came;   OS 23
7 . . . like shame   OS 23
11 . . . were bare;   OS 23; OA; SP
**The Plum Tree by the House**
15 . . . tree.   WA 30
16–17 omitted in WA 28 and WA 29
16 Or . . .   WA 30
26 . . . earth . . . air:   WA 30
31 . . . the Forbidden . . .   OA
32 . . . ah, God . . .   OA
38 . . . may be . . .   SP

43 . . . returned,   WA 30
**Surburban Spring**
Title: another title 'Springtide in Munsey
Avenue' was considered. The following
variants occur in NY 8 May 1943.
11 . . . fresh, . . .
13 . . . that by sleight
16 . . . housetop,
18a and 18b are added here in NY
   version:
   The pear trees' waterfalls,
   Deluge the garden walls,
19 And soft, green, maple rains,
20 Paving the little lanes,
20a and 20b are added here in NY
   version:
   Silence the way until
   You hear the little rill
22 Now . . .
28 and 29 are omitted in NY version
31 . . . faring:
Space between 31–42 in NY version,
   which omits ll 32–41
46 The master said the sap
47 Is once . . . year on tap,
48 And that the whole world taxies
49 All day around its axis,
42–43 space between these lines   P
**Perennial**
The   following   variants   occur   in
*Contemporary Poetry*, II. 3, 1942:
Space between 31 and 32
32 I felt . . .
**Thrush in Ash**
The following variants occur in the *Atlantic
Monthly*, August 1933:
Dedication: (to E.H.)
21 . . . sweetness
22 . . . glows,
40 . . . song,
42 . . . long.
62 . . . blown;
**The Oak Wood**
Tirle: *The Oak-Wood*   WA 30
4 . . . limb   OS 24; SP
6 . . . renew:   WA 30
10 . . . last,   WA 30
**Lullaby**
24 . . . Now and Then, nor Here and
   There   OA
**Angels**

43 . . . nation;   ER
66 . . . Christ-beloved children,   ER;
   ER 42
96 Lane-way and garden   ER; ER 42
414 . . . tomb-stone;   ER; ER 42
143 . . . on Howth . . .   ER
**Song made by Sir Dinadan for Sir
Tristram that an Harper might play
it before King Mark**
Title: Song   H
1. *Incipit citharista* omitted   H
1 . . . Trees . . . close,   H
2 Cock-a-doodle-doo! . . .   H
3 . . . than those,   H
4 . . . with care,   H; *Contemporary Poetry*,
   III. 2, Summer 1943
5 . . . heart of the wood *Contemporary
   Poetry*, III, 2, Summer 1943
7 . . . protrude,   H
8 . . . is happy!   H
9 . . . tree,   H
10 Cock-a-doodle-do! . . .   H
14 Cuckoo! Cuckoo! Look who old!   H
15   Cuckoo!   Cuckoo!   Cuckoo,
Cuckold!  H
15   Cuckoo,   Cuckoo.   Cuckoo   . . .
   *Contemporary  Poetry*,  III. 2,  Summer
   1943
16 . . . is happy!
17 *Hic calcibus citharistam ejiciunt:* omitted
   H
The following variants occur in a version
in Gogarty's hand in S:
1 . . . close –
2 . . . And, who . . .
3 . . . those,
4 . . . care.
5 . . . heart . . .
7 . . . protrude
8 . . . Sappy . . .
9 . . . was . . .
10 Cock-a doodle do! And, who . . .
11 . . . be;
15 Cuckoo! Cuckoo! Cuckoo! Cuckold!
**Dunsany Castle**
4 . . . breathe;   OS 23
5 . . . sheath;   OS 23
6 . . . glows;   OA
7 . . . royallest . . .   OS 23; OA
10 . . . espoused   OS 23; OA
12 . . . song:   OS 23

**Croker of Ballinagarde**
2 . . . floor, P; *Poetry: A Magazine of Verse*, November 1942
3 . . . yard. P; *Poetry: A Magazine of Verse*, November 1942
5 . . . was mares . . . *Poetry: A Magazine of Verse*, November 1942
13 . . . but brewed P; *Poetry: A Magazine of Verse*, November 1942
15 . . . more than the man?
20 You could see that, by Croker of Ballingarde P
20 You could tell that, by . . . *Poetry: A Magazine of Verse*, November 1942
26 . . . Scrant . . . P; *Poetry: A Magazine of Verse*, November 1942
29 . . . drove . . . P; *Poetry: A Magazine of Verse*, November 1942

**New Bridge**
31 . . . once  OA
38 . . . ridge  OA
44 . . . down necks . . . OA

**Glenasmole**
The following variants occur in *Contemporary Poetry* V. 4, winter 1946:
Foreword added. See notes p. 671–72
11 . . . armor . . .
26 . . . cooled.
30 . . . stream,

**Anachronism**
The following variants occur in *NYT*, 5 January 1939:
1 . . . great-bearded, black . . .
3 . . . upright,
7 The sunlit rhythm . . .
8 . . . long vanished . . .
10 . . . market-place
11 . . . race
12 With waves translucent . . .
13 . . . wrath;
14 . . . Achilles's . . .
15 . . . fling,
17 Ulysses . . .
18 . . . Safety First,
22 For Song when . . .
23 . . . lane,

**Sub Ilice**
38 . . . river beeches . . . OA
43 . . . Idylls' ilex . . . OA
This reading has been adopted in the present text instead of CP's Idylls "ilex

**Connemara**
54 . . . done  SP; OA

**High above Ohio**
Subtitle: (To Alfred and Patricia Flesh) P
4 . . . pleasant . . . ER 42; *Contemporary Poetry*, winter 1942
6 . . . move;  ER 42
7 . . . go;  ER 42
10 . . . advance,  ER 42
12 . . . end . . . beginning.  ER 42
14 . . . stream;  ER 42
16 Free American . . . ER 42
20 . . . trees.  ER 42
22 . . . there, –  ER 42
24 . . . lot: *Contemporary Poetry*, winter 1942
25 . . . bears,  ER 42
30 . . . Down,  ER 42; *Contemporary Poetry*, winter 1942
37 . . . earth  ER 42
939 . . . , in time, . . . ER 42

**The Phoenix**
9 . . . linden . . . WA 29
12 . . . X-ray;  WA 29; OA 38; SP
24 . . . a lid;  WA 29; OA 38; SP
24 . . . out: WA 29; OA
37 . . . gone.  OA
38 . . . dawn  OA
52–53 no space between these lines WA 29
60–61 no space between these lines WA 29

**Fresh Fields**
2 . . . gold.  WA 29
8 . . . Un-walked in . . . SP

**High Tide at Malahide**
12 . . . strand;  OA
23 . . . root,  OA . . . roots  P
39–68 set in italic OA; 39–74 P; *Poetry: A Magazine of Verse*, May 1944
56 . . . turn *Poetry: A Magazine of Verse*, May 1944
65 . . . armor . . . *Poetry: A Magazine of Verse*, May 1944
75 . . . odor . . . *Poetry: A Magazine of Verse*, May 1944
80 . . . azure time.  OA
95 Is stored . . . OA
80 space after this line  P

97 space after this line   OA; *Poetry: A Magazine of Verse*, May 1944
**The Isles of Greece**
This title was also used for a poem included in H and in SSDS. The title in ER is 'Applied Poetry; Lecture I. Sappho'. The first 16 lines are printed under this title p. 269 *CP* uses the title 'The Isles of Greece' with a sub-title 'Applied Poetry (Lesbos)'. It follows ll. 17–27 with II, 36 lines beginning with 'Ah, those Isles of Asia Minor'. The following variants (with different line numbering) occur in ER:
17 (l. 1 in *CP* and correspondingly hereafter) . . . city,
20 . . . there:
21 . . . island,
25 Kindly make . . .
26 . . . fount of lyric glee
28 . . . hetarai;
32 But . . .
37 . . . menfolk, but . . .
39 Lies . . .
43 Yes; my Dear, we may be certain
Variants in ER 42:
8 . . . form
9 Lady, make . . .
9–11 The rhyme of 'nota bene' and 'Mitylene' echoes ll. 22–24 of the earlier poem in H and SSDS
15 . . . emulated:
16 But this . . . missed
24 Yes; . . .
34–35 these lines set in italic.
**The Waveless Bay (Kiltymon)**
9 . . . drives   WA 29; OA 38; SP
**Fog Horns**
30 . . . grey   ER; ER 42
66 . . . war-horns . . .   ER; ER 42
67 War-ships . . .   ER
**Between Brielle and Manasquan**
Variants in *Poetry: A Magazine of Verse*, May 1942
15 And when they talked you . . .
17 . . . *they* . . .
20 . . . upon;
23 . . . store
27 . . . wares;
29 . . . throttle;
30 . . . schooner, full-rigged, . . .

32 . . . was . . .
34 . . . old, brass-barreled flintlock pistol
35 . . . failed . . .
36 . . . *Spumy Nancy* . . .
39 . . . Cathay,
40 . . . thought:
46 . . . win.
48 . . . sea and . . .
60 . . . bay.
61 . . . marooned;
66 . . . flagstaff's . . .
**Earth and Sea**
3 . . . tips   OS 23
5 . . . Ahoy',   OA
9 . . . spars   OS 23
12 . . . word by which . . .   OS 23
Variants in *The Free State*, November 1922:
1 It does me good . . . (This opening line also used in OA)
6 . . . journey done
7 Who . . .
8 Of sea and wind and moon and sun
10 . . . earth's . . .
11 . . . heaven . . .
12 . . . hell . . .
**The Ship**
2 . . . furled,   OS 23
3 . . . her name   OS 23
6 . . . wet   OS 23
10 . . . young,   OS 23
15 . . . deep   OS 23
18 . . . City . . .   OS 23
**Off Sicily**
The following corrections were suggested by W.B. Yeats
4 And land and strand and all are fair – MS correction,   OS 24; WA 30
8 And who shall dare to call it home – MS correction,   OS24; WA 30
9 . . . it . . . – MS correction,   OS 24; WA 30
10 . . . found the fleecy tome, – MS correction,   OS 24; WA 30
11 The curling characters that deck – MS correction,   OS 24; WA 30
**'Kingdoms'**
5 . . . teacups   OA
5 . . . butterflies;   WA 29; WA 30
10 . . . pool;   WA 29
11 . . . sunlight   WA 30

NOTES ON THE TEXT PAGES 109–117

14 . . . light,   WA 30
14 . . . light;   OA
18 . . . then,   WA 29
18 . . . And then   WA 30
20 . . . long-shoremen.   WA 29; SP; OA
20 . . . long-shore-men.   WA 30

SATIRES AND FACETIAE
**O Boys!, O Boys!**
Title: O Boys, O Boys!   WA 29
3 . . . been,   OA
**Ringsend**
Title: Aphorism   WA 28
      Aphorism (after reading Tolstoi)
      WA 30
      Ringsend   WA 29
3 . . . fanlight   OA
7 . . . steels . . .   WA 29
14 . . . wrongs   WA 30
15 And peace at length comes,   WA 30
19 . . . back garden   OA
**After Galen**
6 . . . roar or . . .   WA 30
**To a Boon Companion**
This poem first appeared in *T.C.D. A
College Miscellany*, 3 June 1920 with the
following variants:
Title: To Seumas. An Epigram
1 If Medals . . .
4 . . . you'd soon be decorated,
6 . . . your medals on!
There are other variants:
4 By heavens, you'd be decorated!   OA
6 . . . ribbons on!   OS 23
**To an Old Tenor**
The following variants occur in *Poetry: A
Magazine of Verse*, October 1943: Dated
'October 20th 1943' by Gogarty in a
copy of the journal
20 . . . honors . . .
33 first then . . .
**To a Mushroom**
An earlier version of this poem, in H, is
printed on p. 202
5 . . . start up   H
6 . . . when thou wert,   H
8 O my sudden . . .   H
13 Like a baby . . .   H
16 . . . o'er his head.   H
17 . . . the oddest:   H
18 . . . sudden seen,   H

19 . . . and immodest,   H
20 . . . stocking-skin!   H
20–48   H; not included in *CP*
57–60   H; these lines become the last
    quatrain in *CP*
61–64   H; these lines become the
    penultimate quatrain in *CP*
65–76   H; not included in *CP*
77 Dedication   H: 'To Francis Ledwidge'
    omitted in *CP*
**To the Maids not to Walk in the
Wind**
1 . . . blows walk . . .   SSDS
2 For maids, you . . .   SSDS
4 Me, when . . .   SSDS
6 In double . . .   SSDS
9 . . . thighs,   SSDS
11 . . . to rise   SSDS
12 Like Venus . . .   SSDS
14 Unless Ye . . .   SSDS
15 . . . dead *and changed to air*   SSDS
**A Pithy Prayer against Love**
6 Flourishing skyward   WA 30
7 The gardener's staff,   WA 30
8 Flourish it, raise it,   WA 30
9 Raise it and flourish it,   WA 30
10 . . . upon her,   WA 30
10 Give her a clout of it,   WA 30
11 'That for her honour.'   WA 30
11a Give her a clout of it,   WA 30; not
    in *CP*
14 Think how, in boisterous   WA 30
16 Ridiculous Love looks   WA 30
20 . . . disparage:   WA 30
25 (Quaint as the cordax)   WA 30
30 . . . surmount . . .   OA; misprint in
    *CP*
31 with *oú* . . .   WA 30
31a Shaking his love-locks   WA 30; not
    in *CP*
33 . . . courage!   WA 30
**New Forms**
The following variants occur in a letter
written by Gogarty on 15 Ely Place,
Dublin, notepaper in a letter of 24.xi.1932
to Professor E.H. Alton. (Gogarty
remarked of it in a letter 'And here's one
contra Gentiles [?Gentile] and Yeats.')
T.C.D.:
3 . . . 'For . . .
4 . . . the air.'

5 . . . broke in . . .
6 They showed the wreckage to a Professor,
7 Who cried, 'New forms' New forms.' And wrote a thesis
**Choric Song of the Ladies of Lemnos**
Subtitle: '( . . . *which carries* . . . )'   OA; SP
7 . . . honeycomb,   OA
8 . . . winter tend . . .   OA
22 . . . left is . . .   OA
**Europa and the Bull**
105 Gamboling . . .   SP
**Job's Healer**
The following variants occur in *Contemporary Poetry*, IX. no. 2, summer 1949:
19 You were very nearly right
20 . . . night

LOVE AND BEAUTY
**Dedication**
4 . . . to Love;   WA 30
4 . . . Love.   SP; OA
5 . . . you; with you   WA 30
7 . . . rare and few   WA 30
10 . . . lovely and strong:   WA 30
12 Venus, Muse, . . .   WA 30
**Thinking Long**
Title: To Parmenis   NYT, 11 October 1939
1 . . . , grandmama,   NYT
2 . . . thin, dark-veined . . .   NYT; dark veined . . .   ER; . . . dark-veined . . .   ER 42
3 . . . their hair that, Ah,   NYT
4 Recalls . . . smoldering bands   NYT
5 . . . brow   NYT
6 And one . . .   NYT
7 . . . it as . . . it low   NYT
10 . . . past:   NYT
11 'Its Love . . . decay,'   NYT
13 . . . at the . . . ,
15 . . . gray-haired,   NYT
**Tell Me Now**
4 . . . the air   OS 23
5 . . . Triumvir   OS 23
7 .·. . bay,   OS 23
12 . . . brunt   OS 23
13 . . . Trojan men;   OS 23
Variants in a TS signed OG and dated

12.iii.1920, and inscribed 'To S O'S' [Seumas O'Sullivan]:
14 . . . again   OS 23
6 . . . away,
7 . . . bay,
8 Kings . . .
10 . . . taunt.
12 marginalia in MS suggests 'withstand' for 'endure'
14 . . . again,
15 . . . hour;
16 Test his pleasure, . . .
**Concerning Hermione**
Title 'Seven concerning Hermione'   OS 24
I
4 . . . gentle prattle   OA
5 Under half-intended words – MS correction   OS 24; WA 30
6 Shone the memory of Fame – MS correction   OS 24; WA 30
11 'Though . . .   OS 24; WA 30
15 . . . overbold, – MS correction,   OS 24;   WA 30
16 Gallant hearted . . .   OS 24
17 . . . forebears   OS 24; WA 30; OA
18 . . . foothold . . .   OS 24; OA
II
Title: 'The Exorcism'   WA 30
6 . . . dart:   WA 30
9 'Beauty . . . me,' I cried:   WA 30
10 'By Beauty . . . dislodged.'   WA 30
14 . . . worth:   WA 30
16 'I have . . . fourth.'   WA 30
21 . . . song,   OS 24; WA 30
III
22 . . . quarrel   WA 30
5 . . . stand apart   WA 30
6 Though equal of the best who died;   WA 30; . . . to the best . . . – MS correction,   OS 24
8 . . . or by . . . undefied   WA 30
V
Not included in WA 30
VI and VII
Not included in *CP*
**'Release'**
Subtitle: (To Calypso) omitted   WA 30
1 . . . Beauty, as . . .   WA 30
2 . . . faced;   (WA 30)
4 . . . be, at once, displaced   WA 30

5 . . . idea . . .   WA 30
6 . . . some day;   WA 30
7 . . . Messenger, descried   WA 30
9 . . . and as he . . .   WA 30
15 I, for . . . love,   WA 30
16 . . . the sea.   WA 30
**Melsungen**
10 . . . lamp-light while . . .   WA 29;
  OA; SP; . . . of noon,   WA 29; SP;
  OA
**Leave Taking**
Title: Visitation *Contemporary Poetry*, III.
3, 1943
Title: 'Leave-Taking'  P
**Begone, Sweet Ghost**
Title: 'Begone Sweet Ghost'   OS 23
Variants in OS 23:
1 Begone sweet . . .   OS 23
2 . . . body on:   OS 23
4 . . . day;   OS 23
6 . . . Sweet . . .   OS 23
7 O do but clothe . . .   OS 23
9 . . . loveliness   OS 23
10 withheld   OS 23
**Gaze on Me**
Variants, under the title 'Two Songs' (the
other poem is 'My Love is Dark') in *The
Venture* ed. Lawrence Housman and W.
Somerset Maugham (1905)
2 . . . turn your eyes to me;
3 . . . borne,
4 . . . lights I see:
5 For who is there if . . .
6 That will . . .
1 . . . in scorn,   OS 23
2 . . . those eyes;   OS 23
**Good Luck**
3 . . . Atlanta running stopt,   OS 23
10 . . . was what the juice . . .   OS 23
17 Aye; and . . .   OS 23
A TS version, with the title 'Song,' in
HRHRC initialed by Gogarty has the
following variants:
2 . . . outstript
3 . . . Atalanta running stript
5 . . . moment, . . . stride
7 . . . strong
9 . . . long
11 And Tristram gained before he kissed
12 That without help might have
  missed.

13 . . . gold
14 . . . fire
16 . . . desire:
17 Ever to wish, ever to strain
18 For what without good luck is vain?
**Applied Poetry**
34 . . . dear . . .   OA
59 . . . me,   OA
115 . . . undetected   OA
**To Shadu 'L-Mulk**
5 . . . rebellion   OA
5 Thus when the dam's a fighter   SP
  (US edn)
6 The ostlers often use   SP (US edn)
7 A jackass to incite her,   SP (US edn)
8 Till the blood-horse is let loose.   SP
  US edn)
Corrections suggested by Yeats in
Gogarty's hand   SP:
5 as in   OA
7 . . . jackass, ere . . .
**Leda and the Swan**
5 . . . freshness   OA
17 . . . flag-lead; *An Anthology of Irish
  Literature*, ed. David H. Greene (1954)
38 . . . gilded   P; OA; *An Anthology of
  Irish Literature*, ed. David H. Greene
  (1954)
126 . . . water;   P; *An Anthology of Irish
  Literature*, ed. David H. Greene
  (1954)
128 . . . winged . . .   SP; OA; P; *An
  Anthology of Irish Literature*, ed. David H.
  Greene (1954)
134 . . . hardness?   SP; OA; P
138 . . . basket, –   SP; OA; *An Anthology
  of Irish Literature*, ed. David H. Greene
  (1954)
**Faithful even unto Freud**
10 . . . keep:   OA
21 And in marble . . .   OA
26 . . . infidel,   SP; OA
**Farewell to the Princess**
10 . . . 'twould . . .   WA 30
13 . . . proud:   WA 30; OA; SP
**Women**
1 . . . sub-conscious . . .   SP
**I Wonder**
32 . . . and Bounty's paradigm; –   OA
**The Image-Maker**
3 That guided . . .   WA 30; OA

**With a Coin from Syracuse**
25 . . . Arethuse;   WA 30
27 . . . to her   OA 38
28 . . . lovelier,   WA 30; SP
38 . . . lime-stone . . .   SP
42 . . . high, like her own;   WA 30
**Perfection**
9 . . . stir;   OS 23
15 . . . movemnet;   OS 23
23 . . . curved . . .   OS 23
24 . . . action –   OS 23
**Portrait with Background**
3 . . . the water   WA 30
4 . . . and Henry,   WA 30
10 . . . time, –   WA 30
11 . . . submarine-men . . .   WA30
14 . . . their effront'ry;   WA 30
16 . . . country?   WA 30
18 . . . lordly houses –   WA 30
20 . . . Steel it arouses   WA 30
22 Slave . . .   OA
29 . . . the vision   WA 30
32 Awestruck . . .   OA 38
**To Ethne**
These alternatives were suggested by
W.B. Yeats:
TS corrections in ink,   OS 24:
6 . . . golden star,
7 So did . . . goddess come
**Golden Stockings**
4 . . . weather   OS 23
6 . . . delight:   OS 23
14 . . . sun:   OS 23
**A Prayer for his Lady**
Variants in NYT, 24 January, 1940:
4 . . . Yours;
6 . . . Your . . .
8 . . . Love . . . through,
10 . . . to the . . .
12 . . . for Your . . .
**I tremble to think**
Title: 'Portrait'   WA 1929
**To an Old Lady**
7 . . . the rose . . .
9 . . . the thoughts . . . portal, NYT, 30
    May 1940

LIFE AND DEATH
**The Airman's Breastplate**
The following variants occur in a TS in
S: Title: The Pilot's Breastplate. Subtitle:

. . . famous Lorica . . . intó modern
prosody for an Airman's prayer . . . of a
member of the Army Air Force
2 Armoured . . .
4 . . . can hold . . .
6 . . . splenor . . .
14 . . . me bearing.
**The Bubble**
Variants in *Contemporary Poetry*, Vol. 8.
no 2, 1948
3 . . . colors . . .
4 . . . stone . . .
5 . . . broken,
7 . . . up, rounded,
9 . . . tops,
10 . . . breeze, fanned
13 . . . water!
19 . . . water:
20 . . . Immortality.
**Panurge**
Subtitle omitted in H
8 . . . Panurge,   H
17 Such laughter lore . . .   H
25 . . . bent,   H
26 Where sea and sky converse   H
27 Those Isles . . .   H
29 . . . crack,   H
29 . . . Cannons'   OA
30 . . . purge,   H
31 The boar cat Rodilardus back,   H
33 Bring back the virgin, fighting Fryar   H
Dedication: 'To Seumas O'Sullivan'   H,
    omitted in   P
**Time, Gentlemen, Time!**
4 . . . shocks,   ER; ER 42
15 . . . a battleship   ER
71 . . . pleasure   ER
The following variants occur in NY, 8
May 1943:
1–28 omitted
31 Of all the woe Time . . .
34 . . . Heaven . . .
41–44 omitted
46 Which turns . . .
47 . . . piecework . . .
49 . . . errors
50 . . . checks
56 . . . leap year,
62 . . . takes
63 . . . laneway
67 . . . Guinness

69 So make . . .
70 Because the . . .
71 . . . pleasure
76 'Tis then the more we live
**Centaurs**
6 Till God . . . OS 24
**Anglers**
11 . . . river mosses, . . . OA
**The Old Goose**
14 . . . comforts . . . OA
34 . . . down OS 24
62 . . . truth, OS 24
62a Who found in fighting truth, OA
70 . . . sword. OS 24
86 . . . barred . . . OS 24; OA
**Non Blandula Illa**
3 . . . wonder as . . . OS 23
4 . . . wanderings; OS 23
7 But far off . . . OS 23
8 A sea-gray . . . OS 23
9 . . . Bersarks . . . OS 23
11 . . . calls; OS 23
13 . . . Nature falls, OS 23
**The Ho Ho Bird**
The following variants occur in *Good Housekeeping*, November 1951:
6 . . . spring;
7 and 8 omitted
9 . . . slept and . . .
10 . . . heads,
12 Afar, the . . .
16 . . . bird –
18 . . . wings –
**The Emperor''s Dream**
20 Was seized . . . OA
42 How, one . . . OA
**Lullaby**
23 Nor Now or Then, nor Here nor There; OA
**The Mill at Naul**
4 . . . mill, OA; *Atlantic Monthly*, May 1934
24 space after this line OA; *Atlantic Monthly*, May 1934
26 no space after this line OA
30–31 no space between these lines OA
53 . . . lie, till, . . . *Atlantic Monthly*, May 1934
56–57 no space between these lines OA
72–73 no space between these lines OA; P; *Atlantic Monthly*, May 1934

89 . . . alert, *Atlantic Monthly*, May 1934
92–93 no space between these lines OA
116 . . . glowed through with . . . OA
119 . . . go: OA; P; *Atlantic Monthly*, May 1934
132 . . . miller . . . OA; *Atlantic Monthly*, May 1934
**Palinode**
6 . . . palinode. OA
**Domi**
7 . . . thought, OA
25 . . . course OA
**Elbow Room**
The following variants occur in NYT, 19 May 1938:
2 . . . space,
6 And, fainting, . . .
7 . . . this,
8 Chinese . . .
12 . . . anywhere) –
15 Oh, . . .
18 Alone, beyond (also in ER 42)
**All the Pictures**
25 NYT 2 March 1938 omits l.25: 'And woman's love not any mo'
26 Oh, then 'tis surely time . . . NYT 2 March 1938, also ER
An alternative title 'Shadow Show' was used in a version in T.C.D.
**Sund apud Infernos tot Milia Formosarum**
The alterations in lines 6 and 7 (OS 24) were suggested by W.B. Yeats
Title: 'Tot Milia Formosarum' WA 30
6 To Marco Polo; or the West WA 30; also MS correction in OS 24
7 A-bloom beyond those icy walls WA 30
7 Blooming beyond the icy walls – MS correction in OS 24
**Per Iter Tenebricosum**
6 Or heroes, . . . WA 30
**Marcus Curtius**
2 . . . pride and . . . WA 28
**Non Dolet**
8 . . . from Age not Time OS 23
10 . . . drives home; OS 23

ELEGIES
**To Petronius Arbiter**
1 . . . Bithynia OS 23
2 . . . to day OS 23

5 . . . expense    OS 23
5 . . . the soul's expense,    OA
**Farrell O'Reilly**
The following variants occur in *Poetry: A Magazine of Verse*, May 1946:
3 . . . the hard, . . .
5 . . . father, what . . .
7 They say when
9 . . . maybe because . . . ground,
14 . . . cartridge
20 . . . time!
22 . . . plow . . .
23 . . . Tara, . . . way,
26 . . . green,
31 . . . mezzotint,
32 . . . gun,
33 Top-hatted, . . . squint
34 . . . sun);
35 . . . clear, . . . Farrell,
37 . . . men:
38 . . . me, looking . . .
41 . . . wrong though . . .
43 . . . light, I . . .
46 . . . nothing but glanced . . . father,
49 . . . laurels,
50 . . . rimmed,
51 . . . liss . . .
56 And see . . .
57 . . . again:
58 . . . understand.
60 . . . cutaway . . .
62 Alert lest
67 . . . well, the . . . fields,
68 . . . liss . . .
69 . . . early; and . . .
70 . . . morn.
**Aeternae Lucis Redditor**
Subtitle: (To . . . Tyrrell)    OA
1 . . . Friend . . .    ER 42
9 . . . restore    OA
The poem appeared in *The Irish Times*, 26 March 1937 under the heading 'A friend remembers Robert Yelverton Tyrrell.' The title was 'Aeternae Lucis Redditor' (To the memory of R.Y. Tyrrell)
**'Elegy on the Archpoet William Butler Yeats Lately Dead'**
30 . . . authorized    P
31 . . . me,    ER 42
35 . . . flesh;    ER 42

36 . . . rhymes;    ER 42
55 . . . track,    ER 42
79 . . . in the tower *Contemporary Poetry*, I. 3, Autumn 1941
79 . . . in the tower,    ER 42
84 . . . fear,    ER 42
94 . . . about *Contemporary Poetry*, I. 3, Autumn 1941
101 . . . egg Herodotos *Contemporary Poetry*, I. 3, Autumn 1941
106 Or, linking . . .    ER 42
119–120 Gogarty referrred to a change in these lines in *Contemporary Poetry*, I. 4, Winter 1942; he wished the lines to appear thus:

> Straight lines of Burns as plain as prose   P
> On Matthew Henderson, not Grose: P
> 'For Matthew was a queer man';

119 . . . Matthew Grose ER 42; Matthew Grose: *Contemporary Poetry*, I. 3, Autumn 1941
120 CP's l. 120 – 'No, no! on Henderson, not Grose' – is omitted in ER 42; *Contemporary Poetry*, I. 3, Autumn 1941
140 . . . horse    ER 41
145 Return, Dean . . .    ER 42
146 . . . state    ER 42
155 . . . from the . . .    ER 42
174 . . . meseems)    ER 42
175 . . . tragedy.    ER 42
190 And through my loss grow . . .    ER 42
For footnotes added to the text see notes, p. 194
The following opening for IV was not included in the final version in CP, probably as being too concerned with Gogarty's own upbringing:

> When I was young my Master tried
> By Death to make me terrified
> And by Eternal Pain until
> They overdid the terrible
> And all the glowing picture spoiled
> Because from it the mind recoiled;
> But yet by thinking on Life's end
> I almost missed Life's main, a friend

## PART TWO

### POEMS FROM HYPERTHULEANA (1916)

**The Feast**

An early version of a poem which appears in *Collected Poems*, p. 44 under the title 'To my Friend the Rt. Hon. Lorcan Galeran (A Great Householder)'. The text is sufficiently different to justify the earlier version of the poem being included in Part Two.

**To a Mushroom**

This early version of the poem contains eight stanzas more than the version in *Collected Poems*, and reverses the order of the last two in *CP*; it has, therefore, also been included here as well as in *CP*, p. 114.

**To his Friend the Apothecary Poet**

The version in *The Irish Review*, February 1912, written under the name Selwyn Merle, contains the following variants:

12 . . . sly sonnet
13 Send naught to me like Herbert's home
15 Send me no thought of Newman's back
21 . . . well,
25 Send me a Syrop to give me
27 . . . Mind . . .

Versions in NLI contain the following variants:

6 And undefined essence
17 Nor brisk . . .
20 . . . The merrie Mermaid crew,
29 . . . the wine;

**The Isles of Greece**

The later version in SSDS differs from that of H in the following lines:

23 . . . nota bene
46 . . . heresies.
62 . . . Greeks.
69 . . . beautiful'
70 . . . Sunday-school –
71 Oh, your . . .
72 . . . Arnoldising

Variants in MLTT:

69 . . . your 'Greece, the . . . '
70 . . . Sunday-school,
72 . . . Arnoldising!

**To Kasimir Dunin Markievicz**

Variants in a TCD MS:

1 . . . a name . . .
2 . . . dullards, and . . . Joy!
3 . . . , you great incorrigible boy!
6 . . . here:
7 . . . Stallion and Seer,
8 . . . the Trojans' overlord.
9 . . . cringe in Arts and Ethics. You're above
10 . . . Painting Poetry and Love:
11 And this the faint hearts . . .

These variants are repeated in T.C.D. 4648/4148 where the poem was included under the heading RL [Reality League] entitled 'To Kasimir Dunin Markievicz.' (I being 5 lines by S.O'S [Seamus O'Sullivan]) and II by OG [Gogarty]

**On first looking into Kraft-Ebing's *Psychopathia Sexualis***

A version (source not given) in O'C has these variants:

4 . . . bawds connived . . . policeman hold
5 I too have . . .
6 . . . Pure obscene –
7 . . . clean –
10 . . . Macran,
11 . . . and doubts did rise,
13 With love . . . towards . . .
14 . . . Ann?

**'Memento Homo Quia Pulvis Es' (at La Trappe)**

Variants in O'C:

2 . . . darkness and . . .
5 Ah no! Those . . .
9 . . . return.
12 . . . life,
13 . . . If dust . . .
15 . . . His breath . . .
16 . . . clay:
18 . . . Freewill anyway
19 . . . foul.
21 . . . undone,
23 . . . thereon.
29 . . . lurk,
30 . . . free,
31 . . . shirk?

39 . . . pray.
40 I said 'If . . . trim,
42 'O Thou, Lord . . .

### To a Bearded Dealer in Old Objects of Art
1 MS correction in Gogarty's hand in copy no. 2 of H alters 'the beautiful' to 'the curious'

### Helen's Lamp
A letter from Gogarty to James Starkey NLI (see also L) contains these variants:
1 . . . lamp: . . .
3 On me these kisses Paris traced
4 . . . by night light looks best.

### A Line from Rabelais
Gogarty intended to include a version of this poem (containing only stanzas 1, 3 and 6) in his unpublished *Penultimate Poems* (pp. 289 *et seq.*) and sent the following corrections to the text in a letter to Michael Sadleir, a director of Constable and Company (undated, from 45 East 61st St., N.Y.).

He intended this version of the poem to end with a subheading 'His Epitaph' (see p. 491):
Let not Death confuse You all;
Death is not unusual.
3 . . . interval
4 . . . brains,
6 The priest should rest . . .
7 . . . not; but . . .
9 line set in Roman, enclosed by inverted commas
18 . . . Cathedral . . .
19 . . . mediate;
20 . . . dose,
21 . . . the women . . . gate,
22 . . . remonstrate
23 Or watch . . . Brothers . . .
25 . . . Convent . . .
26 line set in Roman, no inverted commas
45 With murmurs . . .
47 . . . besmirch
48 . . . Life . . .
50 . . . punished . . . Rabelais
51 omitted
52 Has risked . . .
53 line set in Roman, enclosed by

inverted commas
In the version published in *The Irish Review*, May 1911, p. 128, the poem appeared under the name Oscar Grünwald. The second stanza was not included in this version.

### Epilogue
1 Later version of this poem in OS (1923) has altered this line to 'Inheritors of laboured Song'
There is a variant in NLI:
1 With . . . with . . .

POEMS FROM *SECRET SPRINGS OF DUBLIN SONG* (1918)
### A Double Ballad of Dublin
44 . . . 'Mayor, (editorial addition of comma)

### Threnody on the Death of Diogenes, the Doctor's Dog
The version in *T.C.D.*, 14 February 1903, has these variants:
1 . . . mouth,
2 . . . tail;
4 . . . doornail
5 . . . hydrophobia – not . . .
8 . . . Greece,
11 And rather were fined ere . . .
14 . . . King,
16 . . . the donor, or owner . . .
18 . . . see yer . . .
19 That'll . . . Dons,
21 And, if . . .
25 . . . me;
27 . . . I shall see
35 . . . is –
36 . . . pork-butcherie,
37 . . . sausage fulfilled . . .
39 . . . Zeus's,
40 A *Bird* . . .
41 (The . . . is,
42 . . . free)
43 To serve as a suitable . . . sign, . . .
45 Mock-turtle . . .
46 myrtles,
48 . . . *élite*, at . . . family-tree.
49 What Bird . . .
52 . . . go –
53 . . . 'conversation,' . . .
57 . . . strand,

## POEMS FROM *THE SHIP AND OTHER POEMS* (1918)
**Castle Corrib**
Variants in OS 24
5 . . . come
7 . . . stored

## POEMS FROM *AN OFFERING OF SWANS* (1923)
**My Love is Dark**
Variants in *The Venture*, ed. Laurence Housman and W. Somerset Maugham (1905)
2 And . . .
3 . . . woodland.
4 Which . . .
5 For she, as shines the moon by night,
6 Can win . . .
Variants in O'C and B:
1 . . . fair,
3 . . . woodland lake water
5 But, as the moon . . .
7 . . . light –
**When the Sun Shines**
Variations in C
Title: Song
1 When shines the sun . . .
2 Her tresses seem
3 . . . rays . . .
4 . . . brown
8 For her is wholly shed
9 . . . from heaven takes the light
10 . . . head:
11 Or that to her I captive fall
12 . . . rainbow . . .
Variants in a letter to G.K.A. Bell written by Gogarty in June 1904 from 5 Rutland Square, Dublin   MLTT
Title: To Mary on Howth's Summit
1 . . . hair
2 Her . . .
3 . . . rays . . .
5 . . . coil . . .
between 6 and 7 no space
7 Then neither wonder . . .
8 On her is wholly shed,
9 . . . heaven's light
11 As in C
The C version adds after the poem:
  we see this in the mystics Blake
  Novalis

**Folia Caduca**
Variants in MLTT
1 . . . falling,
2 . . . that . . .
3 All through the windless air answer her calling
4 Green and russet and . . .
5 They fall the little leaves and wither –
7 . . . he wafts them . . .
8 Go, but they cover the Earth with gold.
9 That men thus seeing the Earth may wonder
10 At golden death which . . .
11 Now bowed down trying to . . .
12 More than is lent to . . .

## POEMS FROM *AN OFFERING OF SWANS AND OTHER POEMS* (1924)
**Early Morning – Germany**
2 . . . food, (MS correction)   OS 24
**To a Trout**
Variants in OS 24:
20 . . . gillie.
W.B. Yeats suggested the following alterations in ll. 21 and 22 (corrections made in Gogarty's hand in a copy of OS 24):
21 I cast . . .
22 And tempting Fate is your employment
**And Now**
Variants in TS in HRHRC typed on 15 Ely Place, Dublin, notepaper: (This version contains a final comment, 'Here is an Epigramophone, Don't ignore it'):
1 For God's sake let us go . . .
3 . . . is
4 . . . grow.
9 Or listen to that . . .
10 . . . daughter
11 Begot . . . Constantine:
12 . . . King . . .
**Relativity**
Variants in TCD:
1 . . . star-light . . .
2 . . . severe,
3 When a thought of . . . Alison,
4 . . . my mind from rectitude and bends it to a curve?
**Medicus Poetae**
Variants in NLI (accompanied by a note:

'I wrote this for you years ago. I found it now and copy it so that if I never sent it before – "Now you have it"'):
2 . . . by meadow and wells of streams
4 . . . spied.
5 . . . hide;
7 . . . stript
8 And thereby grew immortal though they died
8–9 space between these lines
9 . . . bed and crowded lazar-house
10 Where from the Feast they living are debarred,
13 Catch sight of harmonies rare as the stars
14 In the grey morn that makes the blackbird sing,
Gogarty records how Yeats rewrote the last line as it was published in OS 24. See his 'Reminiscences of Yeats', *Mourning Became Mrs Spendlove* (1948), where he comments that Yeats's use of *Leap* gave the line emphasis.

**To Tancred**
A version in NLI reads:
11–14 A thousand years in vain may work their will;
    For I think of them when I think of you,
    Stretched to these days of unheroic things
    Who move as if the steel enclosed you still.
Variants in another version, T.C.D.:
1 . . . such . . . verve
2 . . . undismayed
4 . . . Muses . . .
5 That nothing . . .
6 . . . payed:
7 . . . ridden! – O . . .
8 . . . strictest . . . swerve,
10 For I think of them when I think of you
11 . . . name and lineaments . . .
12 . . . in vain may work . . .

POEMS FROM *WILD APPLES* (1928)
**Portrait. Jane W . . .**
Variants in *The London Mercury*, June 1925, Vol. 12 no. 68:

7 . . . rarely dark eyes . . .
30 . . . Phoenix nest
38 For Life . . .
Title 'Jane W . . . of Grand Rapids' WA 29; B
Subtitle 'Jane W . . . ' omitted WA 30, where the poem's title is 'Another Portrait'
6 . . . rarely dark eyes WA 30; B
7 . . . honey-colored B
19 And, maybe, in WA 30; B
22 with this unmelted . . . B
25 . . . foster-town WA 30
26 . . . is down; WA 30
30 . . . Phoenix . . . B
38 For Life . . . WA 29; B
**To George Redding**
The following variants occur in B:
2 . . . that nowadays . . . reads,
6 . . . emergence,
10 . . . oh, not . . .
14 . . . is:
16 . . . with but with a . . .
**To Some Spiteful Persons**
1 Your Envy . . . WA 30
The following variants occur in *The Irish Statesman*, 3, 267, 8 November 1924:
4 . . . hawk,
4–5 no space between these lines
5 . . . their heads . . .
**The Yacht**
2 . . . on the . . . WA 29
15 . . . imageing . . . WA 29
**Song** ['Dreams bring her back']
5 . . . Times WA 29
**The Crowing of a Cock**
7 . . . may be: WA 29
8 . . . knowledge is . . . WA 29

POEMS FROM *WILD APPLES* (1929)
**Galway**
The following variants occur in *The Free State*, 18 March 1922:
4 . . . green,
9 . . . row!
16 . . . stars.
22 . . . Salthill, from the Square
25 . . . prosperous days,
26 . . . port;
27 . . . City's lovely ways
31 . . . gray walls

**The Weathercock**
The following variants occur in *The Irish Statesman*, 14 February, 3, 1924, 718:
2 . . . laughing. There . . .
4 . . . square
13 . . . would in . . .
14 . . . grass,
28 . . . love:
Last stanza omitted


POEMS FROM *WILD APPLES* (1930)
**To Moorhead, Blind**
The following variants occur in the *Journal of Irish Medical Association* 47, 138, Dec. 1960:
Title: To T. Gilman Moorhead
2 . . . sight,
3 And, long . . .
4 Evening is on us and the daylight flies;
5 . . . were swifter and your . . .
7 That long before the evening fell on light
8 And it shall comfort you to realise
9 That when all we are into darkness sent
10 The dark of which you had more than your share,
11 If there be succour in Time's banishment
12 Pre-eminent again, you'll help us where
13 The sudden dark, the vague beleagurement
14 Calls for such fortitude as you can spare
**The Exorcism**
Variants in *An Anthology of Irish Literature* ed. David H. Greene (1954):
Title: The Exorcism
6 . . . dart;
9 Beauty . . . me, I cried;
10 By Beauty . . . dislodged.
17 . . . War [this reading adopted in the present text]
21 . . . song
22 . . . quarrel,


POEMS FROM *OTHERS TO ADORN* (1938)
**Preface**
This is Preface (i) in *CP*. 'The Poetry of my Friend' by AE becomes Preface (ii) in *CP*. 'Gogarty in the Flesh' by Horace Reynolds becomes Preface (iii) in *CP*. OA also contains:
    Invocation
    Richard Campbell ⎤
    Witter Bynner    ⎬ COME ON!
    David Morton     |
    Horace Reynolds ⎦
**Reflection**
The following variants occur in a TS version in B and C
7 Looks just like an eye . . .
20 Tis from there . . .
24 Bound for . . .
Another TS version (B and C) has the following additional variants:
4 . . . prow,
7 Circles out like . . .
23 . . . hips against . . .
24 'Bound for' . . . cancelled in this TS
31 . . . it
32 . . . may tow it
33 . . . may disturb
35 But were these . . .
36 Why should I exchange at all?


POEMS FROM *ELBOW ROOM* (1939)
**Applied Poetry. Lecture I. Sappho.**
See textual notes on 'The Isles of Greece' p.784


POEMS FROM *UNSELECTED POEMS* (1954)
**Noah's Ark**
The following variants occur in *Atlantic Monthly* 185, April 1950:
9 . . . seasick;
Between 31 and 32 no space
38 . . . orbèd . . .
50 . . . whorlèd . . .
102 . . . doe moose . . .
103 . . . tigers' . . .
121 . . . delectation*
122 Often . . .
124–127 these lines (in AM version) are missing in UP
**Ars Longa**
The following variants occur in B:
5 . . . disease;

8 . . . began.
10 . . . him and . . .
14 . . . apopthegms,
16 For Life . . . Art is long;
17 And the technique takes time to achieve [with alternative to 'achieve' in margin: 'learn']
19 . . . believe [cancelled for marginal 'discern']
20 . . . Life . . . but Art . . . long:
21 Oh, take . . .
22 . . . strong
**One World**
G. The following variants occur in *Contemporary Poetry*, x, 150:
16 . . . great, globorious . . .
20 If I . . .
21 . . . us all! . . .
23 . . . brought again a plastic . . .
24 A gray . . . Age!
**A Report on the Sexless Behaviour of Certain Microscopic Immortals**
The following variants occur in the *Atlantic Monthly*, September 1948
Title: Report . . . Behaviour of Microscopic . . .
2 . . . sex;
4 . . . everlasting
6 . . . copulation,
12 . . . Come;
14 . . . fission,
15 And, while . . . multiplying,
19 . . . tenth
20 . . . until . . . *n*th
24 . . . on . . .
25 . . . would prove . . . thriller;
26 . . . sing:
27 . . . victory?

POEMS FROM *PENULTIMATE POEMS*
(a volume planned by Gogarty before his death but not published as a separate collection) Seven of the poems on Gogarty's list for this projected volume have been omitted from the text under this heading as they appeared in *Unselected Poems* (1954) and are included under that heading in this edition (see pp. 274 *et seq.*). 'Psychoanalysis II' has been added from a TS in B. For abbreviations see p. 657 and

for acknowledgements see pp. 649 and 652. The sources of copy texts are given here after the titles of poems.
**To a Moth**
*Good Housekeeping*, October 1942; G; T.C.D.
The following variants occur in G and T.C.D:
4 . . . flame:
6 . . . quest,
10 . . . wavering . . .
13 . . . I:
16 . . . pain.
18 . . . have all I have, . . .
19 . . . mind when I am gone
21 Therefore in . . .
24 . . . gloom
27 . . . true, for, . . .
28 . . . moth
Variants in B
16 . . . brain TS signed by Gogarty
19 . . . go down, TS signed by Gogarty
**Free Will**
*The Ladies Home Journal*, September 1956; G; T.C.D.
The following variants occur in G:
5 . . . will come . . .
11 . . . apart,
14 . . . no season . . .
Variants in T.C.D.:
3 . . . duresse
5 . . . shall come . . .
7 . . . silences
13 . . . together
**The Village of Plandome**
*Contemporary Poetry*, VI, 2, September 1946; G
The following variants occur in G:
5 . . . white bright . . .
10 . . . each owner . . .
11 That . . .
17 . . . green grocer
18 Each whistling, dawdling messenger
25 . . . comes in
26 . . . appears;
32 . . . the freash . . . salt;
33 . . . ago; . . .
37 . . . young, had
39 . . . unfold,
40 . . . incredulous:
41 . . . now. When . . .

**Sodom and Gomorrah**
G; T.C.D.
The following variants occur in T.C.D.:
2 . . . they didn't oughter;
3 And that . . .
5 . . . of all the lot
After 8 TS inserts the following four lines:
    We look for normalcy in vain
    In the twin Cities of the Plain
    No place to send your son to stay
    Or daughter for a holiday.
9 . . . wonder
10 Made . . . Lot a . . .
12 . . . fully taken . . .
14 When . . .
After 14 TS inserts the following two lines:
    She just looked back and she was
        sore-eyed
    So she was changed to sodium
        chloride.
These lines are followed by the four lines added after 8 above. There follow ten lines:
    Far be from my thoughts to smirch
        ill
    That under belly, Winston
        Churchill;
    But he had both chapter and verse,
    (Could anything on Earth be
        worse)
    For bombing women with such
        daring,
    That he brought on him Hermann
        Goering;
    Both were outdone by Harry
        Truman
    For he spared neither man or
        woman
    But acquiesced when the Big Three
    Tried Goering's lack of chivalry.
**Before Psychiatry**
G; T.C.D.
**Perfection**
G; B; T.C.D.
Variants in B: line 7, 'Exempt alike from victory and grief,' omitted
**A Whodunit Who Didn't**
*The Literary Review*, Winter 1957/58; G
In the copy text the poem consists of 8

lines; the following variants occur in G which has 10 lines:
Title: Whodunit That Didn't
1 . . . that didn't
3 Private . . .
4 And yet their hangovers were not registering.
5 . . . so planned
6 That in it the phone would not constantly ring;
7 In which to the Justice by ways that were lawless
8 The culprit the private eye surely would bring;
9 If I could find a Whodunit so flawless
10 Do you think for a moment I'd read the damn thing?
**Supersonic?**
*Collier's*, 29 April 1955; G; T.C.D.
Variant in G:
Title: Supersonic
Variants in T.C.D.:
2 . . . bars
4 Past barriers . . .
5 Then we . . .
6 Of blaze and blare . . .
**Make us Aware**
G; T.C.D.
The following variants occur in T.C.D.:
5 . . . happiness.
6 . . . is:
9 . . . enjoy
10 . . . those good . . .
12 . . . groan dragooned . . .
13 . . . rest:
15 . . . gate,
17 We freely live . . .
**Full Circle**
G; T.C.D.
The following variants occur in T.C.D.:
3 . . . waters . . .
6 . . . squabbling Europe . . .
7 . . . old History . . .
11 O Life, . . .
12 . . . Death!
Variants in another TS, T.C.D.
2 . . . stand still
3 That, like wild waters through . . .
4 Thundered while Europe lay appalled
6 . . . Europe . . .
7 . . . old History . . .

8 . . . broken wall;
9 Kings slink away . . .
10 And nations weak to nations call:
11 O Life speak out . . .
12 While Europe waits; and waits for Death?
**Misgivings**
Entitled *The Poet to his Soul*, this was sent by Gogarty to Mrs Owings Miller in 1949   G; C; T.C.D.
The following variants occur in C:
1 Latterly . . .
2 . . . keep my body . . . together
3 . . . of weather,
4 omitted in C; included in T.C.D.
5 . . . Death,
6 . . . save it.
7 . . . it
8 . . . breathe my . . . breath
Variants in T.C.D.:
Title: *The Poet to his Soul*
1 Of late I . . . soul;
3 . . . weather
5 . . . Death
6 . . . it
**When**
G; T.C.D.:
Variants in T.C.D.:
Title: When?
1 . . . War . . . Peace . . . Solace
3 . . . Coco Colas,
**A Wish**
G; T.C.D.; B
The following variants occur in T.C.D.:
3 . . . day
4 Or through . . .
**The Eternal Feminine**
T.C.D.; G
The following variants occur in G:
4 . . . Girls . . .
6 . . . lovliest . . .
7–12 omitted
In 2 the reading of G 'bangles' has been adopted here instead of the copy text's 'tangles'
**Psychoanalysis I**
G; *ToMorrow*, December 1946; T.C.D.
The following variants occur in T.C.D.:
1 . . . psychiatrist
3 You are . . .
12 . . . bed;

13 Hence it's . . . you;
14 . . . check's . . .
17 . . . foot
18 . . . yoke
27 . . . unkempt;
29 . . . enplore
30 . . . fallacies
31 . . . done far . . .
(This reading has been adopted in the present text)
**Psychoanalysis II**
B
48–51 'Deed such as . . .
        And bores me still.'
are written in Gogarty's hand in the rt. hand margin of TS, B. It is not clearly indicated whether they were intended to end the poem or be placed before 52–55:
        'Borrow an ax . . .
        Kill your mother and then
        Relax'
52–55 are also the concluding lines of 'Job's Healer'. p. 129
**The Changeling I**
*The Ladies Home Journal*, 71, April 1954; G
The following variants occur in G
3 . . . hillside faeries
12 . . . was mortal . . .
13 . . . gleams, . . .
14 . . . wizened thing
17 . . . his steed . . .
23 . . . light and . . .
**The Changeling II**
*Tomorrow*, January 1951; B; G
A TS in B contains corrections in Gogarty's hand and there are minor variants in another TS, B2:
Subtitle: '(A spray of mountain ash over the door would have saved the human child from the faeries)'   B
2 . . . Square, East;   B2
3 But none knew in Dublin that it ought   B
6 . . . Letter –   B
7 . . . town   B
8 And gently . . .   B
9 . . . to order and lawyer and priest   B
10 To Homestead and Kin of my own   B
11 And gave me a wild will instead of my

own  B
11 I'm no better off by becoming the
debtor  B2
12 Forever, and ever the Good People's
guest  B2
13 . . . Kindred aloof and alone  B
14 Alas I am now made immortal  B
14 It little avails that they made me
immortal  B2
15 If I to mortality . . .  B2
16 They shrivelled . . .  B
17 . . . portal,  B
19 . . . is the yew . . .  B
21 . . . to them . . . curtal, –  B
22 . . . lovers all . . . scarce –  B
26 . . . song.  B
27 Ah, no! There . . . water  B
38 To beauty . . .  B; B2
39 . . . beauty . . .  B; B2

43 . . . living; . . .  B
45 No laughter; . . .  B
47 I changed  B
48 . . . highland inhumanity  B
49 . . . staid  B
     . . . staid;  B2
50 . . . the tides  B
51 Flow back,
52 omitted  B; B2
53 . . . double, that withered  B
63 . . . casement  B
76 . . . eternal,  B
77 praise,  B
78 And dance . . .  B
Variants in G:
4 . . . setter;
9 . . . priest
10 . . . own,
12 Forever and . . . People's guest

# PART THREE

Unpublished Poems and Poems not included in Collections of Gogarty's Poems.
    The sources of copy texts are given after the titles of poems.

## ODES AND ADDRESSES
**Ode of Welcome** *Irish Society*, June 1900. Poem terminates with initials J.R.S.; bottom left hand margin gives an address at Knocklong.
**In Memoriam Robert Louis Stevenson** The Official Guide Ltd., Dublin 1903; also in *Stevensonia* ed. J.A. Hammerton (1903).
63 The copy text's 'éer' has been editorially altered to 'e'er'
**To his Extraordinary Friend, George Kennedy Allen Bell** Written at the Martello Tower, Sandycove D.
**Beginning of a poem to G.K.A. Bell** MLTT
**Foreword** *Ireland*, April 1904.
**Ireland's Welcome to the Fleet** *Ireland*, September 1904.
**Cervantes: Tercentenary of Don**

**Quixote** Privately printed, Dublin, 1905; B. See L, pp 54–55.
**The Horse Show** *Ireland*, September 1908.
**Ode on the Bicentenary** *Souvenir Programme*, Dublin University Dramatic Society, 1912.
III 1.13 The copy text's 'it peers' has been editorially altered (as it seems a misprint) to 'its peers'
**The Injection: To Lord Dunsany** In letter to Lord Dunsany, dated November 1914; O'C; HRHRC.
    The HRHRC version is written from Garranban House, Moyard, County Galway and dated Christmas Eve, 1914. The following variants occur in the HRHRC version:
2 . . . fear
5 But . . .
6 . . . War
7 . . . you,
15 . . . fought.
19 . . . lives
36 fumed is glossed thus: typhoid = smoke-like

**To Her Most Gracious Majesty**
Written on 20 Grosvenor Square, London,
notepaper B.
**To Maurice Baring** HRHRC.
**To Stuart Benson** Sent 'from Oliver
Gogarty with gratitude and esteem' D.
**To Madame Chiang Kai-Shek**
*Montreal Gazette* clxxii, 142, June 1943.
**To the Grand Daughter of Lord
Dunsany, aged two, in the Garden of
Dunsany Castle** B; T.C.D.
  The following variants occur in
  another TS, B.
  Title: 'aged two' inserted in ink, in
  Gogarty's hand
  8 . . . looks!
  17 Erse and . . .
  The following variants occur in TS,
  T.C.D.:
  18 . . . heard,
  20 . . . unstirr'd . . .
  21 . . . bloom and . . .

EARTH AND SEA
**Poem from Oxford** NLI.
**Ringsend** Written on 12 December
1904; this revised version is in a letter
from Gogarty to G.K.A. Bell, of 12
October 1905; privately printed, Dublin,
1905; D; MLTT.
**Ringsend** [earlier version] Letter from
Gogarty to G.K.A. Bell, of 12 December
1904; MLTT; L.
**Clouds** *The Irish Statesman*, 17 August,
1929.
**The Little Dark Wood** *The Ladies
Home Journal*, September 1951; S; B.
  The following variants occur in B:
  Title: *Roisindhu*
  2 . . . neighbouring . . .
  3 . . . where the mountain . . .
  5 . . . the mountain . . .
  6 Was . . . it looked . . .
  7 . . . Water-lilies
  13 . . . Evening the . . . wind, . . .
    motion,
  14 . . . levelled . . .
  16 . . . mountain was . . .
  17 Sometimes . . .
  22 . . . pain;
  23 . . . with its . . .

**Out of Dublin** RL; NLI
**With the Coming-in of Spring** B.
**Lullaby** NLI.
**April** B; D.
**Spring** B
**Chestnut Time** T.C.D.
**Magical Frost** T.C.D.
**Tradition** B.
  The original line of the MS is retained;
  the first two words were cancelled and
  'Resigned' substituted.
**To Nature** T.C.D.
**Spring in the Desert** NYT, 19 April
1940
**Evening Star** Sent to Mrs Owings
Miller, MS dated 21 October 1946;
T.C.D.; C; B.
  Variant in B:
  5 And halfway . . .
**Wind** T.C.D.
**By a Stream in Bergen County** C; CS;
T.C.D.
  Variant in T.C.D.: The poem is
  dedicated to Mrs Arthur Comstock.
**Florida** T.C.D.
  Variants in another TS, T.C.D.:
  1 . . . turn; my
  4 . . . those waters . . .
  6 . . . Else-icy . . . flowers,
  7 And dally . . .
**The Stream** *Contemporary Poetry*, IV. 3,
Autumn 1945; C; CS; B.
  Variants in C and CS:
  4 . . . nook.
  5 . . . fall,
  6 . . . thought: . . .
  8 . . . winnow,
  9 . . . calms,
  10 In currents . . .
  11–12 set as one line
  15 . . . shrink,
  17 . . . I thought: But what . . .
  20 . . . one,
  22 . . . geysers,
  28 And the great potentates
  30 And churches . . .
  36 . . . fish;
  37 . . . up,
  40 . . . flop,
  41 As . . . day
  42 I would heartily wish,

The following variants occur in a TS,
B:
4 . . . little green nook,
7 . . . thought, What . . .
30 . . . flames,
40 . . . day,
**The Green Glint** T.C.D.
**Flyer in Manhattan** T.C.D.
**Conflagration** B; T.C.D.
**To Girls to go Harvesting** CS; B; C
Variants in TS (on Manhasset, Long
Island, NJ notepaper) B
1 . . . planted,
2 . . . waste with . . .
3 Or . . . [This reading has been
adopted in the copy text]
8 . . . land:
9 . . . peach tomato,
10 Dig the far homelier . . .
14 Sterlise and . . .
15 And jerk . . .
16 And whether you be right or wrong
17 . . . to sing a . . .
19 . . . dairy pans, O, girls be blithe.
20 . . . no cookie, pie or light tart
21 . . . heart.
25 . . . harvest fields . . .
26 . . . orchard, when . . .
29 Look like . . .
33 . . . When all we must . . .
34 To save; . . .
37 . . . sure
38 . . . de rigeur
40 . . . toil
43–44 not included in TS
Variants in C
Title: To the Girls
Other variations as in B
**Fishing in Panther Creek** T.C.D.
**Fishing in the Catskills** T.C.D.
**The Hermit Thrush** *Good Housekeeping*,
March 1954; T.C.D.
**And No Farther** First stanza published
in *The Literary Review*, Winter 1957/58;
T.C.D.
Variants in T.C.D.:
3 . . . vital politics . . . or looking at TV
5 . . . and as far as they can be.
**And No Farther** [An unpublished
version] B.
**Fellow Victims** *Contemporary Poetry* II,

2, Spring 1942.
**Before Building** Written on reverse of
letter from Connie [—], Fatima, College
Road, Cork, dated 1 August 1950
T.C.D.
**Air Land and Sea** T.C.D.

SATIRES AND FACETIAE
DISLIKES AND DISAPPROBATIONS
**Epigram on Connolly** B; in James
Carens, 'Gogarty and Yeats', *Irish Literature*,
ed. R.J. Porter and J.A. Brophy (1977).
**A Lock-in** L.
**On his Mother's dishonest Solicitor
being run over by a car, reputedly a
Rolls-Royce** TTY.
**On the Charges of his American
Agent for Lecture Tours** B; L.
**To a Lady Reviewer** HD
**Coming from the Movies** *The Literary
Review*, Winter 1957/58; B; D; T.C.D.
Variants in B and D:
4 . . . swim;
5 raucous crowded street;
7 . . . feet
Variants in T.C.D.:
8 And coloured . . .
Variants which occur in another TS,
T.C.D.:
1 The tufted palms . . .
4 . . . swim
5 . . . the dog bemerded street;
6 . . . that shakes and throngs . . .
8 The coloured taxis . . .
**Anger** T.C.D.
**Copy Writers** T.C.D.
**A Wish** *The Literary Review*, Winter
1957/58; B
Variants in B:
2 . . . drill.
4 . . . up; . . .
5 . . . a place . . . hat,
6 . . . rat-tat!

LIMERICKS
**The Virginal Kip-Ranger** L; in
Stanislaus Joyce, *My Brother's Keeper*
(1958).
**On James Joyce** L (citing Constantine
Curran, *James Joyce Remembered* (1968).
**On James Joyce's Brother, Stanislaus**

L; C; in Stanislaus Joyce, *The Complete Dublin Diary of Stanislaus Joyce* ed. George Healey (1971).
> Variants in C:
> 1 . . . had . . .

**On Parker, the Grinder** HD
**On Ryan, a fellow student** HD
**The Young Man from St. John's** HD papers cited in L.
**Rewritten Classic** BK.
**On Miss Horniman** HD.
> Variants in another TS, HD:
> 1 'Tis a pity . . .
> 2 When obliged to suborn a man
> 3 . . . Yeats,
> 5 And after all isn't . . .

**The Young Lady of Chichester** HD; TTY.
> Variant in another TS, HD:
> 3 One morning of matins . . .
> Variants in TTY
> 2 . . . niches stir
> 3 One morning at Matins
> 4 The heave . . .
> 5 . . . breechesstir

**On being elected to the Irish Academy of Letters** Letter from Gogarty to Shane Leslie consoling him for not being elected O'C.
**On a fallen Electrician** L
**A Lesbian Maid** HD.
**A talented Student** BK.
**Ghostly Feeling** WG; HD.
> Variant from a TS, HD
> 1 One night
> Variants from another TS HD
> 1 One night when I lived . . .
> 2 I tried to make love to a ghost
> 5 Cried – 'Ah, now I feel it – almost!

**The Fussy Boys** C; HD; B.
> Variants in B:
> 1 . . . dizzy boys . . .

**That Exquisite Fellow called Coward** S.
**Sing a Song of Sexpence** HD.
**The Young Maid of Madras** HD.
**Of Daniel O'Connell, who, it is rumoured, begot many bastards** HD.
**Bryan O'Lynn** HD
**The Young Lady from Louth** HD.
**The Young Fellow at Bray** HD.

**The Young Girl of Antigua** HD.
**A Professor of Trinity Hall** HD.
**The End of the World** Written on reverse of letter of 15 January 1957 from Margaret Cousins, Managing Director, *Good Housekeeping* T.C.D.

PARODIES

**Parody of Swinburne's *Itylus*** Letter to G.K.A. Bell, October 1904; MLTT.
**Hymn of Brahma** In letter to James Joyce from 5 Trinity College, Dublin of 3 May 1904, which parodies Lady Gregory's 'Kiltartan' style B; C.
> Variant in another TS, C:
> 16 The Doctor, the Wife and the Nurse

**William Dara thinks of the Sin of his Childhood and is Sorrowful** Letter to James Joyce from 5 Trinity College, Dublin of 3 May 1904 C.
**To Elwood Poxed** Letter 'from the Bard Gogarty to the Wandering Aengus' [James Joyce], from Worcester College, Oxford, of 11 June 1904 C.
**Parody of 'To Althea from Prison'** Letter to James Joyce from Worcester College, Oxford, of 11 June 1904 C.
**The Policeman is bathing – To Girls to have no Fear but Caution** Written 1902/03 NLI; C.
**Lack of Knowledge** Letter written by Gogarty from 5 Trinity College, Dublin on 15 July [1904/05] NLI.
**Languorous Lotus Land** Written c. 1914 NLI.
**Five Parodies** NLI.
**Pax Britannica** NLI.
**Parody of Arthur O'Shaughnessy's 'Ode'** HD.
**A Scotsman speaks to William Shakespeare** NLI; C; B.

LIGHTHEARTED VERSES

**To William Dawson** O'C.
> Variants given by JC:
> 1 . . . well-read:
> 2 . . . rather;
> 3 . . . read, before . . .
> 4 CHAPTERS . . . Sappho': Thus . . . father!

**Note to a Friend** O'C.

**Idea for the Ending of a Poem** Letter to James Joyce of 3 May 1904 C.

**To the Wandering Aengus** Letter to James Joyce from Worcester College, Oxford of 11 June 1904 C; L; O'C.

Variants in O'C:
1 . . . bought for you
2 . . . for ten and six,
3 . . . brow, . . . too
5 . . . yet because of thou
6 . . . leave, lest . . .
7 . . . the stream of quiet flows
9 But O my Knight: . . .
10 . . . gains
11 . . . of Oxenford though on my arse
12 . . . All its pains
Variants in TS version, C (also in L):
7 Far from . . .
11 . . . Oxford . . .

**At Burford** Letter to G.K.A. Bell of 13 December 1904 MLTT.

**The Spud** B Note on MS indicates this poem is addressed to George Redding.

**George Redding's Reply: The Mayo Spud in Paris** B

**McGurk** NLI.

**That City** HRHRC.

**Fragmentary Question** B.

**Ad Priapum** HRHRC dated 30 April 1914 on 32 St. Stephen's Green, Dublin notepaper.

**To One who chews the Cud of Wildish Corn** HRHRC on 32 St. Stephen's Green, Dublin notepaper.

**A Trinity Boat Song** T.C.D.

**T.W. Wilson on Homophony** *The Irish Statesman*, 7 March 1925.
12 Copy text's 'makes' altered editorially to 'make'

**A Rejoinder to George Redding's 'The Quiver'** Letter to J.S. Starkey from 15 Ely Place, Dublin NLI.

**Comment on Thomas Bodkin** Letter to J.S. Starkey of 11 September 1916 NLI. Gogarty suggested the following alternative second line in his letter to Starkey of 11 September 1916: 'Surely the most preposterous is Bodkin'.

**Tom Greene of Gort an Tochain** Written on verso of NLI call slip B.
7 first word indecipherable: either

'Hearty' or 'Healing'?
8 and 9 square brackets in text suggest possible readings of the indecipherable words in these lines

**Impromptu Lines on driving past a Country Wedding** L (1976).

**In the Stud-Farm** Letter to Compton Mackenzie of 9 November 1927 HRHRC.

**Talk** T.C.D. Originally entitled 'Superfluous Cleverness of a Pompous Fool'.

**Diary Entry** T.C.D.

**Part of an Early Love Poem** Gogarty, TTY.

**Logical and Zoological** T.C.D.

**To Mora** HRHRC Written on 15 Ely Place, Dublin notepaper and dated 17 May 1925.

**The Buck** B.

**First Edition** C; T.C.D.
Variants in T.C.D.:
2 And all its stream-fed swell
3 . . . to tell me all
4 It heard before it fell
5 And I cried out, . . .
6 There'd be no . . .
7 If all our . . .

**Noise** Written on envelope T.C.D.

**Stop!** B.

**The Subway – Rush Hour** *The Literary Review*, Winter 1957/58; T.C.D.
Variants in T.C.D.:
Title: *Crush Hour in the Subway*
2 . . . landing:
4 Even men . . . standing!

**Take my Seat Please** T.C.D.

**Aeronautic Sport** T.C.D.

**A Contretemp** T.C.D.

**Barberism** T.C.D.

**A Poem by Simon Swishback** Letter to W.B. Yeats of 1 August 1936 B.

**To a Critic** *Contemporary Poetry*, II, 4, Winter 1943.

SOME MARTELLO TOWER POEMS
**Murray** Letter from 15 Ely Place, Dublin NLI.

**Carmen Carsonii** NLI.

**Carson** NLI.

**McCreedy** Letter from Gogarty, on 5

Rutland Square, Dublin notepaper, of 12 April 1905 NLI.
**McCurdy** Letter from Gogarty to J.S. Starkey, from 17 Earlsfort Terrace, Dublin, of 11 April 1907 NLI.
    4 After this line the NLI MS reads, below 'seafaring':
      sail − (man) − or

SEUMAS O'SULLIVAN POEMS
**Sandycove Lines** On sheet of paper accompanying letter from Gogarty to G.K.A. Bell. MLTT
**Advice to Seumas O'Sullivan** [probably written 1904/05] NLI
**To Stark to leave Rathmines** Letter from Gogarty to J.S. Starkey, on College Historical Society notepaper, of 20 August [1912]. NLI
**To Starkey for the Second Coming** Written by Gogarty [c. 1905] to J.S. Starkey on 15 Ely Place, Dublin notepaper NLI.
**Invitation to my dear Stark** Letter from Gogarty to J.S. Starkey from Garranban House, Letterfrack, County Galway [?1910] NLI.
**In Loco** NLI.
    1 Kochler may be Keohler. See note p. 736. Gogarty sometimes disguised names.
**To Starkey by 'John Eglinton'** NLI.
**A Letter to Starkey from Dresden** Verse letter from Gogarty to J.S. Starkey of January 1908 NLI; L.
    Variants in L:
    8 To break . . .
    9 . . . your poesies . . .
    51 . . . jinks
**At Woodenbridge** A postcard from Gogarty to J.S. Starkey of 13 May 1911 NLI.
**Your Father's Hat** Letter from Gogarty to J.S. Starkey of 9 November 1913 HRHRC.
    10 . . . you healed when . . . These words replace original crossed out . . . you convalesced when . . .
**Limited Edition** Letter from Gogarty to J.S. Starkey of 20 December 1936 HRHRC.

POEMS CONCERNING DERMOT FREYER
**Verse Letter to Dermont Freyer from Nürnberg** Letter from Gogarty to Freyer from the Hotel Maximilian, Nürnberg, Autumn 1907 D; L.
    Dear, Freyer: Editorial omission of comma
**A Villanelle of Thanks** Written by Gogarty to Freyer on 14 October 1907 D; L.
**A Line from Corrymore** T.C.D.

JESTING ABOUT THE SINCLAIR BROTHERS
**To W.A.S.** NLI.
**Lines addressed to William A. Sinclair** L.
**Gretta** NLI.
**Nocturne 7.15 pm** NLI.
**On William Sinclair** Written by Gogarty, on Garranbawn [also spelt Garranban] House, Moyard, County Galway notepaper, on Christmas Eve, 1914 NLI.

CLASSICAL THEMES
**Beyond Hydaspes** NLI.
**To a Sailor** D; MLTT.
    The following variants occur in MLTT:
    13 . . . murkey
    16 . . . Crescent.
    17 . . . I, and
    19 . . . peace.
    54 . . . Cooks!'
    56 . . . Mediterranean,
    57 . . . life a
    60 . . . Greece'
    61 . . . speaks, −
    62 . . . Greeks.
    68 . . . mast,
    69 Time but serves. Reading adopted in text; D reads 'but Time serves . . . '. In the version entitled 'The Isles of Greece' in *Hyperthuleana* (1916) a penultimate stanza was added (see p. 205) and the final stanza altered in the following lines:
    68 . . . serve . . .
    69 . . . to enervate
    71 And you thus lay bare of myths
    72 Ionian thalattaliths.

**Opening Lines of Oedipus Rex** MLTT.

**George Moore's Garden Shrine** In letter to G.K.A. Bell, from 5 Rutland Square, Dublin on 7 March 1905 MLTT.

**In Haven** *Oxford Magazine*, 7 March 1906; MLTT; HRHRC.

Variants in MLTT:
1 . . . spirit . . .
3 . . . brine,
4 . . . fared . . . avers
7 . . . respective,
8 . . . gray . . .
9 O . . .
12 . . . story;
13 The little trumpets . . . hail:

The following variants occur in MS, signed OG HRHRC;
Title: Sonnet
1 . . . stirs:
3 . . . brine,
4 . . . fared . . . avers
7 . . . vespertine,
8 . . . gray . . .
9 O . . .
12 . . . story;
13 . . . hail;

**Foreword for a proposed volume,** *Ditties of No Tone* Letter to Dermont Freyer of 29 July 1909 D.

**Talassio** Written on 15 Ely Place, Dublin, notepaper NLI.

**Four Lines of Sappho's Greek** Letter from Gogarty to Professor E.H. Alton, of 24 November 1932 T.C.D.

**Good Luck** *The Literary Review* Winter, 1957/58; T.C.D.; B; D.

Variants in B and D:
8 . . . splendour,
11 . . . end as . . .
14 Who though not necessarily were . . .

**Happy and Glorious** Sent in lieu of a New Year's card to Professor and Mrs Owings Miller, 1945; S; T.C.D.; C; B.

Variants in C and B:
3 . . . Chiefest Prize;
4 And Glory second comes thereto.
5 For him who . . .
6 . . . own,
7 Life has no greater need: in truth

8 . . . crown.
Variants in TS, B:
1 . . . surmise,
2 . . . ago:
4 Glory, the second of the two
7 Has missed no greater meed. In truth

**The Supreme Crown** *Poetry: A Magazine of Verse*, February 1955.

**Dialogue** Written on Dunsany Castle, County Meath, notepaper O'C.

**'Hesperus, Thou Bringer of Good Things' – Sappho** *Contemporary Poetry*, III, 4, Winter 1944; B.

The following variants occur in B:
2 . . . still,
3 . . . resumes ['heaven' in TS corrected in ink to 'realm']
8 . . . called, The . . .
10 . . . sings:
12 . . . torch of gold.
15 . . . love light . . .
16 . . . apple-green;
17 . . . me,
18 . . . bounty bringer . . .
19 . . . sing though
20 . . . pent up . . .
23 . . . all:
25 . . . sun
26 . . . now comes on . . .
28 . . . unite:
29 . . . star of hope because . . .
30 . . . evening . . . morning star.

A note adds that the poem was sent with 'The Ho Ho Bird' to *Good Housekeeping*, 5 April 1939.

Another TS in B has the following variants:
6 . . . lovely, lonely . . .
8 . . . called, The . . .
10 . . . sings.
15 . . . love light . . .
17 . . . me,·
23 . . . all:
25 . . . sun

**An Epical Tale** B.

The following variants occur in B:
21 The copy text originally read: 'To man's immortal spirit' altered to 'To the divine in their human spirit', then to 'To naked God in the spirit'
22–29 These lines were cancelled in

the TS.

**To Catullus** B; L

The first 6 lines of a version in L are more direct and effective:

> Until I felt, I never knew
> What torture she had put you
>    through
> Who held you on Love's rack.
> How could I sympathise before
> I loved just such a lovely
>    whore,
> A whore and nymphomaniac.

8 'night' editorial emendation for 'might'

**Locusts** T.C.D.

Variants in another TS, T.C.D.:

7 . . . two-peaked Hill . . .
10 . . . teach!
11 . . . screech,
12 . . . rhyme;
14 . . . that few can . . .

RELIGIOUS THOUGHTS

**Samain** T.C.D.

Variants in another TS, T.C.D.:

9 . . . more subtile . . .
27 . . . beneath . . . wave
29 . . . betide him . . .

**Idea for the Beginning of a Hymn** MLTT

**The Song of the Cheerful (but slightly sarcastic) Jaysus** Written in 1905, sent by Gogarty to James Joyce in copy form and used by Joyce in *Ulysses*. In *Letters of James Joyce*, II ed. R. Ellmann (1966). HD

**To Rabelais, the fornicating Friar** HD.

**Celibacy** HD; S.

**Taking the Name** Gogarty SS.

**Why** *The Literary Review*, Winter 1957–58; T.C.D.

Variants in T.C.D.:

3 Below, were . . . full of . . .
8 . . . sties

**Christ and the Money-Changers** T.C.D.; and letter to Denis Johnston *c.* 1950, has another title: *On the sale of St Nicholas Church on Fifth Avenue, New York* L.

Variants in T.C.D.:

2 He scourged the money-changers out
3 Though many a curse and taunt and scoff was his;
4 The money-changers turned about
5 Purchased the place and rented offices

**Jonah and the Whale** *Atlantic Monthly* 185, 4 April 1950.

**Strong Men** S. A note signed Oliver adds: 'Dear Jim, This is what you are accountable for. The 'After-wrath' is a part of the stock-in-trade of the Churches so it had to go in. As "Healy" was somewhat Catholic, I substituted "Heady." It will be of course a misprint of the stenographer.' [The 'Jim' is Gogarty's friend James Augustine Healy].

**For as much as** *Ladies Home Journal*, 7 August 1954; B; C; D.

Variants in B, C and D:

Epigraph: . . . *perfection* . . . *lustre* . . .
4 . . . bear:
5 . . . grows
7 . . . glows:
8 The law . . . unescapable,
9 . . . lustre . . .
10 . . . comfort . . . plain:

**Then and Now** *Good Housekeeping*, May 1955; T.C.D.

The following variants occur in T.C.D.:

14 . . . 'purged';
16 . . . merged;
17 . . . great:
25 . . . wood;
26 . . . stream;
30 Degrade and . . .

POLITICAL POEMS

**Wie geht es Gagenhofer?** Written by Gogarty in a copy of Seumas O'Sullivan's *Requiem* (1917) BL; TS versions in B and S.

Variants in TS version, B:

'Gagenhofer' is replaced by 'Ganghofer' *passim*
5 . . . transformed
6 . . . Spring?
8 . . . man . . .
9 . . . laws,

11 . . . mid-battle . . .
12 . . . staining hand,
19 This line omitted in B
24 In earth in air and sky
25 . . . their equipage
27 . . . up-rides
37 . . . the Fates . . .
40 The Soldier . . .
41 The . . .
43 . . . his Song who sang
45 . . . Archer . . .
46 . . . withstood . . .
47 To you no stain shall cling
48 Of man demeaning ruse
49 O Appollonian King
50 . . . Muses
51–52 omitted in B
53 By Rythm the Gods . . .
54 The Fates . . . its skein . . .
56 . . . by Sound . . .
57 Your millions . . .
58 . . . Guardian Song
60 . . . strong?
61 . . . Fates . . .
65 . . . Sword
68 . . . Word . . .
69 Law, . . . sings,
70 . . . unawed;
73 The Breaker . . .
74 . . . Life . . . Death –
78 . . . the springs new-born
81 . . . War song . . .
82 . . . heart-housed
83 A Word . . . heart-housed
84 Here tell . . . is an . . .
85 Poet, . . .
87 . . . E'er

**To Lord Dunsany** HRHRC written on Dunsany Castle, County Meath notepaper.

**To a German complaining of the Occupation of the Rhineland after 1918** NLI.

**To Erskine Childers** NLI.

**Don't hang Hitler** S (In letter to 'Jim' [James A, Healy]); HRHRC (written on 13 January 1944 by Gogarty on 400 East 52nd Street, New York 22, NY notepaper).
Variants in HRHRC:
3 . . . shall cease . . .
4 . . . reconstruction starts.

5 . . . Goering too shall do his part
6 (Less . . . waist)
7 Mixing tons and tons . . .
8 . . . they . . .
9 Hitler, . . .

**To Ireland befooled** T.C.D.
**Freedom** T.C.D.
**A Reply to Crazy Jane** T.C.D.

ON DRINKING

**Changing Beer** Letter from Gogarty to J.S. Starkey, from the Hotel Maximilian, Nurnberg, of 5 October 1907 NLI.
**Sounds** *Tomorrow*, July 1951.
**Sounds (an earlier version)** CS; D; B.
Variants in D and B:
1 . . . good,
4 . . . tragedy.
5 . . . borne
6 . . . plain:
9 . . . practice . . .
14 And, when . . . hills,
**Driving to the Ward** NLI.
**What might have been** NLI.
**A Large One deep in the Lamb Doyle** Letter from Gogarty to J.S. Starkey NLI.
**The One Before Breakfast (spoken extempore in the Bar of the Shelbourne Hotel)** Written down by a friend and typed by the hotel's typist. B; The TS was signed 'Yours ever O St. J G'. The version in B has these three lines appended:

> And the worst of it is I can't SEE a
>    small whiskey,
> Tout a toi
> Long may you keep your mortal self
>    'unshuffled off'

The following variants appear in L:
1 . . . one . . .
3 . . . fast
10 . . . morning's . . .
12 . . . curse;
15 . . . bucket
A version quoted by O'C (British Library 133371/01) had the following variants:
3 Will slip . . . the neckfast
5 A cup with its nectar
6 Had scarce left . . .

7 When the stomach . . .
8 Its round . . .
**In the Snug** T.C.D.
**A Whiskey below Par** I (p. 91)
**Bona Fides** Written by Gogarty on 15
Ely Place, Dublin, notepaper on 20
September 1932 NLI.
    12 typing error corrected from:
    'Doyles' to 'Doyle's'
    18 . . . 'Wiley' probably not typing
    error for 'Willy'
**Drink** Letter from Gogarty to J.S.
Starkey of 5 September 1934 NLI.
**Hiking** HRHRC; B; C The third
poem, 'III [another version]' appeared
with some differences as 'The Ill Wind
Inn' in *The Literary Review*, Winter
1957/58. B and C omit the Herrick
quotation placed in brackets after the
poem in HRHRC.
**The Wondrous Ties of Bartenders**
*The Literary Review*, Winter 1957/58; B.
    Variants in B:
    16 . . . some wear . . .
    space between 16 and 17
    20 . . . Abstractionists
    22 . . . subtle twists
    29 . . . Silver Shaking . . .
    Variant in another TS, B2:
    25 . . . must order 'Same again'
**The Triumph of 'Time!'** HD; B.
    Variants in TS, B:
    Title: 'Deposed'
    2 At sundown, . . . glow:
    4 My . . . turned;
    6 . . . suddenly – 'Time . . .
**Joyful Bondage** HD; B
    Variants in a TS, B:
    The last four lines are cancelled; they
    have, however, been retained here,
    the last two lines of MS inserted as
    lines 3 and 4

MEDICAL MEDITATIONS
**An Invitation** Sent by Gogarty to
Dermot Freyer O'C
**Song [Medical Dick and Medical
Davy]** Letter from Gogarty to James
Joyce [*c.* 1902–03] written on College
Historical Society notepaper C.
    Variant in a TS, C:

6 . . . comrade medical . . .
**Aide Memoire for Anatomy** L (1976); B.
**Desirable Diet** L (1976).
**Sindbad**
    (i)  *In Situ* TH.
    (ii)  *The NLI Version* NLI.
    (iii)  *A Choral Song* NLI; HD.
    Written by Gogarty from the Devon
    Arms, Teignmouth
    (iv)  *Another Fragment* NLI.
    (v)  *The Voyage of the Morbid Mariner*
    HRHRC.
    (vi)  *The Nenie of Sinbad, the Morbid
    Mariner* GW
(I) *Sindbad in situ*
Variants in stanza quoted on p. 441
occur in version in LJAM:
1 . . . Atlantic's . . . power
2 And . . .
3 . . . heard beyond . . . & roar
4 . . . mallet
5 . . . Coal-Quay . . .
(II) *The NLI version*
Variants in stanza sent to Joyce on 14
June 1906, in version in LJAM:
13 In Virgil there's not anything
    grand –
14 Aeneas 'tossed' . . .
15 . . . city, and
16 . . . depraves;
17 And then to . . .
18 . . . waves . . . etc
Variants in punctuation in letter from
Gogarty to Horace Reynolds HD:
1 paradox!
2 rocks,
4 ashore;
**Delightful Thing** NLI.
**The Prostate** Letter from Gogarty to
Dermot Freyer, written 23 December
1908 D.
**On ENT Specialists, Colleagues in
Dublin** L; O'C.
**Therapeutic Thought** L (1976).
**On looking at a Portrait in the Royal
College of Physicians** L; LJAM.
**Patients** NLI.
    Variants in MS, NLI:
    6 A grisly kind of brown
    8 The girls – but *they* shut down
**To John Kidney who died of**

**Glomerular Nephritis** T.C.D.; O'C; NLI; TH.
Variants in O'C:
1 What's . . .
2 . . . seized:
3 The name . . . appalling
4 For it was . . .
6 The spirit: as
7 . . . urine and mixed . . . urine
9 Thus by . . . unbidden he
10 . . . these clouds . . .
11 Oedema and
12 . . . soul.
13 There came . . . that dies suprema
15 Death, ushered . . . Oedema,
Variants in MS, NLI:
Title . . . of interstitial Nephritis
1 O what's
2 . . . seized?
3 The fact is his fate . . .
4 His name was . . .
A second stanza read
    Could [?] word more completely
        immure in
    The term of his measure of fate,
    When acid gave, mixed with his
        wine,
    A precipitate!?
13 . . . the 'dies suprema'
14 (That comes . . . breath,)
15 Death ushered . . . Oedema
16 . . . and Death
Variants in TH:
6 . . . spirit, . . . lumen,
7 . . . urine, and, . . . urine,
9 And, though . . . unbidden he
11 Albumen . . . Kidney
13 There came on the Dies Suprema
14 That . . .
15 . . . Oedema,
**To his Friends when his Prostate shall have become enlarged** Written by Gogarty on 15 Ely Place, Dublin, notepaper *Contemporary Poetry* III, I, Spring 1943; L.
Variants in version cited in L:
Head note and dedicatory subtitle omitted
2 . . . my mind,
4 . . . postcocious . . .
This stanza (in Gogarty's hand) is

added after 4:
    If I, a philosophic freak
    On 'Cruelty to Children' speak,
    Remember that, in point of fact
    My thoughts may dwell beyond
        Stead's Act
5 When . . . my mind . . .
7 And, from
8 . . . arise,
9 . . . rape,
11 . . . art engrosses me –
17 And I am guarded down the street
18 . . . meet:
19 . . . young, . . . heart:
20 . . . hypotrophic past!
**Poets' Ward** Letter from Gogarty to J.S. Starkey, written from the Meath Hospital, Dublin, Spring 1915 NLI.
A variant version of the third stanza in NLI reads:
    But you wrote of dying vexed
    Before you print or etch it –
    When if you like print the text
    You'll certainly die wretched.
**The Psyching of Mum** T.C.D.
Variants in another TS, T.C.D.:
Lines 4 and 6 from it are used in present text.
**To Poets** Written by Gogarty on 32 St Stephen's Green, Dublin, notepaper NLI; T.C.D.
**Too Late** Mr Petunia (1946); SSE.
Variants in *Mr Petunia*
1 . . . tould . . .
2 . . . tould . . . time,
3 . . . mercury;
4 . . . at the height of me . . .
**Conversation with Tom Casement in the Palace Bar, 1945.** In Lionel Fleming 'Head or Harps' *The Irish Times*, 26 November 1965.

MONTO POEMS
**The Hay Hotel** D; HD; TH.
Variants in HD, presumably Gogarty's alterations, as in l. 11, for publication purposes: (HD2 indicates an autograph version written by Gogarty for Horace Reynolds on 26 October 1941)
1 . . . hay,
2 . . . cast. HD2

6 . . . delectable –
7 . . . past?
8 Maybe you'll find . . . HD2
10 . . . whores
11 Whom we would, perhaps, companion
12 . . . yours?
13 . . . doors,
15 . . . explores –
17 . . . lad
18 . . . down
21 . . . Mecktown HD2, (which glosses Mecktown as 'from Mecklenburg Street')
22 . . . well.   well HD2
25 May Oblong's gone and Mrs Mack HD2
26 Fresh Nellie's gone and Number Five
27 . . . can get . . .   HD2
28 . . . superlative.
29 . . . man alive!
29 oh Man alive   HD2
30 . . . shell.
31 . . . thrive
33 . . . Ruin . . .   (HD2 glosses Ruin with 'The Deserted Village!')
34 . . . roared,
36 . . . love-logged . . .
37 . . . whored
38 . . . fell: –   HD2
39 . . . unencored.   HD2
42 . . . Gates leaves . . . street . . . Hellsgates . . . street   HD2
46 . . . Hell.
H and HD2 omit L'envoi
Variations in TH:
1 . . . hay,
5 . . . mast,
**A Stanza to be added to 'The Hay Hotel'** D.
**Poem attributed to 'Barney'** TH.
**On seeing Athletes in Monto** TH.
**On the Keeper of a Bawdy House** L.
**The Old Pianist** D; HD.
The copy text, a TS of twelve stanzas in D, has been used in preference to that in HD which contains only ten stanzas, presumably as it was, at one stage, edited for intended publication. The explanatory sub-title in HD has,

however, been supplied. HD uses Dublin dialect, in some cases.
  Two alterations have been made in the text printed here, p. 456 from HD:
3 . . . when . . . ['as' in D]
64 . . . Holland ['Europe' in D]
Variants in HD:
3 . . . when the drinks goes round,
4 . . . a rainy night,
5 . . . each, half bred . . .
6 . . . drinks as if . . . feared,
7 . . . was cleared.
Stanza 2 is omitted in HD
17 I mind . . .
18 . . . disguised;
19 . . . sails
20 . . . surprised.
21 Old Mrs Mack . . . paralysed
22 . . . stately
23 And had herself . . .
26 . . . Fresh Nellie
27 . . . yelpin'
28 . . . belly:
29 'Yer . . . damned . . .
30 . . . stickin' up
31 . . . in my quakin' jelly:
32 . . . makin' . . . pup.'
33 . . . said . . .
35 . . . whose . . . back.'
36 . . . laughter
39 . . . I'll tip the rafter,
Stanza 6 is omitted in HD
50 . . . Nellie said 'Yer . . .
52 . . . me modesty . . . shyness.
53 . . . Mrs Mack . . .
54 . . . puke;
Stanza 8 is omitted in HD
66 . . . parlor . . .
67 'Be Cripes . . . near;
68 . . . the best for better feeling;
70 And who's to pay for an hotel?
71 I said as one delights revealing
72 . . . peels,
73 . . . 'short time' . . . going on
74 . . . bould equerry
75 'I'll trouble you . . . one
76 Firm-buttocked
77 . . . stand you all . . . sherry;
79 But, since I'm waiting here on him
80 Except Click Ho or Shattoo Quim
81 . . . here,' says Mack;

82 'And then send up a bottle.
83 You'll find this little cream tart dear:
84 There's nothing knowing what that mott'l
85 Do, or how her little twat'll
86 Besiege you round the pubic hairs
87 . . . brothel
88 . . . Nellie's coolin' . . .
Stanza 12 is omitted in HD, but stanzas 9 and 10 of HD have been added here to the text of D as moving the poem's action further and representing Gogarty's final choice of punchline, HD2, another TS, provides an earlier version, with 12 stanzas, which is generally similar to D. Variants in it are as follows:
3 . . . when the . . .
10 . . . floor
12 . . . whore,
21 . . . paralysed
39 . . . tip the rafter
58 . . . mastered!
62 . . . flea
64 Like Holland . . .
73 . . . 'short time' . . .
93 . . . standing Nappy Tandy'
95 The sun of . . .
**Piano Mary's Fashion of Faithfulness** Letter from Gogarty of 1 August 1936 to W.B. Yeats B; L.
**Forgiveness of Sins** B; L.
**The Days when we were Young** L

LOVE AND BEAUTY
**To —— to powder her Neck** In letter from Gogarty to G.K.A. Bell from 5 Trinity College, Dublin, written in early July 1904 MLTT.
**To Stella** Dana, no. 5, 1904; MLTT.
The following variants occur in a letter from Gogarty to G.K.A. Bell dated 22 July 1904 MLTT.
2 . . . known,
4 . . . outgrown.
5 Tuned to eternity
6 Dear, that . . .
7 . . . thee
9 . . . love
10 . . . sing;

12 . . . Spring,
Variants in another version, MLTT:
2 . . . known
4 . . . outgrown,
5 Tuned to eternity
6 Dear, that my verse may be
8 . . . love
12 . . . Spring.
**To Lilian to cozen Time** In letter from Gogarty to G.K.A. Bell of 22 July 1904 C; MLTT.
Variants in MLTT:
5 If Sun and Moon could but commune
6 And lie as here we lie
7 The golden day would ever stay
12 . . . heaven;
15 . . . spare,
16 Unless that we be one?
**Song** ('Make me a Mirror with those Eyes') Letter from Gogarty to G.K.A. Bell of 22 July 1904 C; MLTT.
**Fragment** NLI.
**Love and Death** Letter from Gogarty of October 1904 to G.K.A. Bell MLTT.
**A Lover's Lament** NLI; B.
Variants in B.
5 . . . frames the bud
9 . . . spring-time . . .
**If Love were all sufficing who would sing?** NLI.
**Enchantment** C; B.
The ink MS has several pencil corrections; with the exception of three lines after l.30 these have been incorporated. The Epigraph has two indecipherable words written above it, followed by 'of.' These have been omitted. l.36 originally read 'And, poising like a bird,'
**Winifred** Dana, no. 7, November 1904.
**Dolly** NLI; B.
Variants in black notebook, B:
10 . . . light:
12 As the dews . . .
20 . . . my tankard . . .
21–24 (As in copy text, NLI) are followed by a final stanza
    When the folks are sitting
    Talking at their ease
    I will talk to Dolly

Down beyond the trees.
**My Love** NLI.
  1 Editorial correction to 'Lily link'
**Molly** *Dana*, no. 10, February 1905
**A Compensatory Poem** TTY.
**Like Thoughts of Youth framed in an ageing Mind** B. It is dated 25 May 1907. The first part of this poem is indecipherable. The title given to it immediately precedes the lines given here.
**Secret Lovers in Vienna** TTY.
**Jack and Jill** B; HD.
  Variants in HD:
  1 Oh, . . .
  4 Replies with, . . .
  5 Oh, Jack . . . down:
  9 Jack . . . gone:
  16 Because right well . . . knew
  17 When . . .
  Variants in red notebook, B:
  1 O come . . .
  3 . . . Parson's . . .
  5 O Jack . . .
  7 But I will never [in TS]
  9 O Jack . . .
  11 But I will . . .
  14 . . . cue,
  15 And bore her mocking meekly
  16 Because right well . . . knew –
  17 Once Love . . .
  24 . . . Jill!
**The Peace of Life** B.
The TS in B has this cancelled stanza before the first:
    It is when I keep my eyes shut fast
    And ears sealed up, I'm at my
      worst,
    For sights and sounds arise to blast
    The peace of life which you have
      cursed.
This stanza was also cancelled:
    The gods are jealous of their seed
    Else why did Aphrodite plan
    To give a Queen of heavenly
      breed
    To some subservient fancy man
**To Helen Beauclerk** *The Irish Statesman*, 7 September 1929.
**For Emily** B.
  Variants in TSS, B:

2 As it played . . .
3 . . . play in . . .
[3a . . . if now in . . . ]
4 . . . flicker of a smile at . . .
5 Quick as her thoughts are her fine
5 a . . . thought . . .
6 . . . in her burns;
7 . . . the falling of . . .
8 Fold . . .
10 . . . meaning is not plain
[11 TS corrected in ink from 'like the buds that' . . . 'to . . . bloom as the colour in . . . ']
12 Wait to bring the rainbows
[14 Shine like all the rainbows hidden in the rain]
**Venus is Dead** Draft written by Gogarty on Renvyle House, County Galway, notepaper T.C.D.
**Goodbye** *The Irish Statesman*, 22 March 1930.
**A Question** B.
**The Blackout** *Good Housekeeping*, February 1943.
**He accounts for the Skyscrapers** *The American Spectator*, I, 5, March 1933.
**The Getting of Gargantua** HD; B.
  Variants in a TS, B:
  6 . . . buttock,
  8 Him down . . .
  10 A marginal note reads 'It becomes cosmic'
  15 . . . the battle . . .
  17 . . . moved.
  19 . . . Lord
  20 . . . winced but . . . wilted;
  21 And when Life's . . .
  24 . . . going:
  25 . . . go
  27 . . . tumoultous . . .
  29 . . . Glue . . .
  30 . . . Buttocks . . .
  32 . . . which held . . .
  35 . . . Us
  36 . . . forged and founded;
  38 . . . cambered;
  39 . . . argument;
  40 . . . me not . . .
  After the poem a line is added 'The blind old bard of Chios rocky isle may not unremembered be.'

**To his Boar Cat Rodilardus** D; B.
Variations in MS (written on Rosenallis, Seamount Road, Malahide notepaper).
Poem is entitled 'To a Cat' and has ll. 1–4, ll. 45–48 of the copy text D. The B MS has instead of ll. 12–15 the following stanza:
Why let the future touch with pain
The time you may not bring again
Why to the moment add the moan
Which we as long as we can postpone?
B omits ll. 17–20; in it l.25 reads 'To a lot of leaves like claws through the sun'
41 in B reads . . . dealt
42 reads . . . 'felt'
49 Despite the maxim *difficilior lectio potior* the copy text's 'coast' has been altered editorially to 'cost'
**For a Collection of Cat Poetry** Written by Gogarty on 29 January 1944; sent to Mrs Owings Miller, 19 May 1944 B; C.
**News** *The Saturday Evening Post*, 216, no. 36, 26 February 1944; CC.
**Love to Anne on Her Wedding Day – April 29, 1944** S.
**On the Pier** Sent by Gogarty to Mrs Owings Miller, dated 17 January 1945 B; C.
**My Dreams** B.
15 This last line is unclear in the copy text TS, 'had' being typed above 'must'.
**The Dream** TCD. Written on notepaper of Frans J. Horah, author's representative, 125 East 57th Street, New York.
Variants in another TS, T.C.D.:
11–14 omitted.
**Tardy Spring** *Atlantic Monthly*, June 1950. This may also be entitled 'Sitting Pretty' as the text of poem with this title has not come to light.
50 The copy text's 'Pardie!' has been retained, though it may have been a misprint for 'Pardi!'
**Amazons: a Fragment** Written on back of a letter from Mary Owings

Miller, *Contemporary Poetry*, 11 August 1954 T.C.D.
**In a Bus** T.C.D.
**Song** ('I played with Love at hide-and-seek'). *Good Housekeeping*, April 1957; T.C.D.
Variants in TS, T.C.D.:
5 . . . as I . . .
12 . . . him;
After 12 TS adds:
Though he was surely out of bounds
For games sight but not of sounds
15 . . . him well . . .
16 If he would say a word for me.
**In the Garden** *Ladies Home Journal*, May 1952.

LIFE AND DEATH
**A Query** Written by Gogarty on 15 Ely Place, Dublin, notepaper, on 8 April 1914 NLI.
**The Land of the Young** Dated 22 July 1915 NLI.
**Upon a Friend who died distraught** *The Irish Statesman*, 5 October 1929.
**A Noble Trace** T.C.D.
**What Else is Joy?** Letter from Gogarty to J.S. Starkey, typed on notepaper headed Siemens-Schuckert (Ireland) Ltd., of [?19] April 1932 NLI.
**Serenity** *Good Housekeeping*, September 1953; B (3 versions); D; a rough draft in NLI.
Variants in B1, B2 , B3 and D:
Title: Serenity (A Thought from Meleager) [A draft had Menander in place of Meleager]:
1 . . . human . . .   B2 and D
2 . . . pain . . .   B2 and D
3 Pray, rather . . .
4 . . . fear and . . .
6 . . . grave,
6 . . . grave;   D
10 palm   B3
7 Witness, King . . . Richard Lion Heart;
10 For you . . .
**Twilight Street** T.C.D.
Variant in another TS, T.C.D.:
7 . . . As Many a . . .

**Reading at Night** T.C.D.
**Where** *The Literary Review*, I, 1, Autumn 1957; D; B; T.C.D.
  Variants in TS, D and B:
  3 And lest . . .
  5 And girls . . . [in T.C.D. also]
  6 . . . feat:
  11 . . . range, and . . .
  13 But we by . . .
**Philosophising** Dated 3 May 1944 C.
  Editorial emendation:
  5 'gere' altered to 'sere'
**Autumnal** T.C.D.
**The Graveyard on the Hill** *Contemporary Poetry*, TV, 4, Winter 1945.
**The Singing Well** *Good Housekeeping*, V, 139, November 1954; B; T.C.D.
  Variants in B:
  9 . . . hours,
  10 And, all their hours, . . . earth
  11 . . . opposite,
  15 . . . clad, in . . .
  B and T.C.D. add at end of poem the remark that 'According to Chinese superstition it was fate to hear the music of a lost kingdom'
  Variant in T.C.D.:
  11 . . . is but Evil's . . .
**Youth and Age** T.C.D.
**The Kaleidoscope** T.C.D.
  Variants in another TS, T.C.D.:
  3 . . . broken ways
  4 . . . Kaleidoscope
  5 That we . . . see when . . .
  6 How lovely patterns . . .
  8 . . . are
  11 . . . wrecked
**Time** Written on an envelope from

*Wisconsin Poetry Magazine*, on 5 September 1957 T.C.D.
**His Epitaph** *The Literary Review*, Autumn 1957.

ELEGIES
**On the Death of a favourite Race Horse** *Ireland*, September 1904.
**Ode for Terence MacSwiney** From MS written out by Monsignor Patrick Browne, President of University College, Galway, on his Presidential notepaper D.
**The Rebels** *Aftermath of Easter Week* (1917), a volume of anonymous verse.
**Arthur Griffith** *An Saorstat. The Irish Free State*, no 27, vol I, 19 August 1922.
**Micheál Coileáin** *An Saorstat, The Irish Free State*, no 28, vol II, 30 August 1922.
**Threnody** Written by Gogarty on 15 Ely Place, notepaper B.
**In Memoriam of my friend Arthur Russell, Soldier and Airman** *The Irish Times*, 4 October 1934.
**George Bonass** Written 1943 B; C. The first typed version of ll. 17–24 (with the handwritten l.20 inserted) has been replaced in the text by a version typed after it. The first version has the following variants:
  25 . . . faces:
  27–28 omitted
  29 Fanning will miss you, so will Rogan Starry
  30 And at the Bailey, William Hogan
**Panegyric on Lietenant Commander Eugene Esmonde of the Fleet Air Arm** *Contemporary Poetry* II, 1, Spring 1942.

# APPENDICES

**The Ballad of Oliver Gogarty**
A version collected by Colm O'Lochlainn in *More Irish Street Ballads* (1965) is entitled 'The Lay of Oliver Gogarty.' It omits ll.33–36 and misdates the kidnapping: 'For tis the tale of a Winter's Night in last December drear.' Variants in

O'Lochlainn's version are:
  1 . . . lay
  3 . . . Tale . . . Winter's Night in last December drear
  5 . . . home
  6 . . . poem
  7 . . . jumped

9 O! . . . 'Now . . . quick
12 As with . . .
13 O! . . . led,'
14 . . . maskéd ruffians . . .
18 . . . say,
20 . . . yer doom.'
22 . . . night's . . .
26 . . . half-bewildered scoundrel . . .
29 . . . fell like
30 . . . gain;
33–36 omitted
37 Then landin' . . . Park,
38 . . . cold and
41 . . . am I,
42 . . . Liffey . . .
43 . . . wink,
44 . . . then . . .
Another version is given in O'C. This
consists of 8 stanzas. The following
variants occur, the most significant of
which is that of l.3 which gives the
correct date for the event.
3 . . . Night last January year
5 . . . in his house,
9–12 omitted
13 'Oh, . . . led.'
14 . . . ruff-i-ans, . . .
15 . . . coat,
18 . . . followed, . . .
20 . . . yer doom.'
21–24 omitted
25 . . . hold,'
26 . . . half-bemoidered ruff-i-an
29 . . . came down like . . .
30 . . . gain;
33 He landed and proceeded . . .
37 am I!

39 . . . the hero . . .
40 Faith, thin,
**Lines on the Sinclairs**
Variants in D:
7 . . . had gaiters on his feet
11 The other's name was Willie
17 . . . sought the sesterces
**As I was going down Sackville Street**
HD
**The Maunder's Praise of his Strolling
Mort** Among Gogarty's papers T.C.D.
**The Worked-out Ward** Published
anonymously by the Talbot Press, Dublin
in 1918.
**Wave Lengths** TS in CC. See footnotes
on editorial emendation in text. Names
have been regularised.
Act II Scene 3
The following passage appears to have
been dropped in favour of 'I have
nothing to hide' . . . p. 611.
I had a formula, a patter a set of set
phrases about love and that he is merely a
third or fourth in the audience. Every
man likes to think that he is the only
husband and that a divorced woman only
married because she wanted to tell her
former husbands how she hated them.
SAM. I have the report here. Your
vibrations are very individual. They could
not be mistaken from anyone else's. That
is to say that they could have been
recovered very easily. The company is
here to protect you. You may regard me
as your bulwark. Your disc may prove to
be too large to be worn as a bangle. It
could be concealed in a large vanity bag.

# ADDENDA

# ADDENDA

(i)

The present edition was about to go to press when Mr Declan Kiely discovered some poems in uncatalogued letters from Gogarty to Horace Reynolds in the Houghton Library, Harvard University. He has very kindly transcribed these, and thirty-four of them, with Gogarty's own comments, form the bulk of these Addenda. They were sent to Reynolds for inclusion in the book of 'bawdy ballads' that they planned (see 'The Editor's Prelude', pp. 303-06) in which Limericks would be intermingled with longer poems, the contents of which were reduced by Reynolds. Other poems sent to Reynolds and intended for this book are included in Part 3.

(ii)

The poem entitled 'Delphi' was Gogarty's entry for the Newdigate Prize in 1904. Its inclusion here is owed to Mr Andrew Goodspeed.     A.N.J.

## On Thought in our Time

(To Dean Inge)

There IS a difference 'twixt Mutt and Jeff.
I write to tell this in case you see a
World in Mutt and Jeff, as Will and Idea:
In urgent Mutt, in All-Too-Human, brief
Inquisitive Jeff. But Oh what a relief
From Zeitgeist, Thing-In-Itself or that chorea
Of Bergson with its saltant onomatopoeia.

Elan Vital, like eggs fried by a chef!
Is Life a tragedy? Then dramatise it!
But gaily let the sorry pageant go:
Black eyes which heal themselves without an ointment,
Jeff unexempt from Love's rich disappointment.
What hope for Mutt? Oh let us then surprise it:
The single curl of else-bald Cicero!

## The Young Lady of Frume

There was a young lady of Frume
Who bolted away with a groom.
He not only fucked her,
But buggered and sucked her
And left her to pay for the room.

## The Young Lady of Stornoway

There was a young lady of Stornoway
Who had all her maidenhead torn away.
She said, 'I don't mind
I have had a good grind,
And I've taken that gentleman's horn away.'

## The Young Parson from Eltham

There was a young parson from Eltham
Who never fucked girls; but he felt 'em.
In byeways he'd linger
And play at stick-finger,
And howl with delight when he smelt 'em.

## The Young Man of Salamanca

There was a young man of Salamanca
Got crabs, buboes, pox and a chancre.
He got them all four
From the same bloody whore;
And he sent her a letter to thank her.

## The Young Lady called Starkey

There was a young lady called Starkey
Who had an affair with a darkie.
The result of her sins
Was triplets not twins:
One black and one white and one khaki.

## A Young Girl of Peoria

There was a young girl of Peoria
Who was raped by Sir Gerald du Maurier;
Next, by three men,
Sir Gerald again,
And the chef at the Waldorf Astoria.

## The Young Lady of Wick: a Limerick with comments

There would appear to be a liberalism about the world of Limerick that not alone deprecates, but forbids, class distinctions. Thus we find young ladies in positions of intimacy which would shock society in its fashionable senses. An example of this familiarity is outstanding in the Young Lady of Wick, a town or hamlet in the North of Scotland. Its locale neither explains nor excuses the democratic intimacy.

There was a Young Lady of Wick
Who was sucking a coal porter's prick;
Said she, 'I don't funk
The taste of your spunk;
But the smell of your arse makes me sick.'

Not once or twice in our rough island story do we find the olefactory nerves overcoming the gustatory. According to anatomists the olefactory was first in sequence. However!

## [More comment on the Limerick world; or,
## The Three Young Ladies of Birmingham]

If you require more proof of the atmosphere that permits young ladies to behave in a way that would be considered, to say the least of it, unladylike, I can refer you to the Three Ladies of Birmingham and to the parody implied on Public Schools in the behaviour which in the Limerick world appears quite natural to the Bishop.

> There were three Young Ladies of Birmingham,
> And this is the story concerning 'em:
> They lifted the smalls
> And they tickled the balls
> Of the Bishop as he was confirming 'em.
>
> But the Bishop was no bloody fool,
> He came from a good public school:
> He opened his breeches
> And regaled those bitches
> With yards of episcopal tool.

As you are aware, public schools in England are, in contradiction to their name, quite exclusive discriminatory and so private after a class distinction which is exigent.

## [Sappho's Niece (early version)]

Have you heard of young Sappho of Greece
Who said, 'I prefer to a piece
To have my pudenda
Rubbed well by the tender
And little pink nose of my niece'?

## Alfred Lawn Tennyson sings, [or, Sappho's Niece (later version)]

Have you heard of young Sappho of Greece
Who said, 'It's my pleasant caprice
To have my pudenda
Rubbed well by the tender
And pink little nose of my niece'?

## [The Geese of Pekin]

Then out spake an old Chinese mandarin,
'It's a subject I always use candour in.
    The geese of Pekin
    Are so steeped in Sin
They'd as soon let a man as a gander in.'

## The Unknown Eros

There were three young girls of Great Grimsby
Who said, 'What on earth can these quims be?
    We're certain of this:
    They're for more than to piss
Else why would the hairs round the rims be?'

## On Parker who 'ground' in Astronomy for the B.A. degree

*i*

There once was a solar eclipse
Which could only be seen from the Kips.
    As daylight grew darker
    I thought I saw Parker
Astride on a prostitute's hips.

*ii*

When caught in this dire disgrace,
He said, with a smile on his face:
    'The height of my pole
    And this young lady's hole
Just equals the lat. of the place.

Axiom: The altitude of the pole is equal to the latitude of the place.

*iii*

Oh, Parker's a jolly old soul,
He keeps mercury in a bowl,
    For the transit of Venus
    Affected his penis
And shifted the point of his pole.


## A Young Man of the Strand

There was a young man of the Strand
Whose tool could contract and expand:
    He could roger a midge
    Or the arch of a bridge;
So between them fucking was grand!


## The Poet of Sciameter
(A Limerick by Reynolds and Gogarty)

A poet who dwelt in Sciameter
Had a prick of enormous diameter;
    It was not the size
    Brought the tears to her eyes;
The rhythm – iambic pentameter.


## A Precautionary Limerick, with Critical Comment

When indulging in sexual contortions
It is wise to employ some precautions:
    My sister, Ermintrude,
    Once let a germ intrude –
Do you know a good man for abortions?

Notice how the prosey opening line topples over into verse only to end
with a rushed staccato question signifying urgency.

## Medical Students' Song

If you're waking in the morning with a big Cockstand,
From the pressure of the Bladder on the Prostate Gland,
You must either have a woman, or use your hand,
Or find a map of Europe in the morning.

Standing on the common, the solitary moke
Would give his eyes and his ears for a poke,
And, when he gets it, he lets it soak –
So here's to Copulation.

The Unicorn, it appears,
Can only get a horn in a thousand years;
But when he does, he makes up for arrears –
So here's to Copulation.

High Church parsons fuck like stoats;
Red-headed women buck like goats;
And all Creation simply gloats
Over Copulation.

The conger eel in his lusty youth
Rubs sand on his stand to make his cock uncouth,
For the course of true love never runs smooth –
So here's to Copulation.

It's generally known that the ostrich bird
Sticks her head in her hole when fucking seems absurd
While the male goes mad with hope deferred;
And crows for Copulation.

## Three Medical Medleys

If ever I marry at all
I'll marry a publican's daughter.
I'll stick a brass cock in her arse
And make her piss brandy and soda.
To show, to show, to show what medicals is.

'I have a song to sing, O.'
'Sing me your song.'
'It's a song of a medical student's pal
Who was going for a whore on the Grand Canal.
In her hand he placed three D;
Lent her arse against a tree;
Opened her cunt with a satisfied grunt,
          All for the love of a lady!'

'I have a song to sing, O.'
'Sing me your song.'
'It's a song K.I. and Hydrarg. perchlor
On the top of a hard Hunterian sore
Which a Medical got from a bloody old whore,
          All for the love of a lady!'

## Suppose

Suppose the Pope had G.P.I.
What would you say to that?
To his Infallibility
Would you write NIL OBSTAT?
And gladly kiss the Pontifical toes
If the Pontifex hadn't got a bridge to his nose?

But symptoms grow intensified
And the meninges thicker,
Do you think he'd be satisfied
With merely being Vicar?
Nor wake one day with the terrible boast
I'm Father, Son and the Holy Ghost?

## Bo-Peep; [or, Lines to be Illustrated]

This should be illustrated: A girl left alone on a ball-room floor while at
some distance stand would-be partners with curly hair and unobtrusive
forehead development.

Little Bo-Peep, she loses sheep
And does not know why they go.
The sheep, alack, will not come back
Till Peep gets rid of B.O.

*Goosey Goosey Gander,*
*censored 'to ridicule the Irish censors'*

Goosey Goosey Gander
Where do you mmmmm
Upstairs and mmmmmmm
In a lady's mmmmmmm?

*To his* Membrum *no longer* virile

In other bellies once you stood;
Now from your own you can't protrude.

*The Game*

Here's to the game of Twenty Toes
That's played in every town;
The women play with ten toes up
The men with ten toes down.

*Song*

I gave my love a Whirling Spray
And not a spray of whorls.
I said, 'It is the cheapest way
To keep her with the girls,
For Nature just to stop our play
To propagate insists,
And often spoils the efforts of
Our best abortionists.'

## See You?

'See you when tea is ready,' wrote
The Royal Mistress whom I quote;
She folded it and sent the note.
Perplexed was the Royal Stoat
His hand upon his brow
And off to her, the giddy goat,
See you? Went he.
She flew to him, and took off his coat.
Loosened the kerchief at his throat:
'And is tea ready then?' 'You goat.
C. U. N. T.'

## Zolande

The habits, Zolande, of stoats
Do not satisfy my need,
So save me, dear, from my wild oats
By swallowing my seed.

## Pic-nic

We shall be both of Luck be reft if
This heat dissolves a contra- ceptive!

## Staboo, Stabella

A Soldier sings.

Landlord, landlord, have you good wine?
Staboo, staboo!
Landlord, landlord, have you good wine?
Staboo!
Landlord, landlord, have you good wine
To suit a soldier from the Rhine,
Staboo, staboo, stiecketyah, staboo?

Oh, landlord, have you a daughter fine?
Staboo, staboo, staboo!
To take on a soldier from the Rhine,
Staboo?

Girl's voice (high pitched)

Oh, father, I'm not too young,
Staboo, staboo.
Oh, father, I'm not too young,
Staboo!
Oh, father, I'm not too young,
For I tried it on with the gardener's son,
Staboo, staboo, stiecketyah, staboo!

★★★★★★★

The soldier followed her up to bed,
Staboo,
And there he took her maidenhead.

★★★★★★★

[Girl's voice]

Oh, father, he is going slow,
Staboo,
Oh father, he is going slow,
Staboo, staboo.
Oh, father, he is going slow
And the reason why I do not know,
Staboo, staboo, stiecketyah, staboo!

[Landlord]

Oh, daughter, you'll feel something warm,
Staboo.
Oh, daughter, you'll feel something warm,
Staboo,
Oh, daughter, you'll feel something warm
For there's always calm before the storm,
Staboo, staboo.

[Girl's voice]

Oh, father, I have a joy divine,
Staboo.
Oh, father, I have a joy divine,
Staboo.
Oh, father, I have a joy divine
For he's squirting gravy up my spine,
Staboo, staboo, stiecketyah, staboo.

[Landlord]

Oh, daughter, I'm off to the cook for a fuck,
Staboo.
Oh, daughter, I'm off to the cook for a fuck,
Staboo.
Oh, daughter, I'm off for a flying fuck,
As the Chinaman said when he buggered the duck,
Staboo, staboo, stiecketyah, staboo.


## [Lines typed at the end of a letter]

The chaplets of old are above us
And the oyster beds out of reach,
Old poets outsing and outlove us
And Catullus makes mouths of our speech.

## Delphi

*'But Greece and her foundations are*
*Built below the tide of war;*
*Based on the crystalline sea*
*Of thought and its eternity.'*

The trees and stars are softened where the moon,
With bow new-bended, ere the night's mid noon,
Has lulled them in her silver soundless song;
And where the level streams move slow along
Between the willows, with a misty noise
Spring whispers in a dream of Summer joys,
Of dappled lake-waters and floating flowers:
And over all the moonlight-muffled towers,
As if they rose in visionary light,
Unbroken hangs a limpid veil of night.
Save only to the southward, save where far,
Clear seen, one lonely and impassioned star
Calls from the meadows of the austrian sky.
And my love winged within me fain would fly
Over these fields whence many a thought has flown
Of theirs who worshipped at thy Delphian throne,
Phoebus, and were thy favoured votaries.
For often underneath our northern skies
Kneeling to thee in many a glorious fane
Built of sweet song by that sweet-singing twain,
Whom thou didst crown with early laurel wreath
And the soft boon of Agamedes' death –
Have I prayed to thee that thou wouldst reveal
The guarded mysteries those hills conceal,
Where sudden Spring the wintry snows o'ertakes
And flame by flame the burning crocus breaks,
Where all the misty blue dim mountain vales,
Stormed by the fiery-hearted nightingales,
Are blossoming bright through many a leafy gloom
Ere English daffodils begin to bloom
Or homestead robins to the greenwood go:
For ever since mine ears have learned to know,
Though far away, its liquid murmuring,
I too have thirsted for the sacred Spring
Whose lustral waves make music in the world
And often towards thy mountain peaks uphurled –

White brows of Hellas with the stars for crown!
I have gone seeking for that little town
Built on the silvern bosom of the hill,
Whence all the forms of Beauty and Joy that fill
Our lives with grace and gladness were revealed
When gods frequented river-side and field,
The song-sweet dingles and the wildwood bowers,
And earth was like a maiden crowned with flowers
New bathed in water and the morning air.

I would fly thither from all slow despair
For this loud coil of disenchanted days
Drowns Earth's voice singing through the astral ways
And no God answers from the deafened heaven.
I would fly thither if the wings be given
Of my soul's love to bear my soul afar
Unto the starlight of that lovely star
That softer than a dew drop seems to burn,
I would fly thither now that I might learn
The grace and grandeur of the period
When ways of Beauty were the ways of God,
And haply find within thy laurel grove
That which all hearts desire – a resting place for Love.

The hour is thine. Thy sister with her bow
Drives far away the mists from heaven, and lo! –
The molten moonlight upon Castaly,
The lustre on the mountain pines. I see
The pillared town and many a colonnade
As if of moonlight and of silence made;
The marble forms that crowd the Winding Way,
The daedal temple and the grove of bay
That drinks the never failing crystal well;
And all the laurels of the Delphian Dell;
Beyond, – the snow lit summits, and, on high –
The stars that voyage on like silver nautili.

It was for this that little Delian isle,
Whose poor fields gladdened in a golden smile
Upon thy birth, was left an empty shore,
And the dark wave swells landward evermore.
It was for this that from the hyaline
Springs of Pieria, Onchestus green

With many a grove and many a yielding lawn,
And Tempe flowering against the dawn,
Thou didst remove, and now thy temple here
Calm with its grand Greek columns stands austere
Like a proud pæan in the marble mood
Of Lacedæmon, when it calmly stood
Amidst the thunders of Thermopylæ.
The mighty hills break round it in array
Sole standing where the valley slope is higher
And it too holds at heart the sacred fire:
The flower of flame, that in the spirit of man
Is folded close since changing Time began,
The sleeping bud that winter makes to bear
A sweeter blossom than the summer air,
The smouldering flame that quenching death inspires
Until its light outlives all earthly fires;
The spark that from the stricken Centre Stone,
Leaped to the supreme sun of Marathon;
The bud the salt, red Salaminian sea
Changed to the stainless flower of Liberty,
That first blew here, a flame, a mountain flower
Within, for snowy brake, the marble bower
Prepared for no incognisable God,
But thine own temple and terrene abode,
The glorious dwelling house and secret cell
Made gracious to receive thine oracle.
And round about it many a wonder stands
To thee, to whom the number of the sands
Is known, the magnitude of waters weighed
And the dumb yearnings as the thought unsaid:
Splendours of brass, and, speaking to the gaze,
Chryselephantine forms' eternal praise,
Silver and ivory and marble pure
And glories of the gold entablature;
Loud spoils that tell how many a fight was won,
And trophies that remember Marathon;
The thirsty beaks that drank a crimson tide,
The shattered relics of a Persian pride,
And works of men whose souls to marble grown
Are gods immortal in the gracile stone.
As sounds of music moulded in the brain
To lovely forms that smile and fade again,
Are these smooth images that do not fade,

But, standing ever, silently pervade
The sacred place with holiness and love,
And all that Beauty is suggestive of.
The calm of triumph of the athlete there
Laying the laurel on his youthful hair
That closer than wild parsley seems to curl;
And that gold body of the Thespian girl
Praxitelean Phryne, like a noon
Incarnate, where the summer roses swoon
In some Idalian lawn or solitude.
O beauteous body with more love endued
Than hers whose beauty lit the sightless eyes,
Troy passed away, but Thebes might re-arise
Hymned into battlements and builded fair!
Here is the chariot-seat, the iron chair
Whence Pindar curbed his Time out-speeding songs
To gain the grace and sweetness that belongs
To him – the honey of the Delphian Bee.
And there are offerings from oversea
The offering of the desert – precious myrrh,
And, from that King whose house is goldener
Than any King's in song or story told,
Vials of silver and great wealth of gold
All overwrought, the tokens of the trust
In thine high truth and in thy judgement just.

Over the columns of the portico
The monstrous shapes of Good and Evil go
(The monstrous shapes that God's long-toiling son
Was fated to encounter ere he won
Serene possession of his painful choice)
Inextricably, but the brand destroys
The Hydra dying by the antique doom
That maidens sing of by their murmuring loom.
Here is the joyful thryse that overthrows
The dark enchantment of its grosser foes;
Heaven's thunder falling on the Giant brood,
Enceladus by Pallas' shield withstood,
And there, above the symbols of the fight,
Shine the Twin Faces with a wondrous light.
Beneath, the porch is graven with a sign:
*Who knows himself has sight of the divine.*

I gaze until the splendour of the sight
Has conquered thought, and through the ages' flight
Recoiling, all my winged senses feel
That ancient day resounding to the peal
That rang out suddenly when noon was stilled:
*Bring feathers birds, and bees your wax to build*
*A nest of song by singing Castaly.*
And some old shepherd heard it, happily,
And to the mountain folk the story told,
How that throughout the echoing vales there rolled
A sudden divine song in accents clear
And ceased, and left him in the tingling air.

Then first they wove for thee of myrtle boughs
And wattles interwined, a mountain house,
Here underneath the hills, a meagre cot
The best accorded to their rustic lot.
But now supreme as that supremest Rhyme
Whose waves are confluent with waves of time:
The rhythmic waves that first on Delphi broke
As if the soul within the mountains spoke,
Or Homer's Spirit was already born;
Thy glory widens with the flame of morn.

O God, enshrined beneath Parnassus' crest!
O God, with whom all truth and judgements rest!
Saviour! and Slayer of all evil things
Whose voice is as the voice of watersprings!
O God of Youth, with forehead golden-curled,
Whose shadow is the splendour of the world!
Teach me to know the image in my heart
That knowing it I know thee what thou art.

★　　★　　★　　★

The light is ebbing and the vision fades,
The darkness gathers slow and overshades
The mountain peaks, and, lenghtening slowly down,
Covers the temple and the antique town;
But here the night grows bright again to bring
The towers — and the star is westering.

A dream! a dream! no longer Delphi shows
The tiers and terraces of old that rose

Crowded and crowned with all that wealth could give
Or sculptor's hand could make adornative.
No more from overseas the monarchs come
To worship at the God of Hellas' home;
No more far o'er the hills the rustics fare
With offerings poor to solve a country care;
No priestess lights again the pine-wood torch,
No laurel trembles in the temple porch,
No Voice is heard, and o'er the sacred close
By tufted stones the wandering shepherd goes,
The springs that whispering gushed no longer pour,
The soul of Greece is audible no more.

Deep-bosomed Delphi! where the heart of Earth
Beat, and the heart of Hellas too went forth
In a more procreant and pure a tide
Than that which lights thy lonely valley-side:
A stream whose faint, aerial murmuring
Could make the Theban Eagle soar and sing;
A tender stream whose maiden mists arose
To soothe the Earth-born in his iron throes;
A stream before whose waters as they moved
White-loamed Colonos that the poet loved
More softlier wove its shelter dedicate
For him whose sorrows moved the heart of Fate;
We owe thee all that lightens age to age
And Time can be enhance our heritage.

They have not gone! thy glories have not gone!
The well is hidden but the waves flow on,
The swelling music drowns the murmuring lute,
The woods are ringing though the nest is mute,
As splendid day conceals the morning sun
Thy glory hides thee and thy work is done.

Here Avon flows more deep than Castaly
To mingle waters with a wider sea;
Here in the vision of a larger throng
Sweeps Pindar hidden in a cloud of song;
Here Phœbus dwells although his roof be down:
The fanes are many but the faith is one.
And here, amid the green, a golden store
Of fruits that were but fabulous before

The Garden of the Western Islands bears.
But ah, the footfall of the careless years
That bring the fruits will trample on the flowers!
And standing in this moted prime of ours
Thought takes me of a clearer, earlier clime
Where morn was shadowless a little time,
A little time before the glorious prime
That was for us as dawn: a country where
Men moved forever through the lucid air
Of noon that cast no shade and never set.
And so without desire, without regret,
I seek the mountains that for ever shine
To bend a moment at an ancient shrine
As one recalls though summer fills the air
The clearer singing when the boughs were bare;
As one recalls though rivers grandly swell
The clear source springing in an upland dell.

# NOTES

## Addenda

### (i)

**'On Thought in our Time'**
*Dedication*: William Ralph Inge (1860–1934), Dean of St. Paul's Cathedral 1911–1934, English theologian, known as 'The Gloomy Dean' for his pessimism.
*Mutt and Jeff*: characters in a popular comic strip.
*chorea*: a distortion of the central nervous system characterized by uncontrollable, brief, irregular, jerky movements.
*Bergson*: Henri Louis Bergson (1859–1941), French philosopher, winner of the Nobel Prize for Literature in 1927, who essayed bridging the gap between metaphysics and science. He argued that change was the stuff of reality.
*Elan Vital*: the creative urge, which Bergson thought was at the heart of evolution. See his *L'Evolution Créatrice* (1907), translated as *Creative Evolution* (1911). His other main work was *Memory and Matter* of 1896, translated in 1911.
**'The Young Man of Salamanca'**
*crabs*: crab-like parasites transmitted by bodily, sexual contact.
*buboes*: inflamed swellings of the lymph glands, particularly in the groin or armpits.
*pox*: syphilis.
*chancre*: a hard syphilitic lesion.
**'On Parker who 'ground' in Astronomy for the B.A.degree'**
  See earlier note on 'Parker the Grinder', p. 751
*Kips*: Gogarty glossed 'Kips' here as 'Dublin's red light district'.
**'Three Medical Medleys'**
*three D*: three pre-decimal pence – D being derived from the Roman denarius, the original penny.
*K.I.*: *Kali iod.* = Potassium Iodide.
 **'Suppose'**
Gogarty sent Reynolds the two stanzas separately, remarking in the letter enclosing the second, 'By the way the one about the Pope should be left out. It might cause offence!' Under the second stanza he wrote 'Delusions of grandeur which are the frequent accompaniment of G.P.I.'
*G.P.I.*: General Paralysis of the Insane, the third and final stage of syphilis.
*meninges*: the three membranes that envelop the brain and spinal cord.

**'Staboo, Stabella'**
In the 'Oxen of the Sun' episode in *Ulysses*, Joyce has his character Punch Costello sing this 'bawdy catch *Staboo Stabella* about a wench that was put in pod of a jolly swashbuckler in Almany...' See *Ulysses* (Penguin edition, 1992), p. 512.

(ii)

**Delphi**
The Epigraph 'But Greece...and its eternity' is from Shelley's *Hellas*, ll. 696–699.
**The austrian sky;** Here Gogarty is echoing Virgil's use of *auster*, in southern, or the south, anglicising it to 'austrian'.
**Thy Delphian throne, Phoebus:** Delphi, a city in Phocis on the southern side of Mount Parnassus at an altitude of 2000 feet, was the main religious centre common to all Greeks. Although Phoebus Apollo was the patron of the Delphic oracle, he had not instituted it but had had to kill a dragon to claim it. This dragon was called Python; the name survived in Delphi's alternative name, Pytho. The centre of the world (or its navel, the *omphalos*) was at Delphi; the priestess, called the Pythia, sat near the stone marking it on a tripod while uttering the oracles in a state of trance when she was believed to be possessed by the god.
**Sweet-singing twain...Agamedes' death:** Agamedes and Trophonius were architects who made the entrance of the fourth temple at Delphi: for this work they demanded from the god the most advantageous gift man could receive. Three days later they died in their sleep. This is the account given in *Consolatio ad Apollonium* reputedly by Plutarch (*c* 46 AD–post 120). Pausanias (fl. *c* AD350), however, had Trophonius cutting off his brother's head when he was caught in a trap lest he give away the secret of their ability to remove treasure from a treasury they had built for Hysieus.
**Thy sister with her bow:** Artemis, the virgin goddess of childbirth and wild animals, a huntress.
**Castaly:** Castalia, a fountain on Mount Parnassus, the water from which was led into a hollow square where it was retained for the use of the Pythia and the oracular priests.
**The Winding Way:** The Sacred Way led up from a road to the sanctuary enclosed within a wall within which were monuments, twenty treasuries, a small theatre and the main temple of Apollo.
**The daedal temple and the grove of bay:** Daedal, meaning skilful or intricate (from Daedalus, the Athenian who built the Labyrinth for King Minos on Crete, and made wings for himself and his son Icarus. The priestess chewed bay leaves and a theory is sometimes advanced that this may have led to the state of trance in which she was believed to be possessed by the God.
**The laurels:** The ancient temple of Apollo was reputedly made of laurel wood.
**Delian isle:** Apollo, the son of Zeus and Leto, a Titaness, was born on the island of Delos, one of the Cyclades.
**Springs of Pieria:** Pieria, a region in Macedonia bordering on northern Thessaly near Mount Olympus was one of the Muses' chief haunts, the others being Mount Parnassus and Helicon.
**Onchestus:** A river in Thessaly.
**Tempe:** A narrow, strategically important valley nearly five miles long in northern Thessaly on the principal route to Macedonia. A Greek force sent to defend it against the invading army of Xerxes abandoned it: there were other passes through which the Persians were able to advance, the Thessalians submitting to them.

**A proud paean in the marble mood of Lacedaemon…thunders of Thermopylae:** In 480 B.C. a force of 300 Spartans under Leonidas (with about 1100 other Greek troops) held the central pass leading from Thessaly to Locris and Phocis; for three successive days they resisted the Persian army, only two of them surviving. Thermopylae (Greek, Hot Gates) is known for its springs; the ground around them emitted a hollow sound as well as a smell of sulphurated hydrogen.

**Centre Stone:** The omphalos at Delphi, a beehive-shaped stone. Two eagles (or swans or crows according to different legends) which flew from the ends of the earth met there.

**Marathon:** At Marathon in 490 B.C. the Athenians defeated the Persian army of Darius.

**The salt, red Salaminian Sea:** In 480 B.C. the Greek fleet decisively defeated the numerically superior Persian navy at Salamis.

**Secret cell:** The adyton or Holy of Holies where the priestess gave the oracles, below the south west corner of the temple.

**Chryselephantine:** Of Greek statues, overlaid with gold and ivory.

**Trophies that remember Marathon:** The Athenians built a Doric treasure house of Pentelic marble at Delphi to celebrate their victory, its sculptures representing the deeds of Theseus and Heracles as well as the battle of the Gods and Giants.

**The thirsty beaks:** The rams of the Greek ships at Salamis.

**The shattered relics:** This may refer to the Persians having sent a force to Delphi to plunder the shrine of the god. The Delphians fled to the heights of Parnassus leaving the treasures in the temple, for the god said he would protect his own. Lightning struck two rocks which crushed many of the Persians, the rest fleeing.

**Wild parsley:** see note on 'the parsley crown' p. 714.

**The Thespian girl Praxitelean Phryne:** Phryne (*fl.* c B.C. 328), a prostitute of Athens, was the mistress of Praxiteles, the 4th century BC sculptor. (See note on him p. 665). His gilded or golden statue of her was at Delphi (and another of her was at Thespiae, hence 'Thespian girl', the chief town of southern Boeotia. Praxiteles' statue of Eros was also there) in the temple of Apollo. Apelles painted his Venus Anadyomene after seeing Phryne naked on the sea shore.

**Some Idalian lawn:** Probably on Mount Ida, a mountain range in west central Crete, where Zeus was reared (In view of the subsequent reference to Helen and Troy it might be argued that this refers to the Mount Ida, south east of Troy, where Paris gave judgement in favour of Aphrodile, his subsequent affair with Helen the cause of the Trojan war).

**Hers whose beauty lit the sightless eyes:** Helen of Troy whose beauty was celebrated by Homer, traditionally blind.

**Thebes might re-arise:** Phryne, well rewarded by her lovers, offered to rebuild Thebes, destroyed by Alexander, at her own expense provided this inscription was placed on its walls: *Alexander diruit, sed meretrix Phryne refecit* (Alexander razed the city but the harlot Phryne raised it again). At one time Gogarty wanted Thebes to rival Troy as a source of literary legend and mythology.

**The chariot seat, the iron chair…Time out-speeding songs:** The line of thought runs naturally from Thebes to Pindar; he was born at Thebes. When Alexander sacked the town he gave orders that Pindar's house should not be destroyed. Pindar (B.C. 518–438) composed odes celebrating victories at the four great Greek festivals, the Olympic, Isthmian, Nemean and Pythian games, which included chariot racing. He was in the habit of visiting Delphi at every celebration of the Pythian games and chanting a paean to Apollo there. The priestess declared it was Apollo's will that Pindar should receive half of the first-fruit offerings annually heaped on his altar.

**The honey of the Delphian bee:** The Delphian bees were well-known; the second temple built there was supposed to have been raised by them from wax and wings. When Pindar was young a swarm of bees settled on his lips and left some honeycombs as a sign of his future greatness.

**That King whose house is goldener:** Croesus (*c.* B.C. 560–546) the proverbially wealthy King of Lydia who presented magnificent golden offerings to the oracle at Delphi.

**The Hydra:** A monster with a hundred heads; as soon as one was cut off two grew to replace it. The result of Echidna's union with Typho, it was destroyed by Heracles with the aid of Iolaus who applied burning irons to the wounds as soon as Heracles cut off each of its heads. Hera later put the Hydra and its friend the Crab among the stars.

**The joyful thryse:** The thrysus was a pole, twined with ivy and grape vines, often surmounted by pine cones, carried by the votaries of Dionysus who gave to those who honoured him the cultivation of the grape and the pleasures of wine.

**Enceladus by Pallas' shield withstood:** A son of Titan and Terra, the most prowerful of the Giants in the war between the Gods and the Giants, he fought against Athena but fled to Sicily, where Zeus or Athena (as Gogarty implies here) piled Mount Aetna on his body. He continued to breathe flames through the volcano.

**The Twin Faces:** Castor and Pollux, the Dioscuri.

**Who knows himself:** One of the two exhortations carved on the temple: 'Know thyself' and 'Nothing too much'.

**Myrtle boughs and Wattles intertwined:** Probably a reference to the early temple built of laurel; the earlier line. **Wings feathers birds, and bees your war** carries echoes of the legend of the bees building the second temple of wax and (birds') wings.

**A mountain house…a meagre cot:** Pausanias stated that the first temple resembled a cottage.

**The Theban Eagle soar and sing:** Pindar.

**White-loamed Colonus that the poet loved:** Colonus is a deme of Attica, north west of the Academy near Athens. It was known in classical times for its olives and nightingales and for the fact that Oedipus was buried there. Sophocles, 'the poet', who was born at Colonus in 496 B.C. set his last play, *Oedipus at Colonus*, there.

**The Garden of the western islands:** The Garden of the Hesperides, located at some far western corner of the world, where the Hesperides, Nymphs who were the Daughters of Evening, guarded the golden apples. These had been given by Ge to Hera as a wedding present; they were stolen by Heracles but restored by Athena.

# NOTES ON THE TEXT

## Addenda

### (i)

All the texts are taken from letters of Gogarty to Horace Reynolds. When firm dates for the letters are established they are given here after the titles of the poems. They do not, however, indicate when the poems were composed; some go back to Gogarty's student days. He was recollecting many of these poems as well as supplying Reynolds with new versions of some and sending him some not published before. Interestingly enough he does not appear in Gogarty's correspondence from New York to his family, recently published in *The Renvyle Letters*, compiled and edited by Guy St John Williams (2000).

**'On Thought in our Time'**: 8 October 1935.

**'The Young Parson from Eltham'**: This is Gogarty's version of the following Limerick which was in circulation from 1879:

> There was a young curate of Eltham
> Who wouldn't fuck girls, but he felt 'em
> In lanes he would linger
> And play at stink–finger
> And *scream* with delight when he felt 'em.

**'The Young Man of Salamanca'**: 19 November 1953.

**'The Young Lady called Starkey'**: 22 December 1953. This familiar Limerick (in American versions the young Lady is called Sharkey) is included here as Gogarty sent it to Reynolds, possibly enjoying a tilt at the Dublin Starkie family. The children of James Starkie, Walter and his sister Enid, were academics, authors and somewhat eccentric. While Enid spent most of her life in Oxford, Walter was a well-known figure in the intellectual world of Dublin. See note on 'Elegy on the Archpoet William Butler Yeats lately dead', p. 703. The Limerick appeared in *The Week-End Book* (Nonesuch Press, 1927), p. 153, under the title 'A Mendelian Theory'.

**'A Young Girl of Peoria'**: 15 April 1954.

**'The Young Lady of Wick; a Limerick with comments'**: 26 October 1952. This is Gogarty's variation of the following Limerick which was in circulation from 1882 onwards.

> There was an old harlot of Wick
> Who was sucking a coal-heaver's prick.

She said, 'I don't mind
The coal-dust and grime
But the smell of your balls makes me sick.'
**'More Comment on the Limerick World; or, The Young Ladies of Birmingham'**: 26 October 1952. Other versions of this Limerick exist. It was in circulation from 1927, for instance:
There were three young ladies of Birmingham
And this is the scandal concerning 'em.
They lifted the frock
And tickled the cock
Of the Bishop engaged in confirming 'em

Now the Bishop was nobody's fool,
He'd been to a good public school,
So he took down their breeches
And buggered the bitches
With his ten-inch episcopal tool.
**Sappho's Niece (early version)**: Another version was current from 1928.
That naughty old Sappho of Greece
Said, 'What I prefer to a piece
Is to have my pudenda
Rubbed hard by the enda
The little pink nose of my niece.'
**Alfred Lawn Tennyson sings, or, 'Sappho's Niece' (later version)**: 5 September 1952.
**'The Unknown Eros'**: September 1952. *The Limerick* (ed.G.Legman) Panther Books, 1974, II, p. 114, provides a version dated 1928-1938:
There were three young ladies of Grimsby
Who said, 'Of what use can our quims be?
The hole in the middle
Is so we can piddle
But what can the hole in the rims be?'
**'A Young Man of the Strand'**: 27 August 1954.
**'The Poet of Sciameter'**: 15 April 1954. This Limerick, probably written by Reynolds, was altered by Gogarty who 'put scansion on it'. He returned to it again the following year, offering, in a letter of 9 March 1955, 'a rhyme of sorts for your Limerick'.
A poet who had not a janitor
Had a tool of enormous diameter
It was not the size
Brought the tears to her eyes
But the rhythm – iambic pentameter!
A little over two years later, in what was probably the last letter, or one of the last, to Reynolds (who died in 1964), dated 14 August 1957, he added a version which he thought he had improved, 'because you no longer have to invent an imaginary place such as, Sciameter:
A man who contemned the hexameter
Had a tool of enormous diameter
It wasn't the size
Brought tears to her eyes
But the rhythm – iambic pentameter!
**'Three Medical Medleys'**: October 1954.

**'Suppose'**: September 1952.
**'Bo-Peep; or, lines to be illustrated'**: 15 December 1938.
**Goosey Goosey Gander, censored 'to ridicule the Irish censors'**: 25 October 1952.
**'To his *Membrum* no longer *virile'***: 31 July 1954.
**Song ('I gave my love a whirling spray')**: 9 September 1952.
**See You**: September 1952.
**'Zolande'**: September 1952.
**'Staboo, Stabella'**: The punctuation and location of the voices have been regularized editorially.
**'Lines typed at the End of a Letter'**: 9 November 1934.

# Some comments on material in these letters to Horace Reynolds

A four line variant of 'On a Fallen Electrician', p. 353, occurs in a letter cast in Cockney idiom

'Ave you 'eard the sad story of Signwriter Joe
Wot fell though a skylight while painting an O'
His friends and relations said, 'Wot could be better?
He went as he came through the hole in a letter!'

Gogarty wrote a note to this version: ' "Letter" equals "French letter", the English name for a condrum [*sic*]'.

In one of the letters he referred to his version of 'The Young Fellow of Bray' (included earlier, p. 355), and glossed 'tabes' as 'locomotori ataxia'.

The Editor has not included here the ten stanzas contained in another letter of the bawdy song beginning 'I gave her inches one', often sung at convivial evenings in rugby and football clubs, barrack rooms and some student parties. The repetition of both the third and fourth lines in each stanza is not characteristic, and Gogarty's version omits the Cockney chorus usually sung between stanzas, 'O Gorblimey how ashamed I was'.

In Part 3 some of the Limericks included were Gogarty's reworkings of older versions; for instance, 'Rewritten Classic' (p.354) was based on a Limerick included in *Anthropophytera* (Leipzig, 1910-11), and 'The Young Girl of Antigua' (p.358) reworks and improves 'The Young Bride of Antigua' which can be dated to 1880:

There was a young bride of Antigua
Whose husband said, 'Dear me, how big you are!'
Said the girl, What damned rot!
Why, you've often felt my twot,
My legs and my arse and my figua!'

In a letter of 4 January 1936 Gogarty added a note to 'As I was going down Sackville Street' (p. 601) remarking that the poem (which he had remembered and written out for Reynolds) dates itself by 'reference to the practice of amputating the primary sore which practice was continued for some years. It is Dublin born because of the wit of the nurse. And it is full of that defiance in distress which we find in "Johnny I hardly knew ye".'

(ii)

**'Delphi'** Bodleian Library, Oxford, 1904.
This copy is inscribed 'To my friend J. Starkey from Oliver Gogarty'.

# INDEXES

---

## INDEX OF TITLES

# INDEX OF FIRST LINES

If the only life we know
Cross from darkness into Spring
Till the Winter lays it low
Does that end its _____ Morrowing?
Say, what Season overbears
Her which hold the seed of years

                              ──ups. are the change forevermore
To ──────ps melancholy lovely curse.
Like thoughts of Spirit flamed in recogising mind
There is such cup in you, a word you'll find
Will set me bursting like an April tree
Forgetful of the full of leaf to be
Unmindful of other leaves that fell before
                    Or their sweetness
thy apple sweetness from a bitter core
                                        25. x.─?

            Tradition
I heard the drovers crying out to keep
The sheep from straying as they drove them by,
And thinking of that inarticulate cry
Heard by the hills before men learnt to sleep,
I wondered at the changeless years that creep
Down from the vales of grey antiquity,
To leave us with the self-same history:
Sheep and drovers' cries, drovers and sheep.
The driven sheep, the drovers and their call!
When one regards their fate and thinks it over,
So little's left to choose, O Jesus Fail,
I am ─ and thus I prove myself your lover,
                                     O Levellzee,─
Because the one tradition ~~covers all~~
~~but~~ ~~i~~ ~~am~~ ~~slave~~ to be sheep or drover.

Resigned and